2ND EDITION
Fully Revised & Updated

Cover artwork by Barbara Moore, born 1964,
Anmatyerre people, Northern Territory
Ngayuku ngura-My Country, 2020
Synthetic polymer paint on linen, 197×198cm
Image courtesy of Tjala Arts

Featuring photography by Wayne Quilliam,
as well as images sourced from AIATSIS
and the National Archives of Australia

WELCOME TO COUNTRY

A Travel Guide to Indigenous Australia

MARCIA LANGTON WITH
NINA FITZGERALD, MARLY WELLS,
TAHLIA EASTMAN, REBEKAH HATFIELD
AND DINO HODGE

Aboriginal and Torres Strait Islander readers are warned that this book includes the names and images of people who have died.

Hardie Grant
EXPLORE

FOREWORD

For years I lived far from my country. I found new homes. New smells, sights and sounds slowly erased the memories of my country.

But then I would fly home. I could feel Australia before I'd even seen it. I would often wake over the Red Centre, looking down on an earth like no other. Like a dot painting it revealed itself: a mosaic of brush and spinifex and red dirt cut with creeks and flat plains and hills.

This country does talk to me. It talks in a language as old as humanity. This is a language that lives in art and music and story. If we open ourselves up, it will speak to us all.

That is what Welcome to Country does, it speaks from somewhere deep inside our land to something deep inside all of us.

Marcia Langton takes us on a journey through this continent. We meet the keepers of sacred places; those who carry the traditions of care for country. They have held it for time immemorial just for us; all of us, no matter where our ancestral journeys may have begun.

It is a story of place and a story of people. It is our relationship to land and our relationship to each other. My blood is buried deep in this place; my kinship winds back thousands of generations and it blends with those who have come here from other lands.

Marcia tells us that kinship matters; culture matters; stories matter. She tells us too that law matters; Indigenous law and the fight to have our place recognised in a country that denied us for too long.

This is an ancient book and a modern book. We live in a globalised world, we are a touch away from anyone anywhere. This is a book of song lines and trade routes; it is also a book of modern tourism in a global economy.

I live now in Sydney, but my real home lies six hours' drive away. I often take that trip, slowly I leave the noise of the city behind and the land opens up to me. There is a place on the Hume Highway where the road rises and dips. Off to my side is a valley leading to the Murrumbidgee River. I come alive here; nothing on earth feels like this.

This is my country. Welcome to country.

STAN GRANT

CONTENTS

1 **PART ONE: INTRODUCING INDIGENOUS CULTURES**

2 Introduction
8 1. Precolonial history
24 2. Aboriginal & Torres Strait Islander cultures & postcolonial history
42 3. Language
54 4. Kinship
62 5. Knowledge
88 6. Art
108 7. Performance
124 8. Storytelling
146 9. Native Title
158 10. The Stolen Generations
169 11. What if your guide is not Indigenous?
176 12. Making a rightful place in the nation for the First Australians
188 13. Business & tourism
198 14. Cultural awareness for visitors
208 15. Looking to the future for Indigenous Australia
219 16. Glossary
229 17. Endnotes

235 **PART TWO: EXPLORING INDIGENOUS AUSTRALIA**

237 1. Northern Territory
301 2. Western Australia
351 3. New South Wales
403 4. Victoria
423 5. South Australia
449 6. Queensland
489 7. Tasmania
505 8. Australian Capital Territory
511 9. Torres Strait Islands

516 Index
527 About the author
528 About the researchers

PART ONE

INTRODUCING INDIGENOUS CULTURES

INTRODUCTION

Australia is alive with the long history of the Indigenous people, our culture and our presence. Nowhere else in the world can you see and experience the oldest living cultures of humankind. This guide to experiencing Aboriginal and Torres Strait Islander places, tourism adventures, art centres and galleries, guided walks and cultural events will help local and international travellers to find their way through our beautiful lands and waters and make a cultural connection with the people who know it best.

There are two distinctive Indigenous cultural groupings in Australia: Aboriginal peoples on the mainland and most islands; and the Torres Strait Islanders, whose homelands are in the Torres Strait between the northern tip of Queensland and Papua New Guinea. People are believed to have settled on these islands about 20,000 years ago. Aboriginal peoples have been living on the mainland for at least 65,000 years; archaeologists have uncovered evidence of people living in Arnhem Land in the Northern Territory 65,000 years ago, with ongoing research in other parts of Australia indicating even longer periods.

The Indigenous footprint can be found across the Australian continent and its islands, but it is often invisible until it is pointed out. Once you see the evidence of Aboriginal life, a whole new world opens up. You begin to see the country around you differently. Keen to share their cultural riches, hundreds of Aboriginal people have found ways to invite tourists into their lives, even briefly, to enjoy the experience of being in Aboriginal Country with the people who know it best: the Traditional Owners. With a deep knowledge of the natural world, they are the ideal guides to show you the extraordinary range of environments across the country.

The opportunity for Indigenous Australians to share their experiences and knowledge with tourists opened up when land rights were recognised and Indigenous people became joint managers of large swathes of our Country. Now there are visitors' centres, art and cultural centres, museums and festivals in even the most remote places, showcasing the fascinating history and cultures of Indigenous societies.

When you are travelling around Indigenous Australia, you will find yourself in extraordinary situations with extraordinary people, whether you are exploring by foot, vehicle, boat, horse or camel; in semi-arid areas such as the Central Desert or the Western Desert; savannah country across

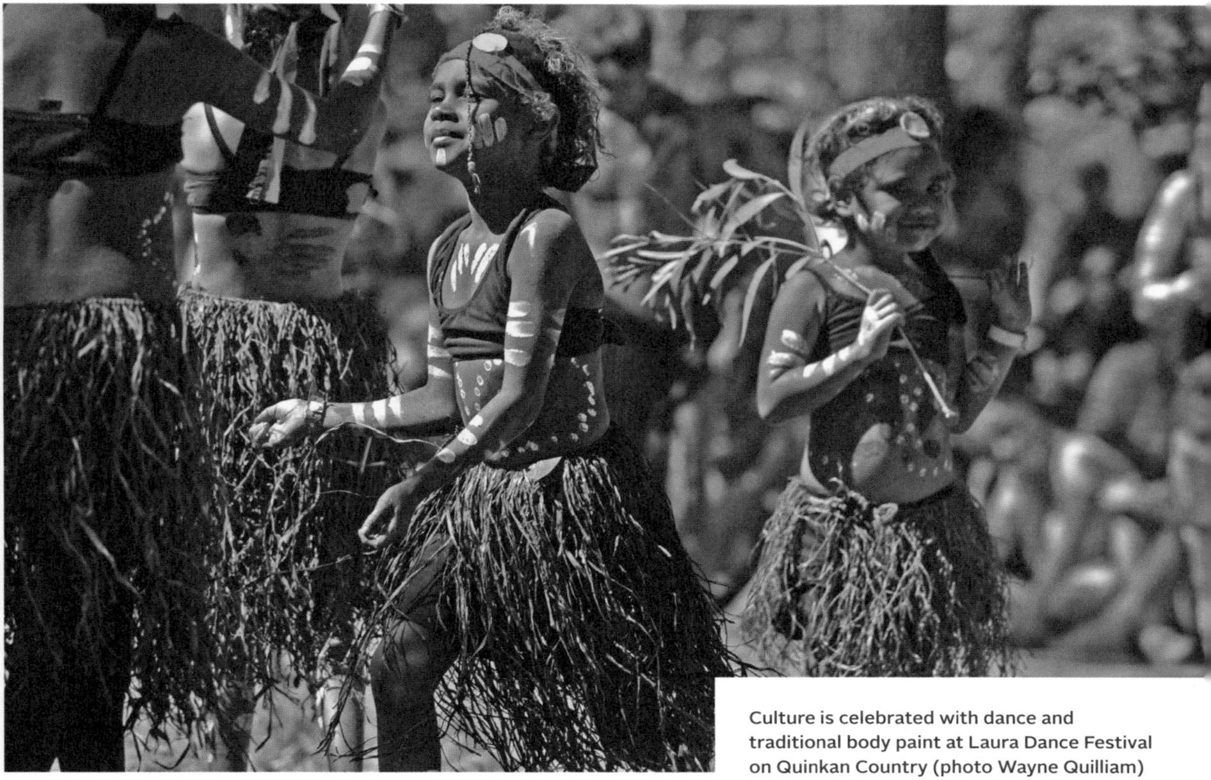

Culture is celebrated with dance and traditional body paint at Laura Dance Festival on Quinkan Country (photo Wayne Quilliam)

north Australia with its many dramatic rock outcrops, escarpments and gorges; or the wet rainforests where fast flowing rivers cascade over mountain ranges; the temperate-zone coastal and riverine plains; the forests; the Great Dividing Range in its many forms; on the beaches, islands and reefs; and in the cities and towns.

Indigenous people have established cultural and natural tourism businesses and opened up their Country for tourists with great energy, determination and a love of sharing the beauty of their culture and heritage. Also, the benefits of tourism to local Indigenous people are many. In large parts of Indigenous Australia, where there are few other economic opportunities, tourism businesses are a pathway for local families to enjoy the benefits of their unparalleled ancestral heritage. With their own tourism projects, local people have the opportunity to work on their Country with their family members. They can also teach their own young people as well as tourists about their culture, history and heritage because Indigenous tourism preserves traditional knowledge and involves the younger generations in its continuation. There are surprises, too, for even the most knowledgeable Traditional Owner. While visiting remote parts of their old estates, where threatened populations were protected from introduced predators and land clearance, Traditional Owners have discovered new species of flora and fauna, and surviving pockets of species thought to be extinct.

The Aboriginal domain was reduced to segregated reserves during and after colonisation and the spread of British settlers and their land clearing for farming and grazing across the continent. The growth of Indigenous rights over the last fifty years has resulted in the return of land areas to the Traditional Owners and resumption of the Aboriginal traditions of management. Free once again to steward the land, Aboriginal people are protecting the biodiversity of Country with a range of strategies. Tourism is one of them, and often it is the Aboriginal rangers who take on the task of conserving the environment as well as working as guides for visitors.

Over the last century, Aboriginal and Torres Strait Islander people, like other Australians, have been attracted to the cities and towns from rural and remote areas. Today, the majority of Indigenous people live in towns and cities. The remainder mainly live in small towns and Aboriginal settlements and communities scattered across the country. Even in the largest cities, such as Sydney and Melbourne, Aboriginal people have retained their traditional ownership customs and established tourism ventures to guide

Sharing of knowledge through cultural dance at Laura Quinkan Dance Festival, Queensland (photo Wayne Quilliam)

Opposite: Walkabout Cultural Adventures provides immersive cultural experiences in the Daintree region, on Kuku Yulanji Country, Queensland

visitors across their land and waters and to understand their culture and history.

The best way to see the Sydney Harbour, for example, is aboard the *Mari Nawi*, or Big Canoe, operated by Tribal Warrior Cultural Cruises. The cruise is hosted by local Aboriginal people who tell the stories of the Gadigal, Guringai, Wangal, Gammeraigal and Wallumedegal peoples of the area as you tour Sydney Harbour. They take visitors ashore at Be-lang-le-wool (Clark Island) to show you their coastal way of life, traditional fishing methods, food gathering techniques, and a cultural performance.

In Melbourne, the Koorie Heritage Trust offers walking tours of the Birrarung Marr (River of Mists / Yarra River) and other sites of cultural significance at Federation Square and within the Melbourne CBD for schools and organisations, and the general public. I also recommend a walking tour of the city with Wemba Wemba-Wergaia man Dean Stewart and his people, who point out the Aboriginal places that remain despite the growth of this city, and explain their history, names and meanings. Dean's knowledge of Aboriginal Melbourne is encyclopaedic, based in both Aboriginal oral history and the records of the colony and the city. The most popular walks are the Aboriginal Yarra River tour: Walkin' Country, Walkin' Birrarung and Ngargee to Nerm: from Ancient Tree to Ancient Sea cultural tour, which goes from a 600-year-old river red gum in St Kilda to the Albert Park grasslands. Dean has guided thousands of students from high school to university level, as well as tourists, around Aboriginal Melbourne and is a regular contributor to classes at the University of Melbourne.

These are some of the hundreds of attractions run by or with Indigenous people that you will read about in the pages of this book.

Many Australians believe that the only 'real' Aboriginal people live in the remote deserts. This is a view based on two centuries of racist ideas that were wrong and should have no place in modern Australia. The official population of Aboriginal and Torres Strait Islander people will reach one million in the next decade. The Aboriginal and Torres Strait Islander peoples want their stories, cultures and history to be understood by all Australians, as well as visitors from overseas, and to be respected. When we see visitors learn about and show respect towards our cultures, histories and arts, a connection is made. This is empowering for our young people.

Pamagirri Dancers perform at Rainforestation Nature Park, Kuranda, Queensland

By building the self-esteem of younger generations of Aboriginal and Torres Strait Islander people through culture, they understand how to survive the racism and discrimination – and importantly refuse to accept the ugly stereotypes – finding their identities, self-worth and futures in our cultural traditions.

We want an understanding of our peoples based in facts, not myths, and to enjoy all the opportunities that Australia offers to other Australians. Offering the experience of visiting our lands, our Countries and sharing our cultures with visitors is one way of overcoming the many misperceptions about us. Learning about the world's oldest continuous living cultures will help all who come to respect our Country and to learn about our achievements.

Aboriginal and Torres Strait Islander peoples maintain knowledge traditions with their own philosophies and epistemologies that originated in ancient Australia, tens of thousands of years ago. Many of these knowledge traditions continue today. They have been transmitted from generation to generation by knowledgeable people and taught throughout each person's lifetime through experience living on Country, learning about the world, the sacred origins of people and traditional estates, their responsibilities for management of the environment, fauna, flora and to the people of the land, and providing for the material needs of their families. The First Australians conveyed understandings of human nature and the natural world, environmental practices and traditions, medicine and healing, and much more, through their teaching systems and practices, sacred narratives, such as song series or songlines, visual designs, rituals and ceremonies, storytelling and in knowledge used regularly in rich but subtle economic lifeways.[1] These lifeways are both highly localised and also spread regionally according to customs.

For over 200 years, Indigenous Australians have hosted and guided scientists and scientific expeditions seeking to understand the environments, flora, fauna and climate of this continent, as well as the cultures of the Indigenous people themselves. This has resulted in a vast literature on Australian life, but until recently much of it was read only by the experts. A growing number of writers, both Indigenous and other Australians, are now publishing more accessible books to show the wonders of this rich heritage to the world, drawing on the literature, films, audiovisual materials and, increasingly, digital objects about Aboriginal and Torres Strait Islander peoples. My aim is to introduce you to some of this material so that you will have a well-founded grasp of the important issues for Aboriginal and Torres Strait Islander peoples and our determination to succeed in keeping our cultures alive and sharing the histories of what happened in Australia in the past.

Our greatest success has been to preserve languages, Indigenous knowledge and land management traditions, and artistic, musical and performance traditions by insisting that we have a right to do so. Now, there is much to share, whereas once, few Australians had access to our Country, our cultures and our own reckoning with history. Most important of all, as all of us face the challenges of climate change and biodiversity loss, learning how to respect Country and to keep our flora, fauna and other species flourishing is best learnt from the stewards of the places you will be introduced to here. They are the descendants of the first people to come here at least sixty-five millennia ago. The Aboriginal history of continuous occupation of this continent over more than sixty-five millennia represents a fifth of the total of human history and the evidence of it should be regarded as a world cultural and scientific treasure. As I will explain, scientists, ecologists and historians are increasingly recognising this and adding to our knowledge. As researchers and scientists come to terms with these impacts, they have been forced to ask the question, What do Aboriginal and Torres Strait Islander people know about the places they have inhabited for very long periods and the life forms that they have co-habited with during this unimaginably long period of time?

The changes to our environments that colonisation and expanding populations and urbanisation have caused cannot be sustained without further extinctions of species and loss of environments and their ability to sustain us. Learning how Aboriginal and Torres Strait Islander people created and managed our environments and biodiversity will inspire you to seek greater care of the natural world we inherited from the ancients and preserve it for the future generations of humanity.

1

PRECOLONIAL HISTORY

Why should we learn about the history of human life and the environment in this country in the time before the British arrived? Because the vast majority of human history on this continent is that of the First peoples, who lived here for tens of thousands of years. Their descendants – the Aboriginal and Torres Strait Islander people – continue to follow and respect the ancient traditions and customs that make this country unique. It is likely that theirs are the oldest continuous living cultures surviving anywhere on the planet.

If we only based the history of Australia on what is known about the way people have lived here since the arrival of the First Fleet in 1788, then we would overlook an estimated 65,000 years or more of human life. Sharing Indigenous knowledge with people beyond the families, clans and language groups that inherited it has given all Australians a rich picture of life in this country before colonisation. It is a very different perspective from the ugly view of Aboriginal and Torres Strait Islander people as 'primitive', 'backward' and unchanging that I was taught in school.

Thanks to many important discoveries, such as those by Chris Clarkson, Associate Professor at the Australian National University, and his fellow archaeologists, we know that human history began many thousands of years before the First Fleet landed. This continent 'is the end point of early modern human migration out of Africa and sets the minimum age for the global dispersal of humans', they write in *The Conversation*, 20 July 2017. 'This event was remarkable on many fronts, as it represented the largest maritime migration yet undertaken and the settlement of the driest continent on Earth, and required adaptation to vastly different flora and fauna.'

Small populations arrived at different times, and their physical attributes were not the same. The historians who studied the small people in the Lake Mungo burials, dated at 35,000 years ago, and the skeletons with large bones discovered at Kow Swamp, in northern Victoria, have documented these physical differences. This diversity is still seen in the many Aboriginal populations across Australia today.

Some archaeologists believe that humans arrived in seagoing vessels on the northern shores of the continent. From there they moved along the coastlines and reached the

This rock art depicts Gwions, described by Wunambal Gaambera Traditional Owner Sylvester Mangolamara: '... Gwion all look different and they dress themselves different for different corroboree and have different job to do like look after trees or special country.' (photo Wunambal Gaambera Aboriginal Corporation/Western Australian Museum)

southern shores about 35,000 years ago. Michael I. Bird from James Cook University and his colleagues wrote an article in 2016 about 'Humans, water, and the colonisation of Australia'. They used satellite imagery and their knowledge of prehistoric waterscapes to show that the migration route most likely followed the 'well-watered routes from northern Australia, through the eastern semiarid and arid zone, to south-eastern Australia and into the rocky arid center of the continent'.

Given that humans arrived here before the last Ice Age, this was the first southernmost human population on the globe. This fascinating history of people living in the world's driest inhabited continent demonstrates great ingenuity.

Modern knowledge about the precolonial history and archaeology of regions around Australia has grown in the last decade. This is partly because of advances in techniques such as radiocarbon and thermoluminescence dating.

In February 2021, scientists announced in *Nature Human Behaviour* that they had dated a 2-metre-long red-ochre painting of a kangaroo on the ceiling of a rock shelter in the Kimberley region of Western Australia at 17,300 years old, the oldest known rock-art date. A new method was used: radiocarbon-dating of ancient mud wasp nests.[2] Scientists have grasped the relevance of the antiquity of Aboriginal culture and have increasingly been bringing their new research findings to the public to great acclaim.

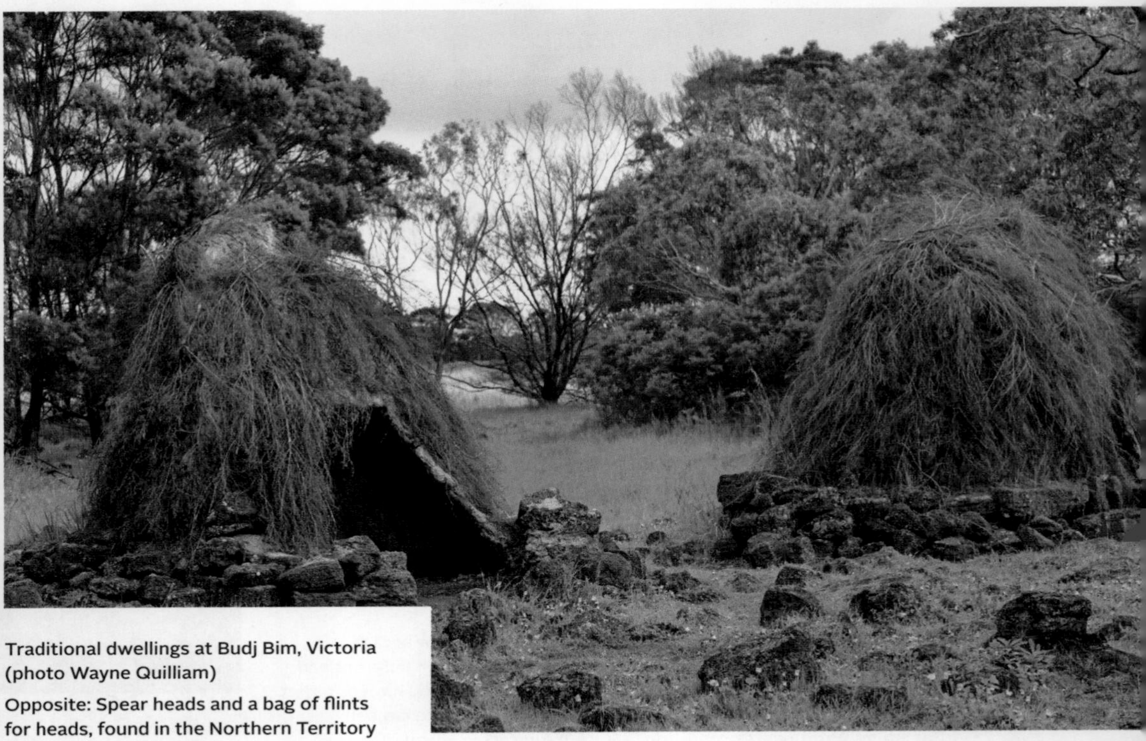

Traditional dwellings at Budj Bim, Victoria (photo Wayne Quilliam)

Opposite: Spear heads and a bag of flints for heads, found in the Northern Territory

However, industry and government have not valued this magnificent cultural heritage in the way it should be. On Sunday 24 May 2020, at the beginning of Reconciliation Week, under orders at mining giant Rio Tinto's Brockman 4 mining lease in the Pilbara, Western Australia, a blast and drill team destroyed the Juukan Gorge caves, sacred places to the Puutu Kunti Kurrama and Pinikura peoples. The blast removed the last remaining evidence of the oldest site of continuous human occupation on the continent and possibly in the world. The Traditional Owners had settled an Indigenous Land Use Agreement under the *Native Title Act* in 2012 agreeing to the terms and conditions of mining on their land with their newly won Native Title rights. Their intention was that the agreement also include mine exclusion zones for the protection of significant sites, as well as waterholes and ecologically sensitive areas, due to the fundamental religious significance of these places to the Aboriginal Traditional Owners. The destruction of their caves, and with them the loss of places of religious significance, is a tragedy for the relevant Aboriginal people, for whom these places constitute a part of their identity and a central place in their social fabric. Their loss is also a travesty, because they held significant evidence for further understanding of deep human history. Along with several other places, they held

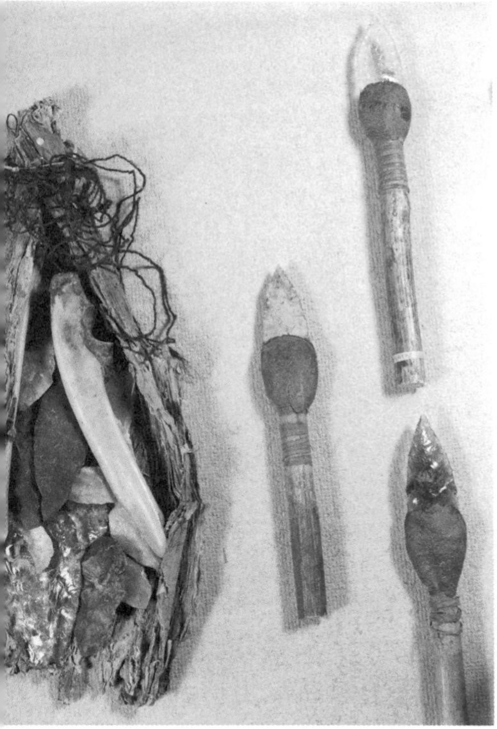

Prehistorians and archaeologists also work with local Aboriginal groups to locate the sites where their ancestors lived. Together, they interpret the rock art, and they discover facts about daily life thousands of years ago. For example, it was discovered that grooves found in some rock surfaces were made by women who were grinding seed to make flour for bread. Archaeologists and the Traditional Owners see the vast array of archaeological finds – wood, stone and bone tools, implements and objects – as evidence of a very different way of life before the impact of colonisation. Through gathering this knowledge, they are changing the conventional – and often mistaken, unfounded and biased – history of the Aboriginal people that has been taught in universities and schools.

The ancient peoples left traces of their lives on the rock faces and in the land everywhere they went. Perhaps their greatest legacy is found in the country's vegetation patterns and in their management of the land. Bill Gammage, a historian and adjunct professor in the Humanities Research Centre at the Australian National University, writes about this in his book *The Biggest Estate on Earth: How Aborigines Made Australia*, which tells us about the country before the British colonisers arrived.

Gammage read through hundreds of historical records and examined decades of scientific research to write this extraordinary history of the entire continent and its islands. In his book he explains the role of Aboriginal land management practices across the entire country. These practices formed the landscapes and vegetation communities that the Europeans saw when they first arrived.

the evidence of the astonishing antiquity of human occupation of this continent. The laws to protect such places had failed in this and thousands of other cases of destruction of sacred places. A federal parliamentary inquiry was established to investigate this particular case and tabled an interim report entitled *Never Again*, but had not tabled its final report at the time of writing.[3]

Archaeological methods used to explore the past of the First peoples include historical studies and field studies. These studies can use landscape surveys, excavation, identification of human tools, materials and food waste, and weighing, categorising and analysing materials found in trenches dug by the archaeologists.

Gammage sounds a note of sadness for what was: 'People made the land beautiful, but settlers took it because it was useful ... The more carefully they made the land, the more likely the settlers were to take it.' He wrote, 'In 1788 [Aboriginal] people used almost every plant in some way.'[4]

Bruce Pascoe, a Yuin, Bunurong and Tasmanian man, in his book *Dark Emu* also writes about the ways the Indigenous people managed the land and water. He reveals the impact that the hundreds of generations of the First peoples who lived here before British colonisation had on the places where Australians live today.

Through their research, Pascoe and Gammage give us insights into what life on the continent and its islands was like before 1788. We know from their writing, based on a range of evidence, that Aboriginal and Torres Strait Islander people produced food using unique agricultural and aquacultural methods. They created homes, structures and tools that were ingenious and appropriate to their lifestyles and environments. They managed the land during changes in climate and geography, including an ice age and significant sea-level changes. They developed artistic and design traditions, and followed legal, religious and social practices.

We also now know that there were extensive trade routes that crisscrossed the country, and some are still used as major roads and highways.

Indigenous knowledge and traditions were essential for survival in this continent's changing environments. Creating the conditions for sustainable human societies meant having a broad and deep understanding of the past and the present, of geography and potential sources of food, water and other material needs, travel routes, and much more. Geographer Patrick Nunn and linguist Nicholas Reid put it this way:

In Aboriginal society, great store is still placed on the learning of traditional knowledge while the geography of the land is taught systematically to new generations, locally through stories about country and totems held within patrilines, and on a larger scale through songs that describe songlines – records of ancestral beings crossing the land performing creative acts that placed totemic sites and language and people into the landscape.[5]

Evidence of traditional Indigenous knowledge is all around us today, and many traditions and practices are preserved, still followed and are now better understood. Books, films, documentaries, art exhibitions, cultural festivals, music, theatrical and dance

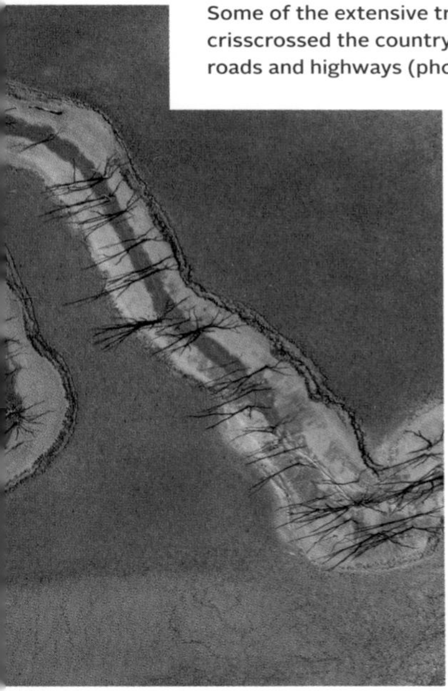

Some of the extensive trade routes that crisscrossed the country are still used as major roads and highways (photo Wayne Quilliam)

performances, and ongoing ceremonial and ritual activities have made this knowledge available to a global audience.

Today, Aboriginal and Torres Strait Islander people tell stories that were handed down to them from their ancestors. These stories help us to understand the past, going as far back as 7000 years and perhaps further.

Geographer Patrick Nunn and linguist Nicholas Reid examined stories belonging to some Aboriginal groups that tell of a time when 'the former coastline of mainland Australia was inundated by rising sea level'. Recording stories from twenty-one locations around Australia's coastline, they found that 'In most instances it is plausible to assume that these stories refer to events that occurred more than about 7000 years ago, the approximate time at which the sea level reached its present level around Australia'.

Nunn and Reid concluded that these individually dateable Aboriginal stories 'appear to have endured since 7250–13,070 calendar years BP [Before the Present]'.[6] In other words, by comparing the details in the stories with scientific investigations, the geographers show that the Traditional Owners have told these stories for more than 7000 years.

Aboriginal knowledge and science have contributed to our understanding of the shape of Australia and the remarkable changes that occurred when the seas rose following the last Ice Age, 7000 years ago. Such collaborations between Aboriginal people and scientists have produced many rich and detailed pictures of the ancient past.

Budj Bim, an Aboriginal cultural heritage landscape in south-west Victoria

Budj Bim is the home of the Gunditjmara people. They have managed this remarkable environment for thousands of years. Their land management agency, Gunditj Mirring, has developed a Master Plan for the Budj Bim National Heritage Landscape, and have also successfully nominated a highly valued part of their Country to the UNESCO World Heritage Listing, citing the cultural values of Budj Bim. The Gunditjmara people are the only Indigenous people in the world to have been successful in making such a nomination.

The 'Outstanding Universal Value' that UNESCO requires to be proved in its

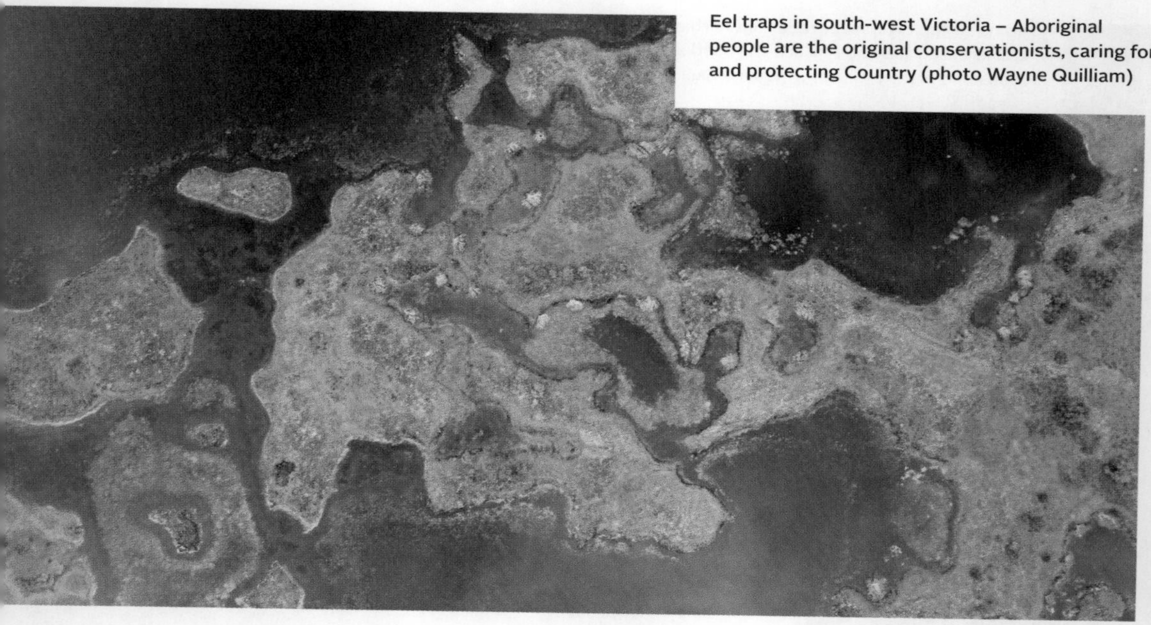

Eel traps in south-west Victoria – Aboriginal people are the original conservationists, caring for and protecting Country (photo Wayne Quilliam)

stringent assessment process is based on 'the three serial components of the property' which contains 'one of the world's most extensive and oldest aquaculture systems'.

The Budj Bim lava flows, which connect the three components, provides the basis for this complex aquaculture system developed by the Gunditjmara, based on deliberate redirection, modification and management of waterways and wetlands.

Over a period of at least 6,600 years the Gunditjmara created, manipulated and modified these local hydrological regimes and ecological systems. They utilised the abundant local volcanic rock to construct channels, weirs and dams and manage water flows in order to systematically trap, store and harvest kooyang (short-finned eel – Anguilla australis*) and support enhancement of other food resources.*

The highly productive aquaculture system provided a six millennia-long economic and social base for Gunditjmara society. This deep time interrelationship of Gunditjmara cultural and environmental systems is documented through present-day Gunditjmara cultural knowledge, practices, material culture, scientific research and historical documents. It is evidenced in the aquaculture system itself and in the interrelated geological, hydrological and ecological systems.

The Budj Bim Cultural Landscape is the result of a creational process narrated by the Gunditjmara as a deep time story. For the Gunditjmara, deep time refers to the idea that they have always been there. From an archaeological perspective, deep time refers to a period of at least 32,000 years that Aboriginal people have lived in the Budj Bim Cultural Landscape. The ongoing dynamic relationship of

Gunditjmara and their land is nowadays carried by knowledge systems retained through oral transmission and continuity of cultural practice.[7]

The remarkable cultural values are cited by UNESCO in addressing one of the criterion for inclusion on the World Heritage List:

The Budj Bim Cultural Landscape bears an exceptional testimony to the cultural traditions, knowledge, practices and ingenuity of the Gunditjmara. The extensive networks and antiquity of the constructed and modified aquaculture system of the Budj Bim Cultural Landscape bears testimony to the Gunditjmara as engineers and kooyang fishers. Gunditjmara knowledge and practices have endured and continue to be passed down through their Elders and are recognisable across the wetlands of the Budj Bim Cultural Landscape in the form of ancient and elaborate systems of stone-walled kooyang husbandry (or aquaculture) facilities. Gunditjmara cultural traditions, including associated storytelling, dance and basket weaving, continue to be maintained by their collective multigenerational knowledge.

This landscape of basalt rises, watercourses and swampland was formed by volcanic lava flow when Budj Bim (formerly Mount Eccles) erupted 37,000 years ago.[8] As UNESCO notes, evidence shows that from at least 6600 years ago, the Gunditjmara manipulated this volcanic landscape, which extends from Budj Bim to the sea and encompasses a series of waterways that include Lake Condah and the Fitzroy River. They built the oldest and largest aquaculture system in the world. In managing and harvesting the short-finned eels whose migratory route bring them to this area annually, they created an economy and culture that thrived due to the great natural wealth that they harnessed. They built houses with stone walls at their base and permanent settlements arranged in family groups along the waterways and channels, expanding them in each generation, and passing on from generation to generation a rich waterworld of engineered channels, ponds and villages. As well as its cultural importance having been recognised by UNESCO, its natural values, sustained and managed by the Gunditjmara people, are also extraordinary. Their determination to preserve and maintain the biodiversity and environmental health of the area is expressed in the vision of the Master Plan in the following way:

Budj Bim Connections aims to improve the condition of native vegetation, increase connectivity of aquatic habitats and foster sharing and integration of Aboriginal knowledge.

Already the project has delivered landholder management agreements to over 60 ha, including fencing and weed management. These works will enhance recreational opportunities along the waterway and benefit rare and threatened species such as Australasian bittern, growling grass frog, Yarra pygmy perch and Glenelg spiny crayfish.[9]

Archaeologist Professor Ian McNiven of Monash University, and many others, have worked with the Gunditjmara people to document their preservation and restitution of this remarkable cultural heritage. As McNiven tells the story, 'In the 1970s, Dr Peter Coutts of the Victoria Archaeological Survey carried out site surveys at Lake Condah (Tae Rak), the centrepiece of the Budj Bim cultural landscape':

Coutts and his team found what local Gunditjmara people had long known about – extensive Aboriginal fish-trapping systems comprising hundreds of metres of excavated channels and dozens of basalt block dam walls constructed over innumerable generations before European contact. Coutts estimated that the volume of basalt blocks moved measured in 'the many hundreds of tonnes'.

Determining how the Budj Bim traps operated was made difficult after European alteration of Lake Condah's water flows through installation of drainage channels in the 1880s and 1950s. Luckily, heavy winter rains in 1977 revealed how some Aboriginal-made channels fed water and eels into natural depressions that Coutts termed 'holding ponds'. In addition, numerous C-shaped basalt block structures, averaging 3–4 metres across and representing house foundations – possibly clustered into villages – were recorded in the same area as the fish traps.

Coutts hypothesised that the fishing facilities were up to 3,500 years old, based on radiocarbon dating of habitation sites in the region such as earthen mounds and shell middens. Reconstruction of ancient water levels in Lake Condah by pollen expert Leslie Head revealed that while some traps could have operated 8,000 years ago, most traps corresponded to water levels of the past 2,000 years.

Working at the same time as Coutts was Harry Lourandos, a PhD researcher from the University of Sydney. Lourandos examined Robinson's journals in detail and investigated a huge Aboriginal fish trap at Toolondo, 110km north of Lake Condah.

Here again was further evidence of Aboriginal people digging an earthen channel (some 3km long) to move eels into a swamp to dramatically increase their range and availability. Lourandos' excavations revealed that it was up to 2.5m wide and over a metre deep. ... Aware of Coutts' Lake Condah holding ponds, Lourandos had the intellectual foresight to call the Toolondo and Mt William facilities for what they were – eel 'farms' associated with eel traps.[10]

The work these researchers undertook with the Gunditjmara confirms the sophistication of the Gunditjmara's economic system and engineering:

These large-scale fishing facilities and associated aquaculture ponds rupture traditional representations of Aboriginal people as simply hunter gatherers.

Rather than living passively off whatever nature provided, the Gunditjmara actively and deliberately manipulated local water flows and ecologies to engineer a landscape focused on increasing the availability and reliability of eels.

Manipulation of the landscape involved stone structures (such as traps and channels) dating back at least 6,600 years. Eel aquaculture facilities (ponds and dam walls) pre-date contact with Europeans by many hundreds (and possibly thousands) of years ...

The Budj Bim cultural landscape provides an outstanding example on a world stage of the scale, complexity and antiquity of a well-preserved Aboriginal fishery that continues into the present. And it is an exceptional example of Aboriginal environmental manipulation and management that blurs the distinction between foragers and farmers.[11]

The staff and members of the Gunditj Mirring Corporation that manage the Budj Bim Cultural Landscape continue to work with scientists, archaeologists, engineers and other researchers to document the aquaculture system, stone houses and settlements, cultural heritage, history and environment and to manage their inheritance and preserve it for future generations. To date, using LiDAR sensing, other imaging technology and drones, as well as on-ground research, five sophisticated fishtrap systems that were built around the lake's edge have been documented. They have also worked with authors to publish a series of books and other material to educate their own children and visitors about their heritage. I highly recommend *The People of Budj Bim: Engineers of Aquaculture, Builders of Stone House Settlements and Warriors Defending Country* by the Gunditjmara People with Gib Wettenhall (em Press Publishing). It was overall winner of the Victorian Community History Awards in 2011 and was reprinted due to popular demand in 2018. The stories of the Gunditjmara people and their deep understanding of their own history brings to life the science and heritage values of the place and its people. With a permanent freshwater supply and an abundance of eels, fish and water plants, the Gunditjmara lived in permanent settlements, unique in Aboriginal Australia. Their way of life was impacted by frontier violence. Their battle against squatters from the mid 1830s until the 1860s, with the most intense period being between 1834 and 1844, was made famous by Rolf Boldrewood as the Eumeralla Wars in his book *Robbery Under Arms*, set in Gunditjmara Country around the Eumeralla River. Thousands of lives were lost, and regaining their ownership and control of their homelands – and ancient rights to stewardship – after the devastation of colonisation has been another long battle over several decades.

There are Gunditjmara-owned-and-managed enterprises and not-for-profit organisations that offer immersive experiences in their fascinating Country, guided by local Gunditjmara rangers who are extremely knowledgeable about Country, its features and biodiversity.

Elsewhere in Aboriginal Australia, other groups of Aboriginal Traditional Owners are maintaining our natural and cultural heritage.

Kimberley rock art

The Kimberley region, in the north-west of Western Australia, has one of the largest concentrations of Aboriginal rock paintings in Australia. This rock art must be one of the oldest continuous art styles practised anywhere in the world. Archaeologist Peter Veth and others, working with Dambimangari and Balanggarra Traditional Owners and rangers, are undertaking studies to determine the age of these paintings. Some are at least 16,000 years old on present evidence, and some could be as old as 50,000 years. There are thousands of paintings in the region. The most famous are the Wanjina (often spelt Wandjina) figures. The distinctive figurative styles are said to span periods of cultural change and major climatic events over thousands of years. These art sites are sacred places for the Traditional Owners, and many artists are continuing these artistic traditions.

Some people believe that the rock art is not just paintings but actually the Wanjina themselves in the rock. The religious belief of the people of this region is that the Wanjina are the sacred creative beings, or sacred ancestor beings. They believe these

Wuuyuru (Bigge Island) is a resting place for Gayarra Wanjina Aarwarrndju – the boss for all this place (photo Wunambal Gaambera Aboriginal Corporation)

beings created the people and the laws, and shaped the geography and climate of their world. They are associated with rain and the seasonal regeneration of the land with each monsoon. It is believed that they and their power are eternal and ever-present.

There are many groups and languages in this region. Mowanjum artist Leah Umbagai has learnt that in her homeland there are three peoples. With Rosita Holmes, the art development coordinator for Mowanjum Art and Cultural Centre, which represents these peoples, Leah explained her artistic depictions of Wanjina.

There are three tribal groups. They are Worrorra, Ngarinyin and Wunambal Gaambera and the tradition of the three tribes is combined under Wandjina, which combines the three in shared customs and the law of country. We believe that Wandjina is the creator. He created the country, the people and the land since the beginning when people were first together.

Rosita added that the 'three groups share a kinship system different from other places in the Kimberley'.

Wandjinas are associated with family groups, tribal groups, even people. It doesn't stop there, it is different in many different ways. It represents different areas. The Wandjinas gave the language, the culture and the laws of the country. They told us how we have to work the country and how we have to live. So all the laws, language and traditions we got from the Wandjinas. This is a very powerful person or spirit being that we believe in. We are here because of the Wandjinas ... The Wandjinas can only be painted by the Ngarinyin, Worrorra and Wunambal Gaambera people. We have had people in the past who didn't know the procedures and protocols for painting Wandjinas. It has really hurt us in the past that people have painted and done all sorts of stuff with Wandjinas. It only belongs to this one area. We were given Wandjina to look after this particular country and it belongs to only the three tribes.[12]

DINNER CAMPS OR SHELL MIDDENS

Middens are mounds of shells and sometimes also of bones and charcoal. They are found in the 'dinner camps' where many generations of ancestors of the local group gathered to feast on their harvest of shellfish and other foods. This makes them important Aboriginal heritage sites and also sites of archaeological significance. They can give us insights into the Aboriginal way of life in particular areas.

The Aboriginal Heritage Tasmania website notes that scientists can analyse the shell, bone, stone tools and charcoal found in them to 'reconstruct past environments, and to understand Aboriginal occupation and land use patterns through time'. The type of information that can be gleaned from such research can include:

... estimations ... about the size of the group that used the site, how long they occupied the region, and whether it was a regular campsite or the product of a single event. Charcoal samples may be tested to determine the age of each layer of occupation, and pollen samples may provide insight into past vegetation within the region.

Middens are a valuable archaeological resource not only for what they reveal about Aboriginal dietary habits, but also the technology that was utilized in gathering and processing food, seasonal trends of species exploitation, and also how humans adapted to environmental changes.[13]

The Aboriginal Heritage Tasmania website also tells us that in some middens, 'Charcoal and hearth stones from fires as well as other cultural items such as stone and bone artefacts can also be present', and that these 'distinct concentrations of shell' contain evidence of Aboriginal hunting, harvesting, gathering and activities to make food. They sometimes contain evidence of 'a more varied diet including fish, seal and kangaroo'.

Aboriginal shell middens are commonly found in estuaries and along the coastlines of Australia and the islands, including in sand dunes and on beaches.

Kudjala/Kalkadoon Elder and educator Letitia Murgha explains that, for thousands of years, 'Aboriginal people caught and ate large numbers of shellfish species in and around the mangrove mud flats and

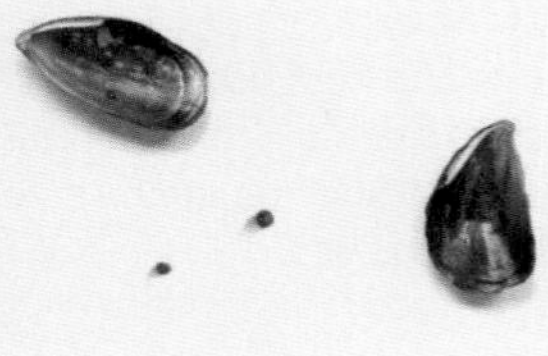

coastal areas along the Queensland coast'. Depending on the type of shellfish, they were cooked or eaten raw. The discarded shells accumulated in these special cooking camps, creating large mounds of shells from one or several species that were harvested in the area. Some types of shells could be used for a number of purposes. For example, by grinding a shell to the right shape and adding a handle, it would become a sharp knife for cutting meat.

As Letitia Murgha says, '[middens] tell the story of the Aboriginal peoples' diet, food sources for that particular area, what species were available, the impact of biodiversity, environmental changes and marine ecosystems'.[14]

Aboriginal shell middens are not easily detected unless you know what you are looking for. They may be 'small shallow discrete scatters to extensive deposits that run along a coastline for hundreds of metres'. They may appear 'on the ground surface as sparse scatters or concentrations of broken shell, and are often associated with dark, ashy soil including charcoal. Middens can also be visible in eroded or collapsed sections of dunes, where they may appear as a dark, ashy band with layers of shell throughout', according to the Aboriginal Heritage Tasmania website.

Shell-wash deposits might look like an Aboriginal midden but they aren't made up of the same shells. They are caused by storms and high tides, and often appear at the high tide mark, but contain only shells from small species, such as Venus clams and dog cockles.

The oldest known Aboriginal shell midden place on the Victorian coast is nearly 12,000 years old. As explained in a Victorian Government fact sheet:

At this time sea levels were lower because icecaps at the north and south poles were much larger than today. The shoreline was many kilometres away from its present position, at times creating a land bridge with Tasmania. Sea levels stabilised between [6000 and 7000] years ago, and most middens along the present coastline were formed since that time. The dates of middens, their location and their contents, indicate that different areas of the coast were used at different times, generally when they were most productive. There were changes in shellfish species that were used, stone tool types and raw materials. The presence of exotic stone in places is evidence of contact between people from different areas.

In Victoria, all Aboriginal cultural places are protected by law. Aboriginal artefacts are also protected. It is illegal to disturb or destroy an Aboriginal place or remove an Aboriginal artefact from a site.

In New South Wales, Aboriginal rangers and New South Wales Parks and Heritage rangers protect Aboriginal sites, including shell middens.

As places with such rich evidence of ancestral life, shell middens are important to Aboriginal people everywhere. All Australians should feel a sense of responsibility to preserve them as part of our national heritage. They are important because they offer clues to the way people lived in this country for thousands of years.

This ancient shell midden is evidence of a 'dinner camp' where many generations of ancestors of the local group gathered to feast on shellfish and other foods, making it an important Aboriginal heritage site. Photo by Melinda Sawers, Birany Birany, Northern Territory, June 2018.

Listening to Country

Elders often say that if you sit quietly in the places where our ancestors left traces of their lives, on middens where they ate seafood in the sand dunes, or in rock caves where they left their paintings, you can hear them and feel them. This sense of being connected to a deep history is at the core of our being. Even if we have grown up with it, coming upon one of these special places always thrills us.

Listening to the stories that Elders tell gives me a feeling of being spoken to from the deep past. In those places where archaeologists look for signs of the past is our history. If all Australians could feel that attachment to our Country, they might respect this great legacy more.

When I was young, I saw so many more animals and birds, the seas and rivers teemed with fish, and the rocks were covered with oysters and mussels. Now it is much more difficult to catch a fish or find oysters. It is important for all Australians to understand what was there, what our ancestors left for us – a beautiful world – and to care for it as our ancestors did.

The modern Australian citizen should know about the history of the First peoples because that is what makes this country distinctive. It should be a source of national identity and pride for everyone. Understanding the contributions Aboriginal and Torres Strait Islander peoples made over at least 65,000 years is also a way of respecting their descendants, their continuing cultural traditions, practices and knowledge. It is a way to recognise their ability to contribute to this country by maintaining those practices that have helped to shape the environment and landscapes since ancient times.

Dancers gather at the 3 Rivers Festival on the Murray River (photo Wayne Quilliam)

2

ABORIGINAL & TORRES STRAIT ISLANDER CULTURES & POSTCOLONIAL HISTORY

It is difficult to define what culture is. We might say, for example, that culture is the set of beliefs, customs and ways of life unique to a specific group of people. This definition is limited, though, because it doesn't tell us how we discover and define what 'beliefs', 'customs' and 'ways of life' are, and how they combine to create a unique culture. Also, these things are constantly changing. They change with the political situation, historical influences and the economy. In modern Australia's multicultural, global society, it is hard to define the cultural beliefs and practices of any group. And if you do, not everyone will agree with the one definition.

What are Australian values? Fairness is often said to be an Australian value, but for many First Australians there's not much fairness. About half the Aboriginal and Torres Strait Islander people are worse off than other Australians in terms of income, access to services, housing, employment and education. It must also be said that although thousands of Aboriginal and Torres Strait Islander people are very poor, they are also the most culturally productive people in the country.

They are celebrated for their performances and artistic creations. Most Australians will have seen at least one example of Indigenous cultural expression, such as an artwork, a 'Welcome to Country' ceremony or a dance performance. However, according to the *The State of Reconciliation in Australia Report* published by Reconciliation Australia, most Australians have never met an Indigenous person. Many people do not know that Indigenous Australia is enormously diverse and complex, both culturally and linguistically.

Many ideas that came to Australia from Britain and Europe led to stereotypes and ignorance about Aboriginal and Torres Strait Islander cultures. These misconceptions started in colonial times and persisted for much of the twentieth century. Even today, many Australians don't understand the full importance of the cultures of the First peoples.

These cultures are thousands of years old and they are always changing. Let's look at some of the historical events that had an impact on our many cultures since the British arrived.

The Landing of Captain Cook at Botany Bay painting by Phillip Fox

In 1770, Captain James Cook declared Britain's possession of the east coast of what was still a mysterious continent to the Europeans. He was standing on Bedanug, which came to be called Possession Island, off the coast of North Queensland. In January 1788, Captain Arthur Phillip, an officer in the British Navy, led a fleet of ships to develop the penal colony of New South Wales. What followed was a brutal upheaval for the Aboriginal people. By the end of the 1940s, only a few Aboriginal groups retained their pre-contact lifestyles.

At the University of Newcastle, a group of researchers led by Professor Lyndall Ryan are researching the frontier violence that led to this terrible outcome. The First Australians were not passive victims: they note that:

From the moment the British invaded Australia in 1788 they encountered active resistance from the Aboriginal and Torres Strait Islander owners and custodians of the lands. In the frontier wars which continued until the 1960s, massacres became a defining strategy to eradicate that resistance. As a result thousands of Aboriginal men, women and children were killed.[15]

Ryan and her team have documented the massacres of First Australians, mapping their locations, 'timelines, and information about massacres in Central and Eastern Australia from 1794 when the first massacre was recorded until 1930'. Their research includes the whole of Australia from the start of British settlement up to 1930 and is based on the most reliable information available on these events which were often concealed: 'Only events for which sufficient information remains from the past and can be verified ...'.

Their findings show that the way massacres were carried out changed over time and involved soldiers, settlers, mounted police and/or native police usually with firearms and sometimes with poison.[16]

In 2021, with more massacres to be added in a later update, their statistics of the death tolls in these incidents are in the table below. There were relatively few massacres of colonists.

Preliminary Statistics

The following statistics relate to massacres of 6 or more people only and are subject to change as more information becomes available. Other factors affect the history of Aboriginal and Torres Strait Islander populations such as disease, loss of land, abduction of children, control of movement, and combined flow on effects to the community.

The statistics are indicative rather than definitive. They are minimum estimates only, and are not estimates of the full extent of massacre. It is likely that more massacres occurred than were reported and recorded and for which we can find evidence.

Recorded massacres between 1788 and 1930 in Australia by current State and Territory borders

	Australia	Tasmania	Victoria	New South Wales	Queensland	South Australia	Northern Territory	Western Australia
Est. Total Massacres	305	36	52	50	72	15	35	42
Est. Aboriginal and Torres Strait Islander victims of massacres	8178	487	1110	1929	2032	255	1350	1015
Est. Colonist victims of massacres	146	0	8	8	96	26	8	0
Est. Average Aboriginal and Torres Strait Islander victims of massacres	28.01	13.16	21.76	39.37	31.26	18.21	39.71	24.17
Est. Average colonist victims of massacres	13.27	0	8.00	8.00	13.71	26.00	8.00	0

The above information was retrieved from the Colonial Frontier Massacres website, 21 July 2021 (https://c21ch.newcastle.edu.au/colonialmassacres/)

RATIONS

The military and, later, free settlers forced many Indigenous people from their land. British graziers and farmers altered most Australian landscapes by clearing trees on a massive scale to make way for their herds and crops. These changes brought to an end the ancient hunting, gathering and fishing economy of the First Australians across most of the continent. It meant that these people had to rely mainly on handouts of food rations in order to survive. The colonial administrators and settlers in New South Wales first started handing out rations to make contact with the Indigenous people and to secure their trust. Later, they gave out food to stop Aborigines from spearing their cattle. In drought times, they were forced to distribute the rations more widely. From the 1880s, government-funded rations were distributed to Aboriginal people in northern Queensland through missions, settler stations and government food-relief centres. The ration system had become widespread in the colonies by the late 1890s.

With little choice but to congregate and wait for rations, Aboriginal people were drawn to the pastoral stations and the missions. Government rations were small and irregular, so the handouts by the missions became a better option. At many missions the local Aboriginal people became a permanent working community, and a 'no work no food' policy was followed. The missionaries' intention was to 'civilise' these people and train them in Christian ways of living.

Relying on rations instead of local food sources brought major changes to the lifestyles and cultures of the Indigenous people from the 1880s through to the twentieth century.

Top: Men at work in a ration store in Delissaville, Northern Territory

Bottom: Collecting the daily milk ration for babies and nursing mothers at the Snake Bay Government settlement on Melville Island, Northern Territory

The Gulag Archipelago: institutional control

After colonisation, Indigenous people continued to live in traditional societies in Cape York, Central Australia and the Western Desert, in some areas of the top end of the Northern Territory and in the Kimberley region of Western Australia. Even there, though, they were now controlled by the Europeans, but this was the case across Australia. Charles Rowley referred to the thousands of scattered reserves and administered settlements to which thousands of Aboriginal and Torres Strait Islander people were confined under legislation as the 'gulag archipelago', comparing these 'institutions of total control' to the Soviet prison camps about which Aleksandr Solzhenitsyn had famously written in 1975.[17]

Elsewhere, the surviving Indigenous populations became involved in the new economy that had taken over from their own. They became cheap or even free workers, and were often exploited by their employers. Despite this, from the hop growers of Coranderrk in Victoria to the pearl-shell divers of the Torres Strait, the ingenuity of the First Australians in these terrible circumstances was seen across the country.

In the first half of the twentieth century, the state and territory governments brought

Children from settlements and missions play tunnel ball at Centralian School Sports Day in Alice Springs, Northern Territory

in assimilation policies that controlled the lives of Indigenous people. They became a low-paid labour force for governments, farmers and businesses. Governments could also regulate whom Indigenous people were allowed to marry, and they removed 'half-caste' children from their families. This way, they were able to control the Aboriginal 'race'.

People who were identified, at least formally, as 'full-bloods' were meant to stay on Crown land – the reserves. The reality, though, was quite different. Reserve populations were mixed and the goal of segregating 'full-blood' and 'half-caste' people was never achieved in practice.

In 1997, the Human Rights and Equal Opportunity Commission published a report about Australia's social security regulations. It documents some of the examples of discrimination that Indigenous people had to live with for decades.

Seven years after federation, national aged and invalid pension schemes were enacted, and in 1912, maternity allowances. However, 'Aboriginal Natives' were disqualified from all payments. Throughout the Great Depression, Indigenous people continued to be excluded from eligibility for any benefit. After World War II, a comprehensive and universal system of social security existed in Australia, except for Aborigines. The first payment to which Indigenous people had access was a child endowment payment introduced in 1941. In 1942, 'Aboriginal Natives' became eligible for Commonwealth pensions, but as the Racial Discrimination Commissioner pointed out, the 1942 amendments excluded 'Aboriginal Natives' who were covered by the 'provisions of a state or territory law relating to the control of Aboriginal natives.' There were also exclusions for Indigenous people who were deemed 'nomadic' or 'primitive' and, despite the existence of entitlements: '... Social Security Act continued to discriminate against Aborigines by adding amendments that restricted access to pensions and allowance payments and placing Aboriginal Australians under the control of non-Aboriginal administrated Aboriginal departments, missions, settlements and pastoral properties.'[18]

This policy of racist exclusion continued until the late 1960s. In 1966, the Department of Social Services removed all specific references to Aboriginal people from the Social Security Act. Indigenous people living in remote communities continued to be excluded from participation in Australia's social security system well into the 1970s. Full, effective access to social security benefits did not occur until the late 1970s and in some remote communities not until the early 1980s.

In the 1960s, Aboriginal people who were in the workforce, or wanted to be, began to fight for equal pay. In 1968, the Conciliation and Arbitration Commission ruled that Indigenous workers in the pastoral industry should be paid the same as other workers. This victory didn't improve the lives of these workers, though, because many employers claimed they couldn't afford to pay the same wages to Indigenous and non-Indigenous people. In truth, many small operators probably could not have afforded to do so. In the upheaval that followed, thousands of Aboriginal people were fired from their jobs and families had to leave the station properties they had lived on for generations.

The Aboriginal Land Commission, established in 1972, purchased pastoral leases for resident or nearby Aboriginal groups. These were the people who had been marginalised by those white pastoralists who refused to pay equal wages to their Aboriginal workers.

When their stake in the industry dramatically increased, Aboriginal pastoralists found that these small holdings could only support an owner-manager and their family. Agribusiness on a much wider scale, or involving more diverse and profitable uses of land, could economically support communities of several hundred Aboriginal people. Today, Indigenous people own and manage huge properties and mix their traditional culture with modern business and farming and grazing practices.

In the late 1960s and 1970s, it became clear that the Commonwealth Government had to invest in desperately needed infrastructure for Indigenous communities. It also had to stop corrupt or poorly informed Aboriginal Affairs officials in the states and territories from managing these communities and controlling people's lives.

Also at this time, missionaries were asked to leave the reserves, and reserve superintendents were replaced by community councils. People's jobs managing cattle, and in sawmills, bakeries, butcheries, on farms and in cottage industries on the missions, disappeared. These businesses had been slowly run down, or simply closed down overnight.

Many families fled from the reserves during the 1960s and 1970s to look for work in larger population centres. However, Aboriginal people had been largely excluded from educational training, apprenticeships and employment. This led to a rapidly growing Indigenous underclass in the towns and cities, where people found it hard to get jobs and accommodation.

Aboriginal communities, in urban areas such as Redfern in inner Sydney and in Sydney's western suburbs, were growing quickly as people moved from the rural areas. New communities were also springing up, such as in Inala in Brisbane. Aboriginal organisations were established at this time to service these highly disadvantaged people.

Young doctors and lawyers who supported Aboriginal rights volunteered to work in the new cooperatives that opened in shopfronts to provide urgently needed services. The model of 'community-controlled' Aboriginal medical and legal services quickly spread across the country. It was a form of popular Aboriginal governance that empowered Aboriginal communities in their dealings with governments and with neighbouring non-Indigenous populations.

Indigenous communities are extremely diverse. Broadly speaking, Aboriginal and Torres Strait Islander people today live in three different types of communities. There are 'urban' Indigenous people who live in the larger cities and towns, although many have come from rural and remote areas to live in towns and cities. This group makes up the largest percentage of the Indigenous population in Australia.

Then there are those who live in small towns and settlements that were established during the 'protection and segregation' era. During that period they were run as Aboriginal reserves, missions or outposts. These communities are usually made up of the descendants of many different Indigenous clan groups, who were forcibly removed from their traditional lands. Over time, Indigenous people living in these communities have been able to gain more control over their lives through campaigns for land rights and political empowerment.

Lastly, there are those Indigenous people who live on their own ancestral lands, usually in remote parts of Australia. Many Aboriginal and Torres Strait Islander people live and move across these three different types of communities, and have family and kinship connections across all three.

The cultural practices of Indigenous Australians in the cities, towns, communities and remote regions vary greatly. They are grounded in different cultures, histories and socio-political conditions.

The notion of community arose out of the administration of Indigenous peoples in remote and rural areas. In Australia today, Indigenous communities are villages where people live and work. Some remote communities are also administrative centres for Indigenous groups who live in homeland centres, and for highly mobile populations. Many originated as missions and government settlements and have been redesigned by Indigenous communities since the 1970s to maintain culture and possession of land. The aim is to survive as distinctive social and cultural entities.

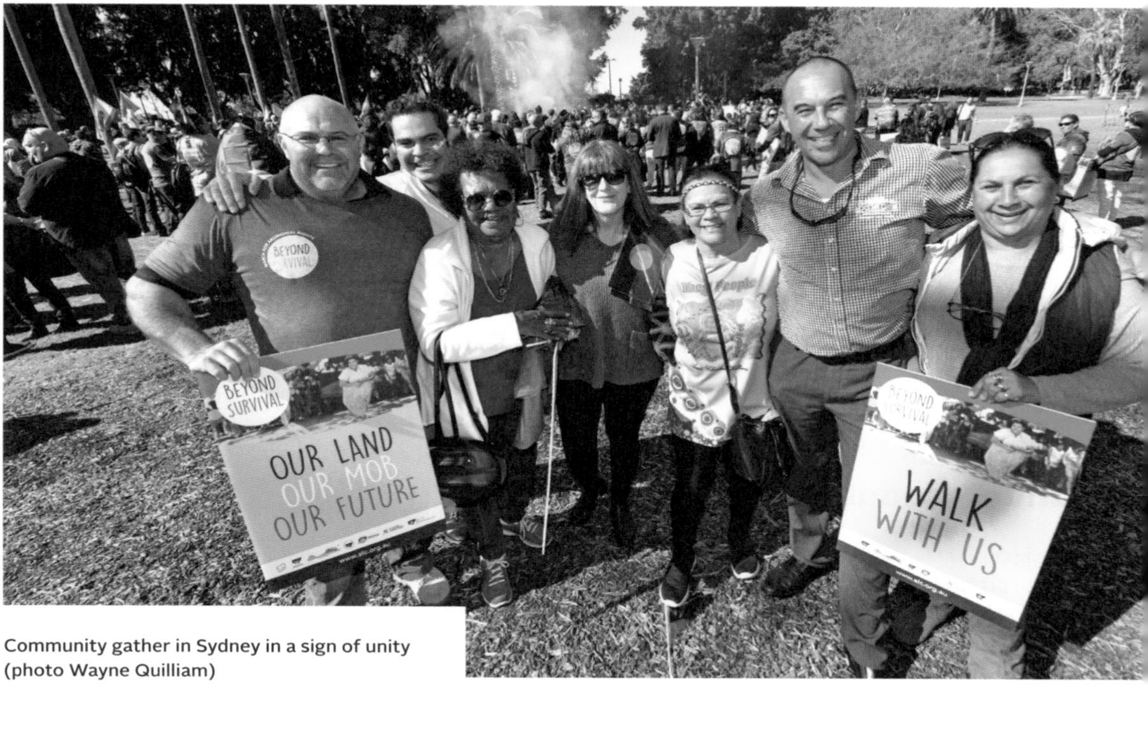

Community gather in Sydney in a sign of unity (photo Wayne Quilliam)

In many remote areas and a few urban and rural areas, precolonial traditions have survived. Many are being revitalised.

Family life is a fundamental aspect of any society, and particularly for First Australians. Colonisation has unfortunately destroyed the old clan systems in many parts of the country. The practice of forcibly removing children from their families to 'assimilate' them as domestic and field labourers has also caused damage to Aboriginal family life that continues today. While strong ties to family often – thankfully – remain, in many areas the kinship systems and the ways that people connect with extended family and 'tribes' have changed dramatically. Chapter 4 on kinship explains some of these traditions and the changes that followed the cessation of Aboriginal societies, as they were forced from their land with heavy losses of life.

Aboriginal and Torres Strait Islander languages, music and performance traditions are also becoming more endangered each year. Events such as the Barunga and Garma festivals have proved very effective in encouraging people to maintain these traditions. Chapter 3 on language and chapter 7 on performance explain more about these aspects of Aboriginal and Torres Strait Islander cultures.

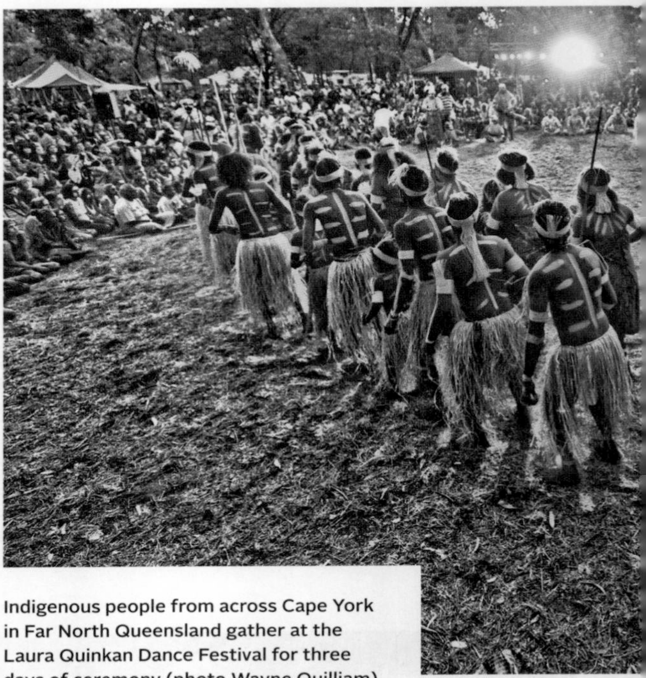

Indigenous people from across Cape York in Far North Queensland gather at the Laura Quinkan Dance Festival for three days of ceremony (photo Wayne Quilliam)

Religious life and rituals continue

Religious life is another area that has been profoundly affected by colonisation. But rituals continue and many have been revived. The idea of the sacred is a strong organising principle, and this is pronounced when people have access to their traditional lands and the important sites where their ancestors are said to remain in the land.

Today, Aboriginal and Torres Strait Islander people around Australia still follow various traditions and carry out important rites and rituals that mark the sacred in everyday life. Welcome to Country rituals for visitors, and some of the rituals of funerals, are good examples. By performing rituals, people bring their sacred spiritual beliefs and traditions into their daily lives. This is the way that Aboriginal and Torres Strait Islander religious life is practised.

A powerful feature of Aboriginal life is the regard that is held for ancestors and supernatural beings that played a part in the creation of the world during a time

that anthropologists call 'the Dreaming' or 'the Dreamtime'. There are terms in Indigenous languages for the sacred world. One such word in some Central Desert languages is Tjukurrpa, which is also spelt Tjukuṟpa or Jukurrpa in some Central Desert languages.

These great spiritual beings are recorded in rock art and are still celebrated in songs and ceremonies today. Some of them travelled, and their sacred travels and the stories that record them are expressed in song series, often called 'songlines', a term introduced by the British writer Bruce Chatwin. The spiritual ancestors, revered as the 'Old People', are sources of great power.

Sometimes this power is dangerous and must be mediated by the Elders, who guide visitors through the landscape where the Old People live in spirit. Because the sacred past resonates in particular places, Indigenous Owners follow traditions that will give safe passage to visitors. That is why the custodians will carry out smoking or water blessing rituals. These rites of mediation are often called 'Welcome to Country' ceremonies. In many places, Elders introduce visitors to the ancestors, because driving or walking to a place where they live eternally without the permission of Traditional Owners can invite their anger.

Traditional Owners perform welcome ceremonies in many different ways. Some groups light smoky fires with wet eucalyptus or paperbark leaves, so that the smoke wraps around the visitors and makes them one with the place. Another type of welcome ceremony involves throwing water on visitors; another involves wiping the sweat of an Elder on the visitor's face so that the visitor will smell like the Traditional Owner.

One rite observed everywhere is the taboo on saying the names of someone who has died recently. Instead, you refer to the deceased with a substitute name, and also, use the substitute name for everyone else with the same name as the deceased. In the deserts, the terms used are Kumanjayi and Kunmanara; Birrinjymal is the word in Arnhem Land in the Gupapuyŋu language; in western Cape York, Tayipity is used; and there are similar terms elsewhere. The deceased are remembered in various ways – with special words, in designs and visual art, funerary objects, songs and dances.

Respect for the spiritual Old People and ancestral beings is strong throughout the cultures of the First Australians. The idea of

Old People corresponds to the perception of stars as being representations of the past. The Old People are encountered in the landscape, just as we see stars when we gaze at the night sky. We know that stars are what can be seen now of some cataclysmic event in the universe many thousands of light years ago. That is, the light of the explosion emanates through time and space, and is visible to our eyes in the present. Likewise, Aboriginal people perceive the spiritual presence of Elders in the landscape as something that has come through time since the ancestor died.

The influence of the ancestors is felt in the Indigenous knowledge systems that tell us about how the world works and how humans should live together and in the world. The ancestors created kinship systems, laws for the ownership of land, sacred sites, and systems of relationship between people and the natural world. All of these are reflected in a variety of ways across Aboriginal and Torres Strait Islander cultures. Some of the different ways are explained in chapter 4 on kinship. Kinship and descent are the main structuring forces that bring people together into clans and 'tribal' groups and customary identities.

Most Aboriginal and Torres Strait Islander people will be required to assert their identity and sometimes to prove that identity. Because of legal and social complexities, many choose to announce themselves by customary or language identities, such as Iman (which I do, as my grandfather was born into the Iman-speaking people in eastern central Queensland). They may also speak of their 'mob' or clan name.

The current legal definition for an Aboriginal or Torres Strait Islander is based on the 1981 parliamentary *Report on a Review of the Administration of the Working Definition of Aboriginal and Torres Strait Islanders*. It is a three-part definition based on (1) descent, (2) self-identification and (3) community recognition. This definition has since been adopted by various federal and state departments.

Debates over the legal wording for an Indigenous Australian rage on. Yet, Aboriginal and Torres Strait Islander people themselves find certainty in following their own family lines or genealogical connections. Stan Grant is a Wiradjuri man from Griffith in New South Wales. His book *On Identity* explains how the idea of 'kinship' is in fact universal for all humans:

Put two or more of us together and it is the first question asked: 'Where are you from, who are your people?' It is genealogy, but it is more than that. It is survival. We all do this in our own way – people everywhere. It is the family crest, the clan's tartan, a sepia-tinged photograph, a convict ship's manifest, a long-dead soldier's pocketbook, the tattooed wrists of the death camps – tangible proof, because we so need it.

Gender identities

Gender identities are also important in the Indigenous world. For example, in the deserts and parts of the Kimberley region, there are women's societies where widows live together. In some cases, the women stop speaking to each other, instead communicating in hand sign language to be used only by widows. Men's ritual groups are similarly rule-bound. Men in these places often have martial arts traditions involving heavy clubs.

Gender roles across Indigenous Australia can also be significantly different from Anglo-Australian practices. In her book *Aboriginal Woman: Sacred and Profane* (1939), Phyllis M. Kaberry writes about her time living in the Forrest River Mission, later known as Oombulgurri (but no longer exists), in the Kimberley between 1935 and 1936. She depicted strong independent women with their own rituals, beliefs and traditions that were the privilege of women. More recent books include Diane Bell's *Daughters of the Dreaming* (1983), which describes a women's society in the area around Tennant Creek, and *Making Aboriginal Men and Music in Central Australia* (2015) by Åse Ottoson, a fascinating account of Aboriginal men in Alice Springs whose manhood is shaped by their love of country, rock and reggae music.

Indigenous LGBTQIA+ cultural life

Now that same-sex marriage is legal, young Indigenous people have felt encouraged to claim their gender and sexual identities, whether gay, bisexual, trans or other. Their important cultural contributions are being recognised and they are flourishing. I have asked some young people who participate

Sistergirl leader, Crystal Johnson (seated), with fellow yimpininnis and allies promoting HIV awareness, Tiwi Islands, 2005

in LGBTQIA+ Indigenous cultural events and happenings – irrespective of their identities – to contribute to this chapter.

But first, it is important to include some history of the fight by LGBTQIA+ people for their rights, because their human rights have only very recently been recognised at law.

The first Pride march or parade to be held in Australia was on 28 June 1970, a year after the Stonewall Riots in New York, which took place in 1969 when, fed up with constant police violence, gay people at the Stonewall Inn in Greenwich Village fought back, and five days of riots ensued, inciting a global movement.[19]

Homosexuality was still illegal in Australia in 1978 when a brave group of gay men and lesbian women organised a street festival to celebrate gay rights. They are remembered as the 78ers and are honoured for their role in fighting for the rights of gay and lesbian people in Australia. The organisers called themselves the Gay Solidarity Group, and after a week of events, on Saturday 24 June 1978, held the first Mardi Gras Street festival. Their aim was to decriminalise homosexuality, and they were also planning the 4th National Homosexual Conference.

Two Indigenous people were among the 78ers – Annie Pratten and Darug man Chris Bourke (deceased) – and Indigenous people have become more visible in the subsequent Pride marches now held annually (except during COVID-19 restrictions) across the country. The first featured Indigenous contingent in the Sydney Mardi Gras was in 1998.

This first Sydney Mardi Gras was a sedate affair, compared to the recent parades that last for hours with float after float of spectacular displays, dancing and music processing down Oxford Street to the noisy adoration of, as 2019 figures attest, half a million people from around Australia and the world. But the night of Saturday 24June 1978 ended in violence, and although the NSW Police have since issued an apology for their behaviour and violence, the horror of the police attack on the festival attendees has not been forgotten. On that night, several hundred gay and lesbian people and their supporters, 'some in fancy dress and some simply rugged up against the cold – gathered at Taylor Square and followed a truck with a small music and sound system down Oxford Street to Hyde Park.' The Sydney Gay and Lesbian Mardi Gras 1978–2020 Timeline is an excellent resource and its account of what happened that night in Sydney, although brief, resonates still, because it inspired thousands to join the 78ers and protest at the discrimination against gay and lesbian people. At the 2019 AGM of the Sydney Gay and Lesbian Mardi Gras (SGLMG), a resolution was passed giving the 78ers Lifetime Membership.

The Mardi Gras in Sydney has evolved since those events in 1978 to become a world-renowned celebration of queerness and it has grown from one night of the grand parade to events held across several weeks. The official title is the Sydney Gay and Lesbian Mardi Gras and for those unable to join in person, the parade is broadcast live on SBS (the Special Broadcasting Service).[20]

In 1982, Narrandera man Roger McKay marched alone in the parade, wearing the Aboriginal flag. This significant moment is widely acknowledged as the first time the Aboriginal flag appeared in the parade.

'He was determined to make the point that, no matter how much Oxford Street was seen as the gay "Golden Mile", it was still on Aboriginal land.' (Colin Clewes, Gay in the 80s)

'The first person to carry the Aboriginal flag up the guts of Oxford Street was Roger McKay from the Sandhills of Narrandera.' (Esther Montgomery, Gay in the 80s)

The parade has also been a means of contesting history-making for the LGBTQIA+ community. Before the 1988 Mardi Gras, a debate over how to acknowledge the bicentenary was resolved by featuring Malcolm Cole, an Indigenous gay man, dressed as Captain Cook. His version of Captain Cook was later commemorated in an exhibition along with Indigenous drag queens dressed as superheroes, and portraits of the well-known Noel Tovey and Raymond Blanco.

In 2019, First Nations Rainbow helped the SGLMG win WorldPride, an international event promoting LGBTQIA+ rights, cultures and issues through sporting events, festivals, conferences, a parade and other cultural events. They were Graham Simms, Gadigal; Ben Graetz, Iwaidja, Malak Malak and Badu Islander; and Joseph Cardona, Iwaidja, Malak Malak and Badu Islander.

Members of the worldwide InterPride network of Pride organisations voted between Sydney, Montreal and Houston as the host city for WorldPride 2023. Sydney won with 60 per cent of the vote. The biennial WorldPride festival will be held over February and March to coincide with the 2023 Sydney Gay and Lesbian Mardi Gras. First Nations Rainbow helped to make the announcement, with a Gadigal man who attended the Athens conference congratulating Australia on its unprecedented win in a video on Twitter: twitter.com/sydneymardigras/status/1185857309479710720

The 78ers inspired a nationwide movement. As the largest Pride event in the Asia-Pacific region, the first parade in 1978 inspired Pride marches throughout Australia, which are held annually. Today the Australian Pride Network is the umbrella organisation for LGBTQIA+ festivals and events for the entire community to celebrate, reflect and promote their cultures and human rights. Across Australia, a diverse selection of festivals and events takes place throughout the year. Events are listed on the Australian Pride Network by state and territory. The Sydney Gay and Lesbian Mardi Gras website also lists all events. The diversity and contributions of First peoples members of the LGBTQIA+ communities are widely acknowledged and respected.

Sydney's Mardi Gras by Luke Pearson

The first Mardi Gras, held on 24 June 1978, in Sydney was an add-on to a demonstration marking the anniversary of the Stonewall riots in New York in 1969. The parade held that night led to an excessive police response in the form of violent arrests, and eventually a riot between police and those participating in the march at Kings Cross. It is believed that a number of Indigenous people were involved in this violent clash, both as participants in the parade and as bystanders who joined in to support the protesters.

While there has been a long history of Indigenous LGBTQIA+ participation in Mardi

Miss First Nation Australia 2018 contestants in the Miss Photogenic shoot at Mrs Macquarie's Chair, Sydney. From left: Shaniqua, Timberlina, Zodiac, MadB, Bailey Legal, Felicia Foxx, Lasey Dunaman.

Gras, it was not until 2017 that an Indigenous float led the parade. Sydney's Mardi Gras has since become a month-long series of events with significant Indigenous inclusion, including Koori Gras, an Indigenous-led event involving performances and exhibitions. There is also an online timeline showcasing the history of Indigenous involvement in the Sydney Mardi Gras parade at tiki-toki.com.

Indigenous LGBTQIA+ culture and lifestyle by Jessie Lloyd

Lesbian, gay, bisexual transgender, queer, intersex, asexual and pansexual people have always been a part of the Aboriginal and Torres Strait Islander community. But due to various religious or cultural practices in some communities, many people are often marginalised or remain 'in the closet'. As a result people migrated to capital cities to connect with other LGBTQIA+ groups or began working in queer-friendly spaces. Indigenous queer folk participate in cultural events such as drag shows, dance and performance works, and pride marches across the country, incorporating their unique cultural identity and themes into the queer space.

There are Indigenous communities that are more open and supportive of LGBTQIA+ members such as Tiwi Island, which has a high percentage of transgender people known as 'Sistergirls'. *Top End Wedding* (2019), starring Miranda Tapsell, features some of the Sistergirls in the film. In other regional places like Broome in Western Australia, community diversity is easily accepted from generations of intermarriage between Aboriginal, Japanese, Malay and Chinese people. Mikka Polina of Broome in Western Australia says, 'Being gay in the Kimberley and Broome is amazing ... You are first accepted as a family member and a community member and ... being gay is not an issue.'

Indigenous LGBTQIA+ people have always had a strong online presence, with Black Rainbow on Twitter and Beautiful, Talented & Deadly on Facebook. There is also the radio program *Rainbow KINection* on Noongar Radio. Issues such as sexual health, suicide or homelessness are the driving factors behind queer programs and support networks.

Melbourne's LGBTQIA+ MIDSUMMA by Mark Nannup and Todd Fernando

Melbourne's LGBTIQA+ MIDSUMMA Festival was established in 1988 after local LGBTIQA+ people became tired of heading to Sydney for the Mardi Gras.

Since 1988, Aboriginal and Torres Strait Islander people have taken part in the festival but 2017 was the first year that the festival was led by Aboriginal and Torres Strait Islander people down Fitzroy Street in St Kilda, with a smoking ceremony from local Traditional Owners, the Boon Wurrung people. It was a huge success and over sixty people turned up to celebrate this special occasion.

MIDSUMMA's organisers now make sure Indigenous people continue to be a part of this festival by working very closely with the Aboriginal and Torres Strait Islander community to make their voices present within it.

Also in 2017, the Victorian NAIDOC Committee decided to incorporate an LGBTIQA+ night in the calendar, to showcase inclusivity within our community. This night came to be because of all the hard work and determination of a group called OutBlack, which has been running the Aboriginal and Torres Straight LGBTIQA+ Pride Night for the last thirty years in Victoria.

Accept and empower our LGBTQIA+ brothers and sisters by Ruby Langton-Batty

A young Aboriginal LGBTQIA+ friend of mine told me that he doesn't think homophobia is a big issue within the Aboriginal community. Unfortunately, there is still some homophobia within the Aboriginal community. I have seen this kind of discrimination firsthand, and I have seen the harm it does. According to the National LGBTI Health Alliance, the Indigenous LGBTQIA+ community 'are an invisible minority ... and there are currently no protocols for identifying them in the suicide and self-harm statistics', but it is understood they are more vulnerable to risk of suicide than other minority populations. I can barely imagine how painful and exhausting it must be to battle daily against both racism and homophobia. We must all stand up against homophobia and racism, and ensure that our LGBTQIA+ brothers and sisters are treated with respect and receive the same rights as any other Australian.

Tiwi Islander Crystal Love-Johnson is the first Indigenous trans person in the Northern Territory to come out as 'Sistergirl' and to live a trans life in a modern way. She has faced incredible hardship and adversity but has fought for her rights and demanded to be treated with respect. She is the first trans person to be elected to a local government in Australia, becoming a member of the Tiwi Shire Council in 2012.

Actor, writer and musician Steven Oliver, of *Black Comedy* fame, makes light of being a gay Aboriginal man in Australia in his brilliant song 'Minority within a Minority'. His lyrics always reduce his audience to tears of laughter. You can watch the song on YouTube. Oliver's work epitomises how the Aboriginal and Torres Strait Islander LGBTIA+ community copes with, and fights against, homophobia and racism: with humour.

TJay 'Lasey Dunaman' and Dallas 'Nova Gina' are the Indigenous drag duo the Dreamtime Divas. These prolific performers travel far and wide around Australia, sharing positivity and acceptance of diversity. One of their stated aims, as they explain on their Facebook page, is to 'raise awareness for youth depression and teen suicide [as a result of] homophobia, violence and bullying'. I have a deep admiration for all drag queens, and especially Black queens, because they are like warriors for love and peace. Their beautiful, glamorous, bedazzling and hilarious resistance is a barrier against all forms of oppression. Even the most complacent and backward audience members can't help but crack a smile.

I went to the Miss First Nation pageant (aka the 'Olympics for Aboriginal drag queens') for the first time in 2017 at the Imperial Hotel in Sydney. The contestants were Bailey Legal, Felicia Foxx, Lasey Dunaman, MadB, Timberlina, Zodiac and Shaniqua. The performances were epic and the competition was fierce. More than anything, it was a powerful explosion of joy. It is incredibly liberating to be in a space where everyone feels safe to truly be themselves, no matter who they are.

It was in this small corner of the world where I glimpsed our possible future. In that future, no one experiences hatred or violence because of who they are. All people and expressions are celebrated. Instead of 'freedom of speech', there is 'freedom of being'. That night, Lasey Dunaman was crowned Miss First Nation Australia.

Our traditions and cultures deserve respect

There are hundreds of Indigenous cultures with many customs specific to those cultures and others that are continent-wide, such as managing fire with fire. Many customs, such as ceremonial practices and rituals, vary greatly across the country. We speak many languages; we are cultural beings. This is the case for humanity universally. We are no less 'cultural' for moving in and out of different cultures.

The Aboriginal and Torres Strait Islander cultures offer unique ways to look at the world. They have been mostly invisible throughout Australian history – misunderstood, denied, vilified and lied about. The price our people have paid for being Aboriginal is not only a tragic and unwarranted loss of life. The frontier deaths,

Aunty Pam feels the love and respect from the young women of our community (photo Wayne Quilliam)

the discrimination and marginalisation, and the stigmatisation are part of the burden that our cultures carry. What is encouraging, though, is the extraordinary resilience of First Australians to maintain and preserve our cultures and tell the world about them.

The increasing interest of students, scholars and historians and others who have investigated our traditions tells us that there are people who prefer the facts over the mythologies. The mythology about First Australians is that we are trapped in the imaginary 'Stone Age' and incapable of change. The facts show otherwise. First Australians have always been innovators, finding ways to create and develop the longest living cultures on the planet throughout tumultuous periods of climate change, radically altered environments, colonisation and more than a century of extreme violence and dispossession. In spite of all of this, traditions that began when our ancestors started to arrive here at least 65,000 years ago continue and are relevant today. There is a great deal to learn about our cultures. This brief chapter explores only a few aspects to show the very different but no less valuable ways of knowing and being in the world of the First Australians.

3
LANGUAGE

More than 600 distinct language dialects and at least 250 languages were spoken across the continent before colonisation. Many of these languages were completely different from one another, and the majority of people spoke more than one language.

There is a strong cultural association between language and land. This means that when the Indigenous people lost their land, in many cases they also lost their language. Australia is one of the world's hotspots for language loss. Many Indigenous languages are no longer spoken; for some languages, only a few words are remembered. Since colonisation, governments and organisations, such as the churches that ran the missions, banned or discouraged Indigenous people from speaking their languages. So it is remarkable that 120 of those languages are still spoken.

Aboriginal languages strengthen the connections people have with their land, their culture and identity. This is one of the reasons why it is important to preserve, record and learn them. The level of information that is available about Indigenous languages varies greatly across the country. Some languages are well supported with stories, dictionaries and multimedia resources in the language. In the case of many others, very little is known about them. Many Indigenous languages are at risk of disappearing as the remaining speakers pass away.

The First peoples are working with linguists and other interested groups to record and revive their languages. They are also teaching them to young people in schools and communities. Some projects that record and share Indigenous knowledge also preserve the language. For example, projects to collect information about Indigenous weather knowledge also preserve the language of weather knowledge, including the words for seasons, weather phenomena and seasonal indicators such as flowering plants.

While it is possible to learn about Aboriginal and Torres Strait Islander languages, it is much more difficult to learn to speak them. They are different from English in every way – in their pronunciation, vocabulary and sentence structures.

William (Bill) Wentworth tape recording Aboriginal words and songs with four Elders from Maree region, Western Australia (image courtesy of AIATSIS, item WENTWORTH.B03.CS-000168946)

Thanks to an innovative policy in New South Wales, Aboriginal languages have a greater chance of surviving there than elsewhere in Australia. In 2017, the New South Wales Government introduced a law to protect the Aboriginal languages within the state's boundaries. The *Aboriginal Languages Act 2017* is the first legislation in Australia to acknowledge the significance of First languages.

This Act seeks to promote, reawaken, nurture and grow Aboriginal languages across New South Wales. It has three parts:

- a preamble that acknowledges the importance of Aboriginal languages. It also recognises the importance of reawakening, nurturing and growing Aboriginal languages and Aboriginal custodianship of languages
- establishment of an Aboriginal Languages Trust to resource local language activities, among other functions
- a five-year Strategic Plan to guide investment and activities in language revival in New South Wales.

The New South Wales Aboriginal Languages Act is the strongest legal expression yet of our right to speak our languages. This right is expressed in the UN Declaration on the Rights of Indigenous Peoples.

One remarkable example of Indigenous language revitalisation has been initiated for the Wiradjuri language, which is spoken in the heartland of Wiradjuri Country around Orange, Parkes and Forbes in the central west of New South Wales. Dedicated Wiradjuri language workers and teachers are introducing their language to students in the state school system, especially in Sydney. St Andrew's Cathedral School in Sydney also has a program for Aboriginal and Torres Strait Islander primary students. The children taking part in this program, which is called Gawura, start Wiradjuri lessons in kindergarten. The other primary school students at St Andrew's start learning Wiradjuri from Year 3.

This revitalisation strongly contrasts with the belief held in the nineteenth and twentieth century by many linguists and anthropologists. They claimed that our languages and cultures would become extinct.

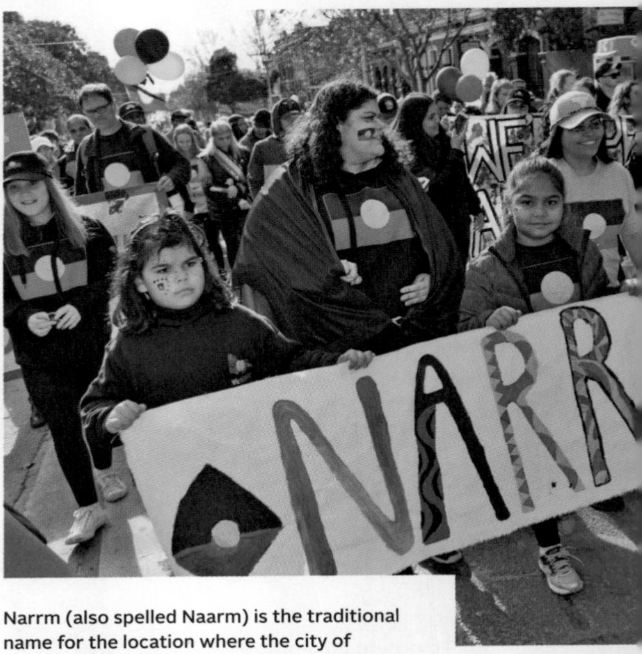

Narrm (also spelled Naarm) is the traditional name for the location where the city of Melbourne is built (photo Wayne Quilliam)

Aboriginal English

Many people assume that speakers of Aboriginal English have not learnt Standard English very well and so they are poor speakers of English. This is not the case: Aboriginal English is a dialect of Standard English in its own right. Dr Diane Eades from the University of New England points out that 'Aboriginal people in areas where there was no pidgin language made English into an Aboriginal English by bringing into it accents, grammar and ways of speaking from their traditional languages'.

Speakers of Aboriginal English can also learn Standard English and switch between the two, depending on the situation. Among other Aboriginal people, instead of saying, 'You are very well dressed', I would say, 'You too flash' or 'You lookin' deadly'.

In some communities around the country, Aboriginal English and several Kriols have replaced the original Indigenous languages, or are spoken in addition to those languages.

Kriol is a language that has developed from a pidgin version of English to become the main language. According to an estimate from the 2011 census, Kriol is spoken across much of northern Australia by around 4000 people. However, the number of speakers is probably higher than that.

Linguist Dr Greg Dickson wrote in *The Conversation* in April 2016 that 'Linguists put the number of Kriol speakers closer to 20,000, knowing that census data struggles to accurately capture high levels of multilingualism in remote Aboriginal communities'. He also tells us: 'Creole, as a linguistic term, is a type of language typically born out of abrupt and often brutal colonisation processes. Creoles are

generally based on the dominant language of the colonisers.'

There are two Kriols that have large numbers of speakers. One is spoken in the savannah regions of northern Australia. The other is spoken in the Torres Strait Islands, where people also speak two Indigenous languages of the Torres Strait and their dialects.

The languages of the Torres Strait Islands

The eastern languages of the Torres Strait Islands are not related to the Aboriginal or, properly speaking, the Australian languages of the mainland, while the western and central languages are.

A handy summary of the languages of the Torres Strait Islands is provided by the State Library of Queensland. It shows the great complexity of language in just one region of northern Australia.

There are two traditional languages of the Torres Strait Islands, Meriam Mir and Kala Lagaw Ya.

Meriam Mir *(also written as Miriam Mer) is the language of the Eastern Islands of the Torres Strait. Linguistically, it is connected to the Papuan languages of the Austronesian family of languages. There are two regional dialects:*

- ***Mer dialect*** *– Mer (Murray), Waier, Dauar.*
- ***Erub dialect*** *– Erub (Darnley) and Ugar (Stephen).*

Kala Lagaw Ya *(also written as Kalaw Lagaw Ya) is the traditional language owned by the Western and Central islands of the Torres Strait. It is linguistically connected to the Aboriginal languages of the Australian mainland and has four distinct regional dialects derived from this language:*

- ***Mabuyag*** *– The dialect of Mabuiag, Badu and St Paul's Village.*
- ***Kalaw Kawaw Ya*** *– The dialect of the top western islands of Saibai, Dauan and Malu Ki'ai.*
- ***Kawrareg*** *– The dialect of the south-western islands of Kubin, Kaiwalagal, Muralag (Prince of Wales), Nurupai (Horn), Giralag (Friday), Waiben (Thursday Island), Keriri (Hammond), Maurura (Wednesday), Moa (Banks). It is also known as Kawalgau Ya.*
- ***Kulkalgau Ya*** *– The dialect of the central islands of Aurid (Aureed), Damut (Dalrymple), Iama (Yam or Turtle-backed), Masig (Yorke), Mauar (Rennel), Naghir (Mt Earnest), Poruma (Coconut) and Warraber (Sue).*

The dialects are determined geographically and developed over time with influences by traditional trade, visits, inter-marriage and kinship ties.

Torres Strait Creole

The contact with missionaries and others since the 1800s has led to the development of Torres Strait Creole; it has developed from a Pidgin and now has its own distinctive sound system, grammar, vocabulary, usage and meaning. Torres Strait Creole (also known as Ailan Tok or Yumplatok) is spoken by most Torres Strait Islanders and is a mixture of Standard Australian English and traditional languages. It is an English-based creole; however, each island has [its] own version of creole.[21]

This map attempts to represent the language, social or nation groups of Aboriginal Australia. It shows only the general locations of larger groupings of people which may include clans, dialects or individual languages in a group. It used published resources from the eighteenth century-1994 and is not intended to be exact, nor the boundaries fixed. It is not suitable for native title or other land claims. David R Horton (creator), © AIATSIS, 1996. No reproduction without permission. To purchase a print version visit: https://shop.aiatsis.gov.au/

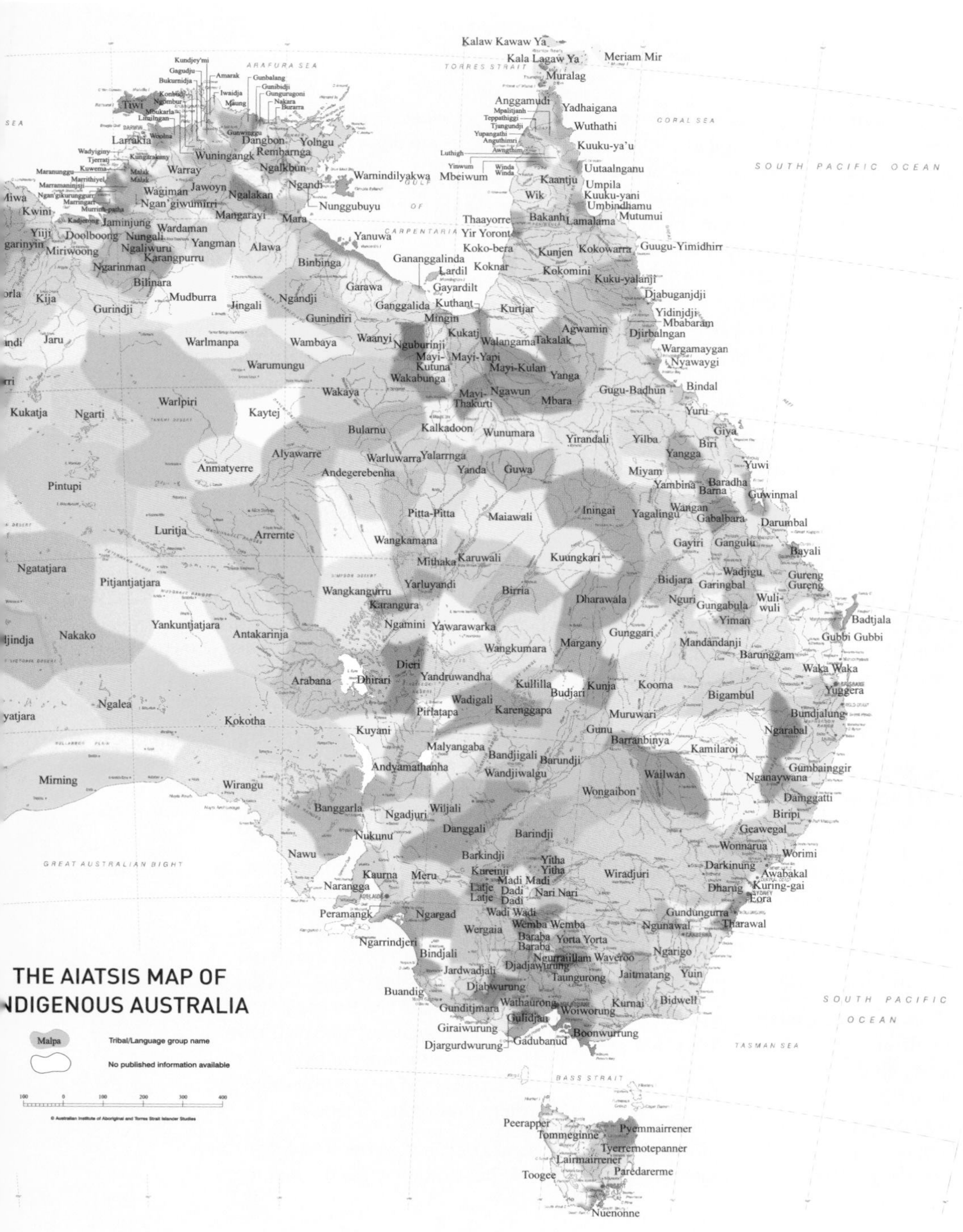

THE AIATSIS MAP OF INDIGENOUS AUSTRALIA

By learning another language, we begin to understand the role of language in our lives. The vocabulary of another language, or the words that make it up, gives us an insight into how other people see the world. Some languages have many terms for rain, for example, because the people live where rain is common. It comes as deluges or drizzles, storms or raindrops. Others have many terms for snow because the people who speak them live in environments that are subject to snowfall for much of the year.

How we speak about something using the words in our language determines a great deal about how we think about it. In many ways, our perception of the world is defined by language. When we lose a language, or our mother tongue is lost to us and replaced by a dominant language such as English, we lose not just the language but all the special meanings that language held for us. This applies to how we understand our environments and our family, our kinfolk and our inner selves.

In many parts of the Aboriginal world, languages are sacred, as they were given to us by the ancestors. Indeed, languages are owned by those people who can claim a sacred genealogical link to an ancestral speaker of that language. Place, identity and the laws that apply among the people who live on the same area of land are bound together by their language.

The different languages spoken around the country, especially in coastal areas, distinguished the many groups of people who lived there. The social relations of language bring people together under one language-speaking identity. They show them as being different from others who speak other, closely related languages in a web of close and distant kin.

The loss of a mother tongue is a destructive burden for Indigenous peoples who are marginalised minorities. Indigenous people face discrimination on the basis of ethnicity, race, lifestyle, religion and especially language. This is why UNESCO has developed tools to help preserve the world's linguistic diversity. To answer the question of why we should preserve languages, the UNESCO project known as the 'Atlas of the World's Languages in Danger' states: 'Languages are vehicles of our cultures, collective memory and values. They are an essential component of our identities, and a building block of our diversity and living heritage.'

To be free to speak our mother tongues is a human right. This right is expressed in the UN Declaration on the Rights of Indigenous Peoples, at Article 13:

1. Indigenous peoples have the right to revitalize, use, develop and transmit to future generations their histories, languages, oral traditions, philosophies, writing systems and literatures, and to designate and retain their own names for communities, places and persons.

2. States shall take effective measures to ensure that this right is protected and also to ensure that indigenous peoples can understand and be understood in political, legal and administrative proceedings, where necessary through the provision of interpretation or by other appropriate means.

Australia declined to become a signatory to this Declaration when the member states of the UN General Assembly voted on 13 September 2007. By eventually becoming a signatory, Australia has indicated a commitment to uphold the rights contained in it.

The Aboriginal and Torres Strait Islander Social Justice Commissioner Tom Calma released a Social Justice Report in 2009. In chapter 3, 'The perilous state of Indigenous languages in Australia', he points out that it was only in August 2009, for the first time in Australia's history, that the Commonwealth Government launched a strategy for preserving Indigenous languages. Called 'Indigenous Languages – A National Approach 2009', it sets out the government's plan to preserve Indigenous languages through targeted actions. Those actions are:

- increasing information about Indigenous languages in all spheres of Australian life
- improving coordination of language centre activity
- supporting language programs in schools
- undertaking a feasibility study to develop a National Indigenous Languages Centre.

While there is still much work to do to implement Article 13 in Australia, there has been some progress. First Languages Australia has developed essential resources for speakers of our languages, and is rescuing endangered languages and those thought to be extinct. First Languages Australia explains that the human rights of speakers of Australia's First languages are a foundational motivation for their work. In 'Why maintain our languages?', which you can find on the First Languages Australia website, the authors cite chapter 3 of the Social Justice Report 2009: 'As Aboriginal and Torres Strait Islander people we know we have a unique place in this country and we value our languages. They are precious to us, and there is a sense of loss amongst those of us who no longer speak our languages.'

Commissioner Calma explains other benefits of maintaining our languages in some detail in his report. They include promoting resilience, improving health, improving cognitive functioning and increasing employment options. He also presents an economic argument about the costs of losing our languages.

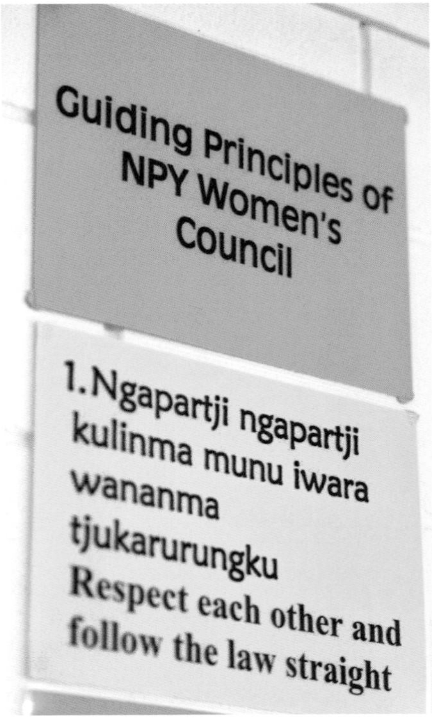

An example of how language is used to convey important values and principles (photo Wayne Quilliam)

THE LANGUAGE WORK OF THE NGANGKA<u>R</u>I TO HEAL

The ngangka<u>r</u>i, the traditional healers of the Pitjantjatjara, Yankunytjatjara and Ngaanyatjarra peoples, have a profound understanding of the meaning and role of their languages. Pitjantjatjara is one of the widely spoken languages in northern South Australia and in the south of the Northern Territory. Some of the neighbouring languages are Yankunytjatjara, Ngaanyatjarra and Luritja.

The women of this region who speak the three dominant languages formed an organisation more than forty years ago to ensure their wellbeing and survival of their cultures. The NPY Women's Council has among its programs the Ngangka<u>r</u>i – Traditional Healers service. Its most innovative project, the Uti Kulintjaku initiative, uses language to strengthen emotional wellbeing. As explained on the council's website, npywc.org.au, uti kulintjaku is a Pitjantjatjara phrase that means 'to think and understand clearly'.

The ngangka<u>r</u>i give young people ways to speak about their feelings in their own language and give their families the language for listening. They do this by providing the words in the languages that describe and name emotional states and states of being, and by doing so in engaging ways. Their tools also give parents the words for understanding the stages in their children's development. Uti Kulintjaku 'works at the interface of knowledge systems and languages to better understand mental health and wellbeing and develops resources to promote this shared bi-cultural understanding more broadly'.

The project is no longer funded but, during its short period of funding support, it brought together:

... ngangka<u>r</u>i, senior A<u>n</u>angu, interpreters, and mental health practitioners in workshops to strengthen communication between A<u>n</u>angu and non-Aboriginal health professionals ... to improve the emotional vocabulary of A<u>n</u>angu children and explain how trauma can affect their behaviour.

The Uti Kulintjaku Project helped 'A<u>n</u>angu address mental health and related issues using their own language and culture, and their knowledge of western mental health'. As explained on the website:

It also strengthens the capacity of local mental health professionals to engage with and communicate more effectively with A<u>n</u>angu people, to 'see through their eyes'.[22]

The Words for Feelings Map is an illustrated poster that is designed to help people to 'find the right words to express different feelings' using words from Pitjantjatjara and Ngaanyatjarra. 'We believe that if people can find the words to express their feelings, then they are better equipped to ask for the help they need.' The map is one item in a set of word tools created by the ngangka<u>r</u>i. Other tools in their kit are posters, magnets and flashcards, children's books such as *Tjulpu and Walpa: Two Children, Two Roads*, and colouring books for meditative practice 'to help improve mental health literacy'. The project also produced the award-winning Kulila! app (*kulila* means 'listen up'). My personal favourite is the set of Uti Kulintjaku magnets. I have them on my refrigerator.

Top: Uti Kulintjaku means 'to think and understand clearly' in Pitjantjatjara. This poster assists the discussion of mental health with 'words for feelings'.

Bottom, left: *Tjulpu and Walpa*, NPY Women's Council 2017, illustration by Katelyn Griffin

Bottom, right: A screenshot of the Uti Kulintjaku Project's dictionary app, designed to help people translate and communicate their feelings

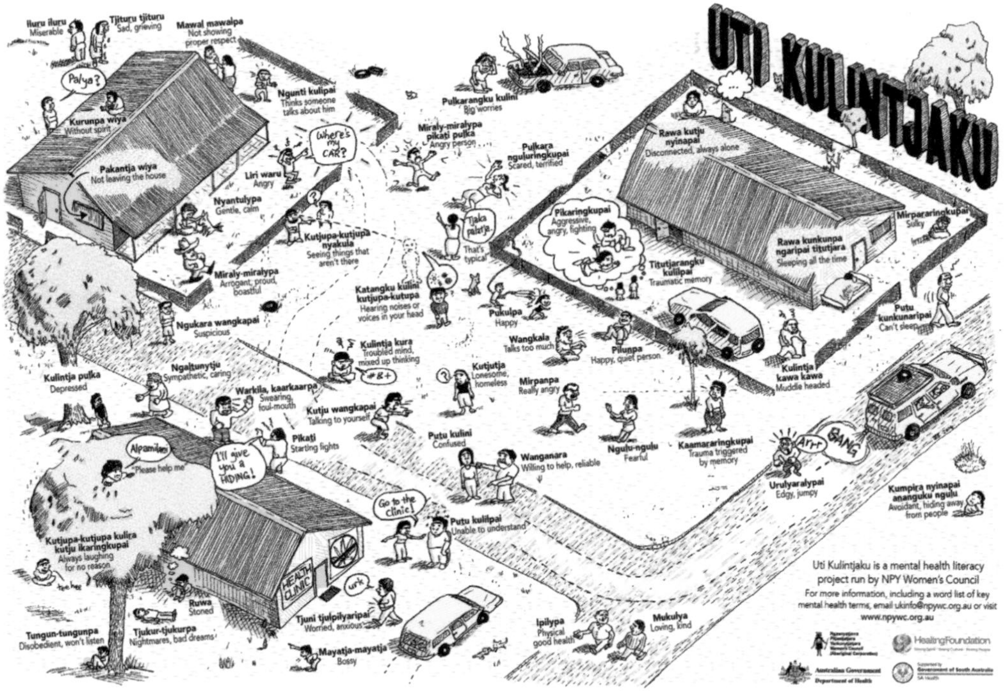

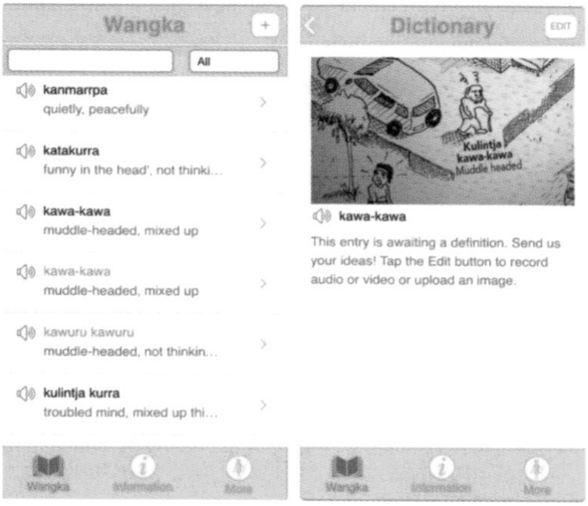

You can watch films made in First languages. In one of my favourite films, *Ten Canoes*, directed by Rolf de Heer and Peter Djigirr and released in 2006, the actors speak entirely in their language, Ganalbiŋu. It is easy to follow as it has some subtitles and is narrated by the awarding-winning actor David Gulpilil.

Ten Canoes is a story of events that took place in the distant past among the Yolŋu peoples of the Arafura wetlands region, in Arnhem Land in the Northern Territory. It involves stolen wives, revenge and war, and, while it is a dark comedy, the storyline is carried by the superb acting of local people. They re-create a Dreaming story within a Dreaming story. It also shows the traditional customs and traditions from one area of Australia.

Many Indigenous musicians sing in both English and their own languages. My favourite band, Yothu Yindi, cut several beautiful tracks in the Gumatj tongue of the Yolŋu matha languages. Their song 'Tribal Voice' is the best example. Several of their most popular hits, such as 'Djäpana: Sunset Dreaming', had fans around the world singing in an Aboriginal language. It is a public ceremonial song in the Manikay style of the Yolŋu musical tradition. Among other things, it is about the sacred sunset. Sunset is the divide between night and day, and is regarded, like dawn, as a sacred event.

The term 'djäpana' refers equally to the yellow colour of clouds at sunset, the particular clans that are linked by the waŋarr (ancestral beings) and their journeys, and other matters. The colour yellow is one emblem of the Gumatj clan, of which Dr Mandawuy Yunupiŋu, the late lead singer of Yothu Yindi, is a famous son. Sunset is when the wind blows through the forest, the leaves rattle, white cockatoos swoop down to their roosts in the branches, and the inflamed sky darkens. It is customary for ceremonies to begin sometime just before sunset; even if the ritual itself is delayed, people gather at this time, waiting for it to begin. Baker Boy (see page 116) is continuing this new tradition of singing popular music in Yolŋu matha, and so too are many other singers. The annual National Aboriginal and Torres Strait Islander Music Awards in Darwin showcase these multilingual singers.

Every time you say the word 'kangaroo' you are speaking an Aboriginal language, Guugu Yimithirr. Captain James Cook wrote down this word at the place called Wabalumbaal, which he named Endeavour River. It was where he moored to undertake repairs on his ship. Cook and his men encountered Guugu Yimithirr speakers, who told him their name for this marsupial that is now on Australia's coat of arms. Each language has its own vocabulary and there are hundreds of words for the animal now called kangaroo. Hundreds of Aboriginal words from other First Australian languages have entered modern Australian English, although some have changed from the original: koala, coo-ee, kookaburra, wallaby, billabong, dingo and wombat are just a few examples.

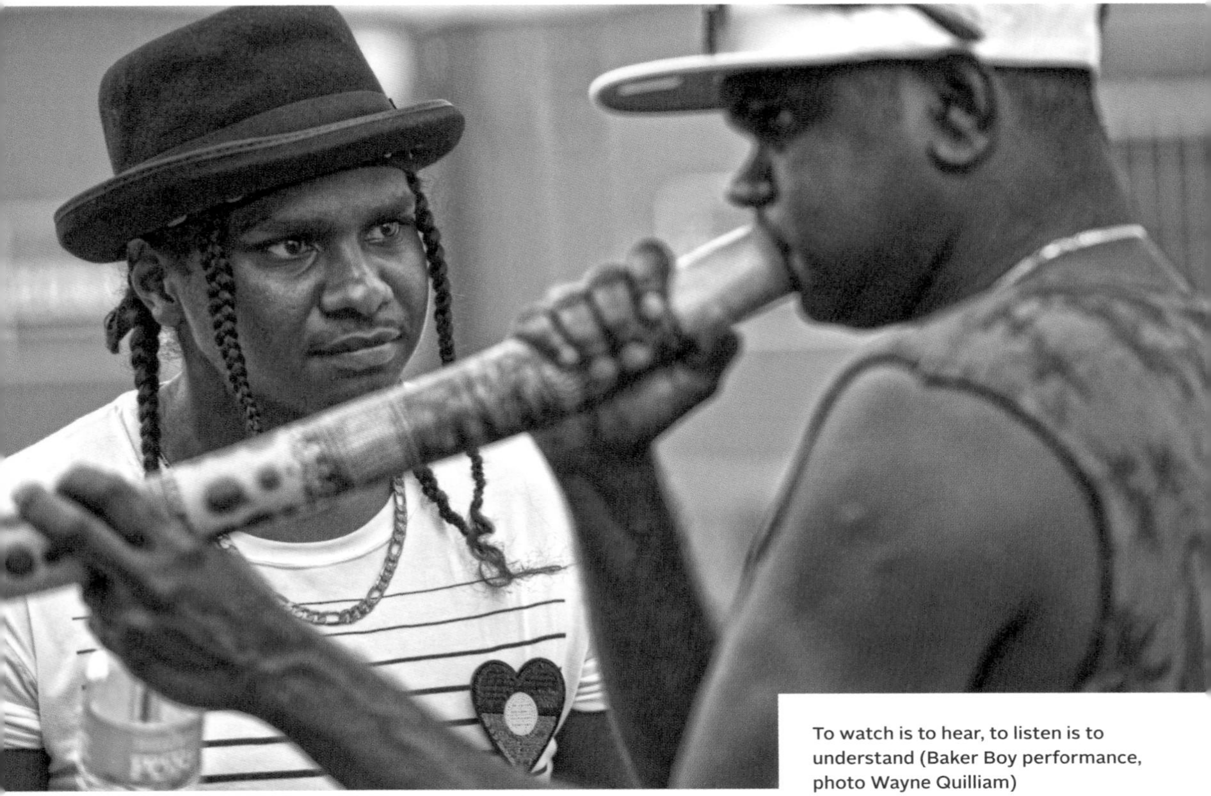

To watch is to hear, to listen is to understand (Baker Boy performance, photo Wayne Quilliam)

4

KINSHIP

The hottest topic in Aboriginal get-togethers is often kinship – how people are related to each other – and determining this by exploring personal histories is regarded as a matter of utmost importance. If a biological kinship link cannot be identified, there are ways to create kinship relationships that are often just as meaningful as close family ties. Many Aboriginal and Torres Strait Islander people follow ancient kinship rules in their everyday relations with others. They believe that these kinship rules are laws left by the sacred ancestors who created the living environment and its people.

Kinship nomenclatures, or the names for kinship status, such as mother, father, etc., and the system of relatedness of each Aboriginal or Torres Strait Islander group are fundamental to a group's identity. A group may be named from a language that was spoken by their immediate or even distant ancestors. Many are named after an English surname that was given to their ancestors who were forced onto reserves. Many Indigenous people in Australia today state their group identity or traditional origins when they introduce themselves. Kinship systems of the Torres Strait Islander peoples are very different from Aboriginal ones. Only Aboriginal kinship systems are discussed here.

Each person is born into a kinship network. It stretches back through the generations, beyond grandparents and great-grandparents into the distant past, and also outwards socially. You may have heard the expression 'He's like a brother to me' or 'She's like a mother to me'. Familial relationships can be created as acts of friendship. These quasi-kin friendship networks have operated throughout human history as people have helped each other and worked together to ensure food and water for all. Aboriginal kinship logic continues to operate in this way, even if the local or regional languages are no longer spoken.

Exclusion from the Australian economy and exploitation for indentured and slave labour created intergenerational poverty for thousands of Indigenous people. It made sense, then, to keep the old traditions of sharing so that no one starved. These traditions have changed, especially in the areas where colonisation impacted first, yet they are still recognisable as Aboriginal kinship and social structures. Helping family and friends in one's social network was, and remains, normal and is often governed by rules in those societies that operated in a more collective fashion, such as tribal and clan-based groups.

All human societies have kinship systems and nomenclature – systems of names – as well as other social structures that bind people together. They vary greatly around the globe. There are several different types of Aboriginal kinship systems operating across Australia. They are far more complex than English or European systems of kinship. Most Aboriginal systems recognise twenty-eight types of kin roles, many more than in the English system of kinship that many Australians use. In the Aboriginal world, everyone is kin, either close or distant. But all relationships, whether or not people are biologically related, are determined by kinship and classification laws. In addition to kinship systems that name kinship roles, there are classifications, such as moieties and 'skin systems'. These classification systems operate together with the kinship system, binding everyone into a world of relatedness and giving them principles of behaviour to live by.

Aboriginal kinship systems are difficult to learn and understand, and it is not expected that outsiders do so. What is important to know is that in all Aboriginal societies, all people and ancestral beings, as well as named and recognised plants and animals, natural features and tracts of land and sea, are part of a structured web of connections that is called kinship.

These systems are governed by rules or laws that prescribe marriage between certain types of kin, and preclude marriage between other types of kin. There are variations to

Aboriginal kinship networks stretch back through generations, and also outwards socially (photo Wayne Quilliam)

these rules that are found to be acceptable, or at least are not considered offensive. There are also ways of referring to people who have married the 'wrong way' or not quite the 'right way'. In many Aboriginal kinship systems, there are also avoidance relationships, especially between mothers-in-law and sons-in-law, who cannot speak to each other. Also, there are rules for showing respect between brothers and sisters and brothers-in-law.

Where the original Aboriginal kinship systems are no longer used because languages are no longer spoken or are spoken only by a few Elders, new Aboriginal ways of addressing people as kinfolk have been developed. You may hear Aboriginal and Torres Strait Islander people refer to Elders as 'Aunty' or 'Uncle' even though they are not related. They are used as terms of address that show respect for Elders and a sense of belonging and identity.

Skin names

In addition to the named kinship roles, such as mother, father, daughter and son, some Aboriginal societies have what anthropologists call a 'section' or 'subsection' system. Aboriginal people call these 'skin names'. Skin names tie

Children hold photos of their family at the Apology in Canberra (photo Wayne Quilliam)

people together as a kind of kinship group, even though there might be no kinship relationship through descent or marriage whatsoever, or only a very distant one. Skin names allow people to identify a kinship relationship between them even if they have never met. 'What is your skin name?' people ask. This is a typical way to engage a stranger or newcomer in those societies where these systems operate.

There are only a few such systems operating, although they are widespread across very large regions. The most famous are:

- the Arrernte section system with its four categories
- the subsection systems (with eight categories divided into sixteen by gendered subsection names) of the Warlpiri people and Western Desert peoples, whose Country extends northwards from the Central Desert
- the Arnhem Land systems. The subsection system is thought to have been introduced into some areas, such as Arnhem Land, perhaps not more than 150 years ago.

When a person from outside these systems is bestowed a 'skin name' by an Aboriginal person, the outsider is incorporated into the wider kinship network in a kind of adoption. A kinship relationship is then established and sanctioned. A local woman will declare to another woman who is visiting, 'You are my sister', and the rules of behaviour among sisters will be explained. The husband of this woman becomes the brother-in-law of this newly acquired sister, and also of her sisters and brothers, and her children will call her 'mother' in the local language.

Where these traditional kinship systems are followed, people often do not refer to each other by their personal names but by kinship terms, as this is considered polite and proper.

A great example of the everyday kinship and skin name structure that underpins Aboriginal societies and connects us to the fauna, flora and all the named phenomena in the natural and spiritual worlds is the story of the white corella of Galiwin'ku. Pets or other domesticated animals, and even semi-domesticated wild animals, often have skin names. The white corella is known by the skin name of Ŋarritj. Ŋarritj achieved fame when he featured in a documentary about his life in the township at Galiwin'ku, a Yolŋu community on Elcho Island in the Northern Territory.

Ŋarritj enjoys a complex network of social relations in the township, speaks Yolŋu matha well enough to make his demands, intentions and thoughts clear to others, and interacts in a variety of ways with his adoptive family, the school children, the police, the shop staff and other residents of the town. Ŋarritj's adoptive family members and the residents of Galiwin'ku refer to him in the appropriate way, using kinship terms or his skin name. Ŋarritj's encounters with people at home, in the shops and on the streets shows kinship and skin names in action.

The use of these names shows respect for the animals themselves and it recognises the close relationship between the human and non-human worlds. The documentary, *Ŋarritj*, has been broadcast on NITV and other broadcast services and is available online.

Gurrutu, kinship

Through my associations with Yolŋu people from north-east Arnhem Land, I refer to my sisters as yapa and my brothers as wäwa, and their mothers and their mother's sisters as my mother, or ŋändi.

In the Yolŋu matha – the languages of the Yolŋu – the term for kinship is gurrutu, but it has a much broader set of meanings. It takes in relationships with traditional land estates, ancestral beings and all things associated with them. The named world is also in a set of kinship relationships with the Traditional Owner groups, members of which refer to neighbouring estates of clan groups in kinship terms.

All named entities in the world are in either the Dhuwa or the Yirritja moiety. This applies to almost everything, including the planets, wind, plants, animals, places and people. The saltwater crocodile is Yirritja, while the crow is Dhuwa, for instance. There are also the spiritual meanings associated with these relationships. As an example, from a female perspective, yothu–yindi means 'child–mother', and gutharra–märi means 'daughter's child–mother's mother'. These terms also express people's relationships to places and are loaded with spiritual meanings.

Clan groupings are the major form of social organisation in Yolŋu society. They are determined by descent from the most distant remembered male ancestor. They operate as the corporation that owns the clan's land estate and other property, both spiritual and physical.

My friends and colleagues ethnomusicologist Aaron Corn and the late Yolŋu elder and scholar Joe Gumbula worked closely together to describe gurrutu through various lenses.

They wrote in the book *Boundary Writing*, published in 2006, that Yolŋu society is an expansive network of more than sixty clans, or mala, that own numerous homelands in north-east Arnhem Land. Children are born into the clans of their fathers, and share in hereditary ownership of the fathers' homelands. All Yolŋu people, clans, homelands, ancestors and bodies of law are classified as being either Dhuwa or Yirritja.

The Yolŋu understand themselves to be 'direct descendants of the *waŋarr* (ancestral progenitors) who originally shaped, named and populated north-east Arnhem Land, and remain sentient and ever-present in its lands and waters'. These sacred ancestral entities are further said to inform the souls of all living Yolŋu people upon conception. They travel through ancestral waters back to their spiritual homes following death. Through this sacred birthright, all Yolŋu are born as owners or wäŋa-wataŋu (Country-holders) of their clan's homelands, and rom-wataŋu (law-holders) in associated canons of names, songs, dances and designs that prove their clan's ownership of its homelands under ancestral law.

Marriage rules are laws in all Aboriginal kinship and classification systems. In the Yolŋu system, as shown in the top diagram on page 59 based on an original painting by Joe Gumbula, a person born into a Dhuwa clan must marry a spouse from a Yirritja clan, and vice versa.

As shown in the bottom diagram on page 59, in addition to being born into one's father's clan (0), Yolŋu people, whether Dhuwa or Yirritja, also use the gurrutu system to trace their relationships to other clans through the mother's lineage.[23]

In this way, a Yolŋu person will also identify strongly with the clans of people from whom they descend and who are

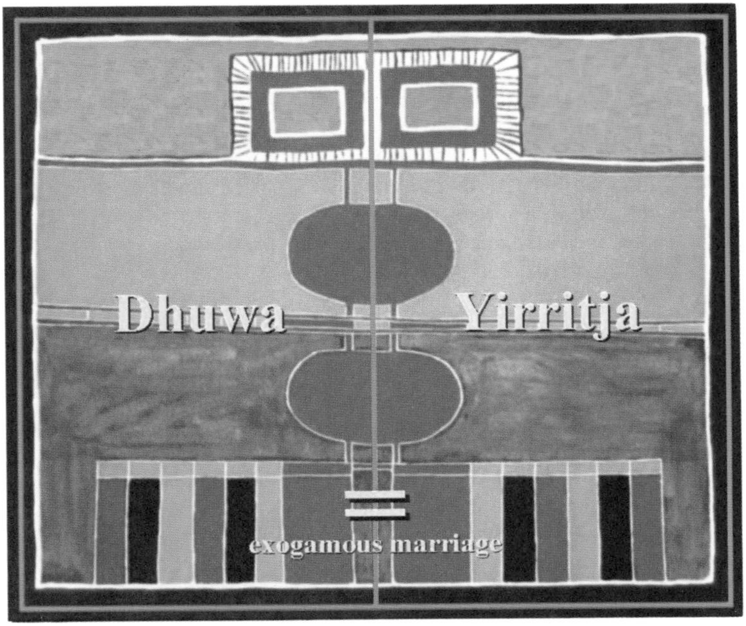
Dhuwa
Yirritja
exogamous marriage

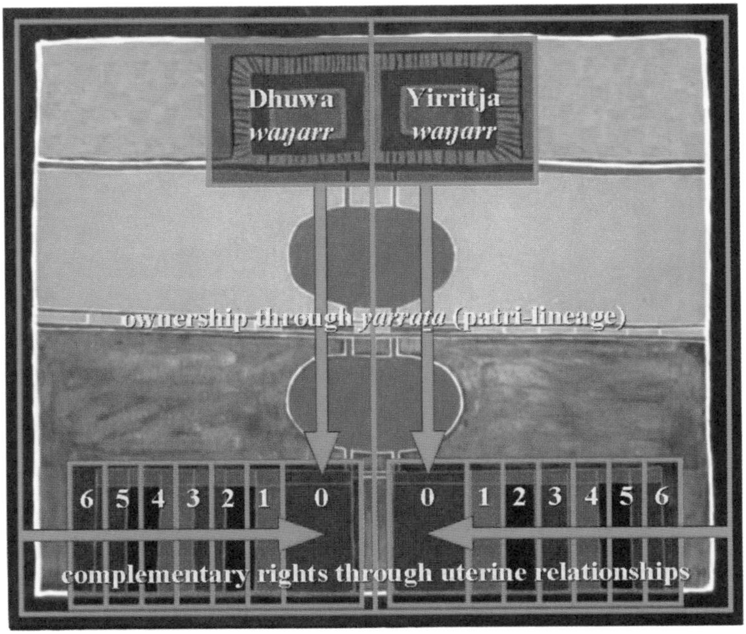
Dhuwa
waŋarr
Yirritja
waŋarr
ownership through *yarrata* (patri-lineage)
6 5 4 3 2 1 0
0 1 2 3 4 5 6
complementary rights through uterine relationships

descended from them in the relationships of mother (1), mother's mother (2), mother's mother's mother or woman's child (3), and mother's mother's mother's mother or sister (4). Father's mother (5) and marriage (6) relationships are also important. A Yolŋu person will also recognise the importance of their father's full female lineage and the complete female lineages of the children of each clan's men.

The diagram below, by Aaron Corn, shows how the Yolŋu recognise such chains of yothu–yindi (child–mother) in relationships between different clans (in red text) and homelands (in black Roman text). These homelands include tracts of sea (in black italic text), which is a distinctive feature of the Yolŋu land-tenure system in this rich coastal landscape. Hereditary knowledge of how the ancestral entities associated with each of these clans passed through each other's homelands is commonly said to bind these clans together in yothu–yindi relationships today.[24]

The Yolŋu place great emphasis on their binary Dhuwa and Yirritja classifications, and less emphasis on their skin system. By contrast, desert peoples, such as the

Yothu-yindi relationships between selected Yolŋu clans and homelands © Aaron Corn, University of Melbourne

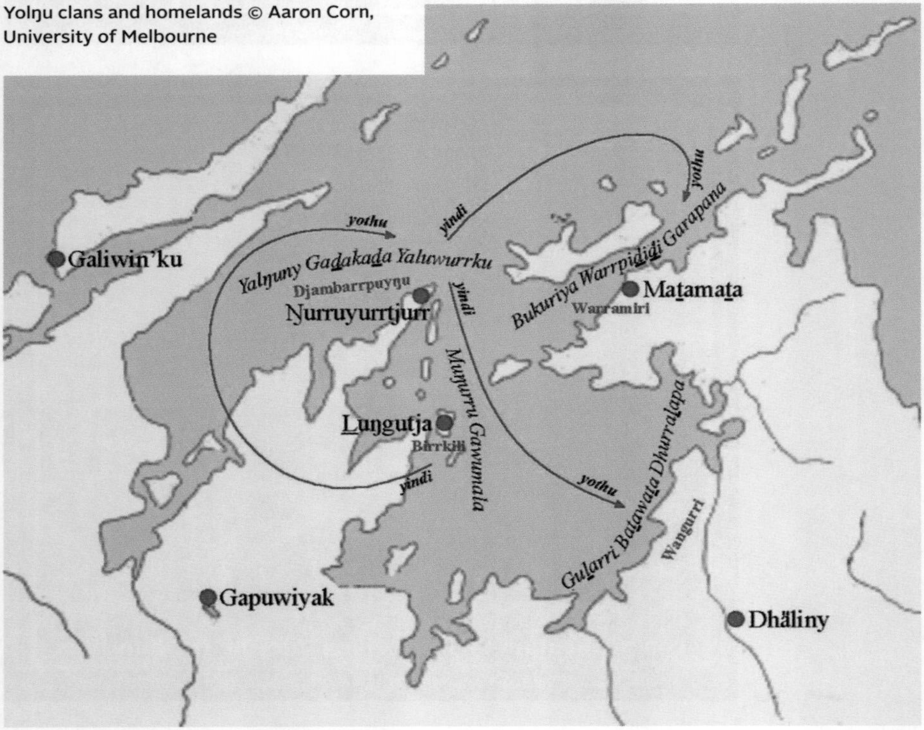

Arrernte and the Warlpiri, place much greater emphasis on skin systems. According to a skin system, each person in society is born with a standard skin name that marks their various kinds of relationships with everyone else. Skin systems are another means of linking people in family relationships. The diagrams on this page, drawn from Aaron Corn's writing, show the ideal Yolŋu mälk (skin name) system for relationships through marriage and descent.[25]

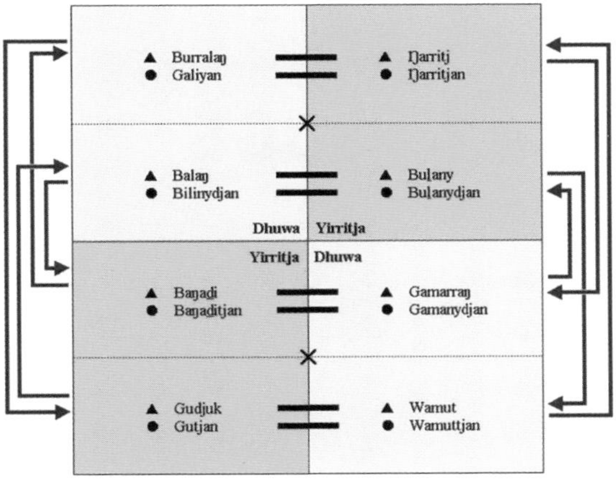

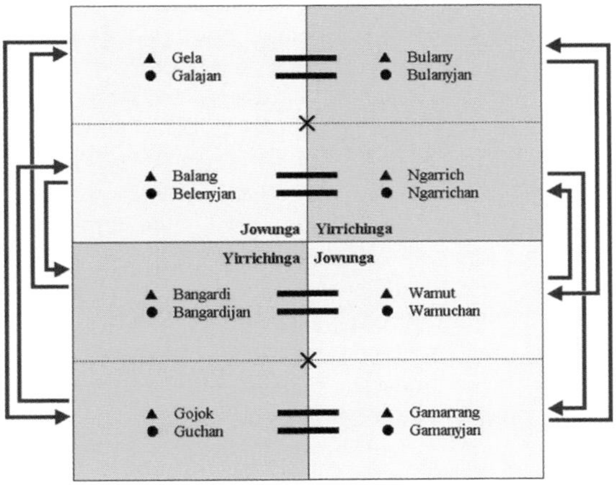

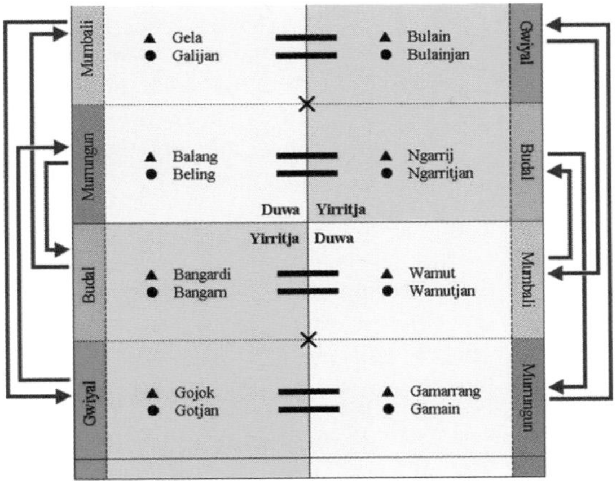

Key

▲ Male ● Female, Mother

➔ Child descent = First-choice marriage

× Second-choice marriages

5

KNOWLEDGE

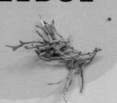

Many Australians have heard of the remarkable abilities of Aboriginal people to track animals and people over very long distances. The character of the Aboriginal tracker has been made famous in novels and films. The tracker in the film *Rabbit-Proof Fence*, discussed in the Storytelling chapter, is perhaps the most well known but there are many others. The tracker has entered the Australian mythology as an especially skilled Aboriginal man (trackers are always male in the mythology, although women read landscapes just as well) with uncanny powers of observation. In reality, trackers were indentured police assistants who had the job of capturing escaped 'natives' and white outlaws, or finding people who were lost. Gradually, non-Indigenous Australians are coming to realise that Aboriginal people also had an encyclopaedic knowledge of their environments and were keen observers of human behaviour.

There are Indigenous knowledge systems that explain how animals and plants survive, how environmental systems work, the movement of the stars and planets, weather systems and climatic change, as well as human relationships with other species.

As the sustainability of human systems and natural environments becomes a key challenge globally, environmental thinkers are looking at the ways Indigenous people managed the land for at least 65,000 years. They needed to be skilled at adapting and innovating: they witnessed an Ice Age, the disappearance of the megafauna, the rising of the seas and the drying up of the continent.

Today, Aboriginal and Torres Strait Islander people maintain their philosophies and knowledge traditions that originated tens of thousands of years ago. They have been passed from generation to generation by knowledgeable people and taught during each person's lifetime. This takes place through experience living on Country and by learning about the world, the sacred origins of people and traditional estates, their responsibilities for management of the environment, and how to provide for the material needs of their families.

The First Australians understood human nature and the natural world, environmental practices and traditions, medicine and healing, and much more. They conveyed this understanding through their teaching systems and practices, the sacred narratives such as song series (or songlines), art and designs, rituals and ceremonies, and storytelling. They also displayed it through

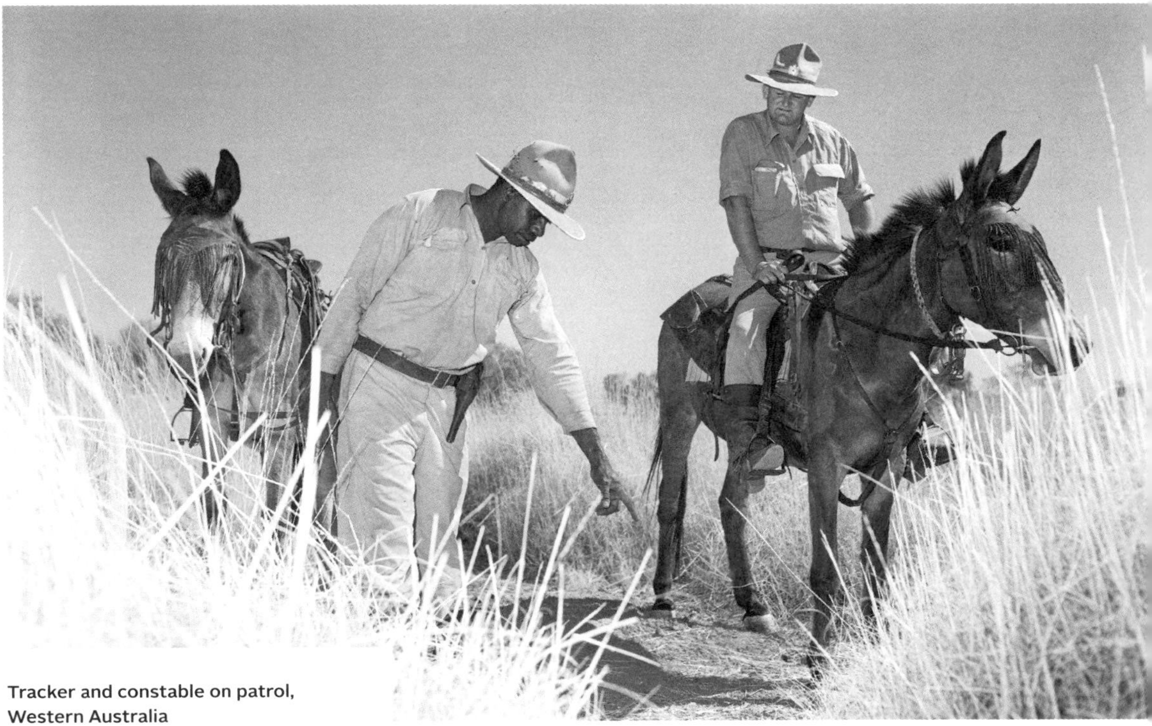

Tracker and constable on patrol, Western Australia

knowledge used in daily life. This knowledge was both specific to local areas and also spread regionally according to customs.

The ever-growing colonising population coming from Britain, with their herds of sheep and cattle and their lust for land and water, changed the environments around the country forever. The impact on the continent-wide Aboriginal land management systems and the knowledge systems that supported them was profound. It is, however, astonishing how much has survived.

As scientists and researchers have come into contact with Indigenous people who practise their ancient traditions, they recognise the importance of these traditions and the elaborate knowledge systems. They acknowledge the relevance of Indigenous knowledge systems for dealing with Australia's many challenges, especially in relation to understanding and living with our environments. There is also greater respect today for the Aboriginal and Torres Strait Islander people who manage land and water. These people are often involved in research projects to help protect the environment and to learn about it.

By the end of the twentieth century, evidence proved that Aboriginal people played a critical role in shaping the environment. It also proved that Aboriginal societies had a co-evolutionary relationship with the continent's landscapes over at least 65,000 years.

As discussed in the Precolonial History chapter, two people, among many others, who have investigated Indigenous knowledge about the environment are Bruce Pascoe and Bill Gammage.

Bill Gammage's book *The Biggest Estate on Earth: How Aborigines Made Australia* (2012) and Bruce Pascoe's book *Dark Emu: Black Seeds: Agriculture or Accident?* (2014) have fundamentally changed the simplistic characterisation of Aboriginal societies of pre-invasion times as 'hunters and gatherers' who harvested their food and basic needs from the 'wilderness'.

Bill Gammage explains in his book that the Australian continent the British encountered in 1788 was no wilderness; rather, it was a managed series of landscapes, much of which looked like 'a gentleman's park'.[26] In his detailed study of the historical records, scientific literature, paintings and images pertaining to Aboriginal use of the land and vegetation, Gammage writes that the Aboriginal people created a continent-wide system of land management.

Two years after Bill Gammage's book came out, Bruce Pascoe's book was published. It set out another body of evidence that changed the way we think about Aboriginal economic practices and their food production, demonstrating that Aboriginal people practised agriculture and developed technological innovations in some areas of Australia. As with Gammage's book, Pascoe showed that the evidence was always there to see, but it had been cloaked in old ideas about Aboriginal people as mere hunters and gatherers.

By examining historical documents written by the very first European people to encounter Aboriginal societies, *Dark Emu* brings to life the Indigenous farming innovations implemented by various Aboriginal societies before colonisation. This is also well before the introduction of colonial farming practices that erased not only the First peoples who starved as cattle and sheep polluted their waterholes and destroyed their grasslands, along with their agriculture, their dwellings and their material culture. Pascoe extends the work of Gammage by including evidence of food production methods, housing construction and even clothing. He says that in his research, he 'came across repeated references to people building dams and wells, planting, irrigating and harvesting seed ... and manipulating the landscape'. Many examples of this community resourcefulness are presented in rich detail in the book.

One such example that shatters the idea that Aboriginal people were merely passive consumers of the land's resources is that of grain production. Pascoe presents evidence that grain was grown and harvested, stored in sheds and then ground into flour for making into bread. Pascoe also highlights evidence of other agricultural practices, including yam and onion production, native grass management that promoted soft and fertile soil, aquacultural infrastructure and dwelling construction. All of this led him to the realisation that 'the hunter-gatherer tag was a convenient lie'.[27]

The second theme of the book is Pascoe's exploration of the reasons why evidence of Aboriginal civilisation has been so comprehensively erased from Australia's national conscience. He describes how the detailed accounts of the very first explorers and pastoralists failed to make it to even the second generation of white settlers.

This is partly because the newly introduced hard-hoofed animals, such as cows and sheep, quickly compacted and destroyed all beneath their feet while Aboriginal villages were burnt to the ground, obliterating the basis for these accounts. It is also partly because what he terms 'cultural amnesia' was necessary to legitimise the wholesale theft of the Australian continent. Pascoe explores this latter idea in some detail, explaining how and why the belief in the 'nomadic, hunter-gatherer lie' was so successfully adopted.[28] His book aspires to introduce an important shift in perspective when examining Australia's precolonial past and its people, and a new respect for its Aboriginal civilisation.

The debates about *Dark Emu* have been ferocious, with many of the contributions reciting hoary old racist myths about Aboriginal people and attacking Pascoe's identity as a person of Aboriginal descent. The formal state records did not always record the details of the birth of Aboriginal children, their paternity or their maternity, as we learnt during the inquiry into the stolen children. Even today, it is estimated that the birth records of about 25 per cent of Aboriginal children born in Victorian hospitals have had their Aboriginality denied on hospital records and birth certificates. Those who have salaciously peeped into publicly available records and denied Pascoe's family history have delivered barbs that are clearly intended to insult and humiliate him. Their concerns have been less with the content of his work and more with policing the boundaries of 'race' as they imagine it. Leaving aside the largely racist attacks on him, the book has also been criticised by several old-school scholars who insist on their own superseded classification of a wide range of economic activities as 'hunting and gathering'. These include anthropologist Ian Keen in a journal article,[29] and linguist Peter Sutton and archaeologist Kerryn Walshe in *Farmers or Hunter-Gatherers? The Dark Emu Debate* (MUP, 2021). They would deny a commitment to the trope of the 'noble savage' but they have clung to a sharp dividing line between humans who hunt and humans who farm, ignoring decades of literature on earlier societies where there is no evidence for any such division but rather contemporaneous hunting and farming and gradual transitions over many centuries from one dominant form of economic activity to another. Such evidence comes from societies across the globe but perhaps most aptly from historian James Boyce in his history of the Fens in eastern Britain, *Imperial Mud: The Fight for the Fens*. Boyce dismissed this 'fateful line' summarily:

The Fens were full of fish, eels and waterbirds, with the wild birds multiplying at the same time as farming was being successfully refined. Both forms of food collection became integral to Fennish life, further evidence as James C. Scott has explored, 'there is no fateful line that separates hunting and foraging from agriculture,' nor any empirical basis to the assumed superiority of farming for economic and cultural development. A predictable and easily countable grain harvest was more efficient for collecting taxes and asserting centralised authority, but this should not be equated with human progress.[30]

At least Keen suspects that there's a racist agenda in the media attacks on Pascoe, while Sutton and Walshe ignore all of the scientific evidence for Aboriginal engineering feats such as the world's oldest

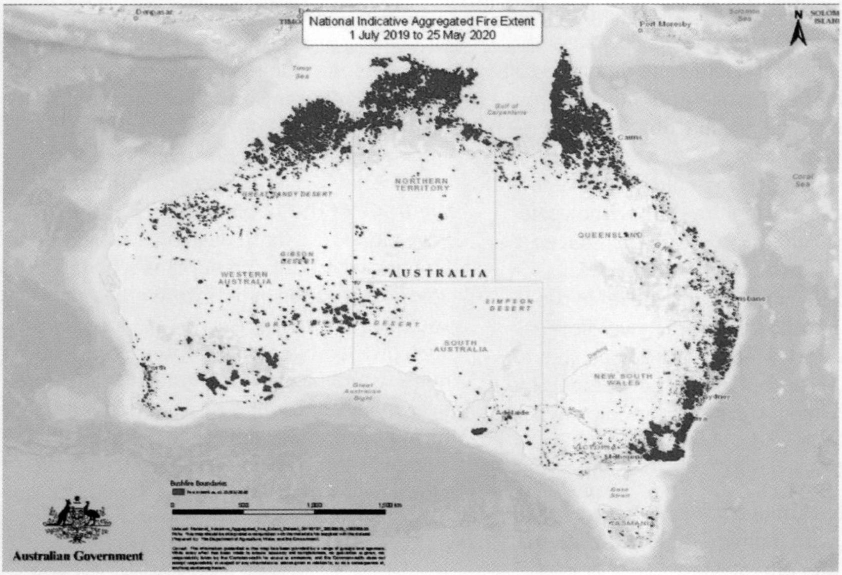

National Indicative Aggregated Fire Extent 1 July 2019 to 25 May 2020. Developed by the Department of Agriculture, Water and the Environment (DAWE). Retrieved from naturaldisaster.royalcommission.gov.au/submissions/summary-submissions, July 2021

and largest aquaculture system at the Budj Bim Cultural Landscape, inscribed by UNESCO onto its World Heritage list in 2019 on the basis of detailed submissions setting out decades of scientific evidence of human engineering and eel farming. Sutton and Walshe ignored not only all of this evidence but that of many anthropologists and others who documented what is often called ‘incipient agriculture’ or the propagation of plants and grains for consumption. Moreover, Sutton and Walshe have no expertise in southern Australia where most of the historical sources that Pascoe cites are relevant, and neither of them are historians. They are clearly not aware that in north Australia, where their work is largely located, Yolŋu make bread from collected and leached cycad seed pods, baked into small loaves for special occasions; it is called ŋathi. I have seen it with my own eyes. I also know that I will be attacked for saying this by those who remain uncomfortable with Aboriginal ideas from the south because this fact blurs the neat racial boundaries of the colonial triumphalist myth of a ‘superior’ race over an ‘inferior’ race. It must be said that those Aboriginal people whose traditional economy includes hunting, fishing with traps, nets and harpoons, gathering shellfish, and harvesting bush fruit, nuts and vegetables have wondered what all the fuss is about. They love their economic practices and their lifestyles.

In these new culture wars between postcolonial and Indigenous versions of our past, one must read diligently and closely to keep up with the battle and the swings and blows against the mounting evidence that Aboriginal economies were varied, mixed and complex. Meanwhile, I continue to recommend Pascoe's *Dark Emu* because it will inspire you to *think critically about the historical sources* and count as part of our Aboriginal traditions: eel farming, propagation of plants and grains for consumption (farming), hunting, fishing, foraging (including shellfish gathering) and food storage of many different types.

The Black Summer

In the Australian summer of 2019–2020, wildfires exploded in the forests and scrublands with fatal consequences for people in the path of the fires, our wildlife and our environments.

In the aftermath of this season of fire that left Australians in a state of shock at the devastation, and recognising that climate change impacts will result in more intense and more frequent fires, on 20 February 2020, the Australian government established the Royal Commission into National Natural Disaster Arrangements. The Royal Commission was established to inquire into the potential for Australian governments to better coordinate their responses to limit the deadly and destructive impacts of bushfires. It published a map of the extent of the fires across Australia from 1 July 2019 to 25 May 2020, which presents a disturbing picture of the loss of our biodiversity and natural resources.[31] The words of the Royal Commission are a stark reminder of that terrible summer:

Over 24 million hectares were burnt. Many Australians were impacted, directly or indirectly, by the fires. Tragically, 33 people died and extensive smoke coverage across much of eastern Australia may have caused many more deaths. Over 3,000 homes were destroyed. Estimates of the national financial impacts are over $10 billion. Nearly three billion animals were killed or displaced and many threatened species and other ecological communities were extensively harmed. Every state and territory suffered fire to some extent. The fires did not respect state borders or local government boundaries. On some days, extreme conditions drove a fire behaviour that was impossible to control ... We heard stories of bravery and camaraderie – and luck. It was a true 'campaign season'. The season commenced in July 2019 and was not declared over until 31 March 2020.

For some species, this was the tipping point, and more have become endangered. Australian extinction rates were already among the highest in the world before the Black Summer.

In the Proceedings of the National Academy of Sciences of the United States of America of April 2015, Woinarski, Burbidge and Harrison write,

The 29 Australian endemic mammal extinctions comprise 35% of the world's modern mammal extinctions. Some 1.5% of the world's 5,500 mammal species are extinct, a proportion substantially less than for Australia. Our assessment of 30 Australian mammal extinctions is also appreciably greater than that recognized

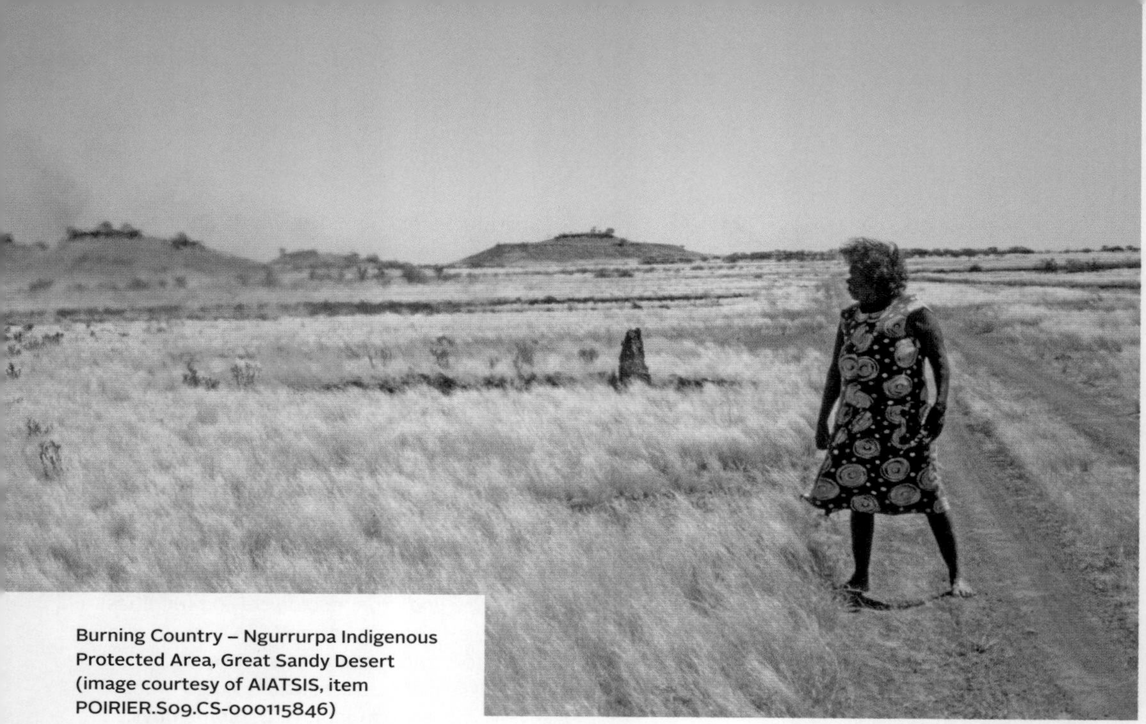

Burning Country – Ngurrurpa Indigenous Protected Area, Great Sandy Desert (image courtesy of AIATSIS, item POIRIER.S09.CS-000115846)

under Australian environmental legislation, which lists 20 Australian mammal species as extinct ...[32]

They describe 'an extent of recent and ongoing loss of its mammal fauna that is exceptionally high and appreciably greater than previously recognized', and they conclude that causes of loss are unlike biodiversity decline elsewhere in the world. While much of the evidence is unclear, there can be no doubt that the colonisation of Australia by the British is correlated with species extinction in 'a broad sequential wave ... beginning from the first settled areas in southeastern Australia ... to the present day in much of northern Australia', and the 'loss of indigenous land management, particularly of fire'.[33] The losses are continuing: a further 56 Australian land mammal species are threatened and 52 species are near threatened. In summary, of the 273 Australian endemic land mammal species, 11 per cent are extinct, 21 per cent are extant but threatened, and a further 15 per cent are near threatened.[34]

Cultural burning – or traditional Aboriginal fire management practices – provide a large part of the solution to this ongoing disaster, as the Royal Commission found. The Royal Commission report is an impressive document, containing 80 recommendations. The Commission Chair, Air Chief Marshal Mark Binskin AC (Retd), presented the report to the Governor-General on Wednesday, 28 October 2020. It was tabled in Parliament on Friday, 30 October 2020.

In two recommendations, the Commission urged that 'Australian, state, territory and local governments should engage further with Traditional Owners to explore the relationship between Indigenous land and fire management and natural disaster resilience' and to 'further opportunities to leverage Indigenous land and fire management insights, in the development, planning and execution of public land management activities'.

These recommendations were based on evidence from across the country about cultural burning. A comprehensive chapter of the report, Chapter 18 on Indigenous land and fire management, presents a compilation of evidence – and the evidence of Aboriginal land managers who fight fire with fire should be required reading for all Australians who live on land at risk of wildfire.

I draw the reader's attention to parts of one submission in particular because of its concise summary of Indigenous knowledge and science in an urgent call for greatly expanded Aboriginal fire management, or cultural burning.

The urgent need for Aboriginal fire management practices

A group of Indigenous and non-Indigenous experts on Australian wildfires and Indigenous fire management made a submission to the Royal Commission that set out a range of urgent recommendations. Their primary concern is the urgent need for traditional Aboriginal fire management practices to be implemented to manage wildfires and limit their impacts in the long term:

... it is fundamental that an implementation of Cultural Burning be planned, led by, undertaken and administered by Indigenous groups that are local to the site of practice. Effort, then, needs to be made to resource and support the formation of Indigenous bodies, such as the highly successful Ranger programs across Australia ... Communities and Elders still hold much information which is not widely known or shared, and in many areas there has never been Indigenous-led initiatives which allow a safe place for knowledges to be activated. Transformational change is required in the way Country is being managed and we assert that resourcing and partnering with Aboriginal knowledge holders to reinvigorate Cultural Fire practice, ensuring empowerment and not appropriation, represents a necessary and powerful piece of the suite of measures required for transformational change ...[35]

They explained how cultural burning will build Australia's resilience to natural disasters:

Indigenous Australians have managed Australian landscapes for more than 65,000 year[s] using a highly effective holistic land management practices and a suite of Country-specific management regimes that have persisted through, and have been shaped by, massive environmental changes ... All Aboriginal land management practices have been the result of intimate knowledge of Country developed over many, many millennia of careful observation, continual interaction and active custodianship (Olsen & Russell 2019). Arguably the most profound influence of Indigenous Australians on the Australian environment was achieved through Cultural Burning. Empirical and ethnographic data clearly demonstrates that the Australian environment of 1788 was radically different to the landscape we see today, and that this difference can be seen as largely as a result of the negation of cultural burning

Victor Steffensen, author of *Fire Country*, demonstrating fire management

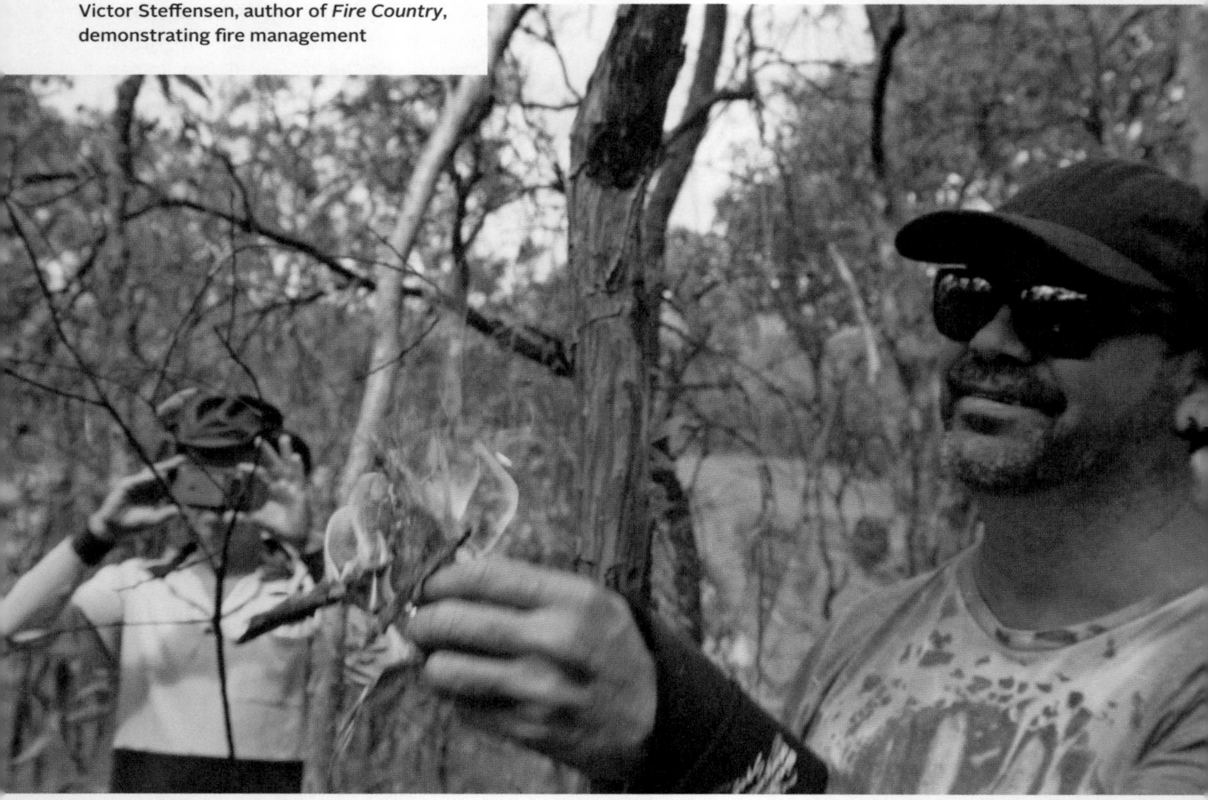

regimes ... This landscape change aligns with significant impacts of colonisation, which have prevented Indigenous Land Management and cultural burning across the region ...

Fire Country

Aboriginal peoples used fire to promote and distribute plant communities, such as grasses or open forest. They also used it to distribute trees and plants, which in turn promoted and protected animals, birds, reptiles and insects. By using fire as an intrinsic part of land management, Aboriginal people managed the wildfire-prone Australian landscapes.

Fire and symbols of fire are important features in Indigenous religious rituals and ceremonies, including many that are still practised today. Fire also features in myths and stories about the sacred past, when life and the world were being created. The video *Yagun Gulinj Wiinj (How Man*

Found Fire), made in 2016, shows a sacred ancestral story about the origin of fire.

Through careful observation of weather and winds, and the seasonal changes in many plant and animal species, Aboriginal people used fire in Country to keep it healthy. Its use was carefully and skilfully regulated so that different parts of Country were burnt in the appropriate season, at appropriate intervals, and with a suitable intensity. Cool burns (that is, low-intensity fires) were used to maintain low fuel loads in the forest understorey without harming the forest canopy, to protect the trees and resident biodiversity.

Burning was also used in relatively small patches of vegetation. This produced a 'mosaic' pattern across the landscape, which meant that when a wildfire started (for example, through lightning) it would be less likely to develop into a large blaze. An occurrence such as a firestorm would have been devastating to Aboriginal society. Fire was also used to maintain grasslands, to ensure the reproduction of fire-adapted vegetation and to protect fire-sensitive plants. In modern terms, traditional Aboriginal fire practices had the overall effect of promoting greater biodiversity. The term 'firestick farming' was devised by prehistorian Rhys Jones in 1969 to indicate that these practices were deliberate and governed by rules.

In his book, Bill Gammage showed that Aboriginal people made fire an ally, not an enemy. Among its advantages, Aboriginal landscape fire:

- gave every species a favourable habitat, letting them flourish and preventing species extinctions
- promoted drought-shielding native grasses and shrubs
- minimised the impact of bushfire ('wildfire') by reducing fuel, and by creating firebreaks to break up or isolate areas with dangerous fuel loads.

In an article in *The Monthly* in 2011, historian James Boyce remarked about Gammage's important book:

Gammage is determined to open our eyes to the fact that in 1788 there was no wilderness, but a landscape that reflected a sophisticated, successful and sensitive farming regime integrated across the Australian landmass. Fire was not an indiscriminate tool of fuel reduction or grass promotion, but carefully employed to ensure certain plants and animals flourished, to facilitate access and rotation, and to ensure resources were abundant, convenient and predictable.[36]

In many parts of Australia, the traditions of using fire came to an end when Aboriginal societies were disrupted – during the colonial period, when many populations were removed from their traditional land, and later, under the protection and assimilation period. Urbanisation, particularly in parts of New South Wales, Victoria and Tasmania, means it is no longer possible in many areas of Australia.

However, Traditional Owners and Indigenous rangers continue to practise these traditions on Aboriginal land, especially in northern Australia. Scientists debate whether the practices can be used to control wildfires in those areas where Aboriginal populations are no longer living on the land. Trials of fire management regimes are run to experiment with burning practices, in order to understand ecological complexity and variation in species response in different communities. And firefighters routinely attend field days to learn Aboriginal burning techniques.

In northern Australia, where traditional management continues to be widely practised, a few communities are harvesting carbon credits by using traditional fire management. This is because, as both Aboriginal and non-Aboriginal experts agree, frequent small fires release less carbon than infrequent, yet larger, wildfires.

Towards the end of the Black Summer of 2020, as the rains came and the fires were finally extinguished, a remarkable book was published that explains cultural burning through the eyes of a man who learnt about this ancient body of Aboriginal traditional knowledge from two Elders in Cape York, George Musgrave and Tommy George. Victor Steffensen wrote *Fire Country: How Indigenous Fire Management Could Help Save Australia* to help 'heal the wounds inflicted on the people and the environment' by 'putting the right fire back onto the land. The fire is just the beginning of an important journey for us all.'[37] Victor first met George and Tommy in the little town of Laura, and their strong presence was immediately obvious:

I could see two old men from a distance, sitting with their families ... I was told that they were brothers and had a reputation as among the most respected and knowledgeable men in the area. I was instantly intrigued by their status and wanted to learn more about them. As I peered over at them I could see that they were watching me. Even when they weren't looking at me, it felt like they were watching me. They had a really strong presence that I was drawn to, but it made me nervous to think of approaching them.

By the end of the day, Tommy George had invited Victor to live in his house, and the story of how ancient knowledge is passed along to the next generation begins in Victor's inimitable bush way with words that are often called 'yarning'. This is a precious written account because it is the only one. Both Tommy and George have passed away, and they were the last Awu-Laya Elders who could give the traditional knowledge and stories of their Country to their young people. Others will do so through the oral traditions and being on Country. This legacy is a fragile one, as Victor explains:

It was an honour to learn from them, but it didn't come without many challenges along the way. You have to develop trust, not just with the old people, but the whole community. It took some time before the old people really started to teach me things. They also found me useful to help them out too around other life matters. The main thing they wanted was to practise culture and get back onto their country. They wanted to apply their knowledge back onto the land, the fire, the water, looking after the story places. But most of all they wanted their younger ones to learn the language and get back onto country. It was vital because the two men were the last of the Awu-Laya Elders who knew the traditional knowledge and stories of that country. They wanted the young ones to inherit the knowledge and take over their role as leading Elders ...The healing knowledge using fire for the land comes from the same knowledge of maintaining country with fire. Healing the environmental problems becomes far more possible if you understand the land through ancient knowledge views. Knowing the values and indicators of each ecosystem allows you to work out ways to adjust the fire management to improve the condition of sick landscapes. Burning outside of the normal times you would burn the country, depending on its identity and condition. The health status of a particular country determines the best possible application of fire. It's sort of like being a doctor for the land, giving a diagnosis and then the treatment.

Cultural burning can only be learnt on Country, and in this excerpt, we are treated to Victor's first lesson:

I will never forget that day Poppy lit the first fire on country in front of me.

We were standing in the middle of a small community of boxwood trees about 20 kilometres out of old Laura town. The ecosystem was only as big as a couple of basketball courts and was surrounded by a small creek and stringybark country. The grass was quite thick, dead and dry, and we were standing in it up to our knees. 'I'm gonna light the grass now, like the old people used to do,' Poppy said loudly and proudly. He walked over to the stringybark country and ripped off a long piece of bark from the closest tree.

'You look now.' He teased one end of the long piece of bark, lit it up and then walked through the boxwood patch in a repetitive, figure eight type movement. He was almost skipping as he dragged the bark along, making the fire follow him around. I watched him dancing through the flames like some kind of fire spirit sprinkling magic dust onto the land. I watched the fire go higher and the smoke fill the space around him until I couldn't see him anymore. There was nothing but fire in front of me, but it was only seconds before it started to calm down. Then he reappeared in the middle of the fire, walking over the flames with his bare feet, giving me the biggest smile.[38]

Scientists, ecologists, historians and many others have given us other versions of the knowledge that Victor shares, but their sources are the written record, not the Elders themselves. When Victor uses the word 'magic' he does so to convey the great subtlety of the practice of cultural burning and the finest understanding of fire and the environment that cannot be learnt from books. Yet, these books are important in their own way, because no Australians will ever again experience the teachings of Tommy and George.

Aboriginal fire management is both an ancient and a contemporary practice, which has altered the Australian landscape. European settlers thought the continent was a wild and harsh environment, but in fact what they encountered was a landscape that had been consciously and deliberately shaped by fire for thousands of years. There is extensive Aboriginal, scientific and ecological literature demonstrating that Aboriginal people have used fire as a technology of powerful proportions and effect to imprint the economic signature of the human species throughout much of the Australian continent. Wherever Aboriginal economic traditions have survived, researchers have discovered ordered, patterned and rule-governed Aboriginal burning practices.

Indigenous rangers: working on Country

Aboriginal and Torres Strait Islander people have continued their tradition of Caring for Country in many ways. One of the most important ways in which they do this today is through the workforce of environmental carers who manage Indigenous land and waters. The Australian government supports these Indigenous ranger projects, which were first funded in 2007 by the Working on Country Program but were established decades earlier by Indigenous volunteers. With government support, these projects acknowledge and reward a traditional practice of Aboriginal and Torres Strait Islander people, and benefit the environment as well.

The Department of Prime Minister and Cabinet has a web page dedicated to the program, now called Indigenous Rangers – Working on Country. In early 2019, it reported that the government supported 123 Indigenous ranger groups across Australia and these employed 839 Indigenous rangers in full-time positions.

The Australian government's recognition of these ancient knowledge systems and environmental conservation and management practices has led to greater awareness of the need to involve Indigenous people in protecting our natural resources. This is acknowledged on the web page:

Indigenous ranger projects support Indigenous people to combine traditional knowledge with conservation training to protect and manage their land, sea and culture. Indigenous ranger groups also develop partnerships with research, education, philanthropic and commercial organisations to share skills and knowledge, engage with schools, and generate additional income and jobs in the environmental, biosecurity, heritage and other sectors.

Aboriginal and Torres Strait Islander seasons and weather knowledge

Unlike the four European seasons, most Indigenous Australian seasonal calendars have three seasons, each with three sub-seasons. These vary across the continent in accordance with the region's climate. In northern Australia, the monsoonal season is markedly wet and the dry season is markedly dry, while in the temperate zones, rainfall varies across the seasons.

While Europeans generally assign whole months to a particular season, Indigenous people say that a season commences and ends with the appearance of particular ecological indicators. This could be the flowering of particular trees or shrubs and the appearance of particular insects. Each season is also associated with particular weather patterns, such as wind directions and speed, temperatures, rainfall, dew or storms, clouds and the time of the day when these occur. There are names for all of these weather patterns as well. Wind patterns are an important part of Aboriginal seasonality and for some groups are the primary indicators of seasonal change.

The Miriwoong seasonal calendar from northern Australia is a good example of an Indigenous seasonal calendar. Miriwoong (Miriwung) is an Australian Indigenous

Miriwoong seasonal calendar, copyright of Mirima Dawang Woorlab-gerring Language and Culture Centre (MDWg), also found at www.mirima.org.au/calendar

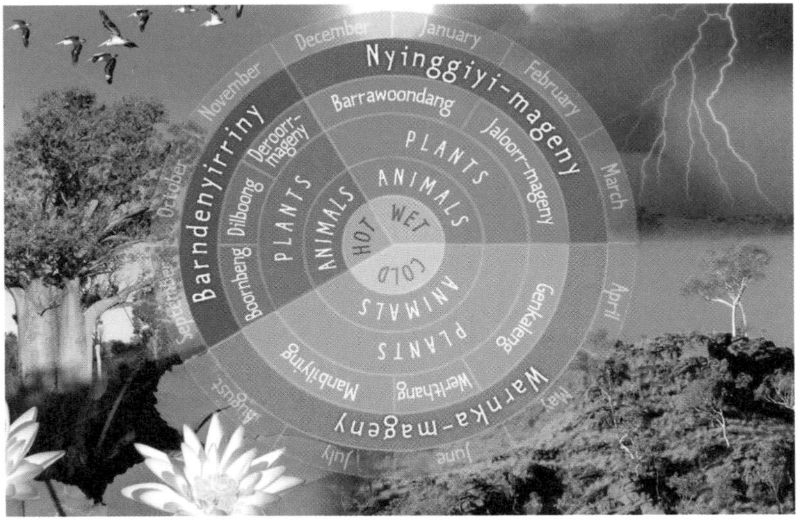

language which is a part of the Jarrakan subgroup of languages, which today has fewer than twenty fluent speakers, most of whom live in or near Kununurra in Western Australia. Miriwoong people have an in-depth knowledge of climatic seasons and weather patterns. This Aboriginal traditional knowledge was documented to produce the Miriwoong seasonal calendar above, showing the links between observed changes in weather patterns and the response of flora and fauna in the landscape. The calendar is being used as a management tool to monitor and evaluate the on-ground impacts of weather events and climate change.

There are many more examples of Indigenous seasonal calendars on the Bureau of Meteorology and CSIRO websites. For example, Bathurst and Melville islands of the Tiwi Islands have three major seasons and thirteen minor overlapping seasons, while Noongar Country in Western Australia has six seasons.

Aboriginal and Torres Strait Islander astronomy

In Aboriginal and Torres Strait Islander cultures, everything on the land is reflected in the sky. The sky serves as a scientific textbook – a map – that is home to a wealth of knowledge for those who are able to interpret and read the information it holds.

This quote comes from Duane Hamacher's contribution to the National Aboriginal and Torres Strait Islander Curricula Project. His Aboriginal and Torres Strait Islander astronomy curricula can be found at: indigenousknowledge.research.unimelb.edu.au.

Did you know that Aboriginal and Torres Strait Islander people paid careful attention to phenomena such as eclipses and meteorite impacts, and could determine the cardinal points to an accuracy of a few degrees? Did you know that they discovered the variability of Betelgeuse, the ninth brightest star in the sky, and made observations of other red-giant variable stars?

Astronomers Professor Ray Norris and Dr Duane Hamacher have led research to document how the traditional cultures of Indigenous Australians include a significant understanding of astronomy. It is explored through storytelling, ceremony and art.

This astronomical component includes a deep understanding of the motion of objects in the sky, and this knowledge was used for practical purposes such as constructing calendars. There is also evidence that traditional Aboriginal Australians made careful records and measurements of cyclical phenomena.

Professor Norris and Dr Hamacher have unearthed this knowledge from historical records and worked with Elders to develop an extraordinary project. Their team includes Indigenous astronomers and astrophysicists Dr Stacy Mader, Karlie Noon, Kirsten Banks, Krystal De Napoli, Peter Swanton, Peter Reeve, Jessie Ferrari, John South and William Stevens. They are documenting the traditional knowledge of the sky, the celestial bodies, their movements and characteristics, handed down over many generations. Their work casts new light on the depth of traditional Indigenous knowledge and has led to new understandings of how Indigenous people organised their economic and social life by observing the sky.

With their knowledge of astronomy, Indigenous people are able to read the weather and climate as it relates to food propagation. They can predict changes in the environment in relation to seasons, weather patterns and the behaviour of plants and animals. Their knowledge is used to manage harvesting, hunting and gathering, navigating across land and sea by the stars, the moon and the sun, and organising social and ritual life.

If you want to explore Aboriginal and Torres Strait Islander knowledge of astronomy, the website aboriginalastronomy.com.au hosts a treasure trove of published and audiovisual records and images of traditional knowledge and cultural astronomy.

Solar points in Torres Strait Islander astronomical knowledge

Duane Hamacher learnt about traditional Torres Strait Islander knowledge of the Sun from Mua artist David Bosun. Bosun's father was a traditional astronomer, or Zugubau Mabaig, and taught him how to observe and interpret the Sun's setting position from the village of Kubin. Bosun explained

people in the village of Kubin observe the position of the setting Sun with respect to the archipelago of islands to the west and southwest throughout the year. This informs them about seasonal change and food economics. [39]

They found further information in the historical records. The notebooks of Peter Eseli (1886–1958) were a treasure trove. Eseli was a Mabuyag man and the son of Peter Papi, one of the three chief assistants to the A.C. Haddon expedition sponsored by Cambridge University in the late nineteenth century.

Eseli's notebooks, translated into English from Kala Lagow Ya, provide a wealth of knowledge about traditional seasonal knowledge in the western Torres Strait.

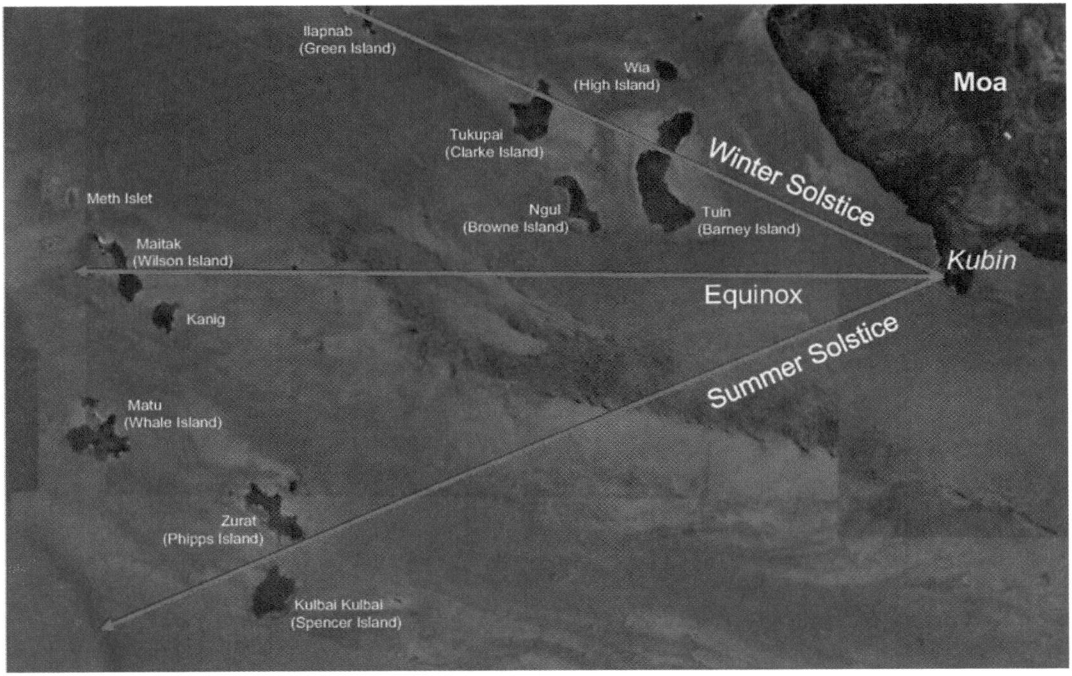

Figure 1: Islands to the west and southwest of Mua Island, western Torres Strait featuring their Western and traditional names (where available), with the solstice and equinox lines in red. Image modified from Google Earth.

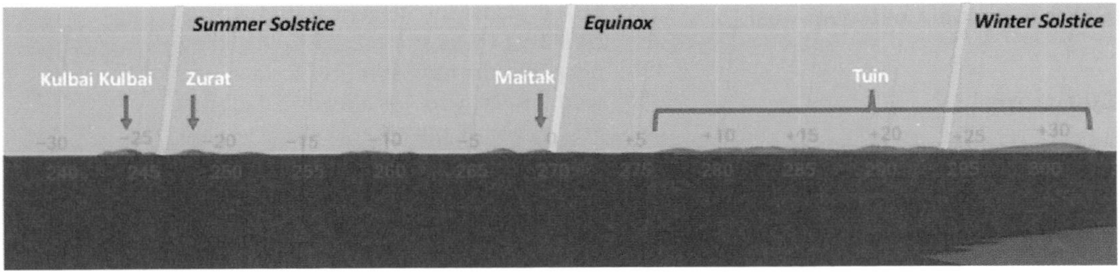

Figure 2: A simulation of the setting Sun as seen from Kubin village, taken from the Horizon software package, developed by Andrew Smith at the University of Adelaide (www.agksmith.net/horizon/)

As the setting Sun moves southward each day, the weather gradually warms, the days lengthen, and the behaviour of the animals changes. It reaches its southerly most point at the summer solstice, when the rains of the monsoon season kick off. The Sun then moves northward each day until it passes the equinox, and the Dry season comes by late April. It reaches its northerly most point at the winter solstice during the Dry season in late June. [40]

They explain in considerable detail the movement of the Sun, the extreme setting position of the Sun at the solstices, and the meanings of these positions, such as the distinctive seasonal implications, the weather, the wind, the turtle mating season, when mating turtles float on the surface of the water, the wet season monsoon, the south-east trade wind in the drier season, the abundance of food at this time and the good conditions for easy travel on the water, and the yam harvesting season.

The diagrams on page 77 show a simulation of the setting sun as observed from Bosun's home, Kubin village on Mua Island, and the solstice and equinox lines as observed from Kubin village when looking towards the islands to the west and south-west.[41]

Star maps

Aboriginal and Torres Strait Islander star maps have been transmitted by Elders over hundreds of generations through stories, teaching, maps and song series, or 'songlines'. They became the subject of research when Euahlayi Elder Uncle Ghillar pointed out a pattern of stars to Robert Fuller, an MPhil student at Macquarie University, as they sat under the clear, starry sky in Goodooga, in north-west New South Wales. Fuller was researching the astronomical knowledge of the Euahlayi and Kamilaroi peoples in 2013 when he became aware of 'star maps' as a way to teach navigation when going outside of one's own local Country.

Ghillar pointed out that the pattern of stars to the south-east was used to teach Euahlayi travellers how to navigate outside their own Country during the summer travel season. They were used not so much as a map but as a memory aid. As you can read on the website aboriginalastronomy.com.au:

Robert did some research, and looked at a route from Goodooga to the Bunya Mountains northwest of Brisbane, where an Aboriginal Bunya nut festival was held every three years until disrupted by European invasion. It turned out the pattern of stars showed the 'waypoints' on the route. These waypoints were usually waterholes or turning places on the landscape. These waypoints were used in a very similar way to navigating with a GPS, where waypoints are also used as stopping or turning points.

After Fuller's lesson from Ghillar, a series of star maps were developed. It became clear that these star maps would guide people to the easiest routes to take, and were probably routes already established in song series and other oral and visual records. Some of the roads and highways used today follow these routes. Again from aboriginalastronomy.com.au:

Drovers and settlers coming into the region would have used the same routes, and eventually these became tracks and finally highways. In a sense, the Aboriginal people of Australia had a big part in the layout of

Gathering of bush medicine in central Australia (photo Wayne Quilliam)

the modern Australian road network. And in some cases, such as the Kamilaroi Highway running from the Hunter Valley to Bourke in NSW, this has been recognised in the name.

Traditional Aboriginal medicine and healing

In many areas of Australia, Aboriginal men and women turn with great confidence to traditional healers to maintain their wellbeing. While scientists have generally dismissed them as being ineffective, Aboriginal people recognise the need to maintain these traditions. In the Indigenous world, the causes of disease are understood in the terms of ancient cultural knowledge that has served thousands of generations well.

We have so much yet to learn from the traditional healers and their techniques, such as the way they use their artistic works, including painting and weaving – healers use images, for example, to focus the patient's attention on ancestral power and the correct balance between the spiritual and ordinary, to achieve social order.

These extraordinary healers are called by many names: clevermen, marrnggitj and ngangkaṟi are just three. Healers, medical professionals and scientists are beginning to collaborate. Health professionals sometimes invite healers into clinics and hospitals when Aboriginal patients are afraid and resistant to health care, as healers bring ancient Aboriginal values to the task. They understand that Aboriginal patients should use Western medical treatments too, and often explain to them that they should go to the clinic or stay in hospital and not fear the doctors and nurses. Healers can be blunt about this, and have said to me, 'I can't help you. Go to the hospital.'

Where there is no hospital, healers use traditional treatments for fever, some infections and wounds, diarrhoea and other common ailments such as mental distress. They are reported to help patients who are overcome with the belief that they will die, and bring them back to a state where they are engaged with life.

Aboriginal medical traditions and treatments are supported by encyclopaedic bodies of knowledge developed in an intimate relationship with the local environment, vegetation, climate and geography. Observations of the cause and effect of particular substances, the transformation of plant material by applying fire, water, smoke or other treatments all helped to build the traditional medicinal knowledge.

More mysterious and difficult to comprehend are the Aboriginal ways of understanding human physiology and psychology. These complex cultural principles and theories involve the idea of the interconnection of people and land, the spirit world and the perceived world. They also involve the many ancestral spirits and their influences on the world. These ideas and principles are such an important part of Aboriginal cultures across the continent, and I have come to understand some of them simply by listening and observing.

That so many Aboriginal people maintain their ancient medical traditions against the odds presents us with an important opportunity. We should study the profound change in Aboriginal health since colonial times through the lens of the repercussions of the widespread destruction of traditional knowledge and practices. With these insights, we should find ways to preserve and reinstate these trusted practices in health care today.

Books about traditional Aboriginal healing

There are many books about traditional Aboriginal healing knowledge and its practice since earliest colonial times.

One book filled with information is the beautiful, award-winning *Traditional healers of Central Australia: Ngangkaṟi*, from the Ngaanyatjarra Pitjantjatjara Yankunytjatjara (NPY) Women's Council Aboriginal Corporation.

Ngangkaṟi are the traditional healers of the Ngaanyatjarra, Pitjantjatjara and Yankunytjatjara Lands – 350,000 square kilometres of the remote Western Desert. As the publisher, Magabala Books, notes, 'To increase understanding and encourage collaboration with mainstream health services and the wider community, the ngangkaṟi have forged a rare partnership with health professionals and practitioners of Western medicine.'

Dark Emu, by Bruce Pascoe, powerfully shows how the derogatory views of our ancient traditions are wrong. Research on these traditions is growing, as are efforts to revive and maintain them. For example, by the production of healing remedies for the market, and programs supporting the healers and their collaborations with the health workforce.

A very useful book is *Body, Land and Spirit: Health and Healing in Aboriginal Society*, a collection edited by Janice Reid. In the article '"Bush Medicine": The Pharmacopeia of the Yolŋu of Arnhem Land', its exploration of how the Yolŋu in Arnhem Land understand human suffering is based on Reid's experience living in and visiting Yirrkala. Reid also wrote the book *Sorcerers and Healing Spirits: Continuity and Change in an Aboriginal Medical System*. Even though so much has changed in the last half-century, many of Reid's descriptions of Yolŋu medicine are easily recognisable today.

She reported very little on the herbal and other remedies that are still offered at women's healing events in north-east Arnhem Land. I suspect that the influence of missionaries drove many of these practices 'underground' or out of sight. But, as my own experience proved, these traditions continue and are a source of great pride for the families who hold the knowledge.

Research on these traditions is growing, as are efforts to revive and maintain them, from the production of healing remedies for the market, to programs supporting the healers and their collaborations with the health workforce.

Indigenous sorcerers

I have met a few sorcerers in Cape York, Central Australia and Arnhem Land – encounters that were fascinating and more than a little frightening. Sorcerers make no claim to the greater good. Sorcerers exist, but so too does fear of imagined sorcerers, who almost always live beyond the social boundaries of one's own group and can never be accurately identified. When I have been told to beware because sorcerers were afoot, the instructions were vague.

When sorcery-removing rituals are conducted, the consequences can be severe: affected families may be required to evacuate their homes, or hand over their worldly goods to their in-laws, while community assets such as stores and vehicles may be put out of action by the taboos that are invoked in ritual efforts to remove sorcery curses. The results of these encounters can be explained by understanding the context of each one.

When I worked for the Royal Commission into Aboriginal Deaths in Custody in the late 1980s, attribution of deaths to sorcery was common. The role of sorcery as an Aboriginal explanation for the rising mortality rates caused by chronic disease, contact with the criminal justice system, alcohol, vehicle accidents and violence was not well understood.

Janice Reid, in her book *Body, Land and Spirit,* writes the accepted view that has been put to me by healers, and one that supports my own observations:

The power utilised by both sorcerers and healers is ultimately from the same source. This power is morally neutral, it is not the nature of the power a marrnggitj possesses which distinguishes him from a sorcerer but the choice which he makes about how he will use it ... this power is held in trust. People believe they use it to heal and to protect others. While the potential for its use to harm people exists, marrnggitj and their families vigorously deny that they work sorcery, even on enemies, and they become offended and angry if anyone suggests such a possibility.[42]

On racist stereotypes of Indigenous people and their origins

Colonial impressions of Aboriginal and Torres Strait Islander societies that cast them as 'simple' or 'primitive' remain the obstacle to understanding the depth of their knowledge. Ideas about the Indigenous people have shifted from insults based on impressions from fleeting observations to a much more profound knowledge of robust, adaptive societies.

From the first recorded encounters of Europeans with Aboriginal people, the idea of a 'backward people' developed. This idea has been remarkably resilient in Australian literature, school textbooks and public commentary. That is despite more than 200 years of experience, scholarship and research that has found to the contrary: Aboriginal and Torres Strait Islander people developed complex systems of social and religious organisation, economic patterns and practices, and artistic, cultural and technological traditions that adapted to life in Australian environments.

English seaman and author William Dampier is credited with being the first European to observe Aboriginal people. His few notes on his glimpses of Aboriginal people have reverberated throughout Australian history. In 1688, he sailed along the coast of what is now Western Australia, in the vicinity of King Sound. In 1699, he sailed his ship

Crude sketch of Bennelong published in 1904 by T Egerton, Whitehall (image courtesy of AIATSIS, item MASSOLA.A01. BW-N02450_11)

5.7 ESTIMATES OF THE INDIGENOUS POPULATION - At 30 June

	1901(a)		1991(b)		1996(c)		2001(d)		2006(d)	
State/Territory	no.	%	no.	%	no.	%	no.	%	no.	%
New South Wales	7,434	8.0	75,020	26.5	109,925	28.5	121,142	28.4	132,716	28.3
Victoria	652	0.7	17,890	6.3	22,598	5.9	24,586	5.8	26,541	5.7
Queensland	26,670	28.6	74,214	26.2	104,817	27.2	118,749	27.8	133,288	28.4
South Australia	5,185	5.6	17,239	6.1	22,051	5.7	24,313	5.7	26,633	5.7
Western Australia	30,000	32.1	44,082	15.6	56,205	14.6	61,505	14.4	66,976	14.3
Tasmania	157	0.2	9,461	3.3	15,322	4.0	16,644	3.9	18,023	3.8
Northern Territory	23,235	24.9	43,273	15.3	51,876	13.4	56,364	13.2	60,610	12.9
Australian Capital Territory	..	..	1,616	0.6	3,058	0.8	3,589	0.8	4,149	0.9
Australia(e)	93,333	100.0	282,979	100.0	386,049	100.0	427,094	100.0	469,135	100.0

(a) Estimates in 1901 based on separate State Censuses. WA number was estimated without an enumeration of the Indigenous population.
(b) Estimate based on the 1991 Census of Population and Housing.
(c) Estimate based on the 1996 Census of Population and Housing.
(d) Projection based on low series, which assumes no further increase in propensity to identify as Indigenous from 1996.
(e) Includes Jervis Bay.

Source: Experimental Estimates of the Aboriginal and Torres Strait Islander Population (3230.0); Experimental Projections of the Aboriginal and Torres Strait Islander Population (3231.0); Population Issues, Indigenous Australians (4708.0).

Australian Bureau of Statistics (2003) '5.7 Estimates of the Indigenous population', 1301.0 - Year Book Australia, 2003, accessed 20 July 2021

the HMS *Roebuck* near Shark Bay, also on that coastline. J. Bach, in the *Australian Dictionary of Biography*, wrote:

Dampier's direct contribution to Australian history was slight; indeed, his own impression of the west coast was unfavourable, since it seemed to him to be a long series of reefs and shoals behind which lay sandhills and barren country, apparently without water and inhabited by 'the miserablest People in the World'. There is nothing in this description of the topography to endanger his reputation for accurate observation. Nevertheless the great interest in the southern continent roused by his books was sustained throughout the century and the final exploration of the Pacific was carried out by his fellow-countrymen.[43]

More than 400 years after Dampier's mistaken impressions were published, it has finally become obvious to non-Indigenous scientists and other researchers that the Aboriginal and Torres Strait Islander peoples' intellectual traditions have been transmitted over hundreds of generations. It's now realised that they are capable of explaining with great clarity and detail their own traditions of knowledge, and they can fully engage in debates about their philosophies and ways of knowing and learning.

When the British arrived in 1788 to found the penal colony at Port Jackson, their first encounters with Aboriginal people were remarkable at first. For a few years, Lieutenant Phillip sought their friendship to gather intelligence about the lands beyond. The records from that time show genuine curiosity on the part of the British. Except for a few individuals, such as Bennelong, the Aboriginal people kept their distance.

Bennelong sought to befriend Phillip to obtain an ally against his British enemies, and he seemed to have a few. Some of Phillip's men were not motivated by the strategy of maintaining good relationships to ease the way to making the colony permanent. His gamekeeper, it can be ascertained from the records, was suspected of assaulting local women, and one of the local leaders sought revenge.

Attacks on the gamekeeper's lodge by Indigenous resistance fighter Pemelwuy were enough motivation for Phillip, by this time dispirited by the difficulties he faced, to order Pemelwuy's head to be brought to him. After that, the relationships turned to war, and massacres of local people became more and more common as free men (as opposed to convicts) set out to stake their claim to what was then entirely Aboriginal land, owned by named clans and governed by a subtle system of laws implemented by a hierarchy of Elders.

The violence was repeated across the continent with terrible consequences. The population decline was rapid. In experimental projections the Australian Bureau of Statistics has estimated that, while the original population in 1788 must have numbered at a minimum 300,000, and some estimates are of a million people, there were about 93,000 Aboriginal people remaining in 1901 (see table on page 83).

The currency in the colony was rum for the convicts and wine for the senior officers. Once alcohol had caught Aboriginal people in its grip, the decline of the Gadigal people in the area we now call Sydney became apparent. Moreover, a smallpox epidemic in 1789 killed more than half the population of the local people and then spread inland.

Some Europeans sought to understand the Aboriginal people. Much of what is known about the First Australians during early colonial times comes from their records, many of them detailed. Paintings, drawings and other illustrations also provide a window on Aboriginal life.

After these earliest encounters, the records present too often a hateful catalogue of unjustifiable opinions. What is often not understood is that these people were documenting the First Australians and their societies after the horrors of the colonial invasion, which was often violent and brutal. Their observations were made after epidemics of disease that also greatly reduced Aboriginal populations, and when the First Australians were being rounded up and confined to reserves and missions. Apart from the few documented accounts of first contact, they were observing people whose social and environmental worlds had already been largely destroyed or permanently altered. This was especially the case in south-eastern Australia where the colonisers arrived first. This pattern of observing people undergoing radical and often violent change continued as the colonists spread across the continent.

They were not observing the lives of the First peoples as they had been before contact, and so the records are often an untrue and derogatory reflection of the Aboriginal ways of life as they were originally.

This is why the work of Bill Gammage and Bruce Pascoe is so important. They correct the false impression that earlier records of Aboriginal life give and inform

Australians today about the ways of life – social, economic and environmental – of the First Australians. By carefully reading the literature, they show that Aboriginal people were knowledgeable and highly skilled in managing their environments and making a dignified and satisfying way of life economically from their resources.

Many Europeans in the colonies were committed to the ideas of a racial hierarchy, and regarded Aboriginal and Torres Strait Islander people as members of 'inferior races'. These ideas distorted their perceptions and their accounts. The nineteenth century fashion for 'scientific racism' has been discredited by reputable scientists. The perception of Aboriginal people as 'simple' and 'backward' has been shown to be a vile and destructive myth.

Many Aboriginal Elders and custodians of our knowledge traditions want all Australians to know about them. They especially want Indigenous children to learn about our knowledge traditions in school, and young people to learn about them at universities. They want teachers to understand that a sound education about Australian life, history, society and environments must include our knowledge systems.

To understand the logic of Indigenous systems of knowledge requires being an Indigenous-born cultural expert. A few dedicated people in each society attain this status through a lifetime of cultural practice. However, it is important for everyone to know about the ancient knowledge traditions that enabled hundreds of generations of the First Australians to live here.

There are teachers scattered across our schools who have enriched their own lives and the lives of their students by teaching Aboriginal and Torres Strait histories and culture. By doing so, they have shown respect for our peoples and given joy and hope to the Indigenous students in their classrooms who want to see themselves reflected in the school curriculum. Also, they have conveyed a deeper understanding of all of Australia's history to students who want to know about our peoples and their traditions.

6
ART

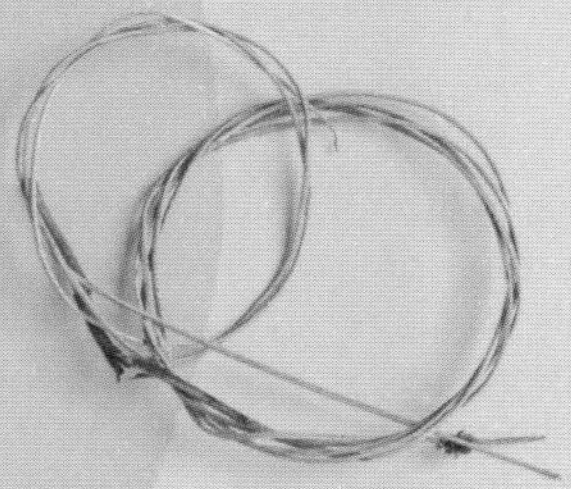

Australian Indigenous artists are acclaimed around the world and their works are held in major public and private galleries locally and internationally. The diversity of artistic styles of Indigenous Australia grows each year as communities, clans and families venture into the art market with renditions of their visual traditions. As well as this increasing diversity in style, the media and materials used by the artists also continue to expand, from bark painting and canvas and acrylic formats, to include fabric and fibre weaving, screen-printing, linocut prints, sculptures in materials such as metal, multimedia presentations using communications technology and computer imagery, virtual reality, photomedia and sound.

There are many more styles of Indigenous art than is generally understood. They range from adaptations of traditional ritual and rock art to the full spectrum of Modernist and Postmodernist art. Some of the regional styles are particularly distinctive, such as the works of the Pintupi art movement and other Central Australian and Western Desert styles, the Arnhem Land bark paintings, and the paintings and sculptures of the Cape York regions; and the artistic community in the Torres Strait Islands creates its own distinctive sculptures and linocuts also.

'Aboriginal art' is an umbrella term for many traditional, adapted and modern styles, forms and genres from diverse and distant regions of the Australian continent and its islands. Many of these places are as remote and isolated as it is possible to be in this world. Yet a painting from a tiny Aboriginal settlement in an Australian desert or on a tropical savannah floodplain can be found in a gallery in a major international city – in New York, Paris or Berlin – and be celebrated as a profoundly important expression of human creativity.

There are hundreds of Aboriginal and Torres Strait Islander artists. Their work can be seen at galleries, art competitions and art festivals throughout Australia. Each capital city has a public art gallery with significant Indigenous collections. There are also collections on exhibition in many leading international institutions, such as the British Museum, the Musée du quai Branly in Paris, and the Kluge-Ruhe Collection at the University of Virginia in the United States of America, to mention just a few. Indigenous works also appear in many important private collections, such as that of Swiss art collector Bérengère Primat. Her gallery and Foundation Opale, in the rural Alpine town of Lens, is dedicated in large part to the artwork of Indigenous Australians.

Many collections in major galleries include artworks that are heavily influenced by classical Aboriginal traditions, as well as the works of Indigenous Modernist, Postmodernist and experimental artists. Museums have traditionally collected precious objects that their curators classify as 'artefacts', but which Indigenous people regard as the property of their ancestors. In this chapter, I will briefly introduce you to some Aboriginal and Torres Strait Islander artists – the Pintupi, Warlpiri and Yolŋu artists – and explain their social and historical contexts.

Aboriginal art circulates in the global market as a kind of commodity, and yet it is difficult to say how its value is determined. This may be because an Aboriginal art object, or commodity, holds many values simultaneously. It is unlikely that any one person would identify both the market and the non-market values embedded in an object. These are discerned by a collection of people in the marketplace, some estimating the object's economic worth and others its cultural and historical significance.

While a painting from a tiny Aboriginal settlement can be found in a major international gallery in a big city, the artist might live in extreme poverty, and die at a young age from a treatable disease or condition. They might never see the world where their art will hang. We cannot ignore this contrast between wealth and poverty that is embedded in the material history of an Aboriginal art object in the global marketplace.

The impact of colonisation on Indigenous people is expressed in much Aboriginal artwork. This impact may not be obvious in the subject matter of the work, but by

Aboriginal artist Wayne Quilliam shares his creations of connection to the land at a major installation in central Sydney (photo Wayne Quilliam)

APY Women's Collaborative, Amata, South Australia, 2017

the way people in Australia and around the world view Aboriginal art images. In each work of art there is a specific personal story grounded in a historical and social past. This is why the contribution anthropologists and historians make to the work of the art historian is valuable. The transition of art traditions and history from ancient societies into the fast-changing world of postcolonial Australian life is complicated. So the input of people in various fields helps the public to understand and appreciate the artwork.

Among other things, it is the meanings within Aboriginal art that make it so profound. And it is in the world of making meaning that the structure and fascination of Aboriginal art are to be found.

Worldwide audiences are attracted to Indigenous art because of the ancient traditions of the First Australians and, I believe, because of its extreme 'otherness': its difference from Western art. The difference is partly to do with the Indigenous treatment of space. An almost universal meaning found in Aboriginal art is the connection between being and place. The idea of place is not of something 'out there' but of something that is part of the nature of ourselves, especially in relation to special places. This is the key idea that many Aboriginal artists offer to their audiences. Modern global living means people might live in a place without having a personal history that is connected to it. Indigenous people have spiritual and religious connections to places over countless generations, and they bring these connections into their art.

Spiritual and religious beliefs are an essential part of Indigenous social structures and the Indigenous interpretation of the world.

When we look at Aboriginal art and images, often it is possible to see the religious beliefs represented in them. The religious symbols sometimes show how Christianity became a part of many Indigenous people's lives after colonisation. The engagement and the conflict between two religious systems since the eighteenth century are sources of inspiration for a great deal of art today.

Art is central to Aboriginal life, identity and culture. One of the results of the unimaginably long period of human presence in Australia – at least 65,000 years – is the vast array of rock art that can be found in most parts of the country. Captured in this ancient art are many of the totemic icons and visual designs – or the 'Dreaming' elements – that appear in modern Aboriginal art and material culture, dance and storytelling. More than art alone, these are the signs of a great human migration across the oceans and the archipelago to our north, and across this vast continent. The remains of ancient Aboriginal life are to be found scattered across landscapes everywhere. Examples include the stone walls of houses in south-western Victoria, the engraved trees on the inland plains of New South Wales and Victoria, the engraved concentric rings in rock faces that signal water sources in the arid areas, and stone tool-making sites.

Artist Michael J Connolly (Munda-gutta Kulliwari) at Dreamtime Kullilla-Art Gallery, Queensland

Artworks by (left to right) Noŋgirrŋa Marawili, Baluka Marawili, Noŋgirrŋa Marawili at Buku-Larrŋgay Mulka Centre, courtesy of the artists, Buku-Larrŋgay Mulka Centre

Painting and engraving rock faces enabled people to write, read and, through time, negotiate the land's cultural meaning. The experience of standing in a rock-art gallery gazing at ancient paintings of people and times long gone is spine-chilling. I have stood on sand in a sandstone escarpment shelter where people had camped tens of thousands of years ago. Gazing up at their paintings, some of them gigantic and elaborate, is a kind of time travel. The paintings seem to resonate with the spirit of the people who made them. The hand stencils made by groups of Aboriginal people record their visits to these rock galleries. Each man, woman and child in the group held their hand up as an Elder blew liquid ochre over them to record their presence.

These beautiful images, often found at the base of large rock-art galleries, are a form of census. We can look at them and imagine the people who marked their presence at these places. Who among them were the artists, we wonder? Who painted the giant kangaroos, the barramundi and saratoga fish, the hunting scenes, and the magical ancestral figures across the walls of the escarpment shelters? Rock art plays a role in the definition of territory and identity. The artists painted themes in styles that portray the particular reality of a world view and a society.

We can imagine families at these rock-art galleries, sitting at night around their campfires, telling the stories of a good season hunting, fishing and harvesting; enjoying their meal cooked on the fire; celebrating a rich season on the grassy plains through their painting and storytelling; and taking shelter from the rain, the thunder, the lightning and storms. The Wanjina paintings in the Kimberley region of Western Australia show the faces of ancestors who came with these storms, and the lightning strikes are painted around their heads to depict their association with the wild storms of the monsoonal season.

When art collectors first approached Aboriginal painters to buy their work, there was no Indigenous art market as we know it today. Very little had been written about Aboriginal design traditions and material culture. The standard view was that only European works could be considered as art. The work of other 'races' was generally seen as merely primitive mark making. Paintings on bark and various funerary sculptures were collected as exotic objects for anthropological study and exhibition. Christian missionaries also collected them as part of their attempts to establish cottage art industries to financially support artists and their families.

Explorers in the eighteenth and nineteenth century collected objects and material culture as exotic trophies and evidence of their travels. Also, some came across rock paintings and revealed them to the world. Sir George Grey, later appointed Governor of South Australia, happened on the Wanjina paintings on sandstone escarpments in the Kimberley region during his exploration of the area in 1838. The Wanjina is the Rain Maker spirit and is often painted with headdresses that represent thunder and lightning.

In 1891, pastoralist Joseph Bradshaw saw ancient rock paintings in the north-west Kimberley region. That is the homeland of the Wunambal and Gaambera peoples. These paintings are now known as the 'Bradshaws', but more correctly should be called by their Aboriginal names, which include *Gwion Gwion* and *Giro Giro*. These are finely detailed paintings of figures, and they are still the subject of research today.

Art historian Andrew Sayers surveyed nineteenth-century Aboriginal artists and their relationships with the European artists they met. He found that in the colonies of New South Wales and Victoria, European artists gave Aboriginal artists paint and other materials, and the Aboriginal men observed the painting styles of the newcomers. The result is a body of drawings and paintings that departs from the men's symbolic traditions.

Adopting to some degree the styles of the European artists they met, they painted and sketched detailed representations of the rapidly changing world around them. Sayers documented drawings by several artists, including works by a man called Black Johnny, which resulted from his meeting with Austrian artist Eugene von Guérard in Victoria's Western District in 1855. Sayers wrote that the work of these Aboriginal artists had two major themes: ceremonies, and traditional hunting and food gathering. Other subjects included encounters with Europeans, such as William Buckley, the 'wild white man', squatters – both sober and inebriated – Chinese men being chased by Aboriginal men, and sailing ships.

In the first half of the twentieth century, Ronald M. Berndt and Catherine H. Berndt documented Aboriginal societies in Western Australia and the Northern Territory, and they also worked briefly in South Australia. During 1947, when they lived in Yirrkala in Arnhem Land in the Northern Territory, they gave some Yolŋu people brown paper and crayons and asked them to draw their world. The works these people produced represent a turning point in the understanding of Aboriginal art. They depict a range of subjects, such as ancestral figures, brightly coloured renditions of traditional ceremonial and body painting, with some variation from the classical forms. Ronald Berndt documented their subjects in detail, and this extraordinary collection is now registered with the Australian Memory of the World Register, a project of the UNESCO Memory of the World Register.

In June 1956, the Czech artist Karel Kupka arrived at Milingimbi in Arnhem Land with the intention of finding Aboriginal bark paintings as examples of the work of 'early man'. Basel Museum had commissioned him to bring back works to add to their small collection. Milingimbi, the oldest Yolŋu town, had become the location of a mission settlement established by the Methodist Overseas Mission. Visiting there, Kupka developed a friendship with artists Tom Djawa and Dawidi Birritjama in order to understand their art. He travelled to other communities as well. The result of his collecting and studying was a short book that told readers very little about these great traditions. It was translated into English as *Dawn of Art*, but its original title, *Un Art a l'État Brut (Art of a Brutish State)*, says a great deal about ignorant attitudes to Aboriginal people in the 1950s.

I have mentioned only a few of the early encounters Aboriginal artists had with Europeans. In the 1960s and 1970s, radical changes took place in the world of Aboriginal art and a better-informed audience and market for art developed with the emergence of the Papunya art movement.

In the early 1970s, an art teacher, Geoffrey Bardon, was sent by the Education

Artists cutting bark in Milingimbi, Northern Territory, to make bark paintings, 1963

Department to Papunya, a remote Aboriginal settlement in Central Australia. He soon found himself witnessing and supporting what was to become a major Australian art form of international standing. Bardon assisted the Luritja and Pintupi Elders to create their religious art with materials readily available on the settlement: acrylic paint on fibro at first, and later canvas. In 1971, he invited some of the men in the community to paint a blank school wall. The men took a great interest in the startling transfer of their ceremonial sand-sculpture designs to modern materials. Soon their works were being exhibited to great acclaim.

Bardon recognised the importance of the old men's wall paintings and encouraged them to paint more. They went on to paint murals on the Papunya school walls. Not satisfied with the results, senior men Long Jack Phillipus Tjakamarra and Billy Stockman Tjapaltjarri painted a Honey Ant Dreaming mural on the wall. This provoked such intense interest among the people living at Papunya that, in the same year, about fifty senior men produced around 620 small paintings on boards, using acrylic paint. In 1972, the artists successfully established their own company, which continues today as Papunya Tula Pty Ltd in Alice Springs. This famous art cooperative brought the art traditions of a small group in the centre of Australia to the world. Their style came to be synonymous with Aboriginal art, despite the long history of many other regional styles.

The images in their paintings, before seen only as sand paintings in ceremonies, sent a clear message that here was a religion with meanings and explanations as deep and as relevant as any that Christian

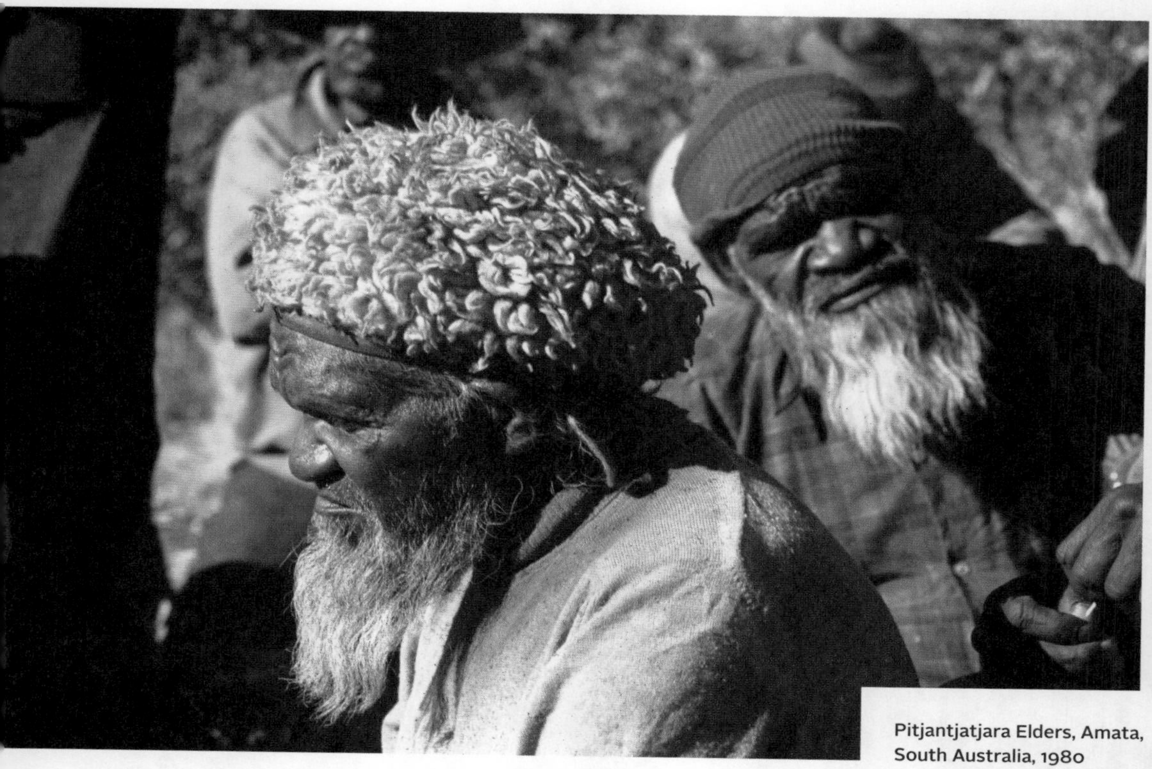

Pitjantjatjara Elders, Amata, South Australia, 1980

missionaries might follow. The paintings were commercially successful but, as anthropologist Fred Myers reported, dispute arose when Pitjantjatjara men from the Warburton Range area of the Great Western Desert saw an exhibition of these paintings in Perth. They did not agree with the sacred designs being put on public display. To overcome this, the sacred symbols were disguised by incorporating them into other designs or omitting them from the final works.

This movement spread throughout most parts of the Central and Western deserts. By the late 1970s, the style was attracting considerable interest in Sydney and Melbourne. It is now classified into a number of 'genres' of the Western Desert acrylic art movement.

From the early 1970s, the Central Desert peoples started to move off government-run Aboriginal settlements, such as Papunya. They returned to the homelands to renew their connections with their sacred places and their histories and meanings. This was an essential step in ensuring the survival of their cultures. They painted their sacred designs for an enthusiastic audience that was prepared to pay for the privilege of seeing the marks of the ancestors. This enabled the leaders of this cultural movement to pursue their philosophical traditions, and to offer the paintings to a marketplace as signs of their ownership of these stories and histories.

A first-hand account of this pivotal period in Australian art history is told in a book by Geoffrey Bardon and his older brother, James Bardon: *Papunya: A Place Made after the Story*. It features images of more than 500 paintings, drawings and photographs from Bardon's personal archive, many of which are 'now regarded as some of Australia's most treasured cultural, historical and artistic items'.

Exhibitions in Paris and the United Kingdom, principally of the Papunya style of art with the distinctive lines and dots that appear to depict a bird's eye view of landscapes, excited the art world. Soon, paintings began to sell for high prices as collectors competed for the rare pieces that reached the northern hemisphere.

The paintings of the Papunya Tula movement tell us that these were people who lived in and knew an immense territory as their home. They journeyed on foot to their far-flung camps within these landscapes. Each camp, or ngurra, was reached after days of walking, sometimes carrying water in wooden vessels. On the way, side journeys were taken to hunt animals, gather vegetable foods or collect firewood. Reaching a ngurra, they cooked in their ground ovens, and before sleep, around their fires in the night, they could gaze at the other great sacred geography in the night sky where ancestors reside among their stellar marvels.

People who live in the open air read the light and shadow of the day, the movements of the stars, the colour, direction and shape of clouds as they traverse the sky, the signs of smoke and dust in the landscape, the level of water in waterholes, the direction of birds flying across the sky in the evening and the tracks and scats of animals. They predict the weather from the rings around the moon, the seasons, and the movement of ants and birds. To eat and live well depends on attention to these details.

Understanding the landscape intimately, living under a vast sky and knowing what lies beyond the horizons is a geographical legacy that is represented in paintings. These graphic designs were formerly marked out in sacred sand sculptures with feathers and sacramental matter, prepared by gatherings of men or women in groupings affiliated with a particular ancestors and sites. They decorated these sculptures as if painting the body of a kinsman.

In 1985, keen to present their own works to the public and distinguish themselves from the Pintupi artists, the Warlpiri people formed Warlukurlangu Artists, now an Aboriginal Corporation. In the Warlpiri language, Warlukurlangu means 'belonging to fire'. In contrast to the subtle colour palette seen in the Pintupi paintings, the Warlpiri artists preferred bold, saturated colours.

The public first saw their distinctive style when the artists painted thirty doors at the Yuendumu school in the Northern Territory. Judith Crispin, who worked with Warlpiri Elders, explains that in 1984, the school principal, Terry Davies, welcomed the approach by the artists, Paddy Japaljarri Stewart, Paddy Japaljarri Sims, Larry Jungarrayi Spencer, Paddy Jupurrula Nelson and Roy Jupurrula Curtis. These men went on to paint the doors with their most important Jukurrpa (the sacred

Warlpiri artists Clarise Nampijinpa Poulson and Michael Japangardi Poulson with son Joel Japanangka Poulson in Yuendumu, 1989

narratives and laws referred to in English as 'the Dreaming') to teach the children about their traditional Country. Twelve years later, the South Australian Museum acquired the doors.

Paddy Japaljarri Stewart's account of painting the doors reveals that the designs, like so much of the art that emerged from the desert communities at that time, were inspired by the sacred ground paintings made for ceremonies. Here are his words, as quoted in an article by Crispin at kurdijiapp.wordpress.com:

We can't leave our Jukurrpa behind, we have to keep it alive.

When my father was alive this is what he taught me. He taught me the traditional ways like the traditional designs in body or head of Kangaroo Dreaming (that's what we call Marlu Dreaming) and Eagle Dreaming. He taught me to sing song for the big ceremonies.

The Warlukurlangu artists' cooperative commenced soon after the artists painted the doors. As recounted on the website, the motivation driving the Elders was their desire to maintain their cultural practices.

In 2014–15, the National Museum of Australia exhibited drawings by Warlpiri people. They had been sketched in the 1950s at the government settlement of Hooker Creek, now the township of Lajamanu, in the Northern Territory, when, in 1953, anthropologist Mervyn Meggitt invited Warlpiri men to draw with crayons on paper. The drawings were deposited with the Australian Institute of Aboriginal Torres Strait Islander Studies. Some sixty years later, the descendants of the artists were shown these works.

At the end of the assimilation period, in the 1970s, Aboriginal artists were encouraged by the Australian government's establishment of the Aboriginal Arts Board of the Australia Council. This was also the time when the government responded to the first Native Title case, brought by the Yolŋu people of north-east Arnhem Land.

When Justice Blackburn handed down his decision in this case, the Yolŋu people and their supporters were shocked. Blackburn found that there could be no recognition of Aboriginal laws, despite the large amount of evidence of their existence submitted to the court. His argument rested on the ceded colony doctrine, better known as the 'terra nullius' doctrine.

The new federal government appointed Justice Edward Woodward to head a commission of inquiry to determine how Aboriginal rights in land could be recognised. He had been the Queen's Counsel representing the Yolŋu clans in the court. At the end of Woodward's hearings of further evidence from the clan leaders, in 1973, the Yolŋu people gave him a number of gifts, including sacred bark paintings and objects. He had become Sir Edward Woodward after a distinguished career, and was chancellor of the University of Melbourne from 1990 until 2001. In early 2003, he entrusted the works to the University of Melbourne's Ian Potter Museum. They are works of art and sacred objects that record the life and history, the sacred narratives and land and sea estates, of the respective Yolŋu clans whose Elders at that time created them.

Art and country

Famous artist and leader of the Madarrpa clan Djambawa Marawili stated the link between art and Country when he spoke at the Garma Forum in 2003: 'Why do I look at arts? What does it mean? It is very

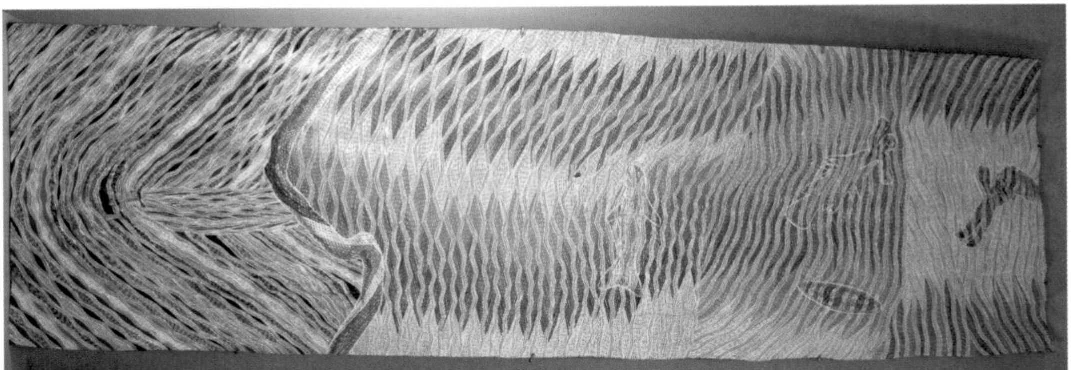

Source of Fire (2014), Djambawa Marawili, earth pigments and sawdust on bark, courtesy of the artist, Buku-Larrŋgay Mulka Centre and the Levi Kaplan Collection

important to me. Because it is the image of the art here in the country. The country is talking to me. We have knowledge.'

His work has featured in many exhibitions, such as the groundbreaking 'Saltwater' exhibition. The exhibition, initiated by Marawili, was part of important evidence of sacred sites that led to the successful 2008 Blue Mud Bay High Court sea rights claim. The authors of the 'Saltwater' exhibition catalogue note that the 'Yolŋu artists had dual motives for selling their artwork: to purchase goods in exchange and to teach Europeans about the value of their culture'.

These beautiful images, as well as the manikay (songs) and buŋgul (dance and performances) associated with them, may be understood in Western thinking as works of artistic and performative expression. For the Yolŋu people they have profound meanings and are associated with matters of law.

The Yolŋu universe has two parts – Dhuwa and Yirritja – and each person, animal and plant, all land or sea estate, sky, water and other beings belong to one or the other. These moieties, or halves, are fundamental in the kinship and marriage system and the general order of things. The maternal connection is especially important in this regard. The yothu–yindi (child–mother link) and the gutharra–märi (daughter's child – mother's mother link) form foundational ties between clans and their estates. The bäpurru is a group of clans linked by songs, dances and designs associated with a particular waŋarr being, who travelled the land when it was first created. Bäpurru also refers to the members of a single clan who come together for ceremonial purposes to celebrate the sacred story that gave birth to them. It is from this story that their shared inheritance of sacred objects and rituals, resources and governing responsibilities comes.

In 1962–63, the clan leaders of north-east Arnhem Land presided over the creation of two large Church Panels painted with clan emblems, representing the Yirritja and Dhuwa moieties and the most sacred designs of the clan waŋarr. They were then displayed in the mission church at Yirrkala. These events marked a turning point in the relationship between Aboriginal people and the Yirrkala missionaries.

Following this, in 1963, in protest at the federal government's decision that bauxite mining could take place on their lands, the Yolŋu clan leaders prepared the famous Yirrkala Bark Petitions. These are sacred paintings that were prepared in ritual fashion, signed in English fashion, and submitted to the Australian Parliament in Canberra. The meetings of Elders to prepare the petitions were the precursor to their litigation in *Milirrpum v Nabalco*. A parliamentary inquiry into the acquisition of the Yolŋu land for mining followed, in 1964. In 1976, the *Aboriginal Land Rights (Northern Territory) Act 1976* was enacted by the federal Parliament to provide inalienable freehold title to Aboriginal land trusts over former Aboriginal reserves and other lands.

In each of the historical events briefly described here, Yolŋu artworks were produced to proclaim the existence of Yolŋu law, particularly land and sea ownership, and the mythological events that resulted in the creation of the land. These paintings represent, in figurative

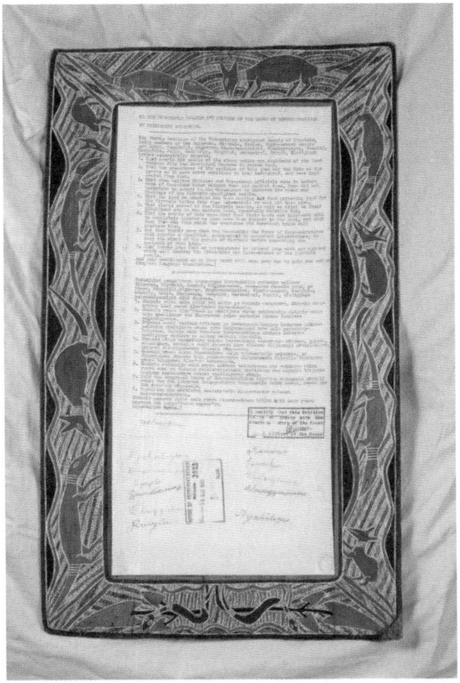

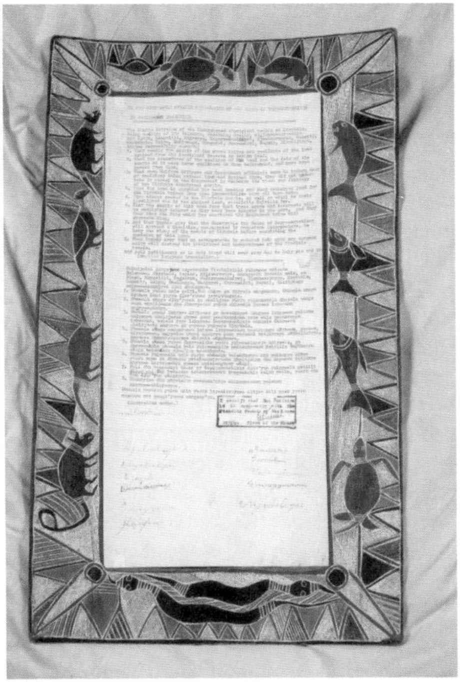

The Yirrkala Bark Petitions presented to Parliament on 14 August (left) and 28 August (right), 1963. Courtesy of the House of Representatives, Commonwealth Parliament of Australia.

and geometric form, the totemic landscape of eastern Arnhem Land. Naming is perhaps the primary act of representation and, in the Yolŋu world, it is a tradition of profound importance. Djambawa Marawili explains this in Andrew Blake's work *Saltwater: Yirrkala Bark Paintings of Sea Country*.

Every individual in this area has a name, small special names, small sacred names, canoe names. Yolŋu have used these names through the ceremonial singing of our ancestors or in the naming of our grandchildren. They are all names in the individual lands; also in the sea. Every small bit of sea has a name.

... There are places there, names there, names that are special, that Yolŋu receive in their heads. And sing and give names to children. Also it explains the country, how they became one, not only the sea but the land too. They became one.[44]

Hence, art serves the purpose of encoding the images that are associated with ancestral names, sacred stories and interpreting people's association with special places and things.

Yolŋu visual representations are intricate and highly structured. The imagery and design of these artworks are rich in metaphor and analogy. If we could read the signs of their culture as they do, a web of the signs of power would emerge from the world around us. Just as the sunset speaks of many sacred elements, so too do flowering plants, which tell us about the seasonality of wild foods; yam leaves, which tell us about an ancestral presence in a clan estate; honey, which tells us about the revolutionary ancestor Ganbulabula; and waterholes, which tell us about souls.

Ethical dealings in First Australians art

It is the special status of art and design in the Aboriginal world that has caused a body of rights to be developed. They are not all recognised by law, but they are observed in the practices of ethical gallery owners and curators. Protection of Aboriginal artists' rights has been the subject of government inquiries, court cases and campaigns over several decades. Crudely manufactured goods made in China or Indonesia, and sold to tourists as 'Aboriginal art', 'boomerangs' and 'didgeridoos', fill souvenir shops and galleries in the tourist precincts of Australia.

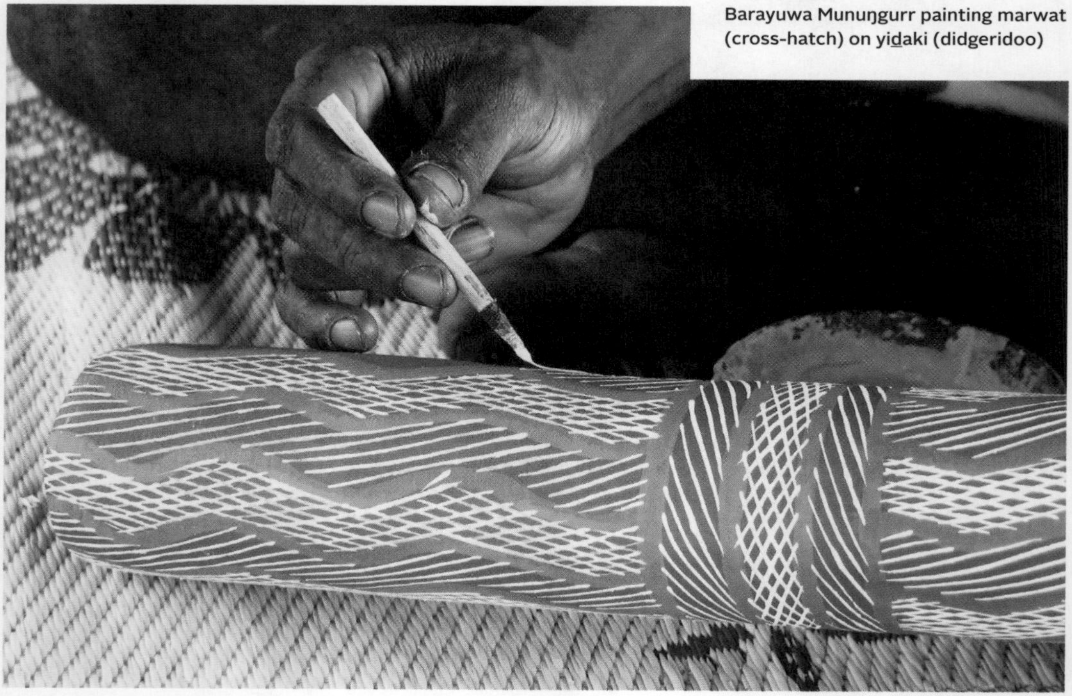

Barayuwa Munuŋgurr painting marwat (cross-hatch) on yid̲aki (didgeridoo)

This trade causes immense harm to Indigenous artists and their families, and brings Indigenous art into disrepute.

Establishing the authenticity of an artwork is important for both the Indigenous artists and the people who buy their art. All reputable and ethical commercial galleries and art cooperatives document each piece and the artist, and provide certificates of authenticity. Even so, fraudsters have copied works or made works in the style of famous artists and sold them to naive buyers. The art centres represented at the Indigenous art fairs are backed by groups such as Desart and the Association of Northern, Kimberley and Arnhem Aboriginal Artists. They are governed by elected councils of Aboriginal artists and advocate for their members.

After several copyright cases in the courts, it was a fraud case in Victoria in 2007 that finally delivered justice to Aboriginal artists whose works had been copied. In the first successful prosecution of art fraud, Pamela Yvonne Liberto and her husband Ivan Liberto were found guilty by a county court jury. They had conned the major art auction houses into selling fraudulent copies. It was reported in the *Age* newspaper in 2007 that:

The Libertos received more than $300,000 after forging and selling four paintings, supposedly by renowned artist Rover Thomas, whose work is keenly sought by collectors across the world and attracted a record price when the National Gallery of Australia purchased All That Big Rain Coming *from Top Side for $778,000 in 2001.*[45]

Scientific examination of the paint and materials to date the works, carried out by the University of Melbourne Centre for Cultural Materials Conservation, provided the evidence of fraud.

Fraud leads to financial losses for the artists and their families, and the artists often feel that their soul has been stolen. Some artists have refused to work again after they discovered copies of their works were sold under their name. Traditional Owners and clans own their traditional designs. Often one person in the group is authorised by their father, mother or grandparent to execute the designs of their people. These designs are inherited, and even though the work of art is intended for the market, the artist feels that they are offering it to the world as a gift with the spirit of their ancestry and special places. Also, the traditional works often depict religious content. In earlier copyright cases in the 1980s and 1990s, aggrieved artists gave evidence to this effect, but these cases did little to protect their rights.

Lawyers Terri Janke and Maiko Sentina have summed up the dilemma succinctly in their work *Indigenous Knowledge*, from 2018:

Indigenous Knowledge is the heart of Indigenous identity. It connects Indigenous people to the lands and seas that they have lived in, and around, for over 65,000 years.

... Indigenous people assert their rights to their intangible heritage and their Indigenous Knowledge to continue their practice of their culture; and to stop misappropriation of their knowledge without consultation or consent, and to stop debasement and loss of cultural practice.[46]

Understanding the laws, customs and traditions of the First Australians is vitally important. Ethical practices and education about Indigenous art, heritage and cultural traditions will serve to protect them. If you know about our cultures, you will be more likely to respect them.

Detail of installation by Gunybi Ganambarrr in the West Australian Indigenous Art Award, Art Gallery of Western Australia, 2013

First Australians art in the global market

Indigenous artists working in non-traditional styles and with contemporary art materials emerged in the nineteenth century, and by the middle of the twentieth century some achieved national fame. Albert Namatjira, an Arrernte man from the Lutheran mission of Hermannsburg, painted exquisite watercolours of his beloved Country in Central Australia. His works were avidly collected and admired, and over time his distinctive style has become recognised as a school of art, with many of his descendants following in his footsteps. The most celebrated today is Vincent Namatjira, who in 2020 became the first Indigenous artist to win the prestigious Archibald Prize for his portrait of champion Australian Rules footballer Adam Goodes. Exhibiting his work both nationally and internationally since 2015, Vincent Namatjira satirises Australia's colonial history in his bold conceptual works 'with recurring references to Captain Cook, the British Royal family and contemporary aspects of Indigenous life'.

Several other Indigenous artists have achieved global fame with their distinctive paintings, motifs, photography and multimedia pieces. Their works often speak back to the highly Eurocentric fine-arts world in Australia. Tracey Moffatt is the first Indigenous artist to have her photographs exhibited in prestigious art galleries in the northern hemisphere. She was chosen to represent Australia at the 2017 Venice Biennale, creating a collection of photographic and video works called *My Horizon*, which was considered a huge success. Moffatt revolutionised the way that Aboriginal art was received and opened the door for the new wave of Indigenous artists experimenting with history, form, media and stereotypes.

Brook Garru Andrew, who claims his Wiradjuri and Celtic ancestors, has similarly achieved global fame. In his own words, his art practice involves deep thinking about the representation of Indigenous people in various media:

His interdisciplinary practice harnesses alternative narratives to explore the

VINCENT NAMATJIRA
Stand strong for who you are, 2020
Acrylic on linen
152 × 198 × 3 cm

Image courtesy of the artist, Iwantja Arts & THIS IS NO FANTASY. Collection of Art Gallery of New South Wales.

legacies of colonisation and modernism. His artworks, museum interventions and curatorial projects challenge the limitations imposed by power structures, historical amnesia, stereotyping and complicity to centre Indigenous perspectives. Apart from drawing inspiration from vernacular objects and the archive he travels internationally to work with artists, communities and various private and public collections.

The rich, research-based interventions and artworks of Brook Andrew have been presented in exhibitions nationally and internationally since 1996.[47]

His pieces use mediums ranging from neon, installation, photomedia and mixed-media, to performance and video. Andrew challenges perceptions and history, often manipulating text and images to address colonialism and the racialisation of minority peoples. Andrew is also the first Indigenous Australian to be selected as the artistic director for the Biennale of Sydney, in 2020. He called the event *Nirin*, which is the Wiradjuri word for 'edge' and acknowledges the importance of Indigenous languages. Sadly, this extraordinary exhibition was only available online after the opening week because of COVID-19 restrictions.

These trailblazers have changed the way we think about Australian art, profoundly and permanently. My own view is their art is the most exciting art in Australia, and if their success is a measure, then thousands of people agree with me. Hundreds of Aboriginal artists have followed them. Misinformed art historians call them 'urban artists', but many are not or were not urban dwellers. The late Ian Abdulla was a Ngarrindjeri artist who's been called Australia's greatest 'naïve' artist with his paintings of his early life in the Riverland region in rural South Australia.

Every major and rural gallery has collected some of the works from the multi-disciplinary Indigenous artists of the last fifty years and many regularly have major exhibitions. One excellent example was the National Gallery of Victoria's highly successful *From Bark to Neon: Indigenous Art from the NGV Collection*, which included a range of artworks across many mediums. It is these kinds of exhibitions that illustrate the diversity of Indigenous art. There is no one type of Indigenous art or artist. The richness of our traditions and the genius of our artists speaks to the survival of great human traditions of representing our lives and our worlds.

Advice on buying authentic art

It is the work of the catalogue writers and art historians, who meticulously document the art styles and the artists' biographies, that offers the best protection for the buyer. To verify authenticity it is possible to find examples of artists' works, their representatives, and the explanations of their works in galleries, published in books, and in catalogues online.

The Art Galleries Association of Australia and the Australia Commercial Galleries Association have websites that list their members.

Reputable galleries subscribe to the Code of Practice of the National Association for the Visual Arts. The Indigenous Art Code (indigenousartcode.org) was set up in 2010 to preserve and promote ethical trading in Indigenous art. Articles on its website discuss buying art ethically, as outlined below, and the harm caused to artists when people buy fakes.

Major Aboriginal art corporations and associations have long had guidelines for ensuring ethical art purchases. Desart in Central Australia has more than 30 member art centres, and ANKA (Arnhem Northern and Kimberley Artists) Aboriginal Corporation in Australia's north serves Aboriginal artists and 47 art centres. These bodies are governed by their members to represent their interests. 'Working together to keep art, country and culture strong' is ANKA's mission statement. The protection Desart, ANKA and similar Aboriginal art associations and corporations offer is vital to Aboriginal artists' art traditions and their livelihoods, as ANKA attests on its website:

Walangari Karntawarra with artworks at the Double Bay Library, NSW

Aboriginal Art Centres provide economic, cultural and social benefits for some of Australia's most disadvantaged communities, they lead the way in caring for the nation's intangible cultural heritage for all Australians.[48]

Many of these local art centres have websites with the online facilities for secure purchase of art. Not all do, however, so the guidelines provided by ANKA on the organisation's website are important in this very tricky market. As many of the Aboriginal art communities have turned to online sale over the years, so too have the 'carpetbaggers'. You can download guidelines for buying ethically in English, German, French and Japanese, from ANKA's website as well as viewing the Indigenous Art Code guidelines, which are summarised further below.

Most Australian artists in all of the media, from music to the visual arts, were placed in a precarious financial state when COVID-19 restrictions were imposed to stop the spread of the coronavirus that had taken the lives of hundreds of thousands in other countries, and posed an existential threat to the highly vulnerable Indigenous peoples who suffer from a range of pre-existing conditions that place them at risk of severe illness and death. The lockdown approach worked, with not only international and state and territory borders shut, but also the borders of Aboriginal and Torres Strait Islander lands and communities. The usual visitors, tourists and art collectors were not permitted to go to the Indigenous art centres, and even in some cities, travel outside of the home was radically limited. The lives of thousands of people were saved but the economic costs were great.

For artists who depend on the precarious market of Aboriginal and Torres Strait Islander art, the impacts of the COVID-19 restrictions included a dramatic decline in their incomes as sales stopped, and the difficulty of obtaining art materials, which also threatened their livelihoods. Exhibitions were cancelled and airlines cancelled most flights, so the shipping of art sometimes became impossible.

In response to the unethical dealers who flooded the website with fraudulent or substandard Aboriginal works, the Indigenous Art Code set up a campaign to assist artists. *Our Art Is Our Lifeline* was launched by the Indigenous Art Code (IartC) in partnership with Macquarie Group to encourage the ethical purchasing of artwork, especially as audiences embraced online sales. Ethical dealing in Indigenous artwork became the primary consideration for these artists, and they explained how involving them in the sale and licensing of their artwork was fundamental to sustaining their art practice.

Those seeking to purchase Indigenous artworks are advised by IartC to 'look for art centres, galleries and licensed product retailers who are members of the Indigenous Art Code'.

The IartC website has a detailed explanation of the things you need to consider to buy ethically. It outlines the questions you should ask an art centre, a gallery, a dealer, an auction or an art fair about the artists and how they are paid; and the importance of provenance, particularly as there are 'some people selling Aboriginal art (and fake Aboriginal art) who respect neither Indigenous culture nor the wellbeing of the artists and their communities':

In Aboriginal and Torres Strait Islander art, provenance is crucial. The origin and history of ownership of a piece of Aboriginal art is both its birth certificate and passport; providing confidence of authenticity and evidence of ethical practices along the value chain.

The remote locations of many artists and art centres compound historical, political and social forces that have created a situation where the relationship between artist and buyer is fundamentally unequal. A moral compass and commitment to ethical trade by both buyers and sellers is the 'finger on the scales' that balance this inequity.

If buying Aboriginal art is stripped of these values, the relationship between artist and buyer is merely a financial transaction, devoid of connections to the artist's heritage and cultural universe – for many, the very things that attracted them to Aboriginal art in the first place.

The IartC requires all Code signatories to issue a Code Certificate for any piece of Aboriginal and Torres Strait Islander artwork sold by a dealer, including art centres and galleries over AUD$250. These certificates 'provide buyers with high levels of confidence in both provenance and fair payment of the artist'. Buyers do need to be aware, though, that 'some unethical dealers have been known to create their own certificates', which are no proof that they have treated Aboriginal and Torres Strait Islander artists ethically or paid a fair price for their work. A buyer can gain certainty by purchasing a piece of art directly from an art centre, but can also gain confidence about purchasing authentic Aboriginal and Torres Strait art when buying from a gallery by asking some questions that 'any reputable dealer will be happy to answer', as the IartC website indicates:

1. Who is the artist?
2. Where is the artist from?
3. How did you get the artwork or product in your gallery or shop?
4. How was the artist paid for their work?
5. If it is a reproduction of an artist's work, how are royalties or licensing fees paid to the artist?
6. How long has your gallery been around?

   If it's suddenly appeared from nowhere, where were they before? And where will they be next week?
7. Is your gallery a member of the Indigenous Art Code?

   If yes, you know it has agreed to follow the Indigenous Australian Art Commercial Code of Conduct.

As IartC emphasises, ethical galleries and dealers will be willing to answer questions about the artist, their work, the community they come from and the art centre they are connected with. Buyers shouldn't believe galleries or dealers that tell 'stories about the art centre ripping off the artist so they now deal direct' – and, just as the artists do, buyers have a right to know the 'money story' relating to an artwork.

Some warning signs of unethical practices that IartC advises buyers to look out for are:

A collection of works unconnected by theme, region, language or culture.

Merchandise, such as bags, scarves, jewellery and artefacts, that is manufactured overseas and does not attribute an artist. A bone China cup manufactured overseas and licensed fairly to the artist is ethical. A bone China cup manufactured overseas which isn't licensed by an Aboriginal artist is not. See Fake Art Harms Culture.

Will the gallery 'do a deal'? Ethical galleries usually work on a fixed price model with a consistent percentage returned to the art centre and artist. Offers of a discount to close the sale can be a cause for concern.

Does the gallery try to prove the provenance of artworks using photos of artists holding the work, rather than official authentication certificates?

IartC also gives this valuable advice to people when buying direct from Aboriginal and Torres Strait Islander artists:

There are many Indigenous artists across Australia who sells their work directly. Some artists might sell their work on the street, others have their own studios which you can visit and some will sell from their own websites. Don't haggle with individual artists selling their work to you, be respectful and understand that this is their livelihood. An individual artist selling his or her own work is not a dealer so the obligations of dealers under the Code do not apply to individual artists.[49]

7
PERFORMANCE

Singing, dancing, composing and making music are at the core of Indigenous cultures in Australia. Indigenous artists work across the full range of performance art – music, drama, dance and multimedia. They perform in many different styles – traditional styles based on their ancient culture, as well as contemporary ones. Many performers also now mix the two – traditional and modern. Both traditional and contemporary Indigenous performance styles often convey connections to culture and Country. They express the artists' ancient hereditary knowledge.

The traditional ways of making music include singing, clapping and keeping the beat by clapping or playing percussion instruments such as clapsticks. Instruments such as the yiḏaki (commonly called the didgeridoo) and, in the Torres Strait, various styles of drums are used. Aboriginal and Torres Strait Islander musicians have also adopted musical instruments and techniques from around the world. For non-traditional performances, Indigenous musicians use guitars, including electric guitars, ukuleles, pianos, most of the orchestral instruments, such as brass instruments, modern drums and percussion instruments, and even gum leaves.

Indigenous artists assert their ownership of traditional music and dance as well as of their new works. They have legal protections for their customary rights, and ownership of their copyright. The global theft of Aboriginal and Torres Strait Islander cultural heritage, music and performance has presented Indigenous artists and Traditional Owners with huge challenges, including legal cases. This has led to changes in government policies, protocols and patenting initiatives, all designed to protect our performance arts and our performers.

The first Aboriginal songs ever recorded were sung by Fanny Cochrane Smith. She was recorded by Horace Watson at the Royal Society in Hobart, Tasmania, on a wax cylinder device between 1899 and 1903. This was less than a decade after this technology first arrived in Australia. These are the only recordings of Tasmanian Aboriginal songs or of any Tasmanian Aboriginal language. Singing in both English and her own language, Fanny recorded 'all of the Tasmanian songs she knew, some in Aboriginal languages, others in English'. In one of the recordings, she talks about being the last of the Tasmanians. Copies are kept in a number of archives, including the National Film and Sound Archive (NFSA) and the Australian Institute of Aboriginal and Torres Strait Islander Studies (AIATSIS) in Canberra.

There is a song whose origins are even older than these late nineteenth century recordings of Fanny Cochrane Smith. It is called 'Ngarra Burra Ferra'.

Many musicians are fascinated by this song, but it was Daniel Browning, host of the ABC Radio National program *AWAYE!*, who discovered its origins and its story. Browning interviewed Professor Gabriel Solis, a music expert of African American Studies at the University of Illinois, about it. Professor Solis says that the story goes as far back as 1887 and could be older. That was when the world-famous Fisk Jubilee Singers from Fisk University, Nashville, Tennessee, USA, visited the Maloga mission near Moama, in Victoria, in the homelands of the Yorta Yorta people. 'Ngarra Burra Ferra' is a Yorta Yorta version of the song 'Turn Back Pharoah's Army', which the Fisk Jubilee Singers sang during their visit to Australia. Professor Solis explained that 'They left a songbook, and one of their spirituals about the escape of the Israelites from slavery in Egypt became "Ngarra Burra Ferra", translated into Yorta Yorta'.

The song was made famous when it was performed in the 2012 film *The Sapphires*, about the adventures of a Yorta Yorta girl group in the 1960s and 1970s. Four young women formed the group at Cummeragunga in Victoria, and travelled to Melbourne and then to Vietnam, where they performed for the Australian soldiers. The version of 'Ngarra Burra Ferra' in *The Sapphires* is sung by cast members Jessica Mauboy, Shari Sebbens, Miranda Tapsell and Deborah Mailman.

Contemporary dancers perform at an international gathering in Darwin (photo Wayne Quilliam)

The first Torres Strait Islander music and dance ever recorded dates from 1898. Alfred C. Haddon, a British zoologist and ethnographer from Cambridge University, filmed dances on Mer (Murray Island). Curated at the NFSA, the exhibition *Torres Strait Islanders (1898)* contains the surviving four-and-a-half minutes of footage A.C. Haddon shot. This is the first field footage taken of Indigenous peoples in Australia and was made just three years after the invention of the cinecamera. Copies of these precious films are archived at the NFSA and can be viewed online. While the film clips are silent, they show the songs and dances that are still performed today. These films were presented as evidence in the famous Mabo case, in the Supreme Court of Queensland. To find out about this case, read the 'Native Title' chapter.

Liz McNiven, the NFSA curator, writes in the exhibition catalogue that the 'film shows Torres Strait Islander men performing three dance sequences ... followed by a demonstration of traditional fire-making practices ... The last part of the film shows two short dances performances [*sic*] by young Aboriginal men'.

The first clip, at just over a minute long, shows 'the spectacular Malu-Bomai ceremony performed by the Torres Strait Islander men of Mer at Kiam, in the eastern Torres Strait'. In the other two dance sequences, 'three men wear traditional headdresses and dance in synchronisation', while the 'final sequence shows four young Australian Aboriginal men performing a shake-a-leg dance on the beach, while another beats the rhythm', McNiven writes.

Many Torres Strait Islander communities and families are committed to protecting and performing the various styles of traditional dancing, singing and drumming. They know that their history and culture are important, and they are preserving them through songs and dances. As the late Ephraim Bani, a noted linguist and expert in Torres Strait Islander culture, explained in 1979:

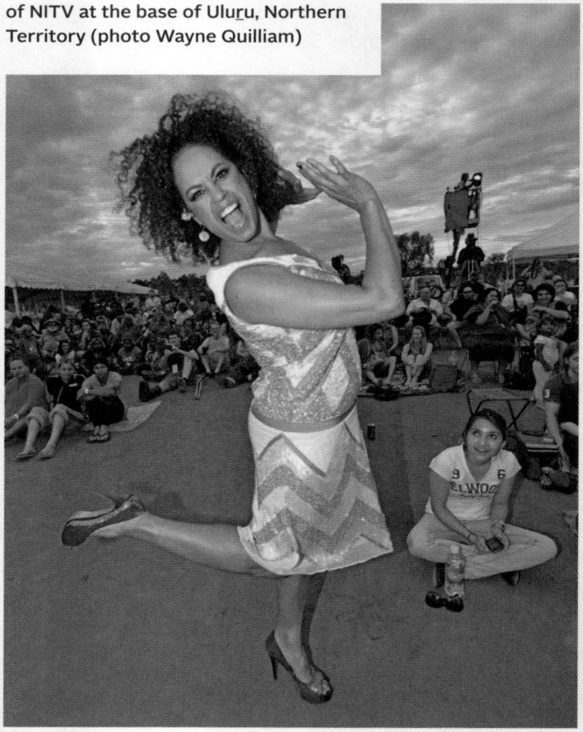

Christine Anu styling up at the launch of NITV at the base of Uluru, Northern Territory (photo Wayne Quilliam)

The importance of dancing and songs in the Torres Strait Islands ... [is not] mere entertainment ... [but] is the most important aspect of Torres Strait lifestyle. The Torres Strait Islanders preserve and present their oral history through songs and dances; in other words, the songs and dances are

Torres Strait literature material. Just like any written materials, which are usually illustrations, the dances act as illustrative material and, of course, the dancer himself [sic] is the storyteller. ('Contemporary Indigenous Dance: Continuing Connections to Culture', yarn.com.au)

Mr Bani was the chief of Wagadagam clan, on Mabuyag Island (Jervis Island), and a cultural ambassador for his people.

The Ilan style of music performed by Torres Strait Islanders combines traditional singing with a variety of introduced styles. In particular, it is mixed with hymns brought by missionaries and songs shared by sailors whose ships stopped among the islands. The songs, accompanied by drums and other percussion instruments, guitars and sometimes ukuleles, celebrate living with the sea, love and adventure. Island songs are performed in two- or three-part harmony and are improvised by the singers.

The best example of modern Torres Strait music is that of the late Seaman Dan – Henry Gibson Dan AM (25 August 1929 – 30 December 2020) – whose work is produced by Karl Neuenfeldt. He was seventy years old when he began to sing publicly. Uncle Seaman went on to release five albums of traditional music and his signature Ilan-style blues and jazz. In his biography, *Steady Steady: The Life and Music of Seaman Dan*, Uncle Seaman told stories of his life in the islands as a pearl diver, and his career as a professional singer and musician.

ARIA award–winning singer Christine Anu also hails from the Torres Strait. She has had success with a number of albums and film appearances, and sang at the Closing Ceremony of the 2000 Sydney Olympics.

Protecting the traditional styles

Today, the traditional styles of music and performance are at risk of being lost or forgotten. Rescue programs, research projects and festivals are working to collect and preserve these musical forms, which are the oldest in the world. Yolŋu musicians, ethnomusicologists and scholars joined forces to stop their decline, forming the National Recording Project for Indigenous Performance in Australia. The Project's 'Garma Statement on Indigenous Music and Dance' of 2002 tells us:

Songs, dances and ceremonial performances form the core of Yolŋu and other Indigenous cultures in Australia. It is through song, dance and associated ceremony that Indigenous people sustain their cultures and maintain the Law and a sense of self within the world.

Performance traditions are the foundation of social and personal wellbeing, and with the ever-increasing loss of these traditions, the toll grows every year. The preservation of performance traditions is therefore one of the highest priorities for Indigenous people.

Indigenous songs should also be a deeply valued part of the Australian cultural heritage. They represent the great classical music of this land.

These ancient musical traditions were once everywhere in Australia, and now survive as living traditions only in several regions. Many of these are now in danger of being lost forever.

Indigenous performances are one of our most rich and beautiful forms of artistic expression, and yet they remain unheard and invisible within the national cultural

TREATY, MUSIC, ART: MANDAWUY YUNUPIŊU AND PAUL KELLY WRITE A NEW ANTHEM

Music and art have been regular companions of politics in our world, and while at least three Australian governments have established formal treaty processes with Indigenous Australians, we should look back into our history to the seminal moment when the demand for treaty was supported by great music and design that drew on ancient traditions. This is how the song 'Treaty' became a new anthem. As Aaron Corn tells the story in *Reflections and Voices*, in 1988, the bicentennial of Australia as a nation, Galarrwuy Yunupiŋu carried on the work of his father, Muŋgurrawuy, who in 1962 was involved with the Yirrkala leaders' campaign against the bauxite mine. Galarrwuy, an elected Chair of the Northern Land Council, collaborated with the late Wenten Rubuntja, Chair of the Central Land Council, to prepare a petition calling on the Australian government 'to enter into a Treaty with Indigenous Australians in recognition of their rights and freedom as Australia's original owners'. They painted a canvas in which typescript was bordered by sacred designs. On the left, were Yolŋu designs for four Yirritja homelands. They were balanced on the right by a Two Sisters Dreaming design common to Central Australia and linked here to Dhuwa ancestors of the Yolŋu. It was called the Barunga Statement and can be viewed at aiatsis.gov.au/explore/articles/barungastatement. In 2017, this form was adopted as the model in 2017 for the Uluṟu Statement from the Heart.

On 12 June that year, the Barunga Statement was presented to Prime Minister Robert Hawke at the Barunga Sport and Cultural Festival under the most sacred of ceremonial conditions. His initial response was overwhelmingly positive and he promised to start negotiations towards a Treaty with Indigenous Australians within the lifetime of his parliament. But by 1990, no progress had been made and the issue had all but faded from public memory.

In 1990, the late Mandawuy Yunupiŋu, Galarrwuy's younger brother and lead singer of the Yothu Yindi band, 'collaborated with Peter Garrett and Paul Kelly to remind everyone of Hawke's well-publicised promise of a treaty at Barunga'.

they composed 'Treaty', which endures as Yothu Yindi's best-remembered song. 'Treaty' was remixed in Melbourne by Filthy Lucre and rapidly gained popularity. It became the first song with lyrics in an original Australian language to top the Australian charts.

'Treaty' won many awards, including Song of the Year from the Australasian Performing Right Association, Song Writing from the Human Rights and Equal Opportunity Commission, Best Australian Single from ARIA, Best Australian Video from the

Australian Music Awards and Best Australian Video from the MTV International Awards. In 1991, Yothu Yindi performed at the New Music Seminar in New York and signed an international recording contract with Hollywood Records.

Aaron Corn explains the deeper significance of the song for Mandawuy and his people:

> *The song's melody comes through its quotation of an historic* Djatpaŋarri *item composed by Rrikin Burarrwaŋa and recorded by Richard Waterman at Yirrkala in the early 1950s. With its youthful calls of encouragement to anyone dancing, the exuberance of the* Djatpaŋarri *style sets the mood and tempo for the entire song, and captures Mandawuy's nostalgia for his childhood on the Gove Peninsula before the advent of mining in 1968.*
>
> *Nonetheless, the ideological heart of 'Treaty' lies in the second verse with its bold affirmation that the Yolŋu have never ceded or sold their homelands to the Crown, and that Yolŋu sovereignty was never affected by the British landing at Sydney Cove in 1788. This second verse also employs the* ganma *'converging currents' model for social equity first used by Mandawuy in 'Mainstream'. Here, he describes Indigenous and non-Indigenous Australians as two rivers running their separate courses, and dreams of a brighter day when a Treaty will make those waters one.*

Mandawuy intended that Treaty would 'raise public awareness about this, so that the government would be encouraged to hold to his promise'. He went on to say:

> *The song became a number one hit, the first ever to be sung in a Yolŋu language, and it caught the public's imagination. Though it borrows from rock'n'roll, the whole structure of 'Treaty' is driven by the beat of the* Djatpaŋarri *that I worked into it. It was an old recording of this* Djatpaŋarri *that triggered the song. The man who originally created it passed away a long time ago in 1978. He was a real master of the* Djatpaŋarri *style.*[50]

MISSION SONGS PROJECT

Jessie Lloyd is a musician and singer whose cultural connections from family who lived on Palm Island are both Aboriginal and Torres Strait Islander. She has researched the song compositions of Indigenous Australians on Christian missions and state-run settlements in the early to mid-twentieth century. Jessie explains that she 'first became curious about the songs from the Aboriginal reserves or the mission days when she heard her Aunties singing an old tune from Palm Island'.

For many decades, the reserve on Palm Island in Queensland was a prison camp for rebellious or non-compliant Aboriginal and Torres Strait Islander people. Indigenous people from across the state and the Torres Strait Islands were forced together under a brutal regime implemented by the Department of Native Affairs.

Jessie's Mission Songs Project is a collection of songs composed by Indigenous people during that time – the assimilation era. 'We're looking at four to five generations of unrecorded song traditions,' Jessie said, when talking about the Project. The song lyrics show what daily life was like for the people herded into these settlements and their concerns about their dispossession and treatment.

Jessie has found rare secular songs that were sung after church. In many cases the descendants of the songs' composers shared the songs with her. Jessie and the singers of the Mission Songs Project perform the songs at music festivals and events in Australia and internationally. Jessie's aim is for audiences to gain 'a deeper understanding about the history of Elders, families and communities, from cultural identity to love and loss'.

During her research, Jessie heard the song 'The Irex'. It is about the boat of the same name that was used to transport children and adults who'd been forcibly removed from their families in the early to mid-twentieth century because of policies related to the *Aboriginals Protection and Restriction of the Sale of Opium Act 1897*. She discovered that it was sung as a lament and farewell song: 'This song was what the families used to sing as they didn't know if they would see their loved ones again'. You can watch a video of this song and others at missionsongsproject.com.

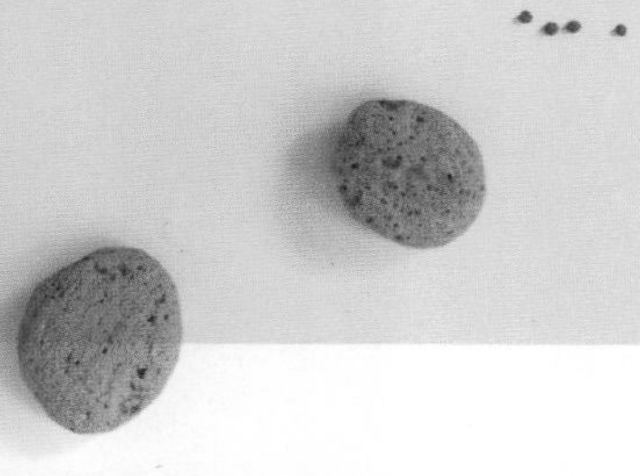

Opposite: Jessie Lloyd of the Mission Songs Project

heritage. Without immediate action many Indigenous music and dance traditions are in danger of extinction with potentially destructive consequences for the fabric of Indigenous society and culture.

The recording and documenting of the remaining traditions is a matter of the highest priority both for Indigenous and non-Indigenous Australians. Many of our foremost composers and singers have already passed away leaving little or no record.[51]

In northern and Central Australia, traditional songs are generally sung in cycles or series. Each song is short but can be combined with others and repeated, and performed throughout a ceremony. When men sing their cycles, there are usually two lead singers, a chorus and a yiḏaki player. In Central Australia, a now rarely seen short wind instrument for ritual purposes was used in the past, and clapsticks and hand-clapping are the usual accompaniments to singing. Each male singer uses clapsticks to keep the rhythm. Women sing in a variety of styles. For example, following a death, a senior woman will lead the keening or high-pitched singing. In the desert, groups of women sing the cycles, led by one or two lead singers, and clap with cupped hands to keep the beat.

The singing style made popular by bands such as Soft Sands, Yothu Yindi, East Journey and many others from Arnhem Land is called Manikay. Ethnomusicologist Aaron Corn explains the powerful force of Manikay in Yolŋu society: 'whenever people sing Manikay, their voices are not their own, but rather mingle with those of the ancestors themselves – all those who have gone before and all those who are yet to be'.

The gospel and country band Soft Sands, from Arnhem Land, started in the 1970s.

Danzal Baker, aka Baker Boy, raps in Yolŋu matha languages and English (photo Wayne Quilliam)

It led the way for Aboriginal musicians to experiment with different styles, fusing traditional Aboriginal music with contemporary sounds, particularly rock music. It was followed by Yothu Yindi, formed in 1986. Yothu Yindi became the most successful and internationally recognised Aboriginal band in that decade. Warumpi Band, with its mix of rock with Arnhem Land and Warlpiri style, also became successful, touring with Midnight Oil. In South Australia, Us Mob and No Fixed Address became popular and toured with several hit songs in Australia and the Pacific region. There are many other bands that have started playing in their communities and tour locally in their regions.

One of Australia's most treasured singers is Archie Roach. His debut and award-winning album, *Charcoal Lane*, was released in 1990. It was his song 'Took the children away' about the Stolen Generations that catapulted Roach to fame in the Indigenous world. Roach is a member of the Stolen Generations. He toured and sang with his late wife, Ruby Hunter, for more than three decades, until she passed away in 2010. In 2012, Archie returned to performing and touring, and released a box set of live recordings called *The Concert Collection 2012–2018 in 2019*. His tour in 2018 featured a new song 'Dancing with my spirit'. His most popular book is his autobiographical *Tell Me Why: The Story of My Life and My Music* (Simon & Schuster, 2019).

Indigenous music today

The National Indigenous Music Awards, held annually in Darwin, celebrate the work of Indigenous performers. Musicians, many of whom sing in their Indigenous languages as well as English, compete for the honour of being named the best in their category or genre, from traditional to heavy metal. Emerging artists such as Gawurra, Apakatjah, Electric Fields, Emily Wurramara, Tia Gostelow and Yirrmal have had their careers launched at this prestigious event.

Many musical artists today bring their traditions into modern genres, such as folk, rock, electronic and rap styles. Danzal Baker, aka Baker Boy, is a Yolŋu artist from Milingimbi and Maningrida in the Northern Territory. His talents span rap, dance, acting and visual art, and include multilingual rapping in Yolŋu matha languages and

A TRIBUTE TO GURRUMUL YUNUPIŊU

The late Gurrumul Yunupiŋu won the hearts of music lovers in Australia and around the world. He was born on Elcho Island on 22 January 1971, the eldest of four children. It was said that his hearing was so acute that it took his family some time to realise he was blind at birth. Despite this, his childhood was much the same as other Gumatj children on Elcho Island, spent running barefoot, playing on the beach and riding bicycles at breakneck speeds. Beyond instructing the other kids to 'keep an eye on him', it was not the Yolŋu way to regard his blindness as a significant limit on his capacity to participate in the life of the island. As a consequence, Yunupiŋu did not grow up regarding himself as someone who was disabled. He never used a white cane, or had a guide dog. He never learned braille. He was a self-taught musician from a young age playing on a toy piano and accordion. His first drum kit was tin cans balanced on sticks.

In his late teens, Yunupiŋu traded in his tin cans for keyboards and a guitar, and embarked on a rock apprenticeship with Yothu Yindi, playing on their worldwide hit 'Treaty'. But Yunupiŋu's time with Yothu Yindi was short-lived – the Elders on Elcho Island were concerned about the impact of a rock 'n' roll lifestyle, so requested his return home. A few years later he would meet long-time collaborator Michael Hohnen. In 2008, Yunupiŋu embarked on his first solo album. While this self-titled recording continued the earlier vein of songs in Yolŋu matha languages backed by contemporary Western instruments, the songs highlighted the ethereal beauty of Yunupiŋu's voice. This album would go on to be triple-platinum, making him the most commercially successful Indigenous recording artist in history. Yunupiŋu released three more studio albums, *Rrakala* (2011), *The Gospel Album* (2015) and the posthumously released *Djarrimirri* (Child of the Rainbow, 2018), and a live collaboration with the Sydney Symphony Orchestra, *His Life and Music* (2013). All of these recordings would win multiple ARIA awards.

In July 2017, Yunupiŋu died after a long bout of illness brought on by liver and kidney disease. During a career that included high-profile international collaborators such as Sting, A.B. Original and Delta Goodrem, perhaps the most notable aspect of Yunupiŋu's career has been a commitment to Yolŋu culture. When culture and a commercial career came into conflict, it was always culture that won out. Royalties and appearance fees were often shared among extended Elcho Island family in the Yolŋu manner. In a continuation of these principles, royalties from the sales of his last album will, in part, be directed towards a foundation that aims to create greater opportunities for remote Indigenous young people.

English. He rose to prominence in 2017 when his work was showcased on Triple J's Hottest 100. Since then, he has been a winner at the National Indigenous Music Awards, received the prestigious Charles Darwin University Art Award at the Northern Territory Young Achievers Awards, and was named 2019 Young Australian of the Year.

Barkaa was tapped on the shoulder to sign on to Briggs's prolific Bad Apples label, who released her songs 'Our Lives Matter' and 'I Can't Breathe' (with Dobby), which became prominent during the 2020 Black Lives Matter protests in Australia. Barkaa's artist name comes from the Barkindji Nation where she is from – 'Barkindji means "river people" and we name our river the Barkaa'.[52] The rapper uses her craft to resist, educate and connect with culture. Some of Barkaa's songs include Barkindji language, and the video clip of her hit song 'For My Tittas' shows Barkaa teaching ceremony and language to her young daughter.

Sydney-based rapper Ziggy Ramo recently collaborated with Australia's celebrated singer-songwriter Paul Kelly on the song 'Little Things', an update of the classic song 'From Little Things, Big Things Grow', written by Kelly and Kev Carmody about Vincent Lingiari and the Gurindji Strike.[53]

Dan Sultan is an alternative rock singer-songwriter and guitarist, and winner of three ARIA awards for his 2010 album *Get Out While You Can* and 2014 album *Blackbird*. In 2009, Sultan appeared in the feature film *Bran Nue Dae*, directed by Rachel Perkins and starring Jessica Mauboy, Geoffrey Rush and Missy Higgins. Like many of the other musicians mentioned in this chapter, Sultan is a member of Black Arm Band, a collection of various Indigenous musicians and performers. He also sings with Paul Kelly, including for the song 'Every day my mother's voice', which featured in *The Final Quarter*, the documentary about Indigenous AFL footy star Adam Goodes.

The most famous Aboriginal rapper is Briggs. A Yorta Yorta man, Adam Briggs owns record label Bad Apples Music, and also writes comedy and acts. He's appeared in various TV shows on the ABC including *Black Comedy*, and is a regular cast member on *The Weekly with Charlie Pickering*. Under the name A.B. Original (which stands for Always Black, Original), Briggs also creates music with Ngarrindjeri man Trials, and together their work is explosive political rap.

Aboriginal women singers and musicians often don't get the recognition they deserve, despite their long history in the music industry and their stellar performances across all genres. Casey Donovan, Thelma Plum and Gina Williams are all headline acts, while emerging talents include Emily Wurramara and Alice Skye. Emma Donovan of the famous Donovan family began singing when she was seven years old. She went on to form the singing group Stiff Gins, and more recently has become famous for her soul music. Dr Lou Bennett, a Yorta Yorta Dja Dja Wurrung woman from Echuca, was one of the three founders of Tiddas, a folk and acapella group with Gunditjmara woman Amy Saunders from Portland, and Sally Dastey from West Heidelberg in Melbourne. They disbanded in 2000 and won a Deadly Award that same year. They returned in 2018, touring across Australia with Archie Roach to celebrate his album *Dancing with My Spirit*. A young woman who will join the stars is Miiesha whose works are available on YouTube. She writes original ballads such as 'Damaged,' 'Drowning' and 'Black Privilege' with a velvet voice and steely lyrics.

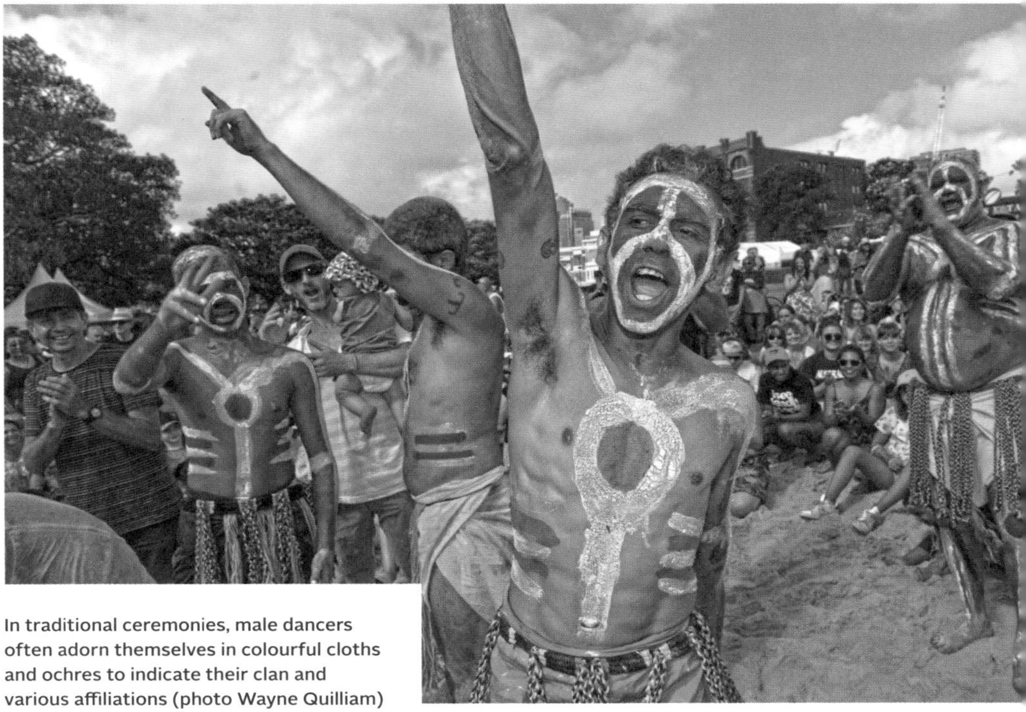

In traditional ceremonies, male dancers often adorn themselves in colourful cloths and ochres to indicate their clan and various affiliations (photo Wayne Quilliam)

Aboriginal and Torres Strait Islander dance traditions

Traditional ceremonies are great spectacles that appeal to Indigenous and non-Indigenous audiences. They are also an important part of traditional Aboriginal life and beliefs. They usually involve dance performances and singing that bring the ancestors to life, and also bring the ancestral stories into the lives of Aboriginal families. Some ceremonies are for man-making, or initiation, while others celebrate particular ancestors.

Funeral ceremonies are often celebrations of the ancestral connections of the deceased. These ceremonies are often now mixed with Christian traditions, and sometimes incorporate other cultural influences as well.

There are ceremonial dance performances that involve men and women, and others that are performed by men only, or by women only. Children often join in public forms of ceremony. Dance performances are also staged for storytelling and for pure entertainment.

Dancers are allowed a great deal of freedom of expression. The movements vary according to the dance style. The performers are barefoot and kick up the sand they are dancing on as a part of the performance. In some styles, dancers keep their feet close to the ground to

Performers in a contemporary dance style (photo Wayne Quilliam)

symbolise their connection with the earth or emotional states of being. Other movements and gestures communicate specific ancestral beings and emotions. Pounding the earth in unison, leaping into the air and imitations of particular animals are some of the movements most Australians will have seen.

Dancers also call out in response to the singers and musicians. This is to express the ancestral events that are part of the performance, and to mark the end of a dance.

Male dancers adorn themselves with colourful cloth wrapped around their bodies, feather headdresses, gum-leaf anklets, and other decorations to indicate their clan and various affiliations. Women wear swaying skirts and, when dancing topless, they paint their bodies with ochre. Both men and women paint their faces with clan emblems. Body painting is a spectacular feature of Aboriginal dances at ceremonies. Each one of the designs painted on the skin has a meaning, and they all tell a story; often it is about Country and ancestral beings. The same or similar designs are used on objects, especially for ceremonies, but also on everyday objects.

Stephen Page, Aboriginal choreographer and Artistic Director of the Bangarra Dance Theatre, explains his own experience with body paint in dance:

For Indigenous Australians, spirituality centres around the land. The nurturing and life-giving capacity of even our hardest terrains has been the mainstay of Indigenous religious beliefs. Incorporating the earth into spiritual ceremonies is done by many tribes using various ochres. Different coloured ochre is applied to various designs according to your totem so that spirituality is awakened during the paint-up. There are no time constraints, no boundaries; there's an apparent timelessness about the ritual.

Festivals and performances of Aboriginal and Torres Strait Islander dancing are held regularly in most cities and in some remote areas. The longest running Indigenous dance festival in Australia is the Laura Aboriginal Dance Festival. It began in the early 1980s near Laura, a tiny town in central Cape York and an important meeting place for people from the area. It is the Country of the Kuku Thaypan and other peoples and is the location of one of Australia's most significant collections of rock art.

Hosted by the Ang-Gnarra Aboriginal Corporation, the festival is held in July every second year. As explained on the website anggnarra.org.au, it is held on 'the site of a very old, traditional Bora ground. It's a respected and sacred site. Here, people from about twenty different communities located across the Cape come together to celebrate with music, dance, singing and cultural performances'. Visitors from other parts of Australia and overseas sometimes present their own dance traditions at the festival.

One of the leading Indigenous performance groups is the Bangarra Dance Theatre. The company was formed in 1989 and is still thriving. American dancer Carole J. Johnson was a founding director of NAISDA (National Aboriginal Islander Skills Development Association) Dance College, and she founded Bangarra with NAISDA graduates Rob Bryant and Cheryl Stone.

Artistic Director Stephen Page has led Bangarra for many years, and it has become one of the most successful performing arts companies in Australian history. Performing nationally and internationally, the company's dancers are professionally trained, and each has an Aboriginal and/or Torres Strait Islander background. Indigenous choreographers and musicians collaborate with the dancers to create works that are both contemporary and draw on at least 65,000 years of stories and culture. Stephen Page has referred to the traditional aspects of Bangarra in this way:

[It's] 'grass roots' in that traditional Aboriginal dance ... is about building a bridge between urban blacks and remote blacks, it's a wonderful marriage for rekindling one's culture and inspiring urban energy ... Without these traditional aspects, Bangarra would not exist in terms of its creative development.[54]

Traditional Indigenous dance draws on songs and storytelling as well as movement. It is part of the First peoples' language and is essential to our culture and our daily lives.

Aboriginal and Torres Strait Islander performers are committed to keeping alive the traditional styles of music, dance and storytelling, and to creating new forms of performance. The peoples whose traditions were all but destroyed by colonisation and assimilation see the traditional forms of dance, singing and music as a precious legacy inherited from their ancestors.

The terrible history of oppression has not stopped the flow of cultural energy and creativity. Events, ceremonies and festivals featuring Indigenous performance styles are held all around Australia. Storytelling through performance is a distinctive part of our First peoples culture. Many Indigenous performers work to maintain and revitalise our culture, offering our young people the opportunity to learn our stories, identify with their traditions and develop their identities and self-respect. Bringing the sacred past and ancestral events to life through performance lies at the heart of our cultures.

DEBORAH CHEETHAM AND THE FIRST ABORIGINAL OPERA, *PECAN SUMMER*

Deborah Cheetham AO is a Yorta Yorta woman who trained in opera and has become one of Australia's most loved sopranos. She wrote and composed the first Aboriginal opera, *Pecan Summer*. In the opera, Deborah performed the role of Ella, the mother of Alice, who is forcibly separated from her family by a police officer under instructions from the Aboriginal Protection Board. This story reflects Cheetham's own life history.

Cheetham was taken from her family at a young age under the government's assimilation policies. This happened during the time when there were efforts 'to breed out the Aborigines' by removing their children and sending them to institutions and white families as domestic servants. In an event that became known as the 'walk-off from Cummeragunga Mission', one group of Indigenous people could no longer stand the white manager's cruelty and so they left, crossing the river into Victoria from the New South Wales side of the Dhungala (Murray River) on 4 February 1939.

Pecan Summer brings this important historical event to life on stage. It weaves together the stories of those people who refused to live under the administration of the Aboriginal Protection Board and led their people to a kind of freedom. Events such as the forced separation of children from their families, and the suffering this caused, led to Cummeragunga. The walk-off and the strong protest movement led by Yorta Yorta leaders are recounted in many books, plays and songs. The late Margaret Tucker (nee Clements) was one of those leaders. A Yorta Yorta (Dhulinyagan) woman born at Warrangesda Mission on the Murrumbidgee River, she was removed at the age of twelve. She told her story in 1983, in the book *If Everyone Cared*.

Realising Cheetham's long-held dream, *Pecan Summer* was performed at the Sydney Opera House in 2016. It has also been performed in Shepparton and Melbourne in Victoria, in Adelaide in South Australia and in Perth in Western Australia, and excerpts have been performed in Europe, the United Kingdom, the USA and around Australia.

Cheetham has established an opera company, Short Black Opera, in order to develop her distinctive approach to music and Aboriginal culture. She and her team have also worked with children's groups in many rural and urban settings. One of the outcomes of her work to strengthen and express Aboriginal cultures is the Dhungala Children's Choir. Most of the choir's members are Yorta Yorta children.

Deborah Cheetham in the role of Ella in *Pecan Summer*

They are often joined by children from other communities from around Australia, when they come together to take part in music workshops.

Cheetham's work *Eumeralla: A War Requiem for Peace* is based on the twenty-three-year Eumeralla Resistance Wars (mid-1840s–1860s) that occurred between the Indigenous people and European settlers along the Eumarella River in Gunditjmara Country in south-west Victoria. In this work, Cheetham adapts the movements and the text of the traditional Requiem Mass. The result is a stirring nineteen-movement work that blends the traditional Latin text, translated by Gunditjmara language custodian Vicki Couzens and linguist Travers Eira into the dialects of the Gunditjmara people. Rather than detailing the atrocities, the text offers poetic references to the violent loss of the people who belonged to the land of the Eumeralla. Cheetham chose to write about the feelings and emotions of the Gunditjmara who were murdered, their unanswered questions, and a hope that they might find eternal rest.

8

STORYTELLING

Storytelling is the original classroom. Through storytelling, history, beliefs and knowledge about people, places and the world are relayed to each new generation. Storytelling is also entertainment, bringing people together to laugh about life, adventures, love, travelling and mishaps. When the best storytellers are in charge, humour and tragedy bring stories to life. Stories can be told through art, song and dance. A traditional Indigenous performance often combines theatre and storytelling.

For a people on the verge of extinction in the early twentieth century due to the frontier wars and introduced diseases, the Indigenous people have shown great resilience. Many of them are cultural warriors who paint, sing, write and tell stories. This is a testament to the power of our culture. Storytelling continues in the same form as before European contact (e.g. oral history), as well as in introduced forms (e.g. literature). Our storytellers can be heard at Indigenous festivals and writers' festivals around the country.

Many collectors of Aboriginal stories are surprised at how little the traditional stories have changed over the generations. There are stories that tell of the rising of the oceans around 7000 years ago, erupting volcanoes 30,000 years ago, and the very different climate, landscapes and animals of the long-distant past.

Aboriginal poets, playwrights, scriptwriters and authors of novels, histories and memoirs continue the tradition of storytelling that has preserved the history and myths of our peoples for thousands of years. Their works have won national and international awards and hold a highly respected place in Australian literature.

Indigenous writers have not always been praised and awarded for their contributions, and they have not always been respected. In fact, it took an outsider to recognise the significance of Aboriginal writing to the world. Adam Shoemaker came to Australia from Canada in the 1980s to undertake his doctorate at the Australian National University. His award-winning doctoral research on Aboriginal literature, *Black Words, White Page*, was first published in 1989. He has published more works on Indigenous literature and writers since then, including as co-editor of the first national anthology of Black Australian writings, *Paperbark* (University of Queensland Press [UQP], 1990) and editor of *Oodgeroo: A Tribute* (UQP, 1993).

Much has been written and published since then. It is time for a scholar of Australian Aboriginal and Torres Strait Islander literature to write another book about the many oral histories and biographies, novels, short stories, poems and plays that Indigenous people have written. Those stories are our history.

One area where Indigenous storytellers are rising up is in traditionally non-Indigenous spaces, such as within museums. Nathan Sentance, a Wiradjuri man, currently works as project officer in First Nations programming at the Australian Museum in Sydney. Nathan argues that museums and other 'memory institutions' have contributed to the many biases and misinterpretations of Aboriginal culture and people.

Galleries, libraries, archives and museums are considered sites of memory, spaces to engage with history and identity, but for me these places are sites of forgetting, erasure and distortion. They are built on stolen land. Their names validate the place names that colonisers used to confirm their occupation of stolen land and to nullify the history that took place before colonial invasion.

My ancestors are in these memory institutions, but their voices are missing from the words written, the art created and the cultural objects taken. All of their cultural knowledge and their history is recorded and interpreted through the colonisers' lens. We are part of the memory conveyed by galleries, libraries, archives and museums, but we have had no say or agency in construction of it.[55]

To help challenge and correct this impact, Nathan attempts to decolonise the museum's exhibitions and demonstrate the complexity and diversity of Aboriginal and Torres Strait Islander cultures. 'This will help us take control of the narrative that surrounds them.'

David Unaipon

The impact of the denial of Indigenous writing and writers over many decades is best told in the true story of writer David Unaipon. A Ngarrindjeri man from the Coorong region of South Australia, Unaipon was born on 28 September 1872, at Point McLeay Mission. He became a writer, inventor and philosopher. The Australian $50 note features a portrait of him in an acknowledgement of his contribution to Australian life.

Unaipon's work was stolen by the publisher George Robertson in 1925 when he sold the complete manuscript to 'the amateur anthropologist and principal medical officer of South Australia, William Ramsay Smith'. In 1930, Smith published the collection under his own name and with a new title: *Myths & Legends of the Australian Aboriginals*. As a result, Unaipon's authorship was not recognised until Australian literature experts, particularly Stephen Muecke and Adam Shoemaker, learnt about this theft and republished the original work under Unaipon's name in 2001. In their introduction to Unaipon's book, *Legendary Tales of the Australian Aborigines*, Muecke and Shoemaker tell the story of this literary theft. Billy Griffiths, author of *Deep Time Dreaming*, a history of archaeology in Australia, provides a good summary of the underhanded treatment of Unaipon in his article in *Australian Book Review* from August 2016:

In appropriating the book, Smith not only denied Unaipon's authorship, he also systematically removed his interpretations and narrative voice from the text. Smith's plagiarism and selective editing speaks volumes for the way Indigenous people were marginalised and oppressed in the early twentieth century.[56]

'Our legends and traditions are all the same tales, or myths, told slightly differently, with local colouring,' Unaipon wrote in his book. From 1924 to 1925, he collected the stories for his proposed collection from his own Ngarrindjeri people from Victoria, on a tour of southern and Central Australia with an Aboriginal translator, and in Queensland. He found many different languages and customs but also, as Billy Griffiths writes, 'a great common understanding running through us all'. According to Griffiths, Unaipon 'infused the stories he collected with his own personal philosophy, and wrote them up in the formal, ornate literary style of the era, overlaid with biblical references and classical tropes'.

Although it has taken a long time, today Indigenous literature is acknowledged as Australian literature. The many awards won by Indigenous writers is evidence of this new attitude.

Many of the recommendations that follow are my own personal favourites, in addition to being widely read and awarded nationally and internationally. My colleague

The Australian $50 note shows writer, inventor and philosopher David Unaipon in an acknowledgement of his contribution to Australian life

Wiradjuri author Tara June Winch

Luke Pearson has also made several recommendations to this chapter. Luke founded and runs the online company IndigenousX Pty Ltd. It has given a voice to many young Indigenous writers, scientists and intellectuals. Luke Pearson and I have suggested here some works that are challenging for any audience, but all are outstanding works by Indigenous writers and creators.

Tara June Winch

A prize-winning author since the publication of her critically acclaimed first novel *Swallow the Air* (UQP) in 2006 and then her collection of short stories *After the Carnage* in 2016 (UQP), Tara June Winch was recognised in 2020 as one of Australia's best writers, winning several major literature awards with the publication of *The Yield* (Hamish Hamilton, 2019), which has also been optioned for production for the screen. Tara was born in Australia in 1983, and has been based in France for many years. In 2008, as part of the prestigious Rolex Mentor and Protégé Arts Initiative, Tara was mentored by Nigerian playwright and Nobel Prize winner Wole Soyinka. In addition to her works of fiction, she wrote the script for the Indigenous dance documentary *Carriberrie*, which screened at the 71st Cannes Film Festival in 2018 and toured internationally. She won the following awards for *The Yield*:

- 2020 Miles Franklin Literary Award, Australia's foremost literary prize
- 2020 NSW Premier's Literary Awards Christina Stead Prize for Fiction
- 2020 NSW Premier's Literary Awards People's Choice Award
- 2020 NSW Premier's Literary Awards Book of the Year
- 2020 Prime Minister's Literary Awards Fiction

She was shortlisted for the 2020 Stella Prize.

The Yield is a profoundly moving and important work of fiction based on Tara June Winch's ancestors who lived on

Wiradjuri Country. A lamentation for her father's language, it is also a story about Wiradjuri people's victory over the traumatic burden of history as her character, August Gondiwindi, returns home from overseas for her grandfather's burial, consumed with guilt that she has not learnt the language. This is a parable for thousands of Aboriginal people whose past involves such painful cultural dispossession.

The publisher has provided Teaching Resources for this book and I highly recommend them to our teachers throughout Australia: static.booktopia.com.au/pdf/9780143785750-1.pdf

Kim Scott

Works by Indigenous writers regularly appear on the short and long lists for major literary prizes, and they are reviewed in newspapers and literary journals. These reviews show us the critics' and readers' appreciation for writing by Indigenous authors. Noongar writer Kim Scott is a case in point. Rohan Wilson, in a review for the *Australian* newspaper in August 2017, wrote of Kim Scott's novel *That Deadman Dance* (Picador, 2010), 'Scott announced himself as the country's most important novelist.'

His novel *Benang* (Fremantle Arts Centre Press, 1999) was the first by an Indigenous writer to win Australia's most prestigious literary prize, the Miles Franklin Award. *That Deadman Dance* also won the Miles Franklin Award, among many other literary prizes. His fifth novel, *Taboo* (Picador, 2017), won four major awards and was reviewed in several journals.

A Companion to the Works of Kim Scott, edited by Belinda Wheeler (Camden House, 2016), deals with aspects of Scott's career in education and literature; and *Kim Scott: Readers, Language, Interpretation*, edited by Philip Morrissey, Ruby Lowe and Marion Campbell (UWAP, 2019) is another useful resource.

Scott's other works include a children's book, short stories and an oral-history account of his family, of the Noongar people from the south coast of Western Australia, *Kayang and Me* (Fremantle Arts Centre Press, 2005). Scott wrote this in collaboration with his aunt, Noongar Elder Hazel Brown.

Scott also founded and is the current chair of Wirlomin Noongar Language and Stories, which has produced six bilingual (Noongar and English) community-authored picture books.

For a list of the awards and commendations Kim Scott has received for his work, go to the Resources section at the end of this book.

Melissa Lucashenko

Melissa Lucashenko is a Goorie writer of fiction, journalism and non-fiction. She lives between Brisbane and the Bundjalung Nation in northern New South Wales. With the publication of her sixth novel, the acclaimed *Too Much Lip*, Melissa joined eminent writers Kim Scott and Alexis Wright in winning the prestigious Miles Franklin Award in 2019. *Too Much Lip* also won the Queensland Premier's Award for a Work of State Significance and was

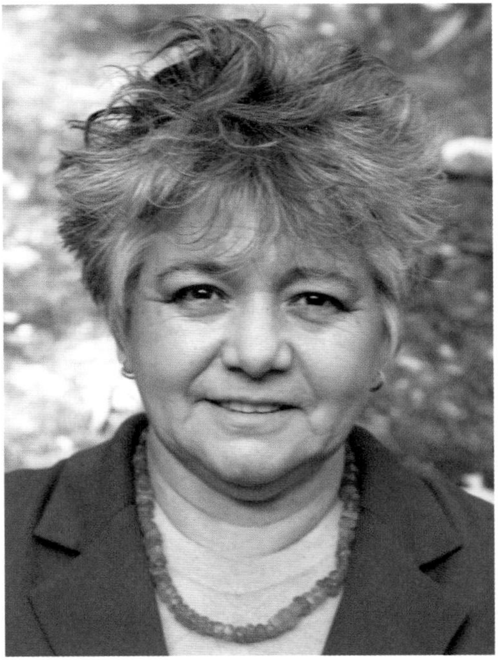

Melissa Lucashenko is a Goorie writer of fiction, journalism and non-fiction

shortlisted for the Prime Minister's Literary Award for Fiction, the Stella Prize, two Victorian Premier's Literary Awards, two Queensland Literary Awards and two NSW Premier's Literary Awards. It was widely reviewed and the article by fellow writer Maxine Beneba Clarke is memorable for its grasp of Lucashenko's subjects, 'sharp defiance' and the power of writing. Having met Lucashenko at writers retreats and events, Clarke observes:

Lucashenko works with Sisters Inside, a Queensland-based organisation that advocates the human rights of girls and women in prison. She is no stranger, personally or in witness, to the scars stories leave. Yet the emotional weight of writing Too Much Lip *was an unexpected drag into the darkness.*[57]

In fact, Lucashenko is a founding member of Sisters Inside, and it was fitting that she should have this recognition in the year before the Black Lives Matter protests exploded, and the sky-rocketing rates of Indigenous incarceration became the subject of public debate after years of being ignored.

Melissa is a Walkley Award winner for her non-fiction, the essay 'Sinking below sight: Down and out in Brisbane and Logan' in *Griffith REVIEW 41: Now We Are Ten*.

Her previous novel, the award-winning *Mullumbimby*, was described by her publisher, University of Queensland Press, as 'A darkly funny novel of romantic love and cultural warfare'. For a more serious understanding of this novel, read the review in *The Sydney Review of Books* by Eve Vincent in which the author's handling of Aboriginal language code switching, the debilitating nature of Native Title processes, and the experience of being on Country are drawn out.[58] It won the Queensland Literary Awards for Best Fiction in 2013.

She has also published fiction for younger readers, *Too Flash* (IAD Press) and *Killing Darcy* (UQP), and short works of fiction, such as 'A saltwater to watch', published in *The Saturday Paper*.

Bruce Pascoe

Acclaimed writer and Yuin, Bunurong and Tasmanian man Bruce Pascoe started a major national debate with his publication of *Dark Emu: Black Seeds: Agriculture or Accident?* (Magabala Books, 2014). Discussed in chapter 5, *Dark Emu* won both Book of the Year and the Indigenous Writer's Prize in the 2016 NSW Premier's Literary Awards and was shortlisted for the 2014 Victorian Premier's Award and the History Book Award in the Queensland Literary Awards. In 2019, we welcomed Pascoe's collected essays and stories, *Salt*. His most recent book, *Loving Country: A Guide to Sacred Australia* (Hardie Grant Travel, 2020), co-written with Vicky Shukuroglou, offers a deeper understanding of Australia from an Indigenous perspective. Pascoe received the Fellowship of Australian Writers' Literature Award in 1999 and the Australia Council Award for Lifetime Achievement in Literature in 2018. His novel *Fog a Dox* (Magabala Books, 2014) won the Prime Minister's Award for Young Adult Fiction in 2013. His stories have won ten national competitions and have been published in six languages and nine countries.

Bruce Pascoe has worked as a teacher, farmer, fisherman and an Aboriginal-language researcher. In the thirty-four books he has written, Pascoe incorporates Aboriginal knowledge and cultural aspects into his storytelling. He believes this way he can educate people about the factual history of Australian colonialism. In addition to his published works, he is also the Director of the Commonwealth Australian Studies Project. Other books by Bruce Pascoe include:

Bruce Pascoe, celebrated author and Yuin, Bunurong and Tasmanian man

Novelist Alexis Wright is a member of the Waanyi Nation of the Gulf of Carpentaria

Fox (McPhee Gribble/Penguin Books, 1988)

Shark (Magabala Books, 1999)

Nightjar (Seaglass Books, 2000)

Convincing Ground (Aboriginal Studies Press, 2007)

Bloke (Penguin Books 2009).

Alexis Wright

Alexis Wright is an award-winning novelist and writer, and member of the Waanyi Nation of the Gulf of Carpentaria. She has written widely on Indigenous rights. Her major novels are:

Plains of Promise (UQP, 1997): shortlisted for the Commonwealth Prize and published in France as *Les Plaines de L'Espoir*.

Carpentaria (Giramondo Publishing, 2006): won five national literary awards in 2007, including the ASAL Gold Medal and the Miles Franklin Award.

The Swan Book (Giramondo Publishing, 2013): won the ASAL Gold Medal.

Her book *Tracker: Stories of Tracker Tilmouth* (Giramondo Publishing, 2017), about Indigenous activist Tracker Tilmouth, won the 2018 Stella Prize. In their award statement, the judges called it 'a new way of writing memoir' and observed:

It is fitting that a book written in the mode and genre of Aboriginal storytelling should win a prize that encompasses both non-fiction and fiction. It is a work, epic in scope and size, that will ensure that a legend of Central Australian politics is preserved in myth.

At around 600 pages, the book features interviews that Wright conducted with people that Tracker chose himself before he passed away in 2015.

Ben Etherington in his review in *The Conversation*, in April 2018, wrote:

It is simply remarkable to hear Tracker's genuinely funny jokes and stories told repeatedly, often word for word and channelling Tracker's unmistakable style, by such a range of different speakers.

Wright is also editor of *Take Power, Like This Old Man Here* (IAD, 1998), a collection of essays and stories celebrating twenty years of land rights in Central Australia, and also wrote *Grog War* (Magabala Books, 1997), a study of alcohol abuse in Tennant Creek.

Claire G. Coleman

Claire G. Coleman is a Noongar woman who has travelled extensively across Australia. Her novel *The Old Lie* was published in 2019. She has received much-deserved accolades

Noongar author Claire G. Coleman

for her book *Terra Nullius*, including the 2016 black&write! Fellowship and the 2018 Norma K. Hemming Award. The book was also shortlisted for the 2018 Stella Prize.

Terra Nullius is a speculative fiction that tells the story of the Australian 'natives' as they fight for survival against the 'settlers', but not in the way you would expect. It creates a picture of an apocalyptic dystopia which forces the reader to confront the idea that what is created as fiction is in fact a reality for all Indigenous peoples who have survived massive upheaval and devastation, and the journey to reclaim culture and identity and have their humanity recognised in the wake of colonisation.

Leah Purcell accepting her Best Play award for her reimagining of *The Drover's Wife* at the 2017 Helpmann Awards

Tony Birch

Tony Birch, a Melbourne Koori man, is an award-winning writer, academic and activist. In 2003, his PhD thesis won the Chancellor's Prize for Excellence at the University of Melbourne, where he lectured for many years. Birch is the inaugural recipient of the Dr Bruce McGuinness Indigenous Research Fellowship at Victoria University and in 2017 he was awarded the Patrick White Literary Award. His recent novel *The White Girl* (UQP, 2019) won the 2020 NSW Premier's Award for Indigenous Writing, and was shortlisted for the 2020 Miles Franklin Literary Prize.

His other novels and short-story collections include:

Common People (UQP, 2017), shortlisted for the 2018 NSW Premier's Literary Awards Christina Stead Prize for Fiction and the 2019 Victorian Premier's Literary Awards Prize for Indigenous Writing

Ellen van Neerven

Ghost River (UQP, 2015), winner of the 2016 Victorian Premier's Literary Award for Indigenous Writing

Blood (UQP, 2011), shortlisted for the 2012 Miles Franklin Award

Shadowboxing (Scribe Publications, 2006)

Father's Day (Hunter Publishers, 2009)

The Promise: Stories (UQP, 2014)

Leah Purcell

Leah Purcell is an award-winning author, playwright and actor. In 2017, her play *The Drover's Wife* (Penguin), a radical re-interpretation of Henry Lawson's short story of the same name, won the Victorian Prize for Literature and the Victorian Premiers Literary Award for Drama, and the Book of the Year Award and the Nick Enright Prize for Playwriting in the NSW Premier's Literary Prize, and associated film and theatre awards. Her other works include:

Box the Pony (playscript) (Hodder Headline, 1999)

Black Chicks Talking (Hodder Headline, 2002)

Purcell now appears on the TV series *Wentworth* in the lead role of Rita Connors. In 2019, she received a Logie nomination in the Outstanding Actress category.

Ellen van Neerven

Winner of three NSW Premier's Literary Awards and the inaugural Quentin Bryce Award for their latest poetry collection *Throat* (UQP, 2020), Ellen van Neerven is of Mununjali Yugambeh (south-east Queensland) and Dutch heritage. *Heat and Light* (UQP, 2014), their first book, is a highly praised short-story collection and received the David Unaipon Award, the Dobbie Literary Award and the NSW Premier's Literary Awards Indigenous Writers Prize, and was shortlisted for the Stella Prize, the Queensland Literary Award for State Significance and the Readings Prize. Ellen van Neerven also writes plays and non-fiction. Their second book, *Comfort Food* (UQP, 2016), a collection of poetry, won the Tina Kane Emergent Award and was shortlisted for the NSW Premier's Literary Awards Kenneth Slessor Prize and Highly Commended for the 2016 Wesley Michel Wright Prize. Their play *Swim* featured at the Yellamundie First Peoples Playwriting Festival in January 2019.

Anita Heiss

Dr Anita Heiss is a prolific Wiradjuri author of poetry, non-fiction and fiction, including chick lit (commercial women's fiction) and children's novels. Her recent work has brought her to greater prominence and includes the novel *Bila Yarrudhang-galangdhuray* and a stage play based on her book *Tiddas*. A collection she edited, *Growing Up Aboriginal in Australia*, was published by Black Inc. in 2018 and her memoir on identity, *Am I Black Enough for You?* (Random House, 2011), won the Victorian Premier's Literary Award for Indigenous Writing and was a finalist in the Human Rights Awards Media (non-fiction).

She lists her other works and prizes on her website.

Her children's literature includes *Kicking Goals with Goodesy and Magic*, co-written with Adam Goodes and Michael O'Loughlin. She also wrote two kids' novels with students from La Perouse Public School – *Yirra and her deadly dog, Demon* and *Demon Guards the School Yard*.

She has been an advocate for Indigenous literacy, working in remote communities as a role model and encouraging young Indigenous Australians to write their own stories.

A selection of the awards she has won includes:

- 2012 Victorian Premier's Literary Award for Indigenous Writing, for *Am I Black Enough for You?*
- 2011 Deadly Award for Most Outstanding Contribution to Literature, for *Paris Dreaming*
- 2010 Deadly Award for Most Outstanding Contribution to Literature, for *Manhattan Dreaming*
- 2008 Deadly Award for Most Outstanding Contribution to Literature, with Peter Minter, for the *Macquarie PEN Anthology of Aboriginal Literature*
- 2007 Deadly Award for Most Outstanding Contribution to Literature for *Not Meeting Mr Right*
- 2003 Inaugural Australian Society of Authors Medal (Under 35) for contribution to Australian community and life
- 2002 NSW Premier's History Award (Audio Visual) for *Barani: The Aboriginal History of the City of Sydney*

She was shortlisted for the 2002 NSW Premier's History Award (Young People's History) for *Who Am I? The Diary of Mary Talence, Sydney 1937*.

Stan Grant

Stan Grant is a Wiradjuri journalist and international relations specialist who has covered events in several war zones throughout his career. He has anchored a number of television radio programs and writes prolifically in newspapers and other media. Since his return to Australia his books have mounted up and he brings an acute compassion combined with a sense of the deep wound that the treatment of his own family has caused. His common-sense balancing of the need to correct the injustices and find a better Australia is his great contribution to the debate about Indigenous history and current affairs.

I recommend his latest books:

Talking to My Country (HarperCollins, 2016)

Australia Day (HarperCollins, 2019)

On Identity (Hachette, 2020)

With the Falling of the Dusk (HarperCollins, 2021)

Poetry

The Aboriginal bent for the poetic and rhythmic is evident in recent anthologies that provide samplings from award-winners and new poets. *Homeland Calling: Words from a New Generation of Aboriginal and Torres Strait Islander Voices* (Hardie Grant

Travel, 2020), edited by Ellen van Neerven with a foreword by rapper Baker Boy, brings together poems created from hip-hop song lyrics in collaboration with Desert Pea Media.

Fire Front: First Nations Poetry and Power Today (UQP, 2020), edited by Alison Whittaker, is challenging in reach and message. Curated under five themes, each introduced in short, powerful essays by Bruce Pascoe, Ali Cobby Eckermann, Chelsea Bond, Evelyn Araluen and Steven Oliver, this book makes available the poetry of our most famous and best writers, some of it half-remembered and no longer in print. Alison includes great poets published in the twentieth century and who have passed: the late Oodgeroo Noonuccal, Jack Davis, Kevin Gilbert and Ruby Langford Ginibi. She also presents us with a clever sampling of present-day stars: Ellen van Neerven, Lionel Fogarty, Ali Cobby Eckermann, Sam Wagan Watson and Evelyn Araluen, while those better known for their novels, biographies, short stories and songs are here also: Archie Roach, Alexis Wright, Tony Birch and Claire G. Coleman. Less well known as poets – and deserving of a wider audience – are Mojo Ruiz de Luzuriaga, Joel Davison, Declan Furber Gillick, Provocalz, Ancestress and Dylan Voller.

Declan Fry in his review of this breathtaking collection writes that it is 'not so much an anthology as a reckoning'.[59] See a video of Alison and Evelyn speaking and readings of the poems at the Wheeler Centre in Melbourne at www.wheelercentre.com/events/fire-front-first-nations-poetry-and-power-today.

Another anthology, *Guwayu – For All Times* (Magabala Books, 2020), edited by Jeanine Leane, is a collection of First Nations Poetry commissioned by Red Room Poetry and produced in a series of workshops.

Desert Pea Media uses contemporary storytelling techniques, including poetry, to foster important social and cultural dialogue

This collection too is curated in sections and includes works in Indigenous languages, including Aboriginal English.

First Australian poets are being supported by the Poetry in First Languages (PIFL) program, developed by Red Room Poetry. During the UN International Year of Indigenous Languages in 2019, the Copyright Agency funded PIFL to expand the teaching of poetry in First Australian languages. This is to ensure that our cultures and languages are strengthened. Published online on the Red Room Poetry website, the contributing poets are Alison Whittaker (Gomeroi), Ellen van Neerven (Mununjali Yugambeh), Matthew Heffernan (Pintupi–Luritja), Melanie Mununggurr-Williams (Djapu), Declan Furber Gillick (Arrernte), Nicholas Paton (Ngunawal), Ethan Bell (Ngunawal), Nicole Smede (Worimi), Jacob Morris (Gumea Dharawal), Paul Collis (Barkindji) and Joel Davison (Gadigal). They are supported by contributing artists and educators including David Cragg (Bundjalung) and Allan Giddy, as well as Elders and cultural knowledge holders Aunty Sharyn Halls (Gundungurra), Aunty Trish Levett (Gundungurra), Jacob Morris (Gumea Dharawal), Aunty Jodi Edwards (Yuin), Uncle Richard Campbell (Yuin) and Joel Davison (Gadigal).

The following poems and collections are also recommended:

Bobby McLeod, *Ngudjung Yugarang 'Mother's Heartbeat'* (BMAC Publishing, 2008)

Alexis Wright, 'Hey Ancestor!' (indigenousx.com.au/alexis-wright-hey-ancestor/)

Matthew Heffernan, 'Ngurrparringu (forgotten)' (indigenousx.com.au/ngurrparringu-forgotten/)

Yvette Holt, *Anonymous Premonition* (UQP, 2008)

Lionel Fogarty, *Yerrabilela Jimbelung: Poems about Friends and Family* (Keeaira Press, 2008)

Scriptwriting and stage production

I was not surprised to learn in 2020 when the Archibald Prize for portraiture prize winners were announced that the self-portrait by Meyne Wyatt, better known as an actor and writer than as an artist, won the Packing Room Prize by popular vote. It is a stunning self-portrait that captures much of Meyne's demeanour and personality. Meyne is a Wongutha-Yamatji actor and writer, born in 1989 in Subiaco, Western Australia.[60] He grew up in Kalgoorlie, the famous gold-mining town, on Wongutha Country inland from Perth. He now lives in Sydney. This is the first time he has entered the Archibald Prize. Simply titled *Meyne*, and painted in acrylic on canvas, it has many of the hallmarks of a mature and technically proficient artist. Painting is a well-hidden talent in this case, obviously learnt from his mother, who is an artist, but few knew of his art practice. He explained more when interviewed by the Archibald Prize staff at the Art Gallery of New South Wales:

My self-portrait is the first painting I've done in over ten years and I decided to enter it at the behest of my artist mother, Sue Wyatt, an Archibald Prize finalist in 2003 for her portrait of writer Doris Pilkington.

I began painting again because I wanted to get back into it at some point, then we went into lockdown [due to COVID-19] and I thought there was no better time than now. Over a span of about four months it took me about five days in total to complete it and I used good old acrylic because it's what I know. I decided to paint myself because there would be no one to offend if the painting wasn't any good.'

I've had no formal art training, just tips from my mum. In 2007 I won an award as part of the Year 12 Perspectives exhibition at the Art Gallery of Western Australia and travelled to Japan, where my painting was on exhibit.'[61]

Meyne has achieved critical praise and fame as a playwright for his debut work *City of Gold*, in 2019. He performed in the play as the main character at the highly successful world premiere at Queensland Theatre. It was transferred to Griffin Theatre Company, where it also sold out. The notes published by the Griffin Theatre Company describe the play as 'a howl of rage at the injustice, inequality and wilful amnesia of this country's 21st century. It's an urgent play for our moment from a vital new voice. As Childish Gambino sings across the Pacific "This is America," Meyne Wyatt calls back loudly "This is Australia."'[62]

City of Gold was shortlisted for the 2020 Victorian Premier's Prize for Drama and for the NSW Premier's Literary Award. At Sydney Theatre Awards, it was nominated for Best New Australian Work. Wyatt won Best Male Actor in a Leading Role and Shari Sebbens won Best Female Actor in a Supporting Role for their performances in *City Of Gold*. The Judges Report of the Victorian Premier's Literary Awards for which City of Gold was shortlisted for the unpublished manuscript prize said:

City of Gold *is an extraordinary cri de coeur; a scream of rage and despair from the heart of First Nations people, it's a work of often breathtaking rhetorical force. Energised by the crisis at the heart of our country, it paints a picture of dire societal pressure and galvanising personal courage. Uncompromising, raw and shocking, it is a play that cries 'Enough! Our people are dying'. Necessary and unforgettable.*[63]

Meyne's career successes since graduating from NIDA in 2010 are astonishing: as the Victorian Premier's Literary Awards notes acknowledge, he was 'just 18 when he was accepted into the National Institute of Dramatic Art and has created a buzz in the industry with non-stop theatre, television and film work since graduating in 2010'.[64]

Meyne's performance in Lachlan Philpott's *Silent Disco* (Griffin Theatre Company) earned him an award for Best Newcomer at Sydney Theatre Awards. Other theatre performances have included *King Lear*, *Bloodland* (Sydney Theatre Company), *Peter Pan*, *Buried* City (Belvoir) and *Gloria* (Griffin Theatre Company). With a sound theatre background, it was inevitable that he would become a star in television and film productions, which include:

- The ABC's tele-movie *The Broken Shore* (2013)
- *Redfern Now* (2013), for which he earned nominations for Most Outstanding Newcomer at the 2014 Logie Awards and Best Led Actor in a Television Drama at the 3rd AACTA Award
- From 2014 to 2016 he also appeared in *Neighbours*, making history as the first Indigenous actor to join the main cast
- *Black Comedy* (ABC, 2016)
- *The Leftovers* (HBO, 2017)
- The AACTA award winning series *Mystery Road* (SBS, 2018) and *Les Norton* (ABC, 2019)

And the feature films:

- *The Sapphires* (2012)
- *The Turning* (2013)
- *Strangerland* (2015), opposite Nicole Kidman and Hugo Weaving

In 2020, he appeared on the ABC television program *Q&A* and delivered a monologue from the *City of Gold* that shocked and thrilled audiences at the height of the Black Lives Matter global protests. It is a powerful statement on racism and his own victory over it, with all the damage it causes to its victims laid bare.[65] (Advisory note: It contains strong language.)

Nakkiah Lui

A Gamilaroi and Torres Strait Islander woman, Nakkiah Lui is a celebrated playwright, television screenwriter, author, actor, performer, comedian and satirist. She is best known in the Indigenous world for her performances in the ABC's *Black Comedy* and *Kiki and Kitty* (2017), the latter which

Lui wrote and stars in. Her theatre pieces include *How to Rule the World* (2019), *Black is the New White* (2017), *Power Plays* (2016), *Kill the Messenger* (2015), *Blackie Blackie Brown: The Traditional Owners of Death* (2013), *I Should Have Told You Before We Made Love (That I'm Black)* (2012) and *This Heaven* (2013). With Indigenous Australian actress Miranda Tapsell, Lui hosts the podcast *Debutante: Race, Resistance and Girl Power* (2020) and the Buzzfeed podcast *Pretty for an Aboriginal* (2017). She now heads up her own book publishing imprint, JOAN, with Allen & Unwin.

Lui was the inaugural recipient of the 2012 Dreaming Award, presented by the Aboriginal and Torres Strait Island Arts Board of the Australia Council, and the 2013 Balnaves Foundation Indigenous Playwright award. Her other awards include the Malcolm Robertson Prize, the Green Room Award for Best Independent Production, the Nick Enright Prize for playwriting and a 2018 NSW Premier's Literary Award for *Black is the New White*.

She is a regular columnist for the *Australian Women's Weekly* and has also hosted Radio National's *AWAYE!* and *NAIDOC Evenings* for ABC Local Radio. She has been a guest on the ABC's panel shows *Q&A* and *The Drum*, a keynote speaker at writers' festivals and has big social media followings.

Jada Alberts is an accomplished playwright, actor, musician and painter

Jada Alberts

Brothers Wreck by Jada Alberts was staged at Sydney's Belvoir Street Theatre in 2014 and Melbourne's Malthouse Theatre and Adelaide's State Theatre Company of South Australia in 2018 to great acclaim. The play centres on Ruben, and the impact on him and his family following the suicide of his cousin. Ruben's family members grapple with this shocking death and work together to bring Ruben back from the feelings of loneliness and anger through compassion and care. The script and staging capture the tension of the wet season in Darwin, where the story unfolds. This insightful writing reflects Alberts's experiences as a Larrakia, Bardi, Wadaman and Yanuwa person from the Top End of Australia.

In addition to being a playwright, Jada Alberts is also an accomplished actor, musician and painter. They have appeared on stage in *Frost/Nixon*, *The Birthday Party*, *Second to None* and *Yibiyung* and the national tour of *The Shadow King*. Alberts also appeared in the feature film *Red Hill* and is widely known for their roles in *Redfern Now*, *Wentworth*, *Rush* and *Cleverman*; they also wrote two episodes for the latter show in season 2. Alongside Aaron Pederson, Alberts starred in the leading role of season 2 of *Mystery Road*. They graduated in 2006 from the Adelaide Centre for the Arts, and in 2007, won the Adelaide Critics' Circle Award for Best Emerging Artist.

In 2013, Alberts won the Balnaves Foundation Indigenous Playwrights Award, and in 2014 they were nominated for Best New Australian Work at the Sydney Theatre Awards for *Brothers Wreck*. In 2015, Alberts was nominated for the Nick Enright Prize for Playwriting, the NSW Literary Awards, and for Best Stage Play in the AWGIE Awards for *Brother's Wreck*. They were a Writers Fellow at Bell Shakespeare from 2016 to 2017.

Beautiful One Day

Beautiful One Day is a theatrical documentary about the death of an Aboriginal man in police custody on Palm Island, Queensland, in 2004. It also explores the aftermath of his death and the demands for justice from the community's residents. The details are told by weaving reports, interviews, transcripts of court hearings and other documents into the script, as well as incorporating audio and video stage elements into the stage performance. It was devised and performed by Sean Bacon, Magdalena Blackley, several Palm Island residents and the Ilbijerri Theatre Company. Much of the play is performed by three people from Palm Island who lived through these events.

Children's literature

Indigenous literature written for children deals with matters of great importance to children and adults alike: freedom, finding one's self and the legacy of the ancestors. *Finding Our Heart* by Thomas Mayor (Explore Australia, 2020), *The First Scientists* by Corey Tutt (Hardie Grant, 2021) and Adam Briggs's *Our Home, Our Heartbeat* (Hardie Grant, 2020) explore both Aboriginal and Torres Strait Islanders' place in Australia today and our past. *Once there was a Boy* by Dub Lefler (Magabala Books, 2011) was a finalist in the 2012 Deadly Awards, in the Outstanding Achievement in Literature category, and was shortlisted in the Speech Pathology Australia Book of the Year Awards (Indigenous Children category) in 2012. *Stolen Girl*, written by Trina Saffioti and illustrated by Norma MacDonald (Magabala Books, 2011), tells the story of a young Aboriginal girl removed from her family and taken to an institution, where 'one day she unlocks the door and takes her first step toward home'.

The following children's books are also recommended:

Amy McQuire, *Day Break* (Hardie Grant, 2021)

Bruce Pascoe, *Found* (Magabala Books, 2020) and *Young Dark Emu* (Magabala Books, 2019)

Aunty Joy Murphy, *Welcome to Country* (Walker Books, 2016)

Aunty Fay Muir & Sue Lawson, *Family* and *Respect* (Magabala Books, 2020)

Bindi by Kirli Saunders (Magabala Books, 2020)

Graphic novels

Brenton McKenna's series of graphic novels bring together oral history and stories about life for a young Aboriginal girl in Broome in the late 1940s. Published by Aboriginal publishing house Magabala Books, the Ubby series shows the Aboriginal and multicultural history of Broome after World War Two, and describes 'adventures full of myths and legends'. Ubby is a smart, street-wise leader of a small gang known as the 'Underdogs'. The first book, *Ubby's Underdogs: The Legend of the Phoenix Dragon* (2011), was followed by *Ubby's Underdogs: Heroes Beginnings* (2013). The publisher's notes tell us that this 'is storytelling on a remarkable scale. It continues with established characters that have links to other worlds amidst an intricate backdrop of Aboriginal and Chinese mythology.' *Ubby's Underdogs: Return of the Dragons*, the final book in the series, was published in 2019.

Digital writing

We are witnessing a generational shift in Indigenous writing and thinking. This is largely brought about by the digital writers in our population who have turned to more immediate styles of storytelling.

Anyone can have a blog these days, but the most important online writing from Indigenous Australia comes from IndigenousX Pty Ltd. I have mentioned my colleague Luke Pearson founded and runs the company with a mission to publish original content from emerging and established Indigenous writers across Australia online and on several social media platforms, such as Twitter, Facebook and Instagram. The company specialises in analysis, commentary and public interest journalism. It has given a voice to many young Indigenous writers, scientists, and intellectuals. Each IndigenousX guest takes over the Twitter account @IndigenousX for a week and publishes an article each Friday in *The Guardian*, which hosts this column to give its readers access to the diverse views in the Indigenous community. I read these articles to stay up to date with our younger movers and shakers and what they believe is important.

Published by IndigenousX, Associate Professor Chelsea Watego's essay 'The irony of the Aboriginal academic' is a defence of Indigenous intellectual work and writing. As a senior academic at the prestigious University of Queensland, she felt compelled to write:

The foundations of our most learned institutions were built upon the premise that the Aborigine was not human, and thus incapable of learning or knowing. Our presence was merely an accessory adding to the aesthetic of white knowing, and to this day as a Black academic, I'm still forced to contest this ideology as an everyday practice.[66]

She concludes her essay about the continual production of racist knowledge in universities with these words: 'there remains both real work, and a real war to be waged in the academy; it just requires a few more warriors to serve'.

Competing strongly with IndigenousX is Blackfulla Bookclub with the maxim, 'Our Ancestors are the original storytellers'. It is an initiative of Teela Reid, who describes herself as a Wiradjuri and Wailwan woman, lawyer and storyteller, and Merinda Dutton, also an Indigenous lawyer. They are 'Sharing stories to heal our nation' on Instagram @blackfulla_bookclub and Twitter #blackfullabookclub.

Film and television storytellers

The new storytellers include the film and television makers who are bringing ancient and contemporary stories to the screen.

Despite the COVID-19 restrictions keeping us away from cinemas for most of the year, 2020 was a great year for Australian Indigenous films. I gave five stars to *High Ground* and *The Furnace*. In 2021, Leah Purcell's *The Drover's Wife: The Legend of Molly Johnson* was screened at its world premiere at Texas's South By Southwest film festival and available to Australian audiences after its premiere at the Melbourne International Film Festival in August.

High Ground, set in the magnificent Kakadu National Park region where the Church Missionary Society established the Anglican mission in 1925, melds the oral and documented history of the wars in Arnhem Land, the savagery of the police and vigilantes who massacred Aboriginal people and the resistance by those who refused to surrender. Travis, a former soldier turned bounty hunter with a moral compass, played by Simon Baker of *The Mentalist* fame, joins Jacob Junior Nayinggul as Gutjuk, a young man from the Christian mission to hunt the renegade warrior (and Gutjuk's uncle) Baywara, played by Sean Mununggurr. It emerges that Gutjuk is the only survivor of a massacre committed by Travis when Gutjuk was a child, when his father, Dharrpa, played by Rirratjingu songman and cultural leader Witiyana Marika, was absent from the family group. Redemption and revenge are the twin themes of this frontier war story. Esmerelda Marimowa is utterly captivating as the rape victim turned guerrilla who joins Gutjuk in the resistance.

The film's title is a double entrendre on Travis's moral epiphany as he confronts his terrible guilt and his mastery of the sniper's high point. It may also refer ironically to the moral failure of the Australians who sought to suppress and control Aboriginal people by brutal means.

As well as his key role as Dharrpa, Witiyana is the producer. He worked with director Steven Maxwell Johnson when he was a member of the band Yothu Yindi, led by the late Mandawuy Yunupiŋu. Johnson directed Yothu Yindi's ARIA award-winning music video 'Djäpana'. *High Ground*'s script was written by Chris Anastassiades who also wrote Johnson's 2001 film *Yolngu Boy*. The idea for the film formed when Witiyana was a young man. He told Belinda Quinn of *NME*:

He first learnt about the white 'horsemen' who massacred his grandmother's clan, Dhalwaŋu, when as a teenager he journeyed to do ceremony with his grandfather, Birrikitji Gumana, on their homeland Gäṉgän.

'I didn't learn it from the school,' he says. 'My grandfather brought all the nephews,

sons and daughters to Gäṉgän. There were over 100 people that had passed away.'

Marika and his dear friend, relative and Yothu Yindi co-founder Dr. M. Yunupingu later returned to Gäṉgän to visit their grandmother, hoping to learn more about the massacre that took place in the early 20th century. 'In the .. early days we were walking and we were searching, researching.'[67]

The police chief Moran – a character based on the vicious first Police Commissioner of the Northern Territory, Paul Foelsche – is played by Jack Thompson, whose Yolŋu name Gulkula was given to him by Mandawuy's eldest brother, Galarrwuy Yunupiŋu. The mesmerising Aaron Pedersen from Central Australia plays the role of a native police tracker from Queensland, the feared and hated assassins that wiped out thousands of their own people.

The cast includes people from many tribes across Arnhem Land, all of whom are acknowledged in the lengthy credits, worth watching to see the list of clans, languages and cultural leaders who gave their permission for the stories to be told and the film locations.

The Furnace by writer-director Roderick MacKay was called a 'brutish western'[68] by a reviewer but this is an entirely glib and incorrect way to describe it. This is a distinctively Australian film that will hold you in its grip with a story that surprises at every turn. It is based on historical events that have been kept largely secret for decades. Why have so few historians told the stories of these events? I knew about some of them because of my friends who have Aboriginal and Afghan ancestry from the days when Muslim cameleers 'moved cargo throughout the vast desert interior' with their camel caravans.[69] Although not the first people of the Islamic faith to come to our country, they left a remarkable imprint. They made friends with Aboriginal people they came to know on the great Aboriginal trade routes criss-crossing the continent and sometimes married Aboriginal women. Set in Yamatji Badimaya Country around Mount Magnet in Western Australia, and with its main characters played by Egyptian star Ahmed Malek, Australian star David Wenham and emerging Yolŋu star Baykali Ganambarr, the story unfolds across the arid lands in a hunt by a young cameleer and a mysterious 'bushman' for stolen gold. For its world premiere at the 2020 Venice Film Festival, the director's notes are illuminating:

Today, Australia has the world's largest wild camel population. Yet, most Australians do not know that, from the 1860s, The British Empire imported camels and handlers from Afghanistan, India and Persia to open up Australia's desert interior. These Islamic, Sikh and Hindu men provided the main form of exploration and freight transport between colonies and gold mining camps. They were vital to the nation's formation, yet experienced much prejudice and were often coerced into indentured labour. The Furnace *is a revisionist frontier mythology that weaves this forgotten history into the tapestry of the Outback. It is my hope that this film enacts a more inclusive sense of Australian identity.*[70]

Rachel Perkins and Warwick Thornton are two of Australia's greatest filmmakers. Both Indigenous, they use the power of cinema and television to tell their stories. They are prolific writers, directors and producers, and have won scores of awards in Australia and around the globe.

Rachel Perkins

Rachel Perkins is an Arrernte and Kalkadoon woman, from Alice Springs, who has been making television programs and films since 1992. She has established her own company, Blackfella Films, and has been a prolific producer of award-winning television series and documentaries, such as *The Tall Man*. Based on a book by Chloe Hooper, *The Tall Man* is the true story of the death of Indigenous man Cameron Doomadgee in police custody in Queensland.

Perkins has directed four feature films: *Jasper Jones* (nominated for Best Film at the 2017 AACTA Awards), *Radiance*, *One Night the Moon* (which received five Australian Film Institute [AFI] Awards) and the musical *Bran Nue Dae*, which screened at the Sundance, Berlin and Toronto film festivals. Released in 2009, *Bran Nue Dae* tells the story of a young man in the 1960s who runs away from the mission school, back to his home in Broome and to his love, Rosie.

In 2012, Perkins directed the telemovie *Mabo*, which screened on ABC1 to mark the twentieth anniversary of the historic High Court decision (of the same name). *Mabo* was nominated for Most Outstanding Mini Series or Telemovie at the 2013 TV Week Logie Awards. Perkins directed three episodes of the landmark television drama series *Redfern Now*, the first Australian drama series written, directed and produced by Indigenous Australians. In 2015, she received the Australian Directors Guild (ADG) Award for Best Direction in a TV Drama Series for *Redfern Now: Promise Me*.

Perkins directed *Total Control* and season one of *Mystery Road* for the ABC. This show premiered in 2018 as a critical and ratings hit. She also wrote, directed and co-produced the seven-hour documentary series *First Australians* (2009), which received Australia's top honours including AFI and IF Awards, the UN Media Peace Prize, TV Week Logie, and the Writers and Directors Guild of Australia Awards.

In addition to all of this, Perkins has worked with Arrernte women who sing the ancient song series and recorded them with linguist Myfany Turpin. Through the Arrernte Women's Project, hundreds of traditional songs were methodically recorded and catalogued, creating an important resource and a national treasure.

Warwick Thornton

The extraordinary filmmaker Warwick Thornton, who hails from Alice Springs, has made several award-winning films. The film that catapulted him to global fame, *Samson and Delilah*, won more than twenty awards, including the coveted *Camera d'Or* at the 2009 Cannes Film Festival.

Samson and Delilah and his other most famous and most awarded film, *Sweet Country*, are not easy to watch but they address truths about life and history in Central Australia in a way that no other Australian filmmaker has ever achieved. In *Sweet Country*, as in Thorton's earlier works, the characters and landscapes are beyond realistic; these films resemble great parables. Inspired by real events, *Sweet Country* is a period western set in 1929 in the outback of the Northern Territory. At its world premiere screening at the 2017 Venice Film Festival, it received a standing ovation, great acclaim from critics and won the Special Jury Prize. It was also the prestigious Platform winner at the 2017 Toronto Film Festival, Best Feature Film at the 2017 Asia Pacific Screen Awards, Best Dramatic Film ImagineNATIVE Festival 2017, the Audience Award at the Adelaide Film Festival, Best Feature Screenplay at Australian Writers Guild, and received Critics' Awards at Camerimage, Luxembourg, Venice and Dublin film festivals.

Tony Briggs

A great example of a modern Aboriginal story is told in the film *The Sapphires*, written by Yorta Yorta and Wurundjeri man Tony Briggs and based on the experiences of his mother, Laurel Robinson. It received standing ovations at its premiere at the Cannes Film Festival in 2012. The British newspaper *The Times* described it as 'the kind of film that makes you want to leap from your seat and shout for joy'. This feature-length film, directed by Indigenous director and actor Wayne Blair tells the story of four young Yorta Yorta women who took their soul music act to Vietnam in 1968 to entertain the troops. Its cast includes strong Aboriginal leading women Deb Mailman, Miranda Tapsell, Shari Sebbens and Jessica Mauboy. It is an adventure story, a love story and a musical. Its historical setting is the Aboriginal community at Cummeragunga on the Murray River, which forms the border of Victoria and New South Wales. Tony is also the curator of the recently established film festival Birrarangga which runs at ACMI in Melbourne and showcases Indigenous films on strength, resilience and the environment from filmmakers around the globe.

Tony Briggs with his mother, Laurel Robinson, on the opening night of *The Sapphires*, New York City, 2013

Ryan Griffen

The gripping television series *Cleverman* was based on an original concept by Ryan Griffen. He created the story idea so that his son would have a superhero that he could relate to. It is a powerful drama depicting a dystopian future in which the Hairy People, a superhuman species based on mythical beings in Aboriginal lore, are persecuted by humans. They are hunted and, when captured, confined in laboratories to change their nature and 'humanise' them.

As a parable of racial politics and policing, it excels in dramatically depicting dangerous myths about science and progress. It also shows the human tendency to dominate other beings. It pits brother against brother in the struggle between the Hairy People and the Containment Authority, recalling the terror inflicted on First Australians during the assimilation period when children were torn from their families.

Doris Pilkington Garimara

The book *Follow the Rabbit-Proof Fence* (1996), written by Doris Pilkington Garimara, was made into a film, *Rabbit-Proof Fence*, in 2002. It is a true, powerful and heart-breaking account of how Doris's mother, Molly, Doris's aunt Daisy, and Molly's cousin Gracie – all Martutjarra girls – were forcibly removed from their families in the East Pilbara in Western Australia in 1931, under the 'assimilation' policy. Molly (aged fourteen), Daisy (eleven) and Gracie (eight) escaped from the Moore River Native Settlement, where they had been taken, and were pursued by an Aboriginal tracker. The girls walked for some 1600 kilometres using the rabbit-proof fence that runs north–south through Western Australia as their guide. Historian Doris Pilkington Garimara used archival evidence and interviews with her mother and her Aunty Daisy to write the story.

The film is gripping viewing, with David Gulpilil in the role of the tracker and Kenneth Branagh in the role of A.O. Neville, the 'Chief Protector of Aborigines', who ordered the forced removal of Aboriginal children in Western Australia. The film won many awards and was screened worldwide.

This story about members of the Stolen Generations helped Australians to understand the suffering that has been caused to thousands of families. Eventually the sentiment around the country led to the National Apology to the Stolen Generations, delivered by then prime minister Kevin Rudd in 2008.

Storytelling is culture

There are Aboriginal and Torres Strait Islander storytellers working across most genres and formats. They are continuing ancient traditions of sharing culture, knowledge, ideas, wisdom and understanding about people and our world, and, above all, entertaining audiences. Now our creators have access to global publication and the broadcast potential of film, television and, increasingly, the worldwide web.

As Indigenous storytelling adapted to new ways of communicating in the twentieth and twenty-first centuries, the positive reception to this creative outpouring has been encouraging. Best of all, our most accomplished storytellers keep our cultures alive and make a living from their talents. Our children and youth, indeed all children and youth, have a right to read and hear these great stories. They will help them to learn about themselves and about the Aboriginal and Torres Strait Islander worlds, and to enjoy them.

9

NATIVE TITLE

Eddie Koiki Mabo had an impact on Australian life that was profound and life-changing for thousands of Torres Strait Islanders and Aboriginal people across the nation. He was born on the island of Mer (Murray Island) in the Torres Strait, in 1935. In 1974, while working as a gardener at James Cook University in Townsville, he met historians Henry Reynolds and Noel Loos. The three men became friends. For so long, writers and historians had ignored the history of Indigenous Australia, but both Henry and Noel wrote groundbreaking books about the Aboriginal resistance to the frontier war in North Queensland that placed Indigenous people at the centre of Australian history.

Through Noel and Henry, Koiki found out that he did not own his traditional land – that it was owned by the state of Queensland. Koiki began teaching, lecturing at the university and writing about his culture and his ties to his land. He wrote about the land ownership and inheritance system on Mer.

He did not accept that the land his grandfather had bequeathed to him did not belong to him by law. In 1982, he met with a group of lawyers in Townsville to begin his legal challenge to the Queensland land laws. That year the case was lodged in the High Court. Koiki was the leading plaintiff and he was joined by other Traditional Owners of Mer as plaintiffs: Father Dave Passi, Mr James Rice and, until she passed away, Mrs Celuia Mapo Salee.

Central to the case was the evidence, written and oral, that the people of Mer had their own laws that were given to them by their god, Malo. This god is often represented as an octopus. The plaintiffs challenged the idea that the entire continent and islands of Australia were given to the British upon 'discovery'. It was wrongly claimed that the Traditional Owners had no laws or system of governance, and that the land was not theirs.

This idea in British law is called terra nullius or 'land belonging to no one'; it was assumed that Aborigines had no laws or governance system and therefore no one for the British to treat with. It was based on arguments by the British legal expert, judge and politician William Blackstone, who, in his *Commentaries* (1765–1770), argued that there were 'ceded' (given) and 'conquered' (taken by force) colonies. Australia was deemed to be a 'ceded' colony until the High Court overruled this legal nonsense in the case known as *Mabo v Queensland* (No. 2) in 1992.

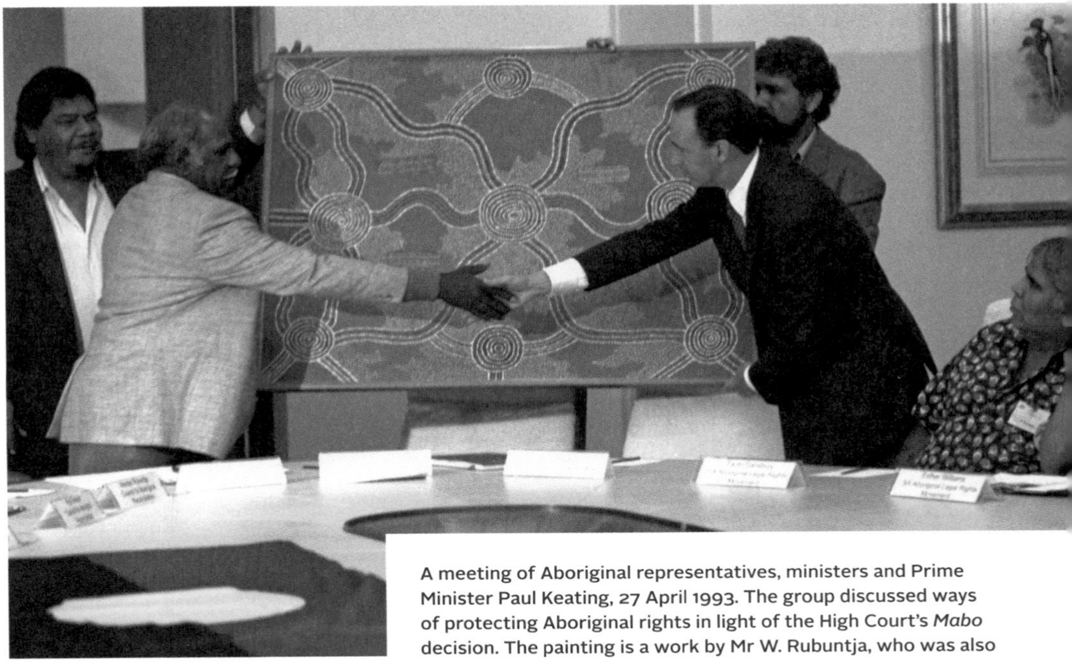

A meeting of Aboriginal representatives, ministers and Prime Minister Paul Keating, 27 April 1993. The group discussed ways of protecting Aboriginal rights in light of the High Court's *Mabo* decision. The painting is a work by Mr W. Rubuntja, who was also present at the meeting.

For Koiki and the other plantiffs, the path was not easy. The Queensland government passed the *Queensland Coast Islands Declaratory Act 1985* in an attempt to overrule any claims Torres Strait Islanders may have had to the land. The Act declared that when the Queensland government took over the Torres Strait Islands under the Coast Islands Act in 1879, title to the islands was transferred to the state of Queensland. This title could not be subject to other claims. In 1992, the plaintiffs from Mer appealed to the High Court, which found the *Queensland Coast Islands Declaratory Act 1985* contravened section 10 of the *Racial Discrimination Act 1975* (Cth) and so it was invalid.

The High Court judges' decision said that if Native Title rights did exist, they should be viewed as part of the human right to own and inherit property. On those grounds, the Coast Islands Act unfairly compromised the property rights of people in the Torres Strait.

To understand why the myth of terra nullius was wrong and was finally dismissed as legal doctrine by the High Court, you can watch *Land Bilong Islanders*. This documentary was directed by Trevor Graham and released in 1989. It features historic film as audiovisual evidence that the Murray Island people's traditional practices have continued over the generations. For example, the dances filmed by A.C. Haddon in 1898 are still performed today. *Land Bilong Islanders* documents the four months of hearings in the Supreme Court of Queensland before the High Court case.

It looks at the evidence about the laws and customs that govern the Murray Island people's land boundaries and ownership of property. Graham and his crew travelled to Murray Island to film sites of significance to the case.

On 3 June 1992, ten years after Koiki, Passi, Rice and Mrs Mapo Salee lodged their case, the High Court of Australia handed down its decision. In a six to one majority, it agreed to the claim that the Meriam people of Mer Island should have their Native Title recognised by law. In this case, called *Mabo No. 2*, the High Court overturned more than 200 years of the legal fiction of terra nullius. It established that rights to land had existed before the arrival of the British and, under certain conditions, survived British sovereignty. Koiki Mabo did not live to see his victory in court. He died of cancer not long before the judges handed down their decision, but his memory has endured in the name given to this momentous decision.

This win in the High Court was a turning point in the long history of governments taking from Aboriginal and Torres Strait Islander peoples their rights to their land.

Following the High Court's judgement in 1992, there was a bitter national debate about the impact of the *Mabo* case on Australian land ownership. After more than a year of difficult negotiations involving Aboriginal leaders and representatives

Eddie Koiki Mabo (with fishing spear) and Jack Wailu on the Island of Mer in the Torres Strait Islands, 1989

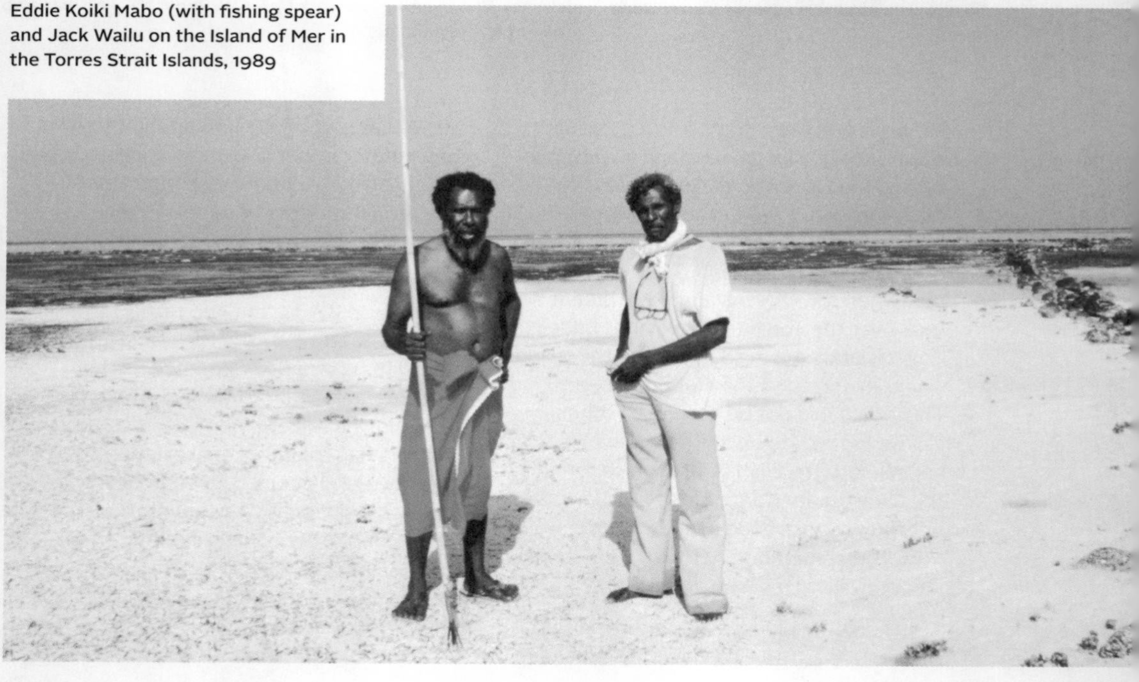

from the farming, grazing and mining industries, *the Native Title Act 1993 (Cth)* was finally passed into Australian law when it received Royal Assent on 24 December 1993. In a speech in Parliament, then prime minister Paul Keating explained that the legislation '[would] make the Mabo decision an historic turning point: the basis of a new relationship between Indigenous and other Australians'.

To see why the High Court's *Mabo* decision was a key turning point in Australia's history, you need to understand how property law works. The most complete form of land ownership is called 'freehold title'. That means the owner has permanent possession of their land and can sell it when they want to. In Aboriginal or Torres Strait Islander people's traditional laws and customs, they had a different relationship with the land. They did not own the land and would never sell it.

In law, the term 'property' describes rights in relation to things. In the 1999 case *Yanner v Eaton*, the High Court of Australia said:

The word 'property' is often used to refer to something that belongs to another. But … 'property' does not refer to a thing; it is a description of a legal relationship with a thing. It refers to a degree of power that is recognised in law as power permissibly exercised over the thing. The concept of 'property' may be elusive. Usually it is treated as a 'bundle of rights'.

The 'bundle of rights' that property involves acknowledges that rights over land can be divided. For example, the rights can be divided between an owner and a tenant. This means that many individuals may be able to claim various bundles of rights over one area of land.

Native Title is also a 'bundle of rights'. What's in that bundle of rights will depend on the Native Title holders' traditional laws and customs, and Australian laws recognising the rights and interests they hold. For example, in *Yanner v Eaton*, the court found that the Gungaletta people had a Native Title right to hunt crocodiles on their traditional lands and waters. That is a limited right. In the 1992 *Mabo* case, the High Court agreed that the Mer people have Native Title to permanently own most of their traditional land.

In 1788, Governor Phillip claimed possession of the entire continent for a penal colony on behalf of the British government. All lands were taken in the name of the Crown, thus the name 'Crown lands'. However, the Aboriginal and Torres Strait Islander people did not sign a treaty with the British. They never gave the land to the British government – and so Native Title continues. Indigenous traditional laws and customs that form the basis of ownership over their lands *co-exist* with the claim of sovereignty by the British Crown.

Since colonisation, much of Australia has come under private ownership, Crown lease or some other private property arrangement. In most cases, the Traditional Owners were forcibly removed from their land. Australian law holds that such acts, which break the Traditional Owners' ongoing connection with their land, 'extinguish' or remove Native Title.

Where the Traditional Owners' rights and interests in relation to their land under the traditional laws and customs are still observed, and they have a connection with their land by those traditional laws and customs, Native Title will be recognised by the common law of Australia.

The High Court of Australia established a form of recognition of Native Title that falls far short of the law in Canada, the USA and New Zealand. While its terms are unjust, *Mabo* was a historic turning point for Australia for two reasons. First, because it gives Aboriginal and Torres Strait Islander peoples the ability to ask for their land rights to be recognised and protected. Second, and most significantly, it recognised Indigenous laws and customs and brought them within the Australian legal system.

The terms of the Native Title Act regulate the circumstances in which Native Title can be recognised and the circumstances in which Native Title over Crown land survives. In many cases these terms have led to bitter disappointment for the Traditional Owners. Courts have dismissed claims when groups of people have been unable to prove their connection to land through an unbroken line of descent to a time before British colonisation. This is because of the lack of historical records. The *Yorta Yorta* case in northern Victoria was such a case.

On 12 December 2002, the High Court handed down its decision in the case of the *Members of the Yorta Yorta Aboriginal Community v State of Victoria and Others*. The Yorta Yorta people claimed their traditional rights in land and waters covering 2000 square kilometres along and around the Murray and Goulburn rivers. They sought to be recognised as the peoples belonging, by tradition, to that Country.

Justice Olney of the Federal Court found that before the end of the nineteenth century the Yorta Yorta people had ceased to occupy their traditional lands 'in accordance with their traditional laws and customs', and relied on a phrase in the *Mabo No. 2* judgement of the High Court: 'the tide of history'. Justice Olney wrote, 'the tide of history has indeed washed away any real acknowledgement of their traditional laws and any real observance of their traditional customs'. The Yorta Yorta plaintiffs appealed to a majority of the Full Court of the Federal Court, which upheld Justice Olney's findings. They then appealed to the High Court, which also confirmed Justice Olney's findings.

This case was widely debated because the courts' findings seemed unjust and discriminatory. Legal scholars turned to arguments about 'tradition', noting the findings of the Chief Justice of the Federal Court, Justice Michael Black, who was in

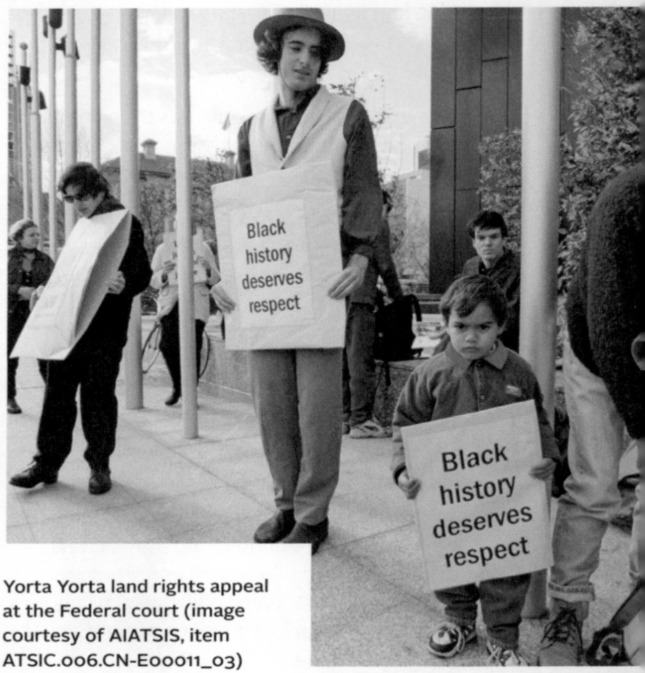

Yorta Yorta land rights appeal at the Federal court (image courtesy of AIATSIS, item ATSIC.006.CN-E00011_03)

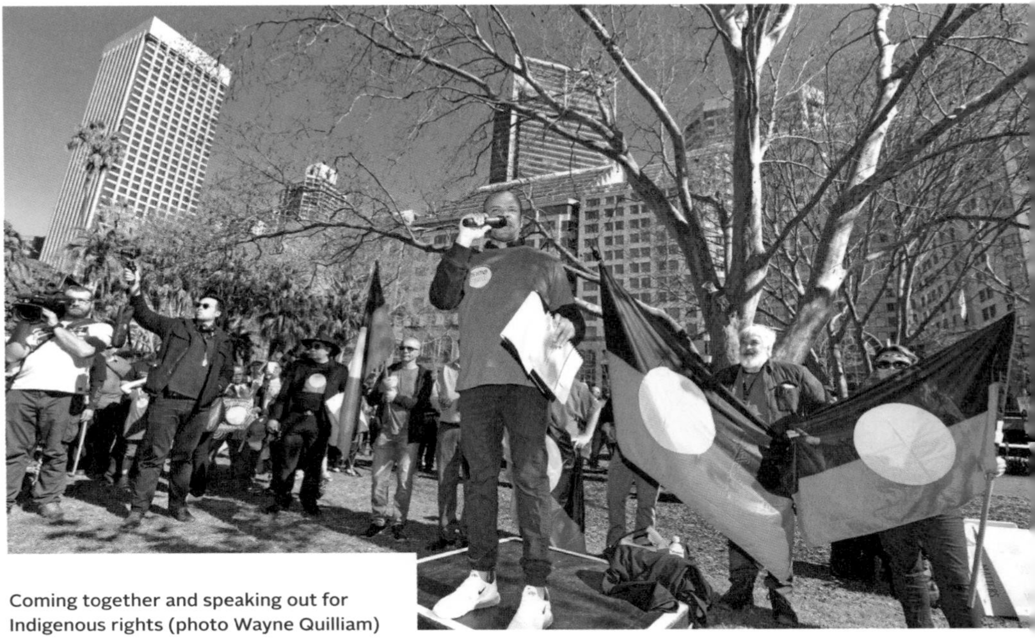

Coming together and speaking out for Indigenous rights (photo Wayne Quilliam)

the minority: 'far from being concerned with what is static, the very notion of "tradition" as involving the transmission from generation to generation of statements, beliefs, legends and customs orally or by practice implies recognition of the possibility of change'.

Indigenous people have a long and brutal colonial history of land being taken from them and people being forcibly moved onto reserves. The Yorta Yorta people, understandably, felt that yet another great injustice had been done to them in their Native Title case.

Native Title has had little impact on the lives of most Australians. After the High Court's findings in the *Mabo* case, opponents of Aboriginal land rights claimed that the outcome would cause enormous damage to the economy. However, this hasn't happened. It is a weak title compared with the usual freehold title that homeowners have, with its exclusive possession and far greater protection at law.

Aboriginal or Torres Strait Islander Traditional Owners usually make a Native Title application to the National Native Title Tribunal (the Tribunal). The Tribunal is an independent statutory body established under the Native Title Act. Its role is to administer and make decisions about matters arising under that Act. This includes matters relating to an Indigenous Land Use Agreement (ILUA) or other agreements made under the Act, or a Prescribed Body Corporate, which holds or manages Native Title.

When a Native Title Claim Group makes an application to the Tribunal, they make a declaration that they 'hold rights and interests in an area of land and/or water according to their traditional laws and customs'. The Claim Group must then mount a case and gather evidence to show that they have a continuing connection with their land by their traditional laws and customs. After making an application, the group can expect to wait decades before the court makes its decision.

If the group is successful, a court will recognise that their Native Title rights and interests exist. The court will do this at an occasion called a 'Native Title determination'. Successful Native Title determinations are usually held on the Claim Group's traditional lands. Many people attend and there are celebrations and ceremonies. Many claims have been successful, but most of those are in the remote areas of Australia.

The Act defines two kinds of acts that affect Native Title. The first are 'past acts', which were done *before* the Native Title Act commenced (on 1 January 1994) and

Representatives of the Aboriginal Land Council attend rallies with sights set on the future (photo Wayne Quilliam)

that were invalid because of Native Title. An example of a past act is where Native Title existed on land leased by a state or territory. The lease becomes invalid because it extinguished, or stopped, the Native Title rights. Under certain limited circumstances, these Native Title holders have a right to compensation.

The second class of acts that affect Native Title are 'future acts'. These are acts done after the Native Title Act's commencement that either affect Native Title or are invalid because of Native Title. For example, the Act provides that a valid lease, licence or permit prevails over any Native Title rights.

A future act is a proposal to deal with land in a way that will affect Native Title by extinguishing or suppressing it. Or it creates interests that are inconsistent with the continued existence, enjoyment or exercise of Native Title. Future acts may include the grant of a mining lease or the compulsory acquisition – for a development, for instance – of land over which Native Title rights exist. The Tribunal explains in 'About Native Title applications', July 2014, that:

Future act processes are based on the principle that in general, acts affecting Native Title will only be valid if they can also be done on freehold land. These processes give effect to the principle that in appropriate cases, these acts should only be done after every reasonable effort has been made to secure the agreement of the Native Title holders. They also provide certainty by ensuring that future dealings with land are enforceable, notwithstanding the existence of Native Title.

The Native Title Act gives Native Title holders rights in relation to certain future acts. This may include the right to negotiate. For some future acts, Native Title holders have no rights. Native Title holders or claimants don't often win under this system. There are many loopholes in the Act that developers can use to avoid having to negotiate with Traditional Owners. The Native Title Act does not allow Traditional Owners to stop any proposal. Where they have a right to negotiate, it is often undermined.

Where parties have negotiated but have not been able to reach an agreement, the Tribunal can host a mediation. Where this fails, the parties may apply to the Tribunal for a determination. The Tribunal will then decide whether the future act may be done; may be done subject to conditions; or must not be done.

The Traditional Owners' rights are often undermined where the government party thinks the future act can be progressed more quickly. This is known as the 'expedited procedure' – a fast-tracking process for future acts that would normally be subject to the right to negotiate, but are considered to have minimal impact on Native Title. If this procedure is used, and no objection is lodged, the future act can be done by a government without following the right to negotiate.

Sometimes, the Act works in favour of Traditional Owners. This happened in March 2018. It involved the Olkolo people, in Cape York Peninsula, who fought the Queensland Government and Gamboola Resources Pty Ltd. Gamboola is a goldmining company that sought an expedited exploration lease on land over which Native Title exists. Gamboola was trying to use this expedited procedure or fast-tracking process to bypass negotiations with the Traditional Owners.

The company claimed that the right to negotiate would not apply.

The Tribunal found against the company because of the evidence that the project would 'interfere with sites of particular significance to the Native Title party', including a sacred 'mound spring area' and a number of matchwood burial sites, and would cause a 'major disturbance' to the land and waters.

The interests of mining companies were at the forefront of the public debate after the Native Title Act was passed. The legislation acknowledged that mining companies and the resource extraction industry would seek access to, and the use of, Native Title land. Thus, the Act defines a range of future acts that, if done by a government, may be permitted to take place on Native Title land. These permissible future acts include:

- the creation or variation of a right to mine, including explorations, prospecting and quarrying
- the variation and extension of the period of a mining right
- the compulsory acquisition by government of Native Title rights or interests to a party other than government.

The Native Title Act provides a right to negotiate the terms and conditions upon which land use and access could occur. For Traditional Owners, the right to negotiate is a beneficial provision of the Act, although it has limitations. For example, Traditional Owners have no right to stop dealings on land held under Native Title.

The right to negotiate has given Traditional Owners the opportunity to sit at the negotiating table with the government and mining companies, and – for the first time in Australian history – negotiate the use of their land and access to it. Its impact is significant because it shows the practical consequences of the rejection of the doctrine of terra nullius. Whereas terra nullius had denied Indigenous people access to the land market, the right to negotiate provides an opportunity for economic participation.

However, the procedures under the Native Title Act make it extremely difficult for Traditional Owners to gain legal recognition of their Native Title. Also, where a state or territory opposes a Native Title application, the Claim Group must face a long and expensive legal process (litigation). The High Court's findings in *Yorta Yorta* and more recent decisions have meant that litigation is often not an effective way to achieve good outcomes for Indigenous people. Only a small minority of successful Native Title determinations have resulted from litigation.

As well as court decisions that have found against the claims of Aboriginal people, the Native Title Act provides the means for Native Title to be 'extinguished' or declared unable to be recognised by Australian law. This aspect of the Act presents Indigenous people with a terrible dilemma: should they appeal to the courts for recognition of their Native Title and risk having it extinguished, or stopped, forever?

In view of these challenges, many Traditional Owners have tried to have their Native Title rights recognised through 'consent determinations'. The Agreements, Treaties and Negotiated Settlements Project in 2015 provided a useful explanation of what a consent determination is:

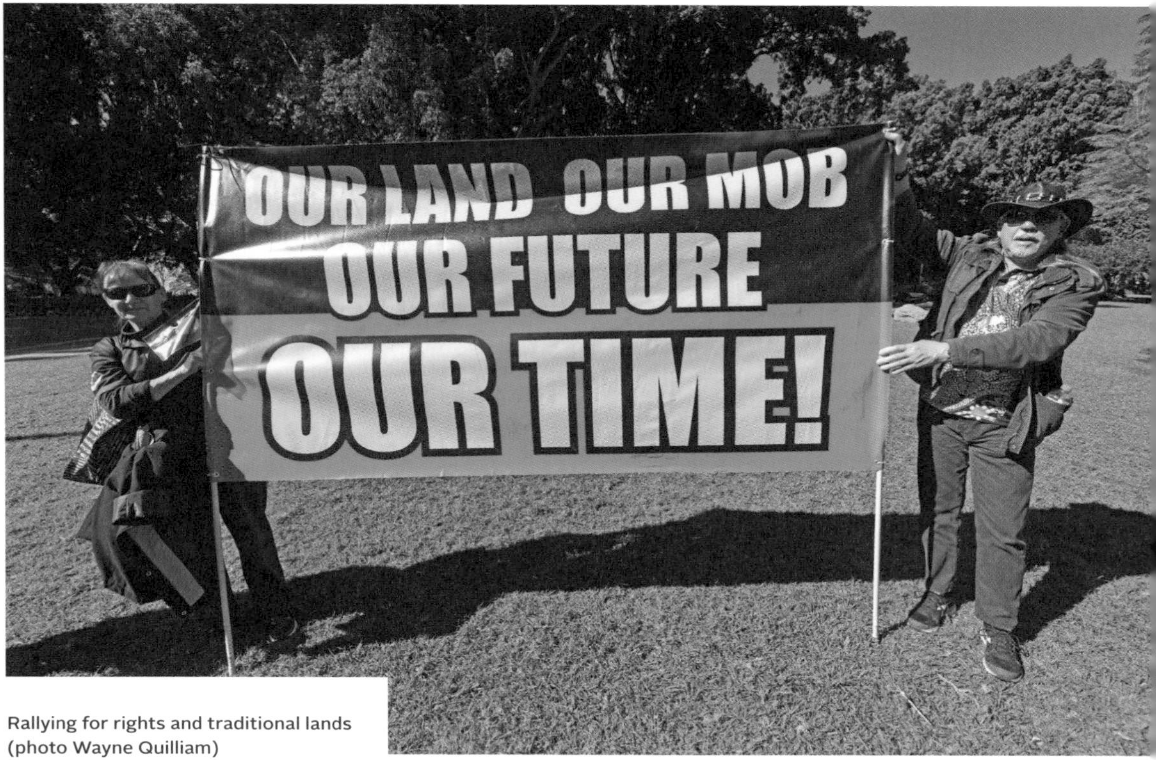

Rallying for rights and traditional lands (photo Wayne Quilliam)

Consent determinations are an alternative to litigated determinations. [They] aim to provide an efficient and resourceful means of settling Native Title issues. The process has been described as: encouraging relationship building between Indigenous communities and others; less intrusive on Aboriginal culture than litigated determination ... In making a determination of Native Title, the court (or recognised body) must:

- *decide whether or not Native Title exists in respect of the determination area;*
- *identify the group that holds Native Title;*
- *state the nature and extent of the Native Title rights and interests; and*
- *set out other rights and interests in the determination area and the relationship between those rights and Native Title*

The court or recognised body is allowed to make a determination without holding a hearing, where there is agreement (consent) between the parties, or where the orders sought by the applicants are unopposed.

Consent determinations are an opportunity for Native Title rights to be recognised through a negotiation process. The advantages of this process include saving time and resources, relationship building, and avoiding the stress and expense of lengthy hearings and cross-examination of witnesses. That is particularly important for Aboriginal people who are elderly and forced to reveal information about sacred sites and ceremonies to secure Native Title.

The National Native Title Tribunal provides maps of determinations and Indigenous estates.

Negotiation has been a more fruitful path for Native Title parties seeking a determination. However, with many hundreds of applications pending, the promise of a full recognition of Native Title through the determination process – either through a process of negotiation or through legal action – is still a long way off.

The content of these determinations varies enormously, with limited economic benefits for the Native Title holders coming from a determination alone. In the years immediately following the *Mabo* case, even consent determinations failed to produce the sorts of outcomes the Native Title applicants hoped for. The majority led to outcomes where Native Title was not recognised.

The amended Native Title Act now provides two main mechanisms for the negotiation of agreements for the use and access of land. They are section 31 and the 'right to negotiate' procedures. These provide that an agreement may be reached between the parties for any development on Native Title land. There is no provision for Native Title parties to stop a future act, only to negotiate its terms. In plain English, Native Title parties do not have a right of veto. Indigenous Land Use Agreements are legally binding on the parties and enforceable as a contract.

Traditional Owners are increasingly looking to other aspects of the Native Title system to secure more meaningful outcomes and to translate the recognition of their Native Title into economic and social benefits for their communities. Economic participation and wealth creation at far higher levels than in the 1990s are the two outstanding outcomes of the right to negotiate.

In 2019, the High Court of Australia ruled that the Ngaliwurru and Nungali peoples, the Claim Group, from the Northern Territory town of Timber Creek be paid for 'the compensation for loss or diminution of traditional attachment to the land or connection to Country and for loss of rights to gain spiritual sustenance from the land'.

This test case was almost as important as the *Mabo* case because it was the first High Court ruling on Native Title compensation. It recognised the cultural loss the Traditional Owners experienced.

The High Court ruled that the Northern Territory government would pay $2.5 million in compensation to the Native Title holders for an area of 126 hectares. The trial judge recorded that 'The Ngaliwurru and Nungali Peoples' connection to Country is unique, deep and broad'.

Until this case, the official view was that Native Title was worthless, and that compensation, if found to be payable at law, would be a pittance or nothing. That view is wrong, not just because of the monetary value of Native Title that is now clarified, but because of the cultural loss that is an integral part of this decision.

To date, governments have settled out of court, but the negotiations and payments have been completely confidential. Clearly, the High Court judgement took into consideration the number of Native Title holders in the Claim Group. It also took into account the acts causing cultural loss that could not be separated from the content of the traditional laws and customs they observed, specifically the 'loss of connection to country suffered by the Claim Group'.

The spiritual loss was captured in the High Court's citation of this passage:

... the connection which Aboriginal peoples have with 'country' is essentially spiritual. In Milirrpum v Nabalco Pty Ltd *[(1971) 17 FLR 141 at 167], Blackburn J said that: 'the fundamental truth about the aboriginals' relationship to the land is that whatever else it is, it is a religious relationship ... There is an unquestioned scheme of things in which the spirit ancestors, the people of the clan, particular land and everything that exists on and in it, are organic parts of one indissoluble whole'. It is a relationship which sometimes is spoken of as having to care for, and being able to 'speak for', country. 'Speaking for' country is bound up with the idea that, at least in some circumstances, others should ask for permission to enter upon country or use it or enjoy its resources, but to focus only on the requirement that others seek permission for some activities would oversimplify the nature of the connection that the phrase seeks to capture. The difficulty of expressing a relationship between a community or group of Aboriginal people and the land in terms of rights and interests is evident. Yet that is required by the [Native Title Act]. The spiritual or religious is translated into the legal.*[71]

This case has implications for governments that have extinguished or impaired Native Title since the Racial Discrimination Act came in on 31 October 1975. There will be litigation to determine whether or not – and if so, how much – compensation is payable to the Native Title groups affected. At the time of the High Court decision, there were 377 Native Title determinations to land over a total area of 2,836,842 square kilometres. They would all be implicated if the states or territories had extinguished or impaired their Native Title.

In the future, governments will be careful to conduct negotiations over 'future uses' or proposals to impose projects or developments on land with determinations of Native Title, and they will be careful to do so within the confines of the law. Each claim in the future will need to be dealt with on a case-by-case basis. This may lead the Commonwealth to amend the Act so that governments don't have to pay compensation.

Unless the Commonwealth Government amends the Native Title Act, the judgement gives force to the present terms of the Act: compensation is payable for acts that impair or extinguish the Traditional Owners' Native Title rights. The compensation must be paid in money on 'just terms' and, subject to the 'just terms', be a maximum of the freehold value of the land.

10
THE STOLEN GENERATIONS

The term 'Stolen Generations' refers to the Aboriginal children who were forcibly removed from their families by the state, territory and federal governments of Australia from 1788 onwards. The children were placed in controlled institutions, or from a young age were made to work without pay in the homes of white people, or adopted or fostered into white families. Most were never able to find their birth families again. This had terrible consequences for the mental and physical health of the children and their parents throughout their lives, and for Indigenous people down through the generations. It also resulted in cultural loss on a nationwide scale for the affected families.

The intention of the policies and laws that led to children being taken from their parents was to 'assimilate' part-Aboriginal people into the general Australian population, leaving the 'full bloods', as these people were called, separated and incarcerated on Aboriginal reserves. Governments regarded 'miscegenation', as mixed racial descent was known, to be a danger to the 'racial hygiene' and health of white Australian society.

For much of the twentieth century, most Australians had no qualms about this cruel practice or were unaware of it. In the 1980s, victims began to challenge the status quo by telling their stories and looking for their birth families. Their efforts led to the revelation that perhaps tens of thousands of children had been removed from their families. Growing evidence from the survivors, who numbered about 13,000, told of the sometimes extreme physical and sexual abuse they suffered at the hands of adoptive and foster families and employers (to whom some were indentured or enslaved). Aboriginal organisations called for a national inquiry.

Eventually, in 1995, the federal attorney-general established the National Inquiry into the Separation of Aboriginal and Torres Strait Island Children from their Families. Two special commissioners were appointed, Sir Ronald Wilson QC, President of the Human Rights and Equal Opportunity Commission, and Professor Mick Dodson, the Aboriginal and Torres Strait Islander Social Justice Commissioner.

After taking evidence from across the entire country, the commissioners presented *Bringing them home: The 'Stolen Children' report* to the Australian Parliament in 1997. Professor Dodson and Sir Ronald Wilson found that the race-based child-removal policies were a special instance of genocide under the definition in the United Nations Convention on the Prevention and Punishment of the Crime of Genocide.

The commissioners wrote:

When a child was forcibly removed that child's entire community lost, often permanently, its chance to perpetuate itself in that child. The Inquiry has concluded that this was a primary objective of forcible removals and is the reason they amount to genocide. [Children are] core elements of the present and future of the community. The removal of these children creates a sense of death and loss in the community, and the community dies too .. there's a sense of hopelessness that becomes part of the experience for that family, that community ... (Lynne Datnow, Victorian Koori Kids Mental Health Network, evidence 135).

There have been similar conclusions in the comparable context of forcible removal to educational institutions of Native American children.

Because the family is the most fundamental economic, education, health-care unit in society and the centre of an

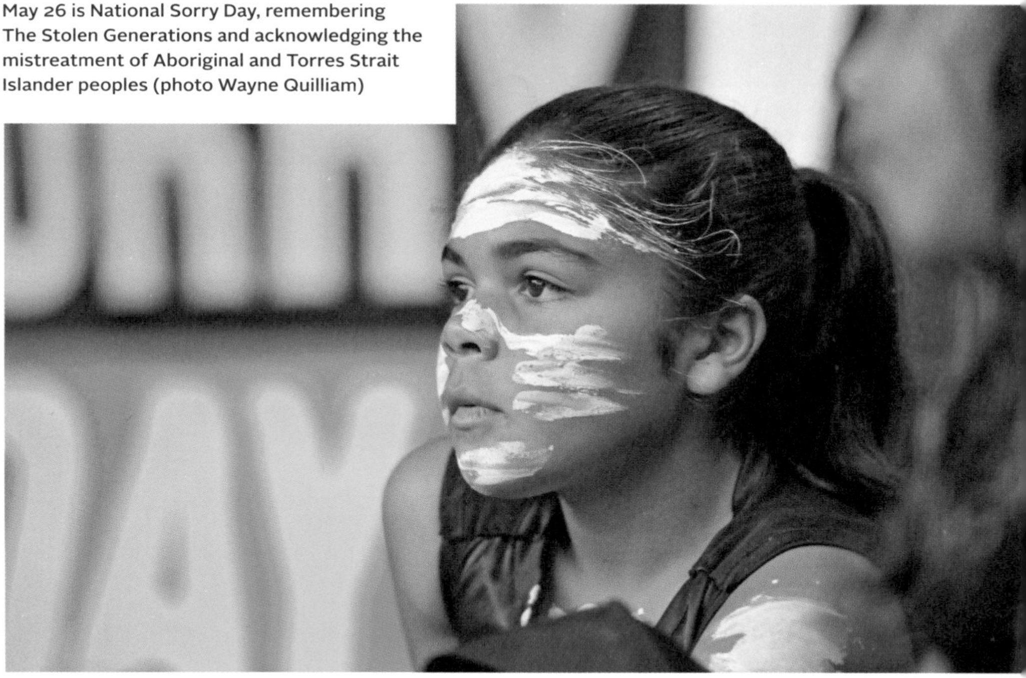

May 26 is National Sorry Day, remembering The Stolen Generations and acknowledging the mistreatment of Aboriginal and Torres Strait Islander peoples (photo Wayne Quilliam)

Moments before Prime Minister Kevin Rudd delivered the Apology (photo Wayne Quilliam)

individual's emotional life, assaults on Indian families help cause the conditions that characterise those cultures of poverty where large numbers of people feel hopeless, powerless and unworthy (Byler 1977 page 8).

A Congressional Inquiry in 1978 found that the removal of Indian children had a severe effect on Indian tribes, threatening their existence as identifiable cultural entities (US Congress 1978).[72]

This was clearly the case in Western Australia, for example, where the instructions and justification were aimed at eliminating the entire 'race'. This incited a national debate among many Australians and in May 1998 the first National Sorry Day was held, one year after the tabling of the report. On Sorry Day, 28 May 2000, around 300,000 people walked across the Sydney Harbour Bridge in the Walk for Reconciliation, and all around the country Australians were demanding a national apology to the Stolen Generations.

From 1996 until it lost the election in 2007, the federal government, led by then prime minister John Howard, refused to acknowledge the facts, and proposed an alternative explanation arguing that the stolen children were 'rescued'. On these – as has been repeatedly proven – grossly false grounds, John Howard refused to apologise. It was also claimed that an apology would establish the grounds for financial compensation; and of course, this would be the case for any other Australian, and is one part of the remedy for genocide set out in international law. In the Northern Territory and South Australia survivors went to court to seek justice. The *Cubillo* and *Gunner* cases were unsuccessful, but a case in 2007 brought by Bruce Trevorrow in South Australia resulted in him being awarded $500,000 compensation. Mr Trevorrow died before the compensation was paid. In a further twist of the knife, the South Australian government ruled that his heirs were not entitled to the compensation payment.

At that time the nationwide campaign for an apology was growing. Tens of thousands of people signed 'Sorry' books to register their own apology and to demand an apology from the Australian government.

On 13 February 2008, then prime minister Kevin Rudd gave an apology in federal Parliament to the Stolen Generations. Here is the parliamentary transcript of his speech:

The Speaker: Prime Minister.

Prime Minister (Hon Kevin Rudd MP): Mr Speaker, I move:

That today we honour the Indigenous peoples of this land, the oldest continuing cultures in human history.

We reflect on their past mistreatment.

We reflect in particular on the mistreatment of those who were Stolen Generations – this blemished chapter in our nation's history.

The time has now come for the nation to turn a new page in Australia's history by righting the wrongs of the past and so moving forward with confidence to the future.

We apologise for the laws and policies of successive Parliaments and governments that have inflicted profound grief, suffering and loss on these our fellow Australians.

We apologise especially for the removal of Aboriginal and Torres Strait Islander children from their families, their communities and their country.

For the pain, suffering and hurt of these Stolen Generations, their descendants and for their families left behind, we say sorry.

To the mothers and the fathers, the brothers and the sisters, for the breaking up of families and communities, we say sorry.

And for the indignity and degradation thus inflicted on a proud people and a proud culture, we say sorry.

We the Parliament of Australia respectfully request that this apology be received in the spirit in which it is offered as part of the healing of the nation.

For the future we take heart; resolving that this new page in the history of our great continent can now be written.

We today take this first step by acknowledging the past and laying claim to a future that embraces all Australians.

A future where this Parliament resolves that the injustices of the past must never, never happen again.

A future where we harness the determination of all Australians, Indigenous and non-Indigenous, to close the gap that lies between us in life expectancy, educational achievement and economic opportunity.

A future where we embrace the possibility of new solutions to enduring problems where old approaches have failed.

A future based on mutual respect, mutual resolve and mutual responsibility.

A future where all Australians, whatever their origins, are truly equal partners, with equal opportunities and with an equal stake in shaping the next chapter in the history of this great country, Australia.[73]

The cruel legacy of the policies of removing Aboriginal children from their families has been felt for generations. Even now, there would not be an Aboriginal person alive who has not been tragically touched in some way, directly or indirectly, by the impact of these policies.

Apologising to the victims of the historical policies of Aboriginal child removal achieved at least two important goals. First, it helped to restore the sense of dignity and legitimacy that the victims ought to feel but were denied. Secondly, it was a national acknowledgement of the wrong and harm done by previous governments to generations of people on the grounds of race-hate, an acknowledgement that should state explicitly that this should never occur again. The victims' inheritance has been denied by their removal. The denial of that inheritance is the key to their suffering and the correct grounds for compensating them: they were denied their family lines and their links to a family past and legacy, their material inheritance, their culture and history, and most importantly, a sense of self shaped by the people who brought them into the world.

The primary significance of an apology must be for the victims of the policies of removing Aboriginal children from their families. But almost as significant is the effect of a formal apology on the citizens on whose behalf the apology was made.

In 2010, the Healing Foundation was established in Canberra to provide trauma support for the victims, assistance with commemorative events and to undertake research. Also, several monuments have been erected around the country to remind us of this tragedy, and families visit them on National Sorry Day every year. As there are so many, it is not possible to mention them all here, nor all the commemorative plaques. For example, the six plaques placed in culturally significant sites around Brisbane – King George Square, Teralba Park in Everton Park, Kalinga Park in Nundah, Orleigh Park in West End, Sherwood Arboretum and the

Wynnum foreshore. Instead I will focus on three of the monuments.

Stolen Generations Memorial

Reilly Lane, Sydenham Green, Sydney, New South Wales

The Stolen Generations Memorial at Reilly Lane, Sydenham Green, is a sandstone sculpture by Aboriginal artist Joe Hirst. Its inscription is taken from Link-Up, the organisation established by victims to find their families.

We may go home, but we cannot relive our childhoods. We may reunite with our mothers, fathers, sisters, brothers, aunties, uncles, communities, but we cannot re-live the 20, 30, 40 years that we spent without their love and care, and they cannot undo the grief and mourning they felt when we separated from them. We can go home to ourselves as Aboriginals, but this does not erase the attacks inflicted on our hearts, minds, and bodies by caretakers who thought their mission was to eliminate us as Aboriginals.

Link-Up (New South Wales)[74]

Stolen Generations Memorial

Phillip Creek Native Settlement, Manga Marda Waterhole, Tennant Creek, Northern Territory

In 1946, sixteen 'part Aboriginal' children were moved from the Phillip Creek Native Settlement at the Manga Manda waterhole to the notorious Retta Dixon Home in Darwin. This kidnapping was authorised by the Native Affairs Department of the Northern Territory government. In 2004, eleven survivors of the group taken from the Phillip Creek mission returned to the place where they were abducted to dedicate a memorial at the long-abandoned settlement. They used the dedication ceremony as a time to distance themselves from their shocking experiences at the Retta Dixon Home and rebuild their ties with their own families. The Phillip Creek mission was opened in 1945 as an interim ration depot for Aboriginal people. They had been displaced from their land after gold was discovered in the Tennant Creek region in the 1930s. By 1956, the mission was abandoned and a permanent site was established at Warrabri.[75]

Stolen Generations Memorial Garden

Beinda Street, Bomaderry, New South Wales

This garden, created on the site of the Bomaderry United Aboriginal Mission (UAM), was dedicated on 21 October 2001. The mission was established in 1908, a year before the enactment of the *Aboriginal Protection Act of 1909*, and became the destination for many of the children in New South Wales who were taken from their families.

The inscription on the plaque at the garden reads:

This plaque and memorial garden is dedicated to 'all' the Aboriginal children of the 'Stolen Generation' who were residents here at Bomaderry, the former 'United Aborigines Mission' (U.A.M.).

Also to honour and respect the children who are now deceased

This site is the birthplace of the 'Stolen Generation' here in New South Wales[76]

Remember the Dead

Advisory note: This section may cause some readers distress.

During the colonial and postcolonial times of massacres,[77] 'dispersion' and forced removals of Aboriginal populations, men and women obtained Aboriginal body parts, skeletal remains (skulls were particularly popular) to serve the eugenicist practice of scientific experimentation on our people, then cast as an 'inferior race' and 'scientific curios.' These ancestral remains were also traded among institutions and private collectors and exhibited to the public. In Australia, ancestral remains were acquired by museums until the 1980s, and there are still thousands of remains in museums worldwide as the international trade in body parts, ethnographic photographs and cultural objects continues.[78]

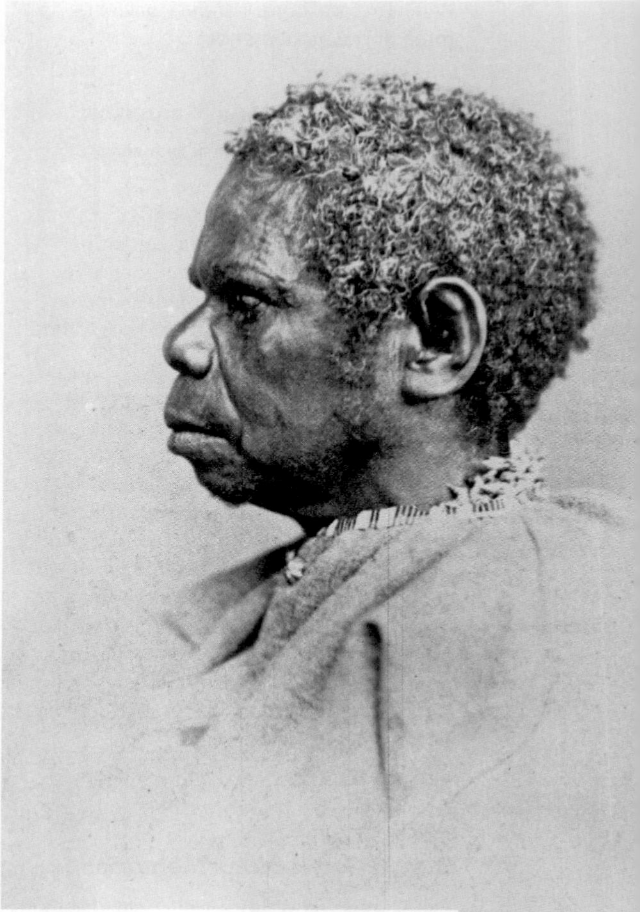

Side profile sketch of Truganini (image courtesy of AIATSIS, item RCS.001.BW-N00701_07)

Truganini, a Nuenonne woman, the most famous of the palawa people of the island now known as Tasmania, witnessed the genocide of her people. She was one of the few survivors. Aware of the terrible practices of the colonists who used Aboriginal bodies for scientific experiments – even stealing them from graves and murdering people for this purpose – she begged that her body not be used in this way. She wanted her ashes scattered in the D'Entrecasteaux Channel. When she died, in 1876, her remains were exhumed and displayed in the Hobart Museum. After many years of demanding that her remains be returned for a proper interment, the museum agreed in 1976, one hundred years after she had passed. A closed service was held at the Cornelian Bay Crematorium on 30 April, attended by then premier of Tasmania, Mr Doug Lowe,

Dr Allen Wallace, Roy Nichols, the state secretary of the Aboriginal Information Service, and other members of the palawa community. On the fortieth anniversary of this event, Dr Stan Florek gathered together the memories of that day.[79] The late Aunty Ida West recounted that it was 'a lovely sunny morning':

The coffin was carried by Mr Roy Nichols and Mr Lowe to the furnace – placed in and Mr Nichols and Mr Lowe waited until cremation had taken place. Under police guard the ashes were taken for safe keeping till the morning of the 1st of May 1976.

The ashes were contained in a Huon Pine casket which was placed in the Egeria's *cabin and carried to a point south-east of the pilot station in the D'Entrecasteaux Channel. Mr Lowe formally handed the ashes to Mr Nichols and the following words were said, 'Truganini, may you now rest in peace'. On the* Egeria *were Mr Lowe, Roy Nichols, Members of the Aboriginal community and a police guard. A flotilla of craft accompanied us down the river ... It was a solemn affair – giving the important person a decent and dignified burial.*

Truganini's ashes were scattered on a lovely sunny morning ... a porpoise was swimming around us when the ashes went down. Truganini had asked for this to be done, but it took a hundred years to come about. My daughter Lennah and another lady were with the casket of Truganini before the cremation. Rosalind Langford made a speech at the cremation and it was very good.

On the 9th of May people from the Aboriginal community and myself all went up to open a park which was dedicated to Truganini. Mr Stephen Walker, a sculptor, made the commemorative plaque for the area which he set into a large stone and it looks lovely. Guest speakers were Mr Doug Lowe, Roy Nichols and Mr Bingham. We had some little children sitting on top of some rocks watching what was going on. My grand-nieces and nephews were sitting there too with a few white children. They had their arms around each other. We were all standing around while they gave their speeches, a big black dog was standing with us too.

This event was one of the first repatriations of Aboriginal ancestral remains, inspiring Aboriginal people across the country to find their ancestors who had suffered the fate of Truganini and have them returned for a dignified burial or interment according to their traditions. Over many decades, Indigenous people have demanded that museums and other collecting institutions return ancestral remains and sacred objects, but around the world and here in Australia most of these institutions remained intransigent, insisting on their ownership and their 'right' to keep them for 'scientific purposes.'[80]

In the twenty-first century, when almost the entire human genome has been mapped, revealing that there is no sound scientific basis for the idea of 'race' and 'racial science', it is difficult to understand why institutions and collectors keep Aboriginal ancestral remains. A group of researchers at the Australian National University have attempted to explain the practice of keeping Aboriginal bodies and body parts. The *Return, Reconcile, Renew* project is a timely response to these practices, with the aim of assisting Aboriginal and Torres Strait Islander people to repatriate their Old People. The project's website informs us that

Ancestral Remains were taken from wherever the deceased can be found. The majority of remains were taken from funerary sites. Indigenous burial grounds were dug up, and remains were taken from caves, burial platforms and other areas of funerary ritual. Indigenous remains were also disinterred from European churchyards and cemeteries. Those seeking to obtain remains also targeted areas where Ancestral Remains had been revealed through erosion, whether through the actions of burrowing rabbits, wind or water. Ancestral Remains were also revealed through construction work when houses and new roads were built.

Some Ancestral Remains were taken from massacre sites or places where people were known to have died a violent death. In some instances, bodies were taken from hospital morgues and university anatomy departments, after executions or from people who had died in jail. Sometimes, as in the cases of Yagan, Kanabygal, Jandamarra, and Pemulwoy, eminent leaders were killed for their part in resistance to colonial expansion and their heads subsequently removed and sent to overseas institutions.[81]

As well, police departments handed over to universities and museums bodies disinterred in excavations and obtained by other means.

Even though those who came from the disciplines of 'comparative anatomy', 'craniology', eugenics and physical anthropology insisted that they took Aboriginal bodies from graves for 'scientific purposes', when Indigenous people have found ancestral remains in institutions, there are no records of who they were, where they came from, and how they got there. So much for their 'science'. Reputable scientists document their work according to the standards of science proper. Because of this gross negligence, there are thousands of unprovenanced ancestral Aboriginal remains that have been returned by overseas institutions to Canberra. Without any records, no one can know who they were nor where to return them. A national Keeping Place is envisaged for these Old People to dignify and memorialise them, although anonymous, and to acknowledge this history of stealing them from their graves and trading them among institutions for the 'racial' entertainment of the audiences of museums and to teach 'racial science' in universities. The University of Melbourne collected thousands of ancestral remains and is a major centre of the study of the now discredited field of eugenics.

In Victoria, the long saga of litigation and campaigning by Aboriginal people to have their Old People returned resulted in a major breakthrough when Gunditjmara Elder Uncle Jim Berg won a significant victory in the courts in 1984. His court injunction against the University of Melbourne and the Museum of Victoria was successful in preventing a collection of Australian Indigenous remains from Kow Swamp and Keilor being sent to America for an exhibition entitled 'Ancestors'. Changes in museum practices followed.

In 2016, the Victorian Aboriginal Heritage Council became the guardian for all unprovenanced Aboriginal ancestral remains and sacred objects in Victoria, but in the 1980s, Jim Berg's injunction, followed by moral persuasion and negotiation, turned the page on this horrible history, as explained by the council's website:

On 22 November 1985, 38 Ancestors were reburied in Kings Domain, Melbourne. The site was chosen in the absence of being able to determine their origins. This monumental event paved the way for collaborative repatriation efforts between Traditional Owners, state government agencies and academic institutions in Victoria. Since then, thousands of Ancestral Remains have been repatriated to their intended resting places. However, the repatriation process is often slow, frustrating and difficult for Aboriginal communities for a variety of reasons.[82]

The eventual repatriation of the Kow Swamp ancestral remains ignited a worldwide debate about the merit of scientific experimentation versus the desires of the communities of origin to have their Old People's remains treated with dignity. This debate continues because collecting the ancestral remains of Indigenous people and non-Western cultures is a global practice and there are many testimonies about how deeply distressing the practice is to descendants. In some cases, the display of the remains of deceased people is permitted in highly restricted circumstances, such as in Cambodia at Choeung Ek (known globally as the Killing Fields).[83]

However, the work of Uncle Jim Berg led to an important change in Victorian legislation: the amendment in 2016 to the *Victorian Aboriginal Cultural Heritage Act* which places all Aboriginal ancestral remains and sacred objects in the ownership of the Victorian Aboriginal Heritage Council, which has the responsibility to repatriate them to their communities of origin.[84] Uncle Jim Berg took a stand against these practices and he tells his story with Aboriginal curator, Shannon Faulkhead, in *Power and the Passion: Our Ancestors Return Home* (2010).

Then in 1984, when Uncle Jim Berg became aware of the George Murray Black Collection in the Anatomy Department of the University of Melbourne, he worked with Ron Merkel of the Victorian Aboriginal Legal Service to prepare

... a number of injunctions which were served against the University for breaches of the Archaeological & Aboriginal Relics Preservation Act *(1972) for being in possession of Aboriginal skeletal remains. Discussions and court proceedings followed, with Berg winning the case and the Murray Black Collection was transferred to the museum.*[85]

The events that followed – particularly audits of the university's collections – resulted in the return of hundreds of ancestral remains for proper burial as instructed by Elders and communities of origin.

The Australian government has worked with Aboriginal and Torres Strait Islander people and institutions such as the Australian Institute of Aboriginal and Torres Strait Islander Studies (AIATSIS) to assist in repatriating ancestral remains from overseas museums, universities and collecting institutions, in compliance with international laws. Some Australian domestic laws, although not entirely adequate, have been useful in bringing them home. As I have pointed out with my colleagues, Brook Andrew and Jessica Neath, in our contribution to the *Handbook on Genocide*:

Despite the widespread acknowledgement of the inhumanity of the practice, still today, some museums like the Natural History Museum, London, and Cambridge University's Duckworth collection refuse

to allow the repatriation of Aboriginal and Torres Strait Islander human remains in their collections.[86]

A National Resting Place for unprovenanced Aboriginal and Torres Strait Islander ancestral remains in Canberra was proposed in a 2014 report by the Advisory Committee on Indigenous Repatriation to the federal government and was the subject of a scoping study by the Australian Institute for Aboriginal and Torres Strait Islander Studies, following Recommendation 4 of the Joint Select Committee on Constitutional Recognition relating to Aboriginal and Torres Strait Islander Peoples:

The Committee also recommends that the Australian Government consider the establishment, in Canberra, of a National Resting Place, for Aboriginal and Torres Strait Islander remains which could be a place of commemoration, healing and reflection.[87]

I have worked with Wiradjuri/Celtic artist Brook Andrew on addressing the need for memorialisation of massacres and other events in which Aboriginal and Torres Strait Islander people lost their lives in the colonial project, acknowledging that many took place in the twentieth century. Andrew established a visual arts research project with funding from the Australian Research Council, *Representation, Remembrance and the Memorial (RRM)*, to address this outstanding moral challenge for all Australians: how to represent the magnitude of Indigenous loss and survival in a national memorial. Andrew has involved a group of local and international peoples (see 'FORUM 2018') to focus on case studies including investigating international examples of monuments to genocide and community approaches to remembering frontier violence.[88] The challenge remains and Aboriginal and Torres Strait Islander people wait for a decision from the Australian government on a formal memorialisation of the Old People who suffered the indignity of being collected as 'scientific curios.' While debates continue as to whether what happened to Aboriginal people after 1788 can be classified as genocide,[89] it is nevertheless important to formally acknowledge the genocidal practices and politics that deem the remains of our ancestors as unworthy of ceremonial funeral services and return to their communities of origin.

11

WHAT IF YOUR GUIDE IS NOT INDIGENOUS?

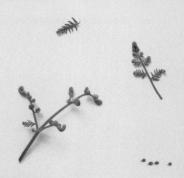

Aboriginal and Torres Strait Islander guides are employed at many places, especially in national parks that have joint management schemes with the Traditional Owners, such as Kakadu National Park and the Uluṟu–Kata Tjuṯa National Park, and at experiences offered by Indigenous-owned companies. However, it is unlikely that you will have an Indigenous guide at most popular tourist attractions. Instead, your guide will usually be a young white Australian. Also, it is sometimes the case that the guides will not mention Aboriginal history and culture at all, or, if they do, they sometimes repeat degrading stereotypes.

In 1997, two Hawaiʻian women visited Australia. One was Mahealani Kahau, an important Hawaiʻian cultural leader, who came to attend the Australian Reconciliation Convention in Melbourne, and the other was her sister. Mahealani told me that her sister had taken a bus to northern Australia because she wanted to meet Aboriginal people in communities there. She was deeply shocked by what she saw, Mahealani said, but even more so when the bus driver, who acted as a guide, repeatedly made extremely racist statements throughout the trip. When she objected, the driver threw her off the bus and she had to find other means to return to Melbourne.

When I worked in Central Australia in the 1980s, visitors told me that tour guides would tell 'jokes' about the 'inferior' status of Aboriginal people. Here's one: 'How do you make a gin squash? You run her over with your road train.' For those initiated into Australian everyday racism, 'gin' is a racist term for an Aboriginal woman. A road train is a truck towing one or more trailers and is used in rural and remote areas of Australia to transport goods. Other jokes are too crude to retell here.

These stories are not common now. The Australian reconciliation movement has brought about changes in attitudes and many racist ideas and habits are being recognised as such and are no longer tolerated. Whereas in the past, Aboriginal people were despised and discriminated against, and excluded from Australian society, reconciliation has enabled many Australians to accept Aboriginal people as a part of Australian life without the fear and anger that typified earlier attitudes – at least for many Australians. Indigenous events, art exhibitions, films and television programs, as well as the National Indigenous Television service, and tourism experiences

The passing of knowledge is integral to the continuance of culture (photo Wayne Quilliam)

have led to greater understanding and awareness of Aboriginal and Torres Strait Islander cultures.

In some parts of Australia, however, rather than the experience of Mahealani's sister, you may find that there is absolutely no information about Aboriginal and Torres Strait Islander cultures and history available for tourists. In 2017, I received an email from an Australian woman who visited Tasmania. This island state across the Bass Strait is infamous for the vicious campaign by British troops from 1824 to 1831, called the Black Wars in some history books, aimed at eradicating Tasmania's entire Indigenous population.[90] They almost succeeded, but you will hear nothing of this genocide from a guide in Tasmania. Historians still debate whether the Black Wars should be defined as an act of genocide. Governor Arthur formed 'roving parties' of civilians to capture Tasmanian Aborigines, offering them a reward of five pounds for each adult and two pounds for each child. The resistance was awe-inspiring. In April 1828, Governor Arthur was forced to defend his colony against the silent guerrillas who attacked the settlers ruthlessly and without warning. He declared martial law and made it illegal for Aboriginal people to go into any British settlement. Seventy years after the arrival of the British, the bloody wars came to an end in 1873. By that time, the sealers and whalers from the northern hemisphere, many from Cornwall, had already wreaked murderous havoc, especially on the smaller islands.[91]

My correspondent wrote this to me:

I am currently holidaying in Tasmania for the first time (I live in mainland Australia), and am visiting many iconic historical and wilderness areas, on occasions on guided tours. What has appalled me is the (almost all) negation in tourist booklets and from tour guides, of information regarding Aboriginal Australians during first contact and beyond.

Although I have questioned tour guides about specific areas relating to the first peoples and their experiences, I have been stonewalled and in one instance told...you do not want to know. Actually, I did want to know and responded accordingly. In another instance on the former penal colony of Sara Island, I was informed that the experiences of Aboriginal peoples during that time could not be spoken about, however there were places on this island that were restricted due to significant cultural Aboriginal heritage (good, re the latter).

Whilst I have furthered my knowledge about the experiences of convicts and their colonial masters, I remain frustrated at the omissions, bordering on negation of the real history of contact, by the rhetoric of the tourist industry.

What has been alluded to in rhetoric, is that contact history stories, are not to be told by non-Aboriginal people. Is this the case? If so, why doesn't the government allocate funding to have Aboriginal Australian guides contest and enrich the rhetoric, with Aboriginal truths?

I feel very uncomfortable in Tasmania because of the complete suppression of this history by the settlers. My limited access to the responses of the palawa – or Tasmanian Aboriginal people – is via palawa artists and academics. Photographer Ricky Maynard, artists and academics Julie Gough and Greg Lehman, and medical leader Ian Anderson have educated me about lives lived in the shadow of their terrible history with dignity and intellectual rigour.

This is too often the challenge of travelling through Indigenous Australia: deciphering the deceit and outright lies about the Aboriginal presence and absence, and seeking out Indigenous people for the story. Occasionally, I have met locals from the settler population who will talk about the history of their area, but the norm is the triumphalist colonial history about 'brave white pioneers'. The fate of Aboriginal people is rarely mentioned, and if it is, the accounts are often brief and inaccurate.

It is best to read the histories on these matters. There is a growing body of rigorous and honest history about the fate of the palawa people and too little space to recommend them all. The best I have read include the list I recommend below. The historians who doggedly told the story of Aboriginal people have been persecuted and hounded for doing so. Henry Reynolds, Lyndall Ryan and a growing body of scholars persist, however. If you are not a reader, there are DVDs, and I highly recommend *First Australians*, an eight-episode series on the history of Aboriginal people since British occupation.

- Henry Reynolds, *Fate of a Free People*, Penguin Books Australia, 1995

- Lyndall Ryan, *Tasmanian Aborigines. A History since 1803*, Allen & Unwin, 2012
- Cassandra Pybus, *Truganini: Journey through the Apocalypse*, Allen & Unwin, 2020
- Cassandra Pybus, *Community of Thieves*, Minerva Australia, 1992
- Ronnie Summers and Helen Gee, *Ronnie: Tasmanian Songman*, Magabala Books, 2009

Our history: what you should know when visiting Australia

I have explained that Aboriginal people were the first humans to colonise the southernmost parts of the planet. Aboriginal people came from what is now Asia and moved across the whole continent before the last Ice Age.

The story that science tells is not so different from the traditional Aboriginal beliefs about our origins. Do the Wandjina tell of ancestral arrivals from the north-west on the monsoonal winds, among the lightning and giant cumulus clouds of the wet season? Rasmus Nielsen and his colleagues, writing in *Nature*, presented their findings in 2017 on likely human migration patterns in the last 60,000 years, confirming the 'out-of-Africa' thesis – modern humans evolved in Africa and expanded out across the world via a series of routes.[92] Using genomic, archaeological and palaeontological methods enabled the direct determination of the genealogical relationships between humans as well as the elucidation of migration routes, diversification events and genetic admixture among various groups. DNA sequencing and methods for the enrichment and extraction of ancient DNA from the remains of ancient humans and our ancient hominid cousins has advanced rapidly and by 'including samples from a wide range of historical times and locations' new understandings of insights into human history have emerged. While there remain unanswered questions, a global picture of paths of migration has been determined from the evidence. Further population movements after the initial migrations may muddy some of the pathways, and several routes are 'controversial'.[93] It seems that our ancestors – who we now know arrived on the continent more than 65,000 years ago – came across the Eurasian continent from what is now the region of Iraq and Iran, and many thousands of years before that from southern Africa, according to this body of evidence.

When the British arrived in force in 1788 with eleven ships under the command of Captain Arthur Phillip and established the first British settlement at Port Jackson on the shores of Eora Country in what is now Sydney, the world of Indigenous peoples across the continent and islands was fated. At the time the penal colony was set up at Port Jackson, the British were losing the War of Independence in North America. The Native Americans were offered treaties, many of which remain legally binding today. After the American Revolution and the Declaration of Independence, the British were no longer permitted to send convicts to America, and sent eleven ships to Port Jackson to establish a penal colony on Gadigal land.

Captain Phillip declaring British possession of New South Wales

The Colony of New South Wales was the first colony, and Arthur Phillip became its first governor, in charge from 1788 to 1792. Governor Phillip and the governors who followed him all failed to control the violence of the frontier. Eventually, six colonies were established, each with its own history of attempts to exterminate Aboriginal people. Unknown numbers of Aboriginal people died in the wake of the frontier, the population falling from an estimated one million at first settlement to less than 50,000 in the early twentieth century.

These colonial beginnings of the nation are a hotly debated issue in Australia, especially on each Australia Day on 26 January. Indigenous people hold their own events, such as the Yabun Festival in Sydney, and in 2017 some local councils voted to celebrate the nation on a different day.

The history of twentieth century Australia was also brutal. So brutal that in many parts of the country, as I have explained, the historical facts have been suppressed and contested, and many still deny the terrible treatment that Indigenous people experienced.

Staff and residents of the Little Flower Black Mission School, Alice Springs, Northern Territory

As the settlers spread out across the lands of Aboriginal peoples, they seized control, assisted by the British troops. Missionaries followed, and Aboriginal people were eventually rounded up and placed in missions and government administered settlements. When people today refer to an Aboriginal community, they are often unaware of the history of these places.

In 1901, Australia became a nation when the six English colonies of Queensland, New South Wales, Victoria, Tasmania, South Australia and Western Australia formed the Commonwealth of Australia under a new constitution. Aboriginal and Torres Strait Islander people were not citizens after the constitution was enacted. At best, they were treated as wards of the state under Acts

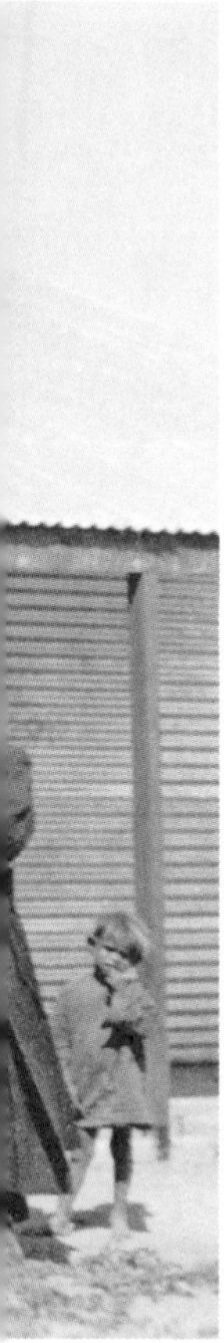

of Parliament in each state and territory that set out the laws for Aboriginal labour, confining Aboriginal people to reserves, and many other rules. In the constitutional referendum of 1967, Australians were asked to vote on whether the Commonwealth Parliament should be able to make laws for Aborigines, and whether Aboriginal people should be counted in the Australian census. After the referendum's success – a resounding 'yes' vote – all the states and the Northern Territory permitted Aboriginal people to vote.

A change of the federal government in 1972 brought about sudden policy changes, including the recognition of Aboriginal land rights, the recognition of distinctive Aboriginal cultures, and the need for Aboriginal organisations. A new prime minister, Gough Whitlam, initiated the legal recognition of Aboriginal land rights by handing over a land lease to the Gurindji people at Wattie Creek, now called by its proper Aboriginal name, Daguragu, in the Northern Territory. Whitlam appointed Justice Woodward to the Aboriginal Land Rights Commission of Inquiry and, in 1976, the Commonwealth Parliament enacted his principles in the *Aboriginal Land Rights (Northern Territory) Act 1976*.

As the century proceeded, the impact of colonisation on Aboriginal people became a major human rights issue. The stealing and removal of thousands of Aboriginal children, incarcerating them in institutions throughout the twentieth century under the so-called 'assimilation' policy became the subject of a human rights inquiry, as discussed in the previous chapter. The *Bringing them home* report was tabled in Parliament in 1997 and eventually, in 2008, led to the government apology delivered to the Stolen Generations.

The practice of jailing Aboriginal people in such numbers that in parts of Australia the imprisonment rate was the highest recorded in the world became another human rights issue. The Royal Commission into Aboriginal Deaths in Custody was established in 1987, and the final report of the commission, published in 1991, remains the most comprehensive survey of Indigenous law and justice issues and of the underlying causes that bring Aboriginal people into excessive contact with the justice system. Despite the Royal Commission's 339 recommendations, Indigenous people are still fourteen times more likely to be imprisoned than non-Indigenous Australians. The Royal Commission recommended a reconciliation process and the Council for Aboriginal Reconciliation was formed, consisting of both Indigenous and non-Indigenous members who initiated programs leading to many changes in attitude and practice. In 1997, a National Reconciliation Convention was held.

National institutions, such as the National Museum of Australia, the Australian Museum, the Australian Broadcasting Commission, and the Australian Human Rights and Equal Opportunity Commission, have produced timelines of the many events in Australian history that are significant to Aboriginal and Torres Strait Islander people in remembering their past, and increasingly to more Australians as historians reveal this past.

The timelines, which can be found on their websites, are a good guide to the history of Australia since 1788.

12

MAKING A RIGHTFUL PLACE IN THE NATION FOR THE FIRST AUSTRALIANS

Australia's state governments controlled the lives of the Aboriginal and Torres Strait Islander people well into the twentieth century. As well as the 'assimilation' policies under which these governments used their legal power to remove Aboriginal children from their families, destroying family life for thousands of Aboriginal people for several generations, across the country Indigenous people were incarcerated on Crown reserves. Superintendents or 'managers' of various kinds ran these reserves as well as the settlements and missions. Indigenous people could not work, travel or even move off these places unless the superintendents gave them permission. Often this permission was not granted, and these people lived on the missions, reserves and settlements as if they were in prison.

Many were in a constant state of starvation. They were given only small quantities of rations, sometimes once a week in the large settlements and less often in smaller ones. As their movement across their land was restricted, many people could not hunt or bring in the food their families had traditionally lived on.

Indigenous people across the country stood up against these racist policies. In the 1920s, the movement for Aboriginal rights started, and it continued to grow over the following years. In Adelaide in 1958, a national body was created: the Federal Council for the Advancement of Aborigines (FCAA). Its aim was to gain 'equal citizenship rights' and to develop a national approach to Indigenous affairs. It campaigned for equal pay and land rights, and to change the Australian Constitution.

In 1964, the organisation's name was changed to the Federal Council for the Advancement of Aborigines and Torres Strait Islanders (FCAATSI). Hundreds of FCAATSI's members, both Indigenous and non-Indigenous volunteers, campaigned for a referendum to remove discrimination against 'Aborigines' from the Constitution.

In 1967, a national referendum was held and the campaign, 'Vote Yes for Aboriginal rights', was an outstanding success. An overwhelming majority of Australians, and a majority of the states, voted Yes, and the Constitution was amended.

Indigenous and non-Indigenous people walk together in the spirit of reconciliation (photo Wayne Quilliam)

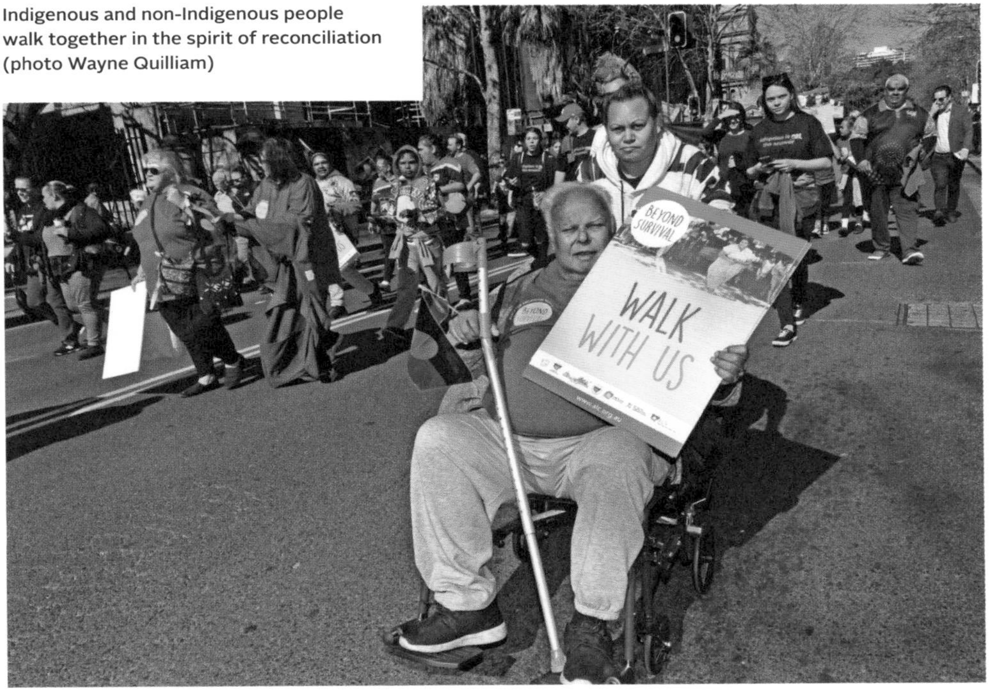

The change to the Australian Constitution meant that Aboriginal and Torres Strait Islander peoples were now included in the national census. Also, the discriminatory clause preventing the federal Parliament from legislating for 'Aborigines' (which was interpreted to include Torres Strait Islanders) was deleted.

Before the 1967 referendum, the Commonwealth Government was unable to legislate for Aboriginal and Torres Strait Islander people. That meant there were no Commonwealth policies governing Indigenous people, only state policies, except for those relating to appointed Aboriginal welfare officers and patrol officers in the Northern Territory.

No other constitution in the world is as difficult to change as the Australian Constitution. As a result, only eight out of forty-four questions voted on in referendums in Australia's history have succeeded. One of these was the referendum in 1967. It fundamentally changed the way Australia as a nation related to Indigenous people.

The question put to the Australian people was:

Do you approve the proposed law for the alteration of the Constitution entitled 'An Act to alter the Constitution so as to omit certain words relating to the people of the Aboriginal race in any state so that Aboriginals are to be counted in reckoning the population'?[94]

This question proposed to delete two parts of the Constitution. First, it proposed

Australians rallying for Aboriginal rights in the 1967 referendum (image courtesy of AIATSIS, item HORNER2.J01.BW-N04612_12)

to remove the words 'other than the Aboriginal people in any state' from section 51(xxvi). Before the referendum, this section read:

The Parliament shall, subject to this Constitution, have power to make laws for the peace, order and good government of the Commonwealth with respect to ...

The people of any race ***other than the Aboriginal people in any state*** *for whom it is necessary to make special laws.*

This meant the federal Parliament didn't have any lawmaking power in relation to Aboriginal or Torres Strait Islander people (Torres Strait Islanders were included in the legal category of Aboriginal people at that time).

Second, the referendum question proposed to repeal section 127, which had prevented Aboriginal people from being included in 'reckoning the numbers of the people of the Commonwealth – that is, the census. Section 127 prevented Aboriginal people from being counted for the purpose of determining the size and distribution of electorates for the federal Parliament. However, in reality the impact of this section on Aboriginal and Torres Strait Islander people was much wider.

As the 'Expert Panel on Constitutional Recognition of Indigenous Australians' reported in 2012:

At the first Australian census in 1911, only those 'aboriginal natives' living near white settlements were counted, and the main population tables included only those of half or less Aboriginal descent. Details of 'half-caste' (but not 'full-blood') Aboriginal people were included in the tables on race. Details of 'full blood' Aboriginal people were included in separate tables. The practice was followed in all censuses up until 1966.

The effect of section 127 was that the government underestimated the number of Aboriginal and Torres Strait Islander people who voted. This reflected the view, widely held at Federation in 1901, that Indigenous people were not entitled to take part in Australia's democratic processes.

In the 1967 referendum, 90.77 per cent of people voted in favour of amending the Constitution, the highest ever Yes vote recorded in a federal referendum. Section 127 was deleted from the Constitution and the words 'other than the Aboriginal people in any state' were removed from section 51(xxvi).

This extraordinary support for Aboriginal rights was a victory for the hundreds of people who had held street marches, written about their situation in newspapers, and campaigned to unions, churches and parliaments for decades. Professor Megan Davis wrote in an essay in *The Monthly* in July 2016 that 'progress on Indigenous rights has never originated in the parliament'. If we have learnt anything from decades of Indigenous campaigns, it is that, as Megan Davis writes:

Indigenous rights, land rights, native title rights have come from indigenous activism – tents on the lawn – and the courts. Parliament is always playing catch-up. The unwavering aspiration of Indigenous people for decades has been a settlement between Aboriginal polities and the state.[95]

The 1967 referendum was a step in the right direction. However, we have a long way to go as a country to make sure that the Aboriginal and Torres Strait Islander peoples are given their rightful place within the nation and are empowered within its legal and political systems.

Many of the men who organised for civil rights leading to the 1967 referendum had served in the Australian Defence Forces (ADF) in World War II. They served overseas and in northern Australia as military and non-military personnel. They fought for the country that discriminated against them.

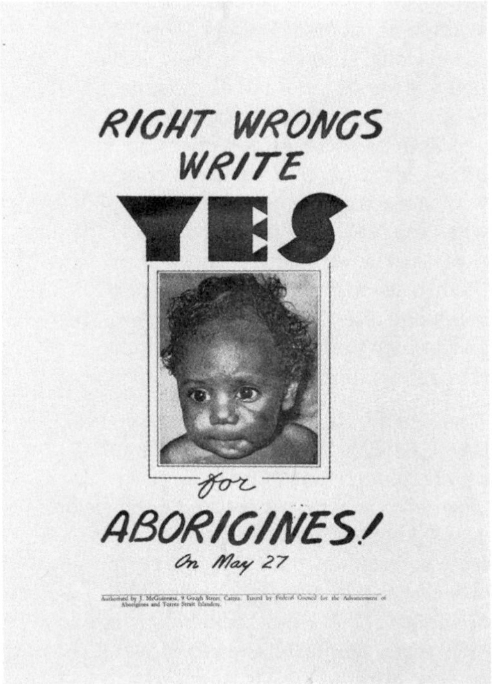

A pamphlet handed out in the campaign for Aboriginal rights in the 1967 referendum (image courtesy of AIATSIS, item DAA.003.BW-N04528_13A)

There was an Aboriginal Reconnaissance Unit in Arnhem Land, established by anthropologist Donald Thomson, who was a commissioned officer after the declaration of war. Also, the Torres Strait Islanders provided a full battalion.

When the war ended and Indigenous Australians who fought for their Country came back home, they faced much the same discrimination as before. Most did not get the right to vote until seventeen years later, and they took part in another long fight in order to achieve that and other citizenship rights.

Aboriginal and Torres Strait Islander people have served in every conflict and commitment involving Australian defence contingents since Federation. The Australian War Memorial records 'even a small number of individual enlistments in the colonial defence forces before that'. Indigenous people served in both world wars, as well as in Vietnam, Afghanistan, Iraq and other deployments. Their contribution was not recognised until the 2000s, when the ADF, the War Memorial and the Australian Government acknowledged them in several ceremonies. That only happened after the Indigenous service men and women themselves campaigned for their recognition.

Then Chief of the Defence Force General David Hurley stated in his 2016 memorial service speech that 'More than 3000 Indigenous Australians enlisted during World War II. Another 150 to 200 served as de facto servicemen, patrolling and performing other military duties along the north Australian coast, while 3000 Indigenous Australians supported the World War II defence effort as civilian labourers'.

NAIDOC Week and the burden of Australia's political history

NAIDOC Week, Australia's annual celebration of Aboriginal and Torres Strait Islander peoples and cultures, is held in the first week of July every year. It is a way to make sure that we never return to the dark days of the Australian colonies, when the efforts to wipe out our peoples almost succeeded.

Originally, the acronym NADOC stood for 'National Aborigines Day Observance Committee', which would organise the activities. From 1991, recognising the distinct cultural histories of Aboriginal and Torres Strait Islander peoples, NADOC was expanded to include Torres Strait Islander people and culture. The committee then became known as the National Aborigines and Islanders Day Observance Committee (NAIDOC). This new name has become the title for the whole week, not just the day.

Now NAIDOC Week has grown to become a part of Australian life. Aboriginal and Torres Strait Islander people in communities and urban areas, as well as government agencies, local councils, schools and workplaces, organise events in towns, cities and rural and remote areas around the country. The celebrations include dancing, singing, storytelling and other events.

Awards ceremonies are held in each state and territory to recognise the achievements of outstanding individuals, young and old, from a wide range of fields. The week culminates in the National NAIDOC Awards Ceremony, hosted by a local NAIDOC committee in a different city chosen each

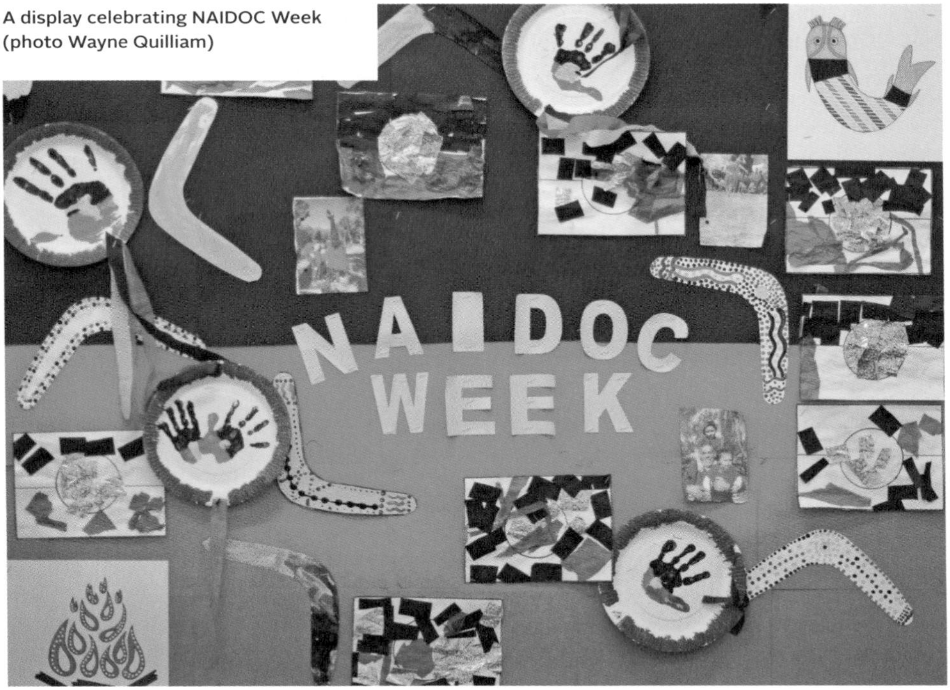

A display celebrating NAIDOC Week (photo Wayne Quilliam)

year. During the week, the Aboriginal and Torres Strait Islander flags are flown across the nation, on buildings and schools and on flagpoles lining avenues and streets. Permission is not required to fly either the Aboriginal or Torres Strait Islander flag. However, it is essential to apply for permission if you want to reproduce the flags in some form.

These celebrations are organised by Indigenous Australians and reflect those issues that matter the most to us: cultural survival, wellbeing, our political rights, our languages and our children. Indigenous people in the host cities form their own local communities and organise the celebrations, including cultural and civic events, and the local and national annual balls. The celebrations are open to all Australians.

Each year there is a different theme for NAIDOC Week. These themes express the concerns of Aboriginal and Torres Strait Islander people. In 2020, the theme of 'Always Was, Always Will Be', recognised that 'First Nations people have occupied and cared for this continent for over 65,000 years', and acknowledged that:

It's about seeing, hearing and learning the First Nations' 65,000+ year history of this country – which is Australian history. We want all Australians to celebrate that we have the oldest continuing cultures on the planet and to recognise that our sovereignty was never ceded.

The 2021 theme, 'Heal Country, Heal Our Nation', is a call for stronger measures to maintain our cultures and heritage.

The first theme was announced by the NADOC Committee (as it was then called) in 1972. This came soon after police violently removed the Aboriginal Tent Embassy from outside Parliament House in Canberra in July that year. The theme of 'Advance Australia Where?' was a response to the refusal by most politicians of the day to consider reforms in the ways our people were treated. They did not agree to negotiating land rights or stopping the ongoing formal racism and racial segregation that most Indigenous people experienced.

The theme of NAIDOC Week 1980 was 'Treat Us to a Treaty on Land Rights'. It showed the Aboriginal people's desire to be formally recognised and treated as First peoples and not as wards of the state, which we had been since colonial days. The demands for a treaty or treaties grew over the years. Many efforts were made to convince governments to consider treaties as a way of overcoming the long history of racism towards Indigenous peoples in our country.

In 2004, the theme was 'Self-determination – Our Community – Our Future – Our Responsibility'. This expressed a widespread dissatisfaction with governments that continued to marginalise Indigenous people and exclude us from policy development. The only national body that gave Aboriginal and Torres Strait Islander people a say in their own affairs was the Aboriginal and Torres Strait Islander Commission (ATSIC). In 2004, the federal government began a campaign in the media to close it down. ATSIC was finally closed in 2005 when then prime minister John Howard's government repealed the legislation that established it.

One of the themes for NAIDOC Week 2012 was 'They dared to challenge', celebrating Aboriginal and Torres Strait Islander people who have encouraged or brought about change.

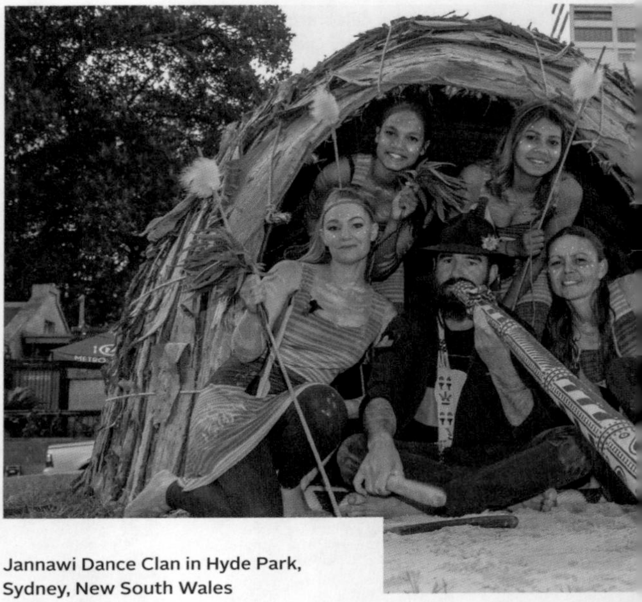

Jannawi Dance Clan in Hyde Park, Sydney, New South Wales

In 2017, the theme was 'Our Languages Matter'. As the National NAIDOC Committee explained, this was to 'emphasise and celebrate the unique and essential role that Indigenous languages play in cultural identity, linking people to their land and water and in the transmission of Aboriginal and Torres Strait Islander history, spirituality and rites, through story and song'.

The National NAIDOC Committee, which until 2008 was chaired by former Senator Aden Ridgeway, has made key decisions on national celebrations each year. It has representatives from most Australian states and territories. From 2008 to 2018, Anne Martin and Ben Mitchell served as co-chairs of the National NAIDOC Committee.

In 2018, Anne and Ben announced the theme, 'Because of her, we can!' A glittering ball held in Sydney that year honoured many Aboriginal and Torres Strait Islander women who served their peoples and the nation. In 2019, under new co-chairs John Paul Janke and Patricia Johnson, the theme chosen was 'Voice Treaty Truth', acknowledging that 'Aboriginal and Torres Strait Islander peoples have ... wanted an enhanced role in decision-making in Australia's democracy'.

We celebrate NAIDOC because of the important contributions that Aboriginal and Torres Strait Islander people make to the Australian nation. We celebrate because we have survived here for over 60,000 years and continue [to] practise our cultures and speak our languages – we want to share this with all Australians. We celebrate because this nation always was, and always will be our land.

NAIDOC Week Committee, 2019

We are not young, we are ancient

For most of Australia's history since the arrival of the British, the First peoples have experienced formal racial discrimination. The Aboriginal and Torres Strait Islander people didn't have any rights as citizens in their own Country. Today, there is still no formal means for our peoples to have a say in their own futures.

The Federation Movement to bring the colonies together under one national government began in 1889. In that year Henry Parkes, the premier of the Colony of New South Wales, gave a speech in the country town of Tenterfield, calling for the six separate colonies to unite and create a national government for all Australia – a federation. At that time the Australian colonies reported to the Home Office in London on matters of state, and were, in most important ways, governed from the Home Office.

Constitutional conventions were held, first in Sydney and then in other cities around the country, to discuss the draft constitution. Aboriginal people were excluded from these conventions in all colonies except South Australia. Nor did they have any right to vote in the referendums on the proposed constitution.

Australia came into existence in 1901 following the enactment of the *Commonwealth of Australia Constitution Act 1900* by the House of Commons in the British Parliament. The Imperial Parliament exercised ultimate authority over the colonies and agreed to the Constitution Act on 5 July 1900. Queen Victoria approved it on 9 July 1900, and it came into force on 1 January 1901.

Although two of several racist clauses in our Constitution were changed in the referendum of 1967, there is still a long way to go.

It is right that the federal Parliament can make laws for Aboriginal and Torres Strait Islander people. But we need to find a way to make sure these laws are fair, and to prevent racist discrimination by the Parliament.

In 2014, Indigenous lawyer and activist Noel Pearson suggested a simple change to the Constitution. This would establish a body of Indigenous people who have the power to review all legislation in Parliament. These people would comment on the effects of legislation on Indigenous people.

This body would be a solution to the problem of our status as a small minority, making up about 3 per cent of the population, and our desire for a rightful place in the nation.

13

BUSINESS & TOURISM

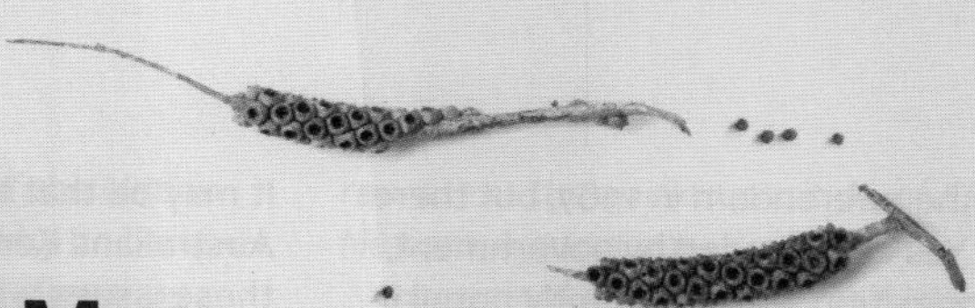

Travellers coming to Australia fifty years ago would have found it almost impossible to visit Aboriginal and Torres Strait Islander communities and lands. Only the most determined adventurers succeeded in obtaining access at that time when government policies of racial segregation and exclusion kept most Indigenous people apart from the rest of Australia. Over the past thirty years, the Indigenous tourism industry has grown from a tiny number to hundreds of businesses today. Since the publication of the first edition of this book, there are many more Aboriginal and Torres Strait Islander businesses and also a new online platform to assist travellers who want to find authentic Indigenous experiences. This new platform is also called Welcome to Country and can be accessed at: welcometocountry.com. It was created by the first not-for-profit online marketplace for Australia's First peoples tourism experiences and products, and was launched on 2 December 2020 with a free virtual event directed by Rhoda Roberts AO, Aboriginal arts leader and festival director. The goal of this online guide is 'to empower Aboriginal and Torres Strait Islander Tourism operators and communities by creating sustainable economic and wellbeing outcomes through tourism and products.' With eighty-seven immersive experiences listed, Welcome to Country online provides an easy-to-use single booking platform.

Tourists are now able to visit Country easily. But the opportunities for Indigenous people to build tourist facilities on their lands and in their communities did not come about so easily. The key industries in rural and remote Australia are mining, pastoralism and tourism – all land-based. As peoples with profound attachments to their land, a large part of the Indigenous population has sought to become involved in these industries. About a quarter of Australia's land mass is Aboriginal-owned and this preference for investment in their own assets and regions is a rational choice. However, to make this happen successfully it was necessary to change the models of economic development that were available to Indigenous communities. A radical overhaul was designed to address the legacy of underdevelopment and exclusion of the previous two centuries.

Business

Changes in attitudes towards Indigenous business came slowly. First the iron-ore miners, then many of the top 200 Australian corporations, and now the Commonwealth Government has created an Indigenous supply chain by procuring goods and services from Indigenous businesses. The growth in the number of these businesses is a core achievement of a new approach to engaging with Indigenous Australians, and all Australians benefit from the outcomes. In 2007, the ANZ Banking Group collaborated with Reconciliation Australia and was the first major private sector company to develop a Reconciliation Action Plan (RAP).

Reconciliation Australia is a non-government body that advises Australians on ways to improve relationships with Aboriginal and Torres Strait Islander people and create opportunities for them. Launched in 2006, Reconciliation Australia's RAP strategy has been enormously successful and has resulted in more than 650 organisations with Reconciliation Action Plans with many more in development. Reconciliation Australia assists companies, government and non-government entities, educational institutions and other bodies to develop

Luke Carroll and Brooke Boney present the Indigenous Businesswoman of the Year award to Petina Tieman (Complete Business Solutions, Queensland) at the Supplier Diversity Awards, 2018 (photo Wayne Quilliam)

RAPs as frameworks to realise their vision for reconciliation. They are practical plans: 'RAPs create social change and economic opportunities for Aboriginal and Torres Strait Islander Australians'. In an evaluation report of their effectiveness by AusPoll in 2012, the RAPs are described as: 'plans that organisations can make to identify clear actions with realistic targets that they can take to improve the relationship between Indigenous people and other Australians both within the organisation and more widely'.

Many major Australian corporations have adopted RAPs and this action has accelerated opportunities for Indigenous businesses as well as encouraging the acceptance of Aboriginal and Torres Strait Islander people in workplaces and recruitment strategies. During the mining boom, companies moved quickly to develop Indigenous business opportunities to demonstrate their commitment to the local Traditional Owners of land where they operated. The results were outstanding. In 2011, Fortescue Metals Group announced its Billion Opportunities program 'to generate business opportunities for Aboriginal people' and to recognise that 'economic opportunity and participation is the key benefit to flow from Native Title agreements'. Since then, the company has awarded 244 contracts and sub-contracts valued close to $2 billion to 105 Aboriginal-owned businesses and joint ventures. In the last decade, Australian governments have caught up with the private sector and developed Indigenous business policies and programs.

Indigenous entrepreneur Michael McLeod and his non-Indigenous business partner Dug Russell were inspired by the National Minority Supplier Development Council in the USA. They developed the idea of creating the Australian Indigenous Minority Supplier Council (AIMSC) to achieve parity in the procurement of Indigenous goods and services, and made a submission to the inquiry by Australian Parliament's Standing Committee on Aboriginal and Torres Strait Islander Affairs in 2008. Their submission outlined the creation of the council and focused on the development of Indigenous enterprises in Australia. One year later, the government announced it would invest $3 million to pilot AIMSC over three years. It was launched on 15 September 2009 at Parliament House in Canberra. In 2013, after successfully completing the pilot phase, AIMSC rebranded to become Supply Nation and has developed the largest membership in Australia of corporate, government and non-profit organisations committed to

Fortescue Metals Group wins Corporate Member of the Year at the Supplier Diversity Awards, 2018 (photo Wayne Quilliam)

Evolve FM wins Registered Business of the Year and Outstanding Impact Award at the Supplier Diversity Awards, 2018 (photo Wayne Quilliam)

supplier diversity and Indigenous business development. It certifies Indigenous suppliers and registered businesses in every state and territory. Then it partners these businesses with companies and governments seeking to buy Indigenous goods and services. Through the work of Supply Nation, private sector expenditure on Indigenous business services has grown dramatically. However, Indigenous business ingenuity, market forces and new government policies on Indigenous procurement account for much of this growth.[100]

In 2015, the Australian government recognised that Indigenous businesses had been largely excluded from its enormous purchasing power and announced a revised and improved Indigenous procurement policy. This led to the increase in federal government spending on Indigenous goods and services from $6 million in 2013 to $594 million in 2017, with the awarding of 4880 contracts to 956 Indigenous-owned businesses over a two year period from 2015, when the Indigenous procurement policy was introduced. There is great interest in these developments because Indigenous businesses employ Indigenous people at far higher rates than other companies, as much as 100 times more, according to the Forrest Review of Indigenous Employment and Training, undertaken by Andrew Forrest, former CEO of Fortescue Metals Group, for the Australian government. Estimates are that there are between 3000 and 5000 Indigenous businesses nationally.

In 2015, the Community Development Program or CDP, a work-for-the-dole scheme, supported 37,000 people across 1000 communities. More than 80 per cent of the participants were Indigenous. This program has had several name changes in just a few years and many rule changes, none of which have improved the situation. The government's work-for-the-dole scheme applied in Aboriginal Australia has only had a 2 per cent success rate for transitioning its participants to jobs. According to Andrew Forrest's report, 'an additional 188,000 Indigenous Australians will have to find work in the next five years if we are to achieve parity. This will require a doubling of the current number of working Indigenous Australians'.

Indigenous Business Month is held annually in October throughout Australia (follow the Twitter account @IndigBizMonth) and events are held nationally to raise awareness of the Indigenous business sector.

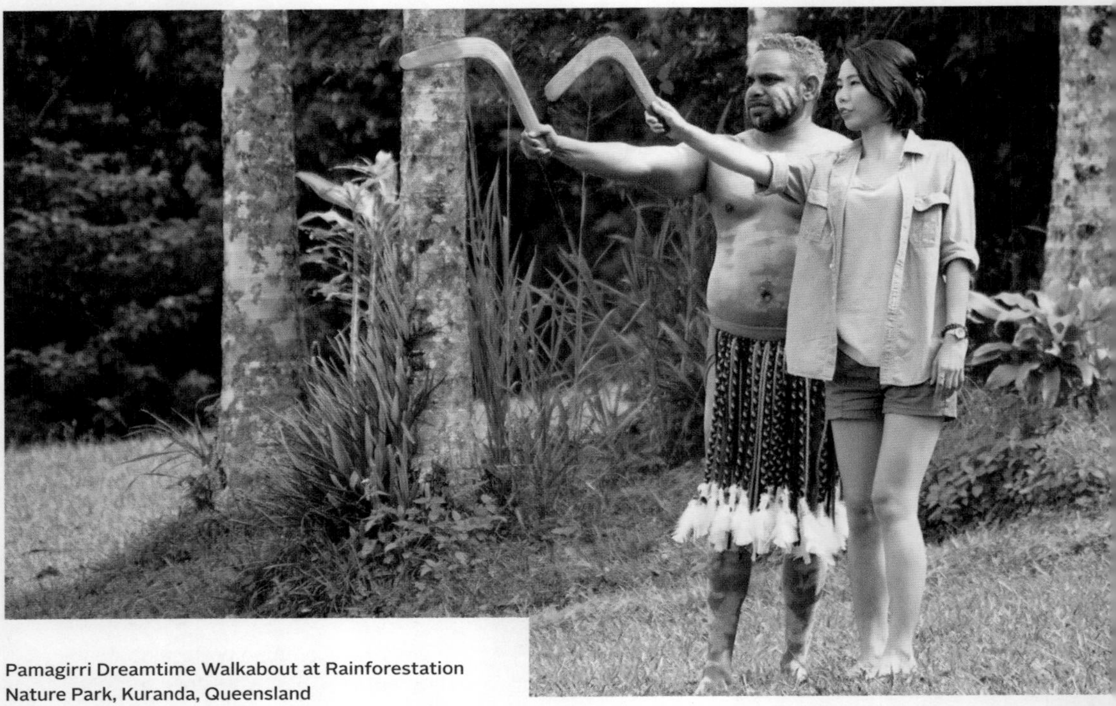

Pamagirri Dreamtime Walkabout at Rainforestation Nature Park, Kuranda, Queensland

The Indigenous tourism sector

The Indigenous tourism sector is small and faces great challenges. For the foreseeable future, it will remain small-scale and attract smaller numbers than the most popular mainstream attractions. The COVID-19 restrictions in 2020, the closing of our national, state and territory borders, and the closing of the borders around Aboriginal lands, has radically changed our access to Aboriginal-owned places of interest, tours and experiences. These measures were necessary to protect our highly vulnerable populations. A majority of Aboriginal and Torres Strait Islander people have underlying health conditions that put them at risk of serious illness and death should they contract COVID-19. Our Indigenous health sector responded swiftly and effectively, implementing pandemic plans in conjunction with Australian governments to protect our most vulnerable from the virus. As the vaccination program is implemented, they will open again and we will be able to travel to them. Before the pandemic, the Indigenous tourism ventures appealed mainly to visitors seeking boutique experiences in art, adventure and environmental experiences. 'There is low awareness amongst the domestic market that Indigenous tourism experiences are available in Australia,' says a research report, *Demand and Supply Issues in Indigenous Tourism*, by Dr Lisa Ruhanen and colleagues from the University of Queensland and Griffith University, which was published in early 2013. The situation has not improved since then. Commissioned by the Indigenous Business Australia (IBA), the federal Department of Resources, Energy and Tourism and the Indigenous Tourism Working Group, the report was based on interviews with more than 1300 international and domestic tourists and more than thirty Indigenous tourism operators. It revealed significant opportunities and challenges for the sector.

Only 5 per cent of international tourists cited Indigenous experiences as an activity they want to take part in while in Australia. Most wanted to stay on the eastern seaboard, especially in Sydney. According to the researchers, 'less than 25 per cent for domestic respondents and less than 20 per cent for international respondents' are aware of Indigenous tourism experiences available to them. 'Preferences for Indigenous tourism experiences declined to 12 per cent and intention/visit to 2 per cent'. Also, the researchers found that domestic visitors have little interest in Indigenous tourism. I hope that readers will see from this book that Indigenous tourism offers opportunities to learn about another side of Australia, away from the mainstream attractions, and to have great fun in the process.

It is important to consider what tourists are looking for. Some people want short, relatively inexpensive, urban activities. This applies particularly to mainstream tour groups. Other types of tourism, such as adventure, art, cultural and environmental tourism, attract far smaller numbers of visitors, but these are the types of tourist attractions run by most Indigenous operators. The researchers found that businesses can tailor their tour to suit particular groups. For instance, if an Indigenous tourism business wants to be included in a Chinese tour company's itinerary, the operators should produce an 'Aboriginal cultural show; bush tucker/story telling; guided nature/environment tours with Indigenous guide'. The researchers also advised that the venues should be 'located in close proximity to major cities/urban areas, have a brochure and interpretation provided in Chinese', and offer souvenir and shopping opportunities. Indeed, there are such offerings to tourists in or near cities and towns, as you will see in the entries in Part Two. Many Indigenous operators in rural and remote areas would find it impossible to achieve all of the points suggested in the report.

IBA is using the information contained in this important report to inform its engagement with Indigenous tourism operators and the advice it provides on product development, particularly to assist potential tourism operators to better understand the domestic and international tourism market. The full report is available from the IBA website at www.iba.gov.au.

The research by Dr Lisa Ruhanen and her colleagues has also had an impact on improving government support for the Indigenous tourism sector. IBA, a government statutory body set up with the purpose of investing in Indigenous businesses, improved its Indigenous Tourism Champions Program thanks, in part, to the report. In 2013, it linked more Indigenous tourism operators to tourism industry expert mentors – from fifteen businesses in 2011–2012 to thirty-seven in 2012–2013. It also provided matched funding so Indigenous tourism operators can participate in trade events and access marketing and other business development services. Although these steps are small, they are essential if Indigenous tourism ventures are to achieve greater success in the future.

Gourmet food and culinary tourism

The high quality of Australian produce makes gourmet tourism experiences very appealing. Mark Olive, aka The Black Olive, was one of the first people to make it easy for tourists to sample and enjoy Indigenous food. This Bundjalung man is Australia's most famous Indigenous chef, and his cooking is highly regarded nationally. His television programs and corporate catering experiences introduced Australians and visitors to the world of wild bush foods and the experience of bush foods in gourmet cooking. Mark's company, Black Olive Catering, based in Melbourne, is sought out for major events all around the country and his series *The Outback Cafe* is

Josh Whiteland, owner–operator of Koomal Dreaming, runs foodie tours and bush-food walks on Wadandi and Bibbulmun Country, Western Australia

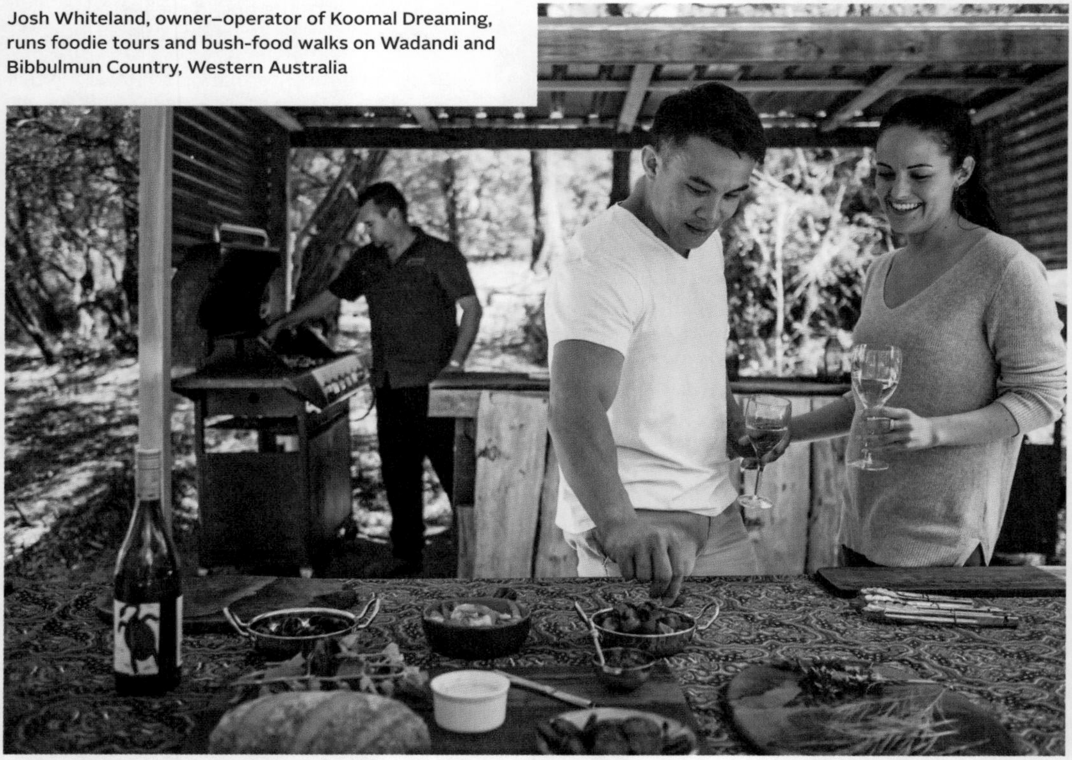

watched around the world. In his role as the Outback Academy Ambassador – Hospitality Programs, Mark has helped many Indigenous people to train as chefs and he has attracted chefs from around the world to experience Australian wild, or bush, food. Chefs looking for exciting new ingredients were not disappointed. Even Heston Blumenthal has experienced Indigenous wild food.

Another Indigenous chef is Clayton Donovan, the only hatted Indigenous chef. He is the star of his *Wild Kitchen* television program. Clayton lives in the Nambucca Valley, northern New South Wales, and brings Indigenous ingredients, both foraged and farmed, to a wide audience at festivals and events.

Roelands Village (p. 336)

Mark Olive, The Black Olive, has worked with the Indigenous bush foods farm Roelands Village in the south-west of Western Australia, to bring their produce to a wide market. Roelands Village is a working farm, producing native bush foods, and a nationally significant heritage site set in a majestic environment surrounded by the rolling Seven Hills. It has accommodation, conference and catering facilities, and is a great food and wine destination. Formerly known as Roelands Mission, it was an institution for the Stolen Generations. From the 1940s to the 1970s, around 500 Aboriginal children were taken to the mission. Now some of those people are transforming Roelands Village into a place of social business, education and healing. In 2004, the Indigenous Land Corporation bought the property on behalf of Woolkabunning Kiaka Incorporated, representing the former residents, and its purpose now is to promote the overall development of the community.

575 Seven Hills Rd, Roelands, Western Australia

Koomal Dreaming (p. 333)

Josh 'Koomal' Whiteland, a Wadandi man, operates Koomal Dreaming at Yallingup, west of Dunsborough in the South-West of Western Australia. Josh offers cultural tours and gives visitors the opportunity to taste native foods, learn about bush medicine and explore the beautiful Margaret River region, three hours south-west of Perth. Sampling the fresh wild food from the sea and the land that Josh knows so much about, as well as swimming at the pristine beaches and walking through the natural environment makes Koomal Dreaming a special experience. Josh took part in the first Margaret River Gourmet Escape in November 2012, along with some internationally renowned Australian chefs. He introduced the chefs and other visitors to the Noongar people's calendar of six seasons and the abundant wild food of the area, including edible flora, kangaroo, emu, abalone and squid. This major annual food festival is a popular attraction for gourmands.

Yallingup Caves Rd, Yallingup, Western Australia

Immersive cultural experiences

The Garma Festival (p. 237)

The Garma Festival is one of the best cultural festivals in Australia. The festival was cancelled in 2020 and 2021 because of concerns about the difficulty of coping

Dancers from Yolŋu clans throughout northeast Arnhem Land take turns to perform at the buŋgul, each adorned in their respective colours and clan designs

with the potential for positive COVID-19 cases in a remote area with extremely limited medical facilities. (However, in 2021, both the Darwin Festival and the Barunga Festival were given permission by the Northern Territory government to proceed.) The Garma Festival has offered a unique combination of traditional Yolŋu ceremonies, held every afternoon, and a forum that pre-COVID-19 attracted a gathering of 2500 political and business leaders from across the globe to share Yolŋu knowledge and culture and to discuss the most pressing issues facing Indigenous Australians. Coordinated and programed by the Yothu Yindi Foundation (YYF), the proceeds are used to improve the lives of Yolŋu people in north-east Arnhem Land through education and community development programs. Garma incorporates visual art, ancient storytelling, dance – including the famous nightly buŋgul, or traditional dancing – and music. As well, important forums are held and education and training programs relevant to cultural tourism, craft, governance and youth leadership are run during the festival. Garma is presented by the YYF in early August each year. YYF is a not-for-profit Aboriginal corporation with tax deductibility gift recipient status. Read more about the Garma Festival in the Northern Territory chapter of this book. It is hoped that in 2022, the Garma Festival will be a COVID-safe event with increased vaccination rates and the numbers of visitors allowed to attend reduced to allow for social distancing and other health measures for the participants. Places will be limited at the festival until the vaccination program is fully implemented in the Northern Territory.

Gulkula, north-east Arnhem Land, Northern Territory

Tourism in the outback: the landscapes of Indigenous Australia

Gariwerd (Grampians National Park) (p. 410)

The ancient landforms in the Gariwerd Grampians National Park date from the Gondwana period, and it shows. These mountains and valleys look and feel old. And they are: about 180 million years old. This is a unique place because of its geological history and also because it is rich in Aboriginal history and culture. The Traditional Owners are the Jardwadjali and Djab Wurrung peoples. The majority of the rock-art sites in Victoria are in the Gariwerd, with some dating back 22,000 years. Their Traditional Owners are still involved in Gariwerd and maintain the culture and the stories of the land. Like other Aboriginal groups, the Jardwadjali and Djab Wurrung peoples have six distinct seasons that have an impact on the times when plants flower and fruit, and on animal behavioural patterns.

You will find information about many other national parks, Indigenous tours and events in the state and territory chapters in this book. These entries prioritise places, events and experiences that are either Indigenous owned and operated or genuinely engage with Traditional Owners and the culture of First peoples. Check with operators directly for updates due to the COVID-19 pandemic.

14

CULTURAL AWARENESS FOR VISITORS

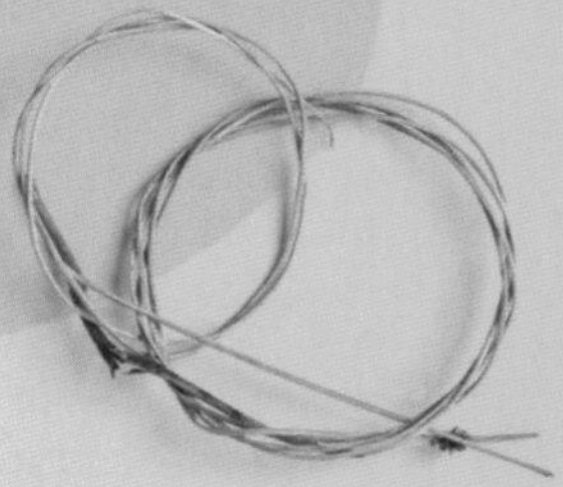

The Aboriginal way of welcoming visitors to their homelands is often a very simple affair, with just a few words of welcome, sometimes in the local language and in English. Some groups light a fire, wetting special leaves such as ti-tree or gum to make a fine smoke and ask visitors to walk through the smoke, while others splash water on their guests. Occasionally, more elaborate ceremonies are held, which involve singing traditional songs. Participating in these rituals is the best way of showing respect for Aboriginal and Torres Strait Islander hosts and guides. Showing respect for Aboriginal and Torres Strait Islander people is often explained in unnecessarily complicated language in cross-cultural awareness programs. As travellers you will probably have met people from many different cultures and usually you will find that it is easy to talk to people in a normal tone of voice and say the usual greetings, such as, 'Good morning. How are you?' Or, 'Hello, my name is...' Also, you will learn a great deal by listening to and observing what your hosts and guides say and do.

In most of Indigenous Australia, English or a form of English is spoken. So there is no need to buy a phrase book that provides translations of everyday expressions such as 'hello' and 'where does the bus leave from?' – if, indeed, phrase books for travellers in Indigenous languages are available. I think it is more fun to get to know people and ask them questions such as, 'How do you say "hello" in your language?'

As I have explained, there are about 120 Indigenous languages still spoken in Australia. This astonishing diversity of languages is one reason why there aren't many, if any, language books for travellers or many other books and guides about Indigenous languages for the general reader.

Many Indigenous people were prevented from speaking their mother tongues during the assimilation period, and were often punished for doing so. That history combined with residual racism has resulted in a great reticence on the part of Indigenous Australians to speak their languages except in their own social settings. Fortunately, there are many grammars and dictionaries published by linguists and language revival programs, but this does not make it any easier for the visitor to engage in basic conversations in local languages.

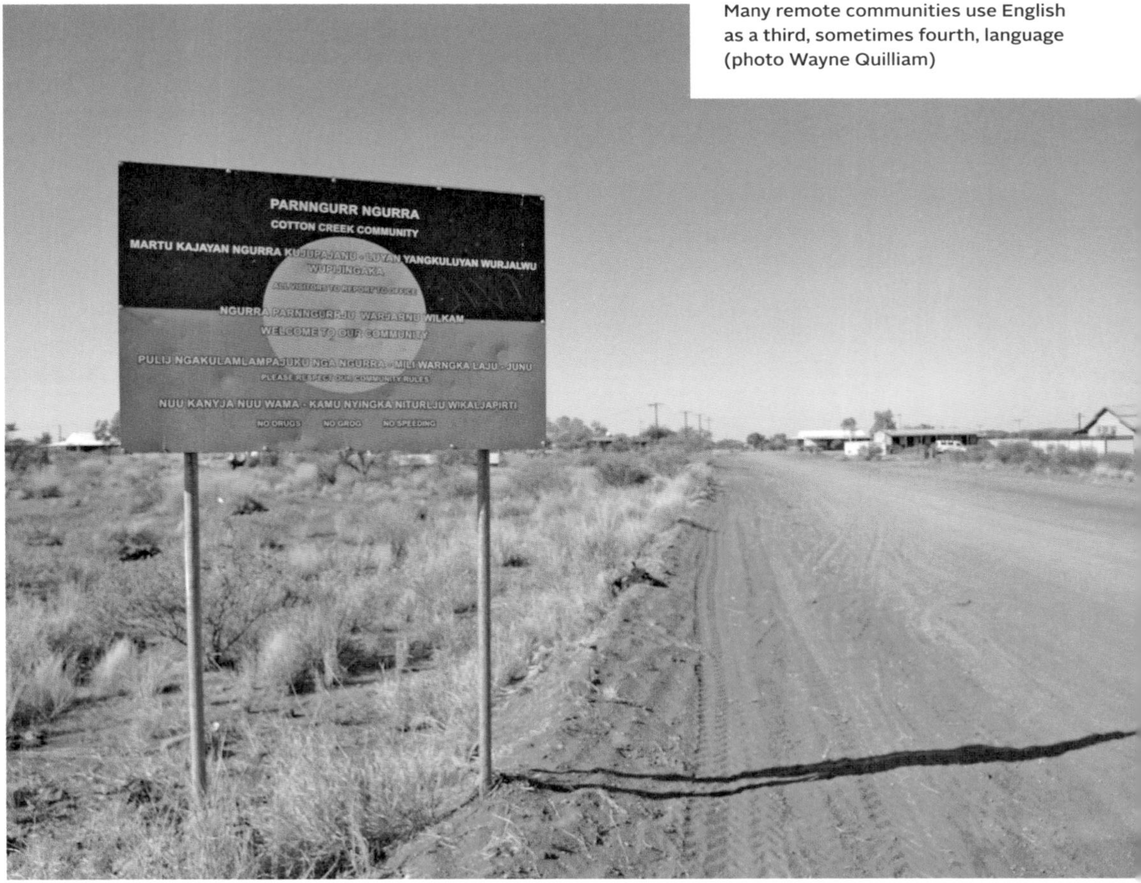

Many remote communities use English as a third, sometimes fourth, language (photo Wayne Quilliam)

Showing respect for your host is as simple as trying to say some words in that person's language, if you meet an Indigenous person who is willing to share their language. Speaking a few words of an Australian language is a great way to make friends, too. Your teacher will want to share more if you show a keen interest. Increasingly, many Indigenous tour guides are very proud and happy to share words about the flora and fauna and their traditional environmental knowledge, such as the names of seasons and weather patterns, and the behaviour of plants and animals during those times. The training provided by Indigenous ranger programs has enabled people to discuss their traditional knowledge openly and without fear.

Nura Gunyu provides experiences ranging from bush food walks to cooking demonstrations in the Budawang bush, New South Wales

Questions

You need to know that not all questions are welcome, even if you are sincerely interested in finding out more about a place or a cultural point. In some areas of Australia, Aboriginal people will not respond to questions. Either the question makes no sense culturally, or it breaches local customs. Often an Aboriginal person – whether a man or a woman – is not permitted to discuss local customs without the permission of their group or clan. Instead of saying, 'I am not authorised to answer that question,' an Aboriginal person will remain silent or answer another question. This is still the Aboriginal way in many areas today. Asking too many questions can be seen as intrusive, even though meant with goodwill. Some trained guides and rangers are accustomed to the inquisitive visitor and deal with questions in a way that the visitor expects of a commercial guide. Aboriginal hosts are not always trained, and even if they are, will not bend their local rules. A good way to get a conversation going is with an observation about what you are being shown.

For example, if you are walking by a forest at sunset and the trees are alive with flying foxes, or bats, you might say, 'That's a lot of bats. I have never seen so many.' This might start a discussion about the bats, the forest they live in, the season and local customs. Or not, but if you are in a different culture, such differences are to be expected.

When to use names of people and places and when not to

Visitors using Aboriginal and Torres Strait Islander names of people and places is not a problem when it is clear that this is allowed because your host has used the names or they appear on signs. Some Aboriginal and Torres Strait Islander names are difficult to pronounce, but it is always worth trying. You may get it right, and no one will be offended if you tried and didn't say it correctly. There are rules about names that cannot be used, but this practice is usually confined to the members of an Aboriginal society. Visitors are not expected to follow these rules, unless the hosts have explained that particular names may not be spoken.

In many areas, when a person dies, the name and images of that person cannot be used at all until the family of the deceased makes a public declaration that the taboo has been lifted. In the case of famous Aboriginal people, it may be some years before this happens. For famous Aboriginal musicians, an elliptical way of referring to the deceased will be used, such as 'that lead singer of the Yothu Yindi band'. Place names that are the same as, or similar to, a deceased person's name will not be used by Aboriginal people in the areas where these traditions are followed. For some years, Alice Springs was referred to as Kumunjayi by local people because of the death of a woman with the same first name as the town. Television stations and websites in Australia that broadcast or publish photographs and videos of Aboriginal people provide warnings at the beginning of the content so that Aboriginal and Torres Strait Islander people will be aware that they are likely to see images of deceased people. These practices have been in place for the last two decades and are commonplace. They show respect for the cultural protocols of the First Australians, and help other Australians to understand these cultural differences.

Language rules

In every language in the world there are rules about what is appropriate to say in public. Aboriginal groups may have words that only women are permitted to use, or that only men are permitted to use. There are words that are not allowed to be spoken in public but are confined to ceremonies. The esoteric languages of many Aboriginal societies are used only in ceremonial or ritual contexts. Visitors may have read in books by anthropologists about Aboriginal cultural practices such as rituals. In many cases, it is not polite or acceptable to speak about these matters in public. When in doubt, don't ask questions about anything that you think might be sensitive, and do not share what you have read in an obscure anthropological text.

I was in Paris many years ago at an international conference on Indigenous cultures when it was the fashion in French universities for students to interpret the 'meanings' of Aboriginal rock art through the lens of European psychological theories about sexual deviation. On a table in the foyer of the conference centre were piles of various documents published by a local publisher. I flipped through a few and my skin crawled. The texts bore no resemblance whatsoever to the meanings of the rock art as explained by the Traditional Owners. One of these texts stated that the art referred to a particular sexual deviation, when in fact the rock art represented a Lightning Ancestor who rouses the world during the monsoon season with thunder and flashes of light. None of the students had been to Australia, and clearly there was a theoretical formula imposed by a Freudian anthropologist in a faraway Parisian classroom. My advice: Don't try out European theories on Aboriginal people.

PHOTO
TRADITIONAL OWNERS
RESPECT THEIR CUSTO
PHOTOGRAPHING LOC
HAVING ONE'S PHOTOGRA
CULTURALLY INAPROPRI
CAPTURED ON FILM, BE
ONE'S SPIRIT, IS REMO
PERSONS CONTROL FO
THANK YOU FOR YOUR

Photographs and videos

You must ask permission before filming or taking photographs of people, especially children. Aboriginal and Torres Strait Islander people do not feel comfortable with visitors taking photographs or videos of them or their family members without explicit permission. Aboriginal hosts at public events and tourist events will make it clear if photography is permitted.

There have been a number of legal cases involving unauthorised photography, commercial use of photographs in publications without permission, and the distribution of photographs and videos. The use of unauthorised photography and video on social media platforms is also becoming a problem, and complaints from Aboriginal people have been acted on by police.

A sign near Uluṟu asking visitors to respect the traditions of the Aṉangu people

Signs and published cultural rules and protocols

Because of the great diversity, culturally and linguistically, in Indigenous Australia, many groups publish their own rules and protocols. A good example is the 'Behaviour protocols' published on the website of the Garma Festival hosted by the Yolŋu people of north-east Arnhem Land in the Northern Territory. It is a thorough and useful guide to the rules and protocols in the area. There are some differences from area to area, so keep in mind that something that is acceptable in one area or at one event might not be elsewhere.

At Garma, you are requested to observe and work within Yolŋu protocols.

Remember you are on Yolŋu land and entering Yolŋu time. Yolŋu perceptions, priorities and preoccupations are different from those of mainstream Australia. Be patient, and try to leave at home your expectations of how things are learnt, and how events should run. Traditionally Yolŋu learn by observation, by looking and listening. Asking too many questions can be

This exhibition contains images and references to deceased people which may cause sadness or distress, particularly to Aboriginal and Torres Strait Islander peoples

Example of warnings displayed in respect for Aboriginal and Torres Strait Islander peoples

inappropriate. So, when you have questions, choose them carefully and thoughtfully.

Respect Yolŋu people's personal space, particularly in the camping areas and each individual guest's tent. Sticking to the walking paths provided is important to ensure you're not stumbling across cultural space.

Avoid strolling around and visiting Yolŋu campsites unless specifically invited and accompanied by Yolŋu.

Please exercise courtesy and sensitivity when taking photographs – seek the permission of the Yothu Yindi Foundation and the subjects if taking close-ups, or photographs of small groups, particularly in the women's programs and men's programs cultural and health sessions. The Yothu Yindi Foundation has enforced strict Intellectual Property policies that safe guard both individuals and Yolŋu families when posting Garma to social media channels. You are reminded that we are working in a realistic environment of high mortality. Cultural protocols are strict for that matter and we ask guests to respect this process. If you wish to use Garma imagery, you will need to seek approval from our Director of Media media@yyf.com.au.

Visitors should NOT leave the Gulkula site on their own and should only walk along specifically marked Festival trails. This is about showing respect for land and is also a safety issue. Wild buffalo wander this country and organisers spend considerable effort in monitoring their trails prior to Garma each year. Please ensure someone knows your travel plans.

Treat the old people with the greatest of respect – they hold the knowledge and the power.

Please be conscious that dress standards may often vary from what is considered acceptable at your home. By dressing conservatively you will avoid the possibility of causing offence. Too much skin on display draws inadvertent attention not appropriate for this event. Schools attending the festival should advise their students of this policy. Our dress standards also protect our participants from sunburn, sunstroke and dehydration. Plan a sensible wardrobe, practical and covered shoes and include a hat to protect you from the elements.[101]

You might wonder how practical advice about wearing hats and covered shoes might be cultural protocols. This is a good question. Aboriginal people become very upset if their visitors are injured or become sick while visiting their homeland, because they feel a great sense of responsibility for visitors. They might think that they have not done their job well as responsible Traditional Landowners by reassuring the spirits of the land about their visitors. Other Traditional Owners may blame them for not paying attention if someone becomes sick or injured while visiting. The cultural belief in the power of the spirits in places is still very strong in many parts of Australia.

In November 2017, the Chairman of the Uluru–Kata Tjutu National Park Board of Management, Sammy Wilson, an Anangu Elder and Traditional Owner of the land, announced his intention to the board that the climbing of Uluru should cease. Sammy Wilson's full statement to the board can be read on the Parks Australia website: https://parksaustralia.gov.au/uluru/pub/uktnp-climb-closure-words-from-chair-nov-2017.pdf

In 2019, the Traditional Owners of the Uluru–Kata Tjutu National Park were finally able to achieve their long-held desire to stop visitors climbing Uluru. Their representatives on the National Park Management Board worked with the board to announce well in advance their intention to close the climb. In 2019, the board announced that it would close the climb to the top of Uluru on 26 October 2019. The board's public statement said:

The date of 26 October is significant to the park's traditional owners, as it was the date in 1985 the park was handed back to them.

In 2010 the Board committed to giving the tourism industry at least 18 months' notice to adjust any itineraries or marketing strategies. With their decision to close on 26 October 2019, people can continue to climb if they choose and it is safe to do so, for the next two years if they wish.[102]

Some forty years before, they had expressed their desire to stop the climbing of this sacred place, but the opposition was extreme at that time, as was the opposition to the hand back of their land under the terms of the Aboriginal Land Rights Act. Once they had received title to their land, they leased it to the Commonwealth to create this national park to allow access to other Australians under the management of the Management Board. They had given up their rights to their land – any say about who could come onto their land and their right as owners as to its use – in order to have legal title. Even though the Federal Court judge who heard their case as the Aboriginal Land Rights Commissioner recommended the return of their land to them, the Commonwealth Government would only return it if they agreed to the complex leasing arrangements to created this Commonwealth controlled National Park. They placed a sign at the commencement of the climbing track established many years before by non-Indigenous people. The sign stated:

Please don't climb.
We, the A̲nangu traditional owners, have this to say
Uluṟu is sacred in our culture. It is a place of great knowledge.
Under our traditional law climbing is not permitted.
This is our home.
As custodians, we are responsible for your safety and behaviour.
Too many people do not listen to our message.
Too many people have died or been hurt causing great sadness.
We worry about you and we worry about your family.
Please don't climb.
We invite you to walk around the base and discover a deeper understanding of this place.

Sign erected at Tjukatjapi, Uluṟu, Northern Territory

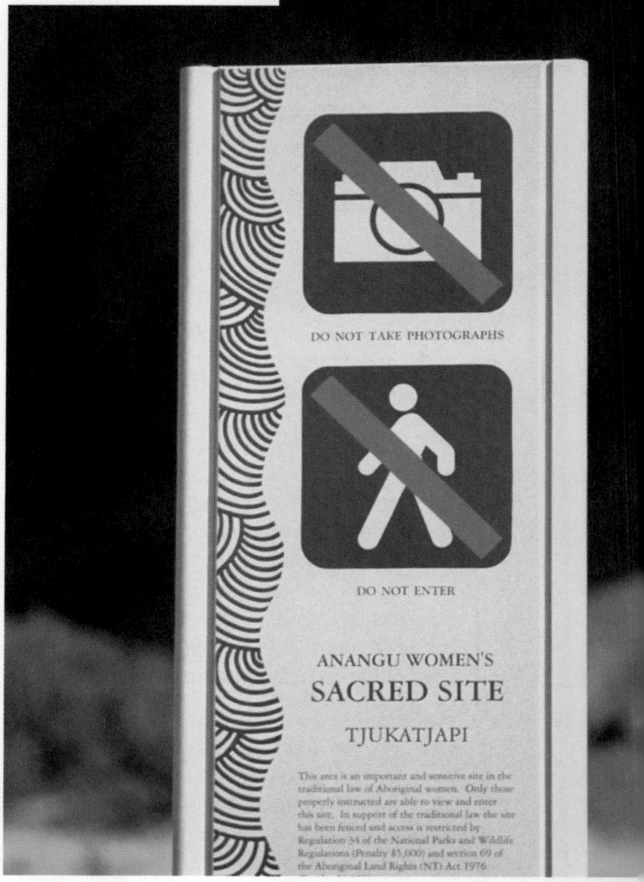

In late October 2019, hundreds of visitors lined up to climb Uluṟu for the last time, some behaving in disgusting ways to show their disrespect for the Traditional Owners. On 25 October, the last person 'permitted to ascend Uluru … reached the base of the climb.'. Rangers permanently closed the climb at 4:00 pm at Australian Central Standard Time and (ACST) and stopped the hundreds still waiting from proceeding. The Traditional Owners celebrated at the base of the rock as a new sign was set up notifying visitors the climb was permanently closed. Australian law had finally respected their wishes.[103]

Rarely do Aboriginal Traditional Owners have the opportunity to set out their protocols as clearly as the Yolŋu in their Garma protocols or the A̲nangu in closing the climb to the top of Uluṟu. In some places the Traditional Owners assert their rights to state what should and should not

happen on their land, which they own under Australian law. In other areas, even when the Traditional Owners legally own the land, they might not have the means to erect signage about their protocols.

In many places there are hidden dangers that Traditional Owners and custodians know about, but non-Indigenous guides are unaware of. So when rules and protocols are explained in signs and publications, everyone should observe them for their own safety.

In most national parks and conservation areas, government authorities install signage for visitors' safety. In north Australia, for example, there are the ubiquitous signs warning about crocodiles and the dangers of swimming as sharks, stingray, stone fish, gropers, fresh and saltwater crocodiles, sea snakes, eels, poisonous jellyfish, 'stingers' and other dangerous creatures inhabit the seas, rivers and waterholes. In other parts of Australia, Aboriginal custodians and government authorities are particularly concerned about the dangers of drowning, people being washed out to sea and bites or injuries from the many dangerous creatures. In view of these and other hazards, signs warning against swimming are common in some areas and should always be taken seriously.

There are many protocols that are not mentioned in tourist guides. I have learnt about fishing protocols, for instance, from Traditional Owners. In northern Australia, when Traditional Owners have taken me on fishing trips, they would speak to the ancestral spirits or hold the fishing line over a smoky fire, and tell me a few rules. It is forbidden to gut fish near water and leave the entrails near bodies of water or on beaches. Clearly this is a practical safety rule because of the constant presence of saltwater crocodiles and wild boar. The smell of fish entrails will attract them very quickly and present an immediate danger. I never sleep or camp near water for the same reason. There are religious rules about this practice as well: it is an offence to the ancestral spirits to leave the remains of fish or other animals near water bodies. There is the constant concern of Traditional Owners that fresh water should not be contaminated, and the traditional way to drink from scarce fresh water sources, especially in arid areas, is to kneel at the edge of the water and sip it, or carefully fill a container without contaminating the water. Most visitors will not encounter these situations, but if you are travelling in the outback, it is good to know the basic Aboriginal rules, for your own safety as well as out of respect for the Aboriginal custodians.

In all cases right around Australia, my advice is: Do not ignore the safety signs.

15

LOOKING TO THE FUTURE FOR INDIGENOUS AUSTRALIA

In his remarkable essay 'Moment of Truth', Mark McKenna observes:

It is not only the absence of any acknowledgment of the country's violent foundation that makes the silence palpable, but also 65,000 years of Indigenous occupation. If it were not for the Tent Embassy and the easily missed Reconciliation Place, Indigenous Australia would have no obvious presence within the Parliamentary Triangle.[104]

This absence of Aboriginal and Torres Strait Islander people, their histories and cultures from the story of the Australian nation cannot be understated. I watched with interest on 26 January 1988 as Australians – not all, but most – celebrated 200 years of the Australian nation. Without any irony, but with some slight and insincere acknowledgement of the existence of the First Australians, the official bodies organised re-enactments of the arrival of the British. Tall ships sailed into Sydney Harbour, and proud white Australians dressed up as convicts and colonists.

There was an Aboriginal protest and a march in Sydney – with several thousand people walking down the main thoroughfare behind a banner that read, 'We have survived'. The slogan was borrowed from the title of Bart Willoughby's song, performed by No Fixed Address, and released in 1981. It quickly became an anthem throughout Indigenous Australia as the nation prepared for its 1988 bicentennial celebrations of the arrival of the British on our shores. The song was first heard on the award-winning film *Wrong Side of the Road*, in 1981, and on the soundtrack album. This film was a tribute to Us Mob, Coloured Stone and No Fixed Address, which were among the first Aboriginal bands to play rock or reggae with a strong political message, while most Aboriginal musicians were playing country music.

The march moved on to La Perouse, where the 'We Have Survived' Festival was held on 26 January each year to counter the propaganda of the Australia Day celebrations. The festival eventually became the Yabun Festival in 2001. Yabun means 'music to a beat' in Gadigal language. It is a free event that features traditional Indigenous cultural performances, music and activities for the Aboriginal and Torres Strait Islander community in Sydney. Similar festivals are curated in other cities and towns.

More than thirty years later, little has changed. The Indigenous protests against

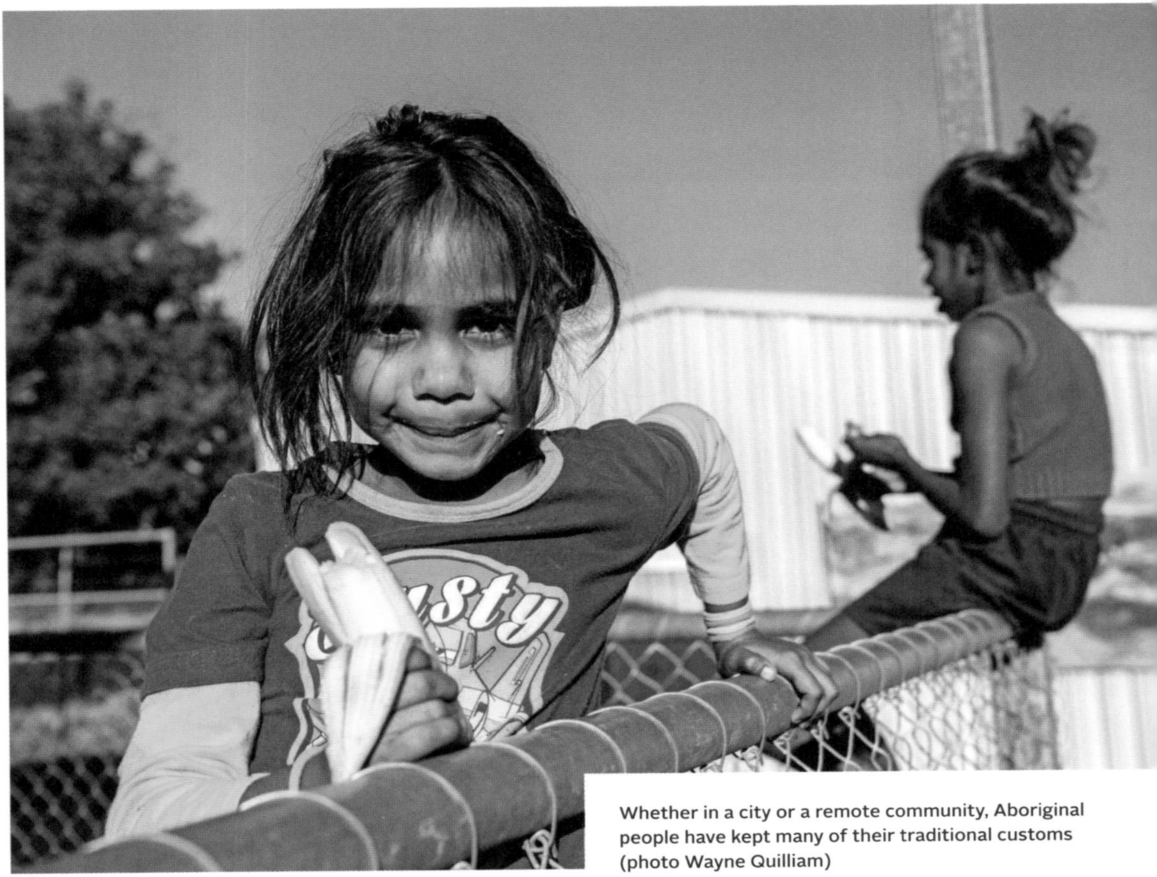

Whether in a city or a remote community, Aboriginal people have kept many of their traditional customs (photo Wayne Quilliam)

the idea of Australia's national day being a celebration of British colonisation grow larger. Indigenous festivals on the day remain distinctly separate and unrelated to the celebrations of many non-Indigenous people for their idea of our nation. The pall of 1950s-style racialist segregation hangs over the day.

Holding the national day on the date that the British established a penal colony at Port Jackson, rather than on 1 January, which was the date in 1901 when the Constitution of Australia was proclaimed by Queen Victoria, presents Australia's citizens with a convenient but troubling myth about the foundations of the nation. In the past, only a few stopped to consider the implications of this for their sense of what it means to be Australian; now, the number is growing.

Television presenter and political journalist Stan Grant, in the following edited extract from his book *Australia Day*, asked all the questions that Australians should ask on the national day, 26 January.

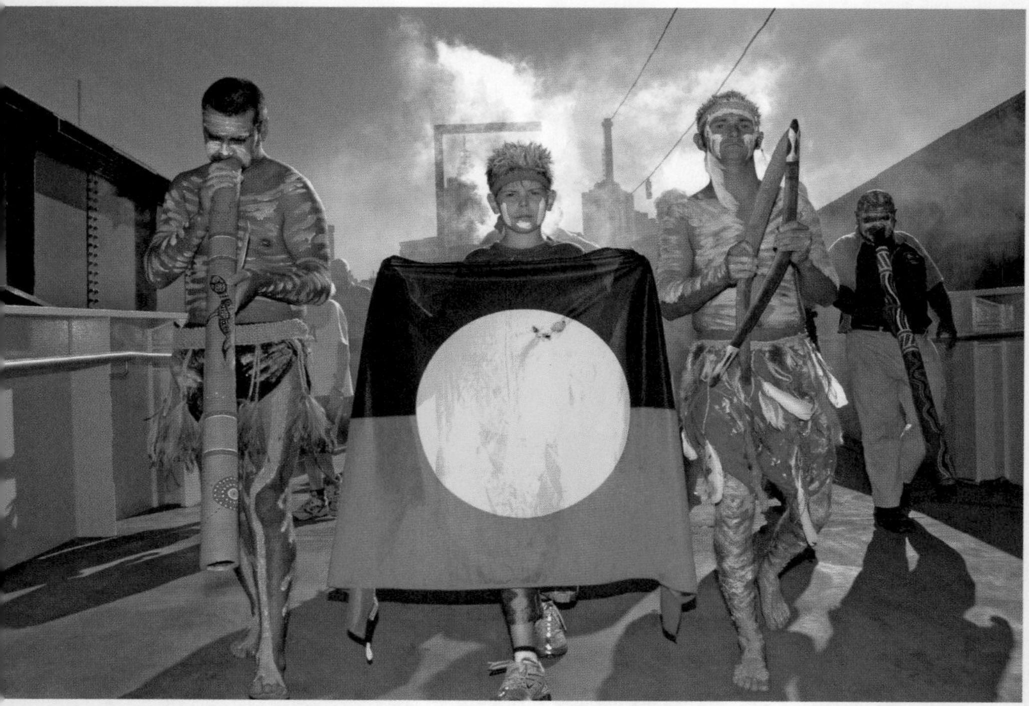

Rallies and marches bring Indigenous and non-Indigenous Australians together to celebrate and work towards a future for Indigenous Australia (photos Wayne Quilliam)

We all seek identity: which communities we belong to; which football club we follow; what music we like; how we dress; where we live; religion; race; culture. All of this gives us a sense of who we are, somewhere to belong. But there is a darker side to identity, a stifling conformity; an us and them; identity that pits us against each other. It keeps returning me to that question: am I Australian? Am I Aboriginal? Can those things be the same?

As a Wiradjuri man himself, Grant turned to Thomas Keneally's famous novel *The Chant of Jimmie Blacksmith*, about a historical Wiradjuri character, Jimmy Governor, to draw out the 'puzzle not easily explained, nor simple to comprehend' that these questions leave us with:

As modern Australia celebrated its birth at Federation in 1901, the historical inspiration for Jimmie Blacksmith, the real Jimmy Governor, sat in a Darlinghurst jail cell, alternating between singing songs in his traditional Wiradjuri language and reading the Bible – the synthesis of the old and new worlds that collided here so violently, given form in a man soon for the gallows. It is a synthesis Thomas Keneally saw as contradiction; and yet it is the essence of being Australian.[105]

It would be superficial to say that Australians have got the date wrong, yet it should be obvious that it is wrong. Australia did not come into existence as a nation for another 112 years after Arthur Phillip unloaded his convicts at what is now Darling Harbour. How could the choice of this date, which commemorates the founding of a penal colony, be seriously considered as providing the foundational myth of this robust, multicultural nation with a history of human society that commenced here at least six millennia ago?

Writers have referred to the British-born or British loyalists who are afraid to cut the 'apron strings' with their motherland. Nicholas Reece, writing in *The Guardian* on 7 June 2015, pondered on the significance of the Queen's Birthday holiday to Australians. It is celebrated each year on different dates across the Commonwealth, few of which are the Queen's actual birthday: 'In truth, the Queen's Birthday holiday is a meaningless excuse for millions of Australians to have a day off work. It is a sorry hangover from a bygone era when Australians clung to the apron strings of the Mother Country.'

Such sentiments usually come from republicans, such as Greg Barns, who chaired the Australian Republican Movement from 2000 to 2002. He wrote, on 9 April 2018 in *The Mercury*, on the occasion of a visit of Prince Edward to Tasmania, that the survival of the British monarchy in the Australian constitutional structure 'is inconsistent with the notion of equality. It does not befit a nation that purports to assure its citizens the impediments of birth or title do not prevent a citizen rising to high office'. Further, he wrote:

There is also the projection of Australia in the 21st century. We live in the Asia-Pacific region and one of the major roadblocks to being embraced by other nations is Australia maintains anachronistic links to its former colonial master.

We may hold republican views or remain loyal to the British monarchy. Either way it makes no sense that our national day should not be on the day that Australia came into existence, even if it was a political artefact of the British Parliament, on 1 January.

It is clear that the First Australians have been excluded from Australian constitutional, political, social and economic life for most of its history. Most likely, this comes from a sense of loyalty to the British motherland as the foundation of the colonies, if not the nation. The Indigenous people are relegated to the status of permanent enemy – if not declared as such, then certainly treated that way. There has been no formal end to this, except perhaps for the creation of the Council for Aboriginal Reconciliation that was formed in 1991 following the recommendation of the Royal Commission into Aboriginal Deaths in Custody. The council was established as a statutory body under the *Council for Aboriginal Reconciliation Act 1991*, passed by the Commonwealth Parliament, with unanimous cross-party support. It ceased to exist on 1 January 2001 in accordance with the Act. As stated in section 5 of the Act:

The object of the establishment of the Council is to promote a process of reconciliation between Aborigines and Torres Strait Islanders and the wider Australian community, based on an appreciation by the Australian community as a whole of Aboriginal and Torres Strait Islander cultures and achievements and of the unique position of Aborigines and Torres Strait Islanders as the indigenous peoples of Australia, and by means that include the fostering of an ongoing national commitment to co-operate to address Aboriginal and Torres Strait Islander disadvantage.

In 2001, after the council was closed, concerned citizens created Reconciliation Australia. As explained in its vision statement, Reconciliation Australia was to be an independent, not-for-profit organisation to lead the reconciliation project and build 'relationships, respect and trust between the wider Australian community and Aboriginal and Torres Strait Islander peoples'. The founders envisioned national reconciliation as based on 'five critical dimensions: race relations, equality and equity, institutional integrity, unity and historical acceptance'.

The work of Reconciliation Australia has made a profound difference to Australian life. It has helped to build relationships of respect between Indigenous and non-Indigenous people. Narragunnawali, a program of Reconciliation Australia, as noted on its website narragunnawali.org.

au, 'supports all schools and early learning services in Australia to foster a higher level of knowledge and pride in Aboriginal and Torres Strait Islander histories, cultures and contributions'.

As I have discussed earlier, among Reconciliation Australia's many other programs, the Reconciliation Action Plans (RAP) have been extraordinarily successful. A RAP is 'a strategic document that supports an organisation's business plan. It includes practical actions that will drive an organisation's contribution to reconciliation both internally and in the communities in which it operates'. Hundreds of institutions and companies, including most major Australian companies, have Reconciliation Action Plans with targets for engagement with Indigenous people, employment and supply-chain goals, and other goals that are relevant to their operations.

I have written about the proposals advanced by Indigenous Australians, such as the Uluru Statement from the Heart, which calls for Voice, Treaty, Truth. The grounds for this proposal, like many others, are the historical injustices that plague our politics, governance and relationships.

Australia, unlike other former British colonies, has no treaty with its Indigenous people. Customary systems of law pre-date the arrival of the British by many thousands of years and survive, often in highly adapted forms, in many parts of postcolonial Australia. Native Title was recognised in Australia only in 1992. This is in contrast to other common law jurisdictions, such as New Zealand and Canada, where Native Title has been recognised for at least 150 years. These countries have superior legal and political regimes for recognising and dealing with Indigenous systems of law and governance. In part, this is because of the treaty rights that were negotiated in their colonial period.

For more than a decade, Indigenous leaders have sought the agreement of successive governments to hold a referendum to change the Australian Constitution to recognise Aboriginal and Torres Strait Islander peoples and their cultures.

It was Galarrwuy Yunupiŋu who gave form to this existential crisis facing all the First peoples in Australia. In 2008, as leader of the Gumatj clan in north-east Arnhem Land, he presented the then prime minister, Kevin Rudd, with a petition. It asked that Australia recognise the right of the Yolŋu clans to exist, and to be acknowledged in the Constitution.

We, the united clans of East Arnhem land, through our most senior dilak, *do humbly petition you, the ... Prime Minister of Australia, in your capacity as the first amongst equals in the Australian Parliament, and as the chief adviser to Her Majesty ... to secure within the Australian Constitution the recognition and protection of our full and complete right to:*

Our way of life in all its diversity;

Our property, being the lands and waters of East Arnhem land;

Economic independence, through the proper use of the riches of our land and waters in all their abundance and wealth;

Control of our lives and responsibility for our children's future.[106]

It is important to acknowledge that 250 Indigenous leaders taking part in the National Indigenous Constitutional Convention held in May 2017 at Uluṟu, one of the most sacred and iconic places in

Aboriginal Australia, unanimously supported the Uluru Statement from the Heart. The Australian government did not agree to the approach outlined in this elegant statement, which calls for the establishment of a First Nations Voice in the Australian Constitution and a Makarrata Commission to supervise a process of agreement-making and truth-telling between governments and Aboriginal and Torres Strait Islander peoples. In response, the government issued a cursory statement in November 2017. But the Indigenous leaders are committed to pursuing their goal, just as their forebears did. And, in 2019, Indigenous Australians minister Ken Wyatt made his pledge to find a 'consensus' that would lead to a referendum to recognise Indigenous Australians in the Constitution within three years.

This is one of the reasons for learning about Aboriginal and Torres Strait Islander histories and cultures in schools. Better understanding of the issues, and better understanding of the cultural riches of the First Australians, will contribute to the intergenerational change of which people such as Megan Davis, Noel Pearson, Stan Grant, Mark McKenna, Bruce Pascoe, Bill Gammage and so many other Australians are a part. Their intellectual contributions explain the growing impatience with the resistance by governments to righting the fundamental injustice of excluding First Australians and our ancient legacy from the idea of the nation.

Noel Pearson, in his essay 'A Rightful Place', written in 2014, refers to this predicament as 'fragmentation': it is the legacy of settler colonialism that created similar grievances around the world, capturing Indigenous peoples in the imperial grasp and denying their right to exist. Pearson states that there are 'four focuses of grievance: identity as a people; the territorial lands of a people; language; and culture. Peoples hold hard to these four things'. He asks the crucial question: 'So the problem of the world is: how do 10,000 distinct peoples live well and prosper – and get along with each other – within 200 nation-states?'[107]

Two events in 2020 made us aware of the fragility of our existence, the Black Lives Matter movement and the COVID-19 pandemic. The implications of these events will be long-lasting and the changes to our ways of life –and what we have taken to be 'normality' – will be profound.

Black Lives Matter

Throughout the first half of 2020, as people chanted 'Black Lives Matter' across the world in protest at the killing of George Floyd and too many others, *Guardian Australia* conducted a study of Aboriginal deaths in custody in Australia. After reading 589 coronial reports, the team at *Guardian Australia* found a record of systemic failure and neglect and reported on a number of key issues that are too often ignored by police and the criminal justice system. There are too many myths about trends in death and incarceration rates and how Aboriginal people in custody are treated both by the police who charge them and when they are in custody, whether in police custody or in a correctional facility:

The key finding of the royal commission was that Aboriginal people are more likely to die in custody because they are arrested

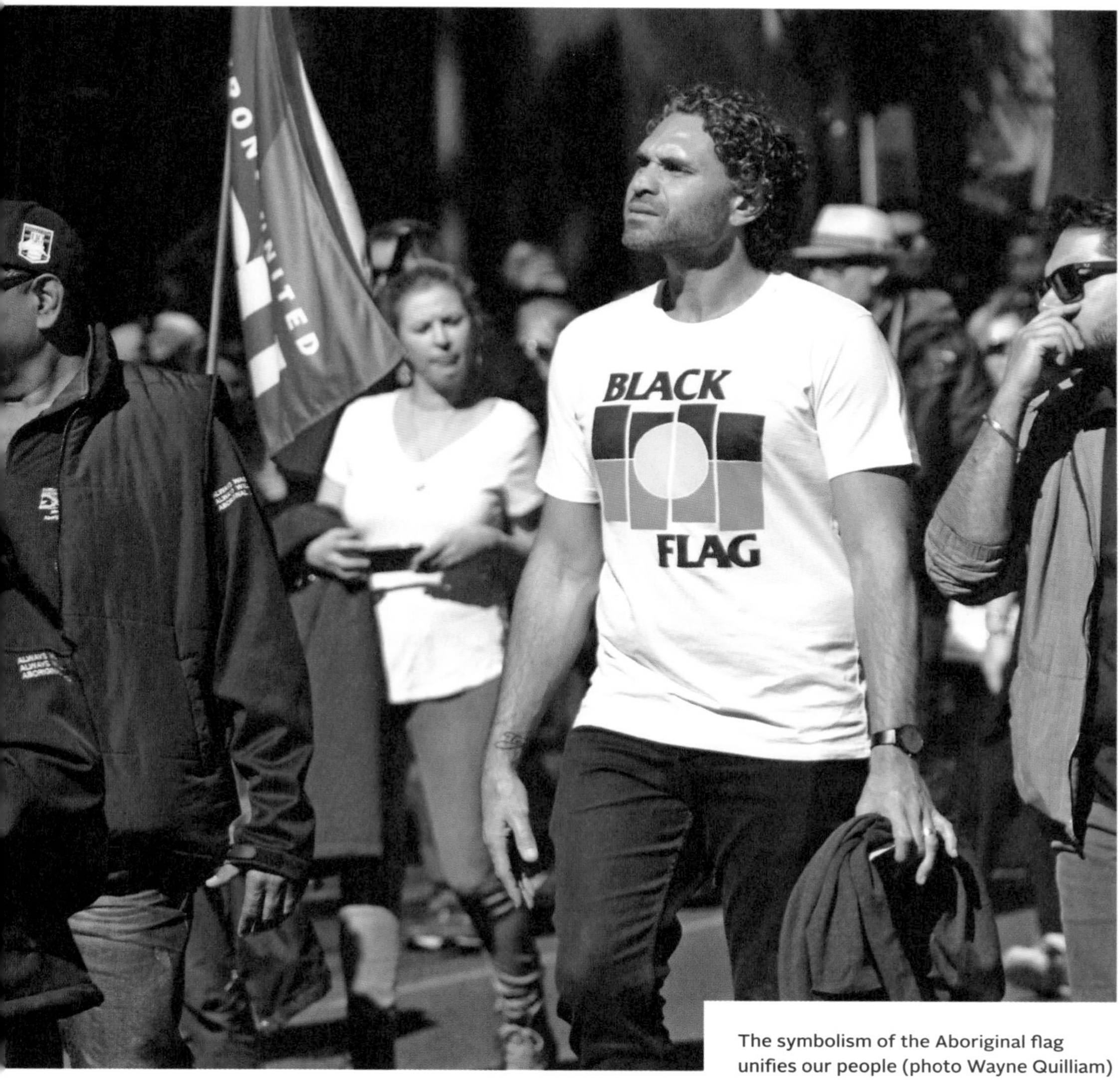

The symbolism of the Aboriginal flag unifies our people (photo Wayne Quilliam)

and jailed at disproportionate rates. That remains as true in 2020 as it was in 1991.

In 1991, 14.3% of the male prison population in Australia was Indigenous. In March 2020 it was 28.6%. And, according to data released by the Australian Bureau of Statistics this month, 4.7% of all Indigenous men are in jail compared with just 0.3% of all non-Indigenous men.[108]

After the primary recommendation of the Royal Commission into Aboriginal Deaths in Custody that investigated ninety-nine cases from 1989 to 1990 – that incarceration (or arrest and imprisonment) of Aboriginal and Torres Strait Islander people should be a last resort, the key recommendation pertained to the principle and implementation of duty of care by all involved in the criminal justice system, from police to correctional service officers. We can see from the evidence unearthed by the *Guardian Australia* team that the failure of police and correctional service officers to exercise duty of care remains the primary contributing factor to Aboriginal deaths in custody. No police officer or correctional services officer involved in these Aboriginal deaths in custody has been convicted of a crime and none has been held responsible. The situation gets worse because of an intransigent culture of blaming Aboriginal people when every Australian should be entitled to be released from custody or prison alive. Non-Indigenous people die in custody too, but the disproportionate rates of arrest and imprisonment – the result of racism and discrimination – make Aboriginal people particularly at risk, especially given their underlying health conditions. There has been no justice, no prosecutions, just a cold silence from the authorities. Until the Black Lives Matters movement, only their families, volunteers with the Change the Record campaign, a few journalists and a very small number of people holding vigils have brought these matters to our attention. These deaths are the tip of the iceberg. Most others have passed without any public attention or anything like justice.

Aboriginal women are also being increasingly arrested, held in remand and imprisoned and are dying in custody. There are too many cases of Aboriginal women who have died in police custody to recount here. Their lives were cut short by violence compounded by what seems to be a contempt for Aboriginal women that can pass for normal and acceptable across all classes and cultures in Australia.

There have been several harrowing cases in recent times, and among them the death of Tanya Day in a police cell in Victoria is notable because while there was no justice for her family, their campaign for the decriminalisation of public drunkenness was successful, thirty years after the Royal Commission into Aboriginal Deaths in Custody made this recommendation.[109] Among the coroner's findings, summarised by the Human Rights Law Centre, were these:

The Coroner found that the decision-making process of the V/Line train conductor – who formed the view that Ms Day was 'unruly' and organised for the police to attend the train station – was influenced by Ms Day's Aboriginality and the train conductor's unconscious bias. This was in part because Ms Day was the first sleeping passenger ever removed from a train by that V/Line train conductor.

Treatment by Victoria Police

The Coroner found that the decision of the police to arrest Ms Day was not influenced by her Aboriginality … The findings of the Coroner did, however, detail a 'culture of complacency regarding intoxicated detainees' within Victoria Police and found that there is a systemic failure to recognise the medical dangers of intoxication and comply with the mandatory terms of the governing policy and procedures regarding the management of persons in care or custody. This shows 'the power of stereotype and its resistance to correction'.

The Coroner also found that the physical checks conducted by the police on Ms Day were 'illusory' and that the police officers did not take proper care of Ms Day's safety, security, health and welfare as required by the Victoria Police Manual and the Standard Operating Procedures.

The Coroner notes that if the physical checks had been done by the police in accordance with the relevant requirements, Ms Day would have been checked 10 minutes after her fall.

The Leading Senior Constable was found by the Coroner not to be a credible witness and the findings noted that the accuracy of his custody module entries (regarding the observation and monitoring of Ms Day) are concerning.

The Victorian Charter of Human Rights and Responsibilities Act 2006 *is relevant to how police carry out their duties, including 'ensuring appropriate monitoring and supervision of people in detention and providing appropriate medical care'. The Coroner made a finding that Ms Day was 'not treated with humanity and respect for the inherent dignity of a human person as required by the Charter'.*

Top: Traditional clapsticks held high during a NAIDOC March on the steps of Parliament House, Melbourne (photo Wayne Quilliam)

Above: Aunty Tanya Day

This is why the Black Lives Matter movement is important. That Aboriginal and Torres Strait Islander people should be 'treated with humanity and respect for the inherent dignity of a human person' by police and the criminal justice system needs to stated repeatedly to remind the authorities that their actions that lead to the deaths of our people are not acceptable. The Human Rights Law Centre also reports that 'the Coroner did find that the totality of the evidence supported a belief that an indictable offence may have been committed. Accordingly, the Coroner directed that the Director of Public Prosecutions be notified.'[110] The Director of Public Prosecutions, however, decided not to prosecute the two police officers and did not provide any reasons for this decision.

Throughout the inquest, the Day family had submitted that an offence of negligent manslaughter may have been committed by the Sergeant and Leading Senior Constable involved in Ms Day's death, who the Coroner found failed to monitor and observe Ms Day in accordance with the relevant guidelines.[111]

This is a rare case of a coronial inquiry into a death in custody resulting in an acknowledgement of our humanity and right to be treated with dignity and in accordance with the laws of this country.

At the very least, the recommendations of the Royal Commission tabled in the federal Parliament 30 years ago should be implemented to avoid deaths such as Ms Tanya Day's:

That Governments must ensure that:

a. Police Services, Corrective Services, and authorities in charge of juvenile centres recognise that they owe a legal duty of care to persons in their custody;

b. That the standing instructions to the officers of these authorities specify that each officer involved in the arrest, incarceration or supervision of a person in custody has a legal duty of care to that person, and may be held legally responsible for the death or injury of the person caused or contributed to by a breach of that duty; and

c. That these authorities ensure that such officers are aware of their responsibilities and trained appropriately to meet them, both on recruitment and during their service.[112]

There are many different ways of coming to an understanding of Aboriginal and Torres Strait Islander cultures and histories. This book presents just a few. The understanding might one day lead to justice – justice for the First peoples whose polities have been suppressed and whose right to exist and be acknowledged is one of the outstanding challenges that Australians must eventually face.

16 GLOSSARY

A comprehensive glossary of terms that apply to Australian Indigenous people, events, laws and practices is available online at the Agreements, Treaties and Negotiated Settlements Project website.

AIATSIS map

A tool often used for teaching about Aboriginal and Torres Strait Islander languages is the Australian Institute of Aboriginal and Torres Strait Islander Studies (AIATSIS) map of Indigenous Australia (see pages 46–47). The map will give you an idea of the many languages that are spoken in Australia, although, for some of the language names on the map, the spellings now widely adopted do vary. As the AIATSIS website notes:

The map is an attempt to represent all the language, tribal or nation groups of the Indigenous peoples of Australia. Aboriginal and Torres Strait Islander groups were included on the map based on the published resources available between 1988 and 1994 which determine the cultural, language and trade boundaries and relationships between groups.

The map was created by David Horton and is based on data collected by AIATSIS, Aboriginal Studies Press and others. The team at AIATSIS also produced *The Encyclopaedia of Aboriginal Australia: Aboriginal and Torres Strait Islander history, society and culture*. I recommend it as a resource if you want to read more about Aboriginal Australia.

You can hear one of our First languages being spoken through various online language resources. One such resource is Arrernte language online (arrernte-angkentye.online/ECALL.html?v=1.3). Another important language resource is the online compilation of language varieties by First Languages Australia on the website gambay.com.au. This is a living archive with an interactive map to which language speakers contribute new materials in many formats, including audio and video, regularly. One that I follow is the 50 Words project of the Research Unit for Indigenous Languages at the University of Melbourne (https://50words.online). This is a resource for students and teachers to learn 50 words in the local languages, and for the general public to discover the diversity of languages around Australia.

AUSTLANG

The AIATSIS website also provides AUSTLANG. AUSTLANG is an online, interactive language resource developed at AIATSIS. On the website, it is explained:

AUSTLANG provides a vocabulary of persistent identifiers, a thesaurus of languages and peoples and information about Aboriginal and Torres Strait Islander languages which has been assembled from referenced sources.

The alpha-numeric codes function as persistent identifiers, followed by a 'string of changeable text'. This allows changes to the name or spelling of a language variety, according to community preference. In cases where there is more than one preference, two or three versions of the name are included, e.g. E6: Dhanggati / Dunghutti^.

This vocabulary of persistent identifiers supports archives, libraries, galleries and other agencies to identify materials or projects in or about Indigenous Australian languages and peoples, without the confusion of a multitude of language names and spellings. The codes maintain an identity if a change is made to the spelling or the name.

AUSTLANG can be searched with language names (including a range of spellings); the codes, for example E6: (note inclusion of the colon); placenames and via the map. AUSTLANG has links to MURA the AIATSIS catalogue and other online resources.

Pathways

AIATSIS also provides a search engine called the Pathways thesauri for Australian place names, Indigenous language groups and subject relating to Aboriginal and Torres Strait Islander studies.

Terms for Aboriginal and Torres Strait Islander people

Aboriginal

People who have cultural and ancestral lineage from mainland Australia (including Tasmania) preceding colonisation by the British.

Also defined, for legal and technical reasons, as a person 'who is a member of the Aboriginal race of Australia, identifies as an Aboriginal and is accepted by their identified Aboriginal community as Aboriginal'.

Aboriginal people, Torres Strait Islander people, Indigenous people, First Australians, First Nations people, First people

These terms are all generally acceptable when referring to Australia's original inhabitants. In international law, the term 'indigenous' refers to those peoples who predate colonising peoples. While the term 'Indigenous' is widely accepted in Australia, some would prefer, for personal reasons, that other terms are used.

Aboriginal Tent Embassy

The Aboriginal Tent Embassy was established in 1972 in front of Parliament House in Canberra as part of the land rights protest movement. It is still established as a permanent protest site.

acknowledgement of Country

Any person – Indigenous and non-Indigenous – can acknowledge the Traditional Owners of the land at the start of a speech or an event. This is considered to be a sign of respect.

ancestors

For Indigenous people, the term 'ancestors' has two meanings. Firstly, it can refer to the ancestral beings who created every aspect of the landscape, and the laws by which people still live (see 'Dreaming'). Secondly, it can also refer to any deceased person(s) from whom an individual or group is descended. In Aboriginal culture, it is expected that ancestors are treated with reverence, just as Elders are revered.

ancestral

When a place, natural phenomena, spiritual being, word or thing is regarded as being made by or inherited from an ancestor or ancestors. See also 'songlines', 'Tjukurrpa' and 'Dreaming'.

anthropologist

A person who studies human behaviour and social structures. Historically, some anthropologists in Australia, the colonial anthropologists and some in the twentieth century, misrepresented Aboriginal cultures, people and communities in ways that have caused immense harm and contributed to racist beliefs about Aboriginal people. A. P. Elkin's contribution to eugenicist and assimilationist policies, building on the work of physical anthropologists such as Norman B. Tindale, is a case in point. Most Australian anthropologists today are bound by ethical guidelines if they work at universities or receive research funding and engage with the communities they study in an ethical way.

assimilation

A policy implemented by the Australian state and territory governments between the 1920s and late 1960s that aimed to integrate Aboriginal people into white Australia, by removing children from their families and confining people considered to be 'full blood' to Aboriginal reserves or under the control of 'native superintendents' in order to achieve 'racial purity', and with the intention of eradicating Aboriginal people and culture in the belief that the 'race' was 'dying out'. The policy was described at the time as 'smoothing the pillow of the dying race'.[113] This policy was couched in terms of concern for Aboriginal people's welfare. See also 'Stolen Generations'.

cleverman

A Kriol term meaning traditional healer, doctor or spiritual healer.

See also 'Kriol', 'marrnggitj' and 'ngangkaṟi'.

Country

'Country' is an Aboriginal Kriol (Creole) term that refers to the traditional estate of an Aboriginal group or clan. This may mean a specific area inherited from ancestors and belonging to a descent-based group of people, or a larger, more general region from which that person's ancestors originate. It may also be referred to as 'place'. See also 'Kriol'.

culture

The term 'culture' is used in many different ways. In the context of Indigenous people, it refers to the collective social, economic and artistic manifestations of the society, and encompasses their ideas, customs, languages and the distinctive material expressions of their society.

Dreaming

'Dreaming' (also 'dreamtime') is a term devised by anthropologists Francis Gillen and Baldwin Spencer to describe the religio-cultural worldview of the Central Australian Aboriginal people they studied. 'Dreaming' is not a direct translation of an Aboriginal word. The English language does not have an equivalent to express these complex Aboriginal spiritual concepts.

The term 'Dreaming' has become popular in the English language for a key religious concept, but there are others and they vary across the continent among the hundreds of Aboriginal and Torres Strait Islander societies. There are many different words across Australia that describe Aboriginal spirituality and beliefs, such as 'altjeringa' (Arrernte people, Central Australia), 'wongar' (north-east Arnhem Land) and 'bugari' (Broome, northern Western Australia).

In *The Aranda's Pepa*, Anna Kenny describes 'Dreaming' as a body of sacred laws and narratives that reveal 'how the landscape was created and imbued with meaning by ancestral beings' and how 'this landscape represents ancestral connections to the land and the mythical beings that created it'. The stories of these ancestral beings are passed down through singing, dancing, painting and teaching songlines. See also 'Tjukurrpa' and 'songlines'.

Elder

Elders are Indigenous people who are held in high esteem and have a position of authority within their community. In Aboriginal society, generally the older a person is, the more respect and authority they have because knowledge is passed down to each generation in a gradual way, often at ceremonies. As a sign of respect, Elders are usually addressed as 'Uncle' or 'Aunty'. Elders don't necessarily have to be old, but they must have earned that title as a result of their knowledge of culture and/or contribution to their community.

freehold title

This is the most complete form of property ownership in Australia. The land holder (owner) owns the land in perpetuity. It allows the land holder to deal with the land including selling, leasing, licensing or mortgaging the land, subject to compliance with applicable laws such as planning and environment laws. Freehold title is referred to as Torrens title by lawyers. Torrens is the mechanism used in all Australian states and territories to record who owns which land.

gurrutu

A concept at the heart of the Yolŋu social system and system of governance. It can be described as the complex networks of kinship that link individuals and groups to each other.

indentured

An 'indenture' is a legal contract that binds someone to another person in order to pay a debt or purchase obligation. An indentured servant or indentured labourer is a worker within a system of exploitative (often forced) labour. The worker is bound by a signed or forced contract to work for a fixed time.

Indigenous Australian

In the 1980s the Commonwealth Department of Aboriginal Affairs defined an Indigenous Australian as 'a person of Aboriginal or Torres Strait Islander descent who identifies as Aboriginal or Torres Strait Islander and is accepted as such by the community in which he or she lives'. The capital 'I' specifically refers to Aboriginal and Torres Strait Islander people from Australia, as opposed to indigenous people of other nations.

Indigenous Land Use Agreement

According to the National Native Title Tribunal website, an ILUA 'is a voluntary agreement between a native title group and others about the use of land and waters. These agreements allow people to negotiate flexible, pragmatic agreements to suit their particular circumstances.'

kinship

The Indigenous kinship system is a complex social system that determines how people relate to each other, and determines their roles, responsibilities and obligations in relation to one another and Country. This feature of social organisation and family relationships exists in various forms across Australia. See also 'moiety', 'totem' and 'skin name'.

knowledge

Aboriginal and Torres Strait Islander knowledge systems are among thousands of indigenous knowledge systems in the world. They share common characteristics and are protected under international law in the Convention on Biological Diversity at Article 8 (j). UNESCO provides a useful description of indigenous knowledge systems:

Local and indigenous knowledge refers to the understandings, skills and philosophies developed by societies with long histories of interaction with their natural surroundings. For rural and indigenous peoples, local knowledge informs decision-making about fundamental aspects of day-to-day life. This knowledge is integral to a cultural complex that also encompasses language, systems of classification, resource use practices, social interactions, ritual and spirituality.

Often, the term 'knowledges' is used to reflect this great diversity and an initial capital is used in technical terms such as Traditional Ecological Knowledge (TEK) and Traditional Environmental Knowledge (TEK).

Kriol

Kriol is a modern, post-contact Aboriginal language, spoken widely across northern Australia. Linguists class Kriol as a 'creole' language, which is a language typically born out of colonisation. Creole languages are largely derived from the dominant language (such as French, English, Portuguese or Spanish), but speakers of creole languages adapt and innovate upon the dominant language to such an extent that they create a separate dialect. Kriol is the second most common language in the Northern Territory.

land rights and Native Title

These are legal concepts that developed with the advent of human rights law in Australia. They mean different things in law, but both refer to legal recognition of Aboriginal rights to land. Land rights laws usually grant title to Aboriginal groups to be held in trust. See also 'Native Title'.

Indigenous languages

Estimates differ, but the consensus is that before colonisation there were between 250 and 500 Indigenous languages in Australia. These languages are often based on connections to Country, with specific words to describe weather patterns in the particular region (see also 'seasons'). Unfortunately, Australia can also lay claim to being a nation with one of the highest number of lost languages. Today, only about 120 languages are still spoken and often only by a handful of people that may include non-Indigenous linguists.

language group

A 'language group' is the community of speakers of a language. The primary members speak the language as a 'mother tongue' or home language. Many speakers of Indigenous languages are multilingual, that is, speaking more than one Aboriginal and/or Torres Strait Islander language.

lore

The term 'lore' is an Aboriginal Kriol term that stands in place of expressions in Indigenous languages that cannot be properly explained in English. Lore encompasses the religious, spiritual and practical laws that Indigenous people observe in their own cultures. See also 'Tjukurrpa'.

makarrata

A Yolŋu word meaning a coming together after a struggle, facing the facts of wrongs and negotiating peace. The term has been used as an alternative name for a treaty process in Australia, notably in the Uluṟu Statement from the Heart.

manikay

A Yolŋu word meaning 'songs', in particular, public clan songs accompanied by clapsticks and yiḏaki.

marrnggitj

The Yolŋu word for doctor. 'Marrnggitj' are traditional healers who diagnose and treat complaints, and advise on physical and spiritual wellbeing. Marrnggitj have a deep knowledge of Yolŋu medicines based mainly on native plants and ancient techniques. See also 'ngangkaṟi'.

midden

Shell middens are places where the debris from eating shellfish and other food has accumulated over time. Shell middens are studied by archaeologists to find out about Indigenous activities in the past.

missionary/mission

A 'missionary' is a person who is sent to another place, usually to 'spread the word of God' or convert people to the Christian religion ('mission' relates to the vocation or calling of a religious organisation). In Australia, when First peoples were forcibly removed from their land, they were often sent to missions which had been established in cooperation with the government. Missions were also notoriously often brutal places for Indigenous people, who were often punished for practising their culture or speaking their languages.

moiety

A Latin word meaning one of two equal parts. The term is used to describe how the Indigenous kinship system is organised into groupings. The word has been used in Australia by anthropologists to describe the first level of the Aboriginal kinship system, which divides everything including people, plants, animals and the environment into two halves. Each half is a mirror of the other, and to understand the whole universe these two halves must come together. Each Aboriginal nation has its own term for their moiety. For example, the Yolŋu moieties in north-east Arnhem Land are called Dhuwa and Yirritja. See also 'kinship'.

NAIDOC

An acronym for the National Aborigines and Islanders Day Observance Committee. NAIDOC Week celebrations are held across Australia each year between the first Sunday in July until the following Sunday. NAIDOC Week celebrates the history, culture and achievements of Aboriginal and Torres Strait Islander peoples.

Native Title

Native Title is the legal doctrine that includes the recognition of Aboriginal and Torres Strait Islander rights to land and water. The *Native Title Act 1993* (Cth) requires these rights to be based on proof of an Indigenous group's traditions of owning specific land before colonisation, and for this land custodianship to have been inherited from forebears according to local descent principles. Native Title rights have been recognised in limited circumstances, such as when no other title has been issued by an Australian government or colony.

ngangkaṟi

The Pitjantjatjara word for doctor. The 'ngangkaṟi' are traditional healers who, according to the Ngaanyatjarra Pitjantjatjara Yankunytjatjara Women's Council, for thousands of years 'have nurtured the physical, emotional and social wellbeing of their people. These traditional healers are esteemed for their unique ability to protect and heal both individuals and communities from harm'. See also 'marrnggitj'.

non-Indigenous

By definition, non-Indigenous Australians are those people who cannot be defined as Aboriginal or Torres Strait Islander because they are not descended from an Aboriginal or Torres Strait Islander ancestor.

old people

A Kriol term for 'ancestors' generally referring to First peoples who lived in traditional ways prior to colonisation. See also 'Kriol'.

oral histories

Oral traditions and oral histories in Aboriginal and Torres Strait Islander families and communities are the records of their peoples, and they should be regarded as a significant part of Australian history.

Reconciliation Place

An urban landscape located in Canberra that contains a number of public artworks. This symbolic area recognises the importance of understanding the shared history of Indigenous and non-Indigenous Australians.

referendum

A direct vote in which an entire electorate is invited to vote on a particular proposal. The Australian Constitution can only be changed by referendum. Section 128 of the Constitution sets out certain rules that must be followed in order for a change to be approved. There have been forty-four referendums held since 1901 and only eight of these have been successful.

republican

In the Australian context, this term refers to a person who supports constitutional change to remove the British monarchy as Australia's head of state.

seasons

Seasonal calendars and seasons vary in different Aboriginal and Torres Strait Islander communities due to the specific land and weather patterns in the region. Most Indigenous seasonal calendars have three large seasons with two or three sub-seasons, or six seasons.

segregation

This word generally refers to racial segregation – the formal or informal separation of a population on the basis of race and/or skin colour. It is usually just one part of a system of racial oppression. It is well known that this occurred in the US; however, Australia's 'White Australia Policy' that led to the Stolen Generations is also an example of segregation. Charlie Perkins famously campaigned against this in his 1965 Freedom Ride.

skin name

Indigenous people are given 'skin names' that determine where they fit within the kinship system. See also 'kinship'.

social order

Social order is a concept used in anthropology and sociology that refers to the way various social structures or behaviours create or maintain a society.

song series or songlines

A 'song series' is a body of songs that are sung sequentially or in repetitive groups, or in repetition by authorised Indigenous singers. These songs are intended to convey a sacred narrative. The term 'songlines' comes from the title of the popular travelogue by British writer Bruce Chatwin.

Stolen Generations

Refers to Indigenous children who, under various Australian federal and state government policies, were forcibly removed from their families. These policies were implemented between approximately 1905 and 1967, but continued illegally into the 1970s. These policies were justified by the now discredited pseudo-science of eugenics, which assumed the superiority of white people over all other races. It was believed that children referred to as 'half-caste', 'quarter-caste' and 'quadroon' had enough European lineage to be assimilated into white Australian society, thus 'breeding out' Indigenous people from Australia. On 13 February 2008, then prime minister Kevin Rudd issued a formal apology to the Stolen Generations.

terra nullius

A Latin term which translates literally as 'land belonging to nobody'. When Captain Arthur Phillip claimed the continent of Australia for the British Crown in 1788, he did so on the basis of this doctrine. This act was a denial of the (approximately) one million Indigenous people who inhabited the continent, as well as their cultures, customs and tenure of the land. Terra nullius was used for over 200 years to justify the dispossession of Indigenous people. In 1993, the High Court of Australia overturned the doctrine of terra nullius in the case of *Mabo (No. 2)*, which granted the people of Meriam Island (in the Torres Straits) rights 'as against the whole world to possession, occupation, use and enjoyment of the lands of the Murray Islands'. This decision paved the way for the Native Title Act to be passed.

Tjukurrpa

The Pitjantjatjara word which describes their sacred narratives and law. Tjukurrpa refers to a way of seeing and understanding the world in which Country, places, objects, songs and stories embody sacred power and knowledge. Most Australians would know this as the 'Dreamtime', but that term was invented by British explorers and does not properly capture the Aboriginal religio-cultural worldview.

Torres Strait Islander

People who have cultural and ancestral lineage from the Torres Strait Islands preceding colonisation by the British. Torres Strait Islanders were often defined in the same terms as 'Aboriginal' people and included under the legal definitions of 'Aboriginal', even though they comprise a different cultural, linguistic and ethnic group.

totem

In the Australian Indigenous context, many people use this term to refer to those revered spiritual ancestors that manifest themselves in non-human forms. Depicted in sacred traditional designs, they are the emblems of particular clans or other social forms. Totems often appear in contemporary visual art, although traditionally they were depicted in rock art and ceremonial body painting and objects. The word is a version of 'doodem' borrowed from Ojibwa, an Algonquian language spoken by a native American people from the regions around Lake Superior. Anthropologists use the term to refer to the sacred emblems in 'animistic' societies, but the common use by Indigenous people worldwide refers to ancestral spiritual beings.

traditional

In Aboriginal and Torres Strait Islander cultures, traditional practices have been passed down through generations and form an important part of their identity. Traditions are adapted to changing circumstances in all societies, and Aboriginal and Torres Strait Islander people also adapt their traditions to ensure their survival in the modern world.

Traditional Owner(s)

Indigenous people or persons who, as a result of their ancestral heritage, cultural ties and/or customary laws, have authority and custodial obligations over a particular area of land and/or clan group.

Wangarr

The Yolŋu term for 'Dreaming'. It refers to both the ancestral past as well the ancestral beings themselves.

Wanjina/Wandjina

To Aboriginal people in the Kimberly region, 'Wanjina' is the supreme creator and a symbol of fertility and rain. Aboriginal people in the Kimberly have been painting Wanjina (also spelled 'Wandjina') in rock art sites for millennia.

Welcome to Country

This is a custom among many Indigenous groups to ensure the safe passage of visitors through their Country. It is now extended to include Traditional Owners giving a welcome at the start of a speech or an event.

yiḏaki

The Yolŋu word for the long wooden wind instrument more commonly known as the 'didgeridoo'. The word 'didgeridoo' is thought to be an onomatopoetic word invented by English settlers, describing the instrument's unique resonances. There are numerous names for the instrument among the First peoples of northern Australia. Yolŋu customs require that only men play the yiḏaki.

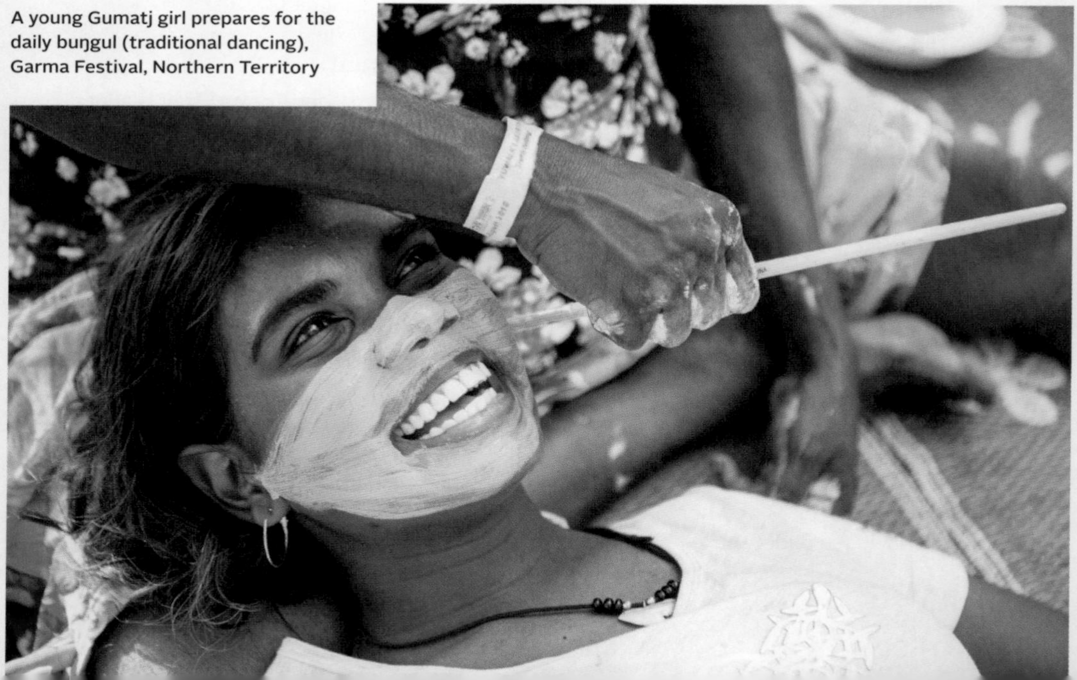

A young Gumatj girl prepares for the daily buŋgul (traditional dancing), Garma Festival, Northern Territory

17 ENDNOTES

1 See, for instance, Nancy Williams, *A Boundary is to Cross*, Routledge, 1982; Nancy Williams, *Intellectual Property and Aboriginal Environmental Knowledge*, Centre for Indigenous Natural and Cultural Resource Management, 1988; Nancy Williams, *The Yolŋu and Their Land*, Stanford University Press, 1986; Nancy Williams, *Two Laws*, Australian Institute of Aboriginal Studies, 1987; Nancy Williams and Eugene Hunn, *Resource Managers*, Westview Press, 1982; Nancy Williams and Graham Baines, *Traditional Ecological Knowledge*, Centre for Resource and Environmental Studies, ANU, 1993; Janice Reid, *Sorcerers and Healing Spirits*, ANU Press, 1983.

2 Damien Finch et al., 'Ages for Australia's Oldest Rock Paintings', *Nature Human Behaviour* 5, 2021, 310–18.

3 Joint Standing Committee on Northern Australia, *Never Again*, Commonwealth of Australia, December 2020: aph.gov.au/Parliamentary_Business/Committees/Joint/Northern_Australia/CavesatJuukanGorge

4 Bill Gammage, *The Greatest Estate on Earth*, Allen & Unwin, Sydney, 2011.

5 Patrick Nunn & Nicholas Reid, 'Aboriginal memories of inundation of the Australian coast dating from more than 7000 years ago', *Australian Geographer*, 47:1, 2015, 11–47.

6 ibid.

7 UNESCO, World Heritage List, 'Budj Bim Cultural Landscape: Description': whc.unesco.org/en/list/1577/

8 Colin Barras, 'Is an Aboriginal tale of an ancient volcano the oldest story ever told?' *Science*, 11 February 2020: www.sciencemag.org/news/2020/02/aboriginal-tale-ancient-volcano-oldest-story-ever-told

9 Gunditj Mirring Traditional Owners Corporation, *Budj Bim Master Plan*: gunditjmirring.com/budj-bim-master-plan

10 Ian J. McNiven, 'The detective work behind the Budj Bim eels traps World Heritage Bid', *The Conversation*, 8 February 2017: theconversation.com/the-detective-work-behind-the-budj-bim-eel-traps-world-heritage-bid-71800

11 ibid.

12 Rosita Holmes and Leah Umbagai, 'Wandjinas, ochre and the art of Mowanjum people', Japingka Aboriginal Art: japingkaaboriginalart.com/articles/wandjinas-ochre-and-the-art-of-mowanjum-people/

13 Tasmanian Department of Primary Industries, Parks, Water and Environment, *Tasmanian Coastal Works Manual*, chapter 5: dpipwe.tas.gov.au/Documents/Tasmanian_Coastal_Works_Manual_Chapter_5_Aboriginal_Heritage_Management.pdf

14 Letitia Murgha, 'Indigenous science: shell middens and fish traps', Queensland Museum, 8 October 2012: qmtalksscience.wordpress.com/2012/10/08/indigenous-science-shell-middens-and-fish-traps/

15 Lyndall Ryan et al., 'Colonial Frontier Massacres in Australia, 1788–1930', The Centre for 21st Century Humanities, The University of Newcastle: c21ch.newcastle.edu.au/colonialmassacres/

16 ibid.

17 Charles Dunford Rowley, *A Matter of Justice*, Australian National University Press, 1978.

18 Human Rights and Equal Opportunity Commission, *The CDEP Scheme and Racial Discrimination*,

A Report by the Race Discrimination Commissioner, December 1997.

19 Further information can be found in the history and timeline of the gay rights movement by Arisa White, 'From midnight raids to same-sex marriage: what's changed in the 50 years since Stonewall': refinery29.com/en-us/lgbt-gay-rights-movement-history-timeline; and Erika W. Smith, 'From Stonewall to Pride 50: the history of the Pride Parade': refinery29.com/en-us/when-was-first-gay-pride-parade-origin

20 To find out more, see: mardigras.org.au, and mardigras.org.au/mardi-gras-parade-2019, and especially see the AGM and annual report at mardigras.org.au/agm; further history of the Evolution of the Mardi Gras can be read in the 2018 annual report of Sydney Gay and Lesbian Mardi Gras Ltd, which also celebrates the 40th anniversary: mardigras.org.au/images/uploads/images/mg19-annual-report-final-artwork-v3-web.pdf

21 State Library of Queensland, 'Aboriginal and Torres Strait Islander languages': www.slq.qld.gov.au/discover/aboriginal-and-torres-strait-islander-cultures-and-stories/languages

22 Ngaanyatjarra Pitjantjatjara Yankunytjatjara Women's Council, 'Ngangkari – Traditional Healers': www.npywc.org.au/what-we-do/ngangkari-traditional-healers/

23 Aaron Corn & Joseph N. Gumbula, 'Rom and the academy repositioned: binary models in YolÐu intellectual traditions and their application to wider inter-cultural dialogues' in L Russell (ed.), *Boundary Writing*, University of Hawai'i Press, 2006, pp. 170–179.

24 Aaron Corn, 'Dreamtime wisdom, modern-time vision,' PhD thesis, The University of Melbourne, 2003, vol. I, p. 219.

25 Corn, 'Dreamtime wisdom,' vol. II, pp. 148–50.

26 Gammage.

27 Bruce Pascoe, *Dark Emu*, Magabala Books, 2014.

28 Pascoe.

29 Ian Keen, 'Foragers or farmers: *Dark Emu* and the controversy over *Aboriginal agriculture*', Anthropological Forum, 31:1, 2021, 106–28.

30 James Boyce, *Imperial Mud: The Fight for the Fens*, Icon Books, 2021.

31 The map is available at: naturaldisaster.royalcommission.gov.au/submissions/summary-submissions

32 John C. Z. Woinarski, et al., 'Ongoing unraveling of a continental fauna: Decline and extinction of Australian mammals since European settlement', in *Proceedings of the National Academy of Sciences*, 112(15), April 2015, 4531–4540: pnas.org/content/pnas/112/15/4531.full.pdf

33 ibid.

34 ibid.

35 Submission to the Royal Commission into National Natural Disaster Arrangements by a collective of Indigenous and non-Indigenous academics primarily from the University of Melbourne, but also from Deakin University and Griffith University: indigenousknowledge.unimelb.edu.au/news/our-submissions-into-the-black-summer-bush-fire-inquiries/full-submission-to-the-royal-commission-into-national-natural-disaster-arrangements2

36 James Boyce, The Biggest Estate on Earth' by Bill Gammage, *The Monthly*, January 2012: www.themonthly.com.au/issue/2011/december/1322699456/james-boyce/biggest-estate-earth-how-aborigines-made-australia-bill-g

37 Victor Steffensen, *Fire Country*, Hardie Grant, 2020.

38 ibid.

39 D. W. Hamacher, et al., 'Solstice and solar position observations in Australian Aboriginal and Torres Strait Islander traditions', *Journal of Astronomical History and Heritage*, 23(1), 2020, 89Ð99.

40 ibid.

41 ibid.

42 Janice Reid (ed.), 1982. *Body, Land and Spirit*, UQP, 1982.

43 J. Bach, 'Dampier, William (1651–1715)', *Australian Dictionary of Biography*: https://adb.anu.edu.au/biography/dampier-william-1951

44 *Saltwater: Yirrkala Bark Paintings of Sea Country: Recognising Indigenous Sea Rights*, Buku-LarrÐay Mulka Centre in association with Jennifer Isaacs Publishing, 1999.

45 Kate Hagan, 'And this is the Libertos, who thought they'd get away with it', *The Age*, 3 November 2007: www.theage.com.au/national/

and-this-is-the-libertos-who-thought-theyd-get-away-with-it-20071103-ge67mm.html

46 Terri Janke and Maiko Sentina, *Indigenous Knowledge: Issues for Protection and Management*, IP Australia, Commonwealth of Australia, 2018: www.ipaustralia.gov.au/sites/default/files/ipaust_ikdiscussionpaper_28march2018.pdf

47 See Brook Andrew's website biography: brookandrew.com/bio/

48 ANKA, 'How to buy ethically': www.anka.org.au/art-centres/buy-ethically/

49 Indigenous Art Code, 'How to buy ethically': indigenousartcode.org/how-to-buy-ethically/

50 See Aaron Corn, *Reflections and Voices: Exploring the Music of Yothu Yindi with Mandawuy Yunupiŋu*, Sydney University Press, 2009.

51 The National Recording Project for Indigenous Performance in Australia, 'Garma Statement on Indigenous Music and Dance': www.aboriginalartists.com.au/NRP_statement.htm

52 Declan Byrne, 'Bars behind bars: how jail and motherhood forced rising rapper Barkaa to turn life around', *triple j*, 10 November 2020: www.abc.net.au/triplej/news/musicnews/bars-behind-bars:-how-having-a-child-in-jail-forced-rising-rapp/12866456

53 Al Newstead, 'Ziggy Ramo's update of a Paul Kelly classic is a history lesson every Australian should hear', *triple j*, 31 May 2021: www.abc.net.au/triplej/news/musicnews/ziggy-ramo-paul-kelly-little-things-every-australian-should-hear/13366924

54 Stephen Page is quoted in Fiona Magowan, 'Dancing with a difference: reconfiguring the poetic politics of Aboriginal Ritual as a national spectacle', *The Australian Journal of Anthropology*, 11:3, 2000, 1–14.

55 Nathan Sentance, 'My ancestors are in our memory institutions, but their voices are missing', *IndigenousX* on *The Guardian*, 6 March 2018: www.theguardian.com/commentisfree/2018/mar/06/my-ancestors-are-in-our-memory-institutions-but-their-voices-are-missing

56 Billy Griffiths, 'Reading Australia: "Legendary Tales of the Australian Aborigines" by David Unaipon', *Australian Book Review*, 31 August 2016: www.australianbookreview.com.au/reading-australia/legendary-tales-of-the-australian-aborigines-by-david-unaipon

57 Maxine Beneba Clarke, 'Author Melissa Lucashenko aims for the heart', *The Saturday Paper*, No. 235, 15–21 December 2018.

58 Eve Vincent, 'Country matters: Mullumbimby by Melissa Lucashenko', *Sydney Review of Books*, 17 May 2013: sydneyreviewofbooks.com/review/country-matters/

59 Declan Fry, '*Fire Front: First Nations Poetry and Power Today*, edited by Alison Whittaker', *Australian Book Review*, no. 423, August 2020.

60 Australian Plays Transform, 'Meyne Wyatt': australianplays.org/playwright/CP-an136

61 Art Gallery of New South Wales. Archibald Prize 2020. Archibald Packing Room Prize, accessed 5 March 2021 at: artgallery.nsw.gov.au/prizes/archibald/2020/30255/

62 Griffin Theatre Company, '*City of Gold* by Meyne Wyatt, 26 July – 31 August 2019': griffintheatre.com.au/whats-on/city-of-gold/

63 Victorian Premier's Literary Awards, '*City of Gold*': wheelercentre.com/projects/victorian-premier-s-literary-awards-2020/city-of-gold

64 ibid.

65 Meyne Wyatt, 'Monologue from *City of Gold*', *Q&A*, 9 June 2020: youtube.com/watch?v=ys2FTUmOnlg

66 Chelsea Watego, 'The irony of the Aboriginal Academic', *IndigenousX*, 20 May 2018: indigenousx.com.au/chelsea-bond-the-irony-of-the-aboriginal-academic/

67 Belinda Quinn, 'High Ground' producer Witiyana Marika: "I would like to show Australia to the world", *NME*, 27 January 2021: www.nme.com/en_au/features/film-features/high-ground-movie-producer-witiyana-marika-yothu-yindi-australia-interview-2865665

68 Xan Brooks, '*The Furnace* review – brutish western is tough as old leather and good as gold', *The Guardian*, 5 September 2020: www.theguardian.com/film/2020/sep/04/the-furnace-review-brutish-western-roderick-mackay

69 *Screenwest*, 'Acclaimed WA film *The Furnace* premieres at Perth Festival', 11 November, 2020: www.screenwest.com.au/news-and-events/latest-news/acclaimed-wa-film-furnace-premieres-perth-festival/

70 La Biennale di Venezia, 'The Furnace': www.labiennale.org/en/cinema/2020/orizzonti/furnace

71 *Northern Territory v Mr A. Griffiths (deceased) and Lorraine Jones on behalf of the Ngaliwurru and Nungali Peoples* [2019] HCA 7.

72 Human Rights and Equal Opportunity Commission, *Bringing them home: Report of the National Inquiry into the Separation of Aboriginal and Torres Strait Islander Children from Their Families*, Commonwealth of Australia, 1997: humanrights.gov.au/sites/default/files/content/pdf/social_justice/bringing_them_home_report.pdf

73 Australian Government, 'Apology to Australia's Indigenous Peoples', 13 February 2008: info.australia.gov.au/about-australia/our-country/our-people/apology-to-australias-indigenous-peoples

74 Monument Australia, 'Stolen Generations Memorial': monumentaustralia.org.au/themes/culture/indigenous/display/23125-stolen-generations-memorial

75 Monument Australia, 'Stolen Generations Memorial': monumentaustralia.org.au/themes/culture/indigenous/display/80245-stolen-generations-memorial

76 Monument Australia, 'Stolen Generations Memorial': monumentaustralia.org.au/themes/culture/indigenous/display/20437-stolen-generations-memorial

77 See Lyndall Ryan et al., 'Colonial Frontier Massacres in Eastern Australia 1788–1872': The Centre for 21st Century Humanities, The University of Newcastle: c21ch.newcastle.edu.au/colonialmassacres/

78 RRR Project Team, 'Why were ancestral remains taken?', *Return, Reconcile, Renew*: returnreconcilerenew.info/ohrm/biogs/E002083b.htm

79 Dr Stan Florek, 'Fortieth anniversary of returning to Truganini land (and water)', Australian Museum, 22 July 2016: australian.museum/blog-archive/science/our-global-neighbours-remembering-truganini/

80 Paul Turnbull, 'Managing and mapping the history of collecting Indigenous human remains', *Australian Library Journal*, 65:3, 2016, 203–12. See also Ros Langford, 'Our heritage—your playground', *Australian Archaeology* 16, 1983, 1–6.

81 RRR Project Team, 'Why were ancestral remains taken?': https://returnreconcilerenew.info/ohrm/biogs/E002083b.htm

82 Victorian Aboriginal Heritage Council, 'An historical overview of the desecration of Aboriginal burial places and repatriation of Ancestors back to Country': aboriginalheritagecouncil.vic.gov.au/historical-overview © Copyright State Government of Victoria

83 Display of human remains for memorial purposes is sensitive in many cultures. See the debate about human remains displayed at Choeung Ek Killing Fields in Brigitte Sion, 'Conflicting sites of memory in post-genocide Cambodia', *Humanity: An International Journal of Human Rights, Humanitarianism, and Development*, 2:1, 2011, 8; the debate about displaying human hair in the US Holocaust Memorial Museum in Timothy Ryback, 'Evidence of evil', *New Yorker*, 15 November 1993.

84 Rob McWilliams, 'Resting places: a history of Australian Indigenous ancestral remains at Museum Victoria', Museums Victoria, 25 August 2016: museumsvictoria.com.au/media/4273/resting_places__history_of_ancestral_remains_25_aug_2016.docx

85 McWilliams.

86 B. Andrew, M. Langton, J. Neath, 'Making visible the Frontier Wars and comparative memorialization', in J. Barrett, A. Alba and D. Moses (eds), *The Holocaust, Human Rights, and the Museum*, University of Pennsylvania Press, 2021.

87 Report of the Joint Select Committee on Constitutional Recognition relating to Aboriginal and Torres Strait Islander Peoples, List of Recommendations: aph.gov.au/Parliamentary_Business/Committees/Joint/Former_Committees/Constitutional_Recognition_2018/ ConstRecognition/Final_Report/section?id=committees%2freportjnt%2f024213%2f26813

88 Brook Andrew, '*Representation, Remembrance and the Memorial (RRM)* – Introduction', accessed 28January 2020: rr.memorial/introduction/

89 For informed discussion of the concept, instances of and laws relating to genocide, see Donald Bloxham and A. Dirk Moses (eds), *The Oxford Handbook of Genocide Studies*, Oxford University Press, 2010.

90 Henry Reynolds, *Fate of a Free People: The Classic Account of the Tasmanian Wars*, Penguin, 2004; Lyndall Ryan, *The Aboriginal Tasmanians*, UQP, 1981.

91 N.J.B. Plomley, 'The sealers of Bass Strait and the Cape Barren Island Community', Tasmanian Historical Research Association, 1988.

92 R. Nielsen et al., 'Tracing the peopling of the world through genomics', *Nature* 541, 2017, 302–10.

93 ibid.

94 Matthew Thomas, 'The 1967 referendum', Parliament of Australia, 25 May 2017: www.aph.gov.au/About_Parliament/Parliamentary_Departments/Parliamentary_Library/FlagPost/2017/May/The_1967_Referendum

95 Megan Davis, 'Seeking a settlement', *The Monthly*, July 2016.

96 From the Heart, 'Explore the Uluṟu Statement': fromtheheart.com.au/explore-the-uluru-statement/

97 Thomas Mayor, *Finding the Heart of the Nation: The Journey of the Uluṟu Statement towards Voice, Treaty and Truth*, Hardie Grant Travel, 2019.

98 NAIDOC, '2019 theme': www.naidoc.org.au/get-involved/2019-theme

99 See further information at Australian Government, 'Indigenous Voice': voice.niaa.gov.au/

100 See the University of Melbourne, 'Indigenous business booming: new data reveals sector's success', 30 April 2021: about.unimelb.edu.au/newsroom/news/2021/april/indigenous-business-booming-new-data-reveals-sectors-success

101 Yothu Yindi Foundation, 'Garma event info: protocol and conduct': www.yyf.com.au/pages/?ParentPageID=116&PageID=120#Protocol

102 Parks Australia, 'Uluṟu climb to close in 2019': parksaustralia.gov.au/uluru/news/uluru-climb-to-close/

103 Chelsea Heaney and Samantha Jonscher, 'Uluṟu climb closed permanently as hundreds scale sacred site on final day', *ABC News*, 25 October 2019: abc.net.au/news/2019-10-25/uluru-climb-closed-permanently-by-traditional-owners/11639248

104 Mark McKenna, 'Moment of truth: history and Australia's future', *Quarterly Essay*, 69, March 2018.

105 Stan Grant, *Australia Day*, HarperCollins, 2019.

106 Yirrkala bark petition, 1963: www.foundingdocs.gov.au/resources/transcripts/cth15_doc_1963.pdf

107 Noel Pearson, 'A rightful place: race, recognition and a more complete commonwealth', *Quarterly Essay*, 55, September 2014.

108 The research and reporting on Aboriginal deaths in custody by *The Guardian* and *Guardian Australia* have been exemplary. See, for instance, Lorena Allam, Calla Wahlquist & Nick Evershed, 'Aboriginal Deaths in Custody: 434 have died since 1991, new data shows', *The Guardian*, 6 June 2020: theguardian.com/australia-news/2020/jun/06/aboriginal-deaths-in-custody-434-have-died-since-1991-new-data-shows. 'Deaths Inside, Indigenous Australian Deaths in Custody 2020' is an interactive database, researched and published by *Guardian Australia*: theguardian.com/australia-news/ng-interactive/2018/aug/28/deaths-inside-indigenous-australian-deaths-in-custody

109 The Human Rights Law Centre in Melbourne represented the family of Yorta Yorta woman, Ms Tanya Day, in the coronial inquest into her death, and the website provides information and a chronology of events: hrlc.org.au/tanya-day-overview

110 Human Rights Law Centre, 'Tanya Day inquest: summary of findings', 9 April 2020: hrlc.org.au/human-rights-case-summaries/2020/9/8/tanya-day-inquest-summary-of-findings

111 Coroners Court of Victoria, 'Finding of the inquest into the death of Tanya Louise Day', 9 April 2020: www.coronerscourt.vic.gov.au/sites/default/files/2020-04/Finding%20-%20Tanya%20Day-%20COR%202017%206424%20-%20AMENDED%2017042020.pdf

112 For an explanation and analysis of these recommendations, see Chris Charles, 'The Royal Commission into Aboriginal Deaths in Custody and the duty of care owed to prisoners in South Australia', *Australian Indigenous Law Review*, 15:1, 2011, 110–16.

113 See, for instance, 'Our Aboriginals. Smoothing the pillow of dying race. Missionary's efforts', *The Cairns Post*, 6 May 1925: trove.nla.gov.au/newspaper/article/40497593

PART TWO

EXPLORING INDIGENOUS AUSTRALIA

THESE ENTRIES PRIORITISE PLACES, EVENTS AND EXPERIENCES THAT ARE EITHER INDIGENOUS OWNED AND OPERATED OR GENUINELY ENGAGE WITH TRADITIONAL OWNERS AND THE CULTURE OF FIRST PEOPLES. CHECK WITH OPERATORS DIRECTLY FOR UPDATES DUE TO THE COVID-19 PANDEMIC.

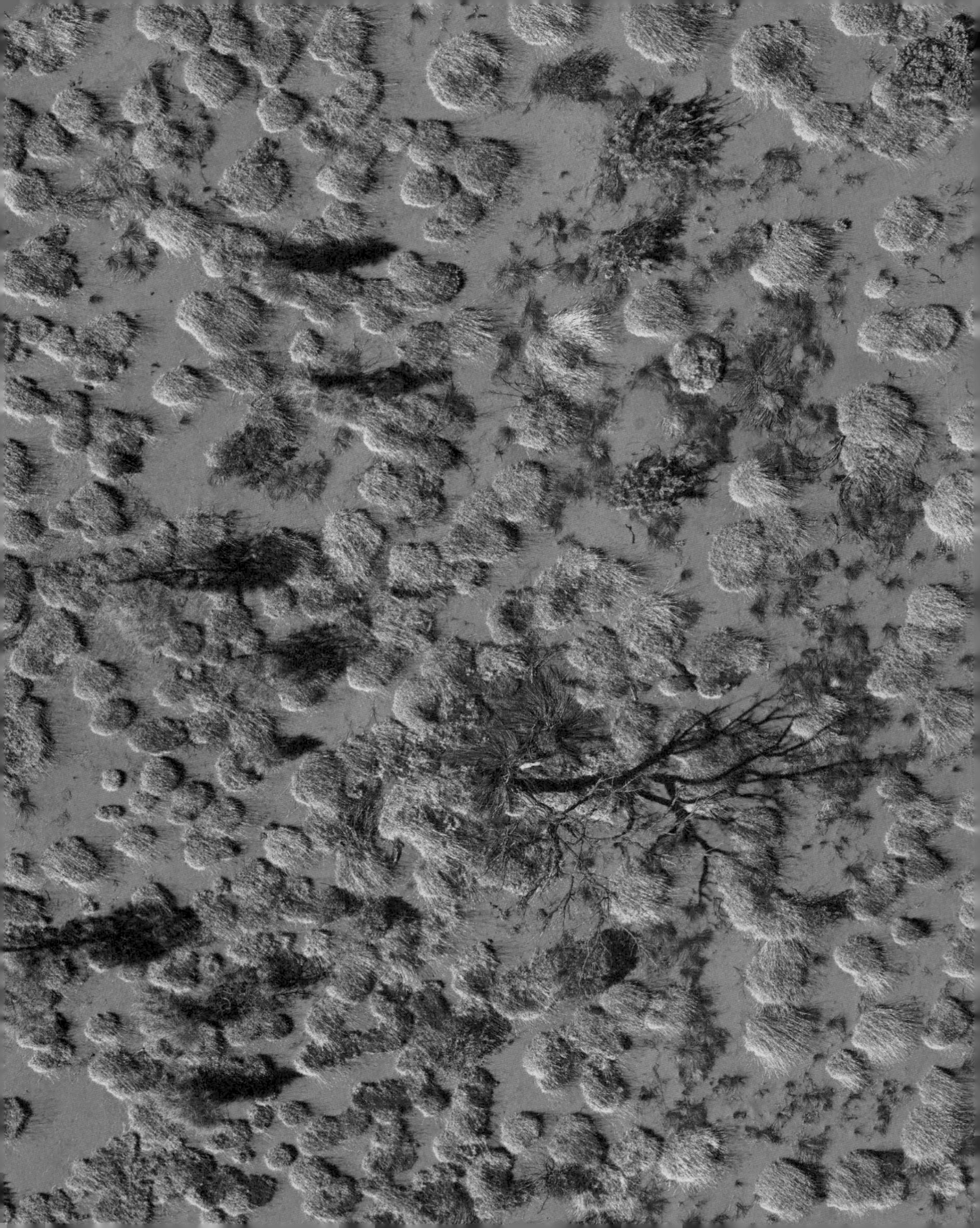

1 NORTHERN TERRITORY

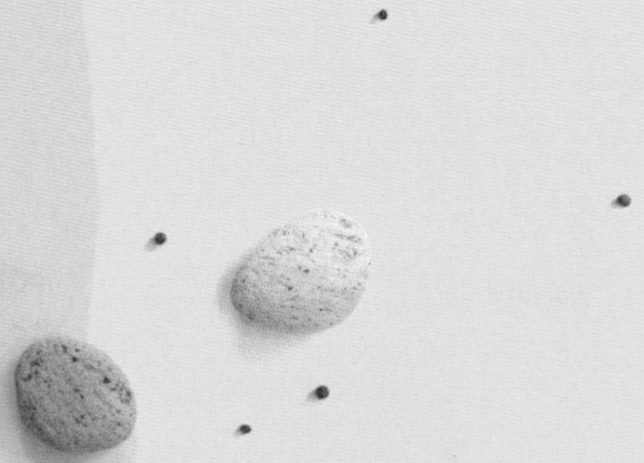

FESTIVALS

Barunga Festival

First held in 1985, Barunga Festival is one of regional Australia's longest running community festivals. It showcases the Indigenous cultures and communities of the Katherine region. Today, about 4000 visitors descend on the small community of Barunga to participate in a 3-day program that is rich in traditional arts, cultural activities, music and sport. The festival provides an exceptional opportunity to engage with remote Indigenous community life.

WHERE: Barunga community is 80 km south-east of Katherine. The festival can be accessed by car.
WHEN: Queen's Birthday Long Weekend, June.
CAMPING AND ACCOMMODATION: Camping sites are available in Barunga, or hotel/motel accommodation in Katherine.
PERMITS: Guests do not require permits to enter the community as tickets enable access for the duration of the festival.
CONTACT: 08 8941 8066

Garma Festival

This world-renowned festival is an extraordinary cultural event. Over 4 days in August the Yolŋu people of north-east Arnhem Land share their knowledge and culture. Each year it attracts about 2500 people, including prominent political and business leaders, academics, philanthropists and journalists from around the globe. A celebration of visual art, dance, music and ancient storytelling, Garma aims to foster economic opportunities for the Yolŋu people through community development, education, self-governance, enterprise and youth leadership. As well as discussing the challenges and solutions to economic issues Aboriginal and Torres Strait Islander people face, Garma also aims to strengthen, preserve and maintain ancient Aboriginal culture and foster a greater understanding between Aboriginal and non-Aboriginal Australians.

Festival tickets cover an all-inclusive package deal. For registered guests, airport shuttles, camping (with assembled tent, sleeping bag and air mattress), and all meals are provided, as well as access to basic tea and coffee making facilities.

Festival features

THE KEY FORUM: Addresses a theme of national significance to Australian Indigenous people. It combines the wisdom, experience and vision of Indigenous peoples from around the country with those of political leaders and policy makers. The local people and everyone taking part in the forum

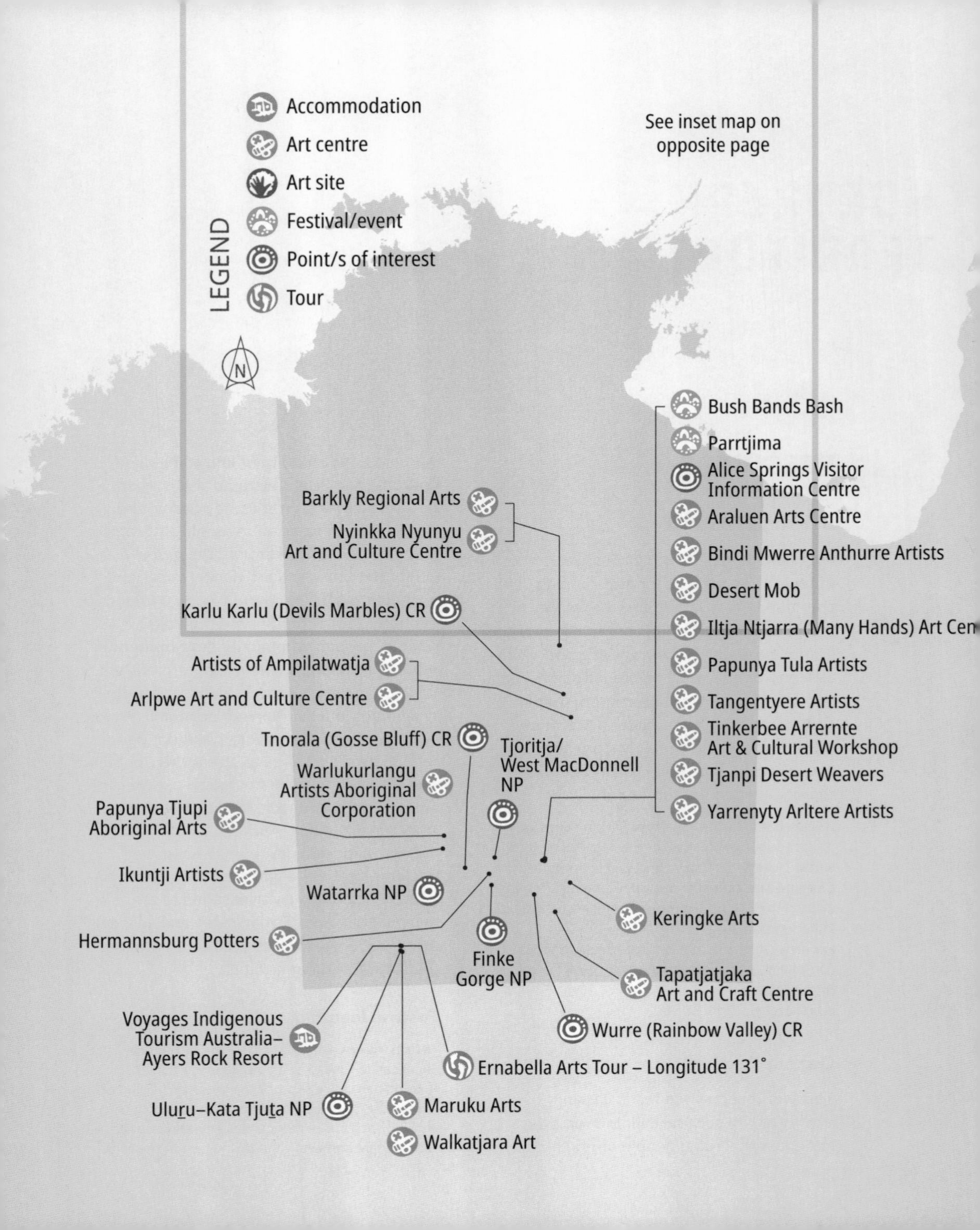
LEGEND
Accommodation
Art centre
Art site
Festival/event
Point/s of interest
Tour
N
See inset map on opposite page
Bush Bands Bash
Parrtjima
Alice Springs Visitor Information Centre
Araluen Arts Centre
Bindi Mwerre Anthurre Artists
Desert Mob
Iltja Ntjarra (Many Hands) Art Cen
Papunya Tula Artists
Tangentyere Artists
Tinkerbee Arrernte Art & Cultural Workshop
Tjanpi Desert Weavers
Yarrenyty Arltere Artists
Barkly Regional Arts
Nyinkka Nyunyu Art and Culture Centre
Karlu Karlu (Devils Marbles) CR
Artists of Ampilatwatja
Arlpwe Art and Culture Centre
Tnorala (Gosse Bluff) CR
Tjoritja/ West MacDonnell NP
Warlukurlangu Artists Aboriginal Corporation
Papunya Tjupi Aboriginal Arts
Ikuntji Artists
Watarrka NP
Keringke Arts
Hermannsburg Potters
Finke Gorge NP
Tapatjatjaka Art and Craft Centre
Wurre (Rainbow Valley) CR
Voyages Indigenous Tourism Australia–Ayers Rock Resort
Ernabella Arts Tour – Longitude 131°
Uluru–Kata Tjuta NP
Maruku Arts
Walkatjara Art

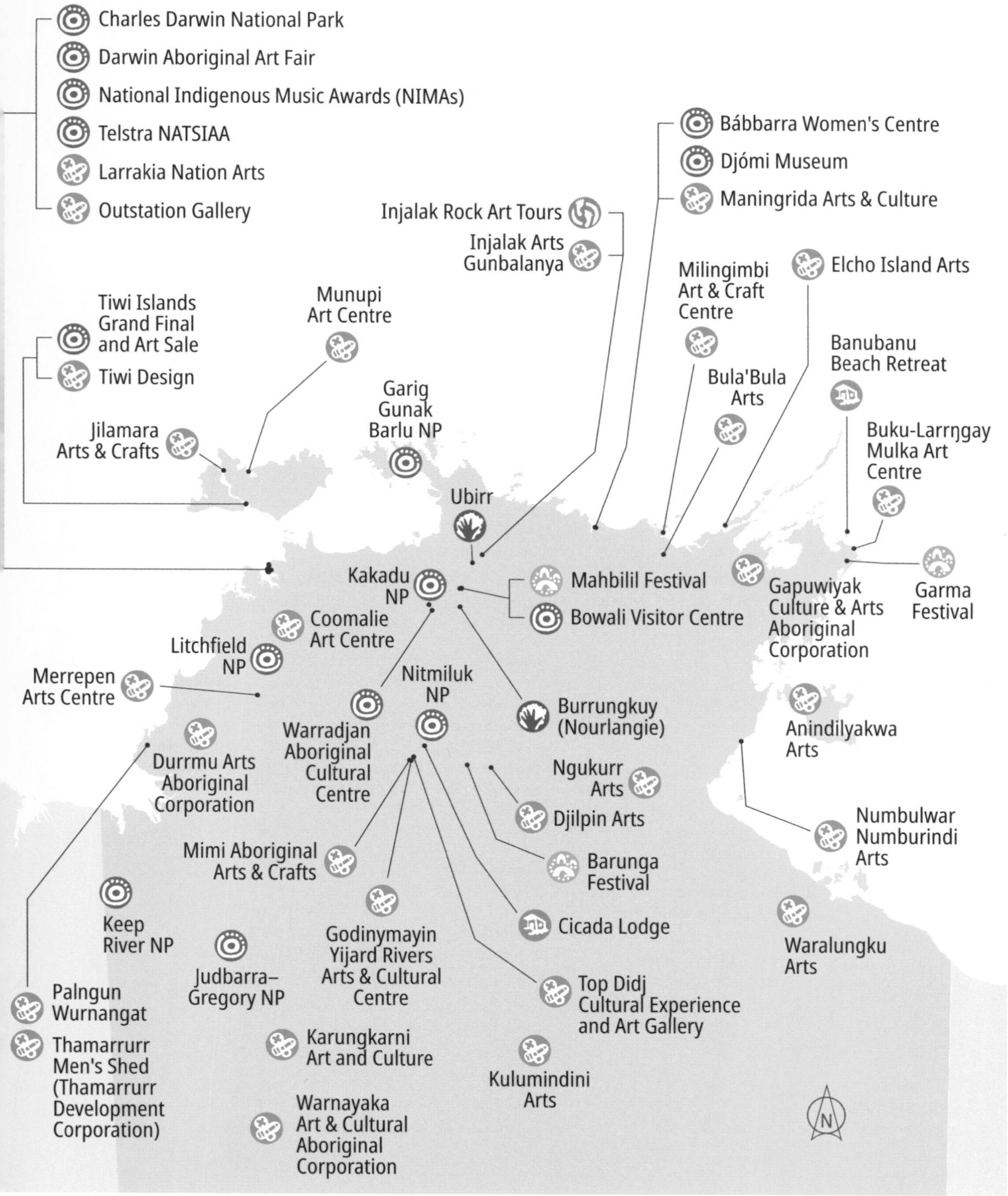

Charles Darwin National Park
Darwin Aboriginal Art Fair
National Indigenous Music Awards (NIMAs)
Telstra NATSIAA
Larrakia Nation Arts
Outstation Gallery
Bábbarra Women's Centre
Djómi Museum
Maningrida Arts & Culture
Injalak Rock Art Tours
Injalak Arts Gunbalanya
Milingimbi Art & Craft Centre
Elcho Island Arts
Tiwi Islands Grand Final and Art Sale
Tiwi Design
Munupi Art Centre
Banubanu Beach Retreat
Bula'Bula Arts
Garig Gunak Barlu NP
Jilamara Arts & Crafts
Buku-Larrŋgay Mulka Art Centre
Ubirr
Kakadu NP
Mahbilil Festival
Bowali Visitor Centre
Garma Festival
Gapuwiyak Culture & Arts Aboriginal Corporation
Coomalie Art Centre
Litchfield NP
Merrepen Arts Centre
Nitmiluk NP
Burrungkuy (Nourlangie)
Warradjan Aboriginal Cultural Centre
Anindilyakwa Arts
Durrmu Arts Aboriginal Corporation
Ngukurr Arts
Djilpin Arts
Numbulwar Numburindi Arts
Mimi Aboriginal Arts & Crafts
Barunga Festival
Keep River NP
Cicada Lodge
Waralungku Arts
Godinymayin Yijard Rivers Arts & Cultural Centre
Judbarra–Gregory NP
Top Didj Cultural Experience and Art Gallery
Palngun Wurnangat
Thamarrurr Men's Shed (Thamarrurr Development Corporation)
Karungkarni Art and Culture
Kulumindini Arts
Warnayaka Art & Cultural Aboriginal Corporation
N

are committed to producing practical solutions to improve Aboriginal and Torres Strait Islander lives.

THE YOUTH FORUM: Aims to foster the leadership capacity of the next generation, both Indigenous and non-Indigenous. Workshops, art, music, film production and social media activities are designed to educate the youth in the avenues available to improve the state of Aboriginal and Torres Strait Islander disadvantage. Students from 8 to 18 years of age participate in this forum, which brings together students from schools both near and far, metropolitan and remote.

EVENING BUŊGUL DANCE: This is arguably Garma's major attraction. From 4 pm until sunset, significant traditional ceremonies are performed by men, women and children from the various clans of the Yolŋu people. The performances showcase the unique traditional ceremonies of north-east Arnhem Land and combine breathtaking song and dance.

CULTURAL WORKSHOPS: Designed to give attendees an experience of some unique Yolŋu cultural practices, these workshops are run by local Yolŋu hosts. Attendees can participate in workshops on a wide range of subjects including cultural education, traditional bush medicine, pandanus basket weaving and spear making.

LIVE MUSICAL PERFORMANCES: Artists and bands provide the entertainment each evening. The list of performers is announced by June of each year.

GAPAN GALLERY: Works by highly respected Arnhem Land Yolŋu artists are exhibited in an open-air gallery in a grove of stringybark trees.

WHERE: Gulkula site, 30 minutes from Nhulunbuy on the Central Arnhem Hwy. Airnorth runs direct flights to Nhulunbuy from Darwin and Cairns. A shuttle service is provided from Nhulunbuy airport to the Gulkula site. Alternatively, hire car companies operate in Darwin and Nhulunbuy, including: Manny's Car Rentals: 08 8987 2300; Gove Rentals: 08 8987 1700; and Nhulunbuy Ute Hire: 08 8987 2872.

WHEN: Annually in August.

PERMITS: The official Garma ticket becomes the permit to enter the traditional Yolŋu lands of the Gulkula site and the township of Nhulunbuy. In buying a ticket, all guests are permitted to enter these lands and no further permit application is required. However, permits are required for any side trips and are strictly regulated. These must be applied for separately.

CONTACT: Yothu Yindi Foundation: 08 8945 5055

Mahbilil Festival

The Mahbilil Festival celebrates the rich culture and community of Kakadu's Mirarr people. Mahbilil is the name of the cooling afternoon breeze that occurs in Kakadu's Gurrung season. This is a time of regeneration, with warm days and cool nights, and hence a perfect time to celebrate. Running from midday to midnight, the festival includes various activities, children's workshops, Indigenous art exhibitions, weaving and painting demonstrations, traditional dance performances, and much more. When the sun sets, the festival becomes a buzz of activity, with spectacular light shows and a diverse program of music and dance. Food is a prominent feature of the festival, with bush food, such as buffalo, barramundi and the specialty of the region, magpie goose, which is cooked in large earth ovens for guests to sample. There is even a magpie goose cook-off.

WHERE: Jabiru, 300 km from Darwin along the sealed Arnhem Hwy. The town of Jabiru, which was recently handed back to the Mirarr Traditional Owners, is a fantastic base from which to explore the wonders of Kakadu National Park. There is a supermarket and other essential shops to stock up for camping trips.

WHEN: Late August to early September.

CONTACT: info@mahbililfestival.com

Parrtjima

Watch an ancient landscape come alive under the desert skies in the heart of Central Australia as the annual Parrtjima Festival connects everyone who takes part in the story of thousands of years of culture. First held in 2016, Parrtjima (pronounced parr-chee-ma) is a spectacular 10-night festival in light that is held in Mparntwe (Alice Springs) on the lands of the Arrernte people. This unique festival is Australia's

Above: Youngsters learn the actions for different dances by observing and copying the movements of the elders at Garma Festival

Below: The Ebb and Flow of Sky & Country, Parrtjima 2020

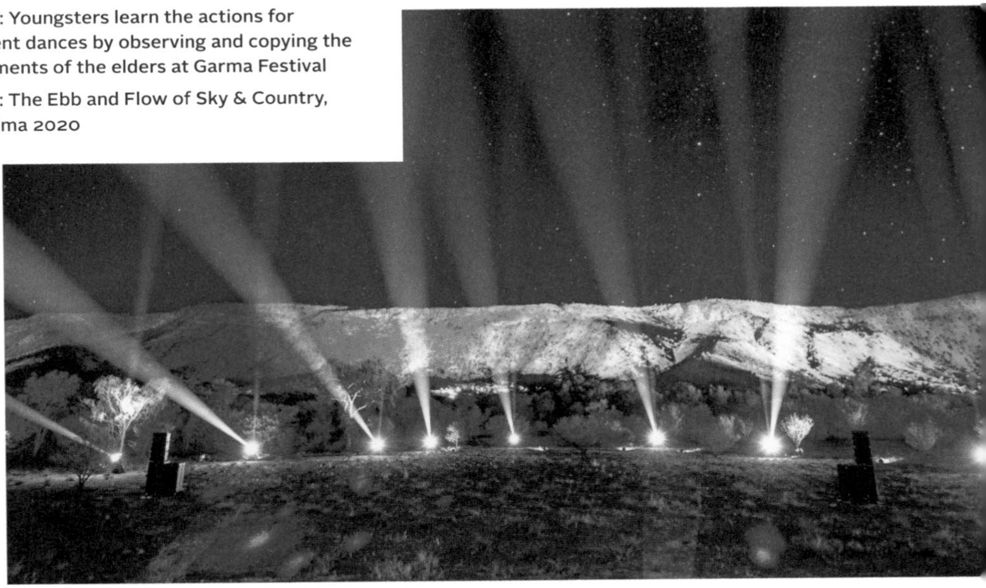

only Aboriginal-dedicated event using the latest light technology to celebrate the world's oldest living culture. From immersive Aboriginal artworks, larger-than-life installations and the magical illumination of the majestic MacDonnell Ranges, to a diverse public program of live music, talks, interactive workshops and films, Parrtjima provides an exceptional opportunity not only to learn about Aboriginal stories, culture and art but to ensure this knowledge is kept relevant in the 21st century through newly developed mediums.

This free event is for all the family to enjoy. Features of the festival include: the MacDonnell Ranges Show – arguably Parrtjima's major attraction as 2 km of the MacDonnell Ranges illuminate with extraordinary effects of colour and movement. The show is best viewed from 7 pm at the earliest due to the levels of daylight. The signature installations – a fresh series of larger-than-life light installations to greet visitors each year – include a dynamic interactive game of discovery that is fun for children (and adults) of all ages, and the crowd favourite, Grounded, which projects animated artworks onto the red sands of Alice Springs Desert Park. Other features include the Youth Outreach Program – a dedicated program which provides activities and opportunities to engage Aboriginal youth in the annual event and, from 2021 on, the Merne Desert Dinner, an unforgettable experience that offers a contemporary take on traditional bush foods, plus special performances and entertainment under a canopy of stars. Parrtjima is a magical bucket-list adventure that is as unique as the Red Centre itself.

WHERE: Alice Springs Desert Park. Mparntwe (Alice Springs) is the gateway to the heart of Central Australia, and is a fantastic base from which to explore the wonders of the Red Centre, no matter your timeframe.
WHEN: Annually in April.
CONTACT: Northern Territory Major Events Company Pty Ltd: 08 8999 5256

MUSIC

Bush Bands Bash

Bush Bands Bash is a massive celebration of contemporary remote Indigenous music presented annually by MusicNT.

Bush Bands Bash is held in Mparntwe (Alice Springs) each September, bringing Indigenous musicians together from remote communities throughout the Territory and tri-state regions to perform and showcase their music to an enthusiastic crowd of over 3000 people, many of whom have travelled from across Australia. Since it began in 2003, Bush Bands Bash has become one of Mparntwe's musical and cultural highlights of the year. It's also an alcohol-free, family-friendly event which sees Indigenous and non-Indigenous people coming together for a fun-filled time, starting with a smoking ceremony and continuing on with awesome sounds and deadly dance moves.

Each band or act performs original music and brings their own mix of unique sounds to the concert, including Desert Reggae, Rock, Soul, RnB, Hip Hop and Country, with many bands singing in their first language. The music conveys these songwriters' personal journeys, culture, life in remote communities and experiences as First Australians.

The concert is preceded by 4 days of workshops at a camp where musicians rehearse together for the Bash and receive professional mentoring in all aspects of the Australian music industry.

If you love what you're hearing from remote Indigenous Australian musicians and want to be immersed in 6 hours of dynamic entertainment from the heart of Australia, this event is for you!

WHERE: Alice Springs Telegraph Station, park at Speedway and buses run frequently to the event.
WHEN: Annually in September.
CONTACT: 08 8952 0322

National Indigenous Music Awards (NIMAs)

The NIMAs are a platform for the rich musical talent of Aboriginal and Torres Strait Islander people from around Australia. They are a special celebration, and showcase up-and-coming artists alongside those who have gained international acclaim, such as Archie Roach, Jessica Mauboy, Yothu Yindi and the late Dr G Yunupingu. The NIMAs have been held beneath the stars in Darwin for the past 16 years. The night's electric atmosphere attracts audiences from all around Australia, and it is a must-see event for music lovers of all ages and cultures. For ticket prices and other information, visit the NIMA website.

WHERE: George Brown Botanic Gardens Amphitheatre, Darwin.
WHEN: Annually in August.
CONTACT: Music NT: 08 89811996

SPORT

Tiwi Islands Grand Final and Art Sale

This unique sporting and cultural event attracts thousands of locals and tourists to Bathurst Island each year. The passion for football engulfs the entire community of the Tiwi Islands and the grand final is the highlight of the season. The day has moved beyond the football match alone and has become a celebration of Tiwi Islands' culture. The Jilamara Arts and Crafts Association is joined by smaller art centres from other communities on the islands to showcase the work of many local artists at the primary school. A large selection of paintings, prints, carvings and woven pieces is available for tourists to purchase at reasonable prices.

WHERE: Bathurst Island, about 80 km north of Darwin. SeaLink ferries run return trips to the Tiwi Islands, with the trip just under 3 hours each way. For more information visit the SeaLink website. Fly Tiwi charters light planes to Bathurst Island, which take 30 minutes each way.
WHEN: March.

NATIONAL PARKS

Charles Darwin National Park

Named after the world-famous scientist Charles Darwin, this national park provides stunning views across the mangroves and harbour to the city of Darwin. It is an ideal place to catch a late-afternoon storm in the early Wet season or to watch the morning light bathe the city. The park lies on Frances Bay in Port Darwin, and protects part of the Port Darwin wetlands, which is one of the largest wetland areas (48 sq km) of any city in Australia. Thirty-six of the Northern Territory's 51 mangrove species grow here and there is an abundance of wildlife.

Ancient Aboriginal middens, piled high with the skeletal remains of shellfish and other marine life, attest to the long occupation by Indigenous people. Today, the Larrakia people are recognised as the Traditional Owners of an area that stretches as far east as the Adelaide River.

There are short walking trails and cycling paths through the tropical woodland. However, visitors are warned that biting insects, such as mosquitoes and midges, are part of the mangrove and tidal system and can be a problem around sunset and sunrise (numbers are highest around the full moon, later in the year). Visitors are advised to wear protective clothing and use insect repellent. The park is open daily, 8 am–7 pm.

WHERE: 5.5 km east of Darwin via Tiger Brennan Dr to Winnellie.
CAMPING: No camping.
CONTACT: Park information, PWCNT: 08 8999 4555; PWCNT Charles Darwin: 08 8947 2305

Finke Gorge National Park

The Finke River is the oldest watercourse in the world. The usually dry riverbed runs for more than 640 km before it disappears in the Simpson Desert. The Finke Gorge National Park is best accessed by 4WD vehicle, and the drive itself becomes part of the adventure.

This is land belonging to the Western Aranda people, with Aboriginal artist Albert Namatjira perhaps the most famous person to come from this area (he was born at Hermannsburg community in 1902).

Highlights of this national park include a walk through some of the world's oldest trees at Palm Valley, and the vast and magnificent view over the desert from the Kalarranga Lookout. There are multiple short walking trails which lend themselves to spectacular photography and sightseeing. There are some harder bushwalking trails including Mparra, Arankaia, Mpulungkinya and Kalarranga. These range from walks of 20–30 minutes up to 2 hours return.

WHERE: 138 km west of Alice Springs; 20 km south of Hermannsburg.
CAMPING AND ACCOMMODATION: There are campgrounds at Palm Valley, and the nearest hotel accommodation is in Alice Springs.
CONTACT: PWCNT Alice Springs: 08 8951 8250; PWCNT Finke Gorge: 08 8956 7401

Garig Gunak Barlu National Park

Covering the entire Cobourg Peninsula, the surrounding waters of the Arafura Sea and Van Diemen Gulf, as well as some neighbouring islands, this national park is one of northern Australia's most spectacular areas. The park lies within the traditional lands of the Iwaidja-speaking Arrarrkbi people of Western Arnhem Land. Ownership of the area is shared by 4 clans – the Agalda, Madjunbalmi, Muran and Ngaindjagar – who engage in management of the land and sea through independent traditional management practices, and are also employed as park rangers. The Arrarrkbi people have proven links to the land and sea that date back 40,000 years. Numerous sacred sites and large middens testify to their long-term occupation. The remote and rugged lands of Garig Gunak Barlu are fringed by pristine beaches with brilliant white sand and sparkling turquoise waters.

The park is a fantastic location for camping, boating, bushwalking, observing wildlife and birdwatching. Barramundi and mangrove jack can be found in tidal creeks and estuaries, but the area is better known for blue water fishing.

Visit the Black Point Cultural Centre, within the Black Point Ranger Station, for an insight into the diverse history of the peninsula. As well as the Aboriginal people, the Macassan traders and European explorers also played a role in the area's history.

WHERE: On the Cobourg Peninsula about 570 km north-east of Darwin. Drive from Darwin via

Ngurrungurrudjba (Yellow Water), Kakadu (photo Wayne Quilliam)

Arnhem Hwy through Kakadu, then through Arnhem Land via Oenpelli and Murgenella rds, 4WD only; the unsealed road is open only during the Dry season (May–October). You can also travel via air charter to Smith Point or via boat (2-day sail from Darwin). **PERMITS:** Bookings are required in advance to travel through Arnhem Land and also to camp; for permit applications contact: Permits and Concessions Unit, GPO Box 1448, Darwin NT 0801; 08 8999 4814; pwpermits@nt.gov.au. Additional permits are required to travel further into Arnhem Land. **CONTACT:** 08 8979 0244

Judbarra–Gregory National Park

Judbarra–Gregory National Park lies in the transitional zone between the tropical and semi-arid regions of the NT. Encompassing a huge 13,000 sq km area, the park includes soaring escarpments with spectacular range and gorge scenery, tropical woodlands and magnificent river systems. Within the national park there are significant Aboriginal sites, and evidence of European pastoral and exploration history.

CULTURAL HERITAGE: The land here is of high spiritual significance to the Traditional Owners and is still used for traditional ceremonies and rituals. Indigenous language groups associated with the park are the Wardaman, Ngarinyman, Ngaliwurru, Nungali, Jaminjung and Karrangpurru people. One of the largest rock-art sites in Australia is found here, and it depicts the ancient history of Aboriginal occupation in the park area. The most common motifs are human figures, which appear in a style unique to this particular region.

THINGS TO DO

Private tours of the Victoria River can be organised in Timber Creek and at the Victoria River Roadhouse. There are challenging and rewarding 4WD tracks and plenty of opportunities for bushwalking.

BUSHWALKING: Most walks in the park are well marked and start close to the Victoria Hwy.
FISHING: This is a popular activity in the park. Regulations do apply, so make sure you are familiar with them before trying any fishing.
WHERE: 160 km west of Katherine; 220 km east of Kununurra. From Katherine or Kununurra via the Victoria Hwy; from Halls Creek via the unsealed Buntine Hwy; from Top Springs via the unsealed Buntine Hwy or unsealed Buchanan Hwy and Victoria River Downs Station. From December to April, the Wet season rains may make all roads, including the Victoria Hwy, impassable. Road conditions should be checked before any travel.
CAMPING AND ACCOMMODATION: There are numerous campgrounds around the park. Most have basic facilities, including toilets, fireplaces, and picnic tables. Sullivan Creek Campground is 17 km east of the Victoria River, on the banks of a permanent waterhole. Big Horse Creek campground is 10 km west of Timber Creek and is popular with anglers for its boat ramp and accessible fishing areas. Limestone Gorge campground is well situated for access to the calcite flow walk, the Limestone Creek Billabong and fishing in the East Baines River. Bullita campground is 60 km south of Timber Creek, near the historic Bullita Homestead and close to the East Baines River. A fee deposit box is located at each campground, with fees assigned based on the facilities provided. Accommodation is available at the Victoria River Roadhouse and Bullita Homestead.
PERMITS: Permits are required for overnight bushwalking and are available from Timber Creek or Bullita ranger stations.
CONTACT: PWCNT Katherine: 08 8973 8888; Kununurra Visitor Centre: 08 9168 1177

Kakadu National Park

World Heritage-listed Kakadu National Park is a landscape of unsurpassed beauty, with world-renowned wetlands attracting extraordinary numbers of birds, thundering waterfalls that plunge from towering escarpments into natural rock pools, and open woodlands that offer a refuge for a wide range of native animals. It is Australia's largest terrestrial national park and has entire ecosystems within its extensive boundaries. More than one-third of Australia's bird species are found in Kakadu, along with hundreds of plant, animal and marine species that do not exist anywhere else on the planet. Kakadu is also a very spiritual place, with a rich cultural heritage that reflects the unique relationship between the Aboriginal Traditional Owners and the land itself.

CULTURAL HERITAGE: Kakadu is a landscape of living culture. Rock art of the region indicates Aboriginal people have occupied Kakadu for at least 65,000 years, the longest record of continual human occupation of any area on Earth. The rock-art galleries show that early Indigenous groups had a strong culture based on deep spiritual beliefs. This spiritual connection to the land is recognised globally in the World Heritage status of Kakadu.

The name Kakadu comes from an Aboriginal language, Gagudju, spoken in the north of the park at the beginning of the 20th century. In 1978 the Gagudju people were granted title of their land, which they then leased for use as a national park. Kakadu is jointly managed by the Bininj/Mungguy people and Parks Australia. Although Gagudju is no longer spoken by Aboriginal people in the area, surviving dialects include Kunwinjku (in the north), Kundjeyhmi-Kundheyhmi (in the centre) and Jawoyn (in the south). Aboriginal people of the region know themselves as Bininj (pronounced Bin-ning). Languages, kinship, ceremonies and Caring for Country have been passed on through the generations from the time of Creation when important ancestral beings crossed the landscape and created the plants, animals, landforms and the people who live there today.

A major creator acknowledged in the region is the Rainbow Serpent, which is known Australia-wide by various Aboriginal groups. As the Rainbow Serpent moved through the land, she formed the features of the landscape in Kakadu, such as waterways, waterholes and hills. Her role in creating the cultural obligations of the Bininj/Mungguy people is very important, as is her creation of the plant and animal life cycles and the seasonal changes. In the Kakadu region she is also known as Almudj in Kundjeyhmi, Ngalyod in Kunwinjku, Nama'rdeedjurr in Gagudju, Bolung in Jawoyn and Lulydjudjan in Limilngan. Other important ancestral beings that feature in Creation stories and rock-art depictions include Bula (Jawoyn ancestor), Namarrkon (Lightning Man) and Warramurrungundji (Earth Mother).

The main Aboriginal rock-art sites are at Ubirr, Nanguluwurr and Burrungkuy (Nourlangie), while an excellent understanding of Kakadu's Aboriginal culture can be gained by visiting the Bowali Visitor Centre and Warradjan Cultural Centre.

THE SIX SEASONS OF KAKADU: The Bininj/Mungguy people divide the year into up to 6 seasons to account for the dramatic changes in weather in Kakadu.

- Kudjewk, from December to March, is the monsoon season or the true Wet. There are thunderstorms, heavy rain and flooding, a vibrant growing season and abundant wildlife. Temperature range is 24–34°C.
- Bangkerreng, in April, is when the rain clouds disperse and the clear skies return. Floodwaters and streams recede and start to run clear again, and plants are fruiting. Windstorms occasionally occur early in the season, but otherwise the air is clear and the winds warm. It is a beautiful time to visit the park and is very popular among visitors. The temperature range is 23–34°C.
- Yekke, from May to mid-June, is cooler with relatively low humidity. Waterlilies cover the wetlands and billabongs, and early morning mist hangs above the plains and waterholes. The Bininj/Mungguy start burning patches of land to encourage new growth. The temperature range of 21–33°C is perfect for visitors.
- Wurrkeng is the cold weather season, from mid-June to mid-August. Creeks stop flowing and floodplains dry up, and an abundance of waterbirds crowd shrinking billabongs. The Yellow Water Billabong is an explosion of activity. Controlled burning continues and birds of prey patrol fire lines in their hundreds, looking for small animals fleeing the flames. The humidity is low and the temperature range is 17–32°C.
- Kurrung, from mid-August to mid-October, is the hot, Dry season. The Country has been cleansed from the burning and is now ready to regenerate. Magpie geese are still numerous, laying their eggs in the wetlands, but Bininj/Mungguy also hunt long-necked turtles and file snakes. Waterfalls have less water, and the drier heat is perfect for touring and trekking. Days are warm, but nights are still cool; with a temperature range of 23–37°C.
- Kunumeleng is the pre-monsoon storm season. It generally runs from mid-October to late December, but exact dates vary each year. Humidity rises and scattered thunderstorms bring the flow of streams and the filling of floodplains. Traditionally Bininj/Mungguy had to move camp to the stone country, to shelter from the storms. With all the water, dramatic changes in the landscape occur across the park and it is a captivating time to visit. Temperature range is 24–37°C.

NATURAL FEATURES: The eastern boundary of the park follows the East Alligator River and the 140-million-year-old Arnhem Land escarpment, which is the western edge of the Arnhem Land Plateau, an imposing geological feature that stands some 300 m above the tropical woodland of the park and extends for more than 500 km.

The escarpment is the edge of the stone country of Arnhem Land and many rivers in the Top End have their headwaters here, including the East and South Alligator, which flow through the tropical woodland of Kakadu, across the floodplains and out to the Van Diemen Gulf. The plains are broken up by impressive rocky outcrops, or 'outliers'. Areas of the escarpment and massive rock formations, such as Burrungkuy, were shelters for Aboriginal people, who often used the rock walls and overhangs as a canvas on which to depict their daily lives and spiritual beliefs.

Compared to the escarpment, which dominates the landscape in the east of the park, the rivers and coastal areas are more modern formations, built up over thousands of years as silt was carried out of Arnhem Land. During the Wet season, rivers and creeks break their banks and flood the plains, creating Kakadu's famous wetlands that also include monsoonal rainforests, swamps and billabongs. It is these areas, rich in plant and insect life, which make Kakadu National Park one of the most abundant areas for wildlife in Australia. There are over 280 bird species, more than 50 fish species, over 120 reptile and amphibian species, 60 mammal species, 100 termite species and more than 300 ant species in the park. Also, biologists have recorded more than 2000 plant species in the area.

THINGS TO DO

BUSHWALKING: One of the best ways to experience Kakadu is on foot. Throughout the park there are various walks that cater to a wide variety of fitness levels and trip itineraries, including shorter day walks and more challenging full-day hikes. There are also overnight walks, which require high levels of experience and careful planning as you walk through unmarked and rugged country. Permits are required for all overnight walks.

BURRUNGKUY AREA: In this area is the picturesque Anbangbang Billabong and the renowned Burrungkuy Rock, a vast, ancient rock-art gallery and an inspirational place that projects a sense of how Indigenous people once lived. The turn-off to Burrungkuy is 19 km south of Bowali, on the Kakadu Hwy. A circular walk (1.5 km) winds through some of Australia's most spectacular art sites and ancient living areas. Other walking trails include Nawurlandja Lookout walk (1.2 km return, 40 minutes, medium difficulty), involving a moderate climb for views of the escarpment and Anbangbang Billabong; Nanguluwurr Art Site walk (3.4 km return, 2 hours, easy), through open savannah woodlands to a secluded art gallery; Kubara walk (6 km return, 4 hours, easy) through woodlands into the stone country and along a string of lovely forest-rimmed rockholes; Bubba walk (3.5 km circuit, 2 hours, easy) starting at Djarradjin (Muirella Park) camping area and trailing through wetlands. A longer trail in the Burrungkuy area, Barrk walk (12 km loop, 6–8 hours, difficult), traverses the sandstone country, passing the Nanguluwurr art site along the way.

JIM JIM FALLS AREA: This area is 43 km from Kakadu Hwy along a 4WD road and is only accessible during the Dry season. Jim Jim Plunge Pool, at the end of a 1 km walk from the carpark (1–2 hours return, difficult – it involves some rock-hopping), is one of the most beautiful swimming areas in Kakadu. It is surrounded by 200 m-high cliffs and fed by a powerful waterfall that stops flowing during the Dry season. Nearby, Budjmi Lookout walk (1 km return, 45 minutes, medium difficulty) is a Dry-season trail that starts near the Jim Jim Creek crossing and involves a moderate-grade climb to the top of a rocky outcrop for expansive views of the Arnhem Land escarpment. Barrk Marlam walk (6 km return, 5–6 hours, difficult) is another Dry-season track that branches off the Jim Jim Plunge Pool track and goes through rugged sandstone country. A further 10 km on from Jim Jim Falls is Twin Falls, where a spectacular waterfall feeds a beautiful plunge pool and creek, rimmed by a white sandy beach. Access is by a boat shuttle service. Swimming is not allowed because of saltwater crocodiles, but there is a lovely walk, Twin Falls escarpment walk (6 km return, 5 hours, difficult), that climbs the cliffs above the falls.

MARY RIVER AREA: The belief of the Jawoyn Aboriginal people is that powerful Creation ancestors rest here and should not be disturbed. Access to Gunlom is via a gravel road and an unsealed dirt road (check Wet season access). The Gunlom plunge pool is wide, deep and scenic, and with its wispy Dry-season waterfall, this is the most popular place in the southern part of the park. A steep trail (2 km return, 1.5 hours, medium difficulty) leads to the top of the falls. Up here some beautiful rock pools, including an infinity pool, provide stunning views of the southern areas of Kakadu and are probably the safest places to swim in the park. The Yurmikmik walks are several separate, but interconnected, walks that are accessible year-round and provide a wonderful experience in the southern hills and basins of the Mary River region.

SOUTH ALLIGATOR AREA: Turn south off the Arnhem Hwy (7 km east of the South Alligator River) to reach Mamukala Wetlands. Mamukala is open most of the year but is at its most dramatic in September and October when thousands of magpie geese and other birds gather to feed as the waters dry up. There is an excellent observation platform and a 3 km walk

(1–2 hours, easy) along the wetlands. Another option is Kungarre walk (3.6 km circuit, 2 hours, easy), which leads through shady monsoonal vine forest, then along the edges of a waterhole.
JABIRU AREA: Bowali Visitor Centre, on the Kakadu Hwy just west of Jabiru, is the park headquarters and a wonderful starting point for learning about Kakadu and Aboriginal culture. There are audiovisual displays and staff are on hand to answer questions. Bowali walking track (4 km return, 1.5 hours, easy) starts opposite the Crocodile Hotel and winds its way through open savannah woodland to the visitor centre (the track is also a bike trail).
EAST ALLIGATOR AREA: Ubirr is one of the best rock-art sites in the park; good views of the art are provided by a 1 km circuit walk. Branching off the loop walk and involving a steep climb, the track (500 m return, 1 hour, medium difficulty) leads to a rocky vantage point with a spectacular view – particularly at sunset – over the Nardab floodplain. The Bardedjilidji walk (2.5 km, 2 hours, easy) is a short, but fascinating, trail that meanders through the sandstone outliers.
NGURRUNGURRUDJBA (YELLOW WATER): This is one of the most accessible and beautiful wetland areas in northern Australia. When the waters recede in the Dry season the wildlife is concentrated in this one area that is part of the South Alligator floodplain. Commercial boat tours travel through the wetlands and guides provide commentaries about the landscape and wildlife. A boardwalk offers another perspective of the wetland during the Dry season. Warradjan Aboriginal Cultural Centre near Ngurrungurrdjba is a fascinating place with outstanding displays of Aboriginal culture. It really is a must-see for visitors to learn about the culture of Kakadu's Traditional Owners.
WHERE: 235 km east of Darwin to the Bowali Visitor Centre. Drive from Darwin via Stuart Hwy then Arnhem Hwy; from Pine Creek via Stuart Hwy then Kakadu Hwy.
PERMITS: A fee applies to visitors entering Kakadu National Park. NT residents and children under 5 years of age are exempt. Camping permits are required for some camp sites. Some camp sites have a quota for camping, so organise permits well in advance of your visit.
CONTACT: Kakadu National Park, Bowali Visitor Centre: 08 8938 1120

Bowali Visitor Centre

The visitor centre, near the town of Jabiru, is a great first point of call before entering Kakadu. Staff at the centre can assist you with travel plans in the park. Interpretive displays show different views of Kakadu's significance and detail its many sights and activities in the park.

The Marrawuddi Gallery, within the centre, displays fine art from Aboriginal artists from Kakadu. The design of the building itself is inspired by an Aboriginal rock shelter and is internationally acclaimed. Bowali is the name locals give to the area where the centre is located.

WHERE: 235 km east of Darwin to the Bowali Visitor Centre, one entrance of the park.
CONTACT: Kakadu National Park, Bowali Visitor Centre; 08 8938 1120

Warradjan Aboriginal Cultural Centre

Located in the heart of Kakadu at Cooinda, Warradjan is an interactive gallery that tells the story of Kakadu from the perspective of the Bininj/Mungguy, the region's Traditional Owners. Warradjan is the pig-nosed turtle, and the building's circular shape reflects this and the local Indigenous ways of sitting in circles to communicate.

The narrative that weaves through the centre and the exhibits focuses on the theme 'Our land is our life' and was developed by the different clan groups across Kakadu. It takes visitors on a journey of 65,000 years of heritage, sharing a powerful understanding of the evolution of Kakadu and the relationship the Bininj/Mungguy have among themselves and with one of the most remarkable natural landscapes in the world. Visitors move through the display as the Rainbow Serpent Creation ancestor moved through the Country, first through lowlands in the drier months and then the stone country in the Wet.

The centre incorporates curated displays with traditional artefacts, as well as using contemporary techniques, such as videos. The centre also regularly hosts art and crafts activities, allowing visitors to watch, talk with, and often participate in aged-old activities.

WHERE: Located at Cooinda, a 40-minute drive from Jabiru.
CONTACT: 08 8979 0525

Burrungkuy (Nourlangie) and Ubirr

Burrungkuy and Ubirr are the best-known rock-art sites in Kakadu. Located in environments rich in natural resources and comprising several large rock outcrops with numerous caves and overhangs, these sites were important centres of pre-contact Aboriginal occupation.

Traditionally, Aboriginal people camped in the rock shelters at Ubirr, where the smooth surfaces were ideal for painting. Over 120 rock-art sites here display a range of styles, including large naturalistic portrayals of extinct animals, simple stick figures with large headdresses, X-ray paintings of fauna such as turtles and fish, and animated and ornamented figures in motion. One painting depicting a Tasmanian thylacine is considered to be around 3000 years old.

Other more recently executed post-contact art portrays the trading period with Macassan fishermen and the arrival of Europeans. One of the most amazing paintings is that of a sailing ship, depicted in white ochre, which chronicles the early contact with Europeans. Such ships were seen in the area between 1880 and 1950, when they brought supplies to buffalo-hunting camps on the floodplains of the Alligator Rivers, and returned to Darwin with hides. Many Aboriginal people worked in these camps.

At Burrungkuy, shell and animal-bone fragments found in an archaeological dig in one of the shelters suggest occupation over the past 6000 years. The most visited site is the Anbangbang gallery, where evidence of occupation dates back 2500 years. The main rock art you can see today is the work of the artist Nayombolmi, who decorated the walls in 1964. In an effort to preserve his Indigenous culture, he painted spirit beings, family groups and people travelling to a ceremonial gathering. Nanguluwurr also has X-ray paintings of barramundi and a short-necked turtle, painted in 1964 by a friend of Nayombolmi.

On the northern side of Burrungkuy is a smaller gallery, Nanguluwurr, which displays most of the rock-art styles found in Kakadu. There are depictions of Alkaihko, the fire woman, one of the First people who created the world. She planted the yellow swamp banksias in the woodlands and used their smouldering flower spikes to carry fire.

High up on the rock face are hand stencils, the subject of rock art in this area since Aboriginal people first came here around 50,000 years ago. On some hands, the three middle fingers are held together and separated from the outer fingers, a style of hand stencil that is often found alongside 'dynamic art' estimated at over 20,000 years old. High on the ceiling of the shelter are small depictions of people, painted in the dynamic style. These figures, adorned with headdresses, carry boomerangs used for hunting about 20,000 years ago when the climate was drier and open grasslands were prevalent. Boomerangs are of little use in the woodland forests of today.

Burrungkuy is accessible by an easy 1.5 km walking track that includes 2 lookouts, and Ubirr by an easy 1 km circuit track (allow at least 45 minutes). From Ubirr, an additional 250 m, moderately steep climb gives an unforgettable panoramic view across the vast Nadab floodplains of the East Alligator River. Time your walk to the top of Ubirr rock to catch an incredible sunset over the floodplains. Also, later in the Wet season, when the rain is not as heavy, the floodplain is still an explosion of plant and animal life. The view across the floodplains is particularly striking at this time. The 12 km Barrk sandstone walk over Burrungkuy is challenging, and should not be attempted solo.

WHERE: Ubirr is 39 km from Jabiru via the Arnhem Hwy.
CAMPING: Djarradjin (Muirella Park) is a camping area with showers and toilets. Fees apply and are collected on site. Check seasonal access. Djirrilba (Sandy Billabong) is a simple bush camping area with basic toilet facilities. Fees apply and are collected on site.

Karlu Karlu (Devils Marbles) Conservation Reserve

Karlu Karlu is one of the most iconic outback destinations in the Northern Territory, with massive red and orange boulders precariously piled atop each other in a broad, desert landscape. At sunset and sunrise, the rocks and boulders are bathed in magnificent orange light. The area is culturally and spiritually significant for four Aboriginal groups: the Alyawarr, Kaytetye, Warumungu and Warlpiri people. Karlu Karlu is the Alyawarr name for the area. Since 2009, the reserve has been jointly managed by the Traditional Owners and the Parks and Wildlife Commission of the Northern Territory. Today it is protected under Northern Territory law as a Registered Sacred Site.

CULTURAL HERITAGE: Traditionally, certain parts of Karlu Karlu were off limits to the local Aboriginal people. Many parts were considered so dangerous that only the Elders could visit them for important ceremonies. The only areas open to all Aboriginal people to gather bush foods and medicines and to hunt were the central areas.

The Dreaming stories are reserved for Aboriginal people only, though there is one version of a women's story available to the public. The entire area is a sacred site for both men and women. Local Aboriginal women often visit the reserve to gather wild figs. Small waterholes found in the northwest creek are also very valuable to Aboriginal people for collecting water.

NATURAL FEATURES: The granite blocks from which the marbles were shaped were originally a solid mass of granite. Over millions of years, flaking and erosion gradually rounded the corners so many of the boulders are now spherical or egg-shaped. Ranging in size from 50 cm up to 6 m in diameter, the boulders continue to flake and erode, creating a landscape that is ever changing.

Animals, birds and plants of the arid zone are found in the area, and the shadows and nooks of the boulders provide a cool refuge for them in summer months. Attached to the underside of overhanging rock are clusters of bottle-shaped mud nests, home to fairy martins; small dragons and lizards live in the crevices.

THINGS TO DO

A short self-guided walk (15 minutes return, easy) leaves from the carpark, with signs giving geological information. A network of tracks meanders through the rock formations, with on-site interpretation developed in consultation with the Traditional Owners. As you wander around, you can find new viewpoints to admire. The Traditional Owners have requested that you remain on the walking tracks and do not climb the boulders.
WHERE: 390 km north of Alice Springs; 100 km south of Tennant Creek via the Stuart Hwy.

CAMPING: A simple bush camping area with fireplaces and pit toilets is located at the southern end of the reserve. No water or firewood is provided, so bring your own.
CONTACT: PWCNT Alice Springs: 08 8951 8250; PWCNT Tennant Creek: 08 8962 4499

Keep River National Park

Keep River National Park sits 3 km east of the border the NT shares with WA, 468 km from Katherine. It is one of the NT's best kept secrets, with Aboriginal rock-art sites and spectacular geological wonders. The striking beehive-shaped sandstone formations that define the park are commonly referred to as the 'mini Bungle Bungles'.

CULTURAL HERITAGE: The Miriwoong and Gajirrabeng people have inhabited the region for thousands of years, with sites containing evidence of their occupation scattered through the park.

THINGS TO DO

WALKING: The unique geological formations of the park are best seen from the walks offered from both campgrounds.
GINGER'S HILL WALK: An easy 200 m return walk to an nteresting Aboriginal structure, typical of groups of the region.
GOORRANDALNG WALK: A moderate 2 km walk that weaves through the sandstone country, providing magnificent views of rock formations and the sandstone habitat.

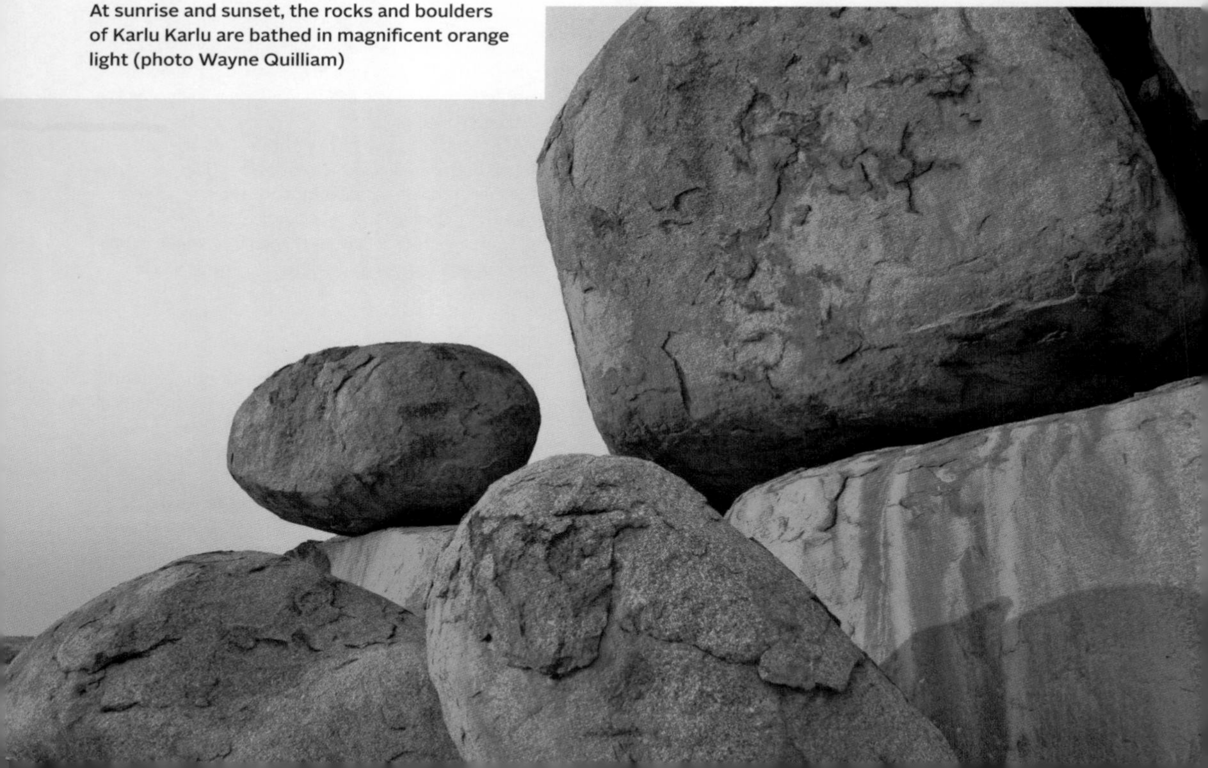

At sunrise and sunset, the rocks and boulders of Karlu Karlu are bathed in magnificent orange light (photo Wayne Quilliam)

JENEMOOM WALK: A moderate 3 km walk that follows the Keep River bed to a Wet season shelter site once used by the Miriwoong people. Evidence of their occupation can be seen in a many-layered midden.

JARNMEN WALKS: There are 3 options for this 7 km loop track, which explore the mini Bungle Bungles sandstone formations. The Jarnem Lookout walk is the most challenging but offers spectacular views of the Keep River Floodplain and the Jarndu escarpment.

The Dry season months of May to August are the most comfortable times to visit, with temperatures of 10–35 °C. However, in the Wet season, provided the park is open, the wetlands and woodlands become lush and particularly beautiful.

CAMPING: Camping areas are available at Goorrandalng, 18 km from the park entrance, and Jarnem, 32km from the park entrance. There are a range of facilities and fees are collected on site.

CONTACT: 08 9167 8827

Litchfield National Park

Litchfield National Park is a true gem. Its 146,000 hectares of diverse landscapes include most types of Top End habitats. Spring-fed waterfalls flow from atop the plateau, creating beautiful, crocodile-free swimming holes, and outliers of imposing, weathered rock rise from grassy plains dotted with massive termite mounds.

CULTURAL HERITAGE: Aboriginal people have lived in the region for thousands of years. In the park are the traditional lands of the Koongurrukun, Marranunggu, Werat and Waray clans.

NATURAL FEATURES: The park is dominated by the Tabletop Range, from which spring-fed waterfalls plunge over its sheer escarpments and craggy rock faces. The constant flow of water from springs and Wet-season floods has gouged out ravines and large rockholes at the base of the range. Creeks spill into the Finniss and Reynolds rivers, which meander westwards across the floodplains to the coast.

Two eucalypt species dominate the tropical woodland, the Darwin woollybutt and stringybark. Banksias, grevilleas, acacias and other flowering species attract birds and insects. Carpentaria palms and aquatic pandanus are common around monsoonal rainforests and along the creeks. Some of the carpentaria forests are extremely tall, with each tree competing for sunlight. Cypress pines grow on the upper slopes around Florence Falls.

In and around the rock pools, water monitor lizards are common. The golden silk orb-weaving spider is also common around waterways, where you will notice their large shimmery, golden webs. Bats inhabit the caverns of the sandstone escarpment. At Tolmer Falls live several colonies of the rare orange leaf-nosed bat and of the ghost bat. The moist tropical vegetation is also home to a range of python species, which are not venomous.

In the woodland environment there are agile wallabies, antilopine wallaroos, common brushtail possums, quolls, sugar gliders and dingoes. The prolific birdlife includes honeyeaters, rainbow bee-eaters, rainbow lorikeets, olive-backed and yellow orioles, dollarbirds, common koels, red-tailed black cockatoos and figbirds. The river floodplains are also important breeding sites for birds such as magpie geese and are home to saltwater crocodiles.

In the Dry season, from May to September, the weather is generally sunny and clear, and the temperature is warm but not too hot. This is the most popular time to visit Litchfield. However, do not overlook a visit in October and November. As the rains begin for the Wet season, the falls become magnificent torrents of water and the rainforests and woodlands become lush and green. Tourists are also fewer. Please take precautions in wetter weather and check the local forecasts – if the rains have been heavy, roads and many waterholes may be closed.

THINGS TO DO

WALKING: Clearly marked trails leave from carparks in most popular areas. At Wangi Falls, a beautiful walk (1.6 km return, 1 hour, medium difficulty) leads around the pool via the top of the falls and includes a boardwalk with wheelchair access. At Tolmer Falls, a 20-minute walk (1.6 km return, 45 minutes, easy) leads from the carpark to an observation platform overlooking a massive rock pool with magnificent Tolmer Falls spilling into the void. Tjaynera Falls (Sandy Creek) and a delightfully cool rock pool are at the end of a rocky track (3.4 km return, 1.5 hours, medium difficulty). Leading from the carpark, the track follows the creek past ancient cycads. An easy stroll around magnetic termite mounds in the north-east of the park is enhanced by a boardwalk with information panels, while one of the best walks in Litchfield is among the sandstone pillars of the Lost City. The Tabletop Track (39 km, 3–5 days, difficult) is a circuit that links many of the park attractions and can be accessed at Florence Falls, Tjaetaba Falls (Greenant Creek), Wangi Falls and Walker Creek. Overnight campers must stay at designated campgrounds; there are 3 on the track.

SWIMMING: Florence and Wangi are impressive waterfalls that plunge into rock pools. They are ideal for swimming and safe from crocodiles during the Dry season. At Buley Rockhole, water cascades over rocks into a series of small plunge pools, offering visitors a range of swimming spots. Another good swimming spot, at the end of a 20-minute walk, is above Tjaetaba Falls. Surprise Creek Falls and Tjaynera Falls are delightful and rarely visited sites just off 4WD tracks. Cascade Falls is a hidden gem. Not as crowded as its famous neighbours, it is reached by an access road off Litchfield Park Rd. The 30-minute walk (medium difficulty, sturdy shoes required) follows Cascade Creek and leads to a series of pools and waterfalls. The falls are almost always closed in the Wet season, as the entire track and carpark gets inundated. The Finniss and Reynolds rivers are off limits to swimmers because they are saltwater crocodile habitats.

WHERE: 100 km south of Darwin. Drive from Darwin via the Stuart Hwy then through Batchelor. The roads to Litchfield are clearly signposted.

CAMPING AND ACCOMMODATION: Camp sites are located throughout the park and generally have both 2WD and 4WD access. There is caravan access at Wangi Falls but no power. Litchfield Tourist Park is the closest commercial accommodation to the national park, with a range of options to suit various budgets.

CONTACT: Litchfield Tourist Park: 08 8976 0070.

Nitmiluk National Park

Nitmiluk National Park is the spectacular Country of the Jawoyn people, who are made up of 17 clans. Impressive stone country, towering escarpments with hidden caverns and caves, gushing waterfalls, broad valleys and a myriad of wildlife are an idyllic backdrop to the many Aboriginal art sites and the rich cultural heritage of the land. The powerful Katherine River, rising in Arnhem Land, has cut through the ancient sandstone to create a series of spectacular gorges.

An outstanding feature of the park is Leliyn (Edith Falls). The Edith River comes off the Nitmiluk escarpment to create the falls. Located 40 km north of Katherine, down a 20 km bitumen road from the Stuart Hwy, the falls descend into the large Leliyn plunge pool. The nearby campground has a small kiosk, a BBQ area, toilets, showers, a laundry and disabled access.

CULTURAL HERITAGE: Nitmiluk, pronounced 'nit-me-look', is the Jawoyn name for the Katherine Gorge. It literally means 'cicada place'. The name was given to the area by Nabilil, a dragon-like Creation-time figure who heard the 'nit, nit nit' song of the cicadas as he travelled through the land. Many other places in the area were also named because of the local wildlife. Nabilil came from the west carrying water in a dilly bag and firesticks.

Bula, the most important figure in the Jawoyn Dreaming story, created this land. He arrived from the north and his actions transformed the landscape. The area where he eventually went underground is today called 'Sickness Country'. The Jawoyn believe that if this country is disturbed fire and earthquakes will wreak havoc on the world. The Rainbow Serpent, called Bolung by the Jawoyn, still inhabits the second gorge, making it a sacred area and Jawoyn people are very careful not to disturb her.

In the traditions, ceremonies, relationships and stories of the Jawoyn people, the Dreaming characters play significant roles. While not all the Dreaming places are dangerous or sacred, all must be approached with care, as they are all significant for the Traditional Owners.

Katherine Gorge was handed back to the Jawoyn people in 1989, and they established Nitmiluk National Park in joint management with the Parks and Wildlife Commission of the Northern Territory.

NATURAL FEATURES: The park lies at the junction of three geological formations – the Pine Creek Geosyncline and the McArthur and Daley basins. Katherine Gorge is a series of 13 gorges that cut through an ancient sandstone plateau formed some 1400 million years ago. Monsoonal waters have eroded the sandstone over the last 20 million years, creating the massive gorge and countless ravines.

More than 450 plant species have been recorded in the area, with some, such as the wattle *Acacia helicophylla*, endemic to the park. The narrow ravines shelter small pockets of monsoonal rainforest plants, while the open plains and valleys have common eucalypt species such as Darwin woollybutt, fan-leafed bloodwood, river red gum and the beautiful salmon gum. Speargrass and native sorghum are widespread and spinifex clumps grow in the high rocky terrain.

The waterways of Nitmiluk are a habitat for fish and other marine creatures, the most common being barramundi and freshwater bream. Archerfish can be spotted near the riverbanks, along with the northern snake-necked turtle. Freshwater crocodiles are common, with the occasional 'salty' finding its way into the gorge during a big Wet season. Gould's sand goanna, the frilled-neck lizard and a variety of frogs are common, while the cane toad is a relatively recent invader. Agile wallabies, antilopine wallaroos and dingoes roam the tropical woodland, while elusive rock wallabies haunt the high rocky outcrops. Most Top End bird species are here, with the rare and colourful Gouldian finch nesting in salmon gums in the Yenberrie Hills, near Leliyn.

THINGS TO DO

BUSHWALKING: There is an excellent network of walking trails in the Nitmiluk National Park. Many walks around the Nitmiluk Gorge itself start from the visitor centre and begin with a climb onto the rocky escarpment. Day walks range from 3½ hours to 9 hours and include the Lily Ponds, Butterfly Gorge, Windolf, Baruwel and Smitt Rock walks. Longer 2–3-day hikes include the Eighth Gorge, Waleka and Jawoyn Valley walks.

The Leliyn Trail (2.6 km return, 2 hours, medium difficulty) is a well-marked loop track that climbs to the top of the escarpment then down to the Edith River, via 2 beautiful pools. Sweetwater walk (8.6 km return, day walk or overnight, moderate to difficult) follows the Edith River to Sweetwater Pool, a good spot for camping and swimming. The track is the last section of the Jatbula Trail. Campers must check the availability of the Sweetwater campground as it is preferentially reserved for Jatbula Trail hikers.

THE JATBULA TRAIL: is a 62 km one-way hike between Nitmiluk Gorge and Leliyn Falls, named after Peter Jatbula, the Jawoyn Traditional Owner instrumental in securing land rights for the Jawoyn people. The trail follows the footsteps of generations of Jawoyn people who traditionally traversed through sections of the track. Following the western edge of the Arnhem Land escarpment over striking sandstone plateaus and through diverse forest and riverine landscapes, the Jatbula Trail passes Northern Rockhole, Biddlecombe Cascades, Crystal Falls, the Amphitheatre and 17 Mile Falls. It is considered to be one of the best walks in northern Australia.

The trail can be completed in 5 days and 4 nights, or 6 days and 5 nights, with each overnight camp set near a cascade or spring. It is graded medium to hard, and requires a reasonable level of fitness.

Booking is essential as numbers are strictly limited. The hike books out months in advance most years. See the PWCNT website for booking information, and when to book.

CANOEING: Canoe hire (per hour or for several days) is available from Nitmiluk Tours. A scenic boat ride takes canoeists through the first gorge to the second gorge, where canoeing can commence. Canoeing through the second gorge and beyond is self-guided and canoeists must carry their own canoe between gorges. Generally, in the time permitted in a day trip, canoeists go as far as the third gorge. For trips further up the gorge, camping is recommended. Canoeists may only camp at the designated camping spots. Overnight trips to the higher gorges are a spectacular and rewarding experience away from the crowds. Late in the Dry season, the river is languid and the water level low so portage becomes strenuous. It is better to plan your trip for earlier in the season. Canoeing is banned during the Wet season. For more information see the Nitmiluk Canoe Guide on the NT Government's national parks webpages.

SCENIC TOURING: Nitmiluk Tours run cruises up the gorge, ranging from 2-hour trips to half- and full-day safaris. In the Wet season, a jet boat travels through the rapids to the third gorge. Helicopter rides leave from a helipad within the park and provide an excellent overview of the area. Nitmiluk Tours also offer accommodation options, from camping to chalets to a luxury lodge. See the Nitmiluk Tours website.

SWIMMING: There are delightful swimming holes at Southern Rockhole, Northern Rockhole, 17 Mile Falls, Biddlecombe Cascades and Crystal Falls. Check with the rangers before swimming in Leliyn and Katherine Gorge because saltwater crocodiles can be present after the Wet season. Always watch for closures.

WHERE: 345 km south-east of Darwin; 30 km north-east of Katherine.

CAMPING AND ACCOMMODATION: Camp sites with facilities are located at Nitmiluk Centre and non-powered sites are available at Leliyn (Edith Falls). Bush camp sites are located along the longer walking trails and the Katherine River. Campers must register and fees do apply – contact the visitor centre. Nitmiluk Tours also offer accommodation options, from camping to chalets to a luxury lodge. Numerous accommodation options are also available in and around Katherine.

PERMITS: Permits are required for camping, walking and boating. Contact the Nitmiluk Visitor Centre.

CONTACT: Nitmiluk Visitor Centre: 08 8972 1253; PWCNT Nitmiluk: 08 8972 1886; PWCNT Leliyn (Edith Falls): 08 8975 4852; PWCNT Katherine: 08 8951 8250

Tjoritja/West MacDonnell National Park

The MacDonnell Ranges are an ancient landscape of parallel ridges sculpted by the elements over millions of years. They rise dramatically from the flat terrain of Central Australia. In one of the oldest and driest regions of the world, hidden gorges and waterholes in Tjoritja/West MacDonnell National Park provide a refuge for plants and wildlife, while the range tops are covered in spinifex and hardy drought-tolerant shrubs.

CULTURAL HERITAGE: The Arrernte people have lived in this area for over 30,000 years and Tjoritja plays a major role in their spiritual beliefs. The desert people lived well here, walking throughout the Country to gather food from underground larders, picking fruit and seeds, and hunting animals and birds. Over generations they accumulated knowledge about plants and animals and where to find water. Conflict arose when Europeans arrived and vied for the best watering areas. Bloody battles ensued and during the dispossession that followed, many Aboriginal people were sheltered by missionaries and influenced by Christianity. Today, important Dreaming trails and sacred sites in the MacDonnell Ranges are still visited for ceremonial purposes.

NATURAL FEATURES: Some 850 million years ago, Central Australia was covered by an inland sea; around 600 million years ago, massive uplifting occurred which formed the chain of mountains now known as the MacDonnell Ranges. Steady erosion by wind and water has carved out spectacular gorges and canyons, some of which retain pools of water throughout the year. Narrow, steep-sided chasms such as Redbank, Glen Helen, Ormiston and Serpentine gorges intersect the 'West Macs', as they are known locally. At 1380 m, Mt Sonder is a landmark of the park. The 1531 m Mt Zeil in the extreme north-west of the park is the highest peak in the Northern Territory.

Eucalypt and acacia trees dominate the lower terrain of the park while mallee, mulga and spinifex grasses cling to the dry rugged hills. The MacDonnell Ranges are a refuge for rare and threatened plants and up to 40 species can be traced back to times when Central Australia was wetter and covered in lush rainforest. These ancient species include the MacDonnell Ranges cycad (*Macrozamia macdonnellii*), maidenhair fern, skeleton fork fern and mountain hakea. Some common trees include the desert she-oak, river red gum, corkwood and coolibah. Here, too, is the beautiful smooth white-barked ghost gum (*Corymbia aparrerinja*), which often features in Aboriginal mythology and was made famous in the paintings of Albert Namatjira. After heavy rains the desert comes alive with wildflowers including mulla mullas, the desert rose, native hops and daisies. With Europeans came a variety of feral animals, including cats, foxes, rabbits, horses, donkeys and camels, which either preyed on small mammals in Central Australia or severely degraded their habitats. Twelve mammal species have disappeared from the region since European contact and others, such as the bilby, rufous hare wallaby, mulgara and black-footed rock-wallaby are endangered. The latter has dramatically declined since the 1930s, and has vanished completely from Uluṟu–Kata Tjuṯa National Park. Red kangaroos, other rock wallaby species, goannas and a variety of other reptiles are still common in the West MacDonnells.

The park has more than 160 bird species. Emus, spinifex pigeons, painted finches, western bowerbirds and dusky grasswrens are common, while at places such as Ellery Creek Big Hole, river red gums are home to Australian ringnecks and pied butcherbirds. Zebra finches, honeyeaters and pigeons drink from the rock pools alongside water birds such as grebes, darters and white-faced herons.

THINGS TO DO

Walking, cycling and 2WD touring are all good ways to become acquainted with the park. Also, an aerial view from a fixed-wing aircraft or helicopter is stunning. There are numerous bushwalks available all over various sections of the park. Swimming is a possibility at many of the waterholes but be mindful as the water can be extremely cold.

SOME OF THE MANY PLACES TO VISIT ALONG THE MACDONNELL RANGES INCLUDE:

SIMPSONS GAP: Sacred to the Central Arrernte Aboriginal people, the Gap is known as Rrengetyirpe. The Dreaming stories of the area involve the goanna, eagle and rock wallaby. The Gap, located 18 km from Alice Springs, is open daily, 5 am–8 pm. There are several well-marked trails including Ghost Gum walk (<1 km, 15 minutes return, easy), a short trail that starts at the visitor centre and takes in the vegetation of the area. Cassia Hill walk (1.8 km, 1 hour return, easy) leads through clumps of witchetty bush and mulga, and rewards visitors with views over Simpsons Gap and the surrounding Country. Woodland Trail (17 km return, 7 hours) passes through mulga woodlands and leads to Bond Gap, a narrow chasm with an ice-cold pool. This part of the national park can be busy during the peak season, but the gap has a permanent waterhole and there is the opportunity to see the black-footed rock-wallabies that live in the boulder-strewn gorge. There is a small camp site but it is only for use by those walking the Larapinta Trail.

ELLERY CREEK BIG HOLE: Called Udepata in Arrernte, this area is sacred to the Eastern Arrernte and Western Aranda people. The Honey Ant Dreaming is the main Dreaming story of the waterhole, although there is also a Fish Dreaming. There are easy walks around this large waterhole, which is located 92 km from Alice Springs. It is a beautiful place to swim, picnic and to view the birdlife. If you want to swim across to the small sandy 'beach', take an inflatable li-lo for safety, and then float back on the still, deep water, marvelling at the blueness of the sky. The permanent water here made it an important meeting place for the Arrernte people.

SERPENTINE GORGE: Called Ulpma by the Western Aranda people, Serpentine Gorge is considered a sacred site. The Dreaming story of the gorge is associated with the Eaglehawk ancestor, but the full story can only be told by traditionally initiated Aboriginal men. There are special Arrernte ceremonial places on the western cliffs and in the gorge itself. A short, steep walking track from the carpark takes about 25 minutes to reach this sheltered oasis. The narrow gorge extends for about another 2 km and there is an easy, well-marked trail that leads to a lookout. The water attracts birdlife, including tiny fairy martins, and insects such as dragonflies skim across its surface. The Centralian flannel flower and the MacDonnell Ranges cycad are rare and endemic, and both grow in the gorge.

OCHRE PITS: For thousands of years Aboriginal people gathered red and white ochre from the banks of a sandy creek at this site, 110 km west of Alice Springs. The ochre was used for medicinal and cultural purposes and for trading with other clans. Red ochre mixed with grease can be applied

Wurre's (Rainbow Valley) sandstone cliffs and tessellated claypan (photo Wayne Quilliam)

as an ointment and can relieve congestion when mixed with eucalyptus leaves. White ochre can be mixed with water and blown from the mouth to abate the heat of the sun, and it was also used as a charm. Ochre can also be used on wooden weapons to increase the success of hunting and to protect them from termites.

ORMISTON GORGE AND POUND: This gorge is located 135 km west of Alice Springs and has a near-permanent 15 m-deep waterhole framed by sheer 300 m-high cliffs. To the Western Aranda people it is a sacred site known as Kwartatuma. The Dreaming story of the area involves the hunting of a group of emus that journeyed to the waterhole from the east. The Pound is a huge rock-walled amphitheatre almost 10 km across. There are a number of walks including Waterhole walk (500 m, 10 minutes one way), a short stroll from the carpark around the waterhole; Ghost Gum Lookout walk (20 minutes one way, easy); and Ormiston Pound walk (8 km circuit, 3–4 hours, moderate), which winds around the slopes of the gorge, descending to the floor of the Pound and returning along the gorge past the waterhole. The long-tailed dunnart and central rock-rat were rediscovered here in 1996.

REDBANK GORGE: Located 165 km west of Alice Springs, Redbank Gorge is also a sacred site for the Western Aranda people. Known as Yarretyeke in Arrernte, the Dreaming story of the area is connected to the euro, a small kangaroo species. However, the full story is restricted to traditionally initiated Aboriginal men only. The Gorge walk (2 km, 1.5 hours return, moderate) is a short hike up a stony creek bed from the carpark to the gorge, which is little more than a small slit between two towering quartzite walls. During dry periods, a path of fine sand marks the bottom of the gorge and it is easy to walk through, but at other times a deep pool of icy water greets visitors. It is advisable to swim in wet suits or to take an air mattress to navigate the waters. Redbank Gorge marks the beginning of a marked trail to Mt Sonder (16 km return, 6–7 hours, moderate), which lies to the east.

LARAPINTA TRAIL: This is an award-winning walking trail (231 km, several weeks) considered one of the best walking tracks in the world. It runs along the backbone of the West MacDonnells, from the old telegraph station just north of Alice Springs to Mt Sonder in the north-west of the park, and is divided into 12 sections. People with basic bushwalking experience can easily traverse section one from Alice Springs to Simpsons Gap, but some other sections are more difficult. For further details contact PWCNT: 08 8951 8250, or visit: www.larapintatrail.com.au

WHERE: The Western MacDonnells stretch 170 km west from Alice Springs. Drive from Alice Springs via Larapinta and Namatjira drives; from Kings Canyon and Yulara via Mereenie Loop Rd, also known as the Red Centre Way.

CAMPING AND ACCOMMODATION: Camp sites with full facilities, 4WD-only sites and basic walk-in sites are scattered throughout the park. Glen Helen Lodge, 08 8956 7489, is the commercial operation closest to the park and offers caravan and motel accommodation. There is a wide range of accommodation available in Alice Springs.

PERMITS: A permit is required for Mereenie Loop Rd, which passes through Aboriginal land; available from Alice Springs Visitor Centre: 08 8952 5800 or Kings Canyon Resort: 08 8956 7442. Permits are required at some camp sites.

CONTACT: Simpsons Gap ranger station: 08 8955 0310; Ormiston Gorge ranger station: 08 8956 7799; PWCNT Alice Springs: 08 8951 8250: Glen Helen Lodge: 08 8956 7489.

Tnorala (Gosse Bluff) Conservation Reserve

Western Aranda people believe that Tnorala was formed in Creation time, when a group of women who were dancing across the sky as the Milky Way were holding a wooden baby carrier which fell to Earth and formed the circular rock walls. Scientists believe that more than 130 million years ago a comet crashed to Earth and blasted a crater about 20 km in diameter, creating Tnorala – one of the largest sites on Earth to be impacted by space debris. The comet would have been over 600 m across, and the mushroom cloud created from the force of the landing is thought to have spread around the world.

A 4WD track leads to the inner crater, where visitors can stand or picnic on the spot where the massive terrestrial body crashed. Interpretive signs give an excellent explanation of the event, while a walking trail circuits Tnorala and a lookout on a ridge provides great viewing.

WHERE: 175 km west of Alice Springs.

CAMPING: No camping; day use only.

PERMIT: A permit is required to access the park via Mereenie Loop Road; available from Alice Springs Visitor Centre: 08 8952 5800, or Kings Canyon Resort: 08 8956 7442.

CONTACT: PWCNT Alice Springs: 08 8951 8250

Uluṟu–Kata Tjuṯa National Park

Located in the red heart of the Central Desert, the ancient forms of Uluṟu and Kata Tjuṯa lie geographically, spiritually and symbolically at the centre of the Australian continent. Rising majestically above the red-sand plains, they dominate the landscape and are shrouded in myth and mystery. Their colours and moods are ever-changing with the interplay of light from the sun, cloud and rain.

Protected within Uluṟu–Kata Tjuṯa National Park, Uluṟu (Ayers Rock) and Kata Tjuṯa (The Olgas) rise like giant red icebergs from the flat 'sea' of the surrounding desert. At around 350 m high, Uluṟu is the world's largest monolith, higher than the Eiffel Tower, with a circumference measuring 9.4 km and an estimated depth of 6 km below the Earth's surface.

For the local people, the Yankunytjatjara and Pitjantjatjara Aṉangu (Aṉangu meaning people in a number of Central Australian languages), Uluṟu and Kata Tjuṯa are far more than just rock formations. They make up a living cultural landscape that is sacred to them.

On 26 October 1985, Uluṟu and Kata Tjuṯa were handed back to the Aṉangu, who are the Traditional Owners of the land, in what remains one of the most significant moments in Australia's Aboriginal land rights movement. It had taken over 35 years of campaigning for the Aṉangu to be recognised as the park's Traditional Owners and given the deeds to their land. From that day, the Aṉangu agreed to lease the park to the federal government for 99 years. This allows public access and also provides funds for the local community. The national park is jointly managed by the Aṉangu and Parks Australia.

In 1987, the area won World Heritage listing for its natural wonders. In 1994, Uluṟu–Kata Tjuṯa National Park became the official park name and the next year it won another World Heritage listing for its cultural value. The park is ranked as one of the most significant arid-land ecosystems and is classified by UNESCO as a Biosphere Reserve.

CULTURAL HERITAGE: Uluṟu is a site of ceremonial significance for many Aboriginal groups of Central Australia, including the Pitjantjatjara and Yankunytjatjara Aṉangu, who have lived in the region for at least 10,000 years. There are more than 40 sacred Aboriginal sites in the area where ancestral spirits still reside, making the land deeply important to the cultural identity of the Aṉangu. The Pitjantjatjara and Yankunytjatjara people still abide by ancient laws and traditions, referred to as Tjukurpa, which provide the foundation to their unique culture.

Before the arrival of Europeans, the Indigenous people moved around this land, which varied from mulga flats and sand dunes to rocky hills and pockets of vegetation around the base of rocks such as Uluṟu. Each of these environments was used at different times of the year, depending on the food and water available. Water was present in claypans, rockholes, soaks and springs. Around the base of Uluṟu are rock shelters and caves, decorated with hundreds of rock paintings – some executed as late as the 1940s – but the ravages of weather and over-visitation by tourists in the past have resulted in severe deterioration. The art sites at Kata Tjuṯa, where there are more engravings than paintings, are better preserved. Today some of the most important cultural areas in the park are out of bounds to non-Indigenous people.

NATURAL FEATURES: Uluṟu and Kata Tjuṯa are remnants of a huge bed of sedimentary rock, worn down by nature over some 40 million years after an inland sea retreated. It is believed Kata Tjuṯa may have been a single rock bigger than Uluṟu before it was weathered back to 36 separate but dramatic rock domes, one of which is almost 200 m higher than Uluṟu.

Between Uluṟu and Kata Tjuṯa lies an ancient valley comprising sand layers that hold water, much of which seeps out into Lake Amadeus, about 40 km north of the national park. Some of this water is estimated to be 7000 years old. The surrounding dune Country is even older, with dunes unchanged for 30,000 years, apart from the loose sand on the dune crests.

Uluṟu and Kata Tjuṯa are among the most photographed and filmed destinations on Earth; the red rock changes colour quickly during the day, and particularly around sunset. Both areas are spectacular during storms and after heavy rain.

The arid landscape around the park comes alive after soaking rains, and vivid wildflowers of white, pink, yellow and blue contrast against the red earth and azure sky. Daisies, desert fringe-myrtle, emu bush and parrot peas are common. Spinifex and other grasses form a thick layer on the desert floor, while mulga is the dominant tree species, tangled and black during dry times, lush and green after a flood. After rains, the green-grey bush tomato flowers and produces small purplish fruit highly prized by the Aboriginal people. The seeds of desert oak, umbrella bush and bloodwood provide food for desert animals, while honey grevillea flowers provide sweetness and energy for a range of birds and insects.

Once 46 species of mammals were found in the park, but today this number has been reduced by more than half. Recently, the mala was reintroduced and moves are being made to reintroduce other locally extinct animals. The insect-eating mulgara, which lives in burrows on the dry sand plain area of the park, is the only mammal currently listed as vulnerable. It shares its habitat with numerous dunnart species and the unadorned desert-skink; watch for this reptile around clumps of spinifex, where it likes to forage. Here, too, is the spinifex hopping mouse, although it prefers to shelter in its burrow during the day, emerging at dusk to zigzag between grassy clumps on the desert floor. Seven species of bat live in the caves and rock crevices of the park. More visible mammals are common wallaroos (euros), red kangaroos, and herds of feral camels, all seen grazing on the plains. Around the rocks you might glimpse dingoes and emus, while rock wallabies hop around the escarpments.

Reptiles are abundant, with some 73 species recorded. Along with numerous skinks, there are sand monitors, the awesome 2 m-long perentie, geckos, and a range of snake species, such as the venomous king brown and the desert death adder. In the shrublands and grassy tussocks watch out for the fierce-looking, but harmless and somewhat delicate, thorny devil.

There are 178 bird species recorded in the park, including some species that are rare in the area such as the elusive striated grasswren, a spinifex dweller. Some of the special birds to be seen at Uluṟu include the oriental plover, princess parrot, grey honeyeater and western bowerbird, while the chiming wedgebill and grey falcon may be seen at Kata Tjuṯa. Other desert birds, such as cockatiels, budgerigars, little button-quails, zebra finches, crows and honeyeaters, are also common. Wedge-tailed eagles and other raptors including black-shouldered kites glide effortlessly on the thermals looking for prey.

THINGS TO DO

A visit to the cultural centre to learn about Aṉangu history and culture, and the arid-zone landscape, will add value to your trip and will give you a better appreciation of the park. You can also visit the Walkatjara Art Centre, which is owned and directed by the Aṉangu of the Mutitjulu community. It showcases their vibrant paintings, which depict traditional stories from the area.

There are parking areas at Uluṟu and Kata Tjuṯa where visitors will have good views of the landscape at sunrise and sunset. Arrive early, especially to watch and photograph the changing colours of Uluṟu, as crowds can be heavy during the peak tourist season. Off the Kata Tjuṯa Rd there is a 30-minute return walk to the dune viewing area, which provides seating, shade and panoramic views of Kata Tjuṯa and the sand dunes (tour groups only after 4 pm).

There are a number of walks that lead to areas around the base of Uluṟu. Kuniya walk (1 km, 45 minutes return, easy), on the southern side of the rock, is a short stroll that leads past rock-art sites to a picturesque waterhole, home of Wanampi, an ancestral water snake, and for centuries an important camping place for Aboriginal people. Before taking the walk, pick up a self-guiding brochure at the cultural centre, which explains Aboriginal cultural and spiritual beliefs of the area that are accessible to the public. Mala walk (2 km, 1.5 hours return, easy), on the north-western side of the rock, is an easy trail that passes several caves used by the Aṉangu until recently, then ends at Kantju Gorge. Signs along this walk give explanations of Aboriginal Creation times. A free ranger-guided tour of Mala walk is conducted daily from the base of Uluṟu during the Dry season – departure times vary depending on the seasons. A self-guiding brochure is also available for this walk at the cultural centre. Both of these walks are wheelchair accessible.

Two longer walks allow visitors to appreciate the immensity of Uluṟu and Kata Tjuṯa. The Base of Uluṟu walk (10.6 km circuit, 3–4 hours, moderate) leads around the base of the rock. The walk takes in the Mala and Kuniya trails, and you are asked to walk in a clockwise direction. The Valley of the Winds walk (7.4 km circuit, 3 hours, medium difficulty) in Kata Tjuṯa is spectacular. The track is steep and rocky in places as it leads through deep canyons and broad valleys, and there are 2 lookouts along the way.

Several shorter walks include Walpa Gorge walk (2.6 km, 1 hour return, moderate), a gentle, rising track in Kata Tjuṯa that leads to the end of a gorge where vine-like spearwood (*Pandorea pandorana*) flourishes amid the rocks. When in flower, this shrub is covered in large, creamy white bells. The long

stems, tough and flexible, were used by Aboriginal people to make spears.
SACRED SITES: Maps provided by the cultural centre clearly mark the sacred sites of the park. Out of respect to the Aṉangu and their culture, some sites may not be visited, filmed or photographed. Please respect the wishes of the Traditional Owners. **Uluṟu itself is a sacred site.** From 26 October 2019, coinciding with the 34th year of the return of Uluṟu to its Traditional Owners, climbing the rock has been banned, out of respect for the cultural and spiritual beliefs of the Aṉangu.
WARNING: High temperatures at Uluṟu can cause heat stroke and exhaustion. Walkers are advised to wear a hat and strong shoes, use sunscreen and drink plenty of water. Avoid wearing lycra and other fabrics that do not breathe, because the red rocks create more heat in already high temperatures and wearing clothes made of these materials can lead to heat stroke.
Stay on marked trails and walk in the cooler hours of the day – preferably early morning.
WHERE: The park is 440 km south-west of Alice Springs. The 450 km drive to Uluṟu–Kata Tjuṯa from Alice Springs takes roughly 5 hours via the Stuart and Lasseter hwys. The highways are sealed roads, so a 4WD is not required. Jetstar, Virgin Airlines and Qantas fly to Uluṟu.
CAMPING AND ACCOMMODATION: There are no camping or other accommodation options within the national park itself. Yulara, 20 km from Uluṟu, is the closest base to explore the park. There are hotels to suit all budgets, as well as camping and caravan facilities.
PERMITS: A park-use fee is charged per person. This is valid for 3 days; annual tickets are also available. All tickets are payable at the park entry station.
CONTACT: Culture Centre: 08 8956 1128; Ayers Rock campground: 08 8957 7001: Ayers Rock Resort: 1300 134 044

Watarrka National Park

This rugged landscape is endlessly fascinating, though the most famous and remarkable feature is Kings Canyon, an imposing, massive cut of red sandstone over 100 m tall. Rock formations which have been shaped by wind and water over thousands of years rise from the top of the rock.

The Traditional Owners are the Luritja people, who now jointly manage the park with PWCNT. The park is named for the acacia (umbrella bush) tree known as watarrka in Luritja, as Kings Canyon has long been an oasis of cool, wet gorges and shade during the long, hot summers and droughts.

Kathleen Springs is another attraction of the park, as well as the Garden of Eden. There are bushwalks of varying length and levels throughout the national park, with the Kings Canyon Rim Walk offering an especially stunning view. The Giles Track is 22 km long and the most intense walk on offer, and visitors must register with the Overnight Walkers Registration Scheme on 1300 650 730.

There are regularly scheduled ranger talks on nature between May and October at both the Kathleen Springs carpark and the Canyon carpark shelter.

WHERE: 302 km south-west of Alice Springs.
CAMPING AND ACCOMODATION: Camping in the park is available at Kings Canyon Holiday Park Caravan Park & Campground: 08 8956 7442, 7 km from the canyon, or Kings Creek Station: 08 8956 7474, aworking cattle and camel station located just outside the park's eastern boundary, with a range of other accommodation options available at these properties. Bush camping is not permitted. Kings Canyon Resort offers a range of accommodation styles, from deluxe spa rooms to private and shared lodge rooms.
PERMITS: A permit is required for the Mereenie Loop Rd, which passes through Aboriginal land; available from Alice Springs Visitor Centre: 08 8952 5800 or Kings Canyon Resort: 08 8956 7442.
CONTACT: PWCNT Watarrka: 08 8956 7460; PWCNT Alice Springs: 08 8951 8250

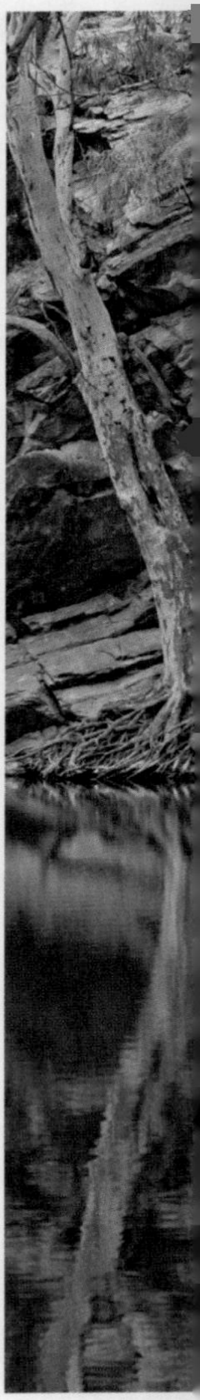

Red sandstone gorges drop into swimming holes, an iconic feature of this landscape (photo Wayne Quilliam)

Wurre (Rainbow Valley) Conservation Reserve

Cliffs of sandstone catch and reflect light over the desert during sunrise and sunset, making this conservation reserve one of the most beautiful outback experiences close to Alice Springs. Erosion and weather have shaped the valley and sculpted the sandstone, with different coloured rock shining throughout the day. After rain, the desert floor becomes a magnificent explosion of wildflowers, and the claypans around the cliffs will hold water long after the surrounds dry up. Aboriginal culture is seen in the rock art and ancient petroglyphs, and scattered artefacts from the early pioneering days can be viewed through the rocks and ridges. A marked walking trail goes to Mushroom Rock from the camping ground.

Temperatures can be quite extreme so adequate clothing cover and water is necessary.

WHERE: 97 km south-west of Alice Springs.
CAMPING: Camp in designated areas; basic facilities.
CONTACT: PWCNT Alice Springs: 08 8951 8250; PWCNT Alice Springs Telegraph Station: 08 8952 1013

TOURS AND STAYS

Alice Springs Visitor Information Centre

Right in the centre of town, the information centre has friendly and knowledgeable staff who are happy to help you plan your itinerary, share their backyard secrets, and share all they know about the NT. There is the most current information on Indigenous tours, as well as a walking tour which allows visitors to peer into Alice's past, learn about Aboriginal culture, bush foods and medicine, and the way of life in the outback.

The centre can help with comprehensive booking services, whether it be tours, unlimited car hire, or accommodation. With up-to-date information about all on offer – your outback adventure will be better for walking into this lovely, air-conditioned building. There is a small gift shop with souvenirs, and plenty of regional maps and brochures available to help you wherever you go in this vast Territory.

WHERE: Cnr of Todd Mall and Parsons St, Alice Springs.
CONTACT: 1800 645 199, 08 8952 5800

Ayal Aboriginal Tours Kakadu

Local Aboriginal guide, Victor Cooper, is a Traditional Owner and former park ranger who knows the area of Kakadu well and enjoys sharing his knowledge and stories with visitors during his small-group tours. They include the Kakadu Aboriginal Rock Art Tour, which visits Ubirr, one of Kakadu's major rock-art sites; and Buffalo Camp History and Wildlife Tour, in which visitors travel in an air-conditioned 4WD along the Arnhem Hwy towards the Alligator River floodplains. Ayal Aboriginal Tours also offer private tours that provide an exclusive Kakadu National Park experience for up to 4 people in a 4WD vehicle or up to 12 in a bus.

CONTACT: 08 8979 0483; 0429 470 384

Banubanu Beach Retreat

Located on Yolŋu Country, eco-friendly Banubanu Beach Retreat enables guests to experience the remote majesty of tropical East Arnhem Land in an intimate way. The Traditional Owners have permitted the Banubanu Beach Retreat to operate on the land in exchange for a permit fee – going directly to the Traditional Owners – which all guests are expected to pay. Stay in luxury beachfront accommodation that showcases the pristine aqua waters, vibrant sunsets and diverse local fauna in an area rich with ancient culture. Enjoy a meditative and restorative pace while snorkelling, exploring the unique landscape by foot or reading on the beach. Dine on local produce, including freshly caught seafood. The Dry season (May to October) provides warm days and cool nights, while the Wet season (November to April) turns the landscape a lush green with dynamic lightning shows.

WHERE: Banubanu Beach Retreat is on Bremer Island, in the waters off Nhulunbuy, East Arnhem Land. It is accessible by air or water, with multiple transport options available on the website.
CONTACT: 08 8987 8085

Cicada Lodge

A unique luxury lodge overlooking the Katherine River within the Nitmiluk National Park. The lodge is open all year round, apart from February when it is closed for scheduled maintenance, and is designed to provide a base from which guests can explore the unique history, beauty and culture of the lands of the Jawoyn people, within Nitmiluk and Kakadu national parks.

FACILITIES: The lodge has 18 modern air-conditioned rooms, all with private balconies opening out into the natural surrounds. All rooms are decorated with local Indigenous artwork. Facilities include an outdoor pool, restaurant, room service, concierge and airport transfers on request.
DINING: The Cicada Lodge restaurant is regularly featured as a winner of the prestigious Gold Plate Awards, and in 2018 won Gold at the QANTAS Australian Tourism Awards for Best Restaurant and Catering service. The restaurant is all about the total experience, with guests invited to taste and experience Indigenous Australian and fresh local foods in a vibrant, contemporary menu. Dishes are truly unique to the region.
WHERE: Nitmiluk National Park, 330 km south of Darwin.
CONTACT: Within Australia: 1300 146 743; International: +61 8 8971 0877

Davidson's Arnhem Land Safaris

Set at Mt Borradaile, the idyllic 700 sq km area that is home to Davidson's Arnhem Land Safaris is a registered Aboriginal sacred site, with caves that have seen 50,000 years of Indigenous occupation. While the area is managed by the Traditional Owners, the Amurdak people, Davidson's was given the great privilege of an honorary custodian status when, in 1986, the Traditional Owners asked Max Davidson if he would start a tourism venture at Mt Borradaile. Davidson's Safaris now provides the Amurdak people with a valuable source of income, and their style of eco tourism is helping to preserve the many significant and sacred sights in the area.

Davidson's Safaris offer something for every taste, such as a billabong cruise, visiting ancient rock art and catacombs, fishing, or exploring for rare species of animals. There is a modern eco lodge on site which includes a pool and lounge area, with a range of cabin facilities and a first-class dining experience. Guests often take a few of the tours on offer and really explore this restricted area of Arnhem Land.

WHERE: Mt Borradaile, Arnhem Land.
PERMITS: Access to Mt Borradaile is restricted and permits are required to enter the lands. When you book with Davidson's, permits will be organised for you and the price included in your accommodation fees.
CONTACT: 08 8979 0413

Injalak Rock Art Tours

Injalak Hill boasts a series of outstanding rock-art galleries that range from 100 to 8000 years old. Injalak Arts has been given exclusive permission by the Traditional Owners to facilitate rock-art tours led by trained and experienced local guides who have detailed knowledge of the rock-art sites. The tour runs for 2½ hours. Visitors need to wear good walking shoes and a hat, and bring water, insect repellent and sunscreen. Tours leave Injalak Arts at 9 am Monday to Saturday. Tours operate in the Dry season only when Gunbalanya is accessible by road.

WHERE: Tours depart from Injalak Arts Gunbalanya (see p. 287).
PERMITS: Permits to visit Gunbalanya must be arranged in advance via the Northern Land Council in Darwin or Jabiru.
CONTACT: 08 8979 0190

Kakadu Cultural Tours

Kakadu Cultural Tours are fully owned and operated by the Djabulukgu Association, which represents the Traditional Owners of Northern Kakadu and parts of Western Arnhem Land. This enables their tour groups to have access to exclusive Country and sites. Kakadu Cultural Tours specialises in Aboriginal cultural and nature-based cruises, tours and wilderness lodge accommodation. Small tour groups are escorted by predominantly Aboriginal guides and this ensures a unique cultural experience. Kakadu Cultural Tours offer the following packages:

GULUYAMBI CULTURAL CRUISE: Enjoy a boat tour along the East Alligator River. Scenically spectacular, this river is a fine example of Kakadu's pristine wilderness. A local Aboriginal guide provides guests with an insight into the river system and its abundant food chain, as well as their own culture and ancestral history, traditional uses for plants and animals and bush survival skills. The tour includes a display of traditional hunting and gathering implements. With a limit of only 25 guests, the cruise is an intimate and personalised cultural experience.
WHERE: The tour departs from the upstream boat ramp on the East Alligator River. Follow the Arnhem Hwy 5 km west of Jabiru and turn north onto the Oenpelli Rd. After approximately 36 km, turn right and follow the signs for Guluyambi Cultural Cruise and Upstream Boat Ramp (East Alligator River). The road is sealed all the way. Allow 45 minutes to drive from Jabiru. Allow 4 hours to drive from Darwin.
ARNHEMLANDER CULTURAL AND HERITAGE TOUR: This 4WD day tour of Arnhem Land and Northern Kakadu is an outstanding way to experience the world-famous landscapes of sandstone outcrops, rock-art sites, forests, floodplains and billabongs. The tour crosses the East Alligator into Arnhem Land and takes guests to Injalak Arts Gunbalanya, where you can see traditional painting and pandanus basket-weaving techniques, as well as the Mikkinj Valley, with its stunning scenery of billabongs, wildlife and towering escarpment.
WHERE: The tour departs from Jabiru, with pickups from all accommodation in Jabiru.
HAWK DREAMING WILDERNESS LODGE: Experience a beautiful and remote area of Kakadu that is restricted to guests and local Indigenous residents only. The lodge is located at Cannon Hill, a very special and well-renowned part of Kakadu. The whole area is a registered sacred site and is important to the local Aboriginal people, many of whom live near the lodge. Sandstone outliers surrounding Cannon Hill are sites of significant rock art, which date back thousands of years. As well as the cultural significance, Cannon Hill is an area where you can see a wide diversity of vegetation in Kakadu, with abundant wildlife and untouched bushland making it a breathtaking place to visit.

Guests stay in comfortable tented cabins, with ensuite facilities and decks. These are spread out nicely through the shady grounds. Knowledgeable and experienced camp hosts and guides take guests on evening tours to explore rock-art sites and to watch the sunset from the escarpment. The cost includes breakfasts and 3-course home-style dinners. There are 2 and 3-day tour options available, which include the Guluyambi Cultural Cruise and the Arnhemlander

Cultural and Heritage Tour. See the Kakadu Cultural Tours website for more details.
CONTACT: 1800 525 238

Kakadu Tourism Adventure Tours

This full-day 4WD adventure tour provides access to various less accessible parts of Kakadu, allowing you to visit the stunning waterfalls and waterholes of Kakadu's stone country. Depending on the time of year, weather and road conditions, the tour itinerary varies, so each day is an adventure. The tour has a fleet of 4WDs; meals and refreshments are provided throughout the day.

CONTACT: 08 8979 1500

Karrke Aboriginal Cultural Experiences

At the south-eastern edge of Watarrka National Park, Karrke Tours offers an interactive walking tour. Owned and operated by Christine Breaden and Peter Abbott, Karrke Tours was established to preserve the cultural knowledge, language and heritage of the Luritja and Pertame Southern Arrernte people. Karrke is the Arrernte name for the western bowerbird. The one-hour walking tour gives an insight into numerous cultural practices of the local people from the community of Wanmarra. The tour includes education about bush medicine, bush tucker, important flora and fauna, language, and traditional painting. It is an ideal tour to do after exploring the nearby Kings Canyon.

WHERE: Karrke is located next to Kings Creek Station on the Luritja Hwy; turn off onto a dirt road, then drive 2 km to the Wanmarra Community.
CONTACT: 08 8956 7620

Lirrwi Tourism

The Yolŋu people of East Arnhem Land often say the land is their mother. It nurtures, heals and guides their lives. Homelands are the ancestral lands and seas of various Yolŋu clans, built around a family group. They are sacred places rich in culture, remote and incredibly beautiful. You can learn of this unique culture with Lirrwi Tourism's homeland experiences. A visit to these homelands is unique. Each day is in sync with the environment, wildlife and climate. Expect the unexpected every day, and immerse yourself in Yolŋu culture, and knowledge acquired over many thousands of years. The tours on offer include day tours and multi-day tours.

BAWAKA HOMELAND HIGHLIGHTS: A 4WD adventure to Bawaka Homeland, 60 km south of the community of Yirrkala. This tour provides an insight into Yolŋu homeland life and lets visitors experience traditional spear fishing and crab hunting. You can learn about moiety – Yirratja and Dhuwa (kinship) – and how this connects Yolŋu to the land and to each other in one big balanced Earth, and also hear about the 7 seasons associated with this homeland and see what the environment is telling Yolŋu. This unique experience departs from Nhulunbuy or Yirrkala, with each day offering something different.
GULULU DAY TOUR: Gululu means 'Welcome to our Country'. This tour is a Welcome to Yolŋu Country, the region of Miwatj. This land has been passed down to Yolŋu from generation to generation. They are the Traditional Owners of the sea and of the inland areas, and they invite you to come and explore their culture, sit with them, hear their stories, walk with them, and share some knowledge.

This 1-day tour of Nhulunbuy and surrounds takes participants to a range of spectacular and culturally significant coastal locations in the East Arnhem Region.
PERMITS: A Dhimurru visitor permit is included in the price of this tour.
MULTI-DAY TOURS: A multi-day tour ensures a thorough cultural immersion in Yolŋu life. There is a

range of options available. Multi-day trips include the 4-night, 5-day Yolŋu homeland stay, educational tours for school groups, and women's tours. Specialty tours can also be organised on request to suit visitors' interests and timeframe, including art centre tours and photography tours. Contact Lirrwi Tourism for more details.
CONTACT: 08 8987 2828

Pudakul Aboriginal Cultural Tours

The Limilngan-Wulna people are the Traditional Owners of the land at the forefront to Kakadu National Park. Pudakul Tours operate on the area of the Adelaide River floodplains and the Mary River, and give visitors an opportunity to learn about the cultural practices and spiritual beliefs of these Aboriginal people. Pudakul is the name of the macaranga tree, or freshwater hibiscus. Traditionally, the Limilngan-Wulna people use the plant to make spears.

LIMILNGAN-WULNA CULTURAL TOUR: This tour offers an educational experience set around the Adelaide River floodplains. It provides a connection to culture, with the opportunity to learn the techniques used in basket weaving and dilly-bag making. Visitors can have a go at spear throwing, play a didgeridoo and clapsticks, go on a bush-tucker walk and learn about local bush medicine. The 2-hour tour is an enjoyable introduction to the area, and ideal to do on the way to Kakadu or Litchfield national parks. There is also an all-day tour on Country, where participants make spears, clapsticks, collect, gather and strip fibres, cook damper and enjoy the Country while listening to cultural stories.
WHERE: 45 minutes' drive from Darwin along the Arnhem Hwy. Transfers can be arranged from Darwin at an additional cost; minimum numbers apply.
WETLAND DISCOVERY TOUR: Learn about the magnificent and unique wetland region through the cultural lens of the Limilngan-Wulna people. The guided tour begins with a scenic boat cruise along the picturesque Corroborree Billabong. The billabong is part of the Mary River Wetlands and is home to a spectacular range of bird life, crocodiles and other wildlife. The tour then travels 30 minutes to the Pudakul Aboriginal Cultural Tours centre for a 90-minute experience learning about the local history and culture.
ACCOMMODATION: Pudakul offers accommodation on Country. There is no better way to truly engage with your experience than to stay on Country with the local family in an air-conditioned, self-contained unit after enjoying a tour experience with them; there is a good-size saltwater swimming pool and you can enjoy the picturesque billabong from your own stilt porch.

Book and stay for a day or 2 and ask Pudakul to build an itinerary for the family. There are 5 cabins, with double, single and queen sized bed options. You can ask about Pudakul's roll-away bed for a child or a third person per room.
CONTACT: 08 8984 9282

Rainbow Valley Cultural Tours

In Southern Arrernte language, Rainbow Valley Reserve is referred to as Wurre. This tour, run by Traditional Owner Ricky Orr and his family, is an introduction to culture and Country. Ricky's tours allow visitors to access places in the Rainbow Valley Reserve that are not open to the public, including an ancient rock-art site and other archaeological sites. The tours also inform visitors about the cultural significance of the Rainbow Valley landscape, including information on Dreaming stories and bush foods and medicines. The tours end with a viewing of spectacular sunsets over the sandstone ridges and bluffs – a perfect opportunity to take photographs.

WHERE: Rainbow Valley is located 97 km south of Alice Springs. The turn-off to the reserve is 75 km south of Alice Springs along the Stuart Hwy. From here, it is a 22 km-stretch east along an unsealed road that has some sandy patches. Access is recommended for 4WD only.
CONTACT: 08 8956 0661 or 0427 075 963

SEIT Outback Australia

SEIT Outback Australia takes its name from an acronym of some of the key words that

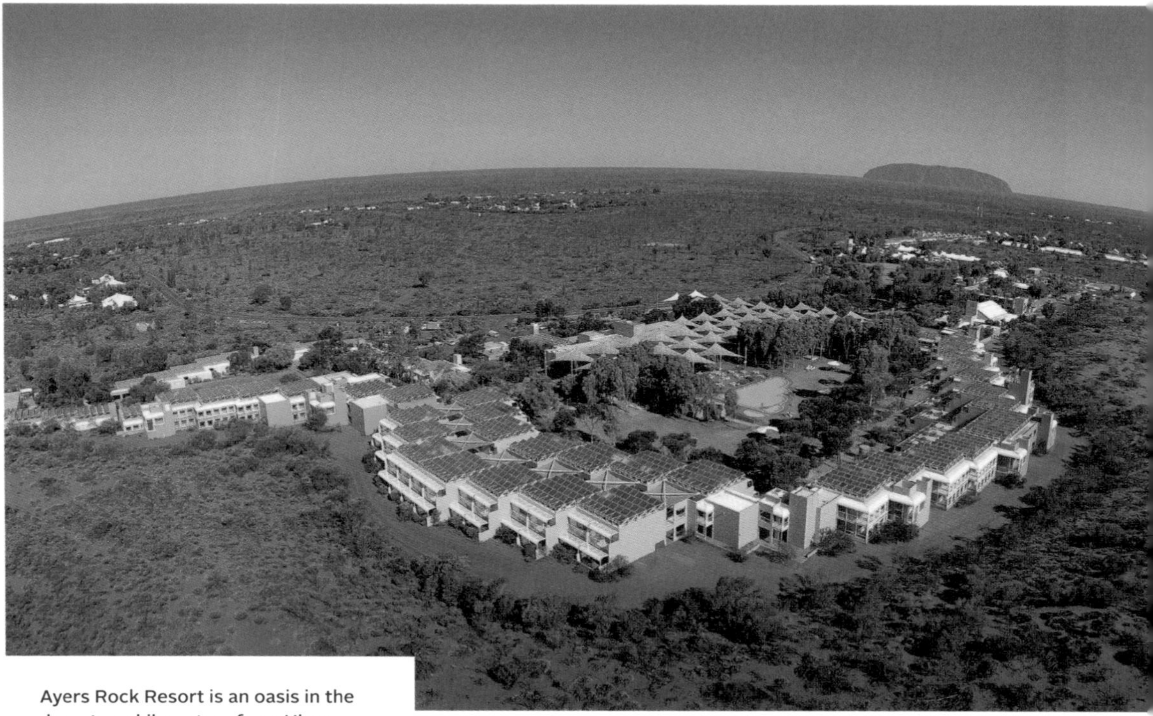

Ayers Rock Resort is an oasis in the desert, 20 kilometres from Uluṟu

describe the kinds of experiences it offers: Spiritual, Emotional, Intellectual and Task-oriented (hands-on). SEIT promises to engage guests in these 4 ways through its large range of tours showcasing the Uluṟu–Kata Tjuṯa region. Experience Australia's most famous landmark, Uluṟu, in the way of your choosing: a 2-hour sunset tour; a 6-hour guided trek around its base, exploring waterholes and Aboriginal rock-art sites as you go; or a Fork and View or Billy Tea experience, during which you will be served quality meals onboard a converted double-decker touring bus as you enjoy views of Uluṟu.

SEIT also offers the option of private touring for those who would like to customise their experience. These tours can include airport transfers and visits to the West MacDonnell Ranges, Rainbow Valley, Alice Springs, Kings Canyon and the Uluṟu Fork and View experience. SEIT tours are run in English, but free iPods are offered featuring audio guides in French, Italian, Spanish, German, Mandarin, Portuguese and Russian. The audio guides will be provided at the beginning of the tour.

WHERE: Yulara.
CONTACT: 08 8956 3156

Venture North Safaris

Family-owned Venture North Safaris is a multi-award winning tour company that specialises in small-group tours exploring the rich cultures and environments of the Northern Territory. Venture North offers

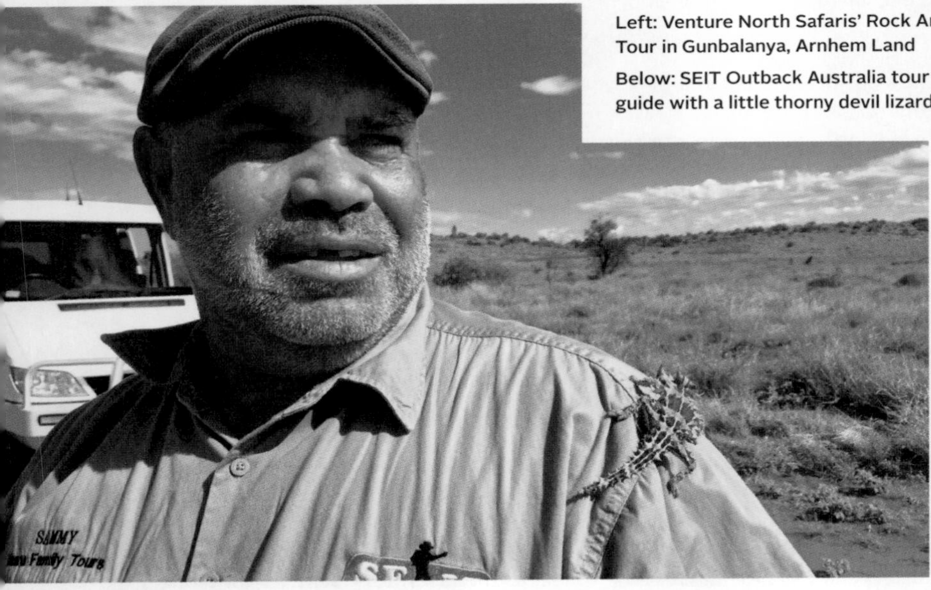

Left: Venture North Safaris' Rock Art Tour in Gunbalanya, Arnhem Land

Below: SEIT Outback Australia tour guide with a little thorny devil lizard

a range of multi-day, 4WD tours around remotes areas of Arnhem Land, Kakadu, Garig Gunak Barlu, Litchfield and Nitmiluk national parks as well as the Kimberley. For those who love fishing, there are also multi-day fly in/fly out fishing packages available, where guests are flown from Darwin to Cobourg Coastal Camp (flights take 1 hour), and are given an exclusive fishing experience in one of Australia's true wilderness areas.

WHERE: Venture North tours operate out of Darwin.
CONTACT: 08 8927 5500

Voyages Indigenous Tourism Australia – Ayers Rock Resort

Ayers Rock Resort is an oasis of hotels (including the Longitude 131 Lodge), tour providers and cultural and natural experiences located right in the heart of Australia, just 20 km from Uluṟu. The resort is owned by the Indigenous Land Corporation (ILC), and has implemented an Indigenous Training and Employment Strategy, aiming to employ Indigenous trainees at the resort each year and to empower a growing Indigenous workforce. All profits from business activities go towards supporting the ILC's Indigenous programs across Australia.

Ayers Rock Resort and the hotels situated there offer a wide range of accommodation and tourism opportunities to suit any needs, from family holidays to culinary, adventure and luxury experiences. The resort also hosts functions, has a variety of dining and restaurant options, and provides a wonderful place from which to explore the Uluṟu–Kata Tjuṯa region. Details on all accommodation and tour packages are available on the website, including hotel-specific phone numbers and contact details.

WHERE: Ayers Rock Resort is located approximately 20 km from Uluṟu along the Uluṟu Rd/Lasseter Hwy.
CONTACT: 02 8296 8010

Watjan Guided Tours

Discover the untouched lands west of the Daly River, visiting secluded stretches of stunning coastline, picturesque waterfalls, authentic Aboriginal fossils, local artwork, local attractions and more. On this 4WD only, self-drive, self-catered experience, you journey through Joe and Lucy's home community of Daly River with the option to visit the neighbouring communities of Nauiyu, Woodycupaldiya, Peppimenarti and Wadeye. Watjan (which means wild dog or dingo) Guided Tours also includes accommodation as part of their tours. You can pitch your tent at their base camp, where you'll find showers and toilets, or if you prefer to spend your nights in a more traditional camp alongside a watering hole in the middle of the bush, this can also be arranged. Ensure you bring everything you need for your trip, such as tents, food and camp gear. Tours run during the Dry season (April to November). Check the website to help organise your trip.

WHERE: Tours depart from Woodycupaldiya or by arrangement.
CONTACT: 0498 572 727 or 0448 036 773

Yellow Water Cruises

Yellow Water Cruises operates year round and provides up to 6 cruises a day, of 90 or 120-minute duration. Located at the end of the Jim Jim Creek, Yellow Water is part of the South Alligator River system. This river system is unique, being included in its entirety within the UNESCO World Heritage-listed Kakadu National Park. Kakadu Tourism has exclusive use of the spectacular Yellow Water

Billabong, providing the ultimate opportunity to experience Kakadu and its abundance of wildlife with their knowledgeable guides.

WHERE: Cruises depart from Cooinda (55 km from Jabiru).
CONTACT: 08 8979 1500

ART GALLERIES AND MUSEUMS

The art centres that are included in this section are all Aboriginal owned and operated. They preserve and support culture, offer new opportunities, develop artistic skills and provide meaningful employment and a source of income for the artists and their families. The art at these centres is sold ethically.

Visitors to the art centres are asked to show their respect to the Traditional Owners by wearing modest clothing, requesting permission before taking photographs, especially of people and artworks, and taking into consideration the importance of the sacred images and stories in all the artworks.

As many of the art centres are on Aboriginal land, visitors should always contact the centre in advance to make an appointment, and to check if permits are required. If so, they must be organised before travel. In many areas in Central Australia, visitors need permits to drive on the roads, even if they are not stopping. This is because the land is Aboriginal owned and it is important to regulate the number of people on the roads and going through these areas.

Driving to the art centres that are in remote communities can be challenging. Before leaving major towns, visitors are advised to get up-to-the-minute reports on road conditions, and pick up current maps and safe-driving tips from tourist information offices. Ensure that you are well-prepared with sufficient fuel, water and emergency supplies. It is also advisable to let someone know where you are driving to before you set off.

Araluen Arts Centre

An integral part of the Araluen Cultural Precinct, this hub of entertainment and art presents an annual program of film, exhibitions, and performances, with Indigenous events featuring strongly. The Cultural Precinct is home to some of the most significant cultural, historical and artistic experiences in Central Australia. Within the four gallery spaces that make up the Araluen Galleries you can peruse works from Araluen's collection of more than 1000 works of art, 55 per cent of which are Indigenous works. A dedicated gallery showcases the Contemporary Aboriginal art movement through time, with featured artists such as Albert Namatjira and the Hermannsburg School. The Araluen Art Centre has a culture garden that includes 7 registered sacred sites and trees of significance to the Two Women Dreaming Track. Take advantage of the opportunity to immerse yourself in the culture and heritage of Central Australia, and learn about Indigenous Dreaming and connection to land. The opening hours of the centre differ in tourist and summer seasons. If you are lucky enough to be a local, admission to the art centre is free; otherwise an entrance fee applies.

WHERE: 61 Larapinta Drive, Araluen.
CONTACT: 08 8951 1120

Darwin Aboriginal Art Fair

Held annually in August, The Darwin Aboriginal Art Fair (DAAF) showcases the diverse work of more than 2000 Aboriginal and Torres Strait Islander artists, from more than 70 Aboriginal and Torres Strait Islander owned art centres around Australia. The event promotes the production of authentic Aboriginal art and its sale within an ethical and sustainable business environment. Attracting more than 17,000 visitors to the Fair and ancillary events in 2019 alone, over the past six years DAAF has generated more than $14 million for the Aboriginal and Torres Strait Islander art sector. Taking no commission on art works sold, the DAAF Foundation ensures that 100 per cent of all sales generated go directly back to the artists and art centres. Both emerging and established artists display their work, which includes paintings on canvas, bark and paper; sculpture; fibre art; textiles; cultural artefacts and regalia. DAAF boasts a program filled with artist workshops and demonstrations, public talks, traditional dance performances, children's activities, fashion and more. Visitors can immerse themselves in this vibrant and dynamic contemporary Indigenous art scene and engage with the artists themselves.

The DAAF Foundation is proud to align itself with the Garma Festival, National Aboriginal and Torres Strait Islander Art Awards, National Indigenous Music Awards and the Salon Art Projects. Together these art, culture and music events create a week of cultural excellence, and mark the most significant national celebration of Aboriginal and Torres Strait Islander art in the world.

Country to Couture

One of the highlights of DAAF each year is Country to Couture – where First peoples textiles and fashion collide in a colourful showcase of wearable art and design.

A celebration of Aboriginal and Torres Strait Islander textiles and fashion design, Country to Couture is a contemporary way of cultural storytelling and sharing knowledge. The event builds on the growing textile design movement in remote Indigenous communities, and has been showcased alongside DAAF since 2016.

The high-energy runway presents innovative collections from Indigenous designers and artists across Australia, as well as unique collaborations between Indigenous communities and well-known Australian labels.

Country to Couture is brought to you by the Darwin Aboriginal Art Fair Foundation (DAAFF) as part of Indigenous Fashion Projects.

National Indigenous Fashion Awards

The National Indigenous Fashion Awards, launched in 2020 to run alongside DAAF, are also presented by the DAAFF Indigenous Fashion Projects.

The awards provide a vibrant platform to celebrate the innovation, diversity and ethical practices of Australia's First peoples in fashion and textiles, while helping to develop the sector.

Recognising and showcasing excellence across six categories, the awards ceremony is a unique opportunity for the Australian and international fashion community to connect to the world's oldest living cultures.

WHERE: During fair dates: The Darwin Convention Centre, 10 Stokes Hill Rd, Darwin.
CONTACT: 08 8981 0576

Julie Shaw of MAARA Collective, winner of the 2020 Fashion Design NIFA, with models Charlee Fraser and Billie-Jean Hamlet. Charlee and Billie wearing MAARA Collective, 2020.

Desert Mob

One of Australia's major Aboriginal art events, Desert Mob represents artists from more than 30 remote desert communities in Central Australia. The annual event, held in September, has been running for more than 30 years and provides a snapshot of life in the art centres of the remote Northern Territory, South Australia and Western Australia. This unique gathering includes an arts symposium, exhibition and marketplace. It is the most immediate interface between remote desert community artists and the wider world, and is an exhilarating testament to the dynamism of Aboriginal art. The exhibition displays paintings, sculpture, weaving, woodcarvings, ceramics, prints, photography and work on paper. It includes hundreds of new works each year.

WHERE: Desert Mob is held in Alice Springs, in 3 galleries in the Araluen Art Centre precinct, 61 Larapinta Dve, Araluen.
CONTACT: Araluen Art Centre: 08 8951 1122

Telstra NATSIAA

The National Aboriginal and Torres Strait Islander Art Award (NATSIAA) is Australia's most prestigious Aboriginal and Torres Strait Islander art award. It celebrates the significant contribution of Indigenous artists from around the country and working in a range of traditional and contemporary mediums.

Originating in 1984, the NATSIAAs provide a platform that deepens the understanding of Indigenous culture. The awards are now an important event on Australia's cultural calendar and attract a wide audience of keen observers. They are delivered and exhibited by the Museum and Art Gallery of the Northern Territory (MAGNT).

The Telstra Art Award, worth $50,000, is presented to the artist of the work deemed by the judges as the most exceptional across all categories. The Telstra Emerging Artist Award, worth $5000, is awarded to an artist within their first 5 years of practice who has not exhibited in a major institution. Prizes of $5000 are awarded in another 5 categories, including the Telstra Bark Painting Award, the Telstra General Painting Award, the Telstra Works on Paper Award, the Wandjuk Marika

Memorial Three-Dimensional Award and the Telstra Multimedia Award. The award ceremony is held in mid-August, but the work of all shortlisted finalists is displayed at MAGNT until late November.

WHERE: Museum and Art Gallery of the Northern Territory, 19 Conacher St, The Gardens, Darwin.
CONTACT: Museum and Art Gallery of the Northern Territory: 08 8999 8264

Top Didj Cultural Experience and Art Gallery

Top Didj has been offering its authentic Aboriginal Cultural Experience since 2000, and is now also the home of the Katherine Art Gallery. Indigenous artists and guides run the 2-hour Aboriginal Cultural Experience, teaching guests about local Indigenous cultures, as well as traditional skills such as boomerang throwing and painting. All the artists and guides working at Top Didj are local to the Katherine and Red Centre regions.

The Katherine Art Gallery, opened in 1997, showcases works that reflect the cultures of the Jawoyn, Dagoman and Warlpiri peoples, Traditional Owners of the lands surrounding Katherine, as well as works by artists from Arnhem Land and the Kimberley. The gallery holds a range of artworks across many mediums, including traditional artefacts and didgeridoos.

WHERE: Cnr Gorge and Jaensch rds, Katherine. Katherine is located 300 km south of Darwin along the Stuart Hwy and is accessible by car. There are 3 main roadside stops between Katherine and Darwin where visitors can restock and refuel. Katherine is also a major stop on both Greyhound bus and Ghan rail trips coming from Central Australia, and is accessible by air with Airnorth.
CONTACT: 08 8971 2751; 0414 888 786

PLACES

Tinkerbee Arrernte Art & Cultural Workshop

Tinkerbee Eastern and Central Arrernte Cross-Cultural and Interpretation Services is owned and operated by Kumalie (Rosalie) Riley – an Elder with a lifetime of experience and stories to share. Aboriginal art in Central Australia is unique, and in the Arrernte Art & Cultural Workshop class, you can learn to paint and understand traditional Arrernte symbols and designs. The ancient art can be explored in these laidback, interactive 2-hour sessions. Bookings are essential, and classes are held regularly on Saturdays and Sundays.

CONTACT: 0457 132 153

ART CENTRES

Anindilyakwa Arts

Anindilyakwa Arts promotes the Aboriginal artists of the Groote Archipelago and helps them to sell their works. Their Alyangula Gallery Shop displays work made on country at Art Centres in Angurugu, Umbakumba and Milyakburra. Works are made from a range of mediums, including ochre and acrylic paintings on canvas, bark and shell; wooden objects such as yiraka (didgeridoos) and clapsticks; carvings; traditional weavings using pandanus and natural dye methods; weavings using reclaimed ghost net and fabrics and traditional and unique jewellery design. The women of Anindilyakwa Arts have also developed a keen interest for fashion, and have become well known for their unique collections of textiles and garments made using dyed silk, cotton and linen, which rely on resources found on the island. Bush-dyed garments, screen printed fabrics and digital printed fabrics are available to purchase, and have been showcased at Country to Couture at the Darwin Aboriginal Art Fair for multiple years, where they are highly regarded. Before visiting, check their website for opening times.

WHERE: Groote Eylandt, 50 km from the eastern coast of Arnhem Land. The airport is located at the northern end of Groote Eylandt, near the Angurugu community. Groote Eylandt is a 90-minute flight from Darwin.
CONTACT: 08 8987 6667

Arlpwe Art and Culture Centre

Arlpwe Art and Culture Centre is comprised of an Aboriginal art gallery, 2 art centres and a pottery studio. It services the local Aboriginal artists of the small Central Australian community of Ali Curung. The Kaytetye people are the traditional custodians of the area, with Alyawarr, Warlpiri and Warumungu language groups also forming the local community. Central Desert–style paintings, including distinct dot painting landscapes and ceremonial body designs, feature prominently in the works on display here. The pottery studio was introduced as a new medium to the community. It has stimulated a unique creative development in the artists, who can express their culture in new ways. The pottery training school also involves classes for children at the primary school, engaging the next generation in the process of artistic communication. Artists here are proud of their work, and their authentic Aboriginal paintings, artefacts and artworks help keep the Indigenous culture alive for all future generations. For details on when the centre is open, see the website.

WHERE: Ali Curung, 350 km north of Alice Springs. From Alice Springs follow the Stuart Hwy and turn right at the signpost. A sealed 22 km road east leads to the community. The drive takes about 4–5 hours.
CONTACT: 08 8964 1640

Artists of Ampilatwatja

The Ampilatwatja (pronounced um-bludder-witch) community is the cultural heart of the Alyawarr nation. For the Alyawarr people, art is an important way to express connection to Country. The works produced at this community are distinct from any other Aboriginal art, even that from nearby communities in Central Australia. The depiction of the land is generally done with bold, bright colours and fine dots. The artists mostly paint Arreth, which means 'strong bush medicine'. Every plant and animal plays an irreplaceable role in the ecological system of the land that has sustained the Alyawarr people for generations. Artists pay homage to their Country, demonstrating their deep connection to it. The stories in their art of the landscape transcend surface meaning. Through the delicate layered dots of the paintings, artists only reveal the 'outside' stories to the general public. However, through the lens of their own deep cultural foundations, the artists and their people interpret the 'inside' stories of information that is held sacred. It allows us all an insight into the rich lives of the Alyawarr people, without encroaching on any religious laws of their culture. Please contact the art centre to arrange a visit.

WHERE: Ampilatwatja community is a 3½-hour drive from Alice Springs (322 km) via the Stuart and Sandover hwys, and is about 10 km in from the turn-off on the Sandover Hwy.
PERMITS: One-day visits do not require entry permits and all visitors are welcome.
CONTACT: 0437 426 549

Bábbarra Women's Centre

Founded in 1983, Bábbarra Women's Centre strives to support new economic opportunities for women, and to create higher outcomes for themselves and their families. The centre supports women of 12 distinct language groups in the Maningrida area of Arnhem Land. Bábbarra is the name of a sacred billabong.

Bábbarra Designs, the centre's textile business, is one of the oldest continuously operating Indigenous textile enterprises in Australia. In the 1990s, the women began working with etching, lithography and screen-printing, steadily building an archive of screens. Eventually, the centre acquired a printing press so that the women could work with this medium onsite and consolidate their printing skills.

Today, Bábbarra textiles are highly regarded and sought after both nationally and internationally, found in the collections of major institutions across Australia, such as the National Gallery of Australia, as well as in exhibitions in France, China, Mexico and the US.

WHERE: Maningrida Community (500 km east of Darwin).
PERMITS: Permits for travel to Maningrida are required before entering the community. They are free and can be arranged through the Northern Land Council.
CONTACT: 08 8979 5775

Barkly Regional Arts

Barkly Regional Arts is the hub for the arts in the Barkly region. The organisation currently provides 50 annual programs or projects to over 800 musicians and artists throughout the Barkly region. Barkly Regional Arts is based in Tennant Creek, from which one of its five operational art centres runs, together these five art centres incorporate The Artists of the Barkly, a collective of artists working across five locally owed art centres in communities across the remote Barkly region: Tennant Creek, Wuntungurru (Epenarra), Owairtilla, (Canteen Creek), Kulumindini (Elliott) and Mungkarta. Each art centre operates as its own grassroots cultural enterprise working through artist-led decision-making processes, supporting culture and respecting protocol. Since 2012, Barkly Regional Arts has supported these art communities through employment of community arts workers, visits from outreach staff, professional and artist development opportunities. Having developed independently, each art centre bares their own distinctive visual language, leading to the diverse range in style seen within the Artists of Barkly collective.

WHERE: The Barkly Region covers 283,648 sq km of vast and diverse country.
CONTACT: 08 0962 2799

Bima Wear

Bima Wear is a women's creative enterprise, proudly owned and operated by Tiwi women. The label was founded in 1969, when the women began creating clothes first and foremost for themselves, and the people of the Tiwi Islands. Bima Wear is designed, printed and manufactured daily, with fabrics that feature and celebrate the distinct Tiwi culture, language, traditions and Country. The enterprise supports Tiwi women and girls to have leadership, autonomy and valuable skills. Bima Wear fabrics are renowned and highly sought after both nationally and internationally. Collections from the centre are often featured in Darwin Aboriginal Art Fair's annual *Country to Couture* fashion show.

In 2020, Bima Wear released a limited edition collaboration with the cult Australian denim brand Nobody Denim. Artist Tara Munkanome's Tunga design was printed onto

Stanalisha modelling Bima Wear x Nobody Denim

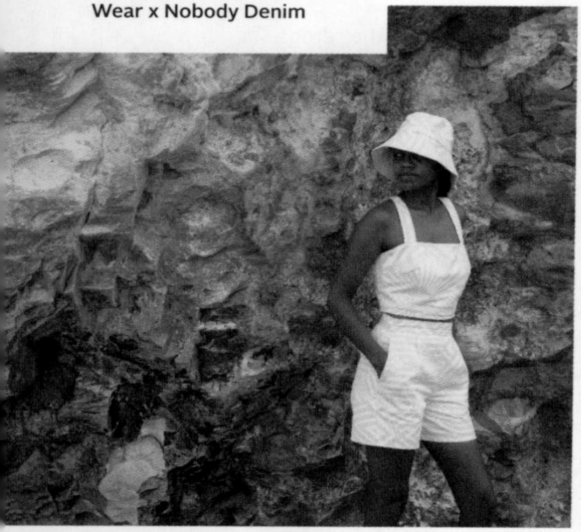

a collection of denim jeans, shorts, a skirt, top, bag and bucket hat.

WHERE: Wurrumiyanga, Bathurst Island.
PERMITS: Permits to visit the Tiwi Islands can be organised through the Tiwi Land Council.
CONTACT: info@bimawear.com

Bindi Mwerre Anthurre Artists

Established in 2000, Bindi Mwerre Anthurre (pronounced 'bindi moora andura') Artists supports Aboriginal artists in Alice Springs living with a disability. The studio ensures these artists receive employment and development opportunities, including working space, design contracts, multimedia collaborations and access to various art fairs and exhibitions, for their artistic practice. Bindi artists come from right across the Central Desert region and most live in Alice Springs. Artworks are often a reflection of self, and an intrinsic link to Country, and include paintings and drawings. Some artworks are also made into witty short films, and more recently a series of striking lampshades. Several artists have large national and international profiles, and their artworks are highly sought after by galleries and private collectors alike.

WHERE: 47 Elder Street, Alice Springs.
CONTACT: 08 8958 6215

Buku-Larrŋgay Mulka Art Centre

Buku-Larrŋgay means 'the feeling on your face as it is struck by the first rays of the sun' – that is, when facing east. Mulka means 'a sacred but public ceremony'.

This large Yolŋu community-controlled art centre in the small community of Yirrkala in north-east Arnhem Land supports many award-winning Yolŋu artists. It is home to some of Australia's most significant artworks. In 1976, the Yolŋu artists established Buku-Larrnggay Arts in the old mission health centre. Today Buku supports traditional and contemporary art across the wide range of media that the Yolŋu artists work in. This centre is comprised of a print workshop, numerous gallery spaces, a museum, and The Mulka Project, a digital production and archiving studio housing tens of thousands of historical films and digital images.

Art from this region has a rich history. There is strong evidence to suggest that art from the Yolŋu people of Yirrkala was the catalyst for a growing interest in Aboriginal art in the 1970s, particularly the profound realisation that traditional Aboriginal art is unique on a global scale. Additionally, it was artists in Yirrkala who first recognised the potential of Aboriginal visual art as a political tool. In 1963, the now famous Yirrkala Church Panels were hung in the Methodist church at Yirrkala to recognise the local clans and their lands. These title deeds can still be seen today at the art centre's museum. Later in that same year, the Yirrkala Bark Petition was presented in Australian Parliament in a bid by Yirrkala Elders to hold the rights to their own traditional lands.

Buku-Larrŋgay Mulka Art Centre services the Yirrkala community and also about 25 homeland centres in a 200 km radius. Yirrkala is the traditional home of the yidaki and some of the world's finest examples of the instrument come from this art centre. Other art and cultural works on display, and for purchase, include larrakitj, which is a traditional memorial pole used in funerary ceremonies; gunga djäma, woven pieces such as baskets, mats and dilly bags; dharpa, wood sculptures; and nuwayak, sacred clan title deeds painted onto the bark of the stringy-bark tree.

Artists from this region are well known for their traditional carving and barks. Their works are consistently selected in competitions and awarded major prizes across the country, including in the prestigious Telstra National Aboriginal and Torres Strait Islander Art Award in a range of categories. Their art is also exhibited in major galleries around the globe, including the Musée du Quai Branly in Paris. Yirrkala is home to the famous artists of the Yunupingu, Marika and Maymuru families, among others. There is also a group of younger, emerging artists. Art from Buku-Larrŋgay Mulka retails from $200 for a smaller work, to thousands of dollars for larger, very detailed pieces. It is fine art and the prices reflect the skill in these traditional pieces. For details on when the art centre is open, see the website.

Adjacent to Buku are the newly built Yirrkala Guest Houses, which provide contemporary accomodation to visitors of Yirrkala and the art centre. There are 8 rooms available and all are individually equipped with kitchenette, private bathroom, a television and air conditioning.

WHERE: 138 Tuffin Rd, Yirrkala. Qantas and Airnorth fly to Nhulunbuy. The road is impassable in the Wet season (from December to May). Car hire recommendations include Manny's Car Rentals: 08 89872300, Gove Rentals: 08 8987 1700 and Nhulunbuy Ute Hire: 08 89872872.
PERMITS: While the community is on Aboriginal land, no permit is required to visit the art centre when coming from the nearby town of Nhulunbuy or the Gove airport. Permission from the Northern Land Council (08 8920 5100) is required to drive there from Darwin or Katherine (about 10 hours). Yirrkala is a dry area where alcohol is forbidden without a permit.
CONTACT: 08 8987 1701

Bula'Bula Arts

Bula'Bula Arts is the cultural heart of Ramingining, the small community located in the heart of the heritage-listed Arafura Wetlands, in north-east Arnhem Land. While an art centre has existed in the community since the 1970s, Bula'Bula Arts Aboriginal Corporation was formally established in the 1990s. The centre is not-for-profit, and its main objective is the preservation and cultivation of Yolŋu culture. Bula'Bula is the voice of the kangaroo, and refers to the song cycle of the area's main creative being, Garrtjambal, the red kangaroo.

Bula'Bula Arts supports approximately 150 artist members from Ramingining and its surrounding homelands, with a core group of around 30 artists. The community sits on the traditional lands of the Djadawitjibi people of the Djinang group, but is now home to more than 16 clans speaking 14 different languages. The work of these artists is captivating, with deep spiritual and ritual connections to the sophisticated social structures of Yolŋu culture. The centre is world renowned for the hollow-log memorial installed at the National Gallery of Australia, which was created there. Many of the leading artists have featured in movies such as *Ten Canoes* and *Charlie's Country*.

Traditional painting by Roy Burnyila of Bula'Bula Arts

Bula'Bula Arts represents a strong group of weavers and painters with both traditional and contemporary styles. Works includes bark and canvas paintings, hollow logs, prints, and traditional fibre work, such as woven dilly bags, bush string bags, mats and baskets. Visits can include participatory art experiences such as weaving or bark painting and visits to artist's homelands. Contact Bula'Bula for more information.

Accomodation is available at the art centre for visitors.

WHERE: Ramingining is located in the Arafura Wetlands. It is 580 km east of Darwin, 435 km west of Nhulunbuy, and 30 km inland from the Arafura Sea. Fly Tiwi flies between Darwin and Ramingining on Monday, Wednesday and Friday. The road to Ramingining is only accessible during the Dry season, and only by 4WD.

PERMITS: Ramingining is Yolŋu land and permits must be obtained before travelling to the community. They may be obtained from the Northern Land Council.
CONTACT: 08 8979 7911

Coomalie Art Centre

Part of the Batchelor Institute of Indigenous Tertiary Education (BIITE), Coomalie connects arts, culture, education and training. It is located on the traditional lands of the Kungarakan and Warrai peoples near Litchfield National Park. Their shared stories and songlines link the area to various Aboriginal and Torres Strait Islander communities further afield, with the art centre showcasing of a range of artworks. Through engagement and participation in visual arts, Coomalie aims to continually foster these interlinking relationships, and the artistic and cultural expression of artists.

WHERE: Cnr of Awilla Street and Nurndina Road, Batchelor (100 km from Darwin).
CONTACT: 08 8939 7404

Djilpin Arts

Established in 2002, Djilpin Arts aims to maintain, develop and promote the local art and culture of the Wugularr (Beswick) community. Wugularr is on the traditional lands of the Jawoyn people, although people from a multitude of language groups and clans reside in the community. A vibrant and thriving cultural enterprise, the art centre fosters various expressions of cultural knowledge, supporting spiritual wellbeing and sustainability as well as purposeful employment and independence for its artist members. Artists express their culture and identity through both traditional and contemporary mediums, including fibre weaving, paintings on bark, paper and canvas, textile design, jewellery and carvings.

The art centre offers cultural tours in the spectacular country surrounding Beswick, workshops, traditional dance performances and concerts. Follow the art centre on Facebook or contact them directly to learn more and book the various experiences available.

Accommodation is available adjacent to the art centre, in the form of four modern elevated pavilion rooms, each equipped with a queen bed, fridge, tea and coffee making facilities, air-conditioning and verandahs. Camping is also available. Check the art centre website for more information.

WHERE: Wugularr (Beswick) is 113 km from Katherine on a sealed road.
PERMIT: Permits for travel to Wugularr (Beswick) are required before entering the community. They are free and can be arranged through the Northern Land Council.

Durrmu Arts Aboriginal Corporation

Renowned for fine contemporary art, particularly fibre work and brightly coloured acrylic paintings, Durrmu Arts is forging a new narrative of contemporary culture, songlines and stories, alongside the age-old traditions of the Ngan'gikurrunggurr people. Durrmu refers to the traditional dot-painting body designs which form the basis of many paintings to come out of Durrmu Arts. Artists also draw painting inspiration from the traditional weaving for which they are renowned. Paintings are intricate, layered and abstract mark-making, some clearly reminiscent of woven baskets and others resembling fine tapestries. Regina Pilawuk Wilson, senior artist, master weaver and winner of the 2003 General Painting Telstra National Indigenous Art Award, leads a team of highly skilled established and emerging artists.

WHERE: Peppimenarti (300 km south-west of Darwin) is only accessible by 4WD during the Dry season (May to November).
PERMITS: Permits for travel to Peppimenarti are required before entering the community. They are free and can be arranged through the Northern Land Council.
CONTACT: 08 8978 1322 or 0487 085 846

Elcho Island Arts

Elcho Island Arts is a Marthakal Business Enterprise, located in Galiwin'ku Community on Elcho Island. More than 200 Yolŋu artists residing in north-east Arnhem Land are supported by Elcho Island Arts to create yiḏakis, larritjs, traditional bark paintings, carvings, paintings, prints, mats, baskets, bags and a wide range of jewellery.

Fibre art from Elcho Island is some of the most spectacular in Australia, with natural grasses and fibres traditionally dyed and woven together to form baskets, dilly bags, mats, sculptures and jewellery. Over 30 Elcho Island weavers have collaborated with Koskela to create more than 280 bespoke interior design products sold through Koskela in Rosebery, NSW.

Elcho Island is also the home of the late Mr G Gurruwiwi, an internationally acclaimed maker of the Banumbirr or Morning Star Pole. Though made for public viewing, these poles are held sacred by their makers and celebrate the importance of the Banumbirr creation story. The poles are made from the wood of a specific tree, decorated with carvings and various coloured ochres and adorned with woven string and feathers.

Elcho Island Arts collaborates with artists to provide a range of assistance including training opportunities, marketing and distribution of art to national and international museums and art buyers and dealers. Elcho Island Arts is usually open Monday to Friday 12–5 pm.

WHERE: Lot 109 Galiwin'ku Community, Elcho Island, which is serviced by Air North Monday–Saturday.
PERMITS: Elcho Island is Indigenous Land and requires a Northern Land Council (NLC) permit to visit. Further information can be found on the NLC website.
CONTACT: artcentre.manager@marthakal.org

Ernabella Arts Inc

Ernabella is Australia's oldest continuously running Indigenous art centre. Located in Pukatja community on the APY Lands, it was founded in 1948 as a craft room attached to the local mission, before being incorporated as an Aboriginal-owned enterprise in 1974. Artists initially made uniquely patterned hand-loomed woven fabrics and hand-pulled knotted floor rugs, and today they are skilled in a range of contemporary applications, including handmade ceramics and bold paintings that typically reflect Tjukurpa (sacred stories of law and country). Ernabella is a culturally strong contemporary art centre that promotes and supports the cultural aspirations and self-determination of the A<u>n</u>angu people. It has a national and international reputation for fine art.

WHERE: Pukatja (Ernabella) community, APY Lands (330 km from Alice Springs).
PERMITS: Permits are required for entry onto the APY Lands. They are free and can be arranged through the APY Permit Office.
CONTACT: 08 8956 2954

Ernabella Arts Tour – Longitude 131°

In A<u>n</u>angu language, tjungu waakarinyi translates to 'working together'. It's a sentiment that underpins the treasured partnership between Ernabella Arts and Longitude 131°.

Longitude 131° (located adjacent to Ulu<u>r</u>u-Ka<u>t</u>a Tjuta National Park) offers guests private tours to the Ernabella Arts studio with a chance to meet the artists and make a real connection. Operated under exclusive arrangement, the cultural adventure includes a scenic charter flight to reach the community, which lies 665 km by road or 155 km by air from Longitude 131°.

Longitude 131° takes guests to visit Australia's oldest continuously running arts centre, Ernabella Arts

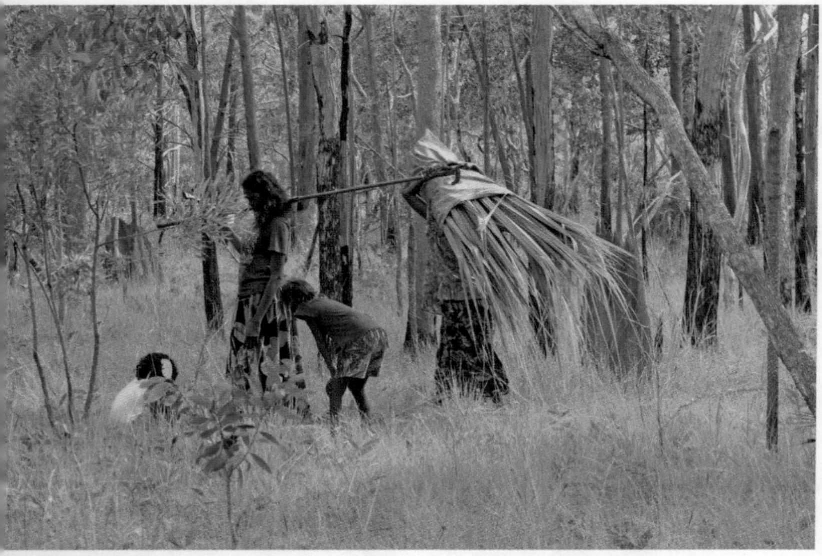

Bush trip collecting pandanus and dyes, Gapuwiyak Culture and Arts Aboriginal Corporation

Visitors arrive in the remote Aboriginal community and discover the arts centre, a hub of vibrant activity where the community's Elders and young people work side by side creating artworks and sharing their culture and knowledge. Guests learn about the symbols used in Aboriginal artworks, meet the artists and try their hand at painting a take-home ceramic tile. Tours operate seasonally from April to October.

WHERE: Tours depart from the Longitude 131°, located in Yulara.
CONTACT: 02 9918 4355

Gapuwiyak Culture and Arts Aboriginal Corporation

The arts corporation of Gapuwiyak, in remote East Arnhem Land, is a recent initiative set up to support the cultural practices of the Yolŋu people living in the region and provide them with leadership opportunities, meaningful employment and professional development. Gapuwiyak is located on the traditional lands of the Gupapuyngu clan; however, people from all major Yolŋu clan groups live in the community and the surrounding homelands. Artists are inspired by the deep and powerful connection to their land and their ancestors, which is continually strengthened through cultural practices such as buŋgul (ceremony), manikay (singing), giritjirri (dance), miny'tji (sacred designs), and dhäwu (stories). The art centre houses its own collection and sells locally produced works. It is particularly well known for its vibrant fibre work, which traditionally uses pandanus leaves and kurrajong bark. There are also fine examples of bark and canvas paintings, yiḏakis and larrakitj (painted ceremonial poles). It also has a media centre, which has a growing archive of old and new media relevant to the community. Check the website for more details.

WHERE: Gapuwiyak is a small Yolŋu town on the shore of Lake Evella in East Arnhem Land. It is

approximately 200 km west of Yirrkala and 250 km south-east of Ramingining. Fly Tiwi operates a daily flight from Darwin to Gapuwiyak. There are also charter companies based in Darwin and Nhulunbuy. Driving from Darwin takes around 12 hours and 4WD is recommended.
CONTACT: 08 898 79110

Godinymayin Yijard Rivers Arts and Cultural Centre

Godinymayin Yijard Rivers Arts and Cultural Centre (GYRACC) was built as a meeting place for both local Indigenous and non-Indigenous people to gather and share art and culture. The centre offers exhibitions, live music, song and dance performances, workshops and education programs, and is often the setting for cultural celebrations as well. Communities in the Katherine region are remote, and GYRACC cites their main goal as connecting these communities through a sharing of art, cultures and a 'two-way' learning philosophy, respecting both the Indigenous and non-Indigenous perspectives and histories in the region. The centre holds regular events and exhibitions, and all details and an events calendar can be found on the website.

WHERE: Stuart Hwy, Katherine East. Katherine is located 300 km south of Darwin along the Stuart Hwy and is accessible by 2WD. There are 3 main roadside stops between Katherine and Darwin where visitors can re-stock and re-fuel. Katherine is also a major stop on both Greyhound bus and Ghan rail trips through Central Australia, and is accessible by air with Airnorth.
CONTACT: 08 8972 3751

A performance of *The Shadow King* production in 2014 at GYRACC

Hermannsburg Potters

Pottery has become a famous feature of the Western Aranda community of Hermannsburg, in the remote foothills of the Western MacDonnell ranges in Central Australia. It was introduced to the community by missionaries in the 1960s. In 1990, the Adult Education Office employed practitioners to teach pottery to community members and people living in surrounding outstations. From these initial lessons, community members began the collective of Hermannsburg Potters. Today artists translate their cultural and artistic heritage into their unique and exciting style of ceramics. Terracotta clay and hand building and coiling methods are used to make the distinctive pots. These are then decorated with animals, plants, people and historical and contemporary scenes, which are moulded, carved and painted into the body and the lid of the pots. The artists paint stories of contemporary life as well as their lived histories, speaking to their strong cultural beliefs, traditions and values. Hermannsburg Potters and the innovative design of their pots have become internationally renowned. Hermannsburg pots are shown in galleries across the country and worldwide. To visit Hermannsburg Potters' gallery, please phone ahead to book a time. Contact Hermannsburg Potters to make an inquiry.

WHERE: Hermannsburg, about a 1½-hour drive (130 km) from Alice Springs via Larapinta Dr.
CONTACT: 08 8956 7414

Ikuntji Artists

Ikuntji Artists has been the cultural hub of the Haasts Bluff community, within the Western MacDonnell Ranges, since 1992, reinforcing and reinvigorating cultural practices. Ikuntji Artists was the first art centre established by Western Desert women. It was a feminist response to the Papunya Tula Art movement, which many of the fathers, brothers and husbands participated in. Artists from Ikuntji Artists draw their inspiration from their Ngurra, or Country, and their Tjukurrpa, or Dreaming stories. The artists use bold colours and decisive brush strokes in their paintings, which show an innovative, contemporary take on a rich cultural heritage. The artworks are diverse, from traditional symbolism and iconography to highly abstract paintings. Many artists who work at this art centre are highly acclaimed and exhibited both in Australia and internationally. In 2017, Ikuntji Artists began exploring the medium of textile design and printing. In 2019 and 2020, the first collections of screen-printed textiles drew national and international attention, and were shortlisted for the inaugural National Indigenous Fashion Award 2020. For details on when the art centre is open, see the website. Day visitors are welcome but it is necessary to make an appointment.

WHERE: Haasts Bluff is 230 km west of Alice Springs. The most direct route is from Alice Springs via Larapinta Dr. The road includes 170 km of sealed bitumen but 60 km is unsealed. 4WD is recommended.
PERMITS: While public spaces in the community do not require a permit, travelling on Aboriginal land may. See the Central Land Council website for more information.
CONTACT: fineart@ikuntji.com.au

Iltja Ntjarra (Many Hands) Art Centre

Iltja Ntjarra (Many Hands) Art Centre supports new, emerging and well-established contemporary Aboriginal artists from Central Australia. The art centre is a place for Western

Aranda artists to come together and paint, sharing new techniques, ideas and stories and in doing so preserving their ancient culture.

Iltja Ntjarra has a particular emphasis on supporting the artists of the Hermannsburg school, who paint in the watercolour tradition of their famous grandfather and relative, Albert Namatjira. Namatjira painted in the 20th century and was famous for painting his native desert Country in western-style watercolour paints. He is arguably one of the most celebrated Australian artists of the 20th century. He passed his unique style on to his children, who have since taught their children, creating a legacy of outstanding watercolour artists from the Central Desert region. The Hermannsburg school artists are a living part of history.

Town-based artists also come to the centre to work on their paintings. A visit to the centre is a chance to see a wide range of artworks and to meet the artists. It is also a unique way to learn about Central Australian Aboriginal culture and art. For details of when the art centre is open and when artists paint on site, see the website.

WHERE: 29 Wilkinson St, Alice Springs, about a 15-minute walk from the centre of Alice Springs town.
CONTACT: 08 7979 3452

Injalak Arts Gunbalanya

Injalak Arts is a non-profit Aboriginal Corporation based in the remote community of Gunbalanya. It started in 1989 as a screen-printing studio and developed into one of the largest art centres in Arnhem Land. The art centre has over 200 active members, with most living in Gunbalanya. Members are Kunwinjku, Mengerrdji and Erre people. Artists create many different kinds of work, including Dolobbo (bark paintings), Mako (didgeridoos) and wood carvings. However, Injalak's painters specialise in works on high-quality watercolour paper inspired by the rock art on Injalak Hill and in the surrounding areas. These artworks are created as part of a cultural training system, where senior artists oversee the appropriate depictions of stories and designs. Injalak is also renowned for its fibre art. These pieces range from Djerrh (traditional bush string bags), to Bulbbe (twined conical baskets) and coiled baskets, which are a more recent development, as well as Marebu (woven mats), which were often used during ceremony. Some fibre artists also create Mayh (woven sculptures). Injalak fibre art is also known for its unique pink colour, which comes from natural plant dyes collected in the area. Artists from the centre have had works displayed in galleries around Australia and the world, including the Kluge-Ruhe in the USA. The rock art that inspires the artists can be viewed by taking a tour up Injalak Hill (see Injalak Rock Art Tours, p. 266). The centre is open 8.30 am–5 pm Monday to Friday and 9 am–2 pm Saturday (during Dry season). Visits outside of these hours may be possible by appointment.

WHERE: From Jabiru, cross Cahills Crossing on the East Alligator River and follow the 17 km dirt road to Gunbalanya. This is an easy 50-minute drive with stunning views. The turn-off to the community is clearly marked. 2WD vehicles make the trip; however, 4WD is recommended. Road access to Gunbalanya is only possible from May to October. Be sure to check tide times at Cahills Crossing before leaving.
PERMITS: Permits to visit Gunbalanya must be arranged in advance via the Northern Land Council in Darwin or Jabiru.
CONTACT: 08 8979 0190

Jilamara Arts and Crafts

Jilamara Arts is located in the community of Milikapiti on the north coast of Melville

Island and presents Tiwi art from up to 60 local artists. For over 30 years they have contributed significantly to Australia's contemporary Indigenous art industry and are highly respected for work based on jilamara (body paint design), Tiwi creation stories and unique island ceremonies such as Kulama and Pukumani. Jilamara artists use locally sourced natural ochres prepared by hand in the studios for works on linen, canvas, stringybark, paper, tunga (bark bags), ironwood carvings and tutini poles. The centre also produces limited edition prints and hand screen-printed textiles. The Tiwi Islands have been separated from mainland Australia for at least 3000 years, leading to the development of regionally distinct creative practices. Jilmara does not offer cultural tours but is open by appointment for groups of art enthusiasts, by contacting the art centre directly or through the website. Please make note of any current health or travel protocols and visit remote communities with respect.

WHERE: Charter services offer flights from Darwin to Milikapiti (Snake Bay) Airport, which is 4 km from Milikapiti town centre.
PERMITS: Permits are required to visit the Tiwi Islands. They can be obtained through the Tiwi Land Council.
CONTACT: 08 8978 3901

Karungkarni Art and Culture

Karungkarni Art and Culture Aboriginal Corporation is owned and governed by the Gurindji artists of the Kalkaringi and Daguragu communities. The name Karungkarni refers to the important Child Dreaming place for Gurindji people on a hill to the south of the art centre. The corporation, established by Elders in 2011, maintains and strengthens the cultural knowledge of Gurindji people, passing on the art, language, culture and history to the younger generations and the wider world.

Above: Michelle Woody Minnapinni, artist and president of Jilamara Arts and Crafts, collecting ochre for painting

Opposite: This painting by Richard Long Jupurrurla depicts the fruit of the popular fruiting vine, kilipi (Bush banana / *Marsdenia australis*). The fruit and leaves of the plant can be eaten. The young fruit called ngamurrurru are the best to eat as they are soft and crunchy. They are found in the heavy rain time of the wet season. Older fruit become hard and chewy but they can be softened by lightly roasting on hot coals. The flowers can also be eaten. The leaves are called pinti or yurtu. They are good for you and are like eating lettuce or cabbage.

The artwork is distinctive for its precise and vibrant dot-painting style.

Some of the art centre's core artists and directors were part of the Wave Hill Walk-Off, led by Vincent Lingiari. On 23 August 1966, over 200 Gurindji people camped in the Victoria River bed after courageously walking off Wave Hill cattle station to protest their deplorable working and living conditions and, most importantly, to seek the rights to the land of their ancestors. These strong and determined men and women are renowned for the stance they took against the powerful Vestey Company, and Gurindji people now commemorate the Wave Hill Walk-Off in the annual Freedom Day Festival.

Under the direction of its board of eight Gurindji men and women, Karungkarni Art supports the production, promotion and sale of artwork by local artists and is the focal point for cultural and social activities in the community. The art centre is housed in the abandoned powerhouse building on the Buntine Highway at the entrance to Kalkaringi, which lies on the magnificent Victoria River. Visitors are advised to call before visiting.

WHERE: Kalkaringi (480 km south-west of Katherine).
CONTACT: 0427 177 779

Keringke Arts

Keringke Arts is located in the remote Arrernte community of Santa Teresa, 80 km south-east of Alice Springs. In Eastern Arrernte the community is known as Ltyentye Apurte, meaning 'stand of beefwood trees'. The Country is rich in rock art, artefacts and

ceremonial sites. Keringke means 'kangaroo tracks'. It is the Dreaming story of Kathleen Wallace, the custodian of Keringke Arts and one of its senior and most well-known artists. The kangaroo came from the south-east and created a rockhole in the desert. Also known as Keringke, the rockhole is a sacred site with great significance to many Arrernte people.

The art centre was established in 1987 after a 9-week fabric-painting course was run in the community. The following year the women exhibited their work at the Australian Bicentennial Craft Show, a first for Aboriginal artists. In 1989 the Keringke Art Centre was built. The artistic style of the Santa Teresa women is unique and is now referred to as Keringke Style. The artists use bright colours and dynamic patterns and shapes to represent their desert country and culture, and pay close attention to detail in their works. Their work includes canvases, silk prints, ceramics and furniture. It is represented in many collections nationally and internationally. For details on when the art centre is open, see the website. Please contact the art centre before visiting.

WHERE: Santa Teresa, 80 km south-east of Alice Springs. Driving to Santa Teresa from Alice Springs takes 1½–2 hours. The road is open year round. However, it is unsealed and 4WD is recommended.
CONTACT: 08 8956 0956

Kulumindini Arts

Kulumindini Arts is located in North Camp, Elliott, halfway between Darwin and Alice Springs. The centre's artwork reflects the stories of artists and their connection to the Country of the Barkly region. Known for their strong use of line and careful measured use of dots, the Kulumindini artists explore the changes to the landscape and its inhabitants throughout the seasons.

WHERE: North Camp, Elliott (421 km from Katherine).
CONTACT: 08 8962 2799

Larrakia Nation Arts

The Larrakia people are the Traditional Owners of Darwin. Larrakia Nation Arts provides a place for both Larrakia and other urban Indigenous artists of the region to produce a broad range of visual arts in both traditional and contemporary mediums. The art centre supports artistic expression as a means of cultural maintenance and knowledge exchange. Artwork mediums include wood carving, linocut printing, acrylic on canvas, large scale public art, silkscreen printed fabric, and silver jewellery.

WHERE: Darwin.
CONTACT: 08 8948 3488

Maningrida Arts and Culture

Located on traditional Kunibidji Country in Arnhem Land, Maningrida Arts and Culture represents the artists from an area of 7000 sq km of land and sea. This encompasses more than 100 clan estates and more than 12 distinct languages, including the Kunibidji, Kunbarlang, Nakkara, Burarra, Gun-nartpa, Gurrgoni, Rembarrnga, Eastern Kunwinjku, Djinang, Wurlaki and Gupapuyngu peoples.

The art from the centre conceptually displays the natural and spiritual worlds, with a focus on the Country itself and the ancestral beings, such as Ngalyod, the Rainbow Serpent; Yawkyawk and jin-Merdewa, the female water spirits; and Namorrorddo, a spirit being.

Artists use materials sustainably harvested from their clan estates, including ochres and pigments; the bark, wood and roots of various tree species; feathers; and the wax from bush honey. Fibre work from the region has always been highly regarded. It comes in decorative, ceremonial and sculptural forms, including conical fish traps, baskets, string bags, dilly bags, mats and ceremonial regalia. Artists are also known for their bark paintings, yid̲akis, sculptures and prints. Acclaimed senior artists continue to expand their artistic narratives across new mediums, while new artists continually emerge and become nationally and internationally celebrated. For details on when Maningrida Arts and Culture is open, see the website.

DJÓMI MUSEUM: The Djómi museum at Maningrida Arts and Culture houses an extremely valuable and unique cultural collection, with local, national and international significance. The collection has mainly grown through acquisitions from Maningrida Arts and Culture and donations from private collections and people who worked in Maningrida, dating back to the 1940s. The museum includes the works from generations of prominent artists, both deceased and still active today, including bark paintings, sculptural works and weavings. It also houses artefacts and other items of material culture, as well as photographs documenting the historical life and culture of the region. The museum is a fantastic way to learn about the history and the cultural practices of the Maningrida area. Visits to the museum are by appointment only.

WHERE: Maningrida community, 500 km east of Darwin; 300 km north-east of Jabiru. Air North operates flights to Maningrida from Darwin twice daily. The drive to Maningrida is via Gunbalanya. The road is unsealed so 4WD is recommended; it is generally only accessible in the Dry season, from June to November.

PERMITS: Permits for Maningrida are free but must be obtained from the Northern Land Council prior to travel.

CONTACT: 08 8979 6100

Maruku Arts

Maruku Arts is a collective of about 900 artists from 20 An̲angu communities across Central Australia. *Maruku* means 'belonging to black', referring to the ownership and operation of the arts collective by these communities. Maruku Arts is a very accessible way to engage in authentic An̲angu culture from across the Central Desert of Australia. It consists of a warehouse in the Mut̲itjulu community, a retail gallery at Ulur̲u–Kata Tjut̲u National Park Cultural Centre, and a market stall in the Yulara town square. The main works are paintings and pun̲u (wooden carvings). Maruka Arts runs 90-minute dot-painting workshops twice daily at the Yulara town square. A local An̲angu artist and an assisting interpreter teach visitors about traditional An̲angu culture, art, symbols and the Pitjantjatjara language. Visitors can apply this knowledge to create a piece of their own. For details on when Ulur̲u–Kata Tjut̲u Cultural Centre is open and on when the workshops are held, see the website.

WHERE: Ulur̲u–Kata Tjut̲u Cultural Centre. The 450 km drive to Ulur̲u–Kata Tjut̲u from Alice Springs takes about 5 hours via the Stuart and Lasseter hwys. These are entirely sealed roads, so a 4WD is not required. Jetstar and Virgin Airlines fly from Sydney directly to Ulur̲u; Jetstar has return services from Melbourne Tullamarine, and may offer direct flights from other destinations, so check their website.

CONTACT: 08 8956 2558

Merrepen Arts Centre

Merrepen Arts opened in 1986 and is now a well-established art centre. The art centre has taken its name from the Merrepen palm tree, which local women use to make dilly bags, mats and fishnets. It supports 20 to 80 artists who work traditionally and also in contemporary mediums that provide new platforms to express traditional stories. Merrepen Arts is located in the community of Nauiyu, in the Daly River region. While the land is the traditional Country of the Malak Malak people, local people now mainly belong to the Ngan'gi language group, which is made up of the two closely related Ngan'gikurrungurr and Ngen'giwumirri languages. There are 10 minority language groups also still in use, including Malak Malak, and Pidgin or Creole is spoken throughout.

Artists here have become particularly well known for their etchings and award-winning screen-printed textiles. In 2013, Marita Sambono's *Fog Dreaming* design was interpreted into a dress that won the national Myer Fashions on the Field prize at the Melbourne Cup, bringing Merrepen art to national acclaim. In 2014, Kieren Karritpul's textile design, *Yerrgi*, won the Youth Award at the 31st National Aboriginal and Torres Strait Islander Art Awards (NATSIAA). The gallery and workshop are open 8.30 am–5 pm weekdays. For further details, see the website.

WHERE: Nauiyu community, next to the picturesque Daly River. Drive south from Darwin on the Stuart Hwy to Adelaide River. Turn right onto Dorat Rd, just after the Adelaide River bridge. Follow Dorat Rd for approximately 30 km then turn right onto Daly River Rd. Follow this road all the way to the Merrepen Arts Centre at Nauiyu. The road is sealed and is easily accessible for most of the year, although care should be taken in the Wet season (November– April) as the region is susceptible to flooding.
PERMITS: No permits are required to visit the Nauiyu community.
CONTACT: 08 8978 2533

Milingimbi Art and Craft Centre

The Yolŋu artists of Milingimbi Island (off the coast of Arnhem Land) and its regional homelands create unique fibre works including pandanus weavings of dilly bags, mats and fish-trap forms, bark paintings, ceremonial poles and carvings. They also create sculptures and works on canvas. The artists use art to express their rich culture, which is a connection of land, sea, song and ceremony. With more than 150 artists from 12 clan groups, art from Milingimbi is highly regarded around the world.

WHERE: Lot 53 Gadupu Rd, Milingimbi via Winellie. Milingimbi community is 15 km from the mainland and 500 km east of Darwin. The art centre is located on the foreshore of the community facing the Arafura Sea. Access to the island is by air or sea. Fly Tiwi operates a daily service from Monday to Friday to Milingimbi from Darwin. Charter flights are also available.
PERMITS: Permits are required to visit the Milingimbi community and may be obtained through the Northern Land Council.
CONTACT: 08 8987 9888

Mimi Aboriginal Arts and Crafts

Mimi Aboriginal Arts and Crafts houses a collection of artwork from an extensive 380,000 sq km area. This includes Arnhem Land, the entire Katherine region, the Tanami Desert and parts of the Kimberley. Mimi is named after the Mimi Spirits, from the Dreaming. Many still inhabit Arnhem Land, and while some are said to be dangerous and must be avoided, many are harmless and can be heard calling in the night. For details on when Mimi Aboriginal Arts and Craft is open, see the website.

WHERE: 6 Pearce St, Katherine. Katherine is an easy 3-hour drive from Darwin along the Stuart Hwy.
CONTACT: 08 8971 0036

Munupi Art Centre

Munupi is located on the north-west coast of Melville Island, in the Tiwi Islands. It grew from

Kieren Karritpul's *Billabong* (2020), Acrylic on canvas

the merger of the Yikikini Women's Centre and Pirlangimpi Pottery. Today it celebrates Tiwi culture through a range of traditional and contemporary mediums.

Art at Munupi is inspired by the lush environment of the Tiwi Islands, as well as the Creation stories and culture of its people. Tiwi culture is very rich, with traditional hunting, gathering and ceremonial events occurring daily, and the art reflects this lifestyle. Artists use ochre, gouache and acrylic paint and are celebrated for the diversity of their works. These include painting, pottery, weaving, carving, screen prints, lino printing and textile work.

Although Munupi Arts is separate from Jilamara Arts, the 2 centres work closely together and a visit to both is recommended when visiting Melville Island.

WHERE: The Garden Point community on the north-west coast of Melville Island. It is about 125 km from Darwin and 30 minutes by air. Munupi is 1 km from Garden Point airport. Fly Tiwi runs 2 flights on weekdays between Darwin and Garden Point, and 1 per day on weekends. For more information, see the Fly Tiwi website. Charter flights are also available.
PERMITS: Permits are required to visit the Tiwi Islands and may be obtained through the Tiwi Land Council.
CONTACT: 08 8978 3975

Ngukurr Arts

Ngukurr Arts sits adjacent to the banks of the Roper River, in south-east Arnhem Land. Like the town of Ngukurr, the art centre is very dynamic, representing people of many different clan and language groups, including Ngalakgan, Alawa, Mangarrayi, Ngandi, Marra, Warndarrang, Nunggubuyu, Ritharrngu-Wägilak and Rembarrnga, collectively known as Yugul Mangi. Artistic output is wholly unique to each artist's Country and culture, with both traditional and contemporary styles being reconceptualised into high quality and diverse works. While there is no one distinct school or style from Ngukurr Arts, works are often known to be bold, with adventurous use of colour to interpret stories and landscapes. The mission history, which dates back to the early 1900s, and resulted in the convergence of Yugul Mangi people in Ngukurr, is often depicted in artwork.

WHERE: Balamurra St, Ngukkur (321 km from Katherine).
PERMITS: Contact the art centre prior to any visit. Permits for travel to Ngukurr are required if staying in the community overnight. They are free and can be arranged through the Northern Land Council.
CONTACT: 08 8975 4260

Numbulwar Numburindi Arts

Numbulwar community sits on the Rose River, on the Gulf of Carpentaria; the traditional lands of the Nunggayinbala clan. Numbulwar Numburindi Arts (NNA) was established in 2019 in response to a growing desire within the community to create a space of artistic and cultural expression. Artists from NNA have already built their profile as champions of fibre art. Using traditional weaving techniques, they marry naturally dyed local pandanus fibre with bright and bold ghost-net fibre, the abandoned fishing line collected from the community's shoreline. The resulting Wulbung (baskets) and Yir (dillybags) are a uniquely colourful blend of traditional and contemporary styles, very distinct from baskets seen elsewhere in the Northern Territory, or Australia at large.

WHERE: Numbulwar (466 km from Katherine).
PERMITS: Contact the art centre prior to visiting. Permits for travel to Numbulwar are required before entering the community. They are free and can be arranged through the Northern Land Council.
CONTACT: 0408 319 879

Nyinkka Nyunyu Art and Culture Centre

Located on the sacred Country of the Warumungu people, Nyinkka Nyunyu offers an insight into the culture of the Aboriginal people of the Tennant Creek region. It includes an art gallery with changing exhibitions that showcase the art movement of Tennant Creek, a gallery shop, an Aboriginal plant and bush-food garden, and the Jajjikari cafe. Nyinkka Nyunyu will be undergoing major upgrades over 2021 and 2022; during this time there is no entry fee to the site. For details of when Nyinkka Nyunyu is open, see the website.

Nyinkka Nyunyu also offers 1-hour guided cultural tours, run by local Warumungu guides. These include a guided tour of the museum and exhibition space and the bush-food garden, as well as education on the traditional Dreaming stories of the Nyinkka site.

WHERE: 13 Paterson St (Stuart Hwy), the main road running through Tennant Creek. Tennant Creek is about a 5-hour drive (500 km) north of Alice Springs.
CONTACT: 08 8963 2150

Outstation Art

Outstation Art was established in 2008 and supports artists working in rural art centres in the Tiwi Islands, Arnhem Land, the Western Desert, the Kimberley and Central and South Australia. Supporting art from art centres ensures that fair work practices are maintained. Through many years of direct experience with artists, their art centres and community engagement, the gallery observes high ethical standards in its business. Outstation embraces a broad range of works, from traditional media, such as bark paintings, hollow logs and weaving, to contemporary visions in fibre art, photography, soft sculpture and acrylic paintings.

In February each year, Outstation holds a 'Rising Stars' exhibition to promote emerging Aboriginal artists. Each year in August it also presents *Salon des Refusés*, which showcases works submitted to the NATSIAAs but not shortlisted for the award.

WHERE: 8 Parap Place (upstairs, entry via Gregory St), Parap, Darwin. Outstation is located in Parap's gallery precinct. The area is also home to the famous Parap markets, held every Saturday. Parap is a short drive from the city and close to the Museum and Art Gallery of the Northern Territory. The local bus route 4 (Monday to Sunday), route 6 (Monday to Friday), and route 10 (Monday to Sunday) leave frequently from the Darwin Bus Interchange in the city.
CONTACT: 08 8981 4822

Palngun Wurnangat

Palngun Wurnangat ('women together'), formally established in 1990, is an independently owned Indigenous women's organisation based in Wadeye. It builds on a strong history of women's social and economic enterprise for the wider community. A print workshop allows local printmakers to produce vibrant fabrics and homewares. The T-House café and gallery/shop and a Mi Marrarl (Kakadu Plum) harvesting business provide both essential services and employment.

WHERE: Lot 458 Perdjert St, Wadeye (400 km from Darwin).
CONTACT: 0438 200 809

Papunya Tjupi Aboriginal Arts

Papunya is a small Aboriginal community, formed in the late 1960s due to the removal and displacement of Aboriginal people from their land. It is made up of Pintupi, Luritja, Warlpiri, Arrernte and Anmatyerr peoples. The community is famed as the birthplace of the Western Desert dot-painting movement. The current art centre at Papunya, Panunya Tjupi, was established in 2007 and supports 100 artists from Papunya and its surrounding outstations. Many of these artists are descendants of the original artists in the Papunya movement and continue to work in the high standards of their forefathers, while carving out their own unique identity in the world of contemporary Aboriginal art. Art remains an important part of the community and connection to the land.

WHERE: Papunya is 250 km north-west of Alice Springs. From Alice Springs, Papunya is a 3-hour drive via the Larapinta and Namatjira Tourist Route. A 4WD is required.
PERMITS: Permits are not required for day visits. Visitors are welcome to visit the art centre but it is necessary to make an appointment.
CONTACT: 08 8964 7141

Papunya Tula Artists

Papunya Tula Artists are renowned for their innovative work within the Western Desert art movement. In the early 1970s, the school teacher at Papunya encouraged the locals to paint a traditional mural on the walls of the school. The murals inspired a large art collective in the community and in 1972 the artists, originally entirely men, successfully established their own company, Papunya Tula Artists Pty Ltd. Traditionally the people of the Western Desert painted stories in the sand or on the body for ceremonial purposes. The artists adapted their cultural practices to remove sacred symbols and monitor ancestral designs, and also to paint in the western style using acrylic paint and a hard surface. They brought the art of the Western Desert into national and international acclaim. In the 1980s, the Pintupi artists returned to their homelands further west and continued painting for Papunya Tula Artists at art centres the company established in Walungurru (Kintore) and Kiwirrkura. The gallery in Alice Springs represents the Aboriginal artists who are originally from Papunya and the Western Desert region. This includes Pintupi, Luritja, Warlpiri, Arrernte and Anmatyerr peoples.

WHERE: 63 Todd Mall, Alice Springs.
CONTACT: 08 8952 4731

Tangentyere Artists

Tangentyere Artists celebrates the complex cultural diversity of Central Australia. It represents the residents of various Alice Springs town camps, who came from many traditional lands across the desert. The centre aims to share the stories from the town camps. Despite sometimes difficult conditions, the camps are important places that also have many positive aspects. The art is diverse, representing various traditional stories and using a range of styles. Today, Tangentyere is comprised of approximately 400 artists.

WHERE: 16 Fogarty St, Alice Springs.
CONTACT: 08 8951 4232

Tapatjatjaka Art and Craft Centre

Tapatjatjaka Art and Craft is located in Titjikala community in the Simpson Desert, south of Alice Springs, and supports local Arrernte, Luritja, Pitjantjatjara and Yankunytjatjara artists. Artists draw inspiration from the striking red sand and desert oak environment surrounding the community to create colourful paintings. They are also known for abstract wire creations, recycling discarded metal wire and miscellaneous objects into sculptural representations of local animals and birds. These sculptures have been exhibited in galleries both nationally and internationally.

WHERE: Titjikala community (120 km from Alice Springs).
CONTACT: 08 8956 0788

Thamarrurr Men's Shed (Thamarrurr Development Corporation)

The Thamarrurr Men's Shed Program has been developed by Wadeye community leaders to improve the health and wellbeing of men in the community, which in turn improves that of Wadeye's women, children and families. By nurturing greater leadership capacity and improving men's health, the program aims to create more positive spaces in Wadeye. One objective of the program is to bring together men of all ages to share and connect to culture, stories and traditional arts, while also exploring new means of creative expression. Some Elders in Wadeye still make traditional ceremonial headdresses, canoes and spears. Within the Men's Shed space, the intergenerational passing of ancient crafting skills occurs alongside upskilling and growth in contemporary mediums. Young men, in particular, are taught how to channel their energy creatively. The gallery also provides a means of income.

WHERE: Wadeye (400 km from Darwin).
PERMITS: Permits are required to visit Wadeye and are available from the Northern Land Council.
CONTACT: 08 8978 1305

Tiwi Design

Tiwi Design promotes, preserves and enriches the culture of the Tiwi people, and supports some 100 local artists. The art centre opened in the late 1960s with exhibitions of wood-block prints. This style of art was a natural link to the traditional techniques of woodcarving. Within a year, the wood-block designs were transferred to silk screens, and textile printing became a major medium of the artists. By the mid 1970s, Tiwi Design artists were creating a wide range of art and craft, including ochre paintings on bark and canvas, ironwood carvings, screen-printed fabrics, ceramics, bronze and glass sculptures, pandanus weaving and limited-edition prints. Today the art centre comprises a pottery studio, screen-printing studio, carver's shelter, a painting studio, plus a retail gallery and administration centre. The work of the artists is as diverse now as it has always been at Tiwi Design.

WHERE: Tiwi Design is located in the community of Wurrumiyanga, on the south-eastern corner of Bathurst Island, 80 km north of Darwin. Fly Tiwi operates a daily, 30-minute flight to Bathurst Island from Darwin. For more information and bookings, see the Fly Tiwi website. On Thursdays, Fridays and Sundays, SeaLinkNT ferries depart from Cullen Bay, Darwin, for Wurrumiyanga in the morning and return in the afternoon. The trip is 2½ hours each way. For more information, see the SeaLink website.
PERMITS: Permits are essential; apply on the Tiwi Land Council website.
CONTACT: 08 8978 3982

Tiwi By Design Tours

Visitors can immerse themselves in the culture of the Tiwi Islands on this cultural walking tour. It begins with a traditional welcome ceremony at Tiwi Designs, followed by morning tea and a tour of the museum, which showcases the culture and history of the Tiwi people. After lunch at Tiwi Designs, a unique screen-printing session with a local artist gives visitors the chance to create their own piece of art. The tour includes a return ferry from Darwin to Bathurst Island.

WHERE: The tour departs from Cullen Bay, Darwin. From the ferry landing, the tour walks up to Tiwi Design.
CONTACT: SeaLink Northern Territory: 1300 130 679

Tjanpi Desert Weavers

Tjanpi Desert Weavers is an Indigenous social enterprise that enables the Indigenous women of Australia's remote Central Desert to earn a regular income from their fibre art. The enterprise was formed by the Ngaanyatjarra Pitjantjatjara Yankunytjatjara Women's Council (NPYWC) in 1995, and now represents more than 400 Aboriginal women from 26 remote Western and Central Desert communities covering an area of approximately 350,000 sq km.

Tjanpi, which means 'wild harvested grasses', is harvested and woven by the women, and then decorated with emu feathers, painted seedpods and coloured raffia. The pieces are beautiful, intricate and whimsical, ranging from conventional basket designs to quirky, colourful animals, teapots and even life-sized figures of people. In 2005, the Tjanpi Desert Weavers earned national and international fame when a group of weavers from Blackstone, 450 km south-west of Alice Springs, won first prize at the NATSIAAs for their woven model of a Toyota 4WD.

Tjanpi has a public gallery in Alice Springs, and regularly exhibits work in various galleries across Australia. They also run public weaving workshops.

WHERE: 3 Wilkinson St, Alice Springs.
CONTACT: 08 8958 2377

Walkatjara Art

Based at Uluṟu, Walkatjara Art is the Aṉangu owned and directed, not-for-profit art centre exclusively representing Mutitjulu community. Artists take pride in their work and in their art centre, and are strong advocates for local culture. Their award-winning artworks, which depict local Tjukurpa (Creation Time) stories, are inspired by the natural beauty and power of this land. The art centre is open 7 days a week, with visitors having the opportunity to meet the artists and watch new work being created in the magnificent purpose-built structure.

WHERE: Cultural Centre, Uluṟu–Kata Tjuṯa National Park.
CONTACT: 08 8956 2537

Waralungku Arts

Waralungku (pronounced 'wharr-a-loongu') Arts represents artists from the Yanyuwa people, the Traditional Owners of Borroloola, as well as three other main language groups of the region, the Garrwa, Marra and Gudanji people. The vibrant contemporary works produced here reflect history, culture and tradition, but also reference current issues and concerns for Aboriginal people. Established artists explore a range of themes in their pieces, ranging from community life, history and the distinctive beauty of the surrounding Country, to wider political views and environmental concerns. A wide range of mediums are used, including acrylic painting, printmaking, sculpture, jewellery and traditional craft items.

WHERE: 191 Robinson Rd, Borroloola (380 km from Daly Waters).
CONTACT: 08 8975 6718 or 0473 064 795

Warlukurlangu Artists Aboriginal Corporation

Warlukurlangu is a vibrant and active art centre that supports artists from the remote Tanami Desert communities of Yuendumu and Nyirripi, and neighbouring communities. These are the traditional lands of the Warlpiri people. Warlukurlangu means 'belonging to fire', and refers to the Fire Dreaming site near Yuendumu. The art centre was established in 1985 and today includes more than 800 artists. They are recognised for creating some of the finest contemporary art in Australia and the world, using coloured acrylic paint to translate traditional cultural designs and stories. Warlukurlangu is also well known for its wide selection of outstanding limited-edition prints. While the art centre is open during the week, visits on weekends are by appointment only.

WHERE: Ral Ral Ave, Yuendumu, 290 km north-west of Alice Springs. From Alice Springs, drive north on the Stuart Hwy for 25 km, before turning west onto the Tanami Rd.
PERMITS: Day visitors do not require a permit. Any longer stays require a permit, which can be obtained from the Central Land Council website. Please contact the art centre before visiting.
CONTACT: 08 8956 4133

Warnayaka Art & Cultural Aboriginal Corporation

Warnayaka celebrates the rich culture of the Warlpiri people, and provides a space

(From left) Mary Katatjuku Pan, Ilawanti Ungkutjuru Ken, Niningka Lewis, Imiyari Frank and Tjunkaya Tapaya of Tjanpi Desert Weavers

for cultural maintenance through creative expression. Historically, the most important Warlpiri artwork was made on wood and in the sand. Later it was transferred onto the body. Today, acrylic paint and canvas is used, with digital mediums fast emerging among the younger generations. The art centre is integral to cultural survival and promotion.

WHERE: Lajamanu (557 km from Katherine).
PERMITS: Permits are required to visit. These can be arranged through the Central Land Council.
CONTACT: 08 8975 0808

Yarrenyty Arltere Artists

Yarrenyty Arltere is a town camp within Alice Springs that is associated with the Dog Dreaming of the Arrernte people. Both Arrernte and Luritja people live there.

Yarrenyty Arltere Artists was an arts training project established in 2000 to combat the chronic social issues faced by residents in the camp. The project quickly became a vibrant hub for the community, rebuilding cultural strength and creating economic opportunities for the people. In 2008, it was established as an Indigenous-owned-and-managed enterprise. The artists have gained national and international acclaim for their soft sculptures. This practice sees recycled woollen blankets dyed with local plants, scrap metal collected from around Alice Springs, and feathers, beads and hand embroidery made into various quirky sculptures of spirits, figures and animals.

Yarrenyty Arltere artists won the Telstra National Aboriginal and Torres Strait Islander Art Award 3D Award in 2013 and 2015, and the Vincent Lingiari Art Award in 2016. Artists were also highly commended in the 2012 NATSIAA 3D award and the 2013 WA Indigenous Art Award.

WHERE: Larapinta Valley town camp, Blain St, Alice Springs.
CONTACT: Art Centre Manager: yalc.art@tangentyere.org.au

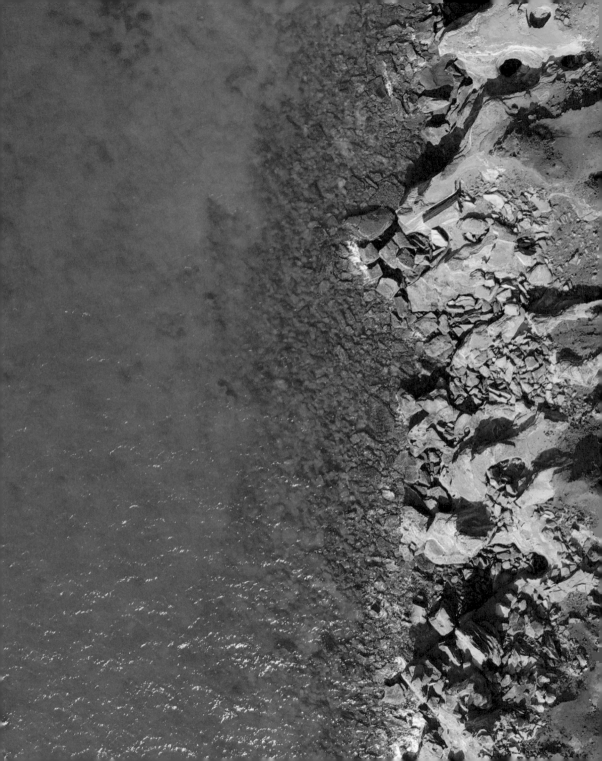

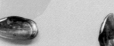

2 WESTERN AUSTRALIA

FESTIVALS

A Taste of Broome

One of the most magical dates on the local calendar, this festival celebrates the multiculturalism of Broome's Indigenous community. A celebration of food, music and culture, A Taste of Broome showcases the diversity of local cuisines, musicians and artists. For a total immersion experience, make sure to attend one of the many cooking workshops and demonstrations. The festival culminates with the Kimberley Indigenous Performing Arts Showcase, which celebrates and shows off the Kimberley's diverse and rich talent. All event and ticket information can be found on the website.

WHEN: Annually in June
WHERE: 7 Blackman St, Broome.
CONTACT: 08 9195 5333

Kullarri NAIDOC Festival

The Kullarri NAIDOC Festival is a ten-day celebration in Broome and surrounding communities recognising the region's diverse Indigenous culture and celebrating the history and achievements of the community. The festival opens each year with the vibrant Reconciliation Walk, a community favourite. Community members, visitors and tourists can experience traditional foods, dance, art and crafts, as well as contemporary music and culture. The interactive events included in the program assist in creating understanding and awareness of Indigenous heritage, and showcase the traditional and contemporary culture of the region's people. Check the website for event information and updates.

WHEN: Annually during June & July
WHERE: 7 Blackman Street, Broome.
CONTACT: 08 9194 9999

Mowanjum Festival

Hosted by the Mowanjum Art and Culture Centre, the Mowanjum Festival celebrates the culture of the Ngarinyin, Worrorra and Wunambal peoples. Held each year in July, the one-night spectacular is one of the largest cultural celebrations in WA and attracts visitors from Australia wide. Open to the general public from 2 pm, the festival includes a variety of free workshops in the afternoon, including painting, didgeridoo playing (for men only) and boab-nut carving, followed by corroborees featuring performers from throughout the Kimberley. The art gallery stays open until 9 pm, with food, drinks and local bush tucker available.

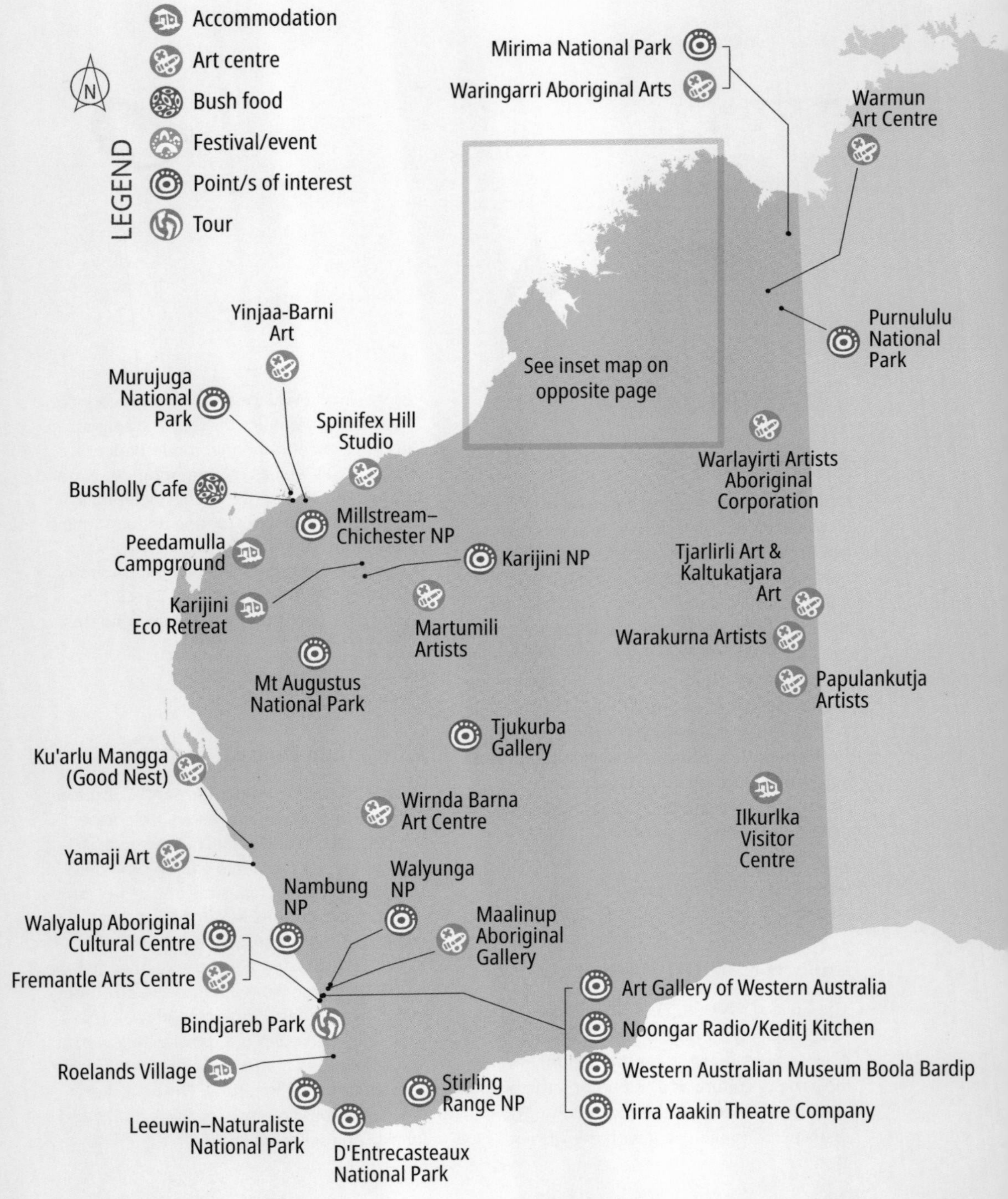
LEGEND
Accommodation
Art centre
Bush food
Festival/event
Point/s of interest
Tour
N
Mirima National Park
Waringarri Aboriginal Arts
Warmun Art Centre
Purnululu National Park
See inset map on opposite page
Yinjaa-Barni Art
Murujuga National Park
Spinifex Hill Studio
Bushlolly Cafe
Millstream–Chichester NP
Peedamulla Campground
Karijini NP
Karijini Eco Retreat
Martumili Artists
Warlayirti Artists Aboriginal Corporation
Tjarlirli Art & Kaltukatjara Art
Warakurna Artists
Papulankutja Artists
Mt Augustus National Park
Tjukurba Gallery
Ku'arlu Mangga (Good Nest)
Wirnda Barna Art Centre
Ilkurlka Visitor Centre
Yamaji Art
Nambung NP
Walyunga NP
Walyalup Aboriginal Cultural Centre
Fremantle Arts Centre
Maalinup Aboriginal Gallery
Art Gallery of Western Australia
Noongar Radio/Keditj Kitchen
Western Australian Museum Boola Bardip
Yirra Yaakin Theatre Company
Bindjareb Park
Roelands Village
Stirling Range NP
Leeuwin–Naturaliste National Park
D'Entrecasteaux National Park

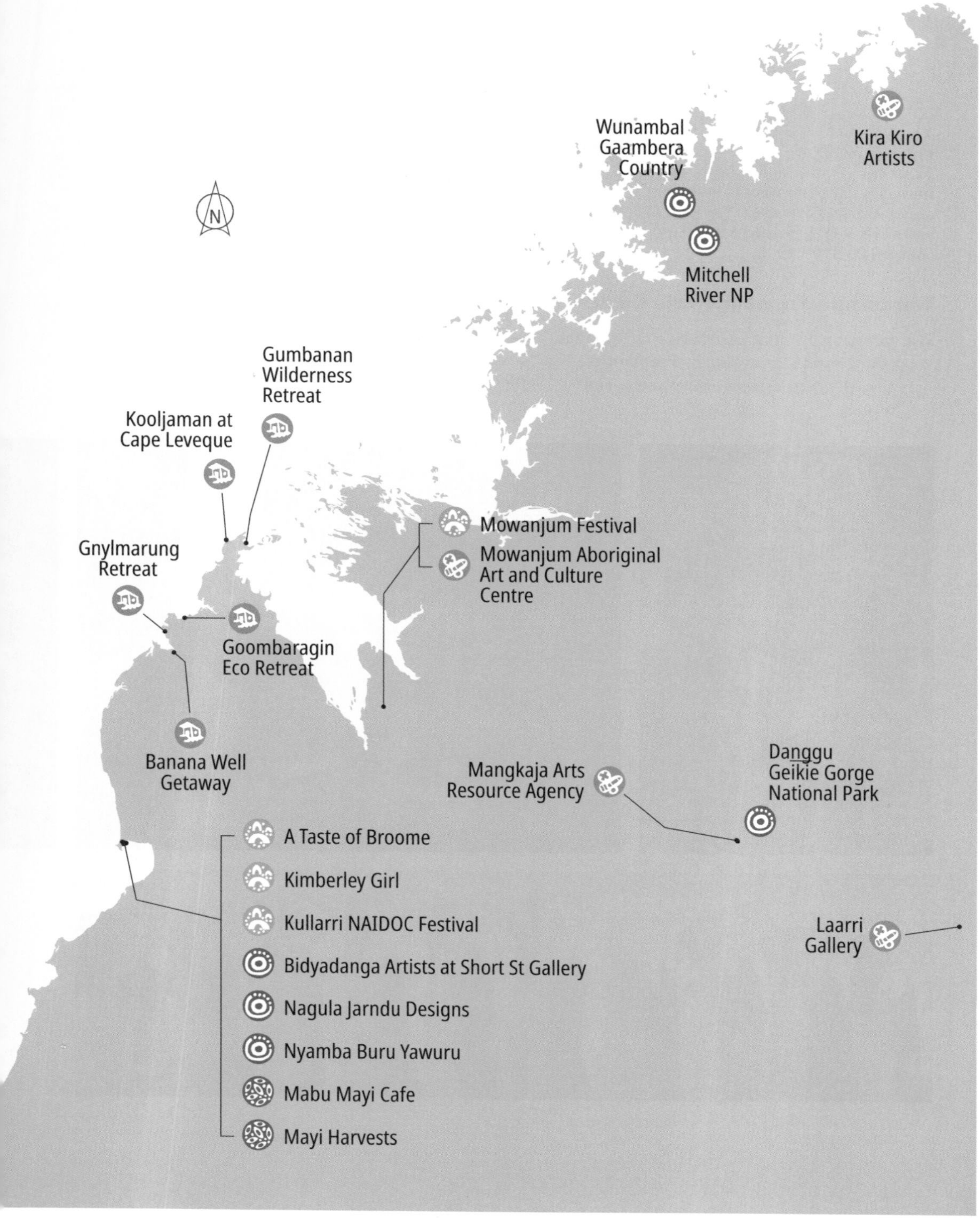

N
Wunambal Gaambera Country
Kira Kiro Artists
Mitchell River NP
Gumbanan Wilderness Retreat
Kooljaman at Cape Leveque
Mowanjum Festival
Mowanjum Aboriginal Art and Culture Centre
Gnylmarung Retreat
Goombaragin Eco Retreat
Banana Well Getaway
Mangkaja Arts Resource Agency
Danggu Geikie Gorge National Park
A Taste of Broome
Kimberley Girl
Kullarri NAIDOC Festival
Bidyadanga Artists at Short St Gallery
Nagula Jarndu Designs
Nyamba Buru Yawuru
Mabu Mayi Cafe
Mayi Harvests
Laarri Gallery

WHERE: Mowanjum Aboriginal Art and Culture Centre, 12 km from Derby, 3 km along the Gibb River Rd.
WHEN: July; check the website for details.
COST: Tickets are available at the gate; adult: $40; youth (12–17): $15; child: $5.
CONTACT: 08 9191 1008

Wardarnji – Fremantle Arts Centre

Wardarnji is a dynamic experience of Noongar song, dance and storytelling on Fremantle Arts Centre's picturesque South Lawn. The free community celebration transports attendees to another place among the beauty of the oldest songs, dances and language in the world, as fires burn long into the evening and people come together to celebrate Indigenous Australian culture.

WHERE: Fremantle Arts Centre, 1 Finnerty Street, Fremantle.
WHEN: November; check the website for specific dates.
COST: Free.
CONTACT: 08 9432 9555

PERFORMANCE

Kimberley Girl

More than just a beauty pageant, Kimberly Girl is a leadership program to support young Aboriginal women between the ages of 16 and 25. Running each year during the September–October school holidays, the workshops and showcases run as part of a program that addresses contemporary issues faced by many young women in the community, empowering participants to overcome the impact of social, economic and isolation disadvantages. This heartwarming celebration of the community's young women unites and pays tribute to their achievements.

WHEN: September–October, annually
WHERE: 7 Blackman St, Broome.
CONTACT: 08 9195 5333

Above: *Hecate* (2020), presented by Yirra Yaakin Theatre Company in association with Bell Shakespeare. A Perth Festival commission.

Opposite top left, top right: A Taste of Broome is a celebration of food, music and culture

Opposite bottom: The Kimberley Girl line-up

Yirra Yaakin Theatre Company

Yirra Yaakin (Stand Tall) Theatre Company is based in Whadjuk country within the Noongar Nation, presenting Aboriginal stories to audiences across the globe. This theatre company was born out of a desire to provide the Aboriginal community with an artistic outlet for positive self-determination and has evolved over the last 27 years from childrens' workshops to showcasing over 50 theatre productions with numerous prizes and commendations. With a solid annual program of contemporary First peoples' performance, the theatre company prides itself on collaborating, commissioning and developing new Aboriginal writing and its dedication to First peoples' employment, engagement and capacity-building. Upcoming productions and ticketing information can be found on their website.

WHERE: 180 Hamersley Rd, Subiaco.
CONTACT: 08 9380 3040

NATIONAL PARKS

The Western Australian Department of Biodiversity, Conservation and Attractions manages over 31 million hectares of national parks and other protected areas. Its Culture in the Parks program supports and encourages Aboriginal people to conduct cultural events and tourism businesses on this land. For more information on these and other parks, see: exploreparks.dbca.wa.gov.au

D'Entrecasteaux National Park

D'Entrecasteaux National Park is a narrow strip hugging the coast for more than 130 km between Augusta and Walpole. This is a significant wilderness area of pristine natural beauty, with long, bone-white beaches, high dunes and spectacular coastal cliffs.

CULTURAL HERITAGE: The traditional custodians of this national park are the South West Boojarah people. Aboriginal artefacts discovered in the park prove Noongar occupation dating back at least 6000 years, although investigations in areas adjacent to the national park indicate occupation as long as 47,000 years ago. Erosion of sand dunes has uncovered a number of sites of significance, including stone artefacts, fish traps, quarry sites and burial sites. The Lake Jasper/Meerup Dunes area is most prolific, with artefacts found 10 metres below the lake's current water levels, indicating that there were major campsites here back when the lake was a prehistoric forest. This is a place of particular archaeological and cultural significance to the Noongar people.

NATURAL FEATURES: The park's outstanding natural features include a series of hexagonal-shaped basalt columns to the west of Black Point, formed by a volcanic lava flow some 135 million years ago, and the 10-kilometre-long mobile Yeagarup Dunes. Inland from the coast is a series of lakes and swamps, including Lake Jasper – the largest freshwater lake in the southern half of the state, and an important habitat for waterbirds and freshwater fish. Major streams and rivers, including the Warren, Donnelly and Shannon, flow through the park.

THINGS TO DO

This is a water-lover's paradise, with swimming, surfing, beachcombing, boating and canoeing on offer at a bevy of beautiful beaches. Photographers will also find themselves spoilt for choice, particularly at sunset and sunrise. Jump in a 4WD and head out along the coast, and you can easily find a beach where the only footprints will be your own.

BUSHWALKING: Point D'Entrecasteaux, accessible by 2WD, offers a selection of walks including the Pupalong Loop Walk (400 m, less than 1 hr, easy) with trailside information on Noongar culture and tradition. A link from the trail provides access to the Point D'Entrecasteaux platform, which offers spectacular coastal views. Coastal Survivors Walk (2.8 km one way, 2 hrs) follows the dunes and cliff tops between Point D'Entrecasteaux and Windy Harbour, and provides information along the way about coastal flora and fauna. The Cliff Top Walk (1.3 km one way, 1 hr, medium difficulty) takes in the impressive limestone cliffs between Point D'Entrecasteaux and Tookulup. More adventurous walkers can tackle the summit of Mt Chudalup (2 km, less than 1 hr return, medium difficulty), which delivers spectacular views. Take care in wet weather as the granite can be slippery.

FISHING: Windy Harbour and Salmon Beach (both with 2WD access) are popular spots for fishing. A 4WD is needed to reach other coastal fishing spots. Coastal fishers should take special care, as dangerous sea surges can occur without warning.

4WD: With 130 km of coastline, much of it remote, this is a fabulous place for remote beach driving. Note this is an isolated national park, so ensure your vehicle is well maintained and you are well equipped for remote driving. Remember to notify someone of your intended route and return.

SCENIC TOURING: The 6-km D'Entrecasteaux Drive enables you to take in the park's diverse landscape and classic vistas over the Southern Ocean, with lookouts at Gardner, Sunset and Salmon beaches.

WHERE: 28 km south of Pemberton.
CAMPING AND ACCOMMODATION: Leaning Marri campground offers six shady single campsites and one group campsite with a shared shelter. Banksia Camp would suit a family holiday, with camping and fishing along with views across to Chatham Island. As Windy Habour is accessible via sealed road, it is the only site in the national park suitable for caravans.
COST: Park entry and camping fees apply. See the website for more information.
CONTACT: 08 9776 1207

Danggu Geikie Gorge National Park

Set in the far north of the Kimberley, the focus of this national park is the spectacular 30-m-deep Danggu Geikie Gorge, with its colourful cliffs and sculptured rock formations carved by the waters of Bandaralngarri, the Fitzroy River.

CULTURAL HERITAGE: The Traditional Owners of this area are the Bunuba people, who maintain ancient spiritual and cultural beliefs. Along with their conservation and cultural work, they also run 1-hour guided cruises from May through to October aboard the *Ms Casey Ross*, named in honour of a late Elder and leader of the Danggu muwayi (clan estate).

In May 2017, the Bunuba people and Parks and Wildlife WA (DBCA) formalised their Joint Management Agreement, which includes Danggu (Geikie Gorge) National and Conservation Parks, Jungi-wa and Guwinyja (Brooking Gorge) Conservation Park, Bandilngan (Windjana Gorge) National and Conservation Parks, Dimalurru (Tunnel Creek) National Park, Balili (Devonian Reef) Conservation Park and Miluwindi (King Leopold Ranges) Conservation Park. And in December 2020, they signed a new Indigenous Land Use Agreement (ILUA) to create the Fitzroy River National Park, which will cover 173,000 hectares, extending up to Jijidu (Dimond Gorge).

Together they are working to create tourism experiences that celebrate the land and history of the Bunuba people across all of their muwayi. At the time of printing, a Bunuba Parks pass is in development, along with myriad tourism endeavours spanning outdoor adventures, performance, art, culture and more. Check Bunuba.com for updates.

NATURAL FEATURES: The gorge is part of an ancient limestone reef system and, on still days, the yellow, orange and grey-white walls are reflected in the waters of the river. Along the riverbanks are thick knots of tropical reeds, freshwater mangroves, native fig trees and pandanus. River gums and cadjeputs provide a welcome home for flying-foxes while the river supports sawfish and stingrays, which over centuries have adapted to the fresh water. Freshwater crocodiles and barramundi are plentiful.

THINGS TO DO

The park offers day use only, from April to November, and restricted entry in the Wet season, between December and March, when the Fitzroy River floods the area. Book a boat tour between May and October and for an insight into the wildlife and geology of the gorge.
BUSHWALKING: Walks include the Jarrambayah trail (4.4 km return, 2 hrs) following the sandbank of the Fitzroy River floodplain to Danggu's West Wall; and the Bun.gu trail (1.2 km return, 30 mins), a signposted walk sharing the Bunuba people's knowledge of plants, animals and landscape.
BIRDWATCHING: Birdwatchers will note the great bowerbird, clamorous reed-warbler, great egret, little pied cormorant and darter, among other species.
WHERE: 20 km north-east of Fitzroy Crossing.
CONTACT: 08 9191 5112

Karijini National Park

Set in the Hamersley Range in the heart of the Pilbara, the vast Karijini National Park is an ancient landscape of massive mountains and steep escarpments cut by spectacular gorges more than 100 m deep. Within these sheer-sided chasms hide crystal-clear rock pools, cascading waterfalls and lush vegetation.

CULTURAL HERITAGE: The Traditional Owners of the Hamersley Range are the Banyjima, Innawonga and Eastern Guruma people. Aboriginal sites more than 20,000 years old have been found here, many of which are still significant to the local Aboriginal community. The park was first known as Hamersley Range National Park, but this name was changed in 1991 in favour of the Banyjima word for the range, Karijini.

NATURAL FEATURES: While much of the southern part of the park is inaccessible, the famous gorges in its northern section attract visitors. Chasms as deep as 100 m scour a steep escarpment, exposing dominant layering and sediments dating back millions of years.

Each gorge has its own particular features. Nestled between the walls of Dales Gorge and shaded by lush vegetation are Fern Pool and Fortescue Falls. Circular Pool can be viewed from the lookout provided. Kalamina Gorge and Pool is the most accessible gorge. At Hamersley Gorge a wave of tectonic rock acts as a backdrop to a swimming hole and natural spa. Joffre Gorge boasts a natural amphitheatre created by an unusual curved wall and, after rain, a 100 m waterfall. Oxer Lookout is above the pool where the Joffre, Hancock, Weano and Red gorges join. Many of these gorges are relatively easy and safe to enter, but some are best undertaken with a guide.

Karijini National Park also contains the two tallest mountains in Western Australia: Mt Meharry at 1250 m; and Mt Bruce, known as Punurrunha by the Aboriginal people, at 1234 m high. A climb to the summit of Mt Bruce gives a panoramic view of the Hamersley Range.

The dusty red earth of the hills, ridges and plateaus of Karijini is covered with spinifex, punctuated by eucalypts such as the drought-resistant snappy gum, with its twisted white trunk. Low mulga woodlands are found on the lower slopes and valley plains. The wildflowers that bloom here vary with the seasons. July to September is the best time to see floral displays, when countless everlastings carpet the landscape, along with the ubiquitous purple–pink mulla mulla. Within the gorges are luxuriant ferns thriving on moist rock ledges and reed-lined pools of water surrounded by river red gums, coolibahs and cadjeputs. The latter, also known as weeping paperbark, are covered with fragrant creamy white flower spikes in spring. Native rock figs grow in seemingly impossible positions on the rock faces of the gorges; birds that eat the fruit leave undigested seeds on the rock ledges, where they germinate in small pockets of soil and leaf debris. The roots of the fig then stretch downwards to reach water, sometimes as far as 10 m below.

Two of the smallest creatures in the park build homes that are a feature of Karijini – look out for the huge termite mounds and, on stony slopes among the spinifex, the rock piles of the rare western pebble-mound mouse. This tiny marsupial uses stones to build a small volcano-like crater for its nesting chamber. These laboriously constructed stone piles serve as entrances to a system of burrows underground. Within, the nesting chambers are lined with leaves and other plant debris. Mounds can cover areas of up to 9 sq m. This little creature is just one of the many species of native rodent to reside in the national park.

Other mammals in Karijini include red kangaroos, euros, rock wallabies, dingoes, echidnas and bats. The park also boasts a variety of birds, which are drawn to waterholes. Spinifex pigeons, distinctive for their sandy-coloured crests, fly between the rocks and through the grasses, and wedge-tailed eagles are a common sight soaring high up on the thermals created by the warm air rising from the surrounding plains. Reptiles abound, with geckos, goannas, dragons and legless lizards scurrying about or lazing on rocks, and pythons and other snakes are common but not necessarily sighted.

THINGS TO DO:

This is a park for wilderness adventurers, nature photographers and keen bushwalkers.

BUSHWALKING: Karijini offers plenty of marked walking trails ranging from easy to difficult. These include the Gorge Rim Trail (5.1 km, allow half a day, medium difficulty), which winds from Circular Pool Lookout along the edge of Dales Gorge to Fortescue Falls lookout.

At Kalamina Gorge a walk leads to the gorge's lush, shaded pool, which can be extended into a 3-hr return walk through the gorge. The trailhead carpark for the walk to Kalamina Gorge has an information board, tables and toilets. Hancock Gorge walk is through a steep narrow gorge that takes you down to Kermit's Pool (1.5 km return, 3 hrs, medium difficulty).

Mt Bruce (Punurrunha) summit walk (10 km return, allow half a day, difficult) is recommended for fit and experienced walkers only. The summit offers good views of the national park and along the way are interpretive signs giving information about Aboriginal heritage, flora and fauna. There are also giant termite mounds in this area. If you are contemplating any of the longer hikes, you must notify a ranger before starting out. Regardless of the length of the walk, remember that the gorges can be extremely hazardous.

SCENIC VIEWS: There are lookouts over most of the gorges, which then lead on to walking trails. A good place to get your bearings is Oxer Lookout, a walk that takes less than an hour from the Weano carpark. The lookout has breathtaking views down a 100 m drop to Junction Pool, the confluence of four gorges – Weano, Red, Knox and Joffre. At Joffre Gorge, rock steps take you down to a lookout overlooking a spectacular curved waterfall, which forms a natural amphitheatre. The 300 m walk down into Knox Gorge to the lookout is best undertaken in the early morning or late afternoon, to witness the full play of light on the view.

SWIMMING: The pools of water in the gorges provide delightful places for a refreshing swim. However, some of the deep pools that remain shaded can be extremely cold, especially between April and September. Take care, as hypothermia can occur; wetsuits are recommended. When swimming in gorges or rivers, watch out for submerged hazards. Most of the gorges have picnic areas.

THE KARIJINI VISITOR CENTRE: Located on Banyjima Dr, the visitor centre is a good place to start any visit to this national park. It offers displays about the flora, fauna and geology of the area, and about the local Aboriginal people and their culture. The design of the building represents a goanna moving through the country; the animal is highly symbolic to the local Aboriginal people. The tail represents their history, the centre or stomach their law, and the head represents the future direction of the Traditional Owners. The high, weathered steel walls of the centre mimic the sheer-sided gorges that are a feature of the park. The building is designed to withstand the fires that are a regular occurrence in the region.

WHERE: 75 km east of Tom Price.

CAMPING AND ACCOMMODATION: There are two campgrounds within the park (one being an overflow campground), with tables and gas barbecues at the nearby picnic area. Bush camping is not allowed. The nearby town of Tom Price offers a range of accommodation from camping and caravan sites to motels.

COST: Park entry and camping fees apply. See the website for more information.

CONTACT: 08 9189 8121

Leeuwin–Naturaliste National Park

This long park makes up a 120 km stretch of the south-west coast of Western Australia between two prominent capes, Cape Naturaliste in the north and Cape Leeuwin in the south. Known as the Limestone Coast, the area boasts a stunning array of natural attractions: wild and rugged coastal scenery, white-sand beaches, some of the state's best surfing breaks, excellent fishing, tall karri forest and magnificent cave formations. Leeuwin–Naturaliste National Park forms the western boundary of the Margaret River region, renowned for its world-class wines and fine craft galleries. Its close proximity to Perth also contributes to its popularity as a holiday destination for Western Australians. The main roads in the park are either sealed or gravel and are suitable for 2WD vehicles; 4WD tracks lead to the more remote coastal areas.

CULTURAL HERITAGE: Bones and teeth found in the park's limestone caves, and implements found at other sites, date Aboriginal occupation of the Leeuwin–Naturaliste area as far back as 40,000 years ago. Many placenames in the region show the strong ties between the local Noongar people and their land. Yallingup translates as 'place of love',

Meekadarribee means 'the moon's bathing place', Boranup means 'place of the dingo' and Cowaramup is 'place of the parrot'. Injidup means 'place of the red pea flower', and in springtime these distinctive plants flourish on the region's limestone cliffs.

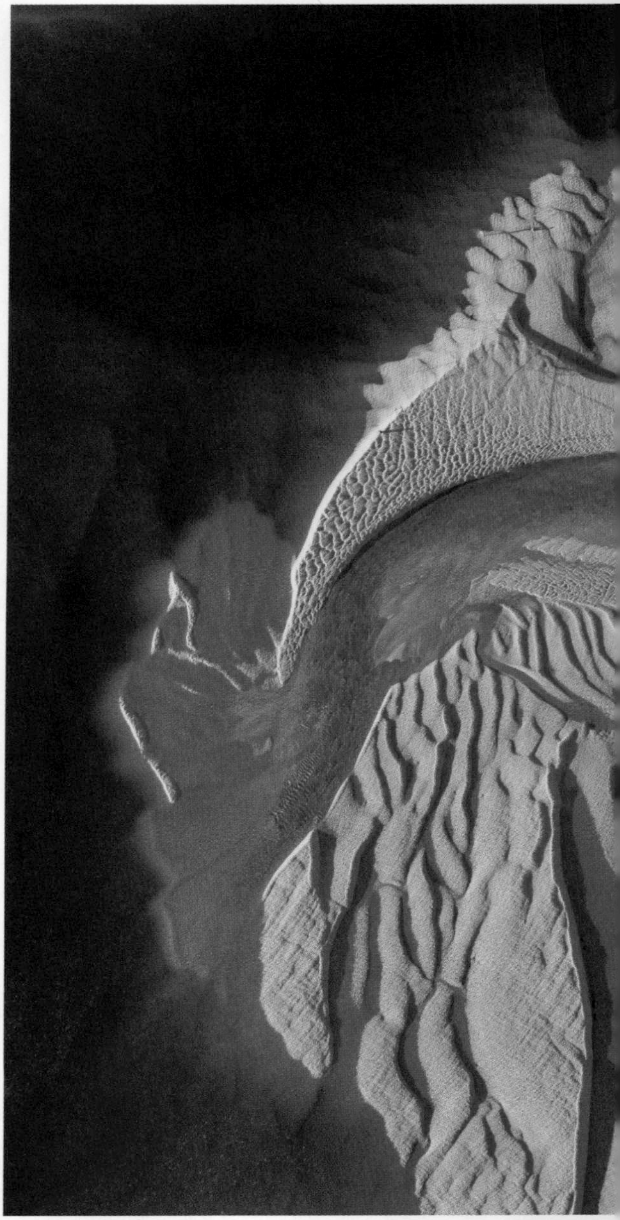

NATURAL FEATURES: The Leeuwin–Naturaliste ridge, which runs from north to south between the capes, is a 600-million-year-old geological formation of granitic rock capped by limestone. Over time, groundwater streams flowing in channels above the granite bedrock have eroded the soluble limestone, forming a system of caves throughout the ridge. The fossils of marsupials long extinct in Western Australia have been found in these caves, including a giant echidna, koala and even, unexpectedly, a Tasmanian devil.

Along the coast are rugged limestone cliffs and granite outcrops, interspersed with sheltered bays and beaches. At Canal Rocks, a natural canal is formed by a series of rocks that extends into the ocean from the headland. The ocean surging powerfully through the canal, viewed from a walkway and bridge, is an impressive sight.

THINGS TO DO

This coastline has so much to offer visitors: bushwalking, sightseeing, abseiling, rock-climbing, caving, fishing, whale-watching and a variety of water sports.

BEACH AND BUSHWALKING: The park's walking trails are many and varied. The Cape Naturaliste Track (4 km, 3 hrs, medium difficulty) leads through small limestone formations to a good vantage point for whale-watching. The ultimate bushwalking experience is the 123-km Cape to Cape Walk Track, which stretches through the park from Cape Naturaliste to Cape Leeuwin. It provides plenty of contrasting terrain, from sandy beaches and cliff-top paths to shady forests and rockstrewn headlands. The track can be broken into shorter sections; for details contact Parks and Wildlife offices or local visitor centres.

CAVE TOURS AND CAVING: Several caves in the region are open to the public with regular guided tours. Ngilgi Cave, near Yallingup in the north of the park, offers a stunning display of stalactite, stalagmite and shawl rock formations. Mammoth Cave is home to

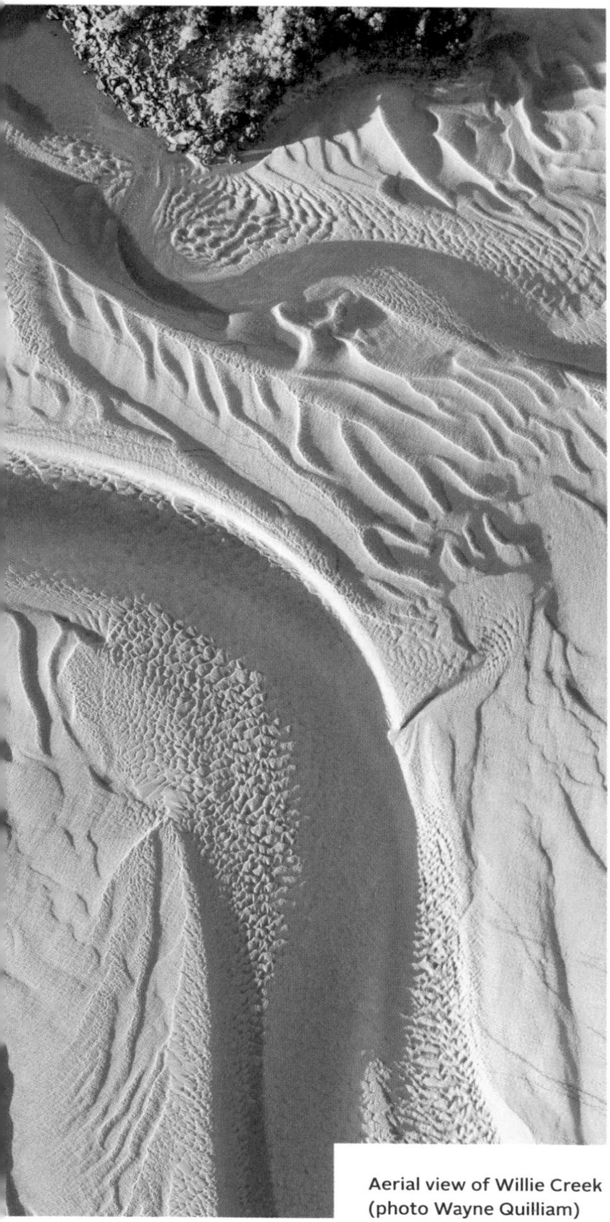
Aerial view of Willie Creek (photo Wayne Quilliam)

the fossil remains of prehistoric animals, and is one of the few caves in Australia with some degree of access for people with wheelchairs.

A few kilometres away is Lake Cave, with its delicate formations and famous reflective lake. The adjacent interpretive centre, CaveWorks, features a walk-through cave model, interactive displays and a boardwalk with views of a collapsed cavern. Further south is Jewel Cave, renowned for its abundant limestone formations, including the longest straw stalactite found in any cave open to the public. Nearby is Moondyne Cave, which offers guided adventure tours.

In addition are two adventure caves, Calgardup Cave and Giants Cave. Torches and helmets are provided to help visitors explore their own way through these unlit caves. Experienced cavers can contact the ranger for access to other caves in the area.

DIVING: Kilcarnup, near Margaret River, offers excellent diving but can only be reached by 4WD. Further south in Hamelin Bay are 11 wrecks, 4 of which form the state's most unusual heritage trail, the Hamelin Bay Wreck Trail. Nearby Cosy Corner has a number of small islands surrounded by reefs, which provide good diving spots.

FISHING: Beach fishing is popular along the shoreline between the capes, but a 4WD is needed to reach the more isolated fishing spots. Between May and June, huge schools of Australian salmon make their way north along the coast to Perth on their annual spawning run, while other species caught from the beach include herring, skippy, tailor, whiting, flathead and mulloway. Offshore the catch includes dhufish, snapper and shark. Sheltered bays scattered along the coast, such as Kilcarnup, Cowaramup Bay and Prevelly, are suitable for launching small boats. However, anglers should note that the ocean waters here are unpredictable and dangerous. Before fishing, check weather conditions and regulations. Contact the Department of Fisheries Western Australia: 08 9482 7333.

LIGHTHOUSE LOOKOUTS: At the northern end of the park is the Cape Naturaliste Lighthouse, built in 1903. With an easy climb of 59 steps, it provides wonderful views over the Cape and Geographe Bay. From here walking trails into the surrounding park offer a variety of routes along the spectacular coastline. A 4WD track leads to good spots on the coast for fishing and surfing.

Just a short drive from Augusta at the southern end of the park is the Cape Leeuwin Lighthouse. The tallest limestone lighthouse in Australia has sensational views. Nearby is the Old Water Wheel which, although originally built in 1895 from timber, has since calcified, giving it the appearance of stone. The windswept peninsula of Cape Leeuwin marks the most south-westerly point of Australia and the place where the Southern and Indian oceans meet.

ROCK-CLIMBING AND ABSEILING: Contact local commercial operators in the area for information on rock-climbing and abseiling. There are also Perth-based companies who have the public liability insurances, equipment and qualified trip leaders who will book permits and conduct safe experiences.

SNORKELLING AND SURFING: In the right weather conditions, some enjoyable and safe places to snorkel along the coast include at Prevelly and Gnarabup. Offshòre from Leeuwin–Naturaliste National Park are world-renowned surf breaks such as Yallingup Reef, Smiths Beach, Three Bears and Super Tubes. The area also boasts a remarkable diversity of breaks: the Huzzas in Cowaramup is perfect for beginners, while Surfers Point at the mouth of Margaret River – where waves up to 5 m are not uncommon – attracts the world's best surfers every April for the annual Margaret River Masters surfing competition. Tracks to the more isolated surfing spots on the coast are often suitable for 4WD only.

WHALE-WATCHING: Between September and November, humpback and southern right whales can be sighted offshore as they head to and from their northern feeding grounds. The best whale-watching vantage points are at Cape Naturaliste, Gracetown Lookout at Cowaramup Bay, Cape Leeuwin and around Sugarloaf Rock. During the season, regular whale-watching boat tours operate from Busselton, Dunsborough and Augusta.

CAMPING AND ACCOMMODATION: There are 4 campgrounds, and 1 privately owned and operated caravan park in the national park, with more accommodation in the nearby towns of Dunsborough, Yallingup, Margaret River and Augusta.

WHERE: 36 km west of Busselton.

PERMITS: Permits required for rock climbing and abseiling.

CONTACT: 08 9752 5555

Millstream–Chichester National Park

Millstream–Chichester National Park in the western Pilbara protects two very different landscapes: in the north lies the rocky, sparsely vegetated Chichester Range, while in the south is the oasis-like Millstream, where a natural freshwater spring feeds beautiful lily-covered pools.

CULTURAL HERITAGE: The Traditional Owners of this land are the Yindjibarndi and Ngarluma people. The broad area of land straddling Yarnda Nyirranha – the Fortescue River – from the Hamersley Ranger through to the Chichester escarpment is the homeland of the Yindjibarndi people. The Ngarluma people's lands run from the Chichester escarpment northward to the sea. Millstream was an important place for inter-tribal meetings. Jirndawurrunha Pool, in particular, was a campsite where the people feasted on fresh fish and bush foods such as the flesh garliwirri, which tastes like coconut, the fruit of the bajila, and the black berries of the bungaa. Yindjibarndi rangers work in the park as part of the Aboriginal Ranger Program.

NATURAL FEATURES: The Chichester Range dominating the park is characterised by basalt ridges, clay tablelands, spinifex-clad hills and rugged plains. It rises abruptly from the coastal plain in the west to form a plateau that sprawls across the Pilbara landscape, with steep escarpments and gentler slopes that extend down to the banks of the Fortescue River, which winds through the south-west corner of the park. At the base of the Chichester escarpment is Python Pool, a deep waterhole that once provided much-needed water for camel drivers; it is still a good place for a swim. Elsewhere in this northern section of the park are sandy watercourses, huge knobs of red rock and hidden gorges. A strenuous walk up Mt Herbert offers stunning panoramic views of bronzed coastal plains.

The landscape in the south is dramatically different. The Fortescue River is generally little more than a dry riverbed except during times of heavy rain, but around Millstream, freshwater springs feed into a chain of natural depressions, creating a permanent wetland and a tropical paradise of cadjeputs and native palms, picturesque pools and lily ponds. An easy walk from Millstream homestead, Jirndawurrunha Pool, shaded by paperbarks and palms, has an oasis-in-a-desert appeal in this hot, dusty region. The lilies and water ferns that adorn it were planted when the area was a sheep station.

THINGS TO DO

Picnicking and swimming are popular at Deep Reach. You can also visit the 100-year-old homestead and learn about life on an early sheep station.
BUSHWALKING: The trails in the park range from short rambles, such as the Wetland Walk (850 m, 30 mins, easy) with interpretive signs and assisted wheelchair access, to Chichester Range Camel Trail (8 km, full day), which crosses the range between Mt Herbert and Python Pool.
SCENIC TOURING: Snappy Gum drive is a 20-km scenic loop road linking the Homestead with Pannawonica Road. It can be accessed by 4WD vehicles year-round and by 2WD vehicles when indicated on signs found at either entrance point. It is not suitable for motorhomes or caravans.
SWIMMING: Swimming is popular at Deep Reach but the water is deep and children should be supervised at all times. Use the platforms provided to access the water.
CAMPING: There are two main camping areas within the park. Water is available at the visitor centre but should be boiled before drinking. The park is remote; visitors must be self-sufficient and bring all supplies with them.
WHERE: 150 km south-east of Karratha.
COST: Park entry and camping fees apply in the national park. Visit the website for more information.
CONTACT: 08 9182 2000

Mirima National Park

Mirima, also known as Hidden Valley, is an ancient limestone range that has been eroded over centuries by wind and the waters of Lily Creek into a broken series of gorges and twisted valleys. Spectacular rock formations in parts of the national park bear a resemblance to the more famous and larger Purnululu (Bungle Bungles) in Purnululu National Park.

CULTURAL HERITAGE: Regarded as a site of special significance, Mirima is the name given to the area by the local Aboriginal people, the Miriwoong. Rock paintings and engravings have been found here, and at Lily Creek, visitors can see indentations in the rocks where axes and spears were once sharpened.

NATURAL FEATURES: Flat grasslands of spinifex surround the range, interspersed with eucalypts, yellow-flowering kapok and boab trees. These bottle-shaped trees even grow on the rock faces here, the seeds deposited in the dung of rock-wallabies. The moist conditions in the valleys favour the long-fruited bloodwood, while woollybutt grows near the cliff bases. Animals include dingoes, echidnas, bats and several wallaby species; Lily Creek provides a haven for frogs and tortoises. Birdlife is plentiful, with species such as the black kite, white-quilled rock-pigeon, double-barred and crimson finches, and brown and king quail.

THINGS TO DO

The park is popular for sightseeing, photography and bushwalking. There are a number of short walking trails: Wuttuwutubin Trail (500 ms return, 30 mins, medium difficulty) follows a narrow track in a gorge to a lookout point over Kununurra; Didbagirring Trail (1 km return, 1 hr, difficult) climbs steep slopes, again with views over Kununurra. Loose rocks can make walking hazardous in some of the places in the park.
WHERE: 2 km east of Kununurra.
COST: Park entry fees apply in the national park. Visit the website for more information.
CONTACT: 08 9168 4200

Mitchell River National Park

The most striking feature of this national park in the Kimberley's far north is Punamii-unpuu (Mitchell Falls), considered by many to be

Australia's most spectacular waterfall. It is at its best after winter rains; by late spring it can be little more than a trickle.

CULTURAL HERITAGE: The Wunambal Gaambera have strong ties with this area and are joint managers of the park, and more information about visiting Country can be found at wunambalgaambera.org.au. (*see also* Wunambal Gaambera Country p. 342)

NATURAL FEATURES: The park protects the Mitchell Plateau, an elevated laterite-capped plain whose limestone margins flow into gorges and waterfalls by the Mitchell River as it flows northwards towards Admiralty Gulf. Walls of white sandstone, 6 m high, tower above the picturesque Surveyors Pool. There are lush patches of rainforest around the edges of the plateau, open woodlands of grey box and white gum in the valleys, pandanus and paperbarks along the watercourses, along with the fan palm (*Livistona eastonii*) – this is one of the few places in Western Australia where palms are such a dominant feature.

THINGS TO DO

The Punamii-unpuu (Mitchell Falls) Walk (8.6 km return, 4–5 hrs, medium difficulty) leaves from the camping area, with some rocky terrain to cross – take care near the many cliffs. Scenic flights by helicopter are available from HeliSpirit. Aunauyu (Surveyors Pool) Walk (2 km return, medium difficulty) starts at Surveyors Pool carpark.

Swimming is not allowed below the Mitchell Falls and at Surveyors Pool. These places hold special significance to the local Aboriginal communities.

CAMPING: There is a large campground with separate generator and non-generator areas near Mertens Creek at the beginning of the walk trail to Punamii (Mitchell Falls), with toilets located at the start of Mitchell Falls Track; campers must be self-sufficient.

COST: Visitors must buy an Uunguu Visitor Pass on the Wunambal Gaambera website before arriving as there is no public internet/phone access on Wunambal Gaambera Country.

WHERE: 500 km north-west of Kununurra.

CONTACT: 08 9168 4200

Mt Augustus National Park

Mt Augustus sits about 700 m above the surrounding plain, 14 km long and 5 km wide. It may not be as famous as Uluṟu but it is twice as high. About 1.6 billion years old, it is also three times older than Uluṟu and is the site of Aboriginal art dating back thousands of years.

CULTURAL HERITAGE: Mt Augustus is known by the local Wajarri Aboriginal people as Burringurrah. The Wajarri people have a number of Dreaming stories relating to the formation of the mountain.

NATURAL FEATURES: Mt Augustus is covered with small, shrubby trees, grasses and spinifex. Open mulga scrubland is dotted with red river gums and acacias and, during winter and early spring, carpeted with softly coloured everlastings. Native mammals such as the red kangaroo, common wallaroo, dingo, long-tailed dunnart, short-beaked echidna and spinifex hopping mouse live here, reptiles abound, and many different bird species have been recorded, including the crested bellbird, white-winged triller, rainbow bee-eater and wedge-tailed eagle.

THINGS TO DO

There are a number of walking trails leading to lookouts, waterfalls, caves, Aboriginal rock-art sites and picnic areas. The Mt Augustus summit hike (12 km return, full day, difficult) is only for the fit and experienced. Take plenty of water and advise the park ranger before departure. The Burringurrah Drive Trail takes you on a 49-km circuit around the base of Mt Augustus.

WHERE: 480 km east of Carnarvon.

CONTACT: 08 9948 2226

Murujuga National Park

Murujuga, which means 'hip bone sticking out' in Ngarluma-Yaburara language, is Western Australia's 100th national park. It is adjacent to the Dampier Archipelago which includes 42 coastal islands making this a popular

The dusty red cliffs and ridges of Karijini are dotted with spinifex and other hardy vegetation (photo Wayne Quilliam)

region for divers looking to explore vibrant coral reefs, or those who just want to swim and relax at the beach. The best time to visit is May to November, when the weather is fine, warm and dry.

CULTURAL HERITAGE: The national park is owned by Murujuga Aboriginal Corporation (MAC) which represents the five traditional custodian groups of the area: Ngarluma, Yindjibarndi, Yaburara, Mardudhunera and Woon-goo-tt-oo, collectively known as Ngarda-Ngarli. It is recognised with a National Heritage listing and has been proposed as a potential World Heritage site for its collection of rock art dating back at least 47,000 years – with over one million artworks, it is one of the largest and most diverse displays in the world. The art depicts humans, as well as extinct animal species such as megafauna and thylacines (Tasmanian tiger) along with existing flora and fauna. Visitors can view some of this rock art via a 700-m boardwalk with information at Ngajarli.

THINGS TO DO

NGAJARLI (DEEP GORGE) TRAIL: A 700-m walk (45 mins) along concrete paths, steel ramps and walkways that takes in some of the national park's prolific rock art, as well as shell midden sites, a grinding stone and medicine plants. Information boards are placed along the trail for visitors to learn more about Ngarda-Ngarli culture and history in the area.

BIRDWATCHING: With a landscape that includes important feeding and resting habitats such as sand bars, rocky shores, beaches, salt marshes, intertidal flats and mangroves, Murujuga provides a popular stop for thousands of migratory birds. The best time for birdwatching here is during spring and summer, when shorebirds escape from their colder breeding grounds in the northern hemisphere winter.
SWIMMING AND FISHING: There are many great swimming beaches around Murujuga, and plenty of spots for recreational fishing. Visitors can also access a number of the park's beaches by boat. Saltwater crocodiles and stinging jellyfish are occasionally spotted in the surrounding waters, so caution is advised.
WHERE: Burrup Peninsula, near Dampier.
CONTACT: 08 9182 2000

Nambung National Park

The unique attraction of Nambung National Park is the strange mysterious landscape, created by thousands of huge limestone pillars rising up out of yellow sand. This is Western Australia's famous Pinnacles Desert, which attracted more than 300,000 visitors in 2020-21.

CULTURAL HERITAGE: Aboriginal artefacts at least 6000 years old have been found in the Pinnacles Desert; strangely, there is no evidence of more recent Aboriginal occupation. One theory is that at some point the Pinnacles were buried by shifting sands, only to be uncovered a few hundred years ago. The park takes its name from the Nambung River that runs into it, which in turn takes its name from an Aboriginal word nambung, meaning 'crooked' or 'winding'. Yued people are the traditional custodians of Nambung National Park.

NATURAL FEATURES: The park is dominated by coastal sand dunes and inland sand plains. Rising out of the plains, the Pinnacles are the remnants of an underlying bed of limestone eroded over time by seeping rainwater. The remnants were then exposed as the overlying sands were blown away, revealing limestone pillars up to 3.5 m tall, which have been sculpted into weird and wonderful formations. Some are jagged and pointed; others appear more like tombstones. A favourite game for visitors and tour guides is to identify recognisable shapes among the pillars; look for the 'Two Nuns' and 'Milk Bottles'.

THINGS TO DO

While exploring the mysterious Pinnacles formations is the main attraction of Nambung National Park, along the coast are beautiful beaches perfect for picnicking, swimming, snorkelling and fishing. Kangaroo Point offers a gas barbecue and toilets. The facilities at Hangover Bay also include gas barbecues and toilets.
FISHING: Hangover Bay and Kangaroo Point are both popular fishing spots for tailor, herring and whiting. Hangover Bay has boat-launching facilities (4WD access only). The offshore islands are all nature reserves and a permit is required to land on them.
PHOTOGRAPHY: The extraordinary landscape created by the Pinnacles is a photographer's delight, especially at sunrise and sunset when the soft light can cast an ethereal glow over the strange shapes.
SWIMMING AND SNORKELLING: Hangover Bay, with its white sandy beach, is an ideal spot for swimming, snorkelling and surfing.
TOURING: The Pinnacles Desert Loop drive is a 4-km, one-way track with bays for cars to park so visitors may explore further on foot. The track is not suitable for caravans or trailers. At the northern end of the loop is a lookout, with excellent views over the Pinnacles. A ramp here allows access for wheelchair users.
WALKING: Although there are no marked trails, the remote desert areas surrounding the Pinnacles, such as the White Desert, the Red Desert and the Painted Desert, are worth exploring by foot. However, before setting out on any desert walk, inform the ranger and ensure you have adequate supplies of drinking water.
CAMPING AND ACCOMMODATION: Nambung is a day-visit park only. Nearby Cervantes offers accommodation ranging from caravan parks to motels. Drinking water is not available so carry plenty for your own needs.
WHERE: 200 km north of Perth.
COST: Park entry fees apply in the national park. Visit the website for more information.
CONTACT: 08 9652 7913

Purnululu National Park

Purnululu National Park lies deep in the rugged east Kimberley region, protecting one of the world's natural wonders, the Bungle Bungle Range. The remarkable tiger-striped, beehive-shaped rock domes have become, somewhat belatedly, one of the iconic images of the Australian outback, and are appreciated worldwide for their exceptional beauty. The region also holds sacred Aboriginal Dreaming stories and a rich culture that has maintained connections to this land for at least 20,000 years.

Purnululu National Park was declared a World Heritage area in 2003, in recognition of it being 'the most outstanding example of cone karst in sandstones anywhere in the world' and for its 'superlative natural beauty and aesthetic importance'. The dramatically sculptured rocks are hailed as being unrivalled in their scale, extent, grandeur and diversity of form. They undergo remarkable seasonal variation in appearance, including striking changes in colour following rain. The adjacent conservation area is a buffer zone established to protect the park's World Heritage values.

Today, the Jaru and Kija people maintain a strong connection and association to the ancient landscape, which holds the stories of their Dreaming. In the Kija Aboriginal language, purnululu means 'sandstone'. Australia is pursuing an additional World Heritage nomination of Purnululu for the remarkable Aboriginal cultural traditions in the area.

The ancient Bungle Bungle Range was the Kimberley's best-kept secret until the early 1980s, known only to local Aboriginal people and a few pastoralists. In 1885 gold was discovered at Halls Creek and the subsequent gold rush brought miners to the region. European graziers followed in the 1880s, marking the beginning of a 150-year period of land erosion. In 1967, the government resumed the leases as part of an erosion-control program throughout the Ord River catchment area. However, it was not until the early 1980s when filmmaker Guy Baskin included aerial footage of the Bungle Bungles in his television series *Wonders of Western Australia* that Australians became aware of this 350-million-year-old natural treasure in the outback. In 1987 the area was gazetted as a national park.

CULTURAL HERITAGE: The area is traditionally the land of the Kija people of the eastern Kimberley region, and their neighbours the Jaru, a group belonging to the desert regions. The Kija people put up fierce resistance to the pastoralists. They killed the cattle (livestock numbers on the Ord River grasslands had reached 50,000 by 1902) and in retaliation there were brutal massacres of local Aboriginal people and punitive police raids. At the height of the violence, many of the Kija took refuge in the Bungle Bungles. They used notched tree trunks to scale the cliffs and pulled these makeshift ladders up afterwards to prevent pursuit. To try to stop the livestock killing, the government provided some refuges and food, but did not stop the land and cultural dispossession, which continued into the 1970s.

Today, descendants of the park's Traditional Owners live in population centres such as Halls Creek and Warmun. The people of Warmun have worked extensively on language and literacy programs for schools and have produced a large amount of teaching material. Some help manage the national park, with a number of Aboriginal people employed as rangers and guides.

The history of the Jaru following white settlement mirrored the history of the Kija described above. Most of the people lived and worked on pastoral properties in the area until 1968, when the introduction of award wages resulted in Aboriginal workers being forced to leave. Many moved to Halls Creek.

Aboriginal rock art adorns some shelters, caves and gorges in the park, with depictions of crocodiles and fish, as well as hand stencils. There is no public access to these sites. There are also many Aboriginal burial sites but these, too, are closed to the public. Living Area leases in the national park for some Traditional Owners have been signed recently with the Purnululu Aboriginal Council.

The relationship of the Indigenous people to the land has been highlighted by the renowned paintings of the Warmun artists. This group emerged in the 1970s, painting ceremonial boards using natural ochres of brown, black and yellow defined by white and black dots. Warmun Art Centre was established in 1998 to represent the Warmun artists and market their work in Australia and overseas. The most famous of the Warmun artists are Rover Thomas and Queenie McKenzie.

NATURAL FEATURES: The national park has 4 major ecosystems: the Bungle Bungle Mountain Range, a plateau that dominates the centre of the park; wide sand plains surrounding this plateau; the Ord River valley to the east and south of the park; and limestone ridges and ranges to the west and north of the park.

The Bungle Bungle Range is a deeply fissured plateau that rises 200–300 m above the surrounding plain. It is distinguished by great cliffs on its western edge that are cut by seasonal waterfalls and pools, numerous narrow gorges, deep gullies, and beehive-shaped domes of rock on its southern edge. Some 350 million years ago, geological activity caused uplifts that formed the ranges to the north and west, and then erosion by creeks and rivers resulted in the transportation of sand and rocks. The rocks were strewn at the edge of the cliffs but the sand was carried further, gradually hardening over time to form sandstone channels. Over the last 20 million years, further uplift and erosion of the sandstone has created the range's distinctive domes. The sandstone is so fine that it crumbles when touched. The dark bands are the more porous layers of rock, where the presence of moisture has encouraged the growth of dark-coloured algae. The less porous layers of the domes are coated with iron oxides that stain the surface orange. These thin layers of black lichen (*Microthelia arterrina*) and orange silica cover and protect the sandstone, giving the domes their distinctive horizontal black-and-orange banding. While sandstone towers are known in other parts of the world, the features of the Bungle Bungles are unrivalled.

Of the many gorges in the range, Cathedral Gorge is perhaps the most awe-inspiring. It is a natural amphitheatre, a quiet place surrounded by sheer rock walls, with a sliver of blue sky above and a still pool of water below.

The vegetation in the park is diverse; closed forests in the park's valleys and gorges change to open forests and woodlands in drier areas. Within the deep valleys and gorges, various palms thrive, along with orchids and delicate ferns. A total of 653 plant species have been recorded in the national park, including 17 different types of fern.

Located in an area where the desert meets the tropics, Purnululu has animal species that typify both environments, including 41 mammals, 149 birds, 81 reptiles, 12 amphibians and 15 fish. In the drier areas on the plateau, reptiles are common, with monitors (including Gould's goanna) and skinks blending in with the colours of their surroundings. Mammals include the short-eared rock wallaby, which roams the grasslands, venturing into the rocky hills and gorges to search for seeds. The northern nail-tail wallaby inhabits the open woodlands, moving onto the grasslands at night to feed.

In the sheltered valleys and damper areas you may glimpse frogs, pale field-rats and the large-footed myotis, a species of bat that roosts close to water – it has exceptionally large feet for its size.

Of the large numbers of birds found in the park, many are migratory species, such as the rare grey falcon, a beautiful white and grey raptor that nests in tall eucalypts overlooking watercourses. More commonly seen in the park are the gorgeous blue and green rainbow bee-eaters and flocks of colourful budgerigars.

Bidyadanga (also known as La Grange) is located on the Kimberley coast (photo Wayne Quilliam)

THINGS TO DO

This remote wilderness offers quiet pleasures such as birdwatching. The only means of access into the gorges is by foot so walking is the main activity. You cannot climb the domes.

BUSHWALKING: Cathedral Gorge walking trail (2 km return, 1–2 hrs) is mostly easy, but has a few short difficult sections, with some rock ledges, waterholes and stony depressions to be negotiated. At the wide still pool at the end of the trail, look for animal tracks near the water's edge. Piccaninny Gorge has no marked track and no defined endpoint, so hikers must rely on their own navigational skills to complete the walk. The 7-km return walk to the gorge entrance (the Elbow) takes a full day. To explore the gorge system, a total of more than 30 km, requires hikers to camp overnight. You must register with the ranger before setting out and again on your return. You must be self-sufficient, carry plenty of water, and a fuel stove for cooking (no campfires allowed). From the Piccaninny Gorge carpark, the short Domes walk (700 m return, easy) leads through sandstone towers.

On the northern side of the park, Frog Hole Trail (1.4 km return, 1–2 hrs, moderate–difficult) leads to a small seasonal pool at the base of the Bungle Bungle Range. After rain a waterfall drops over 100 m into the palm-fringed pool, which is home to a number of frog species. Echidna Chasm Trail (2 km return, less than 1 hr, easy–moderate) involves some rock scrambling and clambering over several large boulders. The chasm is narrow and not for the claustrophobic; at its narrowest part the walls are over 100 m high and barely an arm's width apart, and it ends at a sheer rock face. The challenging Mini Palms Trail (4.4 km return, 1–3 hrs, difficult), leading to a scenic amphitheatre of palms, begins easily then narrows and becomes closed in, with walkers having to clamber over boulders and 'squeeze' between rocks.

The Kungkalanayi Lookout is 3 km from the ranger station and provides panoramic views of the western side of the Bungle Bungles. Sunset is the best time for viewing, when the setting sun intensifies the vibrant colours of the range.

PHOTOGRAPHY: The best times of the day for photography are early morning and late afternoon, when the rays of the fading sun cast a red glow across the landscape, producing a striking richness of colour in the sandstone.

SCENIC FLIGHTS: A scenic flight from within the park, or from Halls Creek, Kununurra or Warmun, is the best way to gain a perspective of the massive size and spectacular scenery of the Bungle Bungle Range. Both helicopter and fixed-wing aircraft operate flights. Contact Slingair Heliwork WA: 08 9169 1300.

WHERE: 300 km south of Kununurra.

CAMPING: There are two campgrounds and camping fees apply. Campers must be fully self-sufficient, bringing in all supplies and water. The nearest supplies available are from Warmun on the Great Northern Hwy.

COST: Park entry and camping fees apply. Visit the website for more information.

CONTACT: 08 9168 7300

Stirling Range National Park

Surrounded by a flat, sandy plain, the Stirling Range rises abruptly to over 1000 m, its jagged peaks sometimes veiled in swirling clouds. Of the many mountains, Bluff Knoll is the most famous, being the highest peak in Western Australia's South West region. A mecca for bushwalkers and climbers, Stirling Range National Park attracts thousands of visitors every year.

Stirling Range National Park is also significant for its wildflowers. Some 1500 flowering plants thrive here, 87 of which are found nowhere else in the world. This incredible richness of flora is set against the breathtaking beauty of the ranges, which rise sharply from the surrounding plains.

CULTURAL HERITAGE: The Aboriginal people who originally occupied this area of the South West were the Minang and Goreng people. Unlike their northern counterparts, they dressed for the cold mountain weather in knee-length kangaroo skin coats and built small, conical huts out of sticks thatched with paperbark, rushes or leafy branches to provide shelter from the rain. Wagyl Kaip people are the traditional custodians of Stirling Range National Park.

Aboriginal people believe that in the Dreaming, the mountains were formed by the ancient kangaroo people who once lived in the area. According to legend, a male kangaroo killed its female partner and was in turn killed by its joey. The range is the body of the dead male kangaroo, and its knees form the mountain peaks. The mountains were once considered a place to be wary of – the mists that shroud the peaks of Bluff Knoll were believed to be the only visible form of an evil spirit called Noatch. The Noongar people, the traditional Aboriginal custodians of the region, call Bluff Knoll both bular mial, meaning 'many eyes', and bala mial, meaning 'his eyes', because the rocks on the bluff are said to be shaped like the eyes of the ancestral master spirit.

The Minang people were living around King George Sound when Captain Phillip Parker visited the area in 1821. He recorded that the Minang used taap knives, hammers and spears, producing them for bartering purposes with the Europeans. The large taap knives – over 40 cm long – were made of wood and quartz flakes, cemented together with gum, probably made from the sap of grasstrees. These taap knives, unique to the South West region of Western Australia, were used by the Aboriginal people to cut up the flesh of seals and other animals.

A renowned Aboriginal interpreter and guide of this area, Mokare (c. 1800–1831), was a Noongar man of the Minang people. He accompanied a number of European explorers on various expeditions through the South West region of the state.

NATURAL FEATURES: 'The Stirling Range burst on our view in great magnificence as we rounded the crest ... the whole extent of the conical summits were spread before us.' So wrote Surveyor-General John Septimus Roe in 1835 and, over 160 years later, visitors to this national park undoubtedly have similar first impressions. Stretching some 65 km in an east–west direction, this spectacular range of jagged mountain peaks rises abruptly from the surrounding heath-covered sand plains. In the eastern half of the park is Bluff Knoll, a towering 1095 m above sea level. The main face of the bluff rises, at one bound, over 950 m above the plain. Other notable features are Toolbrunup Peak, and a silhouette called The Sleeping Lady, which is visible from the Porongurup Range to the south. The mountains of the Stirling Range, and particularly the craggy summit of Bluff Knoll, is one of the few places in Western Australia where snow falls – the mountain peaks are often shrouded in distinctive cloud formations.

THINGS TO DO

Stirling Range National Park is one of the best bushwalking locations in the state. Apart from the challenging mountain climbs, there are stunning views from the peaks and, in spring, wildflowers in abundance – only matched by the number of photo opportunities. Stop at one of several scenic picnic areas dotted around the park for a spot of lunch. Birds Australia operates dawn and dusk bird walks in spring.

ADVENTURE SPORTS: Abseiling may be undertaken at the North West Bay on Bluff Knoll. Enthusiasts must register with the ranger before setting off. Stirling Range Retreat, outside the park's northern boundary, organises adventure activities including abseiling, rock-climbing, hang-gliding and gliding; for further details call: 08 9827 9229. (The retreat also has guided wildflower walks and slide evenings focusing on flora and fauna of the Stirling Range.)

BUSHWALKING: There are a variety of marked walking trails in the park, from easy wildflower trails to more challenging hikes in the mountains. There are also countless other trails in more remote sections of the park.

For daytrippers, the more popular trails include the demanding climb to the 856-m Mt Magog summit (7 km return, 3–4 hrs, difficult), which is rewarded by great views at the top. Walkers should note that there is no path for the final 1 km to the summit. Talyuberlup Peak Trail (2.6 km return, 2 hrs, medium difficulty) has interesting caverns and rocky outcrops along the way, while Mt Hassell walk (3 km return, 2–3 hrs, medium difficulty) is a good manageable trail for adults with children in tow. The ascent of Toolbrunup Peak (4 km return, 3 hrs, difficult) is regarded as the best trail climb in the park, with its spectacular scenery of dramatic rocky outcrops and 360-degree views.

The most popular trail in the park leads to the 1098-m summit of Bluff Knoll . After an energetic walk and climb (8 km return, half a day, difficult), hikers are rewarded by breathtaking views from the cliff-top lookout. However, experienced bushwalkers might prefer the challenge of the Ridge Trail (26 km one way, 2–3 days), which leads from the base of the range via Ellen Peak to the Bluff Knoll carpark. This trail requires overnight camping, and walkers must register with the ranger before setting out.

Many of these walks are steep and rough, so for safety reasons they are not recommended in wet or windy conditions. Walking is also not advised on days of extreme heat. At all times of the year, walkers must carry plenty of drinking water and be prepared for abrupt changes in the weather; the range is subject to sudden drops in temperature, driving rain and sometimes snow.

SCENIC TOURING: The Stirling Range Drive Trail is regarded as one of the best mountain drives in Australia. It winds through the centre of the park for 42 km, taking in lookouts near Mondurup Peak and Mt Magog on the way. Although the trail can be driven either way, the west to east route is considered the more picturesque.

CAMPING AND ACCOMMODATION: Moingup Spring is a centrally located bush camp set among jarrah and marri trees. Stirling Range Retreat and Mount Trio Bush Camping and Caravan Park, both on the park's northern boundary, offer a range of accommodation and services.

WHERE: 100 km north-east of Albany.

COST: Park entry and camping fees apply. Visit the website for more information.

CONTACT: 08 9842 4500

Walyunga National Park

Set on the edge of the Darling Scarp just north of Perth, Walyunga National Park encompasses a section of the Swan River valley. It is here that the Swan River transforms from a series of pools in summer to a raging torrent in winter; every August, the river's long stretch of rapids becomes the location for one of Australia's best whitewater canoeing events, the annual Avon Descent.

Bidyadanga's Traditional Owners are the Karajarri people (photo Wayne Quilliam)

CULTURAL HERITAGE: The park is also significant as the site of one of the largest known Aboriginal camping grounds in the Perth region. With a history going back 6000 years, the area was still used by the Noongar people until late last century.

NATURAL FEATURES: The parkland is made up of heaths, granite outcrops and woodlands. As the valley climbs, vegetation changes from large flooded gums on the banks of the river, through forests of wandoo, marri and powder-bark, to stands of jarrah on the ridge tops. Late winter and early spring is the best time for wildflowers. Western grey kangaroos, western brush wallabies, short-beaked echidnas, sacred kingfishers, grey fantails, shingleback lizards and carpet pythons inhabit the park.

THINGS TO DO: Activities include canoeing, birdwatching, picnicking and bushwalking. The Aboriginal Heritage Trail (2 km return, 45 mins, easy) gives an insight into local Aboriginal myths and culture; Syd's Rapids (4.6 km return, 1 hr, medium difficulty), a lovely walk under shady wandoo and flooded gum, leads along the grassy flood plain of the river; Kangaroo Trail (4-km loop, 2 hrs, medium difficulty) traverses granite outcrops; Kingfisher Trail (8.5-km loop, 4 hrs, medium difficulty) focuses on flora; and Echidna Trail (10.6 km return, 5 hrs, difficult) offers panoramic views of the Swan and Avon valleys.

COST: Park entry fees apply in the national park. Visit the website for more information.

WHERE: 30 km north-east of Perth.

CONTACT: 08 9290 6100

TOURS AND STAYS

Banana Well Getaway

Banana Well Getaway is situated on rich cultural land known as Burrguk, which means 'high-grounds' or 'high place' in the Nyul-Nyul language. The Burrguk Aboriginal Corporation has a 99-year lease on this property, which is situated on an Aboriginal Reserve, with many community members feeling connected to their surrounds, while simultaneously recognising the deep historical impact of colonisation in the area. The local spring waters have long been celebrated for their fertile properties, with stories of community members visiting Banana Well Getaway and falling boogajin (pregnant). Many animals thrive in this area, so you may see a wild donkey, wallaroo, brahman bull and frill-neck lizard all in the same day. Banana Well blooms with wildflowers including acacias, grevilleas, wild orchids and bachelor buttons. Stay in self-contained cabins and enjoy fishing, trekking along the white-sandy nearby beaches and leisurely soaking in the artesian springs. Bookings are essential.

WHERE: Follow the signs from Cape Leveque Road (15 km south of Beagle Bay; 140 km north of Broome).

CONTACT: 08 9192 2631

Bindi Bindi Dreaming

Aboriginal family–owned-and-operated business Bindi Bindi Dreaming (meaning butterfly in Noongar language) has been running for over 2 decades, providing visitors to Noongar Country with a curated tour experience. As a hunter-gatherer society, Noongar people remain connected to the land and their cultural traditions. Soak in local cultural knowledge that Elders of Noongar Country have allowed these guides to share through a range of activities, including finding bush foods, and the simplicity of seeing, touching and immersing yourself in the local area. Listen to the stories of the bush and get a feel for being on Country with a guided tour of ancient stories and natural wonders that surround the Perth region. Take a cultural learning journey or get your local school involved in the Tucker Bush Schools Program, where students will gain knowledge of the local environment and the many bush tucker species. Bookings are essential.

WHERE: Bindi Bindi Dreaming is based in Perth.
CONTACT: 0417 031 707

Bindjareb Park

Karrie-Anne Kearing, director of Bindjareb Aboriginal tours and cultural awareness activities, is a local Traditional Owner of Bindjareb Nyungar Boodja. Karrie-Anne was educated in Nyungar language and customs by her parents and Elders, and shares her knowledge out of deep respect for her ancestors, fellow Nyungars and all First peoples of Australia. Based in Pinjarra, Bindjareb Park is a 22-hectare nature sanctuary that houses a multitude of wildlife and rare bird species such as the red-tailed black cockatoo. Enjoy a walk in the bushlands and learn about traditional uses of plants, watch films of local history, visit the site that holds remnants of an Aboriginal reserve or eat food made from local native ingredients – with many species of plant food grown right in the park. Tour packages vary in length and content – choose a 5-hour package or a 1-hour enlightening visit – and custom packages can also be arranged. Bookings are essential.

WHERE: 70 Hampton Rd, Pinjarra (21 km from Mandurah and 82 km from Perth).
CONTACT: 0422 818 403

Black Tracks

Trek across the Kimberley on a curated adventure walk with Aboriginal-owned company Black Tracks. Immerse yourself in local Aboriginal history, including a visit to 20,000-year-old rock art, and learn about the evolving area. The trek is guided by local Aboriginal people, when available, including trainees from the nearby town Mount Elizabeth – a company initiative that aims to improve social and economic development as well as increase and enhance cross-cultural engagement. Black Tracks are committed to ethical and responsible tourism, with the maximum of 12 people in each group allowing effective movement between destinations and limiting the ecological impact on the places visited. Treks range from moderate to challenging in intensity, and 3–8 days in length, it is recommended that you train to prepare. Camping supplies are provided, with tents and swags draped with mosquito nets to ensure a comfortable sleep under the Kimberley night sky. Food is also included, catering to all dietary requirements. Tours run from May to September and bookings are essential.

WHERE: Black Tracks are based in the Kimberley region.
CONTACT: 0418 855 548

Boorloo Experience

Boutique Aboriginal-owned business Boorloo (the Noongar name for Perth) was created by husband and wife Olman and Sharna Walley to provide a deeper understanding of Noongar culture. Boorloo offers cultural experiences in performance, education and tourism, with customised and walking tours available to suit participants' needs, and large school, corporate or private groups able to be accommodated. Other services can be arranged, such as cultural awareness training, traditional dance, and didgeridoo performances and lessons. Bookings are required.

WHERE: Boorloo Experience is based in Perth.
CONTACT: 0418 855 548

Boorloo Experience provides a deeper understanding of Noongar culture through performance, education and tourism

Borrgoron Coast to Creek Tour

On the Dampier Peninsula, the Bardi (land) and Jawi (island) peoples' special relationship with their Country includes in-depth knowledge of local bush food and medicine, along with sustainable hunting and fishing practices. Local guide Terry Hunter operates Borrgoron Coast to Creek Tour from Cygnet Bay Pearl Farm, showing you a coastal landscape abundant with wildlife, steeped in ancient stories and cultural heritage. While exploring the mangroves, creeks and tidal flats of King Sound, you will hear stories of life growing up on the remote pearl farm. Forage for oysters and discover a culture that has been caring for this Country for thousands of years. This 2-hour walking tour requires a reasonable level of fitness, as you cross the rocks at low tide under the bright Kimberley sun, with appropriate clothing recommended. Bookings are essential.

WHERE: Cygnet Bay (200 km from Broome).
CONTACT: 08 9192 4283

Brian Lee Tagalong Tours

Brian Lee Tagalong Tours are run by Brian Lee, who shares knowledge of his Country and the traditional ways of Bardi people on the pristine turquoise waters of Hunters Creek. Seasonal bush fruit is on offer as you stroll along listening to stories of people who have walked this landscape for centuries.

Once you have learnt how to successfully catch a feed, the tour concludes as you place yourself under a shady tree and sample the caught fish and crab cooked on a traditional Bardi open fire.

WHERE: Tours depart from Kooljaman (200 km north of Broome).
CONTACT: 08 9192 4970

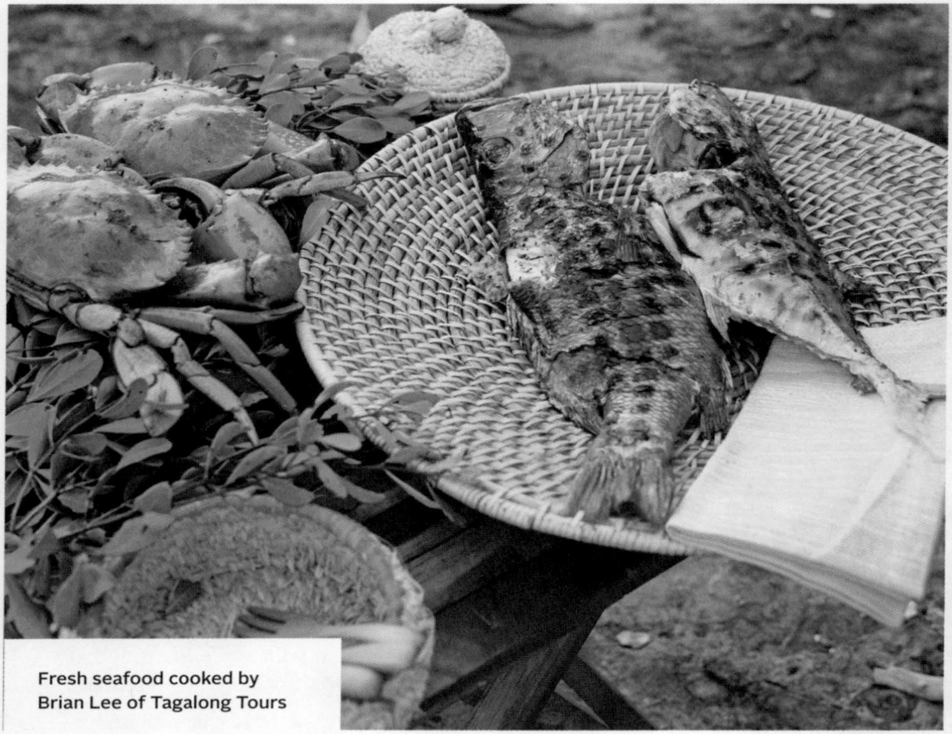

Fresh seafood cooked by Brian Lee of Tagalong Tours

Bundy's Cultural Tours

Bundy's Cultural Tours operate in Bardi Country, at the northern tip of the Dampier Peninsula. As a Traditional Owner, Bundy provides guests with insight into life in this area, teaching you about the region's history and sharing the Dreaming stories of the Bardi people. On the Bush Tucker Tour, join Bundy on a guided walk around Kooljaman and sample some delectable seasonal fruit while soaking in the glorious surrounds. On Bundy's Night Fishing Tour, discover the array of marine life and the colours beaming on the ocean from the wide-open skies above.

WHERE: Tours depart from Kooljaman (200 km north of Broome).
CONTACT: 08 9192 4970

Bungoolee Tours

In the inspiring landscape of the Bunuba country of the Kimberley, Jimmy Dillon Andrews and his family run Bungoolee Tours, sharing their knowledge and powerful spiritual connection to their traditional lands. In addition to the Aboriginal cultural significance of the area, the tours give visitors insights into the history, geography, topography and biology of this region. Tunnel Creek Walking Tour is a 2-hour trek led by a Bunuba guide through this water-worn tunnel beneath the limestone of the Napier Range, a landscape of immense environmental and cultural heritage. Windjana Gorge Rock Art Tour takes guests to see rock art that is only accessible with an Elder like Jimmy. Sites like Jumburrurru (Carpenter's Gap) have shown Bunuba people have been on this land for at least 46,000 years. There are other tours with Bungoolee available, so check the website for more details. Booking in advance is required.

WHERE: Fitzroy Crossing (400 km east of Broome and 300 km west of Halls Creek).
CONTACT: 08 9191 5355

Bush Ghoodhu Wongutha Tours

The Wongutha people have been strongly connected to Kalgoorlie and the surrounding Country for 30,000 years, with family-owned business Bush Ghoodhu Wongutha Tours giving visitors a glimpse into the region's modern and ancient history. Choose from 3 tours, with a tailored on-Country camping experience available. The tours can incorporate team-building exercises, such as food foraging, wildlife tracking, traditional toolmaking or building a wiltja structure, to familiarise visitors with Wongutha culture. The Outback Day Tour teaches you to identify tracks of local wildlife, including kangaroos, emus, goanna and dingoes, as well as gathering bush tucker and learning about ancient medicinal plants while your guide shares Wongutha names of places, animals and plants. The Town Tour visits significant sites and shares ancient Dreaming stories, ending the day with a lesson in traditional Wongutha toolmaking and nyinji (spear) throwing. The immersive Overnight Tour gives you the opportunity to camp under the stars, visit sites of great spiritual and cultural significance, and enjoy local bush tucker cooked the traditional way in an earth oven Bookings are essential.

WHERE: Bush Ghoodhu Wongutha Tours are based in Kalgoorlie.
CONTACT: 0474 971 548

Dale Tilbrook Experiences

Wardandi Bibbulmun woman Dale Tilbrook, whose traditional Country lies in the Margaret River and Busselton area, has spent many years gathering Aboriginal cultural knowledge from her Elders and other sources. Her Aboriginal cultural activities include Bush Tucker Talks and Tastings, where you will explore Aboriginal agricultural practices, learn about different native food and medicine plants, sample bush tucker fruits, nuts, seeds, herbs and leaves, and finish with some savoury and sweet bush tucker dishes. With Aboriginal Art and Dreamtime Stories, experience dot painting river stones while listening to Aboriginal Dreamtime stories and learning about Aboriginal culture and life. Bush Tucker and Wellbeing will teach you about the nutritional value and healing properties of various Australian native food and medicinal plants, allowing you to sample some too. The World's Oldest Continuous Culture introduces you to traditional Aboriginal life, spirituality and social systems, sharing some Dreamtime stories about Creation and events that shaped the landscape and laid down rules for everyday life, with some bush tucker included. Advance bookings are required.

WHERE: 10070 West Swan Road, Henley Brook (30 km from Perth).
CONTACT: 08 9296 0711

Darngku Heritage Cruises

Aboriginal-owned business Darngku Heritage Cruises offers visitors the opportunity to explore the Danggu (Geikie Gorge) around Fitzroy Crossing with a local Bunuba guide, with cruises ranging from 1 hour to half a day in length. Explore the breathtaking geography of the area and gain insight into the Kimberley

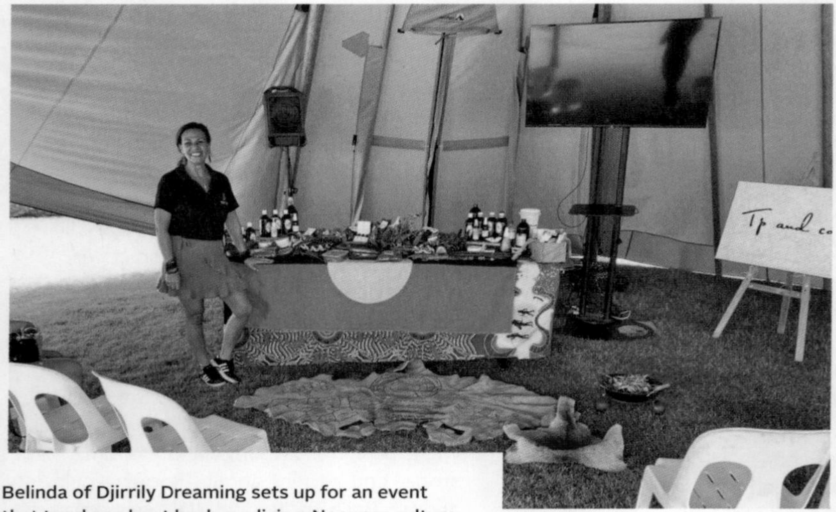

Belinda of Djirrily Dreaming sets up for an event that teaches about bush medicine, Noongar culture and Dreaming stories

region's rich and culturally significant Aboriginal history and culture. Visit sacred and historic Aboriginal sites to learn about the local history and Dreaming stories, while also discovering traditional Aboriginal hunting practices and listening for the sounds of local fauna. Bookings are required.

WHERE: Fitzroy Crossing (400 km east of Broome and 300 km west of Halls Creek).
CONTACT: 0417 907 609

Djirrily Dreaming, Aboriginal Cultural Tours

Belinda Cox, a Kangeang/Bibblemun Noongar woman (Yorga) practised in the ways of traditional cultural medicine plants and natural remedies, is the owner of Djirrily Dreaming – Aboriginal Cultural Tours, curating different experiences of Noongar culture. The Woola Noongar Tour and Dance Tour shares Noongar Dreaming stories, song and dance, ancient tools, mouth-watering gourmet food and stories of ancient Aboriginal Australia and the Noongar Nation. The Mooditch Munda Medicine Tour allows you to discover the Noongar bush pharmacy of seasonal native bush plants and flowers. The Woola Yorga Yokia Tour, for women only, and offers the chance for you to celebrate Noongar women's ways. Bookings for all tours are required. Artisan items are also available at Djirrily Dreaming, such as essential oils infused with native botanicals, smoking smudge sticks made from native plants to cleanse and invigorate, and tapping sticks that are hand-crafted from local bush timber.

WHERE: Djirrily Dreaming is based in Perth.
CONTACT: 0424 525 356

Djurandi Dreaming

Wadjuk man Justin Martin, a qualified tour guide and Aboriginal artworks specialist, owns and operates Djurandi Dreaming, an Aboriginal arts and tour company that showcases Aboriginal culture in Western Australia while conserving culture, language and Country. Dreaming in the Quay offers an interactive tour experience with a local guide sharing Dreaming stories that provide a deeper historical understanding of the Nyungar people of the Swan River. Finding Yagan takes you on a cultural walk through the Perth streets to learn about the Nyungar resistance warrior and leader Yagan, and the past and present history of the Nyungar people. The Traditional Aboriginal Art Workshop encourages you to learn traditional symbols, stories, language, colours and line work used in Aboriginal art – you can even create your own piece. Djurandi Dreaming also take school groups, with yarning sessions, cultural walks and art activities that keep kids engaged in learning about Nyungar culture and history. Bookings are required.

WHERE: Djurandi Dreaming is based in Perth.
CONTACT: 0458 692 455

Echo Tours

Take a cultural guided tour of the Kimberley region, learning about the ancient land and its First people – the Kija people. Aboriginal-owned Echo Tours offer curated experiences of the landscape, immersing you in the area while you enjoy the local knowledge and stories shared by experienced Kimberley stockman and guide Johnny Echo. Discover the Kimberley's wide-open skies, local wildflowers and rugged landscape, while looking out for local wildlife. Bookings are required.

WHERE: Tours depart from Warmun Art Centre, Warmun (160 km from Halls Creek).
CONTACT: 08 9168 7496

Gnylmarung Retreat

This meditative wilderness escape is on a secluded beach in a remote part of the Kimberley region. Relax and watch the turquoise waters of the Indian Ocean, or fish, dive or snorkel off the reef, where the array of ocean life includes trevally, mangrove jack and bluebone. Those who venture into deeper waters might catch sailfish, coral trout, north west snapper and more. The nearby Aboriginal land is private, with permission is required to visit some areas; road signs posted as 'Local Access' are strictly for community residents. Only twenty campsites are available, so book in advance.

WHERE: Gnylmarung (150 km from Broome).
CONTACT: 08 9192 4097

Go Cultural Aboriginal Tours and Experiences

Walter and Meg McGuire own and operate this range of cultural experiences and tours located on Noongar Country. Tours include the Goomup (Elizabeth Quay) Walking Tour, which offers a glimpse into the world's oldest living culture through ancient Dreaming stories, traditional songs and Noongar language – learn how the 6 seasons and elements have influenced the daily lives of Noongar people, determining their unique spiritual connection to this Boodjar (Country). The Wadjemup (Rottnest Island) Premium Experience allows you to explore the iconic island from an Aboriginal perspective, as your Noongar guide teaches the Island's significance to Noongar people, prior to and despite its notorious recent past as an Aboriginal prison. Beginning with a traditional Aboriginal sand ceremony at the first settlement, your walk also includes a Dreaming story and traditional song in Noongar language. The tour concludes with a Noongar smoking ceremony and unique gift. Check the website for other tours and experiences. Bookings are required.

WHERE: Go Cultural Aboriginal Tours and Experiences are based in Perth.
CONTACT: 08 9429 8875

Goolamwiin

Goolamwiin (meaning 'winds blowing from the south west') is an Aboriginal–owned-and-managed tour company and consultancy based in Mandurah, Western Australia, by Nyungar woman Kerry Stack and Nyungar man Trevor Stack. The Goolamwiin Day Tour runs for 3 hours and invites you to explore for bush tucker and medicinal plants and participate in Aboriginal dance. You will experience a Nyungar Welcome, a walking tour, a lesson in identifying bush foods and how to use Aboriginal tools, and a campfire morning/afternoon tea. The Goolamwiin Overnight Tour offers similar experiences as the day tour, with the addition of camping under the wide star-filled skies, with tour guides telling Dreaming stories around a campfire, and waking to a billy tea breakfast in the morning. Check the website for other services on offer at Goolamwiin. Bookings are required.

WHERE: Goolamwiin is based in Perth.
CONTACT: 0417 183 119

Goombaragin Eco Retreat

This coastal retreat is just over 2 hours' drive north of Broome, in the remarkable Kimberley region. Take in the spectacular views of Pender Bay on the Dampier Peninsula, with this site also boasting striking red soil cliffs, beautiful bays and private beaches and wild woodlands. With accommodation options to suit a variety of needs and budgets, choose from campsites and nature tents on raised decking, to eco tents and eco chalets positioned at the edge of clifftops. Relax on pristine beaches with great fishing and snorkelling or enjoy the magnificent beauty of the night's sky. With accommodation placed sparsely on the 10-hectare coastal property, your stay will allow you to unwind and breathe in the fresh air in privacy and luxury.

WHERE: Pender Bay, Dampier Peninsula.
CONTACT: 0429 505 347

Gumbanan Wilderness Retreat

Immerse yourself in an amazing cultural experience for the whole family at Gumbanan Wilderness Retreat. There is a variety of camping choices on this family-run site, including facilities for campers, camper trailers and caravans, as well as furnished safari tents for couples and families. Family Safari Tents include a queen bed, a sofa lounge for the kids and your own outdoor hot water shower with of the nearby islands. A variety of tours are also available from the campground, with guides sharing their homeland, stories and traditions. Tours can include spear making, mud crabbing, bush tucker tours, local cooking, fishing and storytelling. The family are Bardi Jawi people, known to be 'Salt Water People'. They are keepers of traditional culture and stories through song and dance. Their style is very distinctive as they perform with intricate totems depicting coastal life and traditional hunting practices, which have been handed down orally and visually from generation to generation – a strong example of living culture in contemporary society. This location is also the gateway to the Buccaneer

Archipelago, with known attractions such as Waterfall Reef and Horizontal Falls. Bookings for performances are essential; check the website for details.

WHERE: Lot 344 One Arm Point Rd, Dampier Peninsula.
CONTACT: 0499 330 169

Jetty to Jetty Trail

The Jetty to Jetty Trail is a self-guided walk of Broome that explores the rich cultural landscape of the Yawuru people and Broome's pearling era. The trail was developed by Nyamba Buru Yawuru Limited (NBY), the Yawuru Traditional Owners' not-for-profit company responsible for generating long-term economic development for the Yawuru community. The 4-year development process involved deep collaboration with the local community and the signing of a historic accord between the Shire of Broome and the Yawuru.

Participants follow the Jetty to Jetty map to find a series of seats and informative signs scattered from Streeter's Jetty to the Old Jetty at Town Beach. The trail highlights places of significance for Yawuru people and the cultural significance and use of guwan (pearl shell). The trail also describes how, for decades, pearling dominated the life of people in Broome; the ebb and flow of the tides dictated the town's cycles, and the industry brought multiculturalism to the north of Australia.

The trail includes a smartphone app that provides stories and music relating to each location (search for 'Jetty to Jetty' on the Apple App Store or Google Play). The app highlights the voices and Country of the Yawuru people and connects participants with the foreshore of Roebuck Bay – the heart of Yawuru Country – and its many historic and cultural treasures. More than 30 local people contributed stories and images of living and working in Broome to the app. This cross-section of experiences from the Aboriginal, East Asian and European people who lived and worked through the boom years of Broome pearling includes tales of Yawuru Bugarrigarra (Dreaming) beings, police raids on gambling houses, boat-building techniques and outings to the Sun Pictures.

The Jetty to Jetty Trail comes to life with storytelling and music as part of the annual Shinju Matsuri Jetty to Jetty event. Participants should be aware of strong sun and traffic while walking the trail and should bring sun protection, drinking water, headphones (for the smartphone app) and walking shoes.

WHERE: Start the trail at Streeter's Jetty, Broome.
CONTACT: 08 9192 9600

Kaarak Dreaming

Immerse yourself in Nyoongar culture as you join Kaarak Dreaming on a guided bushwalk along ancient dream trails around the small community of Dwellingup in the Darling Range. Learn about the stories of this land accompanied by the didgeridoo and enjoying billy tea and damper. Tours include information about traditional bush medicines and native foods, how to collect materials to create artefacts and cultural objects, and sand mapping demonstrations, where you will be taught the local Nyoongar style, all while learning about the 6 Nyoongar seasons. Walking tours range from 1 to 3 hours in length, catering to all fitness levels. Check the website for tour times.

WHERE: Dwellingup (100 km south of Perth).
CONTACT: 0498 853 544

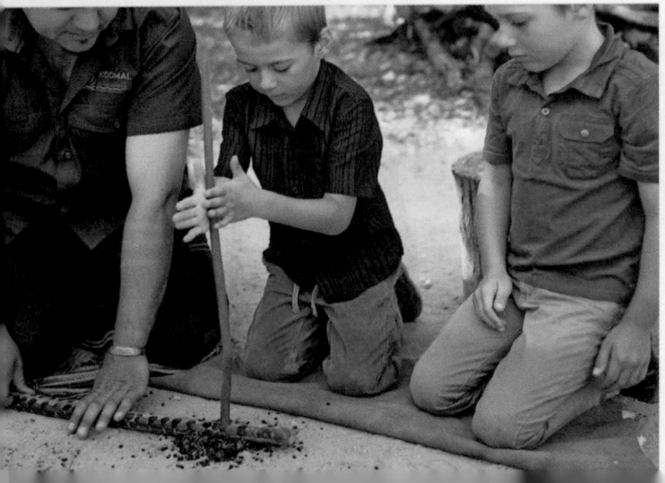

Top: Learn about the Bardi people of the Dampier Peninsula with Indigenous guides at Cape Leveque

Middle: Josh Whiteland, owner–operator of Koomal Dreaming, runs foodie tours and bush-food walks

Bottom: Traditional fire lighting with Koomal Dreaming

Karijini Eco Retreat

Stay in the spectacular Karijini National Park on the edge of Joffre Gorge with easy access to the park's walks and outback-style restaurant. Nestled in the sprawling spinifex and native bushland, the retreat's accommodation offering includes eco tents, cabins and campsites. During your stay, explore the park's wonderland of nature, from red cliffs, gorges and waterfalls to emerald green waterholes. A popular spot for visitors to check out is Joffre Falls, just a short but sometimes steep walk from the retreat. Please note that entry fees apply when visiting the Karijini National Park. Passes are available from the Karijini Eco Retreat or for purchase at entry points to the park.

WHERE: Savannah Campground (off Weano Rd), Karijini National Park (340 km from Port Hedland).
CONTACT: 08 9286 1731

Kimberley Cultural Tours

Connect to the rich culture and spectacular beauty of Broome as you are guided by local Robbi Dann. This tour will give you a hands-on experience of the culture and history of the area. Robbie has a profound love for his Country and culture and is excited to share this with his guests. Each tour runs for 3 hours and includes bus transportation for up to 11 passengers. You will gain a deeper understanding of local history, bush tucker and medicines, visit beautiful beaches, collect ochre, and maybe even track down some dinosaur footprints. Tours run Monday to Friday; check the website for more information.

WHERE: Broome.
CONTACT: 0434 537 639

Kooljaman at Cape Leveque

Kooljaman is the Bardi Aboriginal name for Cape Leveque, in the remote far northern reaches of the Kimberley region, on the Dampier Peninsula. It is also the name of the resort that is owned and operated by the Traditional Owners of the land, the Bardi and Jawi people from the nearby Aboriginal communities of Djarindjin and Ardyaloon. To some people Kooljaman is seen as a luxury resort, as the Traditional Owners have taken care to ensure the resort showcases their country in its natural, unspoilt beauty. Others see it as a wilderness camp: off the grid and sustained by solar power and local bore water. However you see it, staying there is a unique experience in some of the most incredible and isolated country in the world.

The beaches of the Kooljaman are endless stretches of fine white sand and clear, turquoise waters. Accommodation is designed to capture the rugged beauty of the Bardi Jawi country and reflect the traditional values of Caring for Country. Options range from deluxe safari tents, to cabins, beach shelters and camping, with something to suit all budgets and itineraries. Guests can enjoy fishing, swimming, snorkelling, mud crabbing, charter-boat trips, scenic flights, whale watching, bird spotting, or just relax. Unique tour opportunities are also available.

WHERE: Cape Leveque (200 km north of Broome).
CONTACT: 08 9192 4970

Koomal Dreaming Tours

Josh Whiteland takes guests on cultural tours based throughout the Wadandi and Bibbulman Country of the Busselton, Dunsborough and Margaret River areas of South West WA. Wadandi and Bibbulman are two language groups of the Noongar people, whose country stretches from Kalbarri to Esperance. Josh is a Wadandi custodian, and *Koomal*, the Wadandi word for 'brushtail possum', is his totem. He has a deep connection to Country and passion for his culture, and he is committed to sharing his knowledge with visitors. Koomal Dreaming Tours offer guests the opportunity to taste native foods and discover bush medicine, animals and plants, and learn about the ancient Dreaming spirits and culture of Wadandi and Bibbulman people. Tours include the Ngilgi Cave Cultural Tour; the Twilight Didgeridoo Cave Tour; and the Aboriginal Food, Culture, Cave and Didge Tour. The Djiljit Coastal Fishing Experience, guided by a Wadandi cultural custodian, allows you to discover, fish and forage on the spectacular seascape of Meelup Regional Park. On the Cape Cultural Experience, a Wadandi guide escorts you on an easy 2.5 kilometre walk around the tip of Cape Naturaliste, interpreting the seasonal flora and fauna of the landscape. The wheelchair-accessible 'Kaya' Cape Experience shares the deep connection that the Wadandi people have to the Cape-to-Cape region. Bookings are essential.

WHERE: Yallingup Caves Rd, Yallingup.
CONTACT: 0412 415 355

Koorah Koorah Cultural Tours

Koorah Koorah (Long Ago) Cultural Tours celebrates culture on Ballardong Country with Elder Trevor Davis as he guides you along his lifetime journey, to discover your pathway across the heart of the Wheatbelt. This scenic tour captures the true essence of country (Wildflowers, Dreamtime Stories, Native Cuisine and Significant Cultural Sites). Bookings are available from September to March; book by phone or Facebook.

WHERE: Ballardong Country, Wheatbelt, starting from Northam.
CONTACT: 08 6454 8845

Mayi Harvests' Pat Mamanyjun Torres with brother Wayne Jowandi Barker with an artists impression of their maternal granduncle Cassmond Drummond after she received a NAIDOC award from the local Broome NAIDOC committee, 2019

Below: Koorah Koorah's Elder Trevor Davis celebrating culture on Balardong Country

Kurrah Mia

A visit to Kinjarling (Albany) and the Great Southern Region is not complete without taking an Aboriginal Cultural tour with Kurrah Mia to learn about the Menang Noongar People relationship with their country. Throughout these immersive tours, you will understand how the Traditional Owners gathered resources from the land, practised ceremonial rituals, and you will gain insight into community customs. Be welcomed into Menang Boodja (Country) by your tour guides while learning about flora and fauna. Listen to traditional stories on Country and see the land through the eyes of the local people. Kurrah Mia provides a number of beautiful walks catering to various fitness levels and hosts an arts and craft store with a selection of educational books, dual-language stories for young people, bush foods and medicine books.

WHERE: 64 Middleton Loop, Albany.
CONTACT: 0419 320 533

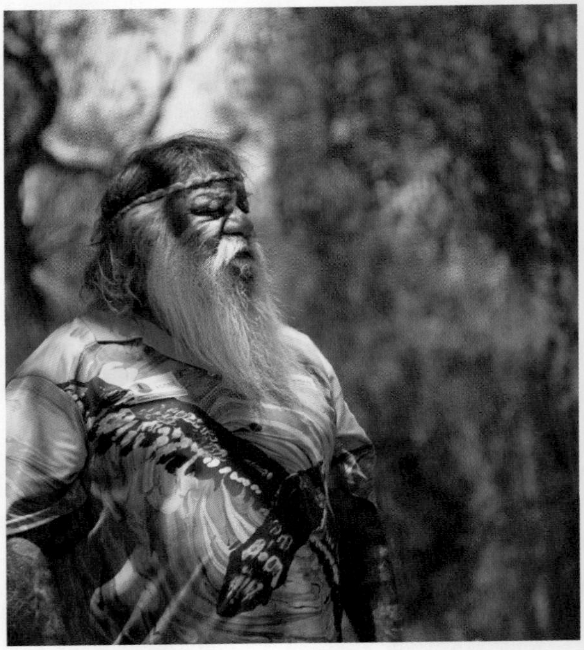

Mandjoogoordap Dreaming

Offering visitors to the Peel region eco bus and walking tours, Mandjoogoordap (meeting place of the heart) Dreaming celebrates and preserve the cultural knowledge of Mandurah and its surrounding area. Stroll along the Mandurah Eastern Foreshore or visit one of the oldest living organisms in the world, Woggaal's Noorook (thrombolites), while learning about the local history and dreaming stories. Make your own rope and bracelets out of river reeds and sticks and discover how local Aboriginal people sourced everything from the land while nourishing yourself with wattleseed and saltbush damper.

WHERE: Tours depart from Mandurah Performing Arts Centre, Mandurah.
CONTACT: 0408 952 740

Mayi Harvests

The Mayi Harvests cultural immersion half-day tour of Ngumbarl and Jabirr Jabirr Country celebrates Indigenous women's ancient traditional ecological knowledge and practices. The tour is led by Patricia Mamanyjun Torres, CEO and founder of Mayi Harvests Native Foods, and specialist in harvesting and processing native food plants including the Kakadu plum. These immersive experiences give you a better understanding of Indigenous culture that you can take back home and share with others.

The tour starts with a Welcome to Country by a Traditional Owner and a cleansing smoking ceremony to bring in positive wellbeing. Experience and be included in ancient family traditions of harvesting off the land (depending on the seasonal availability), then finish with a tasting plate of native foods. Bookings are essential.

Select native produce is also available for purchase from the Mayi Harvests website.

WHERE: Tours depart from Broome.
CONTACT: 0403 486 955

Narlijia Experiences Broome

In the Yawuru language of the Western Kimberley area, *Narlijia* means 'true for you'. This name refers to the authenticity of Narlijia Experiences Broome, run by passionate Yawuru man Bart Pigram. Born and bred on his traditional Country in Broome, Bart has a deep knowledge of his saltwater lifestyle, and shares his Aboriginal perspective with his guests. His stories are rich and fascinating, often drawn from his family's long tradition in the local pearling and music industry. Bart's tours are unique and personable.

WHERE: Narlijia Experiences are based in Broome.
CONTACT: 08 9195 0232

Nyungar Tours with Kerry-Ann Winmar

Nyungar Tours, a fully Aboriginal–owned-and-operated business, was established in 2018 by Kerry-Ann Winmar, a Whadjuk Yorga ('Yorga' means woman) from the Perth region, and won the 2020 NAIDOC Perth Business of the Year award. Kerry-Ann began Nyungar Tours as a way of maintaining and sharing her ancient Nyungar language, heritage and culture.

The South Perth Cultural Walking Tour includes a Welcome to Country by a Traditional Owner with a strong family history of ancient customs and traditions. Listen to traditional stories of Whadjuk Country and the history of the Nyungar people as you walk along the beautiful South Perth foreshore, overlooking the city skyline and scenic Swan River, known as Derbal Yerrigan in the local Nyungar language. This tour is a unique opportunity to learn about Perth's Aboriginal heritage and sites of cultural significance.

The Kings Park Yorga Walk focuses on sacred Yorgas' places in and around the Perth area.

WHERE: Tours operate in South Perth and Kings Park, Perth.
CONTACT: 0400 335 174

Peedamulla Campground

Situated on a 226,000-hectare cattle station crossed by the Cane River, Peedumulla Campground offers spectacular views of the Pilbara sky. Peedamulla's newly built campground has modern amenities with options of powered and unpowered sites. This is the perfect place to stop, camp and relax between Exmouth, Carnarvon and Karratha. Peedamulla means 'plenty water' in the local language and there are lots of opportunities to get wet. Explore the isolated coastline, rivers and wetlands with chances for fishing, boating and hiking close by. The campground is open April–October and takes bookings via its website.

WHERE: 203 km south of Karratha on Peedamulla-Onslow Rd, just off the North West Coastal Highway.
CONTACT: camping@peedamulla.com.au

Roelands Village

Roelands Village is a place of healing and cultural connection on a nationally significant heritage site surrounded by the rolling Seven Hills. Formerly a Mission housing Aboriginal children who were removed from families, and the base for one of Western Australia's most successful citrus fruit exporting businesses, the Mission today has been transformed into a happy, productive and welcoming place which the former 'Mission kids' now run.

Roelands accommodation includes 15 houses located in the central Village precinct, with a large function venue and commercial kitchen that can accommodate up to 100 people. The Blue House offers wheelchair-friendly accommodation with its own specialised bathroom and ground-level accommodation. Book by phone or online.

WHERE: 575 Seven Hills Road, Roelands (155 km from Perth).
CONTACT: 08 9726 3606

Wadumbah Indigenous Dance

Based on Whadjuk Noongar Country in Perth, Wadumbah Indigenous Dance shares its ancient Noongar culture with pride, passion and energy throughout Australia and the world. Wadumbah means 'Big Flood Waters' in the language of the Walmatjerri people from around Fitzroy Crossing, where the troupe's founder, James T. Webb, grew up. This phrase refers the Wet season, when bucketing rain fills up the rivers, which flow in a fury, full and ready to burst their banks. It is with this same energy that Wadumbah share their stories through song and dance. Performances range from 5 to 90 minutes in length. Check out their website for performance times or get in contact if you wish to organise a unique experience for yourself.

WHERE: Wadumbah are based in Perth but are happy to travel to perform.
CONTACT: 08 9313 3056

Wuddi Cultural Tours and Cultural Centre

Wuddi Cultural Tours and Cultural Centre offer tours around the local area, visiting mostly untouched sites and imparting valuable knowledge of the Traditional Owners of the lands through storytelling, demonstrations and hands-on experiences. Visitors learn the history of the region at the Cultural Centre before heading out for a 2-hour, half-day or full-day adventure. Owners Grant and Anne Riley run this small but impressive business and have set up the centre with gardens, artefact and artwork displays and a souvenir shop. All tours can be booked ahead of time, but Grant and Anne try their best to accommodate last-minute and same-day bookings as well. Please note that Wuddi accept cash and cheque payments only.

WHERE: 22 Harvey St, Dumbleyung (267 km from Perth).
CONTACT: 0476 788 139

Wula Gura Nyinda Eco Cultural Adventures

Where the red sand and turquoise waters meet is where real adventure begins. The untouched natural beauty and spectacular landscape and seascape of Shark Bay is home to some of Australia's most unique wildlife and geology. It is a place of immense ecological and cultural significance. Wula Gura Nyinda conduct a range of non-strenuous 'on Country' tours based in this spectacular location, exploring the ancient cultural ties of the region's First people, to the place they call 'Gutharraguda'.

Wula Gura Nyinda translates to 'you come this way', a traditional Aboriginal term for the sharing of stories – both between generations and between cultures. This notion of intercultural sharing extends into every aspect of the tours, which operate under the philosophy of education, understanding and respect.

WHERE: Shark Bay (400 km from Geraldton).
CONTACT: 0429 708 847; 0432 029 436

Wula Gura Nyinda tour at Shark Bay

ART GALLERIES, CULTURAL CENTRES AND MUSEUMS

Art Gallery of Western Australia

Situated in the heart of Perth's Cultural Centre on the traditional land of the Whadjuk Noongar people, the Art Gallery of Western Australia hosts the work of local and international artists. The gallery draws inspiration from the Swan River and other waterways close by, invoking its force and flow throughout its spaces. The Balancing Act gallery features the work of Aboriginal and Torres Strait Islander artists living and working across the state and Australia, aiming to create a balance between traditional stories of Country, culture and identity, and truth-telling. For all exhibition and event information, check the gallery's website.

WHERE: Perth Cultural Centre, Perth.
CONTACT: 08 9492 6600

Maalinup Aboriginal Gallery

'Maali' is the Wardandi word for the black swan, and along the Western and Southern coast of WA, 'up' means place of. So Maalinup is the 'place of the black swan', acknowledging the gallery's location in the picturesque Swan Valley region. Maalinup is an Aboriginal owned and operated enterprise, selling authentic Aboriginal art, gifts and bush tucker, and offering Aboriginal cultural activities. The gallery specialises in art and culture from the South West of WA.

WHERE: 10070 West Swan Road, Henley Brook (23 km from Perth).
CONTACT: 08 9296 0711 or 0411 112 450

Mowanjum Aboriginal Art and Culture Centre

The Mowanjum Aboriginal Art and Culture Centre is the creative hub for the Worrorra, Ngarinyin and Wunambal language groups, who form the Mowanjum community outside Derby in Western Australia. These peoples are the custodians of Wandjina law and iconography, united by their belief in the Wandjina as a sacred spiritual force and the creators of the land. The centre hosts exhibitions, workshops and community projects, as well as the Mowanjum Festival, one of Australia's longest running Indigenous cultural festivals, held each July.

Mowanjum is also home to Western Australia's only dedicated Indigenous museum. The museum provides a sensory learning experience and an insight into the history and culture of the Worrorra, Ngarinyin and Wunambal peoples. The museum features displays on Welcome to Country, Kimberley rock art, Junba (traditional song and dance) and artefacts. The museum also boasts the Selsmark Collection: an exceptional set of dance totems, costumes and musical instruments made in the early 1970s by senior Worrorra, Ngarinyin and Wunambal men and women.

WHERE: Gibb River Road, Derby.
CONTACT: 08 9191 1008

Nyamba Buru Yawuru

The Yawuru people are the Traditional Owners of the lands and waters in and around Rubibi (the town of Broome). The Liyan-ngan Nyirwa Cultural Wellbeing Centre, built on this Country, houses the Mabu Yawuru Ngan-ga Language Centre, other community programs and meeting facilities, as well as a function centre and Mabu Mayi

Cafe (see p. 342). The centre is set within landscaped gardens that were developed with community guidance to reflect Yawuru heritage and culture. Fourteen artworks on the grounds add a deeper understanding of Yawuru cultural philosophy and create a lively and interactive space.

The centre hosts many arts and culture programs and events such as cultural practice and incubation activities; reviving Yawuru material culture; reviving Yawuru Nurlu (traditional song and dance); development of both contemporary and traditional dance and music; respect for elders and ancestors; storytelling; bush cooking; outdoor community events; and, training, workshops and meetings. Nyamba Bura Yawuru also provides a range of cultural services including Welcomes to Country and smoking ceremonies. Event and tour information can be found on the website.

WHERE: 55 Reid Rd, Cable Beach.
CONTACT: 08 9192 9600

Tjukurba Gallery

Tjukurba Art Gallery celebrates the rich culture of the Martu people, and provides a space for creative expression. Since its opening in 2005, it has grown to become an important place in Wiluna community, at the start of the Canning Stock Route, showcasing the locally made artwork of the Birriliburu clan who call the area home. The gallery is not-for-profit, and provides artists with materials, a studio space and access to professional development workshops and activities. Art is ethically produced, and provides an income to artists.

WHERE: 28 Scotia St, Wiluna (720 km from Geraldton).
PERMITS: Permits are required to visit Wiluna and were cancelled in March 2020 to stop the spread of COVID-19 in the region. Contact Kuju Wangka for updates.
CONTACT: 08 9981 8000

Walyalup Aboriginal Cultural Centre

Walyalup Aboriginal Cultural Centre showcases local Aboriginal art, culture, and history through exhibitions, residencies, workshops, film screenings, music performances, and cultural tours underpinned by the 6 Nyoongar seasons. Visit the shop to support Aboriginal artists and makers, with a selection to choose from, including weaving, wood carvings, jewellery and art. The centre is open Thursday to Saturday 10 am–3 pm. Event and workshop information can be found through the website or social media.

WHERE: 12 Captains Lane, Fremantle.
CONTACT: 08 9430 7906

Western Australian Museum Boola Bardip

WA Museum Boola Bardip is a place to share Western Australia's many stories: our people, our places and our role in the world. Boola Bardip means 'many stories' in Noongar language. Situated in the heart of the Perth Cultural Centre, the museum explores the state's rich cultural and natural heritage through 3 major themes – Being Western Australian, Discovering Western Australia and Exploring the World. Woven throughout are the voices of Aboriginal and Torres Strait Islander peoples, recognising the primary rights of Australia's First peoples in practising and expressing their cultural heritage.

WHERE: Perth Cultural Centre, Cnr Francis and Williams sts, Northbridge.
CONTACT: 1300 134 081

PLACES

Bushlolly Cafe

Tucked away in the busy streets of Karratha, the Bushlolly Cafe celebrates food and culture. Infusing traditional cafe favourites like eggs benedict with native ingredients like warrigal greens (native spinach), and amplifying the classic chicken burger with lemon myrtle seasoning and quandong fire chilli sauce, meals can be paired with a range of native iced teas, such as bush plum, lemon myrtle and rosella. If you're looking for a treat, they also have a great range of native-infused smoothies such as strawberry and rivermint or banana and wattleseed. The cafe is open Monday to Saturday 7.30 am–2 pm.

WHERE: 5-15 Sharpe Avenue, Karratha.
CONTACT: 08 9185 1953

Ilkurlka Visitor Centre

The Ilkurlka Visitor Centre is owned by the Pila Nguru Aboriginal Corporation on behalf of the local Spinifex Traditional Owners (or A_n_angu) who mostly live in the Tjuntjuntjara remote community, 135 km to the south. The Spinifex families of Tjuntjuntjara have lived on their Country for at least 600 generations.

Ilkurlka is named after a desert rockhole that is a major site for the Spinifex people's Kalaya (Emu) story.

The Spinifex people are responsible for several significant Western Desert songlines and Dreaming stories that traverse the land area and require frequent visits and close adherence to traditional cultural protocols.

The Spinifex people temporarily left the northern part of their country in the 1950s during a time of severe drought and the British nuclear tests at Maralinga, returning

Left: Ilkurlka Visitor Centre, heart of Spinifex country
Right: Marble gums at Ilkurlka

to settle at Tjuntjuntjara and Ilkurlka in the 1980s. In 1995, they registered a Native Title claim over 55,000 sq km (5.5 million ha) of the Great Victoria Desert.

The visitor centre includes the Ilkurlka Roadhouse, which opened in July 2003 and offers a variety of services to enable tourists to traverse the Great Victoria Desert. The roadhouse operates on a model of sustainability with its buildings designed to fit unobtrusively in the natural environment, embodying passive design principles and fully powered by a solar microgrid.

Day-to-day operation and management are undertaken in rotational two- or three-month shifts by a sole operator, with the only permanent residents being three dogs.

The Ilkurlka Visitor Centre also hosts the renowned Spinifex Arts Project, established in 1997 as part of the Native Title documentation negotiations. The two Native Title paintings, the Men's combined and the Women's combined, document the entire Spinifex area, showing claimants' birthplaces and important stories. After the launch of the two Native Title paintings, the Spinifex people donated 10 major paintings to the people of Western Australia which are housed at the Western Australian Museum.

Spinifex artists paint traditional stories in acrylics, often using a vibrant palette. The Spinifex Arts Project is now an internationally acclaimed art project with paintings in major collections in Australia and overseas. Some works are available for viewing at the Ilkurlka Roadhouse.

Limited visitor accommodation is available at Ilkurlka with a campground and self- contained studios. Studio bookings are essential.

The Ilkurlka Visitor Centre is open 8 am–5 pm Monday to Friday, and by appointment on weekends.

Please note that motor mechanical repairs are not available at Ilkurlka Roadhouse or along the Anne Beadell Highway. A mechanical shed is available at Ilkurlka for limited DIY repairs.

Ilkurlka reopened on 1 March 2021 after a brief closure because of COVID-19, but visitors should call ahead before setting out on the Anne Beadell Highway for an update on the current situation.

WHERE: Anne Beadell Highway (540 km west of Laverton; 770 km east of Coober Pedy).
PERMITS: No permit is required to visit Ilkurlka. Permits are required to transit the Anne Beadell Highway within South Australia. Note that the north-south road passing through Ilkurlka is only available for community use. See the Ilkurlka Visitor Centre website for more details.
CONTACT: Visitor Centre: 08 9037 1147

Mabu Mayi Cafe

The Mabu Mayi Cafe is one of the several businesses established by the Nyamba Buru Yawuru Limited (NBY), the Yawuru Traditional Owners' not-for-profit company, which works towards the sustainable empowerment of Yawuru culture, Country and community.

Mabu Mayi (meaning 'good food' in the Yawuru language) Cafe is fully Yawuru owned and run. It offers healthy and delicious food influenced by Yawuru seasonal produce in a relaxed garden setting, with takeaway and private event catering also available. The cafe is open 7 am–2 pm Monday to Friday.

WHERE: 55 Reid Road, Cable Beach, Broome.
CONTACT: 08 9192 9616

Noongar Radio / Kuditj Kitchen

Transmitting positive, informed and empowering Indigenous programming to the community, Noongar Radio is a community-run station broadcasting across the length and breadth of Noongar Boodjar on 100.9 FM and digital radio. Running alongside the radio station is Kuditj Kitchen, a catering and hospitality training service that hosts corporate functions while serving bush tucker–infused creations. Check the website for catering and bookings.

WHERE: Kuditj Kitchen is located at 201 Beaufort Street, Perth.
CONTACT: 1800 733 322

Wunambal Gaambera Country

With over fifty visitor locations for you to enjoy, experience the rich Wanjina Wunggurr culture while exploring the remote, rugged, awe-inspiring beauty of Wunambal Gaambera Country in the far north Kimberley. Throughout your journey on this beautiful country, you will experience the changing landscapes from savannah to coastline and everything in between. Wunambal Gaambera Country is also home to several North Kimberley icons such as Punamii-Uunpuu (Mitchell Falls), Ngauwudu (Mitchell Plateau), Wanjina and Gwion paintings and World War II history.

The guided rock-art tour with the Uunguu Rangers and Traditional Owners is an excellent opportunity to see the magnificent Munurru Rock Art Sites at Ngauwudu (Mitchell Plateau). When visiting Ngauwudu (Mitchell Plateau) and Punamii-Uunpuu (Mitchell Falls), make sure to stay at Munurru (King Edward River). This serene campsite is run by the Traditional Owners, within a day's trip of waterfalls and rock art sites. All visitors to this area must have an Uunguu Visitor Pass, which you can purchase through your tourism operator or the website. Further information about tour offerings can also be found online.

WHERE: Wunambal Gaambera Country is situated 500 km north-west of Kununurra.
CONTACT: 0439 288 235

ART CENTRES

Bidyadanga Artists at Short St Gallery

Bidyadanga is Western Australia's largest remote Aboriginal community. With a population of roughly 750 residents, it is the traditional lands of the Karajarri people, but also home to the Juwalinny, Mangala, Nyungamarta and Yulparitja language groups. The art centre champions established and emerging artists, and supports the individual mark making, artistic expression and cultural maintenance of artists from all 5 language groups. Inspired by both the desert and coast, artists mix various hues with dramatic contrast. Since getting their land back, the Karrajarri do not encourage visitors to the community. Instead, their artwork and studio can be visited at Short St Gallery in Broome. Short St Gallery (since 1998) is the longest running gallery in Broome, specialising in contemporary artworks from regional Australia. The gallery showcases some of Australia's most respected Indigenous artists.

WHERE: Short St Gallery is at 7 Short St, Broome, and its stockroom is at 3 Hopton St, Broome.
CONTACT: 08 9192 6118

Fremantle Arts Centre – Revealed

Presented on Whadjuk Country by Fremantle Arts Centre since 2016, Revealed celebrates the breadth and vibrancy of Aboriginal arts practice in WA. Originally conceived to support WA's remote and regional Aboriginal art centres, Revealed has expanded in recent years to include a growing number of independent artists.

The program showcases the most exciting new and emerging Aboriginal artists from all over the state, connecting them with a metropolitan Perth audience through a prestigious exhibition and art market. Revealed also includes a series of professional

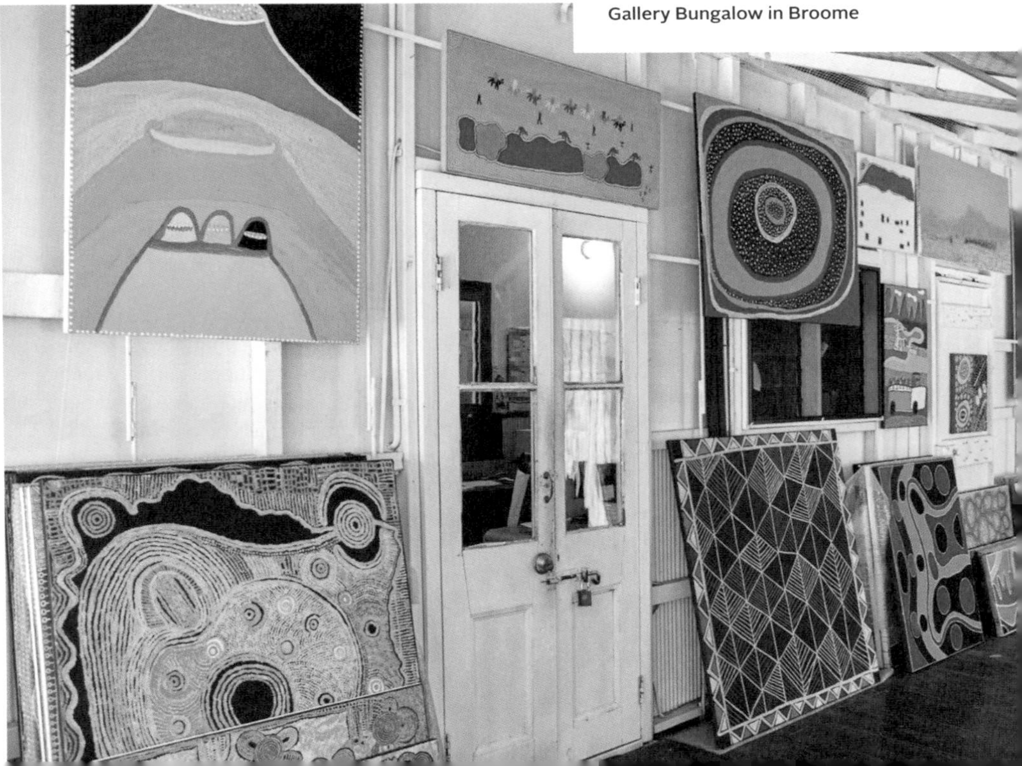

Artworks on display at the Short St Gallery Bungalow in Broome

development workshops for Aboriginal artists and art centre staff.

The Revealed WA Aboriginal Art Market is now one of the highlights on the Perth arts calendar, attracting thousands of visitors each year and generating more than half a million dollars in revenue, which is returned to the artists and art centres.

The Revealed Exhibition presents the works of over 100 new and emerging WA Aboriginal artists each year. Hundreds of new contemporary artworks fill Fremantle Arts Centre's galleries, spanning a range of styles and mediums including painting, installation, textiles, photography, print media, video, jewellery, carving and sculpture.

WHERE: Fremantle Arts Centre, 1 Finnerty Street, Fremantle.
WHEN: March to April. Contact for specific dates.
COST: Free.
CONTACT: 08 9432 9555

Karungkarni Art and Culture

Karungkarni Art and Culture Aboriginal Corporation is owned and governed by the Gurindji artists of the Kalkaringi and Daguragu communities. The name Karungkarni refers to the important Child Dreaming place for Gurindji people on a hill to the south of the art centre. The corporation, established by Elders in 2011, maintains and strengthens the cultural knowledge of Gurindji people, passing on the art, language, culture and history to the younger generations and the wider world. The artwork is distinctive for its precise and vibrant dot-painting style.

Some of the art centre's core artists and directors were part of the Wave Hill Walk-Off, led by Vincent Lingiari. On 23 August 1966, over 200 Gurindji people camped in the Victoria River bed after courageously walking off Wave Hill cattle station to protest their deplorable working and living conditions and, most importantly, to seek the rights to the land of their ancestors. These strong and determined men and women are renowned for the stance they took against the powerful Vestey Company, and Gurindji people now commemorate the Wave Hill Walk-Off in the annual Freedom Day Festival.

Under the direction of its board of eight Gurindji men and women, Karungkarni Art supports the production, promotion and sale of artwork by local artists and is the focal point for cultural and social activities in the community. The art centre is housed in the abandoned powerhouse building on the Buntine Highway at the entrance to Kalkaringi, which lies on the magnificent Victoria River. Visitors are advised to call before visiting.

WHERE: Kalkarindji (480 km south-west of Katherine).
CONTACT: 0427 177 779

Kira Kiro Artists

Kira Kiro represents the art and culture of the Kwini people of the Kalumburu community in north-western WA. Kira Kiro or Kirri Kirri are spiritual figures that feature in the area's rock art galleries. It is believed they were painted by the sandstone strike thrush's beak using blood from its wingtip.

Artistic practice plays a key cultural and economic role in the community, and the art centre supports traditional bark harvesting and painting, local white ochre collection, the production of cultural artefacts and storytelling through contemporary works. Art is grounded in the stories of Wandjina, the 'rain-maker' spirit, as well as secular themes including land animals, sea-life and seasonal bush foods and medicinal plant knowledge. Artists paint with natural ochre pigments on canvas, papers and bark, and are skilled boab nut engravers.

WHERE: 89 Kalumburu Blvd, Kalumburu.
PERMITS: Permits are required to visit Kalumburu lands and are available to purchase at the Community Resource Centre or the Uraro Store on entering the community. An entry permit for access to Aboriginal land is also required and available from the Department of Planning, Lands and Heritage.
CONTACT: 08 9168 2212

Ku'arlu Mangga (Good Nest)

Building on the successes of the original Northhampton Old School community centre, which started operating nearly 30 years ago, the Ku'Arlu Mangga (Good Nest) emerging art centre supports up-and-coming local artists. This vibrant art space hosts a range of programs to support the community's ongoing connection to culture and Country, with art and creative content running throughout all of the community projects. In addition to supporting the production and sale of the community's art, the art centre hosts various events and workshops throughout the year. You can find a range of art here, from textiles and material culture to jewellery and homewares. Stay updated on upcoming events and gallery opening times through their website and social pages.

WHERE: 31 Robinson St, Northampton.
CONTACT: 0437 460 015

Laarri Gallery

Laarri Gallery is a small not-for-profit gallery located in Yiyili community. Established in 1999, the gallery showcases diverse traditional and contemporary art and crafts that detail local culture and history of the Gooniyandi Country of the Yiyili, Ganinya, Girriyoowa, Goolgaradah, Rocky Springs, Kurinyjarn and Moongardie communities. The gallery provides a place for artists to produce and showcase their art, including original works on canvas, artefacts such as didgeridoos, painted boab nuts and various locally designed merchandise. All money from sales is returned to artists, supporting the artists themselves and the community at large.

WHERE: Yiyili community (120 km west of Halls Creek).
CONTACT: 08 9191 7195 or 0459 109 812

Mangkaja Arts Resource Agency

Mangkaja Arts began in the 1980s as a place where community members could paint their personal stories and histories. Mangkaja is a Walmajarri word for the wet weather shelters erected by the Walmajarri people in the Great Sandy Desert during the Wet season. Today the art centre is situated in the centre of the Fitzroy Crossing and functions as a studio space for the artists to work, as well as a fine art gallery and specialty store. It represents the Bunuba and Gooniyandi people of the Martuwarra (river Country), and Walmajarri and Wangkajunga people from the Jilji (sand-hill Country of the Great Sandy Desert).

Artists share their history, culture and Country through their arts practice. With diverse upbringings between the river and the desert, Mangkaja artists showcase a unique range of artistic styles. Their art is bravely innovative, in both aesthetics and mediums, with a full palette of bright colours and bold mark-making resulting in vibrant and unique paintings on canvas and paper, for which the artists are most well known. In recent years, acrylic has also been transferred onto perspex, with works being celebrated both nationally and internationally. Other mediums of Mangkaja artists include printmaking, traditional artefact making, carving and basket weaving.

In 2019, a collaboration between 5 senior Mangkaja artists and the Australian fashion label Gorman was released. The collection celebrated the contribution of artists Ngarralja Tommy May, Sonia Kurarra, Mrs Japulija, Mrs Rawlins and Ms Uhl to the contemporary Australian art scene, showcasing them in the medium of contemporary fashion.

WHERE: 8 Bell Rd, Fitzroy Crossing.
CONTACT: 08 9191 5833

Martumili Artists

Martumili Artists, established in 2006, represents the Martu people from the East Pilbara remote communities of Parnpajinya (Newman), Jigalong, Parnngurr, Punmu, Kunawarritji, Irrungadji and Warralong. Martu people are the Traditional Owners of a large area of land that spans the Great Sandy, Little Sandy and Gibson deserts as well as the Karlamilyi (Rudall River) area. Martu artists are both established and emerging, and showcase the strength and diversity of their culture and lived experiences. Senior artists are well renowned as exceptional painters, working with bold bright colour palettes and strong brush strokes.

WHERE: East Pilbara Arts Centre, Newman Dr, Newman.
CONTACT: 08 9175 1020

Nagula Jarndu Designs

Nagula Jarndu means 'saltwater woman' in the local Yawuru Language of Broome. This women's arts and resource centre was started by Yawuru women in 1987 to preserve the oral history of Yawuru language and culture. It later began to offer training in fabric design and production, screen-printing and dressmaking, and is now renowned for its distinctive textiles inspired by the unique landscapes around Broome. Today the art centre is governed by 8 female Yawuru directors, and has a membership of 130 Aboriginal women. The Nagula Jarndu workshop provides a space for artists to work and produce textiles and other specialty handicrafts, and to earn an income from their artistry. Textiles are printed onto high-quality base fabrics including linen, silk and cotton. The work of Nagula Jarndu is exhibited nationally at various galleries and events.

WHERE: 1/12 Gregory St, Broome.
CONTACT: 0499 330 708

Papulankutja Artists

Papulankutja Artists was established in 2003 as the evolution of the local Women's Centre, which had its origins in painting from the mid-1980s. The art centre focuses on supporting its members, the Ngaanyatjarra people of Papulankutja and nearby Mantamaru, to develop their arts practice and to earn a viable income from their works.

Through painting, artists work to maintain Ngaanyatjarra culture, law and storytelling, which still guide the lives of the people living right across the Ngaanyatjarra lands. The area around the community of Papulankutja has some of the region's most significant sacred sites, and artists share the stories of their Tjukurrpa (Dreaming) and connection to Country and ancestors. Artists are also known for innovative fibre work made for Tjanpi Desert Weavers and local punu (wood) carvings. In 2005, a group of 18 Papulankutja women won the National Aboriginal and Torres Strait Islander Art Award with their large woven 3D Toyota.

WHERE: Papulankutja (Blackstone) (353 km from Uluṟu–Kata Tjuṯa).
PERMITS: A permit is required to visit the region. Contact the Ngaanyatjarra Council for further information and to apply.
CONTACT: 08 8956 7586 or 0477 567 537

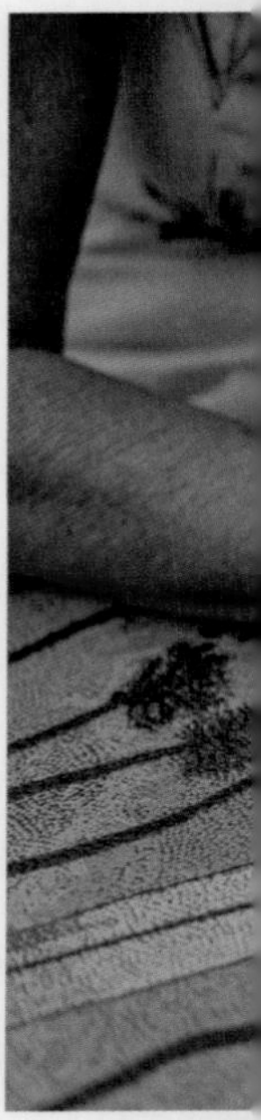

Spinifex Hill Studio artist Lorna Dawson painting

Spinifex Hill Studio

Spinifex Hill Studio is one of the youngest Aboriginal art collectives in Australia's north-west, but its artists are fast gaining popularity in major galleries, art fairs and awards right across Australia and abroad, for their bold and vibrant acrylic paintings.

Located on Kariyarra Country in the Pilbara region, Spinifex Hill was established in 2008. It supports the dynamic Aboriginal creative practice of the region, and provides a platform to promote the traditions, culture and heritage centre of its artists. More than 100 artists, both established and mid-career, regularly use the studio facilities, and hail from language groups including Kariyarra, Banyjima, Mangala, Manyjiljarra, Martu, Noongar, Nyangumarta, Nyamal, Nyiyarparli, Walmajarri, Warnman, Yamatji, Yindjibarndi. This diversity of lived experiences and cultures is reflected in the rich colour palettes and bold brush strokes, for which the artists have become renowned.

WHERE: 18 Hedditch St, South Hedland.
CONTACT: 08 9172 1699

Tjarlirli Art & Kaltukatjara Art

Tjarlirli Art is a fully artist-owned Aboriginal art centre, representing the artists of Tjukurla in the Ngaanyatjarra Lands of Western Australia, and also managing Kaltukatjara Art, which represents the artists of Kaltukatjara (Docker River) in the Pitjantjatjara lands of the Northern Territory. Artists from both centres produce artwork with strong links to the Papunya Tula movement, as families left Kintore and Kiwirrkurra to return to their homelands in the mid-1980s. There are close ties and family links between these communities.

At Tjarlirli Art, artists are from the Ngaanyatjarra and Pintupi language groups, and their art commonly depicts Ngurra (Country), Kungkarangkalpa (Seven Sisters), Karlaya (Emu Dreaming) and Tjarlirli Rockhole. At Kaltukatjara, artists are from the Pitjantjatjara and Ngaanyatjarra language groups, and commonly depict Kungka Kutjarra, Kungkarangkalpa (seven sisters) and Tingarri Tjukurrpa (dreaming).

TJARLIRLI ART

WHERE: Tjukurla, Ngaanyatjarra Lands (350 km from Uluṟu–Kata Tjuṯa).
PERMITS: Entry permit from Ngaanyatjarra Council required. The art centre is open by appointment only.
CONTACT: 08 8956 7777

KALTUKATJARA ART CENTRE

WHERE: Kaltukatjara.
PERMITS: Entry permit from Central Land Council required. The art centre is open by appointment only.
CONTACT: 08 8955 8396

Warakurna Artists

Warakurna is a remote community in the Ngaanyatjarra Lands of Western Australia, near the Northern Territory border. The community has a long history of artistic expression, and the art centre was established to champion this in 2005. It provides services to artists living in and visiting Warakurna, and the neighbouring communities of Wanarn and Patjarr. Artists paint and share Tjukurrpa (traditional law and culture) and contemporary stories, as a critical means of keeping culture vital and strong. The vibrant and diverse paintings reflect the unique style of each artist and their lived experiences. Artists are known for their use of bright colour palettes and bold brushstrokes.

The Ngurra Streetwear project was established in 2014 as a response to requests from within the community to design fashion. In collaboration with Jack Searls of Noap Studio, a week-long design workshop is held each year to create new and original imagery. Participants use paint, textas and photography to develop images from around the community, which are then workshopped for screen-printing. These designs are turned into original T-shirts and marketed online.
WHERE: Warakurna community (330 km from Uluṟu–Kata Tjuṯa).
PERMITS: Permits are issued by the Ngaanyatjarra Council.
CONTACT: 08 8955 8099

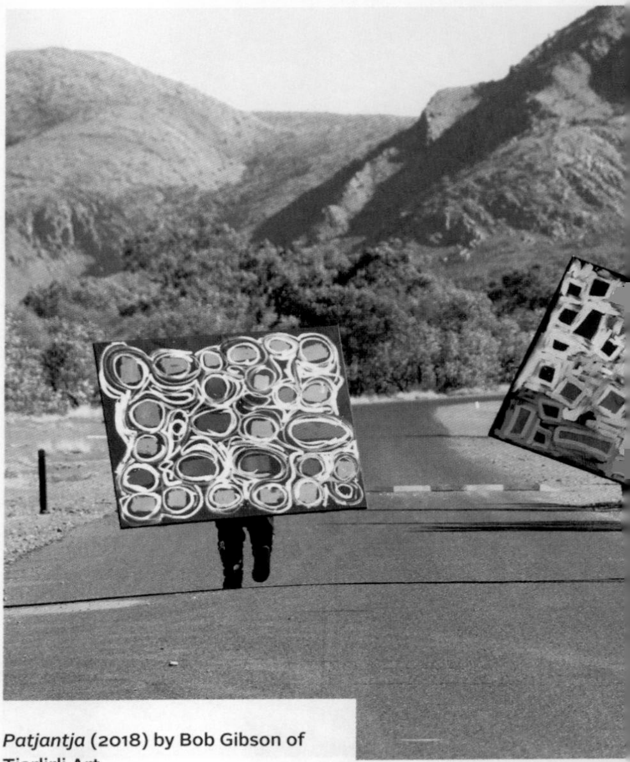

Patjantja (2018) by Bob Gibson of Tjarlirli Art

Waringarri Aboriginal Arts

Waringarri Aboriginal Arts celebrates the uniqueness of the Miriwoong cultural identity in the Kimberley region of Western Australia. Established in the 1980s, it is one of Australia's longest continuously running Aboriginal-owned art centres. Today, it supports more than 100 artists, including those from Kira Kiro in Kalumburu, who work in a range of mediums including painting, printmaking, wood carving, boab engraving, sculpture and textile designing and printing.

The Miriwoong Creation era is known as the Ngarranggarni, and is a time when spirit beings roamed the Country creating all natural features of the landscape, and filling the land with a spirituality that remains vital

to this day. Maintaining the sacred places and stories associated with the Ngarranggarni is, for the Miriwoong people, essential to their cultural survival. Artists share stories of their unique and sacred Country through their artwork, and maintain connection to their rich cultural heritage.

Waringarri Arts includes studio space for artists to work from, a shop, and the Dawang Gallery, a unique cultural information space presenting selected works from the Waringarri collection, complemented by multimedia presentations to share the richness of Miriwoong cultural identity with both community and visitors. Cultural tours and performances are also available for visitors.

WHERE: 16 Speargrass Road, Kununurra (515 km from Katherine).
CONTACT: 08 9168 2212

Warlayirti Artists Aboriginal Corporation

Warlayirti Artists is located in the community of Wirrimanu (Balgo). This is the Kutjungka region of the south-east Kimberley, on the edge of the Tanami and Great Sandy deserts. The community is the ceremonial hub for several Indigenous clans and is a site for the Luurnpa Tjukurrpa (Kingfisher Dreaming). Established in 1987, Warlayirti Artists now supports more than 200 artists from Wirrimanu and the neighbouring Kururrungka (Billiluna) and Mulan communities. Artists represent eight different language groups – Kukatja, Ngardi, Djaru, Warlpiri, Walmajarri, Wangkajunga, Pintupi and Ngaatjatjarra. Art is a part of everyday life here, ensuring cultural continuity for these multicultural and diverse communities.

Warlayirti Artists specialises in fine art acrylic paintings on canvas and linen, with a reputation for vibrant colour palettes, bold brushstrokes and distinctly individual artworks. A wide range of mediums, including works on paper, silk painting, artefacts and glass, are explored by artists. The work of Warlayirti Artists is exhibited widely both nationally and internationally, and is represented in major public and private collections.

The art centre itself functions as a studio space for artists, as well as a large specially built gallery for artwork display and sale. The art centre is also home to a cultural Keeping Place and archive of national significance.

WHERE: Wirrimanu (Balgo) community (260 km from Halls Creek).
PERMITS: Day visitors are welcome to visit the art centre and the community store without a permit, however it is advisable to contact the art centre prior to visiting. Permits are required to stay overnight and accommodation is very limited; please contact the art centre for more information.
CONTACT: 0407 123 478

Warmun Art Centre

Warmun Art Centre was established in 1998 by the founding members of Warmun's contemporary painting movement, including the late Rover Thomas, Queenie McKenzie, Madigan Thomas and Hector Jandany. These Elders saw the need for a community owned and controlled centre to support, maintain and promote Gija art, language and culture.

Warmun Art celebrates and supports the expression of Gija culture, and encourages the continued development of innovative contemporary art by Gija artists. Artists draw on the Ngarrangkarni, or Creation period, to create striking contemporary paintings renowned for their natural ochre hues and textural application. The originality and vibrance of this style transcend cultural and artistic boundaries, placing many senior Warmun artists at the forefront of contemporary Australian art. The work from Warmun Art is loved in galleries and collections, both at home and abroad.

The art centre itself includes a studio, which is the central hub for community life where artists come to share stories and work, and the gallery, which usually attracts thousands of visitors annually to engage with Gija art and culture. At the time of writing, however, the art centre is closed to visitors due to COVID-19.

WHERE: Warmun community (200 km from Kununurra).
PERMITS: Visitors require a verbal permit to enter the community, which the art centre can arrange over the phone.
CONTACT: 08 9168 7496

Wirnda Barna Art Centre

The Wirnda Barna Art Centre supports and represents Aboriginal artists from Badimia and Wajarri Country based in Mount Magnet and Yalgoo. It offers a creative environment where artists can work together to share stories and knowledge to connect with their unique language and culture, and create visual representations of this.

Artists take inspiration from the rich landscape of their Country, including the spectacular spring wildflower season and important cultural sites of the region including the Granites, Australia's largest ochre mine the Wilgie Mia Aboriginal Ochre Mine, and Walga Rock, Western Australia's largest gallery of Aboriginal rock paintings.

WHERE: 79 Hepburn St, Mount Magnet (343 km from Geraldton).
CONTACT: 0438 757 274

Yamaji Art

Yamaji Art is the longest established 100 per cent Aboriginal owned-and-operated Aboriginal art centre in the Mid West of WA. The centre provides professional development services to support and develop Aboriginal artists living in the Lower Murchison region of Yamaji Country, with a focus on sustaining cultural maintenance and arts practice while creating economic benefit.

WHERE: 189 Marine Terrace, Geraldton.
CONTACT: 08 9965 3440

Yinjaa-Barni Art

Yinjaa-Barni Art is a Aboriginal artists collective. Artists predominantly belong to the Yindjibarndi language group, whose ancestral homelands surround the Millstream Tablelands and Fortescue River in north-west Western Australia. Established in 2004, the art centre is based in Roebourne in the Pilbara region, and artists create deeply personal works of collective memory, rendering the wildflowers, river systems and landforms of their Country on canvas. Artistic expression is a means of expressing culture and love and connection to Country, and, along with storytelling, it plays a vital role in sharing knowledge with younger generations. Art from Yinjaa-Barni has been exhibited nationally and internationally.

WHERE: Roebourne (273 km from Port Hedland).
CONTACT: 0439 494 757 or 08 9182 1959

3 NEW SOUTH WALES

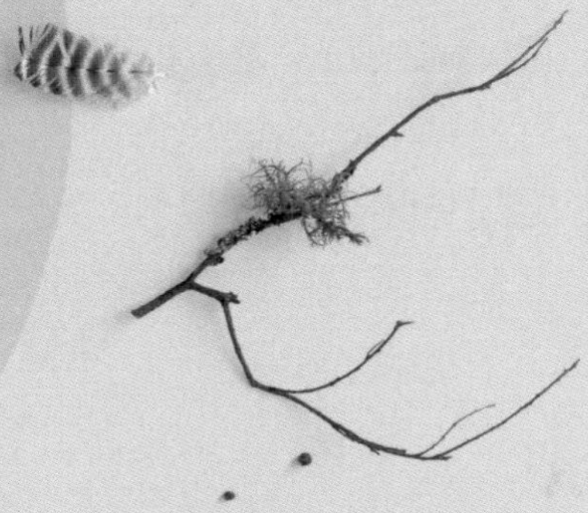

FESTIVALS

5 Lands Walk

Proudly held on Darkinjung country, this spirited celebration of place and people is held annually in June on the weekend closest to the winter solstice. A place where family, friends and the wider community are encouraged to celebrate life, have fun and connect to our deep Aboriginal history, settlement, and who we are today. The walk joins the five coastal villages of Macmasters Beach, Copacabana, North Avoca, Avoca Beach and Terrigal, each bringing its own celebration in and around the surf clubs of the 5 Lands. They are connected by 10 km of beaches, headlands, bush, footpaths and streets. Along the way, you will experience Aboriginal ceremony and culture, music, food, artworks, colourful kites, whales, dance, sculptures on the beach and craft workshops. A free event.

WHEN: Annually in June on the weekend closest to the winter solstice.

WHERE: Macmasters Beach, Copacabana, North Avoca, Avoca Beach and Terrigal, Central Coast – running concurrently.

CONTACT: admin@5landswalk.com.au

Saltwater Freshwater Aboriginal Cultural Festival

The Saltwater Freshwater (SWFW) Festival celebrates and shares authentic Aboriginal living culture with the wider community on Australia Day, making it a positive, inclusive day for all to enjoy. The only Aboriginal cultural festival of its kind in regional NSW, it is a true showcase of Aboriginal arts and culture from the Gumbaynggirr, Dunghutti, Biripi and Worimi nations from the Mid North Coast of NSW. The festival also creates a platform for Aboriginal performers, artists and businesses, unearthing the rich, diverse and living Aboriginal culture from the SWFW region.

The Saltwater Freshwater Festival was first held on Gumbaynggirr Country (Coffs Harbour) in 2010, and since then has moved around the Mid North Coast – to Biripi Country (Port Macquarie, Taree), Dunghutti Country (Kempsey) and, most recently, Worimi Country (Forster).

WHEN: Annually on 26 January (Australia Day).

WHERE: Mid North Coast – the festival travels to a different location each year. Check the Saltwater Freshwater website for details.

CONTACT: 02 6658 1315

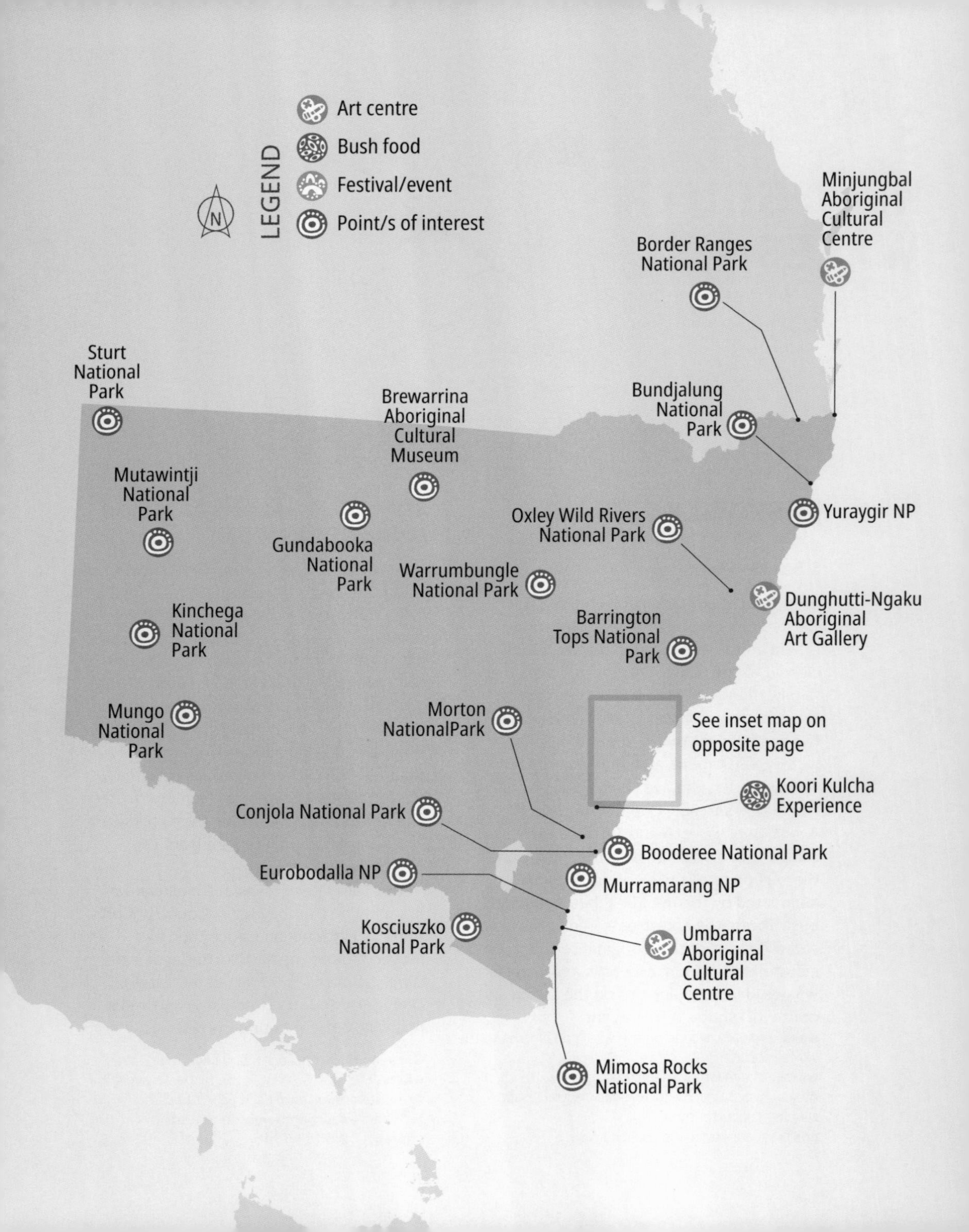
LEGEND
Art centre
Bush food
Festival/event
Point/s of interest
N
Minjungbal Aboriginal Cultural Centre
Border Ranges National Park
Sturt National Park
Brewarrina Aboriginal Cultural Museum
Bundjalung National Park
Mutawintji National Park
Yuraygir NP
Oxley Wild Rivers National Park
Gundabooka National Park
Warrumbungle National Park
Dunghutti-Ngaku Aboriginal Art Gallery
Kinchega National Park
Barrington Tops National Park
Mungo National Park
Morton NationalPark
See inset map on opposite page
Koori Kulcha Experience
Conjola National Park
Booderee National Park
Eurobodalla NP
Murramarang NP
Kosciuszko National Park
Umbarra Aboriginal Cultural Centre
Mimosa Rocks National Park

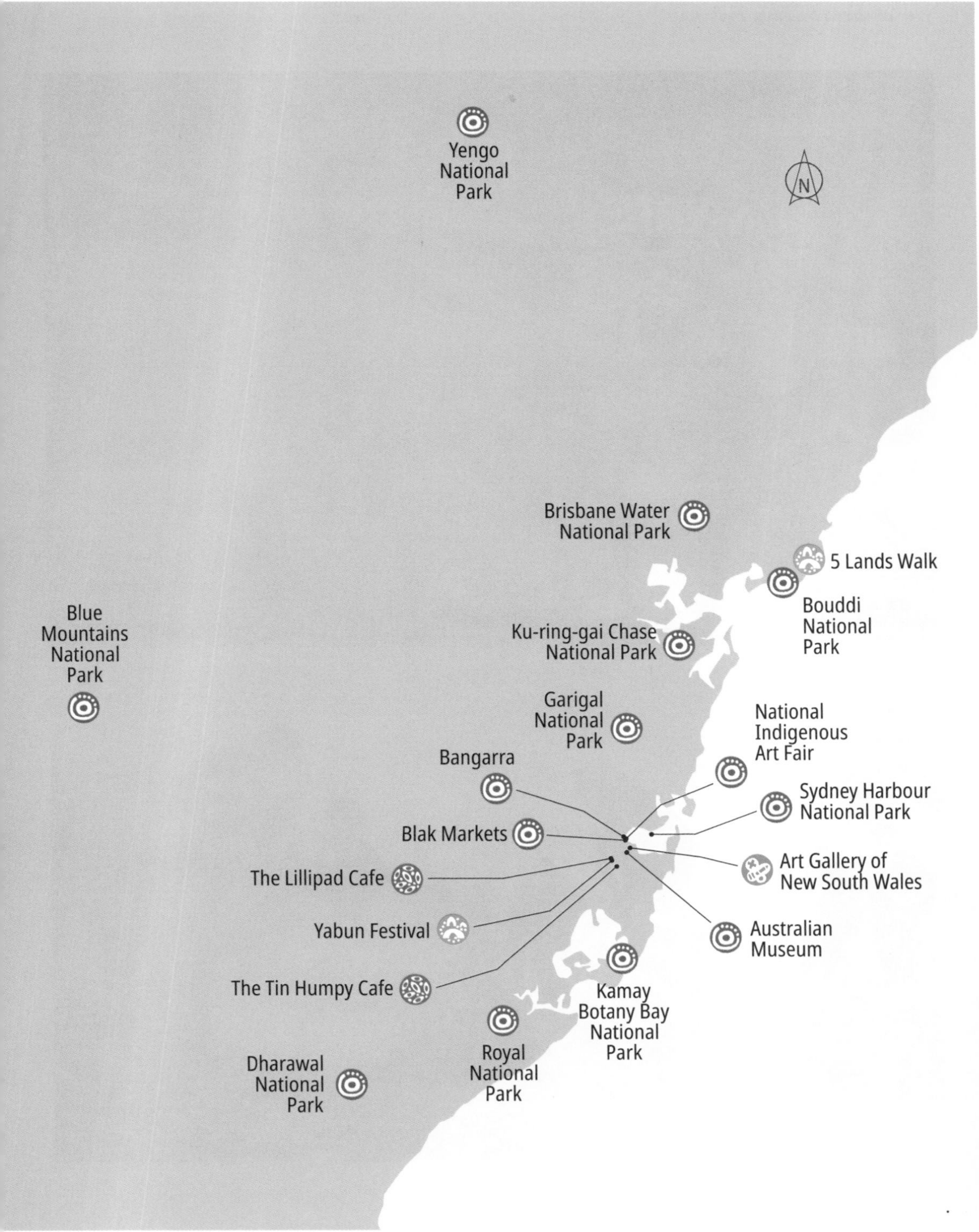
Yengo National Park
N
Brisbane Water National Park
5 Lands Walk
Bouddi National Park
Blue Mountains National Park
Ku-ring-gai Chase National Park
Garigal National Park
National Indigenous Art Fair
Bangarra
Sydney Harbour National Park
Blak Markets
Art Gallery of New South Wales
The Lillipad Cafe
Yabun Festival
Australian Museum
The Tin Humpy Cafe
Kamay Botany Bay National Park
Royal National Park
Dharawal National Park

Top: Performers at Saltwater Freshwater Festival

Bottom: 5 Lands Walk

Yabun Festival

Held every year on Survival/Invasion Day, 26 January, Yabun Festival is a celebration of Aboriginal culture on a day that signifies for many Aboriginal people the beginning of their country's invasion. The festival started in the inner-city suburb of Redfern in 2003 as a way for Aboriginal people to be together for Survival Day. It is now Sydney's largest Survival Day event and a beautiful community gathering where people from all backgrounds come together. *Yabun* is a Gadigal word meaning 'music to a beat' and the festival is filled with live music from the morning to the evening, with performances by Aboriginal artists and a corroboree ground with traditional dancing, as well as more than 100 stalls selling food and merchandise. In the Speak Out Tent, Aboriginal community members conduct panel discussions, while the Jarjums Tent has children's activities, including Aboriginal Elders reading and telling stories. This is a great way for visitors to experience Aboriginal culture, especially on such a significant day in Aboriginal and Australian history.

WHERE: Victoria Park, cnr Parramatta and City rds, Camperdown, Sydney.
WHEN: Annually on 26 January, 10 am–7 pm.
COST: Free admission.
CONTACT: 02 9384 4000

PERFORMANCE

Bangarra

Widely acclaimed both nationally and internationally, Bangarra Dance Theatre is one of Australia's leading performing arts companies. Since it was founded in 1989, Bangarra has inspired audiences nationally and internationally. Its performances of powerful and emotive dance and music bring together the contemporary and traditional duality of Aboriginal and Torres Strait Islander culture. For the artistic director, Stephen Page, the dance company's relationship with Aboriginal and Torres Strait Islander communities and respected Elders remains at the heart of Bangarra. Stories for the company's productions are gathered from around the country and performed by highly skilled artists – each with their own proud Aboriginal and/or Torres Strait Islander background that drives their passion and influences their styles of dance.

Bangarra tours nationally in the major cities and in regional Australia, and also regularly tours internationally. Each production displays the wonderful diversity that is Aboriginal and Torres Strait Islander Australia.

CONTACT: 02 9251 5333

SPORT

The Harvey Norman Rugby League All Stars Match

This is a must see for all Rugby League fans and anyone who enjoys watching great sport. The Harvey Norman Rugby League All Stars Match is a spectacular celebration of Rugby and Aboriginal and Torres Strait Islander culture. The match features the Indigenous All Stars versus the Māori All Stars men's and women's teams. All teams play with vigour and passion, making it one of the most significant NRL (National Rugby League) matches in the season. With traditional Aboriginal, Torres Strait Islander and Māori dancing before the match, the atmosphere of the All Stars Match will excite even those spectators who have never watched an NRL match before. It is essential to book tickets early, so check the website to find out when they will go on sale.

WHERE: The venue changes yearly; in 2021 the game was held in Townsville.
WHEN: Usually held in the second week of February. Details about the date, location and ticket prices will be available on the website in the weeks leading up to the game.

NATIONAL PARKS

Visitors planning to go to a few national parks in NSW can purchase an All Parks Pass; see the NSW NPWS website or call for information about any national park within the NPWS: 1300 072 757 (13000 PARKS).

Bookings are required for all NPWS-managed national parks, and highly recommended in general. All wild, back country or remote 'walk-in' camping is permitted, but requires a Trip Intention Form. This is an online form campers need to fill out via the NSW National Parks website to register their plans to assist emergency services in the event they become lost or injured.

Campers should always check the NPWS website for up-to-date closures and safety alerts and to see if walk-in camping is permitted at their desired national park.

Barrington Tops National Park

World Heritage–listed Barrington Tops National Park spans a world of contrasts, ranging from near sea level to almost 1600 m and including subalpine tablelands and peaks wreathed in swirling mist, to plunging waterfalls and sun-filtered subtropical rainforests in the deep valleys. The dramatic changes in altitude and climate have created an immensely varied terrain, including high plateau areas, steep ridges and deep gorges. The park is the ultimate outdoor destination. It is great to visit year-round, but be prepared for sudden weather changes, snow and subzero temperatures in winter.

CULTURAL HERITAGE: The park occupies the traditional domain of several Aboriginal groups – the Worimi, Biripi and Wonnarua peoples – for whom the land held spiritual significance and also provided good hunting and bush tucker, including edible fruits such as the native cherry, lilly pilly and figs.

Europeans moved into the area in the 1820s and 1830s for logging and farming and were soon clearing the forest. Within 2 decades the natural ecological balance had been destroyed, wildlife had dwindled and the Aboriginal people were driven off their traditional lands. Although there was talk in the 1920s and 1930s of developing the area and turning the Barrington Tops into a resort, and there was ongoing discussion of logging and road building, conservationists lobbied successfully and Barrington Tops National Park was declared in 1969.

Today, Aboriginal history in Barrington Tops exists in oral records and Aboriginal sites in the park, such as ancient camp sites, scarred trees and sacred ceremonial places, all protected by the national park.

NATURAL FEATURES: Barrington Tops is a subalpine plateau between a series of extinct volcanic peaks in the Mount Royal Range. Wild rivers and ridges radiate outwards from the sloping edges of the plateau. In altitude, the park ranges from near sea level to almost 1600 m at the highest point of the plateau, with Polblue Mountain at 1575 m and Mount Barrington peaking at 1556 m. The climate is equally diverse, ranging from subalpine to subtropical in these World Heritage–listed Gondwana

Rainforests. More than three-quarters of the park is declared wilderness, a wonderland of rushing rivers, thundering cascades and pristine, undisturbed bush.

THINGS TO DO

Visitors can walk in the rainforest, enjoy a picnic (there are picnic venues with tables and most have gas or wood-fired barbecues), fish in the crystalline rivers and enjoy the brilliant views. There are many fantastic vantage points from which to survey the park's majestic forested wilderness. In the northern section of the park there are quite a few trails suitable for mountain bikes, ranging from easy, undulating trails to steeper inclines. Cyclists are not permitted on walking tracks or on some specific trails (check with NPWS for details).

The fresh, clear waters of the creeks and waterholes are often chilly and shallow but some are suitable for swimming. Beware of slippery rocks and fast-flowing streams.

The rivers on the eastern slopes of Barrington Tops provide good trout fishing, while in the lower reaches of the Barrington, Moppy and Gloucester rivers, anglers bait for bass, catfish and mullet. A recreational fishing licence is required to fish inland waters in NSW. Contact NSW Fisheries: 1300 550 474, or visit its website for further details. Fishing is not permitted between the June and October long weekends.

WHERE: 300 km north of Sydney; 40 km north-west of Dungog; 65 km east of Scone; 38 km west of Gloucester. Access: from Dungog via Chichester Dam Rd then Salisbury Rd; from Scone or Gloucester via Gloucester–Scone Rd. Park entry is mainly along unsealed roads and most visitors use the Dungog approach. At times of extreme weather some roads in the park may be closed or accessible by 4WD only.

CAMPING AND ACCOMMODATION: In the park's north, high-country camp sites offer wonderful views over wilderness and farmlands and the chance to do a spot of mountain fishing, as well as providing access to walking tracks, good swimming and 4WD trails. Other sites promise abundant wildlife-spotting opportunities. For the fit, there are ample walk-in camping areas.

Camping fees are payable at some sites and bush camping is permitted in the park but keep at least 300 m from roads or tracks. Fuel stoves are recommended. All creek and river water should be boiled before use. Bookings are required; see the NSW NPWS website.The area around the park is well serviced, with a range of accommodation options, such as the Barrington Wilderness Cottages in the park (via Dungog).

CONTACT: NPWS Gloucester: 02 6538 5300; NPWS Scone: 02 6540 2300; NSW National Parks Contact Centre: 1300 072 757 (13000 PARKS)

Blue Mountains National Park

Blue Mountains National Park presents an astounding and unique landscape to its millions of visitors. The terrain ripples and folds, a world of canyons, gorges and bizarre rock formations, with golden sandstone breaking through a dense canopy of greenery. Waterfalls cascade magically from cliff faces and a mystical blue haze hangs in the air. The park is immensely rich in natural and cultural history. Much of the park was affected by the 2019/2020 bushfires, but the forest is regenerating and many walking tracks and sites have reopened.

CULTURAL HERITAGE: The park occupies the traditional lands of the Dharug and Gundungurra peoples, with the wider Greater Blue Mountains World Heritage Area also spanning the Country of the Darkinjung, Dharawal, Wiradjuri and Wonnarua peoples. Evidence of Aboriginal occupation, including rock-art sites, dates back 14,000 years.

The Three Sisters form an iconic landmark, intrinsically linked with Aboriginal ancestral stories, legend and ceremony. One of the local Dreaming stories tells how the 3 sisters Meehni, Wimlah and Gunnedoo fell in love against traditional lore, and amid the tribal war that ensued, they were turned to stone for protection. However, the witchdoctor who performed this magic was killed in the battle, and so the sisters have remained in their rock forms to this day.

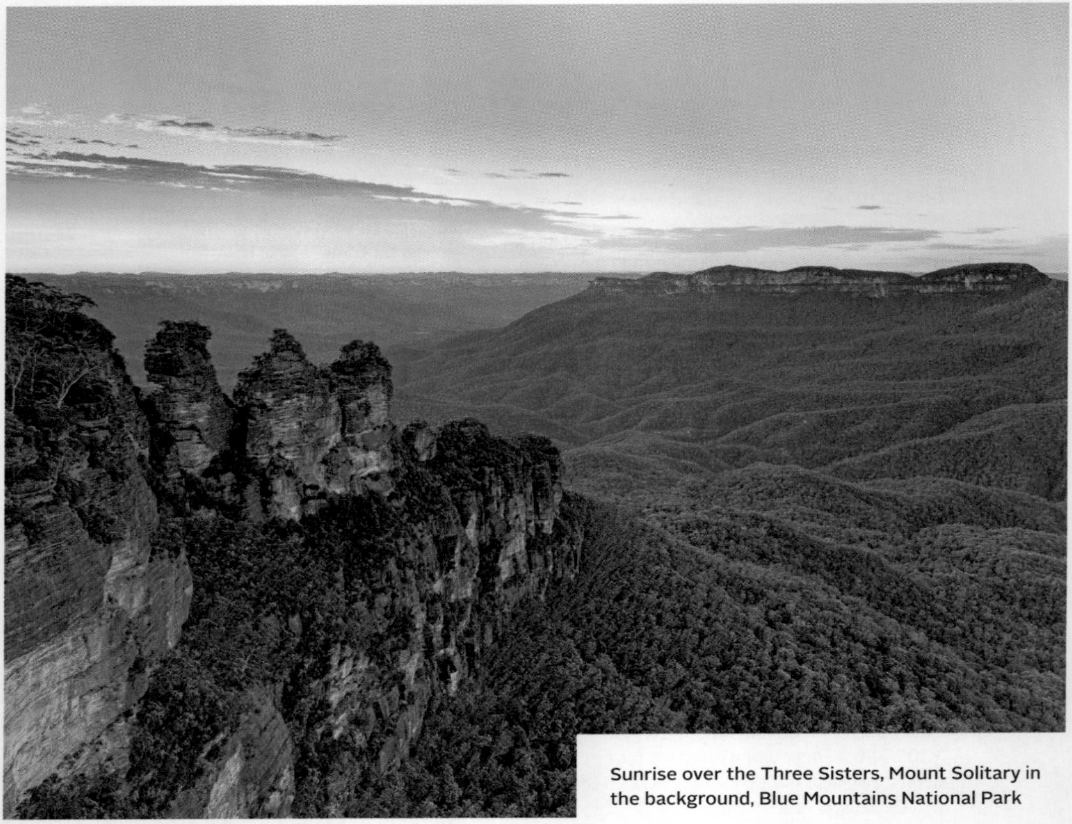

Sunrise over the Three Sisters, Mount Solitary in the background, Blue Mountains National Park

Other significant sites in the national park include The Gully, which contains grinding grooves, camp sites and rock wells as evidence of a permanent residential settlement; Emu Cave, a ceremonial site containing 172 engravings, and likely a placemarker for hunters or a boundary between nation groups; and Red Hands Cave, named after the red, orange and white hand stencils lining its walls, which are estimated to have been painted between 500 and 1600 years ago.

NATURAL FEATURES: High plateaus, sheer cliffs, deep gorges and weathered outcrops (the most famous being the Three Sisters) are all characteristic of the Blue Mountains. Between 190 and 230 million years ago, layers of shale, coal, sandstone and claystone settled into the Sydney Basin, then between 2 and 60 million years ago, those layers were uplifted, buckling and warping to form the Blue Mountains. The sandstone plateau with its peaks of basalt is evidence of volcanic activity, but erosion and weathering have added their own dimension – carving, etching, moulding and relentlessly wearing away. Over time the Grose River has gouged its way through the rock, creating the near-vertical walls of the Grose Valley. The layering is exposed in deep canyons and cliffs that tower up to 200 m. The rivers, creeks and the many waterfalls and cascades are other major features of the park.

THINGS TO DO

With wonderful walks, breathtaking views, idyllic picnic spots and many reminders of the area's Aboriginal and European cultural history, this is one of Australia's most visited national parks. Call in at the Heritage Centre at Blackheath or visitor centres at Echo Point and Glenbrook for detailed information about walking tracks, camping, and Discovery walks, talks and tours (held weekends and school holidays). Wheelchair access is available at various sites and walks, including the Fairfax Heritage Track to Govetts Leap Lookout at Blackheath, and tracks at Echo Point and Katoomba Falls Reserve. Many tours in and around the park are run by private operators – see Aboriginal Blue Mountains Walkabout, p. 283.

This is bushwalking heaven, with over 140 km of walking tracks, from rugged, challenging bushland to paths created for Victorian-era honeymooners. All walkers should carry drinking water and remember that the weather in the mountains can change rapidly, so always be prepared. It is best to pick up a detailed list of walking tracks (there is also 2 km of boardwalk through the rainforest) from the visitor centre and there are some good books available. The following are a few shorter walks. Princes Rock Walk (1.8 km return, 30 minutes to 1 hour, medium difficulty), with its 1890s heritage parapets, leads to one of the national park's impressive lookouts. Mount Banks Track (2.4 km return, 2–3 hours, medium difficulty) lets you take in stunning views, including from the summit of Mount Banks, and an impressive view of the Grose River gorge. Furber Steps–Scenic Railway Walk (2.4 km return, 1–2 hours, medium difficulty) includes a descent via hundreds of steps through luxuriant rainforest with beautiful tree ferns, and past cascades, waterfalls and rock overhangs. Walk to the Rainforest Lookout, where you can gaze over the rainforest canopy. You can then walk to the base of the Scenic Railway, which runs daily, leaving every 10 minutes, so you can ride back up to the starting point.

The park offers a wealth of canyoning opportunities, though many chasms are only suited to those with experience. Rock climbing and abseiling are also extremely popular, as there are some breathtaking sites. These activities are potentially dangerous, so consider joining a group or club. All Aboriginal sites and some other areas are closed to rock climbing and abseiling (ask the NPWS Heritage Centre at Blackheath for more information and details). Canoeing and kayaking offer a peaceful way to explore the park's lower areas, especially after rains, and an excellent chance to observe wildlife.

Cyclists will find a multitude of roads and trails. The Blackheath Tour (10 km) is one of the easiest and takes in splendid views including Govetts Leap, Evans Lookout, Pulpit Rock and Perrys Lookdown. The Woodford-Oaks Trail (27 km one-way, 3.5 hours, medium difficulty) from Woodford to Glenbrook is a classic ride, requiring a little more fitness as you cycle down some steep hills, but you can see Aboriginal rock engravings (at the Circles) and hand stencils (at Red Hands Cave). The ride takes 3–4 hours.

The Grand Circular Tourist Drive (260 km) is one of the country's great touring routes, winding from Sydney up the Great Western Hwy then back through the quieter Bells Line of Road. Spectacular lookouts, access to walking paths, the excellent Heritage Centre at Blackheath, the historic township of Hartley, plummeting waterfalls, sun-dappled glades for picnics and the Blue Mountain Botanic Garden are a few of the highlights en route.

Scenic World in Katoomba combines the Skyway, Cableway and Railway to deliver views of the Blue Mountains from the top of the valley to the rainforest floor. The Scenic Railway, reputedly the world's steepest railway, descends 415 m into the valley and runs daily. For an aerial view, take the Skyway, a 720-m cable-car ride across the startling ravines and waterfalls of Jamison Valley. Fees apply.

WHERE: 50–100 km west of Sydney. Access from Sydney via Great Western Hwy or by train to Glenbrook, Wentworth Falls, Leura, Katoomba, Blackheath or Mount Victoria.

CAMPING AND ACCOMMODATION: There is a host of wonderful camping areas throughout the park that offer a range of activities, including wildlife-watching, swimming, mountain biking, bushwalking, rock climbing and more. Of course, you can opt out of all of these and just relax and take in the bush surroundings and stunning cliff and escarpment views. In the Grose Valley bush camping is restricted to 2 sites. South of the Great Western Hwy, bush camping is permitted but you must keep at least 200 m from public roads and visitor facilities. No camping is allowed within 3 km of the catchment zone of Lake Burragorang. Bookings are required;

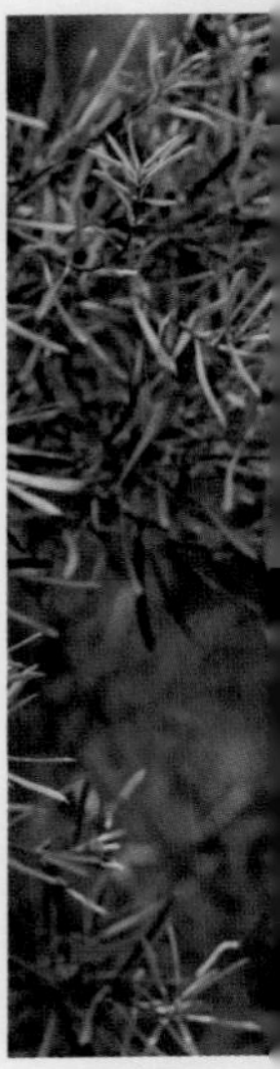

see the NSW NPWS website. There is plenty of private accommodation of all types and standards, including caravan parks, nearby.
CONTACT: Heritage Centre, Blackheath: 02 4787 8877; NPWS Glenbrook: 02 4720 6200; Richmond: 02 4588 2400; Oberon: 02 6336 6200; NSW National Parks Contact Centre: 1300 072 757 (13000 PARKS)

Booderee National Park

Booderee National Park, on the southern side of Jervis Bay, is cloaked in coastal scrub and flowering heath, with crumbling cliffs fronting pale sandy beaches, clear blue waters and a wealth of Aboriginal archaeological sites. Its fascinating landforms, extraordinary diversity of plant and animal life and its lovely beaches make it a favourite holiday destination for Canberra and Sydney residents. The Aboriginal Wreck Bay community lives on the park peninsula and, in association with the Commonwealth Government, administers the national park.

CULTURAL HERITAGE: Koori people have long lived in this area and have strong cultural ties to the region. The former Jervis Bay National Park and adjacent Jervis Botanical Gardens were returned to the Wreck Bay community in 1995. The word Booderee, which the community has chosen for the park, means 'bay of plenty' or 'plenty of fish', and on the southern headland at Wreck Bay, shell middens recall the feasts Aboriginal people had over hundreds of generations. There are also ceremonial grounds, axe-grinding grooves, rock shelters and other sites on the Bherwerre Peninsula.

NATURAL FEATURES: Formidable cliffs and sweeping views are typical of the park. Some of the highest cliffs along the eastern coast, towering 90 m or more, flank isolated Steamers Beach. Most of the peninsula is sandstone and siltstone covered with dunes and sandy soils. It is thought a tsunami may have been responsible for some of the coastal features; for example, the huge boulders along the cliff tops on Beecroft Peninsula and on the fluted rock platform at Stony Creek.

THINGS TO DO

The terrain is gentle and there are many options for walkers. Leaving from Green Patch carpark, Telegraph Creek Nature Trail (2.4-km circuit, 1 hour, easy) loops through eucalypt forest, woodland and heath and across fern-lined creeks. Murrays Beach is ideal for beach walks; for example, at low tide you can stroll along Murrays Beach to Hole in the Wall (1.1 km one way, 30 minutes, easy). Steamers Beach Trail (14.5-km circuit, 5 hours, easy) is a full-day walk, and includes St Georges Head, Whiting Beach and expansive views. There are also walking trails within the Booderee Botanic Gardens. Pick up a detailed list of walks from the visitor centre.

When exposed at low tide, the many rock pools are places to look for sea urchins, crabs, sea stars and other marine life (but be careful not to disturb any creatures). Look out for bottlenose dolphins swimming offshore, and humpback whales on their annual migration north (June–July) and south (September–November). For family swimming, the best beaches are around the sheltered Jervis Bay from Green Patch to Murrays Beach. Surfers should head to Steamers, Cave or Bherwerre beaches. These waters are astonishing for their remarkable underwater scenery, with marine life, underwater cliffs and pristine seagrass meadows. Rock platforms at Murrays Beach and Scottish Rocks are good areas for snorkelling. There is also good line-fishing along the coast (spearfishing and collecting crustaceans and other marine life is prohibited).
WHERE: 200 km south of Sydney; 260 km east of Canberra; 35 km south-east of Nowra; 18 km south-east of Huskisson. Access from: Nowra via Princes Hwy then Jervis Bay Rd; from Huskisson via Jervis Bay Rd.
CAMPING AND ACCOMMODATION: All camp sites are unpowered and the more popular areas book out quickly; apply online at the Parks Australia website. At the time of writing, Green Patch and Bristol Point campgrounds were open, while Cave Beach was closed due to COVID-19. Check the above website for updated information. Fees apply and are payable in advance. Bush camping is not permitted.

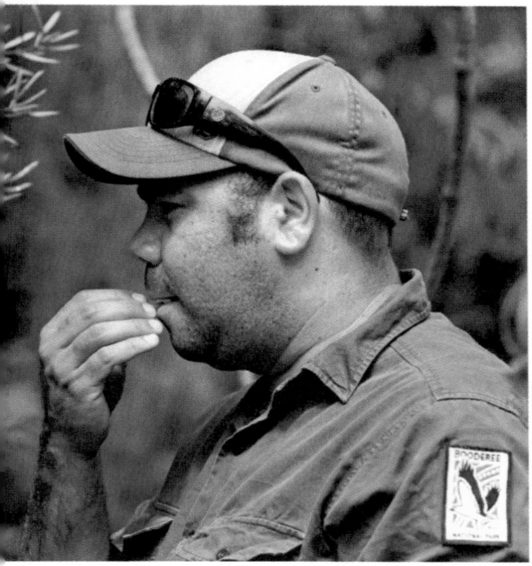

On a bushwalk with Kane Ardler, Booderee National Park

PERMIT: You need a park pass to visit the beaches, landscapes and cultural activities of Booderee National Park. Two-day, 1-year and 2-year passes are available, see the park passes pages of the Parks Australia website for more information.
CONTACT: Booderee Visitor Centre: 02 4443 0977.

Border Ranges National Park

World Heritage–listed rainforest clinging to the edges of an ancient volcano, waterfalls spilling into crystal-clear waterways, and seemingly limitless views are the highlights of the lush wilderness country that makes up Border Ranges National Park. Sprawling across the very northern perimeter of NSW, and extending for 85 km along the Queensland state border, this national park embraces 3 wilderness areas and has World Heritage status. It is an area of great biodiversity, an important haven for native fauna, with the border region said to have the highest concentration of marsupial, bird, snake and frog species in Australia.

CULTURAL HERITAGE: The Githabul language group of the Bundjalung are the traditional custodians of this region but they were driven off their tribal lands at an early stage in European settlement. More recent progress has seen a return of Country in the Border Ranges as part of Githabul Native Title, including transferring care and control of forests and sites within the national park from the Forestry Corporation of NSW to the Githabul people.

NATURAL FEATURES: The park contains part of the eroded remnants of the Wollumbin (Mt Warning) shield volcano, waterfalls and gorges, steep escarpments and rugged ridges. The declared wilderness areas are Warrazambil Wilderness Area in the south-east, Lost World Wilderness Area across the north-eastern section and Levers Wilderness Area in the western section of the park.

THINGS TO DO

A network of excellent tracks crisscrosses the park. The Pinnacle Walk (200 m, 20 minutes, easy) leads through rainforest to the edge of the escarpment and a lookout platform where you can gaze at Mount Warning, the Tweed Valley spread 1000 m below and – on a clear day – as far as the coast. Sunrises here are renowned. On Red Cedar Loop (750 m, 30 minutes, easy) you will see giant rainforest trees encrusted with orchids and staghorns, but the walk's highlight is a grand old red cedar towering 48 m high and said to be 1000 years old. For the more energetic, Booyong Walk (10.5 km one way, 5 hours, medium difficulty) is more demanding, linking Forest Tops and Sheepstation Creek camping areas (start from Forest Tops to avoid a steep climb). You will pass tumbling waterfalls and can even stop for a swim en route. If you choose to cool off in the rocky streams or water pools, do not wear sunscreen or insect repellent: these can contaminate the water for wildlife, including endangered frogs.

The park provides many opportunities for photography, with majestic waterfalls, craggy ridges wreathed in mist and magnificent old-growth

rainforest trees. There are some excellent lookouts. Tweed Scenic Drive (gravel road, suitable for 2WD except in the wet, may be slippery November to May) loops from Murwillumbah to Kyogle and Lismore and offers stunning views. Cycling is permitted on trails and roads and some cyclists ride the Tweed Scenic Drive. There are 7 dedicated picnic areas; all except Brindle Creek have barbecues and most have shelters.
WHERE: 880 km north of Sydney; 27 km north of Kyogle; 40 km west of Murwillumbah. Access: from Kyogle via Summerland Way, Lions Rd, Simes Rd then Tweed Range Scenic Dr (latter winds 64 km through park); from Murwillumbah via Murwillumbah–Kyogle Rd then Creegan Rd to Tweed Range Scenic Dr (unsealed roads).
CAMPING: There are 2 camping areas in the park, Sheepstation Creek and Forest Tops. Access to both includes unpaved roads (accessible by 2WD). Both campgrounds have toilets, picnic tables, barbecues and firewood supplied but there is no drinking water. Fees apply. Bush camping is permitted (keep 200 m from public roads, walking tracks and other facilities) but vehicle-based bush camping is prohibited. Bookings are required; see the NSW NPWS website.
CONTACT: NPWS Kyogle: 02 6632 0000; NSW National Parks Contact Centre: 1300 072 757 (13000 PARKS)

Bouddi National Park

Heavily timbered hills and cliffs rise behind a cluster of lovely beaches at Bouddi National Park south-east of Gosford. The park's attractions include one of Australia's first marine protected areas and even an old paddlesteamer wreck.

CULTURAL HERITAGE: The park is of special significance for its Aboriginal heritage. The Hawkesbury River and the Pacific Ocean provided a rich source of bush tucker with freshwater fish and marine seafood for the Guringai (Kurringgai) people, the traditional custodians of this region. Around 100 Aboriginal sites have been recorded on the Bouddi Peninsula, including shell middens, rock engravings and rock shelters.

THINGS TO DO

Walkers can strike out on a number of tracks through the heathland, eucalypt woodland and open forest. Maitland Bay Track (850 m, 30–40 minutes return), from the visitor centre to Maitland Bay, is worthwhile, but is quite a steep haul on the way back. The more energetic might tackle Bouddi Coastal Walk (8 km, 4 hours return, medium difficulty) from the eastern end of Putty Beach then climb the stairs to Gerrin Point Lookout for panoramic coastal views. Call in at the Maitland Bay visitor centre for advice on other walking tracks.

The park is a mecca for those seeking sun, sand and surf, peaceful camping and a spot of fishing. Putty Beach, crescent-shaped Maitland Bay (ideal for swimming and snorkelling) and Lobster Beach (favoured by boaters) are all popular. None of the beaches are patrolled. The remains of the paddlesteamer *Maitland*, wrecked off Maitland Bay in 1898, can be seen rusting in the surf. A marine extension to the park extends across Maitland Bay, protecting all marine life. Sweeping Tallow Beach is subject to strong rips and currents, but keen surfers will find good breaks, mainly between MacMasters Beach and Box Head. Rock fishing is popular, but take care on rock platforms.
WHERE: 95 km north of Sydney; 19 km south-east of Gosford via Scenic Rd (access is at Putty Beach).
CAMPING: There are 3 campgrounds in Bouddi National Park, ranging from remote with basic facilities (toilets, barbecues) to larger sites well-equipped with barbecues, toilets, showers and drinking water. All have easy access to the park's stunning beaches. Bookings are required; see the NSW NPWS website.
CONTACT: NPWS Girrakool: 02 4320 4200; NPWS Lake Munmorah: 02 4972 9000; NSW National Parks Contact Centre: 1300 072 757 (13000 PARKS)

Brisbane Water National Park

Created as a reserve in 1959, this park embraces a rugged sandstone landscape known for its beautiful wildflowers and Aboriginal sites. Visitors can also enjoy scenic views, bushwalking and water activities like fishing and kayaking.

CULTURAL HERITAGE: The Dharug and Darkingjung people occupied the area for thousands of years and there are outstanding rock engravings at Bulgandry, on Woy Woy Road.

NATURAL FEATURES: Rainforest runs through the valleys and along the streams, with low open woodland and open eucalypt forest elsewhere. The rich flora supports more than 270 animal species and 150 bird species. Threatened species include the diminutive eastern pygmy-possum and the long-nosed poteroo. You will often hear the echoing call of the whipbird, or the carolling of currawongs, and the native brush-turkey can sometimes be glimpsed scraping through the leaf litter beside walking tracks. Somersby Falls, hidden in a cool pocket of rainforest, and myriad wildflowers in spring are other park highlights.

THINGS TO DO

There is a network of walking trails, including part of the Great North Walk (a 250 km trail from Sydney to Newcastle). The Girrakool loop track (2 km loop, 30 minutes–1 hour, medium difficulty) from Girrakool picnic area offers scenic views over waterfalls and colourful wildflowers during late winter and early spring. Check out the Aboriginal rock engravings near the beginning of the walk and stop at Illoura lookout and the shady waterfall at Andamira lookout for a photo. Wildlife watchers will enjoy the Mooney Mooney Nature Walk (4.2 km one-way, 2.5–3.5 hrs, hard), which follows the secluded gorge along Piles Creek. Head to Waratah Trig and Staples Lookout for stunning views.
WHERE: 70 km north of Sydney; 12 km south-west of Gosford via Pacific Hwy then turn off at Kariong for access to Girrakool; via Wisemans Ferry Rd for Somersby Falls; via Woy Woy Rd for Patonga.
PERMIT: You will need a permit to hold a wedding or undertake commercial photography within the park.
CONTACT: NPWS Girrakool: 02 4320 4200; NPWS Lake Munmorah: 02 4972 9000; NSW National Parks Contact Centre: 1300 072 757 (13000 PARKS)

Bundjalung National Park

Bundjalung National Park, on the north coast of NSW, is one of the most beautiful national parks in Australia, with its scenic coastlines and lush bushland. It stretches north from Iluka to Evans Head, and meets the Pacific Ocean on the east. The park is in the land of the Bundjalung people. It can be subject to closure due to bad weather or danger of fires. The NSW NPWS recommends visiting during spring, as this is whale-spotting season. Winter can be nice, to avoid a visit during the scorching summer heat, and it can still be warm enough to swim.

CULTURAL HERITAGE: This park is one of a group (including neighbouring Broadwater National Park) where the Bundjalung people's Native Title rights have been recognised and is one of 4 determinations of Native Title rights in NSW. Native Title rights come from the Bundjalung people's traditional laws and customs and legally recognises their connection to Country. This means that these lands will continue to be places of Indigenous ceremony, learning and inspiration for generations to come.

Dreaming stories tell of how animals helped to shape the land. At the centre of the Bundjalung beliefs is the battle between the Goanna and the Snake. They formed the Evans River as they fought, creating the headland coast known today as Evans Head.

The Gummigurrah area in the park was once used as a winter camp for the Bundjalung people and the remains of a midden can be seen near the end of the Gummigurrah walking track, located close to the Evans Head entrance.

NATURAL FEATURES: The national park extends from Evans Head and the Evans River in the north to the Clarence River in the south. Along the coast the long crescent of Ten Mile Beach stretches between the 2 river estuaries. The park protects a large sand-dune system, heathlands that are part of a discontinuous coastal chain along which animals migrate, coastal wetlands and foreshores, ancient rainforest, and the unspoiled Esk River, which is the largest untouched coastal river system on the north coast. Rocky headlands are a feature of the Iluka peninsula, while in the north some dunes rise to around 70 m above sea level.

WHERE: The closest town is Evans Head. 703 km north of Sydney; 50 km south of Ballina via Pacific Hwy then Woodburn–Evans Head Rd; 60 km north of Grafton via Pacific Hwy then Iluka Rd or further north at Gap Rd.

CAMPING: There are 2 campgrounds, Black Rocks, with 50 sites, and Woody Head, with 94 sites. Bookings are required; see the NSW NPWS website. There is also cabin accommodation in the park: Woody Head cottages and cabins, Forest House, and Swamp House and Bunkhouse, all bookable via the NPWS website.

CONTACT: NPWS Clarence North Area: 02 6641 1500; NPWS Alstonville: 02 6627 0200; NPWS Grafton: 02 6641 1500; NSW National Parks Contact Centre: 1300 072 757 (13000 PARKS)

Stunning sandstone patterns of Bouddi (photo Wayne Quilliam)

Conjola National Park

Located on the state's south coast, Conjola National Park embraces a landscape of woodland and heath, creek and river estuaries, the tranquil beauty of Swan Lake and the sweeping Cudmirrah and Monument beaches. The mild coastal climate and unspoiled natural environment ensure plenty of opportunities for bushwalking, birdwatching, picnicking, swimming and surfing. Areas of the park were affected by the 2019/2020 bushfires, but there are signs of recovery and sites and walking tracks have reopened.

CULTURAL HERITAGE: Budawang and Yuin people have used the area's resources for at least 6000 years and evidence of their occupation include shell middens, scattered artefacts and rock shelters.

NATURAL FEATURES: Sandy beaches lapped by the Tasman Sea are one of the park's biggest drawcards but the lakes and hinterland also have much to offer. The park is especially rich in plant life and almost 430 species have been identified, including a wealth of flowering plants and 35 native orchids. From spring to summer there are masses of wildflowers and in winter banksias come into bloom.

THINGS TO DO

Swan Lake and the surrounding wetlands provide a habitat for waterbirds, in particular the graceful black swan. Elsewhere in the park are significant habitats for the gang-gang cockatoo, glossy black cockatoo, powerful owl and the hooded plover.

WHERE: 208 km south of Sydney; 6 km south of Sussex Inlet; park surrounds Cudmirrah (access via Goonawarra Dr) and Berrara (access to Fishermans Rock); access to Monument picnic area via Bendalong Rd then Cedar Rd; unsealed roads.

CONTACT: NPWS Ulladulla: 02 4454 9500; NPWS Nowra: 02 4428 6300; NSW National Parks Contact Centre: 1300 072 757 (13000 PARKS)

Dharawal National Park

Located south-west of the massively popular Royal National Park (see p. 378), Dharawal is a hidden gem within easy reach of Sydney which offers immersive bushwalks to freshwater swimming holes, chances to spot local wildlife, scenic lookouts, waterfalls and more. Previous to it becoming a national park, it was a water catchment area and then state conservation area, so 70 years of restricted public access has left the natural environment largely untouched.

CULTURAL HERITAGE: Dharawal was declared a national park in 2012, making it one of the newest in NSW. Though this status change is recent, its connection with its Traditional Owners, the Dharawal people, is ancient, and there are many protected sites within the park that serve as evidence to their history there.

THINGS TO DO

Swimming, bushwalking and cycling are all popular in the park, allowing visitors to enjoy their pristine surrounds. The Jingga walking track (2.4 km return, 1–1.5 hrs, medium difficulty) is a short walk and can be challenging for its steep gradient, but very rewarding for those who wish to take a dip in the beautiful freshwater swimming hole found at its end. Jingga means 'nice and sweet' in Dharawal language, and it's no doubt that this little oasis is what that relates to. The Minerva Pool walking track (2.4 km return, 2 hours, medium) takes you on a picturesque journey through the bush, past Sydney golden wattle and mountain devil shrub, both used in Dharawal bush food and medicine. At the end of the track lies the pristine Minerva pool, with its waterfall, sandstone features and a small stone island.

Please note: Minerva Pool is a sacred women's place for the Dharawal people and only women and children may enter its waters. Please move through this important place with respect.

The 10B cycling trail is a 15 km (one way) mountain bike track that's perfect for beginner and intermediate riders and small groups. It starts at the park's southern entry (Appin Rd) and takes you along a sandstone ridge, through open forest and woodland, with the last 3 km proving the most challenging with its final descent into Stokes Creek Gorge and climb back up to the northern entrance at Wedderburn.

WHERE: 48 km south-west of Sydney CBD; 16 km west of Helensburgh.

CONTACT: NPWS Wollongong: 02 4224 4188; NSW National Parks Contact Centre: 1300 072 757 (13000 PARKS)

Eurobodalla National Park

This sliver of national park runs in 3 sections along the south coast between Moruya Heads and Tilba Tilba Lake, just south of Cape Dromedary. It is particularly picturesque, with 30 km of lovely beaches, broken by estuaries and backed by wetlands, lakes and spotted gum forest. At Bingie Bingie Point and Congo Point there are significant Aboriginal artefacts. European settlement dates from the 1870s, and an old pilot station at South Head Moruya, now a meteorological station, remains from the days when coastal steamers plied the Moruya River.

CULTURAL HERITAGE: The park is on the traditional land of the Yuin people, and it served as a rich resource of food, medicine, shelter and weapons. The Bingi Dreaming track leads you along Aboriginal songlines, ancient navigators that link camp sites, fresh water sources and other significant locations.

NATURAL FEATURES: Eucalypts are the dominant species, but there are stretches of banksia woodland and low open grassland with feathery casuarinas and mangroves in low-lying areas near the estuaries. An array of fauna includes possums and gliders and 11 bat species. The ocean, river and freshwater habitats attract many migratory waterbirds including 17 wader species in summer. In season, eastern curlews, whimbrels and godwits can be seen probing in and around the coastal waters. More majestic birds such as the whitebellied sea-eagle and the whistling kite frequent the skies, and black swans and chestnut teals congregate around the lakes and estuaries.

THINGS TO DO

The Bingi Dreaming track (13.5 km one way, 4–6 hours) takes you on a coastal walk through different types of coastal habitat. You can also canoe on Congo Creek, Lake Tarourga and Lake Brou. The park's beaches are beautiful but are not patrolled (there are patrolled beaches during peak season at nearby towns).

WHERE: 320 km south of Sydney; 28 km north of Narooma via Princes Hwy; 10 km east of Moruya via Moruya Heads.

CAMPING: There are 2 campgrounds in Eurobodalla National Park, from which you can choose quiet bush camping or popular family fun. Each is in a great location near the beach, perfect for fishing and paddling. Bookings are required; see the NSW NPWS website. Beachcomber Holiday Park offers camping and well-equipped cabins close the beach and Tuross Lake.

CONTACT: NPWS Narooma: 02 4476 0800; NSW National Parks Contact Centre: 1300 072 757 (13000 PARKS)

Garigal National Park

One of Sydney's small gems, Garigal National Park offers a bush retreat just 12 km from the city's hectic centre, a precious pocket of natural bushland with steep forested slopes, fine water views and terrific walking tracks. The park is in 2 sections, one skimming around Middle Harbour then bordering several creeks, and the East Garigal section protecting Deep Creek catchment area.

CULTURAL HERITAGE: The park was named after a local Indigenous group, and nearly 100 recorded Aboriginal sites in the park, including rock engravings, cave art and shell middens, are tangible evidence of early Aboriginal occupation. Today the park is hemmed in by the ever-increasing urban development.

NATURAL FEATURES: Sandstone ridges and escarpments to the west and north of the park slope gently to the Narrabeen Lakes, ensuring superb views across the bushland. Vegetation is varied, ranging from dry heath to moist forest with unusual eucalypt species and grevillea. Nocturnal mammals are the main animals and birdlife includes honeyeaters, noisy butcherbirds and the hawk-like powerful owl.

THINGS TO DO

Walking tracks wind around the harbour shores and some of the creeks, occasionally past waterholes and small waterfalls, and link with tracks to the area's leafy suburbs. Swimming and canoeing on the calm waters are other possible activities. Bushwalkers will especially enjoy the East Garigal section where short and longer trails enable visitors to delve a little deeper into the tranquil bush (contact the NPWS for detailed walking-trail maps). Horse riding is also allowed on some (signposted) tracks in the north-west section of the park.

Middle Harbour is well known for its boating and fishing (boat ramps open day and night). The Davidson Park Picnic Area is a favourite with families (gates here close at 6.30 pm; 8 pm during daylight saving).

WHERE: 12 km north of the Sydney CDB via Warringah Rd to Davidson Park Picnic Area or via Morgan Rd to East Garigal section of the park.

CONTACT: NPWS Forestville: 02 9451 3479; Bobbin Head Information Centre: 02 9472 8949; NSW National Parks Contact Centre: 1300 072 757 (13000 PARKS)

Gundabooka National Park

The awesome scale and quiet grandeur of outback NSW is laid out before you at Gundabooka National Park, 90 minutes' drive from Bourke in the state's far west. Stretching from the banks of the Darling River to the Gunderbooka Range, this is a majestic landscape of woodlands, floodplains and sandhills, spread out beneath the ancient and watchful eye of 500-m Mount Gunderbooka.

CULTURAL HERITAGE: This is traditional Ngemba country, and traces of their long-held association with the land can be found on the Mulareenya Creek Art Site Track (1 km return, 30 minutes), which leads to an impressive display of Aboriginal rock art.

NATURAL FEATURES: Observant visitors will be rewarded with sights of grazing red, eastern grey or western grey kangaroos. Look to the skies for glimpses of majestic wedge-tailed eagles around Mt Gunderbooka, as well as red-tailed black-cockatoos and brightly coloured eastern ringneck parrots – just a few of the more than 130 bird species recorded in the park.

THINGS TO DO

As well as the Mulareenya Creek Art Site Track, other walks include the Bennetts Gorge picnic area walk (1 km return, easy), which will take you to the foot of Mt Gunderbooka; and Little Mountain Track (4.8 km return, 2–3 hours, hard), which meanders through mulga woodlands and up to the summit of Little Mountain, from where you can gaze across the northern escarpment of Gunderbooka Range. Visitors can enjoy a picnic at Bennetts Gorge, Dry Tank or Mulgowan picnic areas.

WHERE: 830 km north-west of Sydney; 70 km south-west of Bourke via The Kidman Way (State Route 87), from entrance road is unsealed and closed in wet weather.

CAMPING: There are 2 camp sites, Dry Tank and Yanda. Facilities are basic, and you'll need to bring your own water. Bookings are required; see the NSW NPWS website. Comfortable accommodation is available at the restored Belah Shearer's Quarters, or Redbank Homestead, both within the park. Fees apply.

CONTACT: NPWS Bourke: 02 6830 0200; NSW National Parks Contact Centre: 1300 072 757 (13000 PARKS)

Kamay Botany Bay National Park

Kamay Botany Bay National Park, now surrounded by Sydney suburbia, is the site of Captain James Cook's first landing on the mainland of the continent in 1770. In 1788, within days of the arrival of the First Fleet, French explorer Comte de Laperouse also sailed into the bay. The park, occupying the bay's 2 headlands, includes sites of important pre-colonial history, as well as retains significant remnants of the original vegetation. It is split into 2 sections: La Perouse and Kurnell.

CULTURAL HISTORY: Rock engravings are among the 30 or so Aboriginal sites that recall occupation of the Gweagal and Goorawal peoples. Join an Aboriginal Discovery tour with the park, or see Kadoo Tours (p. 389) for a guided walk and an insight into this Indigenous heritage.

NATURAL FEATURES: Heath and scrub spread across the La Perouse section, with banksias, grasstrees, she-oaks, paperbarks and cabbage palms in the northern section, typical of those that botanists Joseph Banks and Daniel Solander studied in 1770. The park's animals are mainly shy and nocturnal but there is ample birdlife, with threatened species such as the powerful owl, along with peregrine falcons and fairy-wrens as well as innumerable honeyeaters and parrots.

THINGS TO DO

The easy 200-m Dharawal Walking Track takes you to Dharawal Resting Place, a significant site where various Aboriginal ancestral remains are buried, and part of the Coast Hospital Cemetery. Take your time to read the headstones and information boards as you wander through to learn more about the stories of both Aboriginal and colonial heritage. There are trails and roads suitable for cyclists, walking tracks that crisscross the park, boardwalks through the scrub, favourite spots for family picnics, and some fabulous views.

Plan your visit so you can take in the Blak Markets, Aboriginal cultural markets that feature dance performances, art and craft stalls and bush tucker (see p. 398).

Swimmers will find sheltered coves and snorkelling and diving spots with reeds, seagrass meadows and a shipwreck off Cape Banks. The bay has good fishing.

WHERE: 15 km south of Sydney via La Perouse then Anzac Pde (northern section) and via Kurnell then Captain Cook Dr (southern section).

CONTACT: Randwick City Council: 02 9093 6190; Kurnell Visitor Centre: 02 9668 2010; NSW National Parks Contact Centre: 1300 072 757 (13000 PARKS)

Kinchega National Park

An hour's drive from Broken Hill in the state's far west, Kinchega National Park is an outback vision splendid, where red and sunburnt plains meet the iconic Darling River and the immense Menindee Lake system. For several years after a flood event, the lakes are vast mirrors reflecting sprawling river red gums, thriving birdlife, brazen blue skies and heart-stopping sunrises and sunsets. Menindee Lakes are a system of ephemeral freshwater lakes fed by floodwater from the Darling River. The 4 largest lakes comprise the Menindee Lakes Water Storage Scheme, and 2 of these – Cawndilla and Menindee – are within Kinchega National Park.

CULTURAL HERITAGE: The region's Traditional Owners, the Paakantji people, occupied the region for tens of thousands of years before European contact. Numerous Aboriginal sites have already been recorded in the park, including shell middens, burial grounds and earth ovens. The close association of the Paakantji people to their Country continues into the present day in the form of joint management of Kinchega National Park by NPWS and the Menindee Aboriginal Elders Council.

NATURAL FEATURES: Kinchega National Park is part arid and part river country. When the lakes are full, the region is a riot of birdlife; as the water recedes, it is replaced by a carpet of green grazed by emus and kangaroos. Huge river red gums stand sentinel over the riverbanks and floodplains. Move away from the river and its floodplains and you'll find yourself among sandplains and dunefields, characterised by that quintessentially outback red soil.

THINGS TO DO

Guided Discovery tours run during school holidays in Easter, winter and spring school holidays. These include ranger talks, billy tea with Paakantji Aboriginal Elders and tours of the old Kinchega homestead.

There are 3 self-guided drives to do in the park. The River Drive winds through the river red gum woodlands on the banks of the Darling River; the Lake Drive takes in lakes Menindee and Cawndilla; and the Woolshed Drive heads out to the historic Kinchega Woolshed as well as the old Kinchega homestead and cemetery.

The most coveted fishing spot in the park is below Weir 32 on the Darling River. Your catch of the day could be European carp, golden perch, Murray cod or silver perch. You'll need a licence to throw a line in, and be aware of relevant regulations pertaining to bag limits and species.

WHERE: 113 km south-east of Broken Hill via Menindee–Broken Hill Rd; 630 km north-east of Adelaide; from Wentworth via Wentworth–Pooncarie Rd.

CAMPING AND ACCOMMODATION: There are camp sites along the Darling River, and at Emu Lake and Lake Cawndilla. Facilities at all these sites include picnic tables, wood barbecues and non-flush toilets. There are gas/electric barbecues at Lake Cawndilla campground. Bring your own firewood and drinking water, and be aware of weather conditions, as rain can lead to road closures. Bookings are required; see the NSW NPWS website. Basic accommodation is available in the heritage surroundings of the restored Kinchega Shearers' Quarters, which sleeps up to 27 people in six bedrooms. Hot showers are available at the Shearers' Quarters by gold coin donation. Book online or call NSW NPWS.

CONTACT: NPWS Broken Hill: 08 8084 2880; NSW National Parks Contact Centre: 1300 072 757 (13000 PARKS)

Kosciuszko National Park

Located in the Snowy Mountains, Kosciuszko National Park boasts Australia's largest and highest continental mountain, Mt Kosciuszko. With 7 adventure-filled areas within the park, visitors who love the outdoors will never be idle here. Areas of the park were damaged in the 2019/2020 bushfires; much of the park has reopened, but at the time of writing, many areas have been scheduled for infrastructure repairs. Please check the NSW NPWS website for up-to-date information before you visit; fees vary for different areas of the park.

CULTURAL HERITAGE: The park is in the lands of the Ngarigo people, around Cooma, and the Bidawal people, from around Bombala. Today there are many people living in south-eastern Australia who have traditional connections to the Australian Alps. Aboriginal camp sites dating back 20,000 years have been found within the valleys of the Snowy Mountains and along the upper Snowy River, and prehistoric burial sites are also found in the Snowy Mountains. In 2011, a memorandum of understanding was signed by Tumut Brungle Gundagai Area Aboriginal community and NSW NPWS to ensure that the local Aboriginal community is involved in the management of culturally significant areas of northern Kosciuszko National Park.

NATURAL FEATURES: Kosciuszko National Park straddles the Great Divide, its altitude ranging from just 200 m in the Snowy River valley to the peak of Mount Kosciuszko at 2228 m. This is the highest part of the continent, where glacial action has left 5 glacial lakes, including the icy Blue Lake, Australia's highest lake. There are many different types of rock, with the oldest marine sediments 450 million years old, but granitic rock such as that at the summit of Mount Kosciuszko is the most common. An outstanding natural feature is the spectacular Yarrangobilly Caves, with their dramatic limestone formations.

THINGS TO DO

The Thredbo-Perisher area is the gateway to Mt Kosciuszko. It is ideal in winter for visitors who love to ski and snowboard in the fresh snow. Lower Snowy River area allows visitors to camp beside the Snowy River and explore the area by walking, cycling or horse riding. Khancoban area is perfect for

New South Wales presents a range of stunning landscapes (photo Wayne Quilliam)

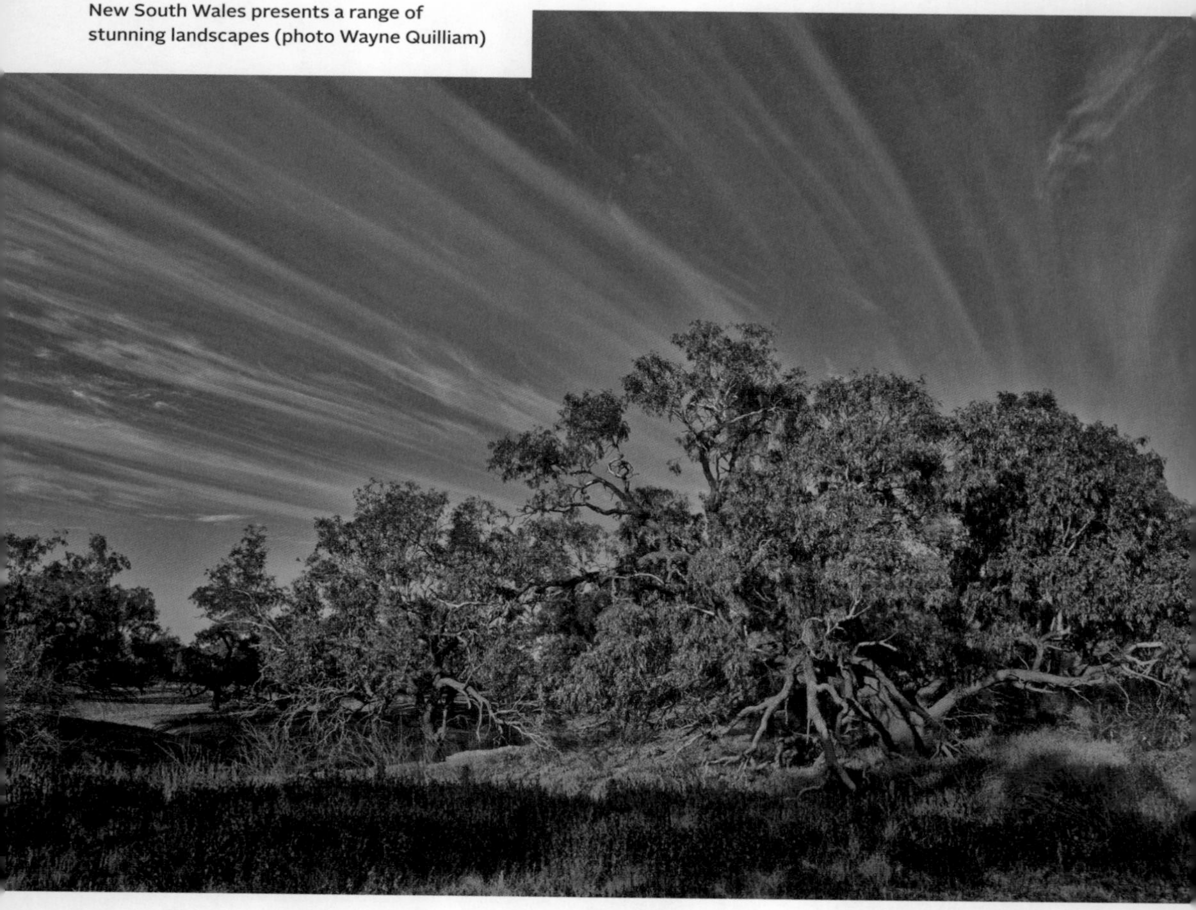

visitors who enjoy fishing and hiking. Selwyn area is where visitors can find the family-friendly Selwyn Snow resort. Yarrangobilly area has incredible caves and thermal pools. The Tumut area is full of walking trails and waterfalls. Visitors can also participate in water sports at the Blowering Dam. The High Plains area is ideal in summer to explore the walking trails and gorges. Located on the north-east side of Kosciuszko National Park, it is the perfect place to camp in summer.

WHERE: Snowy Mountains. For the many entrances to the park check the website.

WHEN: All year round. Some roads and trails may be closed due to park maintenance or poor weather conditions.

CONTACT: NPWS Snowy Region: 02 6450 5600; NPWS Tumut: 02 6947 7025; NPWS Khancoban: 02 6070 8400; NPWS Yarrangobilly Caves: 02 6454 9597; NPWS Perisher Valley: 02 6457 4444; NSW National Parks Contact Centre: 1300 072 757 (13000 PARKS)

Ku-ring-gai Chase National Park

Just north of Sydney, historic Ku-ring-gai Chase National Park constantly surprises with its tree-covered headlands, sheltered coves, wide peaceful estuaries and wonderful blue-water views. It is rich in both Aboriginal and European heritage.

One of NSW's most loved and most visited parks, declared in 1894 and thus the state's 2nd oldest national park, Ku-ring-gai Chase preserves an important stretch of natural bushland as well as the lower reaches of the Hawkesbury River and a number of its tributaries. It is scenically beautiful, provides important breeding and roosting sites for numerous bird species and contains significant Aboriginal sites. It is also an outstanding recreation area, enabling visitors to savour the pleasures of this relatively undisturbed bush so close to Sydney.

CULTURAL HERITAGE: The park takes in part of the traditional lands of the Guringai people, and 800 sites, including some of the state's finest Aboriginal art sites, are found in the escarpment country. Engravings have been etched into the soft, smooth sandstone and drawings, stencils and paintings embellish caves and rock overhangs.

Axe-grinding grooves indicate where stone axes were sharpened and middens can be seen near caves or along the waterways where people fished or collected shellfish. It is a precious legacy dating back 10,000 years. Join a guided tour to discover more about the park's Indigenous heritage (see Guringai Aboriginal Tours, p. 389).

THINGS TO DO

Ask at Kalkari Visitor Centre about the Discovery programs, which include guided tours to see Aboriginal art sites, as well as wildlife and more. Walking is by far the best and sometimes the only way to experience much of the park, including its Aboriginal sites. There are tracks for all different levels of fitness and expertise. Secret beaches, expansive views, birdlife and colourful wildflowers in spring and summer are also highlights. Garigal Aboriginal Heritage Walk at West Head (4.4 km loop, 2.5–3.5 hours, hard) is fascinating. You can also follow Elvina Track (7 km one way, 2.5 hours, medium difficulty) to see Aboriginal rock engravings, waterfalls, water pools and rainforest. Willunga Trig Walk (1.5 km return, 30 minutes–1.5 hours, hard) takes you through heathland and woodland to Willunga Trig, the park's highest point, and some dazzling 360-degree views. Or make the steep climb to the 1881 sandstone Barrenjoey Lighthouse at Broken Bay for tremendous coastal views. There is also a wheelchair-friendly Discovery Walking Trail from Kalkari Visitor Centre. Pick up detailed maps from Bobbin Head Visitor Centre.

Limited climbing and abseiling are allowed at Barrenjoey Head. Swimming at the sheltered beaches and in freshwater pools, fishing (flathead, tailor, mullet and snapper are typical catches) and relaxing at the water's edge are other options.

The deeply indented coastline ensures excellent opportunities for sailing and boating, and there always seem to be dinghies afloat and canoes swishing by on the peaceful waters. There are 2 marinas within the park, at Bobbin Head and Akuna Bay. There are also 15 km of horse-riding trails in the Terrey Hills and Duffys Forest areas.

WHERE: 30 km north of Sydney CBD, from Sydney by road: to North Turramurra then via Bobbin Head Rd; off Pacific Hwy at Mt Colah/Asquith then Ku-ring-gai Chase Rd; from Terrey Hills or Church Point then McCarrs Creek Rd; or by bus, ferry or rail.

CAMPING: Camping (for 400 visitors) is permitted at The Basin only, near West Head. Bookings are required: 02 9974 1011; fees apply. Vehicle parking is a 2.8-km walk from the camping area (most facilities are available including drinking water). There is also access by water via private boat, ferry from Palm Beach Wharf, or water taxi.

CONTACT: NPWS Bobbin Head: 02 9472 8949; NSW National Parks Contact Centre: 1300 072 757 (13000 PARKS)

Mimosa Rocks National Park

At Mimosa Rocks National Park, in the state's south, a ragged coastline of volcanic rock has been hewn by weather and water into sculptural cliffs, rock stacks and jutting headlands. The park offers plenty of opportunities for recreation and relaxation.

Mimosa Rocks National Park lies on the state's far south coast between Bermagui and Tathra. The 16-km coastline, a succession of beaches tucked into coves and small bays, is backed by low timbered hills. Recreational activities are primarily beach-based – swimming, surfing, fishing and snorkelling – although, there are some enjoyable short walks. There is a choice of picnic and camping sites, some more basic than others but offering a little more solitude.

CULTURAL HERITAGE: The park encompasses part of the territory of the Yuin people, who enjoyed its abundance of seafood and bush tucker – the park was an important source of sustenance, shelter and medicine, and its landscape is strongly connected to Dreaming stories. Signs such as shell middens and open camp sites indicate that Aboriginal people lived in this region for at least 6000 years. The Mimosa Rocks walking track is an excellent way to see these sites and learn more about Yuin history here.

NATURAL FEATURES: The park's most distinctive natural feature is its rock formations, a mix of slate, granite, basalt and volcanic rock, folded, faulted and shaped by weathering over millions of years.

THINGS TO DO

There are plenty of short and easy walks. Nelson Lagoon Walk (300 m one way, 18 minutes) is worth doing to see the lagoon and watch for birds (especially in spring). Mimosa Rocks Walk (2 km return, 30 minutes–1 hour, easy) from Aragunnu links the southern and northern picnic areas. From the northern area, a wheelchair-accessible path and boardwalk (250 m) lead to a lookout over the intriguing Mimosa Rocks, scene of an historic shipwreck. The headlands are good spots to watch for humpback whales (June–July when they migrate north, September–October when they return south).

The beaches are lovely but there are strong currents. There is patrolled swimming (in peak periods) at Tathra, Bermagui and Merimbula and some good surfing along the coast. Keen canoeists willing to lug their canoe about 300 m can paddle on Middle Lagoon or Nelson Lagoon (although Wapengo Lake, which adjoins the park, is more readily accessible). Kayaking along the coastline is another option. Or you can try some rock or beach fishing, enjoy a picnic (there are gas barbecues at Aragunnu, Picnic Point, Bithry Inlet, Middle Beach and Gillards Beach), or take your camera and capture some of the coast's unique rock formations and ocean skies.

WHERE: 401 km south of Sydney; 23 km south of Bermagui; 10 km north of Tathra Access from Bermagui or Tathra via Tathra–Bermagui Rd (access via gravel roads, but suitable for 2WD vehicles; take care in the wet).

CAMPING AND ACCOMMODATION: There are several designated camp sites in attractive settings. Bush camping is permitted but due to the small size of the park, not encouraged; camping is not allowed on Bunga Head. Campers should carry drinking water as fresh water is not readily available in the park. Bookings are required; see the NSW NPWS website.

Accommodation at historic Myer House offers self-contained accommodation for up to 12 people and overlooks Bithry Inlet, the mouth of pristine Wapengo Lake.

CONTACT: NPWS Narooma: 02 4476 0800; NSW National Parks Contact Centre: 1300 072 757 (13000 PARKS)

Morton National Park

An expanse of spectacular sandstone country on the eastern escarpment of the Southern Tablelands, Morton National Park is a world of dense bush, its plateau rent by deep gullies and thundering waterfalls, and in the south, mountainous terrain and tracts of wilderness including the rugged Budawang Ranges.

This national park has been a retreat for visitors for more than a century and well-developed visitor sites are a feature in the northern section. In the south, experienced walkers can savour the wilderness.

CULTURAL HERITAGE: This is the traditional Country of the Yuin people, whose occupation dates back over 20,000 years. The area is rich in Aboriginal cultural sites, numbering in the hundreds. Many of the valleys and ridge lines were traditionally part of a route from the hinterland to the coast, and sites such as Didthul and Fitzroy Falls are distinct features in Aboriginal ancestral stories. Visit the Fitzroy Falls Visitor Centre for more information about the local Aboriginal history of Morton National Park.

NATURAL FEATURES: The powerful Shoalhaven River flows through the park, as does a web of smaller rivers and creeks. Vegetation is a patchwork of tall eucalypt forest, mallee woodlands and heathland, with cool temperate rainforest thriving in sheltered aspects and in the moist fertile soil along creeks. Extensive tracts are officially declared wilderness areas.

THINGS TO DO

Call in to the Fitzroy Falls Visitor Centre for helpful information on this park. A wheelchair-friendly boardwalk leads to the falls and excellent views. Ask at the visitor centre for a list of walking tracks – they are numerous. In the northern section of the park are the East Rim and Wildflower walking tracks (6.7 km return, 2–3 hours, medium). Follow the well-marked trail with its interpretive signs and enjoy wildflowers in spring, sheer chasms and panoramic views. Belmore Falls walking track (1.8 km return, 30 minutes–1 hour, medium) from Hindmarsh Lookout carpark, rewards with views across Kangaroo Valley, and past banksia and wattle to the impressive falls. Other walks include those to the Erith Coal Mine, Fern Tree Gully, Glow Worm Glen, Granite Falls Lookout and Long Point Lookout.

In the southern part of the park, Pigeon House Mountain Didthul walking track (5 km return, 2.5–3.5 hrs, hard) is steep in parts (the final ascent is by ladders in the rock face) but a rewarding climb to reach the mountain's stony peak. Large lace monitors sometimes cross the track. All walkers should be well equipped, and carry a compass, topographic maps and drinking water.

A number of trails are suitable for mountain-bike riders. Fire trails around Bundanoon – popular with families – lead to lookouts over Bundanoon Gullies. The ride from Fitzroy Falls to Kangaroo Valley (30 km, leaves from the visitor centre) is a little more challenging, as it includes some steep sections. Register with the visitor centre before departure.

Breathtaking views from many vantage points are an outstanding feature of the park: Long Point Lookout (for a wonderful view of the Shoalhaven River), Bagerys Lookout, Gambells Rest, Fitzroy Falls, Belmore Lookout, Tianjara Falls and George Boyd Lookout are just a few.

There are opportunities for canyoning and rock climbing but written permission from the NSW NPWS is required in advance. Four-wheel drive touring is limited; to undertake the 17-km Tianjara Fire Trail route you will need permission from the NPWS Ulladulla office.

WHERE: 115 km south of Sydney; 18 km south of Moss Vale; 2 km south of Bundanoon; 24 km west of Nowra; from Wollongong via Illawarra Hwy to Belmore Falls and Fitzroy Falls; from Ulladulla and Milton in the east and Goulburn and Marulan in the west (southern section); from Princes Hwy between Ulladulla and Nowra, and from Nowra–Moss Vale Rd (route 79).

CAMPING: There is just 1 camping area in the north of the park (hot showers) and a couple in the park's south. Bush camping is permitted in many areas but not in parts of the Budawang wilderness (check first for details). Campfires are generally not permitted in Morton National Park so campers must be totally self-sufficient and carry a liquid-fuel stove. Bookings are required; see the NSW NPWS website.

CONTACT: Fitzroy Falls Visitor Centre: 02 4887 7270; NPWS Ulladulla: 02 4454 9500; NSW National Parks Contact Centre: 1300 072 757 (13000 PARKS)

Mungo National Park

At the heart of the Willandra Lakes Region World Heritage Area in the state's remote south-west, Mungo National Park is unique, containing a wild and arid moonscape where scattered remains (Aboriginal skeletons of Mungo Man and Mungo Woman were found here) recall human occupation over 40,000 years, making the area one of immense international archaeological significance.

CULTURAL HERITAGE: This remote district has long been part of the traditional Country of the Mutti Mutti, Paakantji and Ngiyampaa people. Old campfires and cooking hearths are extremely well preserved. The Ngiyampaa are still associated with the Willandra region and are involved in the running of the park and interpretation of its rich cultural history.

NATURAL FEATURES: This is semi-arid country with sandplains and sand dunes. During the last ice age, freshwater lakes were strung along Willandra Creek, but there has been no water for 15,000 years or so, and today the ancient, dusty lake beds provide a time capsule of the era when Aboriginal people hunted, fished and foraged around the lakes. One of the most dominant features is the bizarre, wind-and-weather sculpted form of the Walls of China. This 'lunette', a 33-km crescent of orange-and-white dunes, has been exposed, and with it human skeletal remains, tools, middens and the bones of ancient megafauna.

THINGS TO DO

Call in at Mungo Visitor Centre for information on the amazing natural and human history of the park.

The Grasslands Nature Stroll (1 km, 30 minutes, easy) is a signposted walk through the open woodlands of belah and cypress pine. After rain wildflowers will be in bloom and there are interesting lookouts. The walk is suitable for wheelchairs. Foreshore Walk (2.5 km, 1 hour, medium difficulty) starts from the Mungo Woolshed then wends its way across the shallow dip that is the ancient lake bed, with its scrubby bluebush, and then climbs the sand dune on the western shore. At the holding yards and old Mungo Woolshed, a little imagination will conjure up the shearing heydays.

For a scenic drive or cycle, the Zanci Pastoral Loop (10 km) extends from the Mungo Visitor Centre to the site of the old Zanci homestead. You can also

Moon rising over the Walls of China, Mungo National Park

cycle or drive along the road over the ancient lake bed to the Walls of China (20 km one way). Another option is the self-guided drive tour (70 km), a circuit to the Walls of China then over the dunes to the mallee country and around the north-east aspect of the lake. There are shady spots along this route and Belah Camp is around the halfway point. Cyclists in particular must carry plenty of drinking water.
WHERE: 130 km north-east of Wentworth; 104 km north-east of Mildura; 70 km south-east of Pooncarie; 150 km north-west of Balranald; access is via dirt roads, which are impassable after rain.
CAMPING AND ACCOMMODATION: There are 2 designated camping areas at Mungo and there are hot showers at the visitor centre. Camping fees apply. Note that no petrol is available at the park; the nearest fuel is at Pooncarie, 80 km away. Bookings are required; see the NSW NPWS website. An alternative to camping is the privately run Mungo Lodge, which has cabins. It is 2 km from the park entrance. Bookings are essential. There is also the historic Mungo Shearers' Quarters, bookable via the NPWS website.
CONTACT: Mungo Visitor Centre: 03 5021 8900; NPWS Buronga: 03 5021 8900; NSW National Parks Contact Centre: 1300 072 757 (13000 PARKS)

Murramarang National Park

Murramarang National Park rims the south coast for 44 km and includes Durras Lake and several small offshore islands. The park features a string of lovely coves, sandy and rare shingle beaches, intriguing weathered sea stacks, rock platforms and a backdrop of low mountains. Of scientific interest are shell fossils, such as those at Snapper Head.

CULTURAL HERITAGE: Just north of the park is Murramarang Aboriginal Area, where the largest complex of shell middens and stone tools on the south coast is a reminder of the long history of Aboriginal people in this region. Walkers can follow a self-guided track which takes in some superb views of the coast and hinterland.

NATURAL FEATURES: Along the coastal fringe whispering sheoak, geebung and coastal rosemary grow, while elsewhere there is open forest with large stands of spotted gum, and lush rainforest gullies. The relatively undisturbed vegetation provides a habitat for eastern grey kangaroos (see them grazing at Pebbly Beach), red-necked wallabies and swamp wallabies. Nectar-seeking honeyeaters, parrots and finches are common, and seabirds patrol the coast.

THINGS TO DO

Visitors can enjoy a range of different walks. In the north, the climb from Pretty Beach to the top of the 283-m Durras Mountain (7 km, 3 hours) rewards with brilliant views; a stroll around Durras Lake provides some top birdwatching. Families will find good swimming, excellent surf beaches, and plenty of picnic spots. Rock, beach and lake fishing are popular, and canoeing, kayaking, beachcombing, cycling and watching pods of dolphins swim offshore are other activities.
WHERE: 269 km south of Sydney; 25 km south of Ulladulla; 10 km north of Batemans Bay via Princes Hwy.
CAMPING: There are camp sites at Pebbly, Depot and Pretty beaches. Bookings are required; see the NSW NPWS website. As well as camp sites, 8 cabins are available at Depot Beach, 2 cabins at Pretty Beach and 4 beach shacks at Pebbly Beach; bookings are essential.
CONTACT: NPWS Ulladulla: 02 4454 9500; Depot Beach office: 02 4478 6582; Pretty Beach campground: 02 4457 2019; NPWS Nowra: 02 4428 6300; NSW National Parks Contact Centre: 1300 072 757 (13000 PARKS)

Mutawintji National Park

Tranquil valleys and rugged gorges cut through the craggy, burnt-red Byngnano Range, the dominant landform in Mutawintji National Park in the state's outback. On the fringe of the Central Arid Zone, this is a landscape of red dirt and woodlands, where mineral-laced rocky outcrops catch the brilliant light and creeks and waterholes contain precious water. Some of the finest Aboriginal rock-art galleries in the country are found here.

CULTURAL HERITAGE: Mutawintji occupies part of the traditional Country of the Malyangapa and Pantyikali people. The landscape of the Byngnano Range, with its protected gorges, creeks and rock pools, was traditionally a source of shelter, food and water and a home to Aboriginal people for hundreds of generations. Aboriginal rock-art galleries are a physical reminder of the long occupation of these lands by Aboriginal people, but the landforms themselves are also of spiritual significance, tracing the tracks of ancestor spirits. The park was returned to its Traditional Owners in 1998 and is administered in association with them. Access to Aboriginal sites within the historic area is by tour only; some other sites can be seen within the main park.

NATURAL FEATURES: Cutting through the park, the Byngnano Range is rich red in colour, its fragmenting sandstone sculpted by gorges and river valleys, with spidery creek beds and cool, hidden rock pools. Elsewhere are low tablelands, the gentle rippling stony downs around Mount Wright Creek, and arid plains of saltbush and mulga extending to the horizon.

THINGS TO DO

At the heart of the park, lies the Mutawintji Historic Site, where paintings, stencils and engravings offer an insight into Aboriginal culture over tens of thousands of years. The site can be viewed on guided tours only, bookings are essential and fees apply (see Mutawintji Eco Tours, p. 391). There is a cultural centre within the historic site. It is also possible to see rock art elsewhere in the park on various walks.

Thaaklatjika Mingkana Walk (400 m one way, 1 hour return, easy), from the camping ground, leads into gorges and Thaaklatjika (Wrights Cave), where paintings and stencils can be seen on the rocky overhang (the walk is accessible to wheelchairs). Rockholes Loop (5.6-km loop, 3 hours, difficult), leaving from the Homestead Creek Trail, a challenging walk involving some rock-hopping, takes you to areas with Aboriginal art, and also sweeping outback views. Homestead Gorge Trail (8 km, 3 hours return, easy) features Aboriginal engravings on a captivating walk that takes you to Homestead Creek and into the imposing Homestead Gorge. Western Ridge Walk (6-km loop, 5 hours return, difficult) is also fairly strenuous, involving some steep sections, but it is worth it, especially at sunset for the dazzling sight as the light catches the Byngnano Range. Take a torch for the walk back.

SCENIC TOURING: Although only 10 km long, the Old Coach Road Drive is an interesting excursion, following part of the original Broken Hill to White Cliffs coach run. You can stop en route to see intriguing rock formations such as Little Half Dome Rock.

WHERE: 1290 km west of Sydney, via Broken Hill; 130 km north-east of Broken Hill via Silver City Hwy, then gravel roads; check conditions beforehand as roads can be closed in the wet.

CAMPING: There is 1 designated camping area in the park, which includes toilets, showers, picnic tables, an amenities block and gas/electric barbecues. No bookings are taken, there is no fuel or firewood (available in Broken Hill) and fees apply. Bush camping is permitted in some areas of Mutawintji; self-registration is required. Pick up forms from the Broken Hill NPWS office. This is remote country, so ensure you are well equipped and well prepared and carry plenty of water; a fuel stove is recommended.

CONTACT: NPWS Broken Hill: 08 8084 2880; NSW National Parks Contact Centre: 1300 072 757 (13000 PARKS)

Oxley Wild Rivers National Park

Oxley Wild Rivers National Park, much of it World Heritage–listed, is a stunning environment of majestic gorges, deeply incised river valleys and powerful waterfalls plunging over formidable escarpments on the eastern side of the Great Divide. The park encompasses 2 wilderness areas: Macleay Gorges Wilderness (1996) and Kunderang Wilderness (1998). Areas of the park were affected by the 2019/2020 bushfires, but there are signs of recovery and many walking tracks and sites have reopened.

CULTURAL HERTIAGE: The park covers an area once occupied by the Dunghutti people. Their lands centred on the food sources of the Macleay River, the swamps, rainforests and valley woodlands, and there were seasonal movements only between the tablelands and the coast. Archaeological research suggests occupation dating back 4200 years. Along the creeks and on the tablelands there are artefact scatters, scarred trees and axe-grinding grooves. Archaeological sites include burial sites at East Kunderang; ancestral sites include the landscape of the upper Apsley Gorge; and contact sites encompass the rugged falls country, where Aboriginal people undertook their final fight against white settlers, as well as sites along Kunderang Brook, where brutal massacres took place.

NATURAL FEATURES: Located in the New England Tablelands, the park encompasses the catchment of the Macleay River and large tracts of virgin bushland. The Great Dividing Range, which runs through the park, slopes gently to the west, while the steep, eastern escarpment is dissected by streams, spilling over the side. Waterfalls are a prominent feature, with the most impressive – and one of the country's highest – the 240-m drop of Wollomombi Falls. Not so high but still impressive, Tia Falls and Apsley Falls plummet into the gorges below after rain.

THINGS TO DO

Oxley Wild Rivers is extensive but has a range of relatively easily accessible areas as well as memorable lookouts and peaceful picnic spots. There are short walks, as well as challenging trails leading into quiet gullies and along pristine waterways, where native wildlife is plentiful. From East Kunderang Homestead there are easy, 15-minute walks to the river. Apsley Gorge Rim Walk (1-km loop, 30 minutes, easy) takes in some spectacular lookouts, and Oxley Walk (2.7 km, 1.5 hours, easy) is a longer option, offering dramatic views of the gorge. More challenging walks extend between Budds Mare and Riverside camping areas, with one track (14 km return, 6 hours, difficult) passing through rainforests and heathlands and offering a steep climb on the return to Riverside.

Although access is limited, canoeing is possible on the Macleay River. The best launching points are at Kunderang West (4WD access only), Riverside (a permit is required) and East Kunderang Homestead (house guests only). Cyclists can use most park roads and management trails (permission from landowners is required in some cases), but not the walking tracks. Or you can explore the park on horseback along the signposted Bicentennial National Trail, but do not venture to East Kunderang Homestead, as horses are not permitted there. Stay overnight en route in huts at Left Hand and Middle Yards, valued for their cultural heritage. Check conditions with the park office before departing; the trail can be hard yakka, or worse, impassable after rain.

Swimming and fishing (a fishing licence is required and size and bag limits apply) are possible at East Kunderang and Riverside on the Macleay River. If you opt for staying at Youdales Hut, Riverside or East Kunderang Homestead, access roads are 4WD only (a permit and key are required).

WHERE: 560 km from Sydney; 20 km east of Walcha via Moona Plains Rd, or via Oxley Hwy then Kangaroo Flat Rd (walking access only); 18 km south-east of Armidale via Waterfall Way to Wollomombi; from Armidale access roads to the south-east lead to several gorges; there are also other unpaved roads, but some are 4WD only.

CAMPING AND ACCOMMODATION: There are a number of sites suitable for 2WD car-based camping in the park; Riverside and Youdales Hut are only accessible by 4WD. Remote bush camping is also permitted (except at picnic areas). Bookings are required; see the NSW NPWS website. East Kunderang Homestead has beautifully restored heritage accommodation for up to 14 people.

PERMIT: Day-use vehicle permits are required for 3 areas in the park: Halls Peak campground and picnic area, Riverside campground and picnic area, and Youdales Hut campground and picnic area. These can be bought online via the NSW NPWS website. If camping, permits are included in the campground fee.

CONTACT: NPWS Armidale: 02 6738 9100; NPWS Walcha: 02 6777 4700; NSW National Parks Contact Centre: 1300 072 757 (13000 PARKS)

Red dunes of Mungo National Park (photo Wayne Quilliam)

Royal National Park

Royal National Park, Australia's oldest national park, has a rich cultural heritage, both Aboriginal and European. It combines magnificent sandstone country with Victorian-era gardens and memorable views that make it one of the state's favourite parks. The gates to all areas of the park are locked daily at 8.30 pm.

CULTURAL HERITAGE: People of the Dharawal Nation have lived in this region for thousands of years and the park guards important Aboriginal sites and artefacts. The Dharawal and their neighbouring groups had been fishing in the bays and estuaries for 6000 years when Captain Cook arrived at Botany Bay in 1770. Visit Royal National Park Visitor Centre for more information about the Aboriginal sites and stories of this area.

NATURAL FEATURES: The park is situated on a sandstone plateau that is deeply dissected by valleys and in many ways epitomises the distinctive Sydney landscape, both in its landforms and vegetation.

THINGS TO DO

More than 100 km of walking tracks traverse the park. Follow the Coast Track (26 km one way, 2 days, difficult) that snakes along the cliffs and beaches from Bundeena to Otford, through a range of environments – the views along the way are a highlight. The track can be walked in sections, or it is possible to camp (you will need a permit to camp overnight at North Era). Forest Path (4.5-km loop, 1.5 hours, easy), a circuit that starts just south of Bola Creek, is a fine introduction to the park's subtropical and warm temperate rainforests. Karloo Track (10 km return, 4 hours, medium difficulty) is more demanding, winding from Heathcote Station to Uloola Falls; on the way, you pass Karloo Pool, a favourite swimming spot and a pleasant place for a picnic.

Sydneysiders find endless activity in the park. There is a kiosk and picnic pavilion at Audley, and other picnic locations are scattered through the park. You can bring your own boat, or hire a canoe or rowboat at Audley boatshed, paddle up river and stop for a picnic – Ironbark Flat and Wattle Forest are well-known spots. Anglers can drop a line from the coastal rocks or beaches and in the Port Hacking River estuary, but freshwater fishing is not allowed in the park. A fishing licence is required for fishing in NSW. Contact NSW Fisheries: 1300 550 474, or visit its website for more details.

There are some splendid views – Bungoona Lookout and Wattamolla Lookout are favourites – and a network of roads makes car touring and cycling easy. The roads allow you to see the diverse plant environments at a relaxed pace and also offer access to many of the park's highlights and attractions. A number of small, unspoiled beaches nestle in rocky coves along the coast. Bonnie Vale, Wattamolla and Little Marley offer sheltered swimming and there are also freshwater swimming holes. Surfers should head to Garie, North Era, South Era and Burning Palms beaches, on the park's southern coast, for sublime breaks.

WHERE: 32 km south of Sydney CBD: by road via Princes Hwy then Farnell Ave, just south of Loftus, or McKell Ave at Waterfall; by train to Loftus, Engadine, Heathcote or Waterfall (easy access to walking tracks); or ferry from Cronulla to Bundeena.

CAMPING AND ACCOMMODATION: There are 3 designated camping sites in the park. Bonnie Vale has wood-fired barbecues, but at 2 smaller bush camping areas no fires are allowed and drinking water and fuel stoves must be carried in. Bookings are required; see the NSW NPWS website. There are 3 cottages available – Hilltop, Reids Flat and Weemalah – that are excellent bases from which to explore Royal National Park. Park entry fees are not included in accommodation fees.

CONTACT: Royal National Park Visitor Centre: 02 9542 0648; NSW National Parks Contact Centre: 1300 072 757 (13000 PARKS)

Sturt National Park

In the far north-west of the state, in so-called Corner Country, lies one of Australia's driest, most remote national parks. Sturt National Park is a sea of sand, seemingly endless gibber plains, red rock and mulga bushes. Lake Pinaroo, near Fort Grey, was placed on the Ramsar list in 1996 – when it fills, it is a significant refuge for large numbers of waterbirds and waders.

Sturt National Park lies 400 km west of Bourke, the town touted as epitomising the outback. It is tucked into a distant corner, where the borders of NSW, SA and Queensland converge. This is arid, harsh country, intriguing for its vastness, with vestiges of exploring and pioneering history and surprisingly plentiful wildlife.

CULTURAL HISTORY: Among the peoples who survived in this remote area for generations before the arrival of the white man were the Wangkumara, Malyangapa and Karenggapa peoples, and many signs of occupation remain, including shell middens and stone artefacts. Before World War One many of the Aboriginal men worked on the sheep and cattle stations.

NATURAL FEATURES: The red sands of the Strzelecki Desert roll in on the western side of the park, while the east has stony downs of round gibbers and Mitchell grass. Low, flat-topped hills or jump-ups rise up to 150 m above the ground in the centre of the park. Lake Pinaroo is an ephemeral lake, only filling after very heavy rains, but it can retain water for as long as 6 years, attracting an extraordinary number of birds, which seemingly appear from nowhere.

THINGS TO DO

Call in at the visitor centre at Tibooburra before visiting the park to pick up detailed maps of walks and driving routes, and to get an update on closed roads or other information. Ask about ranger-guided tours during school holiday periods. Do not consider walking in the extreme heat of summer. There are short walks at Mt Wood, Olive Downs and Fort Grey, where Charles Sturt built a stockade to keep his party's supplies and secure their sheep on his expedition in the 1840s. The Granites Track (6 km, 4 hours, medium difficulty) passes huge granite boulders and wildflowers in season. There are loop drives suitable for 2WD vehicles or take the 4WD-only Middle Road that meanders across the park, linking the camp sites and letting you appreciate the vastness of the outback. This is remote country, so always carry plenty of drinking water and food. Note that roads in the park are closed after heavy rain.

WHERE: 1504 km north-west of Sydney; 335 km north of Broken Hill via partly sealed Silver City Hwy; 400 km west of Bourke via unsealed Bourke–Milparinka Rd then Silver City Hwy; 22 km north of Tibooburra (check conditions as roads may be closed after rain).

CAMPING AND ACCOMMODATION: There are 4 designated camping areas in the park. At most sites wood fires are not permitted; some have barbecues but a fuel stove is a good idea. It is best to take your own drinking water as only untreated water is available. Bookings are required; see the NSW NPWS website. Slightly more upmarket accommodation is available at the Mt Wood Homestead; visitors must take all food and supplies. Bookings are essential.

CONTACT: Sturt Visitor Centre: 08 8091 3308; NSW National Parks Contact Centre: 1300 072 757 (13000 PARKS)

Sydney Harbour National Park

Sydney Harbour National Park comprises a series of small foreshore areas of great natural beauty and historic importance around one of the world's most stunningly beautiful natural harbours. The park includes South Head with its historic fortifications, sandstone cliffs and 1858 Hornby Lighthouse; Nielsen Park, known for its lovely picnic spots, swimming and picturesque, heritage-listed 1852 Greycliffe House; Bradleys Head, the site of Taronga Zoo and superlative views of the landmark Opera House and Harbour Bridge; Middle Head, where military fortifications date back to the Napoleonic era; Dobroyd Head, with its natural coastal heathland; and North Head, containing the Old Quarantine Station and spectacular views from the craggy cliffs looming 90 m above the water. The park also protects Goat, Shark, Rodd and Clark islands and Fort Denison.

CULTURAL HERITAGE: The harbour area was part of the traditional lands of the Eora, Guringai and Dharug nations. Evidence of their culture and lifestyle was rapidly destroyed following the arrival of the First Fleet, yet even today some Indigenous sites remain and Aboriginal culture lives on.

THINGS TO DO

At Dobroyd Head, the Grotto Point Aboriginal Engraving Site couples fascinating rock art of people, marine and land animals and objects such as boomerangs with information boards describing more about the history and culture of the site.

There are many walking trails, but a fine way to appreciate the harbour is the Manly Scenic Walk (9.5 km one way, 4 hours) from The Spit to Manly, a trail of sweeping views, pretty coves and beaches, Aboriginal sites and pockets of subtropical rainforest. The park has beaches for swimming, good scuba diving (especially around North and South heads), excellent rock and beach fishing, and a multitude of

leafy picnic venues. Sydney ferries cruise the harbour and there are also many ranger-led tours, including fascinating heritage tours of the former convict island prison of Fort Denison and fortified Goat Island.
WHERE: Located around Sydney Harbour and accessible at a number of points by car or public transport.
CONTACT: NPWS Neilsen Park: 02 9337 5511; NPWS Middle Head: 02 9960 6266; NSW National Parks Contact Centre: 1300 072 757 (13000 PARKS)

Warrumbungle National Park

With its strange volcanic terrain, fresh mountain air and excellent camping Warrumbungle National Park is one of the state's most popular parks. Rocky spires emerge from the heavily forested valleys and peaks, and gorges slice deep into the landscape. This is spectacular country, with more than 17 peaks exceeding 1000 m, and a range of unusual landforms and idyllic valleys in a sprawling national park on the edge of the semi-arid interior of NSW. Stargazing, camping, bushwalking, rock climbing and sightseeing are the primary activities.

CULTURAL HERITAGE: When European explorers travelled through the area in the 1800s, the Warrumbungle (or 'crooked') Mountains had been well known to the Gamilaroi people – and other Aboriginal groups such as Wiradjuri and Weilwan – for thousands of years. Archaeological evidence in the park points to extensive occupation by Aboriginal people, and research into their links with this land is continuing.

NATURAL FEATURES: The park is distinctive for its dramatic landforms, the remnants of complex volcanic action that took place 13 to 17 million years ago. Over that period, molten lava and huge volumes of rock spewed out and a vast shield volcano was formed. Erosion has gradually worn away the softer rock, leaving tough volcanic plugs and fissures and the arresting landforms we see today – the shard-like form of the Breadknife, domed Bluff Mountain, Belougery Spire and the majestic Grand High Tops.

THINGS TO DO

Stop at the park visitor centre in Coonabarabran to ask about ranger-guided Discovery tours in spring and autumn and for information on walking, climbing and the park's fascinating geology, flora and fauna. Wambelong Nature Track (1-km loop, 30 minutes, easy) follows Wambelong Creek through a sheltered gorge (ideal birdwatching territory) and then rises to a rocky outcrop with marvellous views over the valley. For more energetic walkers, Breadknife and High Tops Walk (12.5-km loop, 5 hours, medium difficulty) is considered one of the state's top bushwalks. It is a demanding trek, taking in the shaded Spirey Creek valley, eucalypt forest, woodland with wildflowers in spring, the jagged, 90-m-high rocky spur, the Breadknife, the High Tops and dazzling views of the Warrumbungles. White Gum Lookout Walk (1 km return, easy) is a bitumen track suitable for wheelchairs.

You can cycle on the park's many roads and trails but not on walking tracks. Mountain-bike enthusiasts might tackle some of the steep fire trails. Canyon Picnic Area is in an attractive bush setting for a picnic or barbecue. Head to some of the lookouts for outstanding views. The bizarre and rocky volcanic cliffs are outstanding for climbing, but registration is required. Climbing the Breadknife, Chalkers, Square Top and Blackjack mountains is not permitted.
WHERE: 492 km north-west of Sydney; 35 km west of Coonabarabran via John Renshaw Parkway; 80 km north of Gilgandra via Newell Hwy then Gumin Rd.
CAMPING: There are a number of designated camping areas in the park. Only untreated water is available and fees are payable at all sites. Bush camp sites (some with toilets) are located along walking tracks. Bush campers must be self-sufficient and carry a fuel stove. No wood fires are permitted. Bookings are required; see the NSW NPWS website.
CONTACT: Warrumbungle National Park Visitor Information Centre: 02 6825 4364; NSW National Parks Contact Centre: 1300 072 757 (13000 PARKS)

Yengo National Park

Steep valleys, sandstone ridges and a web of creeks and rivers are found in Yengo National Park. European history is evident in the convict-built Old Great North Road, adjacent to the park's east boundary. The varied flora, ranging from dry Hawkesbury forest to melaleuca swamp, creates habitats for around 200 or so animal species. Birdlife is particularly prolific. Areas of the park were affected in the 2019/2020 bushfires, but many sites and tracks have reopened and the land is showing signs of recover.

CULTURAL HERITAGE: Part of the Greater Blue Mountains World Heritage Area, Yengo National Park is rich in Indigenous heritage. Flat-topped Mt Yengo is an Aboriginal sacred site and there are outstanding rock engravings, with Burragurra (Devils Rock) and Finchley Aboriginal Site accessible to visitors.

THINGS TO DO

Bushwalking, mountain-bike riding, 4WD touring, and horse riding (in the south of the park) are popular. The peaceful environment is ideal for watching birds and wildlife. There is the Old Great North Road – World Heritage walk (9-km loop, 3.5–4.5hrs, medium difficulty). For energetic walkers there is the 43-km section of the Old Great North Road, from Wisemans Ferry to Mt Manning (2–3 days). Mountain-bike riders can also tackle this route. The Womerah Range Track is only accessible on foot or by guided 4WD tour.

WHERE: 80–180 km north-west of Sydney via Wisemans Ferry and St Albans (southern section); from Singleton or Cessnock via Broke or Wollombi rds (northern section).

CAMPING: Campgrounds include Blue Gums, Finchley and Mogo, and 4WD car-based camping is available at the base of Mt Yengo (permit is required). Bookings are required; see the NSW NPWS website.

Big Yango House is great accommodation to use as a base for exploring the national park. Note: at the time of writing, areas of the national park remain closed due to the bushfires, including Big Yango House, Blue Gums campground and Mountain Arm campground. Check the NPWS website for updates before you go.

CONTACT: NPWS Bulga: 02 6574 5555; NSW National Parks Contact Centre: 1300 072 757 (13000 PARKS)

Yuraygir National Park

Yuraygir National Park protects the longest stretch of undeveloped coastline in NSW, a glorious sweep of beaches backed by forest and heath. The state's coastal fringe is increasingly busy and increasingly developed, so this park's 60-km tract of largely untouched bushland is an important natural reserve. Areas of the park were affected by the 2019/2020 bushfires, but many sites and walking tracks have reopened. Check the NSW NPWS website for details.

CULTURAL HERITAGE: The name 'Yuraygir' is derived from the Yaygirr language group, who, along with the Gumbaynggirr people, remain the traditional custodians of this land. Signs of past Aboriginal occupation exist within the park, such as the large midden at Station Creek. Aboriginal communities share a deep spiritual connection with many sites in Yuraygir National Park, where their ancestors camped, fished and held ceremonies, and weaved neckbands, dilly bags and baskets from the local pandanus palms. Follow the Freshwater Walk to view this impressive plant in its natural habitat.

NATURAL FEATURES: Yuraygir's pale sandy beaches are punctuated by rocky headlands, sand ridges and cliffs, and broken by river estuaries. Inland are lakes, bogs and swamps, created by changes to sea levels over millions of years. The lakes of Minnie Water and Hiawatha are perched freshwater lakes, encircled by massive dunes.

THINGS TO DO

Most of Yuraygir's walks are comparatively short and easy, though Angourie Walk (10 km, 3 hours return) is a medium-grade track that joins Mara Creek and Lake Arragan. There are some terrific views from Point Dirrigan Lookout as well as good birdwatching. Dolphins are often spotted frolicking offshore, and migrating whales are regularly seen from here in winter. If you would like to camp, you can stop at Shelley Headland. Wilson Headland Walk (3 km, 1 hour return) is an easy stroll from Wilson Head picnic area to Boorkoom camping area, with lovely ocean views.

The waves that crash in bring some of the state's best surf breaks and there are plenty of opportunities for swimming, boating and picnicking along secluded beaches. There are a number of very good picnic areas, most with barbecue facilities. The lake system attracts plentiful birdlife and also provides some excellent canoeing. Of several good venues for canoeing, the Sandon River, with its wide estuary expanse that is particularly picturesque and peaceful, is probably the best, and has a boat ramp, but Wooloweyah Lagoon, Lake Arragan, Minnie Water, Lake Hiawatha and Station Creek in the south of the park are some other options available.

The sheltered coastline and large rock pools at Sandon Bluffs are great for snorkelling, while divers should investigate the underwater delights, including a colony of resident grey nurse sharks at Pimpernel Rock, of the Solitary Islands Marine Park and the North Solitary Island Nature Reserve. The beaches are lovely but not patrolled, so swimmers need to take care, as the currents can be strong. Illaroo and Sandon beaches are generally considered fairly safe.

Angourie and the Mara Creek area are known for their top surf breaks and Grey Cliff (just north of Brooms Head) is another recommended surfing spot. Keen anglers and those just wanting to try their luck will find that tailor, drummer, mulloway, bream and groper are likely catches. The Sandon River camping area, near the mouth of the river, is a fine spot for river and beach fishing.

WHERE: 615 km north of Sydney; 35 km east of Grafton via Pacific Hwy, then either Wooli Rd (Wooli–Illaroo section) or, further south, Barcooongere Forest Way (Station Creek area); 5 km south of Yamba via Angourie Rd to Angourie section; 25 km south-east of Maclean via Brooms Head Rd to Brooms Head.

CAMPING: There are a number of great camping sites enjoying prime coastal positions within the park and facilities include showers, drinking water, toilets, tables and barbecues with wood supplied. Bush camping is permitted at Shelley Headland and Rocky Point (no facilities). Bookings are required; see the NSW NPWS website.

CONTACT: NPWS Grafton: 02 6641 1500; NSW National Parks Contact Centre: 1300 072 757 (13000 PARKS)

TOURS AND STAYS

Aboriginal Blue Mountains Walkabout

Born and bred local Aboriginal man Evan Yanna Muru owns and operates this cultural education bushwalking tour on Darug land. Evan has learned and practised traditional culture throughout his life and has specialised knowledge of local sacred sites. He is also a fully accredited teacher and wilderness guide.

On the tour, visitors are privy to wonderful rock engravings, sandstone caves, rock pools, waterfalls and rainforest, and have the opportunity to connect deeply with Aboriginal Country and culture, as Evan shares the traditional significance of these places.

The tour duration ranges from 3 to 4 hours depending on the season and covers a distance of 2–3 km. It is a medium-grade bushwalk, suitable for those of good health and mobility. Visitors are asked to bring lunch, adequate water, soft soled shoes, a rain jacket, hat, camera, a mat to sit on and a bag for rubbish.

WHERE: The tour starts and finishes in the Blue Mountains, on the Faulconbridge railway station platform.

COST: $95 per person. Payments available online or in cash on the day. No refunds or bad-weather cancellations. Standard tour up to 10 people per day

or private charter tailored to suit your needs can be up to 50. Advance bookings are essential.
CONTACT: 0408 443 822

Bundyi Aboriginal Cultural Knowledge

Owned and operated by Wiradjuri man Mark Saddler, Bundyi Aboriginal Cultural Knowledge, based in Wagga Wagga, offer full and half-day tailored experiences to engage all the senses. Mark proudly shares the local ancient Wiradjuri culture, history and landscape through walks alongside the Marrambidya Bila (Murrumbigee River), a luxurious bus ride or motorcycling the surrounding townships.

WHERE: 7/295 Copland St, Wagga Wagga. Local transfers can be organised at request.
CONTACT: 0412 693 030

City of Parramatta cultural experiences

The Darug people are Parramatta's First people and the traditional custodians of this land. Parramatta's name comes from their word burramatta, meaning 'the place of eels'.

As the site of the extensive government farm and the colony's first land grants, Parramatta was a place where dispossession of land strongly impacted the lives of Aboriginal people, and so it became a major focus for the early frontier conflicts.

As a centre of governance for New South Wales, Parramatta was where the first recorded diplomatic protests against dispossession occurred; where the annual Native Feast was held; and where the Parramatta Native Institute, widely recognised as the site of the first institutional removal of children, was located. Yet it was also a place where Aboriginal people and colonists sometimes found ways to work together to mutual advantage. It became the setting for a range of largely forgotten stories of trade, cooperation, assistance – and even some unlikely friendships.

Visitors can join local Indigenous guides on a number of walks and experiences, including:

Warami Mittigar – Aboriginal Cultural Walk

This easy 2-hour walk along the river and in beautiful Parramatta Park is a wonderful opportunity to spend time on Country with an Aboriginal traditional custodian, learning about connections to land, plant uses, tools, hunting and other aspects of local culture.

This tour is aimed at adults and families with children aged at least 7 years. It follows accessible pathways. In case of rain or otherwise adverse weather, it will become an interactive cultural presentation in the Heritage Centre.

WHERE: Meet at Parramatta Heritage and Visitor Information Centre, 346A Church St, Parramatta.

First Contact – Trade, Friendship and Conflict

Join an Aboriginal guide on this engaging tour to visit the actual sites where hidden histories unfolded, enjoying a rare opportunity to look closely at the lives of individual Aboriginal people and consider the complex nature of first contact.

This 2-hour tour is suitable for adults and families with children aged at least 11 years. It follows accessible pathways.

WHERE: Meet at Parramatta Ferry Wharf, Charles St, Parramatta.

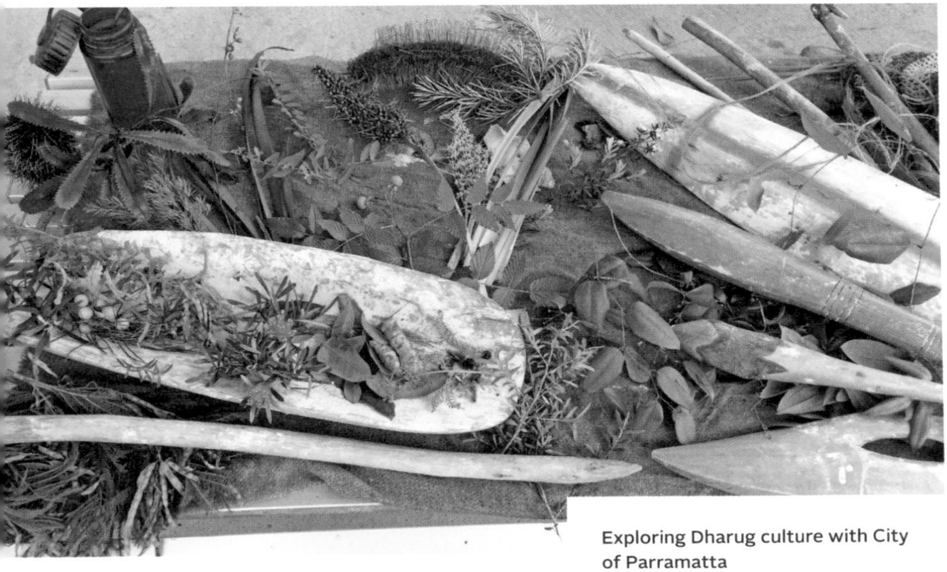

Exploring Dharug culture with City of Parramatta

Top: Dharug tools and plant resources

Bottom: Aunty Leanne King sharing culture

First Contact – The Imbalance of Power

This engaging tour focuses on interactions between the colonial government and the original inhabitants of this land, considering how and why these changed over time.

This 2-hour tour is aimed at adults and families with children aged at least 11 years. It follows accessible pathways.

WHERE: Meet at George St Gatehouse, Parramatta Park.

Aboriginal Ochre Painting Workshop

Join an Aboriginal custodian in this 2-hour interactive workshop, where you will have the opportunity to hear stories of Aboriginal life, uncover the cultural significance of local plants and animals, and pick up the basics of a traditional cultural practice. Weather permitting, participants will assist in painting temporary artworks, in natural ochres, on beautiful eucalyptus trees along the river.

This program is suitable for families with children of all ages.

WHERE: Parramatta Heritage and Visitor Information Centre, 346A Church St, Parramatta.

Bush Tucka Walk – Aboriginal Cultural Activity

On this relaxed 2-hour walk along a beautiful stream you will be introduced to the variety of native plants which sustained the traditional Aboriginal custodians of this area, the Darug people. Learn about the many food and medicinal plants that grow in your local bushland and discover some of the other resources provided by our beautiful trees and shrubs.

This program is suitable for adults and families with children over 7 years of age. Tracks may be slippery, rocky or muddy, and may include a creek crossing.

WHERE: Various bushland reserves in the Parramatta Local Government Area.

Youth Walking on Country

A rare opportunity for youth to join together with Aboriginal guides to discover how the traditional lifestyle of Australia's Indigenous population protected resources while providing for all the needs of their community.

Enjoy a relaxed 2-hour walk, delve into Aboriginal culture and learn how this people's sustainable lifestyle sustained the land. Learn how you can care for Country and walk lightly on the land. Join in some activities that are popular with Aboriginal youth.

WHERE: Meet at Parramatta Heritage and Visitor Information Centre, 346A Church St, Parramatta, or at Lake Parramatta Reserve.

Aboriginal Weaving Workshop

Celebrate Aboriginal Culture by learning some traditional weaving techniques in this 3-hour workshop. A Darug custodian will share the oral history of the coiled weave, and explain natural fibres and their uses. There will be an opportunity to make a bracelet and begin weaving your own coiled basket.

WHERE: Meeting room, John Curtin Reserve, Winston Hills.

Aboriginal Culture Camp

This 3-hour activity is a wonderful opportunity to spend time in nature with an Aboriginal traditional custodian, learning about plant uses, tools and local culture. Listen to traditional songs and stories. Maybe even develop your own bush skills, such as string making. All ages will enjoy the learning circle and a short, easy bushwalk.

WHERE: Various bushland reserves in the Parramatta Local Government Area.

Margret Campbell of Dreamtime Southern X takes visitors to five Aboriginal heritage sites on the Wyanga Malu coach tour

Please note that bookings are essential for all walks and experiences listed. Please arrive 15 minutes prior to the start time for registration. The City of Parramatta recommends wearing a hat and comfortable shoes, and bringing water and a snack.
CONTACT: 02 9806 5050

Dreamtime Southern X

Operating out of central Sydney, Dreamtime Southern X is owned and run by Aunty Margret Campbell, an Aboriginal woman from the Dunghutti and Jirrinjha Countries of mid north and south coastal NSW.

Margret was educated in her traditional custodianship, the Baranbyatti Mirra Buuka (Dreamtime Southern Cross), and encapsulates the living wisdom of her ancestors' Dreamtime. Margret has had a long career as an accredited teacher and has applied this knowledge to Dreamtime Southern X, which offers two cultural experiences: The Rocks Aboriginal Dreaming Tour, departing daily at 10.30 am and 1.30 pm from Cadmans Cottage, for groups of 25 people or more; and Wyanga Malu half-day coach tour, which takes booked groups of 15–25 people.

WHERE: Cadman's Cottage, 110 George St, The Rocks, Sydney.
COST: The Rocks Dreaming Aboriginal Heritage Tour: adults: $59; children: $44. Tours must be booked in advance by phone or on the website.
CONTACT: 02 8394 9940 or 0403686433

Explore Byron Bay

Local Arakwal Bundjalung Elder Delta Kay provides all-encompassing tours of Cape Byron, Broken Head and Bangalow. She shares her knowledge of bush tucker and medicines, tools and artefacts, land and the local history before British settlement through to the present-day Native Title. Top off the experience with a variety of bush tucker delights, a cup of tea and a biscuit. Contact Explore Byron to make a booking.

WHERE: Byron Bay Free pick-up and drop-off for guests within 6 km of Byron Bay's CBD or at the designated meeting place.
CONTACT: 0467 277 669

Giingan Gumbaynggirr Cultural Experience

The Giingan Gumbaynggirr Cultural Experience (Giingan Experience) runs on the second Saturday of each month at the Sealy Lookout, Korora (just north of Coffs Harbour). Launched by the not-for-profit Bularri Muurlay Nyanggan Aboriginal Corporation (BMNAC) in January 2017, it won a gold medal at the 2019 NSW Tourism Awards for Excellence in Aboriginal and Torres Strait Islander Tourism. 'Bularri Muurlay Nyanggan' means '2 Path Strong' in the Gumbaynggirr language and sets the goal of the BMNAC as ensuring that the local Aboriginal community, and in particular Gumbaynggirr youth, are strong in culture and strong in education.

The Giingan Experience is about Gumbaynggirr culture, people and language and is made up of three components:

Giingan Tour

The 2-hour Giingan Tour takes place at Niigi Niigi (Sealy Lookout) within Orara East State Forest, an important cultural site of the Gumbaynggirr people. Take in the 360-degree views and immerse yourself in the stories, songs, language and native plants of Gumbaynggirr culture. By taking part in the tour, guests directly contribute to revitalising Gumbaynggirr language and culture. The tour also provides the Gumbaynggirr community with the opportunity to speak traditional language and practise culture on Country.

Nyanggan Gapi Cafe

Enjoy a coffee with a perfect view or sample traditional ingredients with a new-age twist.

WHERE: Niigi Niigi (Sealy Lookout), Korora (9 km from Coffs Harbour).
CONTACT: 0409 536 670

Girri Girra

Journey with Girri Girra as you connect to beautiful Darkunjung Country. Director Tim Selwyn has a wealth of knowledge and draws on his own experience to share Aboriginal culture, dancing, singing, bush medicine and tucker. While working with a network of experts, Girri Girra provide a unique insight into the culture and landscape of the Central Coast. The guided walking tour of Bouddi National Park is a popular experience, as you walk through the twisted coastal canopy and out onto high rock platforms while discovering engravings and rock carvings. They are committed to sharing this knowledge through first-hand experience, guiding people through this ancient country, its history and customs. For tour times, check out their website.

WHERE: Tours depart from various locations on the Central Coast. Check the website for more details.
CONTACT: 0434 413 643

Guringai Aboriginal Tours

Guringai man Laurie Bimson established this fully Aboriginal–owned-and-operated company in 2009 to provide cultural education and to keep the Guringai traditions alive. Laurie is a descendant of Bungaree, leader of the Guringai tribe at the time of British arrival in what is now New South Wales. The Guringai people are saltwater people and have been the custodians of Guringai Country for about 40,000 years.

Guringai Aboriginal Tours take guests on a journey of discovery in World Heritage–listed Ku-ring-gai Chase National Park, a 45-minute drive from the Sydney CBD, where they learn how the Guringai people used the site as a classroom, caring for the land and having it care for them. The tour includes a Welcome to Country ceremony by a Traditional Owner and a visit to an Aboriginal rock engraving site and the famous Red Hands Cave, where the Aboriginal guides show how the art is done, how the carvings are made and how to read the site.

The tour runs for 3.5 hours daily (excluding public holidays) with a minimum of 10 people for each tour and an optional barbecue lunch for groups of 10 or more. Participants should bring comfortable walking shoes, hat and sunscreen, water and a camera.

WHERE: Ku-ring-gai Chase National Park (27 km from Sydney CBD).
CONTACT: guringaitours@gmail.com

Kadoo Indigenous and Historical Tours

Kadoo Tours is owned and operated by Latoya Brown and Tim Ella, both members of the Yuin–Dharawal nation with bloodline connections to many coastal NSW Aboriginal communities from Sydney to the far south coast, and Grant Hyde, a local writer and historian. They offer a 90-minute walkabout cultural tour to Watsons Bay, which is a 10-minute ferry ride from the centre of Sydney, and a 2-hour discovery cultural tour to historic La Perouse, 14 km from the city, as well as private walking tours. While each tour is different, all visitors have the opportunity to walk along the coastline and through the surrounding bush, try bush tucker, learn about Aboriginal culture, and be welcomed with a traditional ochre ceremony.

WHERE: For details about the meeting place for each tour and other information, visit the website.
COST: Adults: $50; child 5–11 years: $32; a family pass is available.
CONTACT: Latoya Brown: kadootours@outlook.com

Milan Dhiiyaan

Milan Dhiiyaan (One Family) draws on ancient knowledge and aims to empower all in our relationships and healing through mutual understanding and connection to Country, using a mixture of methods, such as workshops, tours and exhibitions. Sit with Milan Dhiiyaan to be introduced to First peoples' culture and refresh your spirit by developing a better understanding of yourself and connection to your surroundings. Immerse yourself in the travelling Winhangaduringya Healing Space, a collaborative effort led by Milan Dhiiyaan, developed as part of the *Unsettled* exhibition at the Australian Museum in Sydney. As you navigate the installations and develop the cultural practice of deep listening, you will be equipped and encouraged to step forward into the future more connected. Guided tours of the Goulburn River National Park, near Mudgee, are also available, which explore Fleur and Laurance's knowledge of local bush tucker and Aboriginal culture. To see the latest

Top left: Tim Ella of Kadoo Indigenous and Historical Tours

Top middle: Milan Dhiiyaan's 'Winhangadurinya' healing space at the Australian Museum's 'Unsettled' exhibition

Top right: Milan Dhiiyaan's dance troupe performing at Sydney's Blak Markets

Left: Traditional smoking ceremony by Ngaran Ngaran in Narooma

of Milan Dhiiyaan, visit their website or contact them directly for more information and bookings.

WHERE: Operating between Orange and Sydney. Check the website for more information.
CONTACT: 0400 409 102

Minga Cultural Experiences

Be guided through picturesque stretches of Yuin Country and coastline following traditional Aboriginal Dreaming tracks and identified pathways. Choose from a wide variety of options, from 2-hour guided walking tours to 2-day overnight camps, and gain insight into both Indigenous and non-Indigenous local history. As you journey, learn about native plants used for food and medicine, significant landmarks and the bountiful seafood and wildlife that sustained the Yuin people for tens of thousands of years.

WHERE: Eurobodalla, Murramurang and Deua National Parks.
CONTACT: 0407 076 511

Mutawintji Eco Tours

Mutawintji Eco Tours is owned by the larger Tri State Safaris, which runs small-group tours through Mutawintji National Park led by accredited Aboriginal guides. Visitors will be shown around the National Park and surrounding sites of significance in air-conditioned 4WDs, with some tours including short walks. All tours have been awarded Advanced Eco-Certification and emphasise leaving as little impact on the ecology of the region as possible. There are a variety of single- and multi-day tours to choose from, and guests also have the option of participating in a tour of their choice with their own vehicle through the tag-along options offered.

WHERE: Mutawintji National Park (75 km from Broken Hill).
CONTACT: 1300 688 225

Ngaran Ngaran Culture Awareness

Ngaran Ngaran Culture Awareness (NNCA) was established in 2011 and is an Aboriginal-owned-and-operated business and Tourism Australia accredited Indigenous Tourism Champion located on Yuin Country on the NSW far south coast. Owner and operator Dwanye Bannon-Harrison created NNCA to pass on the legacies left to him by his family over 17 years of traditional teaching on Yuin Country.

Ngaran Ngaran offers a range of workshops, performances and multi-day tours, including the ever-popular Yuin Retreat, which gives participants a 2-night fully immersive experience on Yuin Country. The retreat includes the option of 2 different on-Country walking experiences, traditional Aboriginal wellness, dance and cooking workshops, and yarning circles. Various accommodation options are available, from belle or safari tents to private cabins or beach houses. The retreats are available for solo travellers or groups of 2 to 8 participants.

WHERE: Narooma and the Tilba region are 4½ hours drive south of Sydney, or 3 hours drive east of Canberra. Bus transfers are available from the local Moruya airport as well as Sydney and Canberra airports at additional costs.
COST: Djirranganj Dreaming Tour: $800 per person; Gulaga Creation Tour: $605 per person. Ngaran Ngaran tours depart on set dates and advanced bookings are essential. Tour dates, booking forms and additional details can be found on the website.
CONTACT: 0408 272 121

Nura Gunyu

Immerse yourself in the beauty of the Budawang bush and abundant wildlife, while only minutes from untouched beaches and lakes, as you learn about the culture of the local people. With experiences ranging from bush food walks and cooking demonstrations to camps, all activities are flexible and tailored to suit your needs and interests. Nura Gunyu also offers onsite accommodation options at Jamanee Gunya (Happy Camp, Yuin). This facility is equipped with dormitory-style accommodation, complete with an eco-friendly shower and toilet block. Alternatively, come prepared to set up your tent within the spacious camping grounds.

WHERE: 501 Wheelbarrow Rd, Morton.
CONTACT: 0405 646 911

Royal Botanic Garden Sydney Aboriginal Heritage Experiences

In addition to the breathtaking views of the Harbour, the Royal Botanic Garden Sydney also offers immersive Aboriginal heritage experiences, presenting the culture of the Traditional Owners of the Sydney city land area, the Gadigal people of the Eora Nation. Regular guided tours give visitors insights into the plants in the gardens and their significance for and use by the Gadigal people, as well as an opportunity to taste some of the fruits and herbs. Those wanting to learn the history of the Sydney region can take the Cadi Jam Ora (First Encounters) walk, which presents information boards and shows some of the plant life introduced by the First Fleet in 1788 in the First Farm Garden.

There are also occasional one-off Aboriginal cultural experiences and tours, such as bush-food foraging or artist workshops. These offer participants a deeper

Top: Glamping tents provided on Ngaran Ngaran's 2-day Djirranganj Dreaming Tour

Right: Fire lighting demonstration with Nura Gunyu

look at certain aspects of Aboriginal life and culture, and are advertised on the Royal Botanic Garden website ahead of time.

WHERE: The Royal Botanic Garden is located in central Sydney.
WHEN: Tours run every Wednesday, Friday and Saturday at 10 am, departing from the Garden Shop.
COST: Entry to the Garden is free; Aboriginal Heritage tours: adult: $42; children under 7 years: free.
CONTACT: 02 9231 8111

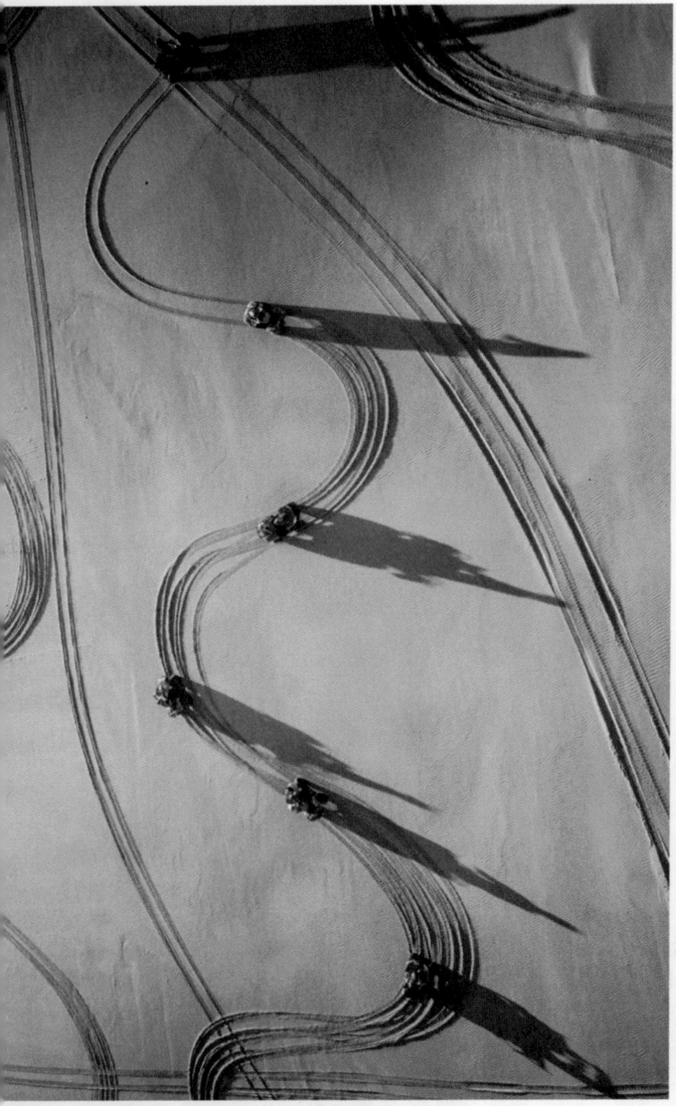

Get out on Worimi Country with Sand Dune Adventures' 400cc quad bikes touring the largest natural moving sand dunes in the southern hemisphere

Sand Dune Adventures

Owned and operated by the Worimi Local Aboriginal Land Council, Sand Dune Adventures is a multi-award-winning tourism operator offering quad bike tours on the sand dunes in the Port Stephens area. Visitors can experience the Worimi stories, culture and heritage through a number of different tour packages, including the quad bike tours ranging from 1 to 1.5 hours, with quad bikes and safety gear. On the tours, visitors will explore the area, which is rich in shell middens, Aboriginal burial and tool-making sites. Experienced guides ensure that visitors have a safe, informative and enjoyable experience.

WHERE: Murrook Cultural Centre, Williamtown, Port Stevens.
WHEN: quad bike tours: Monday to Sunday.
COST: Quad bike tours, depending on length: $110–$135. Book tours in advance; discounts are available on online bookings.
CONTACT: 02 4033 8808

Southbound Escapes

Experience one of the most pristine coastlines in the world with a carefully curated luxury escape, ranging from one to four days in duration. Tour and picnic options are also available, all showcasing the best the South Coast has to offer. These experiences will help you discover some of the most beautiful areas in Narooma and surrounding areas while learning about Aboriginal culture and local history, the area's enchanting nature and wildlife, and the origins of its delicious cuisine as well as some of its passionate producers.

WHERE: Shop A/44 Princess Highway, Narooma.
CONTACT: 0407 106 392

Tribal Warrior

Jump aboard the *Mari Nawi* (Big Canoe) and learn the traditional culture, history, and stories of one of the most beautiful harbours in the world, on this 2-hour cruise and cultural commentary. Hear stories of the Cadigal, Guringai, Wangal, Gammeraigal and Wallumedegal people of Sydney Harbour, and learn the Aboriginal names and meanings of significant Sydney landmarks, before stepping ashore on Be-lang-le-wool (Clark Island). Visitors learn about life pre-colonisation, the Indigenous coastal lifestyle, traditional fishing methods and food-gathering techniques, and may even be surprised with a cultural performance.

COST: Adult: $60; concession: $45; children: $40.
WHERE: Departs from Eastern Pontoon, Circular Quay, Sydney.
CONTACT: 02 9699 3491

Vision Walks: The Bush Tucker Walk with Aunty Delta

The Australian bush is full of edible fruits, roots, nuts, seeds and leaves, which Aboriginal people have gathered, hunted and harvested for centuries. Join Delta Kay, a local Arakwal woman, on a 2-hour discovery walk that will teach you how to identify what's good to eat and what's not.

Finding bush tucker takes special knowledge that comes from living close to nature. Delta has lived on Country for much of her life and is committed to working in genuine partnership with the local community to promote an awareness, understanding and mutual respect between Aboriginal and non-Aboriginal people. After the walk, enjoy a local bush tea, local bush foods and learn how to make bush string.

WHERE: Tours depart from Federal or Mullumbimby (20 km from Byron Bay).
CONTACT: 0405 275 743

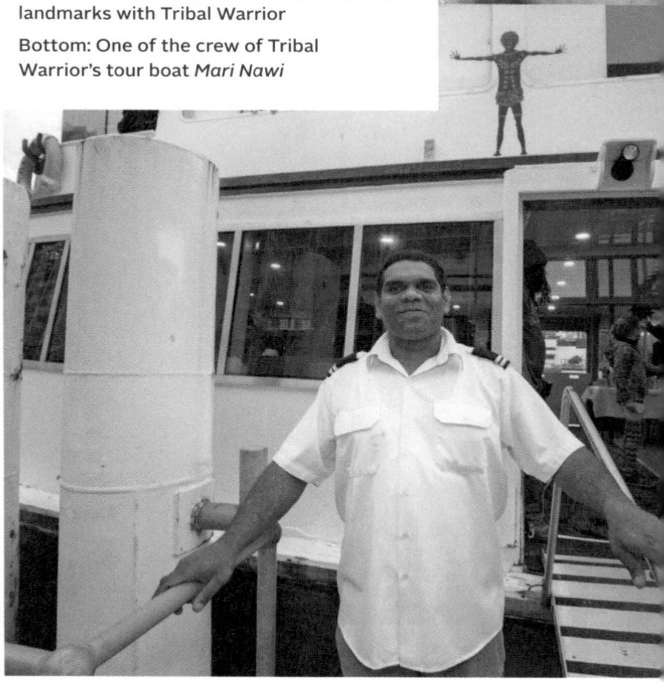

Top: Learn First peoples' history of Sydney landmarks with Tribal Warrior

Bottom: One of the crew of Tribal Warrior's tour boat *Mari Nawi*

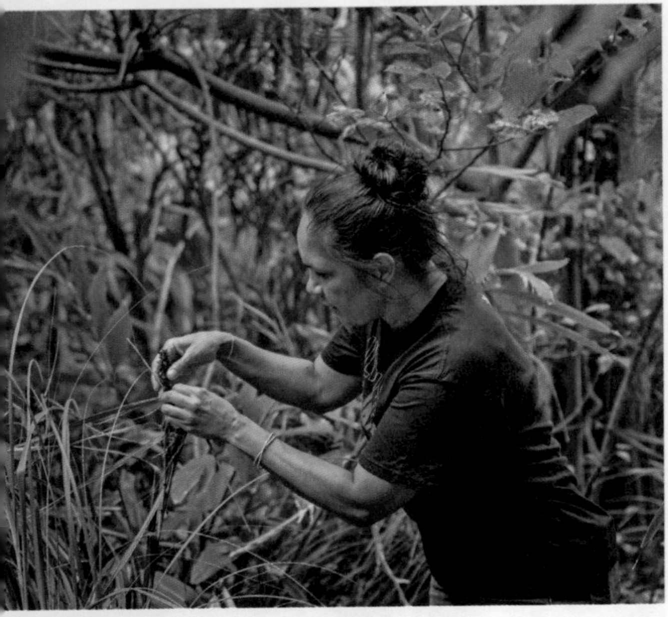

Top left: Aunty Delta showing the kids how to eat the best bush tucker on Vision Walks Eco Tours

Top right: Auntie Leanne King, founder of Wollombi Aboriginal Cultural Experiences and Consultancy

Left: Aunty Delta picking some local bush tucker on Vision Walks Eco Tours

Wajaana Yaam Gumbaynggirr Adventure Tours

Wajaana Yaam Gumbaynggirr (meaning 'from this Country' in Gumbaynggirr) Adventure Tours offer a 2.5-hour tour, using a stand-up paddle board or kayak, in the Solitary Islands Marine Park waterways in Coffs Harbour. Paddle with the direct descendants of the world's first stand-up paddlers, connect to land and sea through stories and language, and collect and taste seasonal bush tucker. No minimum fitness level or experience using a stand-up paddle or kayak is necessary to participate in the tour. Qualified instructors provide a stand-up paddle or kayak lesson at the start of each tour to ensure a highly enjoyable and safe experience for all.

This Gumbaynggirr social enterprise provides an employment pathway for Gumbaynggirr youth and community members through knowledge of language and culture, with a percentage of tour profits invested in Bularri Muurlay Nyanggan Aboriginal Corporation to ensure that Gumbaynggirr youth are '2 path strong' – strong in culture and strong in education.

WHERE: Tours depart from Red Rock boat ramp, Moonee boat ramp and Coffs Creek boat ramp.
CONTACT: 0409 536 670

Walangari Karntawarra

Walangari Karntawarra, artist, educator and performer, and Diramu Aboriginal Dance and Didgeridoo are leaders in face-to-face and online Aboriginal First peoples cultural education and entertainment. Their popular Aboriginal experience packages include traditional dance, didgeridoo performances and workshops, Welcomes to Country, Smoking and Cleansing Ceremonies, art and cultural presentations, guided art tours through Yirribana Gallery at the Art Gallery of NSW, Bondi Aboriginal walking tours, sand paintings and school programs. Check the website for more details.

WHERE: Walking tours run from Bondi Beach.
CONTACT: 0414 932 863

Wollombi Aboriginal Cultural Experiences and Consultancy

Immerse yourself in the world's oldest living culture while visiting and learning about important spiritual and cultural sites in and around Yengo National Park. Leaving from the Wollombi Cultural Centre, tag along in your own vehicle on a half-day or full-day tour exploring significant local sites such as Finchley Trig and Map Site. Your local guides will teach you about local lore and places of significance, such as Mount Yengo and how it came into being. For those looking for a more immersive experience, camps are also available. Ngurrumpa is a 160-acre bush property close to the Yengo National Park with basic camping facilities. During your stay, you'll experience fibre-craft and artefact making, traditional dance workshops, campfire stories and bush walks while learning about local food and medicine.

WHERE: Wollombi Cultural Centre, 2888 Wollombi Rd, Wollombi.
CONTACT: 0409 228 235

ART GALLERIES, CULTURAL CENTRES AND MUSEUMS

Art Gallery of New South Wales

The Art Gallery of New South Wales acknowledges the traditional custodians of the Country on which it is located, the Gadigal of the Eora nation, and recognises their continuing connection to land, waters and culture. The Art Gallery is one of Australia's flagship art museums and a destination for Aboriginal and Torres Strait Islander art. It displays both national and international art in its permanent galleries and major exhibitions. Representing artists from across Australia, the Art Gallery's collection of Aboriginal and Torres Strait Islander art, showcased in the Yiribana Gallery and across the museum, celebrates Indigenous Australia's enduring cultural heritage and its myriad contemporary expressions. Yiribana means 'this way' in the language of the Eora. Visitors can also enjoy the Art Gallery's program of tours, lectures, performances, films, educational program and activities for children. See the website for more information.

WHERE: Art Gallery Rd, The Domain, Sydney.
CONTACT: 02 9225 1700

Australian Museum

The Australia Museum's Indigenous galleries, Garrigarrang and Bayala Nura, boast some of the most significant Aboriginal and Torres Strait Islander collections. Garrigarrang, meaning sea country in the language of the Eora people, explores the richness of Australia's Salt Water People. It showcases the traditional objects and culture that encompass every part of the coastline from the oceans, beaches, plants and animals to the weather, seasons and sky. Bayala Nura celebrates yarning, and the traditional methods of sharing stories and songlines through talking, song and dance. This gallery showcases the vibrance and resilience of Aboriginal and Torres Strait Islander cultures, as well as providing insight into the ongoing impacts of colonisation.

WHERE: 1 William Street, Sydney.
CONTACT: 02 9320 6000

Blak Markets

Blak Markets are art and craft markets that run every few months at La Perouse and Barangaroo in Sydney, featuring artworks and craft created by Indigenous artists from all around Australia. The markets start with a Welcome to Country and a smoking at 10 am. Throughout the day there are various workshops, such as making shell work and weaving, as well as Aboriginal dance performances, cooking demonstrations and children's activities. Blak Markets are also a micro business hub for Indigenous

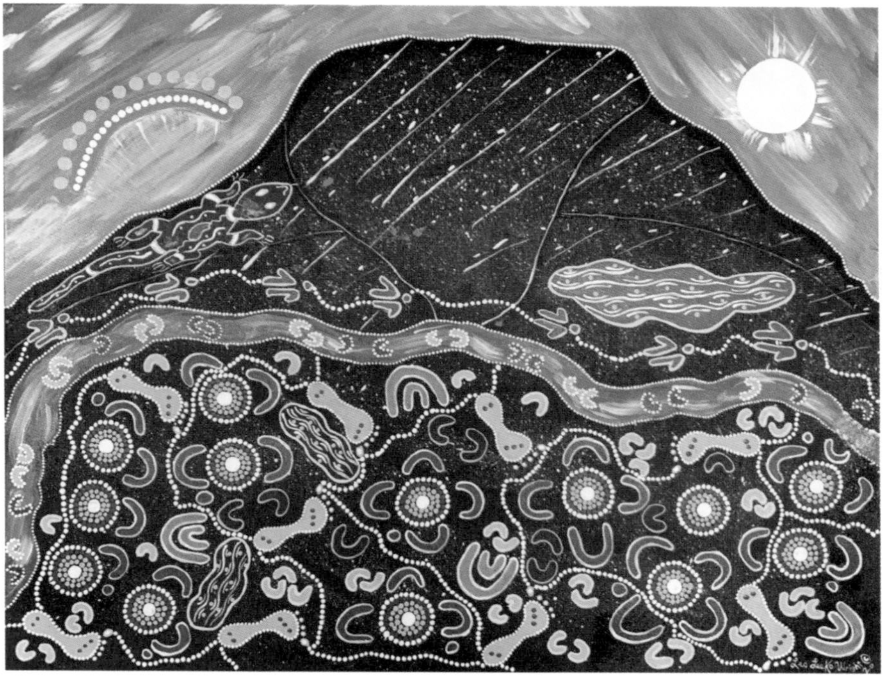

Leo Leeko Wright's *My House – My Site Burrel Bulai*, Dunghutti-Ngaku Aboriginal Art Gallery

businesses, providing economic development opportunities to Indigenous people. As well, Blak Markets train and employ young Aboriginal people in retail, food and coffee preparation and supervision, which allows them to work in the pop-up coffee, food and retail stores at the markets.

WHERE: La Perouse and Barangaroo; also Blak Markets pop-up shops and online store.
WHEN: Blak Markets are held about 8 times a year. For market dates and addresses, see the website.

Dunghutti-Ngaku Aboriginal Art Gallery

This proudly Aboriginal-owned art gallery in South Kempsey displays works from established and emerging artists from the local area and other regions. The gallery, designed by internationally renowned architect Glenn Murcutt, is located on the land of the Dunghutti people on the mid-north coast of New South Wales. It has been operating since 2008 and is also establishing a permanent collection of work by local artists. There are always new artworks and exhibitions on display, and most of the art is available for purchase.

WHERE: Val Melville Centre (next to the Museum), South Kempsey Park, Macleay Valley Way, Kempsey South.
CONTACT: 02 6562 1432

Minjungbal Aboriginal Cultural Centre

The Minjungbal Aboriginal Cultural Centre, at the main entrance of Tweed Heads Historic Site National Park, gives visitors a unique insight into the local Aboriginal culture. Run by the area's Aboriginal community, it is a popular meeting place for Goori people and other Aboriginal peoples. It is also a popular destination for school excursions and for individuals who want to learn about local Aboriginal culture. In the centre are museum exhibits, informative videos, Aboriginal art exhibitions, and occasional outdoor performances of traditional dance and song are held.

Aboriginal guides offer tours through the museum and site, explaining the significance of its relics and sharing information about the local plants and animals. Visitors will gain an insight into what Aboriginal life was like when this area was an untouched paradise of natural forest and mangroves, and learn about the cultural significance of the bora ring located on the Walk on Water track.

The centre is fully wheelchair accessible, and the amenities include picnic tables, barbecue facilities and drinking water. No pets or smoking allowed.

WHERE: Tweed Heads Historic Site, 17 Kirkwood Rd, South Tweed Heads.
COST: Adult: $15; concession: $7.50.
CONTACT: 07 5524 2109

National Indigenous Art Fair

This 2-day art fair and cultural program provides a unique opportunity to buy artwork directly from remote community art centres from the NT, SA and WA, and directly engage with artists. Held annually at the Overseas Passenger Terminal in Circular Quay, the fair includes an exciting public program of workshops and cultural performances, for adults and children alike. Profits are returned directly to the art centres, their artists and their communities.

WHERE: The Overseas Passenger Terminal, Circular Quay.
WHEN: Annually in July; see the website for details.

Umbarra Aboriginal Cultural Centre

Umbarra Aboriginal Cultural Centre is a leading cultural destination on the south coast of NSW. An Aboriginal Art Gallery and shop, the centre is a gathering place for Aboriginal artists and creatives, as well as a space for non-Indigenous visitors to learn about the rich Aboriginal culture of the area. With strong ties to the Wallaga Lake Koori community, the centre strives to keep culture alive.

WHERE: Wallaga Lake (7 km north of Bermagui).
CONTACT: 02 4473 7232

PLACES

Brewarrina Aboriginal Cultural Museum

No visit to north-western New South Wales is complete without visiting the charming township of Brewarrina and one of the oldest man-made structures in the world, the Ngunnhu (Fish Traps). The Brewarrina Aboriginal Cultural Museum is a community-run organisation that teaches visitors about the local area, how the Ngunnhu came into being and how the 8 nations came together on this significant site over 30,000 years ago. The distinctively designed museum is nestled into the side of the riverbank, adjacent to the fish traps, and overlooks the magical Barwon River. It offers visitors the chance to experience Aboriginal culture first-hand, while gaining an in-depth understanding of the area since time began. The Riverbank coffee bar and gift shop inside the museum showcases handmade gift lines, traditional paintings and artefacts all designed by local artists and makers. Tours of Ngunnhu and the ochre pit run daily by captivating and engaging locals who love sharing their culture.

WHERE: 18 Bathurst Street, Brewarrina.
CONTACT: 02 6839 2421

Koori Kulcha Experience

This multifaceted catering and training business has something to offer for everyone. The Bowral premises hosts a mixture of foodie experiences such as a cafe during the week, fine-dining on the weekends, and workshop spaces for corporate events or community classes. Their chefs marry 60,000 years of flavour with new methods of cooking to deliver an unforgettable dining experience, with fusion pieces including crocodile gyoza, kangaroo sausage rolls and emu and fennel chipolatas. For fine dining and community workshop times check out their website. The cafe opens Monday–Friday 9 am–2.30 pm.

WHERE: 15-17 Kirkhan Rd, Bowral.
CONTACT: 02 4858 1754

Mirritya Mundya

This 'Indigenous twist' catering company was created by husband and wife team Dwayne and Amelia Bannon-Harrison. Mirritya Mundya means 'hungry blackfish' in the Ngarrugu language group of south-eastern Australia, and the couple infuse native ingredients into their cuisine. They offer private functions, pop-up restaurant experiences, wedding catering and luncheons that take people on an Indigenous-led food journey.

Pop-up restaurants are run in collaboration with different venues in the Shoalhaven area, and include a 5-course food journey and traditional song.

WHERE: Callala Bay, NSW South Coast.
CONTACT: 0400 285 461 or 0408 272 121

The Lillipad Cafe, Glebe

Be transported from the hustle of Sydney to Far North Queensland as you move through the eclectic, brightly painted interior and end up in the plant-filled garden terrace. Co-owners Nyoka and Laszio create an Indigenous-inspired menu, sharing their knowledge of bush flavours to bring a unique take on contemporary cafe cuisine. Their wonderfully balanced kangaroo burger can be substituted for the equally satisfying plant-based version, the native flora burger. Both incorporate saltbush, wattleseed and pepperleaf seasoned patties with a finger lime mayonnaise. Open 6 days a week: Tuesday–Friday 7 am–4 pm, Saturday 8 am–4 pm and Sunday 8 am–3 pm.

WHERE: 34 Glebe Point Rd, Glebe.
CONTACT: 0423 289 779

The Tin Humpy

Nestled in Sydney's inner-city suburb of Redfern, The Tin Humpy cafe is a quaint family-run cafe and catering business. Known for their made-in-house pastries, the Tin Humpy blends cafe-classics with native ingredients like their lemon myrtle meringue tarts and blueberry and strawberry gum muffins. The cafe welcomes everyone, no matter where you come from. Open 7 am–3 pm Monday to Friday and 8 am–1 pm Saturday.

WHERE: 137 Redfern Street, Redfern.
CONTACT: 0413 789 152

The Tin Humpy cafe in Redfern blends cafe-classics with native ingredients

4
VICTORIA

FESTIVALS

Balit Narrun – Share the Spirit Festival

Held in the heart of Melbourne, this free, family-friendly outdoor concert features an eclectic mix of established and emerging local Indigenous artists, showcasing dancing, music, cultural art stalls and food trucks. Share the Spirit is the largest and longest-running Indigenous music festival in Victoria. Around 5000 people attend each year.

This festival is presented by Songlines Aboriginal Music Corporation and is supported by the City of Melbourne.

WHERE: Treasury Gardens, 2–19 Spring St, East Melbourne.
WHEN: Annually on 26 January.
CONTACT: 03 5350 2204

Belgrave Survival Day

Drawing 2000 to 3000 attendees every year, the Belgrave Survival Day provides an Indigenous perspective of the last 200+ years of European occupation in Australia. As well as information stalls, community groups and the Indigenous sector organisations that attend, a variety of vendors supply food, drink, books and merchandise for people of all ages to enjoy. Various entertainment acts round out the day. Volunteers are welcome.

WHERE: Borthwick Park, Benson St, Belgrave.
WHEN: Annually on 26 January.
CONTACT: 03 9754 8723

Castlemaine State Festival

Victoria's pre-eminent regional art festival is held biennially across several locations with a huge variety of acts that are unique in scope and diversity. There is music, literature, visual arts and film, musical performances, and conversation aplenty. The festival always includes a strong Aboriginal voice and in 2021 this was highlighted in the One Sky Many Stories instalment, a historical live reading – Soul of Possum, with Archie Roach in conversation.

WHERE: Across the city of Castlemaine.
WHEN: March/April; check the website for details.
CONTACT: 03 5472 3733

Deadly Funny

A national comedy competition which gives Aboriginal and Torres Strait Islander people around Australia the opportunity to submit their acts and then work in collaboration with professional mentors before being selected to perform at the Deadly Funny National Final

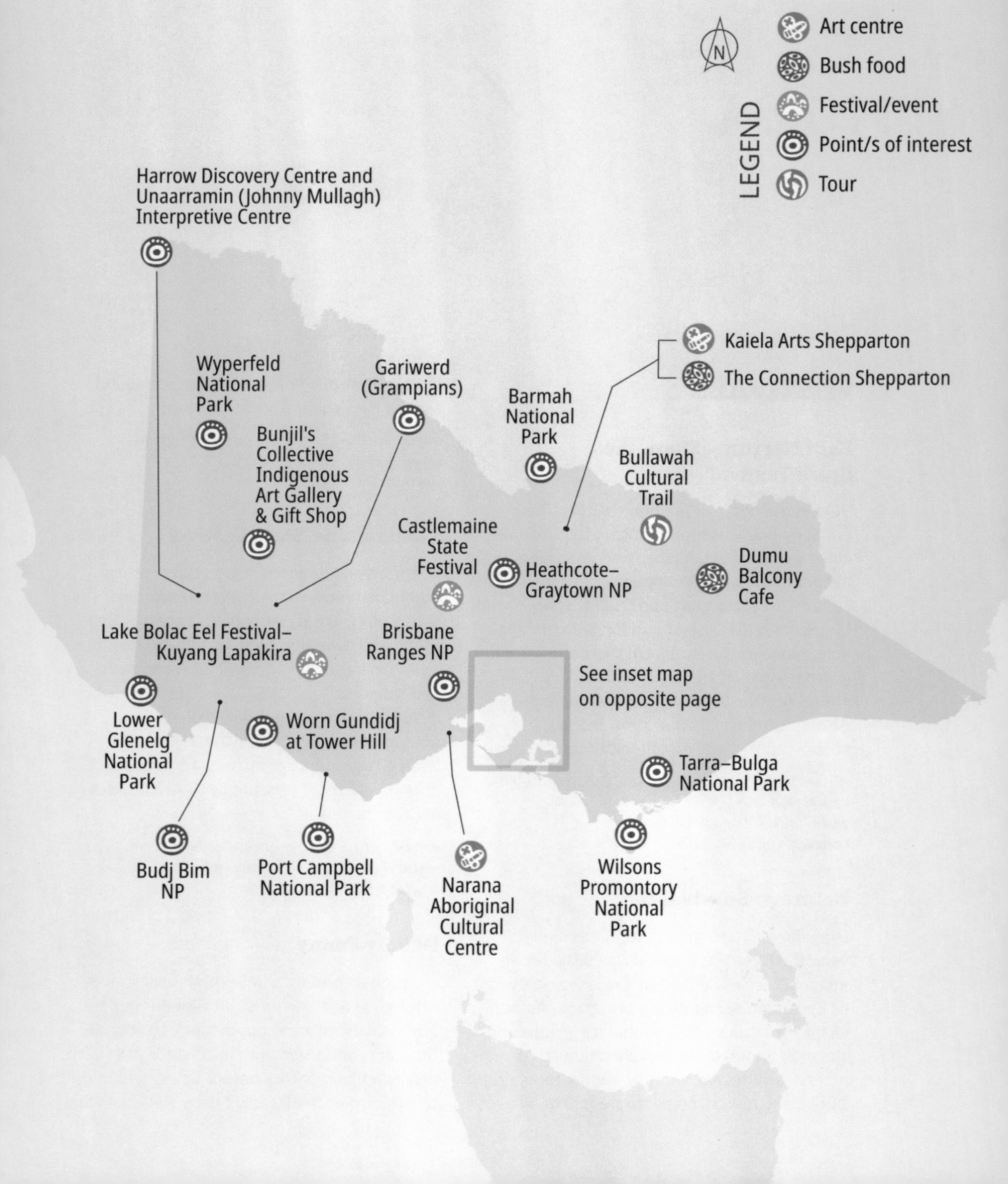

LEGEND
Art centre
Bush food
Festival/event
Point/s of interest
Tour
N
Harrow Discovery Centre and Unaarramin (Johnny Mullagh) Interpretive Centre
Wyperfeld National Park
Gariwerd (Grampians)
Bunjil's Collective Indigenous Art Gallery & Gift Shop
Barmah National Park
Kaiela Arts Shepparton
The Connection Shepparton
Bullawah Cultural Trail
Castlemaine State Festival
Heathcote–Graytown NP
Dumu Balcony Cafe
Lake Bolac Eel Festival–Kuyang Lapakira
Brisbane Ranges NP
See inset map on opposite page
Lower Glenelg National Park
Worn Gundidj at Tower Hill
Tarra–Bulga National Park
Budj Bim NP
Port Campbell National Park
Narana Aboriginal Cultural Centre
Wilsons Promontory National Park

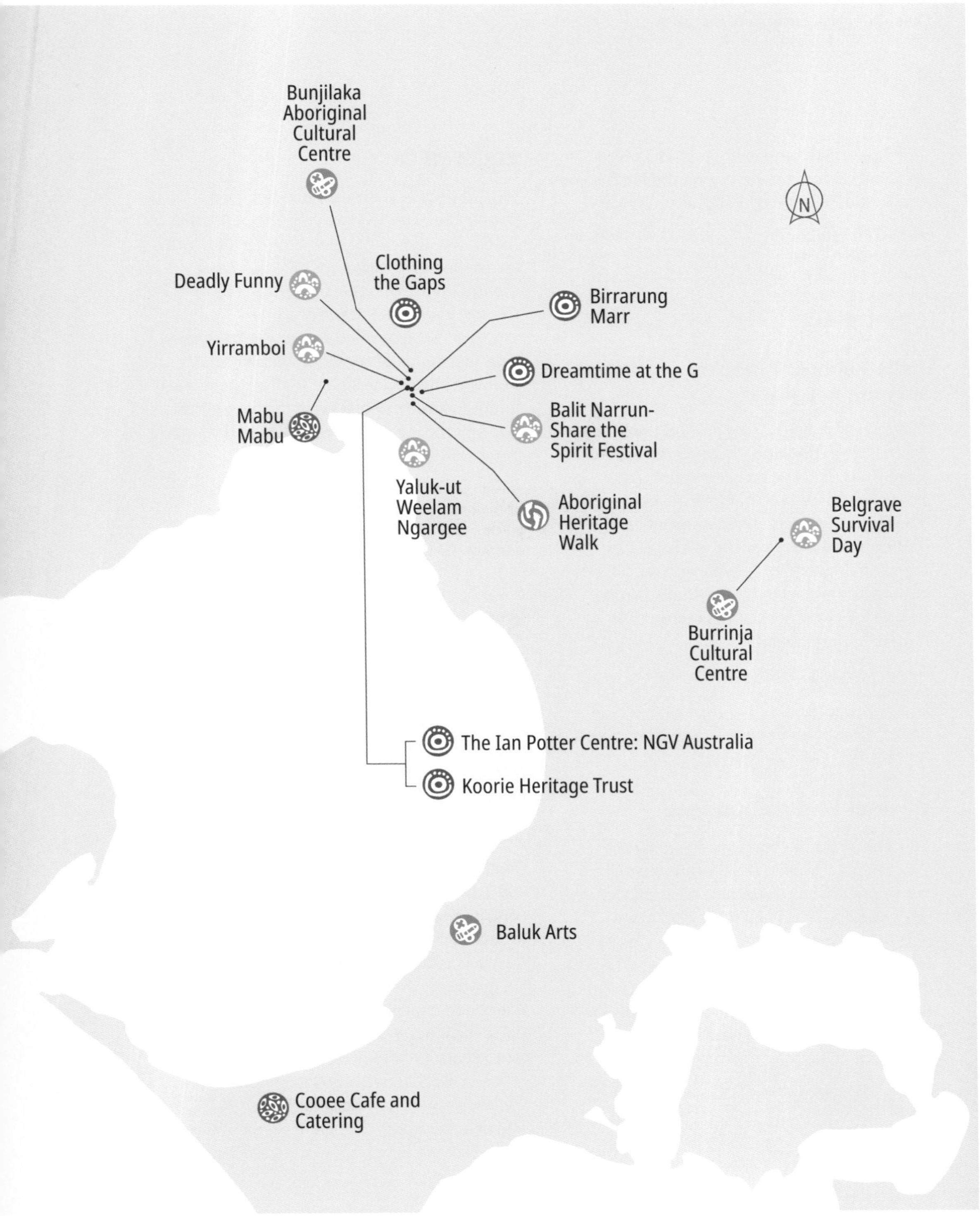
Bunjilaka Aboriginal Cultural Centre
Clothing the Gaps
Deadly Funny
Birrarung Marr
Yirramboi
Dreamtime at the G
Mabu Mabu
Balit Narrun-Share the Spirit Festival
Yaluk-ut Weelam Ngargee
Aboriginal Heritage Walk
Belgrave Survival Day
Burrinja Cultural Centre
The Ian Potter Centre: NGV Australia
Koorie Heritage Trust
Baluk Arts
Cooee Cafe and Catering
N

and Showcase, alongside Australia's best Indigenous comedians, during the Melbourne International Comedy Festival.

WHERE: Comedy Theatre, 240 Exhibition St, Melbourne.
WHEN: National Grand Final takes place each year in March; check the website for details of state/territory performances.
CONTACT: 03 9245 3700

Lake Bolac Eel Festival – Kuyang Lapakira

Indigenous peoples from around the Western District have traditionally gathered around Lake Bolac and the Salt Creek to trade, hold ceremonies and harvest the eels. The festival was created as a significant gathering place for people of all ages to come and enjoy themselves with music, arts, culture and workshops. The Djabwurrung people invite reconciliation, respect and mutual understanding.

WHERE: Lake Bolac Boat Ramp, Frontage Rd, Lake Bolac.
WHEN: Every 2nd year in late March or early April, when the eels' migration to the sea typically begins.
CONTACT: 03 5350 2204

Yaluk-ut Weelam Ngargee

This annual gathering is produced by the City of Port Phillip in collaboration with the Boonwurrung Traditional Custodians of the St Kilda area and local Aboriginal and Torres Strait Islander communities. It features Indigenous artists at various stages of their careers, and a mix of music, dance, technology and film is produced and delivered for diverse audiences. There is usually a footfall of more than 10,000 people.

WHERE: O'Donnell Gardens, The Esplanade, St Kilda (next to Luna Park).
WHEN: Early February.
CONTACT: 03 9209 6490

YIRRAMBOI

YIRRAMBOI is Australia's premier First peoples festival. Every two years, YIRRAMBOI takes over the city of Melbourne in May with an exciting program across music, dance, theatre, film, exhibitions, markets, family-friendly events, talks and more.

YIRRAMBOI means 'tomorrow' in the shared local languages of the Boonwurrung and Woiwurrung peoples. The festival presents a future-focused celebration of the sophistication, diversity and continuous evolution of the longest living culture in the world.

WHERE: Events take place throughout the City of Melbourne.
WHEN: Every 2nd year, in May.
CONTACT: 03 9658 9658

SPORT

Dreamtime at the 'G

Dreamtime at the 'G is held at the Melbourne Cricket Ground (MCG) during the Sir Doug Nicholls Round of the Australian Football League (AFL) Premiership Season. Typically held in the middle of the AFL Season, in late May or early June, the Sir Doug Nicholls Round commemorates all the Aboriginal and Torres Strait Islander players who have contributed to the hugely popular sport of Australian Football. It is a way for all Australians to respect and pay tribute to the Indigenous presence within football and sport. The round itself is named in honour of Sir Doug Nicholls, an inspiring person and former football player who represented the spirit of reconciliation between Indigenous and non-Indigenous Australians.

While there are many games now played in the round, the match between Richmond and

Essendon Football Clubs is the most highly anticipated. The day starts with the customary 'Long Walk', where attendees of the match walk from Federation Square, along Birrarung Marr to the MCG. The atmosphere is that of unity and excitement, with Australians from all backgrounds taking part in the Long Walk in commemoration of former Aboriginal Essendon football player Michael Long, who walked to Canberra to protest for the human rights of Aboriginal and Torres Strait Islander peoples in Australia.

The game itself is opened with traditional dancing and a smoking ceremony conducted by local Wurundjeri Elders. If visitors enjoy sport and a great atmosphere, then Dreamtime at the 'G is the perfect way to see how sport can bring people together for a common cause. Tickets sell fast and are available for purchase online through Ticketek or at the games.

WHERE: Melbourne Cricket Ground.

Harrow Discovery Centre and Unaarramin (Johnny Mullagh) Interpretive Centre

Harrow Discovery Centre presents the largely unknown story of the First Eleven: the first Australian international test cricket team to tour England, and the first team to represent Australia abroad in any sport. The First Eleven was comprised of 13 Aboriginal men from the Jardwadjali, Gunditjmara and Wotjobaluk clans in south-western Victoria. The composite photograph of the players was made into a poster and sold to help fund the tour. Between May and October 1868, the team played 47 matches against English amateur teams, and also taught the traditional skills of their people in the heart of the Commonwealth. The story of these athletes has been told at the Harrow

Statue of Johnny Mullagh standing in the Harrow Discovery Centre and Unaarramin (Johnny Mullagh) Interpretive Centre

Discovery Centre since 2004 and has been adapted into a stage play called Black Cockatoo by playwright Geoffrey Atherden, which premiered at the Ensemble Theatre in January 2020 with Wesley Enoch as director, and is due to be staged in Harrow on the Johnny Mullagh Oval in April 2022. The centre is open 11 am–4 pm daily.

WHERE: 1 Blair St, Harrow.
CONTACT: 03 5588 1387

NATIONAL PARKS

Parks Victoria manages an expanding and diverse estate covering more than 4 million hectares, or about 17 per cent, of Victoria, including 45 national parks. In addition to the national parks included here, visitors can find out about the many other parks at the Parks Victoria website.

Barmah National Park

Situated on the Murray River, Barmah National Park is the Victorian section of the largest river red gum forest in the world. The Yorta Yorta people's long association with this Country is clearly evident in the mounds, stone artefacts, middens and burial sites found here; the Yorta Yorta are joint managers of the park. European exploration and eventual settlement of this area began in the 1830.

Canoeing and boating along the Murray River gives tourists the chance to see the park, which includes many protected rare or threatened plants, and over 200 bird species (including brolgas, spoonbills, sea eagles and azure kingfishers). You may also see grey kangaroos, emus and koalas. Fishing is a popular pastime, as is swimming in the sandy beaches on the river bends. Walking trails are self-guided and

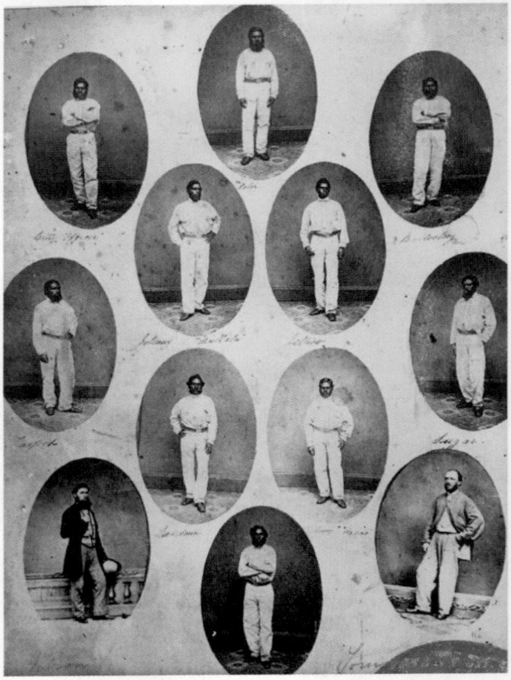

Top: Photo of the First Eleven, Australia's first international test cricket team to tour to England

Bottom: The First Eleven team comprised of 13 Aboriginal men from south-west Victoria – this composite photograph of the players was made into a poster that could be sold to help fund the tour

include views of mature river red gums, and the remains of Aboriginal camp ovens. Heavy rains can mean the park is shut down, so get in contact before you make the trip.

WHERE: On the Murray River, 225 km north of Melbourne; 40 km north-east of Echuca.
CAMPING: Camp sites along the river.
CONTACT: Echuca–Moama: 1800 804 446

Brisbane Ranges National Park

The Wathaurong people traditionally lived in and around the Brisbane Ranges, and their descendants, based in Geelong, still undertake the preservation of the area's Aboriginal heritage. There are over 600 types of native flora, including some rare, vulnerable and notable plants. There are also 170 species of native birds, the greatest population density of koalas in Victoria, swamp wallabies and eastern grey kangaroos bounding. Rugged gorges and hidden gullies splice the low mountains in the park, with the striking animals and plants creating some engrossing picnic destinations. There are some easy walks, as well as some more serious hiking opportunities.

WHERE: 80 km west of Melbourne.
CAMPING: The park has 2 campgrounds with unpowered and fuel stove–only camp sites, as well as overnight bush camps. Bookings are recommended in holiday periods; see the Parks Victoria website.
PERMIT: Permits required for the Old Mill and Little River overnight bush camps.
CONTACT: Parks Victoria: 13 1963; Bacchus Marsh: 03 5367 7488; Geelong: 035275 5797

Budj Bim National Park

Budj Bim National Heritage Landscape, located in the Victorian south-east region, belongs to the Gunditjmara people who have continually cared for this remarkable Country for thousands of years – a time that intimately links the creation story of the Gunditjmara people to the volcanic eruption of Mt Eccles.

Gunditjmara Traditional Owners Aboriginal Corporation – Gunditj Mirring developed a Master Plan for the Budj Bim National Heritage Landscape that brokered a partnership with Parks Victoria to co-manage the land and develop strategies that support sustainable tourism. In 2019, Budj Bim Cultural Landscape was inscribed on UNESCO's World Heritage List for its 'Outstanding Universal Value', acknowledging the cultural richness of the landscape. The Budj Bim Cultural Landscape is the result of a creational process narrated by the Gunditjmara as a deep time story, referring to the knowledge that Gunditjmara people have always been there. The sheer splendour of this area is unparalleled and welcomes visitors to experience all the Country has to offer.

For guests on Gunditjmara Country, Budj Bim Tours offer an authentic guided experience of the land and waters through the eyes of Gunditjmara people. Bear witness to ancient circular stone dwellings and lava flows that have been manipulated over thousands of years to create local hydrological regimes and ecological systems. Immerse yourself in the Budj Bim volcanic features and Tae Rak (Lake Condah), as well as the wetland swamps at Kurtonitj, and Tyrendarra in the south, an area encircled by rocky ridges and large marshes. Explore lava blisters on the Lake Surprise Walk and descend on a journey around the crater lake's edge, soaking in all the dynamic and pristine surrounds have to offer.

WHERE: 813 Mt Eccles Rd, MacArthur (40 km from Hamilton).
CAMPING: Budj Bim National Park Campground is surrounded by twisted manna gum trees, lava rock and hollows. Bookings are essential and can be made via the Parks Victoria website.
CONTACT: Budj Bim National Park: 13 19 63

Gariwerd (Grampians)

Gariwerd (Grampians National Park) is a must see if visiting Victoria. The landscape is timeless, rugged and beautiful. Gariwerd is and always has been a significant place for Victorian Aboriginal people, and their incredible rock art can be seen throughout the park, and at Bunjil's Shelter in particular.

CULTURAL HERITAGE: For the Aboriginal people of this area, Bunjil is an essential spiritual figure and the creator of life. Bunjil created the land, the trees, the people, the food and resources, the waterways, religion and Law. To see Bunjil's Shelter is to gaze upon rock art that is thousands of years old and yet the spirit and beliefs of Bunjil the creator are still evident in Victorian Aboriginal culture today. Many Victorian Aboriginal people continue to respect the stories and artworks about Bunjil that have been passed down through the generations and preserved in art galleries and museums.

THINGS TO DO

Brambuk: The National Park and Cultural Centre is the centrepiece of the Gariwerd cultural landscape. Opened in 1990, the cultural centre was the product of 10 years of work by the Aboriginal communities in the area to create a place to document, share and preserve the Indigenous cultures of the Gariwerd region. While the Cultural Centre is temporarily closed for maintenance, the Visitor Centre in the Brambuk precinct is open, which is a great place to stop for information about your visit to the park and to find out where the rock art sites are. Parks Victoria is currently managing the site with Eastern Maar Aboriginal Corporation, Gunditj Mirring Traditional Owners Corporation and Barengi Gadjin Land Council; see the Parks Victoria website for more details.
WHERE: The park is located in Western Victoria, a 3-hour (260 km) drive from Melbourne; and a 5-hour (460 km) drive from Adelaide. It is easily accessed from the villages of Halls Gap, Wartook and Dunkeld, and is a scenic day trip from the regional

Top: Hanging Rock, near Mount Macedon (photo Wayne Quilliam)

Bottom: Mt William, Boronia Peak in Gariwerd

towns of Hamilton, Horsham, Stawell and Ararat. Brambuk: The National Park and Cultural Centre is located at 277 Grampians Tourist Rd, just south of the Halls Gap township.
CAMPING: A variety of campgrounds are located in beautiful forest surroundings. All have basic amenities including pit toilets, fireplaces and picnic tables; they do not have power. Drinking water is not provided, so bring your own. Book early during busy holiday periods; see the Parks Victoria website.
CONTACT: 03 8247 2058

Heathcote–Graytown National Park

This park is culturally significant, with evidence of Aboriginal occupation over thousands of years. The Taungurung are recognised as the Traditional Owners of this national park and are its joint managers. Boasting the states' largest remnant of box and ironbark forest, there are many types of eucalypt species here, as well as brilliant displays of wildflowers, and large old trees playing host to creatures such as squirrel and sugar gliders and ringtail and brushtail possums. Commonly spotted animals include eastern bearded dragons, barking geckos, swamp wallabies and wedge-tailed eagles. The highest point in the district, Mt Black, provides views of the surrounding countryside, and Mt Ida or Viewing Rock (on the Mt Ida Range) and Melville's Lookout are also good vantage points. At the old gold settlement of Graytown, traces of streets, building foundations and a cemetery are relics from the gold era. Bushwalking, cycling, horse riding and orienteering are popular activities in the park. There is a visitor interpretation centre located at Whroo in the Rushworth–Heathcote State Forest, to the north, between Graytown andRushworth.

WHERE: 110 km north of Melbourne via Hume Hwy then Northern Hwy to Heathcote; or via Calder Hwy to Bendigo then McIvor Hwy to Heathcote; 25 km west of Nagambie.
CAMPING: Camp sites are available, with basic pit toilets; no drinking water is supplied.
CONTACT: Heathcote: 03 5433 3121; Nagambie 1800 444 647

Lower Glenelg National Park

This national park is on the traditional lands of the Gunditjmara and Buandig people, who are involved in the management of the park. Its tranquil waters provide optimal conditions for many outdoor activities. Some of the highlights include canoeing – the headwaters in Gariwerd (the Grampians) weave over 400 km to the Southern Ocean; fishing – salt water in the estuary offers solid and dependable successes; bushwalking – a network of trails of various lengths and experiences; boating and water sports – 2 launch ramps and designated areas and times for water skiing etc.; and tours – including the infamous Princess Margaret Rose Cave, with dripping stalactites and stalagmites.

WHERE: 450 km south-west of Melbourne; 15 km south of Dartmoor and Winnap; 2 km north of Nelson.
CAMPING AND ACCOMMODATION: There are basic camp sites all along the Glenelg River, but vehicle access is only possible to some of these sites. Cabins are available, as well as camping with facilities (but make sure you book), at Princess Margaret Rose Cave. Bookings are required and fees apply; see the Parks Victoria website.
PERMIT: Permit is required for overnight camping. Contact Nelson Visitor Centre: 08 8738 4051.
CONTACT: Parks Victoria: 13 1963; Parks Victoria Portland: 08 8738 4051; Princess Margaret Rose Cave Visitor Centre: 08 8738 4171

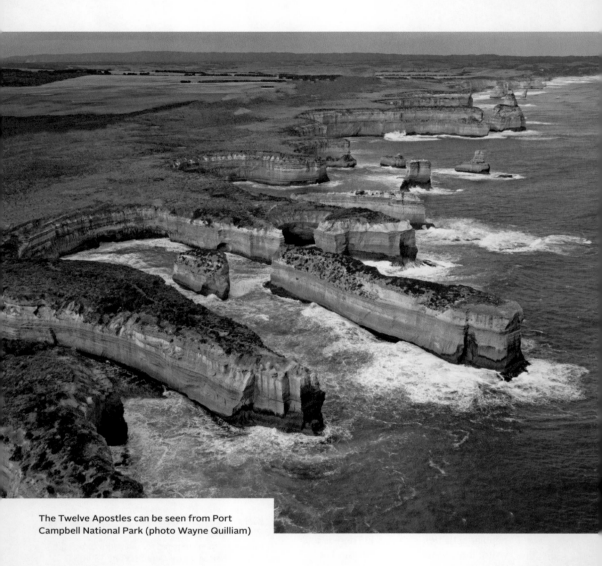

The Twelve Apostles can be seen from Port Campbell National Park (photo Wayne Quilliam)

Port Campbell National Park

This land belongs to the Giraiwurung people, who still live in the area and honour their traditional culture. The coastal region, with its rich natural resources, has long provided food, shelter and tools.

There are a variety of options for exploring – short works ending in viewing platforms, long walks providing the opportunity to see the dramatic effects of the wind and ocean on the coastal cliffs, and intriguing wildlife in woodlands and wetlands. The Great Ocean walk opened in 2006 and covers 91 km between Apollo Bay and Glenample Homestead; specially constructed campgrounds with various facilities now exist for the use of hikers. Registration in advance is required for anyone covering some or all of this distance. Ocean activities you can pursue include fishing, canoeing, swimming and diving, though these activities are best suited to specific locations and different times of the year, so it is always advisable to check with local experts and/or the park office for recommended options.

Special boardwalks provide excellent access for viewing key sights such as the Twelve Apostles, of which 8 stacks now remain. Towards the end of the day, the setting sun turns these ancient shapes into rugged blocks of brilliant colour, rising majestically up from the waves. There are tours (guided and independent) for historic sites and interpretative signage providing shipwreck information, this coastline having been a notorious shipping hazard in earlier days.

WHERE: 250 km west of Melbourne via Colac or 285 km via Great Ocean Road.
CAMPING AND ACCOMMODATION: There is no camping within the park or in carparks. There are camping grounds and caravan parks at Port Campbell, Peterborough and Princetown, as well as a range of other accommodation options.
CONTACT: Peterborough/Port Campbell/Princetown: 03 5598 6059, 1300 137 255; Warrnambool 03 5564 7837, 1800 640 082

Tarra–Bulga National Park

The park's name derives from the Indigenous word 'bulga', for mountain, and 'tarra', after Charlie Tarra, the Aboriginal guide who trekked with explorer Count Strzelecki through Gippsland in 1840. Although European settlement in the 1800s was disastrous for the local Brataualung people, their descendants have maintained their people's cultural heritage. The winding, unsealed Grand Ridge Road hosts one of Victoria's most beautiful scenic tours – mountain ash, myrtle beech and tree ferns are noticeable through the rainforest, with waterfalls, vantage points, picnic areas and walking tracks adding to the unique and striking experience.

WHERE: 200 km east of Melbourne; 30 km south of Traralgon; 30 km north of Yarram.
CAMPING AND ACCOMMODATION: There is no camping in the park, but a range of accommodation options are available in nearby towns.
CONTACT: Parks Victoria: 13 19 63; Parks Victoria Traralgon: 03 5172 2111; Traralgon/Yarram: 03 5174 3199

Wilsons Promontory National Park

Commonly known at the Prom, this beautiful and wild landscape of forests and heathlands, sandy coves and magnificent granite boulders sees over half a million visitors per year. Aboriginal people's occupation of this area of land has been dated back at least 6500 years, with a number of language groups finding spiritual significance here. The abundance of seafood and nutritious vegetation provided an important source of bush tucker, and it has been said that the Prom could have been used as a land bridge to Tasmania. The Gunaikurnai, Bunurong and Boon Wurrung peoples are Traditional Owners with a deep connection to this park, and local Aboriginal communities are heavily involved in its management. At the Prom you can have your choice of crowds or tranquillity, and both are easy to access. Tidal River hosts an outdoor cinema in the warmer months, a general store, a visitor centre with audio-visual presentation, displays and park notes, and lovely beaches. There are opportunities for exploring rainforests, hiking in the wilderness, tours with nocturnal animals, and accessing panoramic views. The turbulent seas of the Bass Strait can influence the wild and windy weather at the drop of a hat. Canoeing, kayaking, fishing, snorkelling and scuba diving are safe for families, with various locations providing calm, sheltered beaches or some good surf.

WHERE: 200 km east of Melbourne; 90 km south-east of Leongatha.
CAMPING AND ACCOMMODATION: There are hundreds of camp sites (limited powered sites and no generators allowed) as well as cabins, lodges and huts at Tidal River. There is a small campground at the park entrance and some campgrounds in the south and north-east. Accommodation is also available in several cottages at the lighthouse. Summer and Easter holiday periods are extremely busy and bookings are allocated via a ballot system (applications accepted during June and drawn on 1 July). Fires, including solid fuel heating compounds, are not permitted in the park; there are free barbecue facilities at Tidal River and Norman Bay. Bookings are essential for holiday periods, with a ballot system operating for peak periods; see the Parks Victoria website.
PERMITS: Permit is required for overnight hikes.
CONTACT: Parks Victoria: 13 19 63; Parks Victoria Tidal River: 03 5680 9555, 1800 350 552

Wyperfeld National Park

Wotjobaluk people have moved through this country for at least the last 6000 years, searching for bush tucker along Outlet Creek, which has flowed only 3 times in the last hundred years. As the Traditional Owners, they are involved in the co-management of this Aboriginal cultural landscape. The harsh conditions of the area ensured the first pastoral run taken up in the 1840s was found to be unsuitable, and the Wyperfeld National Park was declared in 1921. This vast park of open plains and spreading mallee eucalypts is located in the state's arid north-west. Recordings of more 450 plant species have been made, with desert flowers appearing after rain. Black box and river red gum woodlands sprawl across the dry lakes and wide flood plains, mallee scrub, cyprus pine, bull-oak and heath cover the land. Mice, kangaroos and emus are spread far and wide, as well as reptiles such as geckos, goannas and lizards (few snakes live here). Birds are abundant, with over 200 species calling Wyperfeld home. Alongside the 3 self-guided walks – Lake Brambuk Walk, Desert Walk and Tyakill Nature Walk – wildlife-watching is a highly rewarding activity in this park. Brochures and advice are available at the information centre.

WHERE: 450 km north-west of Melbourne via Western and Henty hwys to Hopetoun, then either west on Hopetoun–Yaapeet Rd or north to Baring via Patchewollock; 40 km west or 74 km north of Hopetoun; 85 km south-west of Ouyen.
CAMPING: Camping options are available, including some bush camping. For the Wonga campground bookings are required; see the Parks Victoria website.
CONTACT: Hopetoun/Rainbow: 03 5083 3001; Ouyen: 03 5092 1000

TOURS

Aboriginal Heritage Walk

The Aboriginal Heritage Walk takes visitors through the Royal Botanical Gardens, located in the heart of the city of Melbourne, next to the Yarra River, opposite Birrarung Marr. Tours start at the visitors centre in the Melbourne Gardens, where Ben Church conducts a traditional smoking ceremony. Ben is the local Aboriginal guide and Aboriginal Programs Officer at the Royal Botanical Gardens. The tour teaches visitors about the type of foods Aboriginal people in Victoria traditionally ate, and the different and important functions of plants and trees in the gardens, including which plants do what, and which are medicinal. It is an important and fascinating experience for non-Indigenous people to see how Indigenous people used the land in a way that didn't harm it or take from its resources. Ben also tells visitors how the five clans of the Kulin Nation used natural materials such as wood and stones for various purposes, including as tools or weapons.

The Royal Botanical Gardens is a very peaceful and scenic part of Melbourne. Within its grounds, the Aboriginal Heritage Walk is an empowering and informative introduction to the presence and culture of Aboriginal people in Victoria. The tour finishes with a cup of lemon myrtle tea and reflections on the significance of Aboriginal culture in Australia. Prices and times are available online, and bookings are essential.

WHERE: The tour starts at the visitor centre, Melbourne Gardens, Royal Botanic Gardens.
CONTACT: 03 9252 2429

Bataluk Cultural Trail

The Bataluk Cultural Trail follows significant traditional routes used by the Gunaikurnai people for over 30,000 years. Many Aboriginal organisations in the Gippsland region were involved in establishing the trail, including the Ramahyuck District Aboriginal Corporation, Gippsland & East Gippsland Aboriginal Cooperative, Lake Tyers Aboriginal Trust, Moogji Aboriginal Council and the Far East Gippsland Aboriginal Corporation, with the support of both the Wellington and East Gippsland Shire Councils. Together the organisations worked to identify places that are culturally significant to the Gunaikurnai people, the Traditional Owners of the Gippsland area.

In this self-guided tour, visitors can use the maps and information on the Bataluk Cultural Trail website to go to some or all of the 11 significant sites. They are located throughout the vast Gippsland region, ranging from Won Wron State Reserve to Sale, Stratford, Bairnsdale, Lakes Entrance, Orbost and Cann River. Visitors can drive from one end of the trail to the other or select a range of sites and activities and design a route that suits their timeframe and interests.

WHERE: For a map of the trail visit the website. Bataluk Cultural Trail visitor information centres are located at Orbost, Lakes Entrance, Bairnsdale, Maffra and Sale.
CONTACT: Krowathunkooloong Keeping Place Gippsland and East Gippsland Aboriginal Cooperative: 03 5152 1891; Bataluk Cultural Trail visitor information centres: Orbost: 03 5154 2424, Lakes Entrance: 03 5155 1966, Bairnsdale: 03 5152 3444, Maffra: 03 5141 1811, Sale: 1800 677 520

Budj Bim Tours

Take a guided tour on Gunditjmara Country as the Budj Bim Rangers share their knowledge with you.

The Gunditjmara have manipulated the landscape to build fish and eel traps that have been here for over 6600 years.

WHERE: 598 Henty Hwy, Portland.
CONTACT: 0458 999 315

Bullawah Cultural Trail

This 2.4 km self-guided walking tour follows the Ovens River in Wangaratta. Discover Aboriginal stories, culture, sculptures, food and more from the helpful signage, which includes QR codes to scan with your smart phone for further information via short films. Bangerang is the local language and Bullawah (taken from bulla – meaning two, and wah – meaning water) is significant on multiple levels: there are 2 suspension bridges crossing the river, there are 2 rivers that join, and the area is a place for Indigenous and non-Indigenous people to come together. Please note that the trail is prone to flooding during winter.

WHERE: Bickerton St, Wangaratta.
CONTACT: 1800 801 065

Bullen Bullen Cultural Tours

These walking tours, in the Dandenong Ranges, are operated by the Wurundjeri Woi Wurrung Cultural Heritage Aboriginal Corporation. A range of tours and cultural experiences are available, including an hour-long guided walk, the opportunity to participate in the ancient tradition of Tanderrum, including a Welcome to Country and smoking ceremony, and the chance to learn about the land and Country lore, foods, fibres, and flora and fauna, as the ancestors have passed this knowledge down through generations.

WHERE: Grants Picnic Ground, 70 Monbulk Rd, Kallista.
CONTACT: 0401 902 321

Worn Gundidj at Tower Hill

Tower Hill is an important environmental and historical landmark near Warrnambool. The area is the result of a volcanic eruption that occurred on the site approximately 32,000 years ago, and ancient tools and artefacts of the Traditional Owners, the Gunditjmara people, have since been discovered on the site. In 1892, Tower Hill became Victoria's first national park.

The Tower Hill Visitor Centre is managed by WG Enterprises (formerly Worn Gundidj Aboriginal Cooperative), formed in 1992 with a goal of supporting local Indigenous people by providing economic stability through employment and engagement in Indigenous-operated commercial enterprises. WG Enterprises offers guided tours, nature walks and twilight walks through the Tower Hill Reserve as well as school programs. The visitor centre and tours aim to educate visitors about the heritage of the reserve, its wildlife and environment.

WHERE: Great Ocean Rd, 10-minute drive from Warrnambool.
CONTACT: 03 5561 5315

ART GALLERIES, CULTURAL CENTRES AND MUSEUMS

Bunjilaka Aboriginal Cultural Centre

The Bunjilaka Aboriginal Cultural Centre, located in the Melbourne Museum, draws on contemporary styles of learning to inform visitors about Victorian Aboriginal history. The centre also offers workshops and runs educational tours. It is perfect for visitors with children who want to learn about Victorian Aboriginal culture in an exciting and interactive way. The centre displays walls of artefacts and cases of possum-skin clothing, and projects videos showing the history of the political struggles that Victorian Aboriginal people have faced. There is also a Deep Listening Space where visitors can go to listen to the stories of Elders; these stories bring to life the artefacts on the walls. The cultural centre pays homage to important political figures such as William Barak, Sir Douglas Nicholls and former St Kilda football player Nicky Winmar. There are also interactive activities available on the museum website to encourage learning at home. The museum is open 10 am–5 pm daily; closed Good Friday and Christmas Day and tickets are available online or at the front desk.

WHERE: Melbourne Museum, Nicholson St, Carlton.
CONTACT: 03 8341 7777

Burrinja Cultural Centre

A vibrant hub for creative and community arts in the picturesque Dandenong Ranges. There are multiple gallery spaces, a diverse collection of Indigenous art, a theatre with various performances, meeting and making spaces, an Indigenous cultural garden and many more delights to be found at Burrinja. Reciprocal cultural learning is valued and cross-cultural engagement with the local Aboriginal community is a key aspect of both the management of the collection and the curatorial practices employed throughout the centre.

WHERE: Cnr Glenfern Rd and Matson Dr, Upwey.
CONTACT: 03 9754 8723

Koorie Heritage Trust

The Koorie Heritage Trust offers a rich and complex history of the world's oldest continuous living culture. At the Koorie Heritage Trust, you can take part in a number of cultural experiences, including Building Aboriginal Cultural Competency workshops, Aboriginal walking tours, and an annual exhibition program supporting emerging, mid-career and established artists. You can also purchase authentic gifts from shopKOORIE, supporting local artists and craftspeople. It is a safe space for Indigenous people to learn about culture, and offers basket-weaving workshops and yarning circles; in addition to the exhibitions in the art gallery, it houses an archival collection of oral, photographic and written histories. Also, information services are available via an online reference library that holds more than 4000 items.

The Koorie Heritage Trust is filled with valuable information about Victorian Aboriginal people and their culture, land and history. It even offers family history tracing for Aboriginal people to find out where their families come from.

A visit to the Koorie Heritage Trust is essential for anyone who wants to learn about Victorian Aboriginal culture. Open daily 10 am–5 pm; closed on Victorian and

Koorie Heritage Trust, Yarra Building, in Melbourne's Federation Square

national public holidays. Admission is free, though fees apply for some education and art workshops.

WHERE: Levels 1 & 3, The Yarra Building, Federation Square, cnr Swanston & Flinders sts, Melbourne.
CONTACT: 03 8662 6300

Narana Aboriginal Cultural Centre

A cultural centre located 1 hour's drive from Melbourne, Narana offers guided and self-guided cultural tours, displays of artefacts and a cafe serving Indigenous-inspired meals. The onsite Cultural Exhibition Building and Art Gallery displays artworks by internationally acclaimed Aboriginal and Torres Strait Islander artists that are available for purchase. The site includes Australian wildlife such as wallabies and emus, a native garden and an adventure playground for children. Open 7 days a week.

WHERE: 410 Surf Coast Hwy, 10 minutes from Geelong on the way to Torquay.
CONTACT: 03 5241 5700

The Ian Potter Centre: NGV Australia

A suite of galleries dedicated exclusively to Aboriginal and Torres Strait Islander art form an integral part of the world's first major gallery dedicated exclusively to Australian art. Artists and artworks from the colonial period to the present day are featured, with a selection of artists and artworks often exhibited as part of specially themed exhibitions. Free timed-entry tickets are available online or at reception.

WHERE: Federation Square, Melbourne.
CONTACT: 03 8620 2222

PLACES

Birrarung Marr

Winding along the Yarra River's north bank, next to Federation Square, Birrarung Marr is an urban park for the community. Open-air exhibitions in the park showcase Aboriginal and Torres Strait Islander art all year round. And a pathway winding through it is designed to symbolise the eel, an important traditional food source for Victorian Aboriginal people.

Often hosting major festivals, Birrarung Marr encapsulates what it means to be a multicultural society. The festivals, from the annual Moomba festival to the Diwali festival, commemorate many different cultures. Additionally, each year before the Dreamtime at the 'G match, game attendees walk along Birrarung Marr together, showing their commitment to unity and reconciliation.

During a scenic stroll through the park, visitors should stop to admire the 5 metal shields standing proudly in a semicircle, representing the 5 language groups of the Kulin Nation: Boonwurrung, Dja Dja Wurrung, Taungurung, Wathaurung and Woiwurrung.

WHERE: Batman Ave, Melbourne.
CONTACT: 03 9658 9658

Bunjil's Collective Indigenous Art Gallery and Gift Shop

The Wimmera district is known for its rich and diverse history and culture, so a sweet and simple Indigenous owned gift shop and gallery space in the middle of Horsham is a valuable resource. Art, gifts, books, jewellery and much more are available for your leisurely perusal.

WHERE: 6 Firebrace St, Horsham.
CONTACT: 0432 160 391

Clothing the Gaps

This fashion label and social enterprise was started by Aboriginal health professionals with the aim of encouraging Aboriginal and Torres Strait Islander people to engage with the health initiatives they were running. Originally, T-shirts were designed as a way of funding grassroots health promotion activities. The merchandise has meaning, associated with 4 main values: Elevate, Educate, Motivate and Advocate. 'Closing the Gap' is an Australian government health initiative to help close the life expectancy gap between Aboriginal and Torres Strait Islander people and non-Indigenous Australians. Clothing the Gaps unites all people through fashion and causes. The merchandise has always been sold online, but the business has grown so much that a retail store became viable in 2020. Each product produced – including hats, jumpers, accessories and T-shirts – is labelled with a symbol to help people understand which items have been designed specifically for Aboriginal and Torres Strait Islander people (mob only) and which are for anyone (ally friendly). All of the products are fashionable conversation starters.

WHERE: 744 Sydney Road, Brunswick.
CONTACT: 0413 344 590

Cooee Cafe and Catering

Mornington Peninsula's only 100% Indigenous-owned eatery and catering business is a hub of First peoples culture along the coast. Indigenous ingredients, foods and Native flavours sourced from around the country are served up alongside the Jala Jala range launched during the COVID-19 pandemic. Cooee's catering service is available for groups of 10 to 200+ and

Top: Baby emus join one of Narana Aboriginal Cultural Centre's guided tours

Bottom: Sharon Brindley's Indigenous owned Chocolates (Jala Jala)

delivers to government, corporate offices and businesses, and private clients across the Mornington Peninsula and Melbourne's CBD. Located upstairs, among a carefully curated gallery of original paintings by owner Sharon Brindley's aunties, the Mezzanine Shop is stocked with products from Indigenous-owned businesses.

WHERE: 1/7 Thamer St, Capel Sound.
CONTACT: 03 5986 4414

Dumu Balcony Cafe

A First peoples business focused on delivering delicious, locally inspired dishes while employing and training Aboriginal youth from the Thamarrurr area. Those working in the cafe are given the opportunity to build up their work-readiness skills. This social enterprise has a strong commitment to the local Indigenous people, as well as sourcing native bush foods and produce.

WHERE: 4 Ireland St, Bright.
CONTACT: 03 5755 1489

Mabu Mabu

Mabu Mabu is a saying in the Torres Strait that means 'help yourself'. It's what you say before you dig into a big meal with friends and family. Mabu Mabu's food culture is all about sharing. Whether you are joining them for a meal, an event, or picking up some products in-store or online, you'll be welcomed to the village. The business incorporates two venues in Melbourne, a catering arm for corporate and private events, along with a retail range of small batch teas, spices, and sauces featuring Indigenous and tropical flavours that are made in-house and sourced from suppliers who are passionate about Australia's Indigenous food industry.

Nornie Bero is the head chef and business owner of Mabu Mabu. Originally from Mer Island in the Torres Strait, Nornie has been a professional chef for over 20 years. Bero is on a mission to put Indigenous ingredients in kitchens across Australia. She wants people to be using, eating and celebrating Indigenous ingredients every day.

Mabu Mabu – Big Esso

Big Esso is an all-day bar and kitchen, bringing Indigenous food and culture back to the banks of the Birrarung at Federation Square. Big Esso means 'biggest thank-you' and is a place to meet friends and join the village. Grab a seat at our communal tables, and tune into our 'Island Radio' surrounded by First peoples artworks. While you're there, tuck into bar snacks or a meal featuring seasonal native spices, fruits and vegetables, fresh seafood, and native game meats. Order native spiced cocktails, or a drink from a list of Indigenous owned businesses and certified social enterprises, and have a yarn with the people either side of you. Open for lunch, dinner and drinks 7 days. Bookings encouraged.

WHERE: Yarra Building, Federation Square, Melbourne.
CONTACT: hello@mabumabu.com.au

Mabu Mabu – Tuck-Shop

A small cafe that packs a big punch – fresh, seasonal, native ingredients are not just sprinkled on top of the dishes, they're the main event. With a breakfast-to-lunch menu, Mabu Mabu's Tuck-Shop highlights the flavour and diversity of Indigenous ingredients. Try their wattleseed latte, house damper, as well as seasonal vegan dishes. Open for breakfast and lunch, Thursday–Sunday. Bookings encouraged.

WHERE: 13 Anderson St, Yarraville.
CONTACT: hello@mabumabu.com.au

Street Feast Food Truck and Catering

Catering for parties, corporate events, weddings, anything! Monero Ngarigo man Dale Vocale is a chef from Orbost who, alongside his wife and business partner Jenni, has created a unique menu filled with native flavours and delicious food. The aim of the Indigenous-inspired range of food is to use local, native and foraged ingredients to create modern dishes based on ancient cultural food practices and uses. There are options for grazing platters, food truck service, or a marquee set up.

WHERE: Victoria wide. Arrangements and details are individually tailored and open for negotiation.
CONTACT: 0408 057 002

The Connection Shepparton

Set in picturesque bushland just outside of Shepparton, this venue is open and available throughout the week for everything from conferences and celebrations to simple dinners. The venue is fully licensed and has a strong focus on Indigenous foods. The Connection is also the home of Yurri Catering, whose delectable fare can be enjoyed anywhere in the Goulburn Valley area, with specialised menu options. There are also homewares and delicious treats available to purchase – such as bush spices, sauces, jams and teas, native soaps, beauty products, jewellery and art.

WHERE: 7287 Midland Hwy, Shepparton.
CONTACT: 03 5821 0600

ART CENTRES

Baluk Arts

Baluk supports the artistic and cultural expression of a range of visual artists in the greater Melbourne, Bayside and Peninsula areas of Victoria. Baluk is a local Boonwurrung word that means 'many or group of people', reflecting both the diversity of artists and the work they produce. This urban art centre has supported artists and family groups of the Stolen Generations to reconnect to their heritage and culture, building cultural and creative wellbeing. The range of artworks made at Baluk include wood, stone and bone carvings, painting, jewellery, weaving, kelp works and sculpture.

WHERE: 6 Bruce St, Mornington.
CONTACT: info@balukarts.org.au

Kaiela Arts Shepparton

Established in 2006, Kaiela Arts is an Aboriginal art centre in Shepparton situated on the traditional lands of the Yorta Yorta Nation. It provides an important space for local Aboriginal artists to connect to culture through the arts and share this culture to strengthen both the Aboriginal and non-Aboriginal communities. Kaiela Arts represents some 80 Aboriginal artists who commonly depict the traditional linear and X-ray styles of south-eastern Aboriginal people, using both traditional and contemporary visual art mediums and forms of expression. The public gallery and shop is open to the public Tuesday to Friday.

WHERE: 530 Wyndham St, Shepparton.
CONTACT: 03 5821 9842

5 SOUTH AUSTRALIA

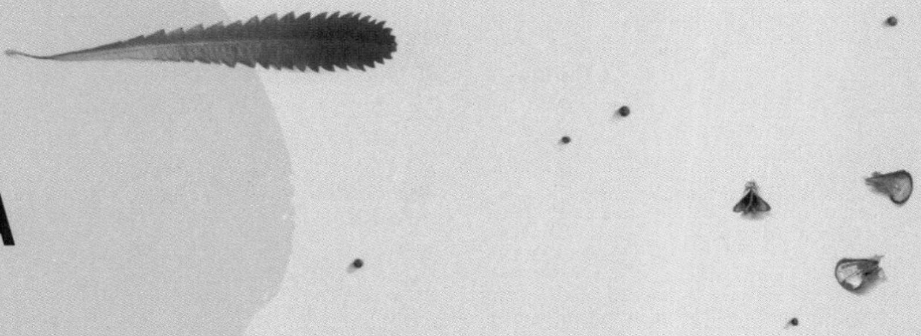

FESTIVALS

Survival Day Festival

This festival marks a time when the whole community celebrates the resilience of the Aboriginal and Torres Strait Islander people. It runs all day and includes live music from Aboriginal singer–songwriters, traditional dances, children's activities, arts and craft, and food stalls. Check the Tandanya website for more details.

WHERE: Tandanya, 253 Grenfell St, Adelaide.
WHEN: Held annually on 26 January.

Tarnanthi Festival of Contemporary Aboriginal and Torres Strait Islander Art and Art Fair

Tarnanthi (Tar-nan-dee) Festival is presented by the Art Gallery of South Australia. The festival showcases aspects of the rich, diverse and ancient cultures of Indigenous Australia by providing the opportunity for significant and unique new works to be displayed. Tarnanthi means 'to emerge', like the sun at first light, and signifies new beginnings. It is a Kaurna word from the Traditional Owners of the Adelaide Plains, and refers to the festival's artistic vision of showing distinctive works that challenge existing notions of Aboriginal art. The inaugural festival in 2015 was extremely popular and successful, and provided a platform for artists to share their stories. Now the festival includes a series of exhibitions, an art fair, artists' talks, performances and events held in key cultural institutions in Adelaide.

WHERE: The Art Gallery of South Australia, North Tce, Adelaide, and various partner locations around Adelaide city.
WHEN: Tarnanthi Festival of Contemporary Aboriginal and Torres Strait Islander Art and Art Fair are held annually in October. Tarnanthi at the Gallery runs from October until the end of January.
CONTACT: Via the Art Gallery of South Australia website.

NATIONAL PARKS

The Traditional Owners of Country associated with national parks in SA request that restricted areas are respectfully left alone, as they represent areas of cultural significance and cultural practice.

Belair National Park

With the historical woodlands and natural bushland this park offers, you might find

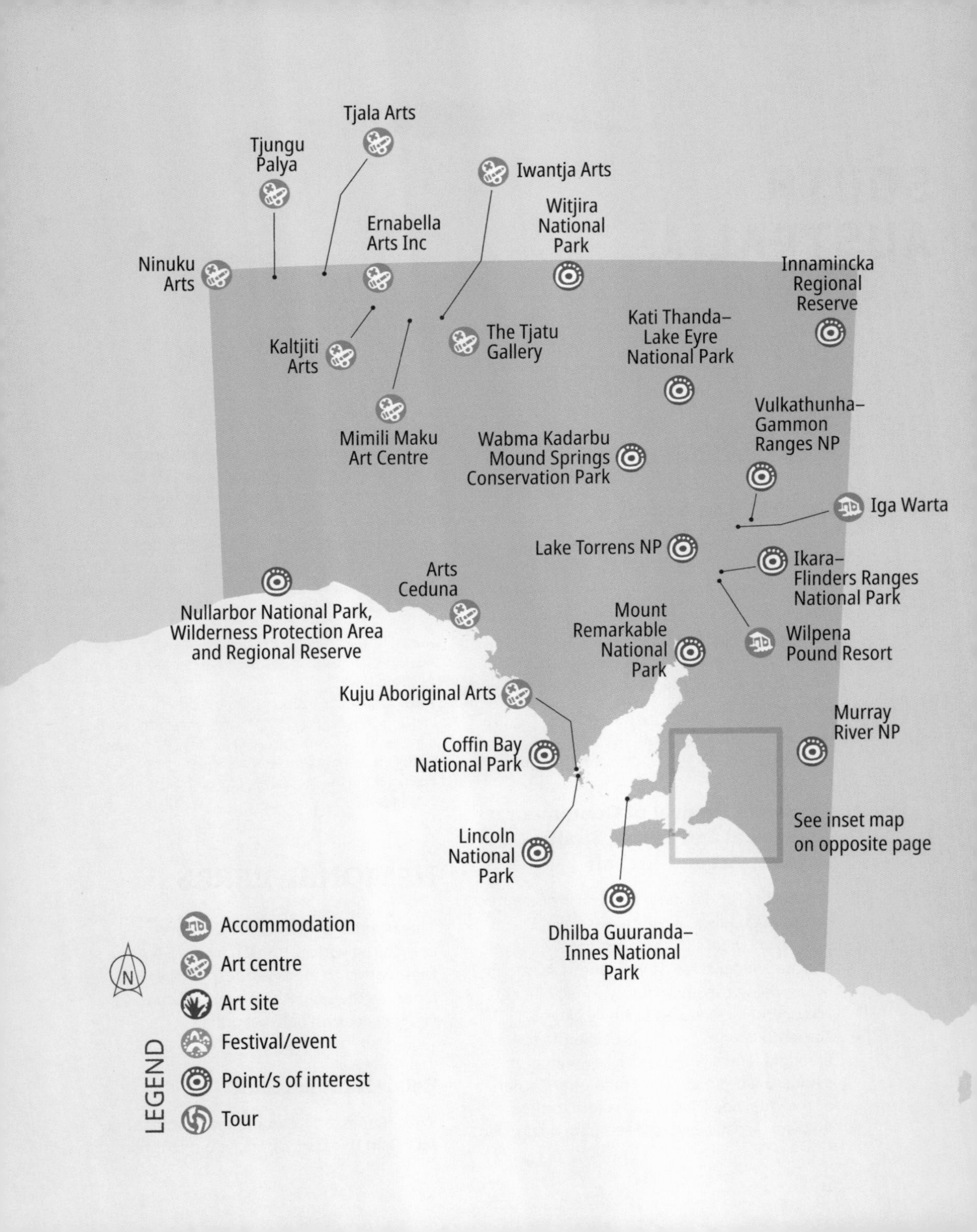

Tjala Arts
Tjungu Palya
Iwantja Arts
Witjira National Park
Ernabella Arts Inc
Ninuku Arts
Innamincka Regional Reserve
Kaltjiti Arts
The Tjatu Gallery
Kati Thanda–Lake Eyre National Park
Mimili Maku Art Centre
Wabma Kadarbu Mound Springs Conservation Park
Vulkathunha–Gammon Ranges NP
Iga Warta
Lake Torrens NP
Ikara–Flinders Ranges National Park
Arts Ceduna
Nullarbor National Park, Wilderness Protection Area and Regional Reserve
Mount Remarkable National Park
Wilpena Pound Resort
Kuju Aboriginal Arts
Murray River NP
Coffin Bay National Park
See inset map on opposite page
Lincoln National Park
Dhilba Guuranda–Innes National Park
N
LEGEND
Accommodation
Art centre
Art site
Festival/event
Point/s of interest
Tour

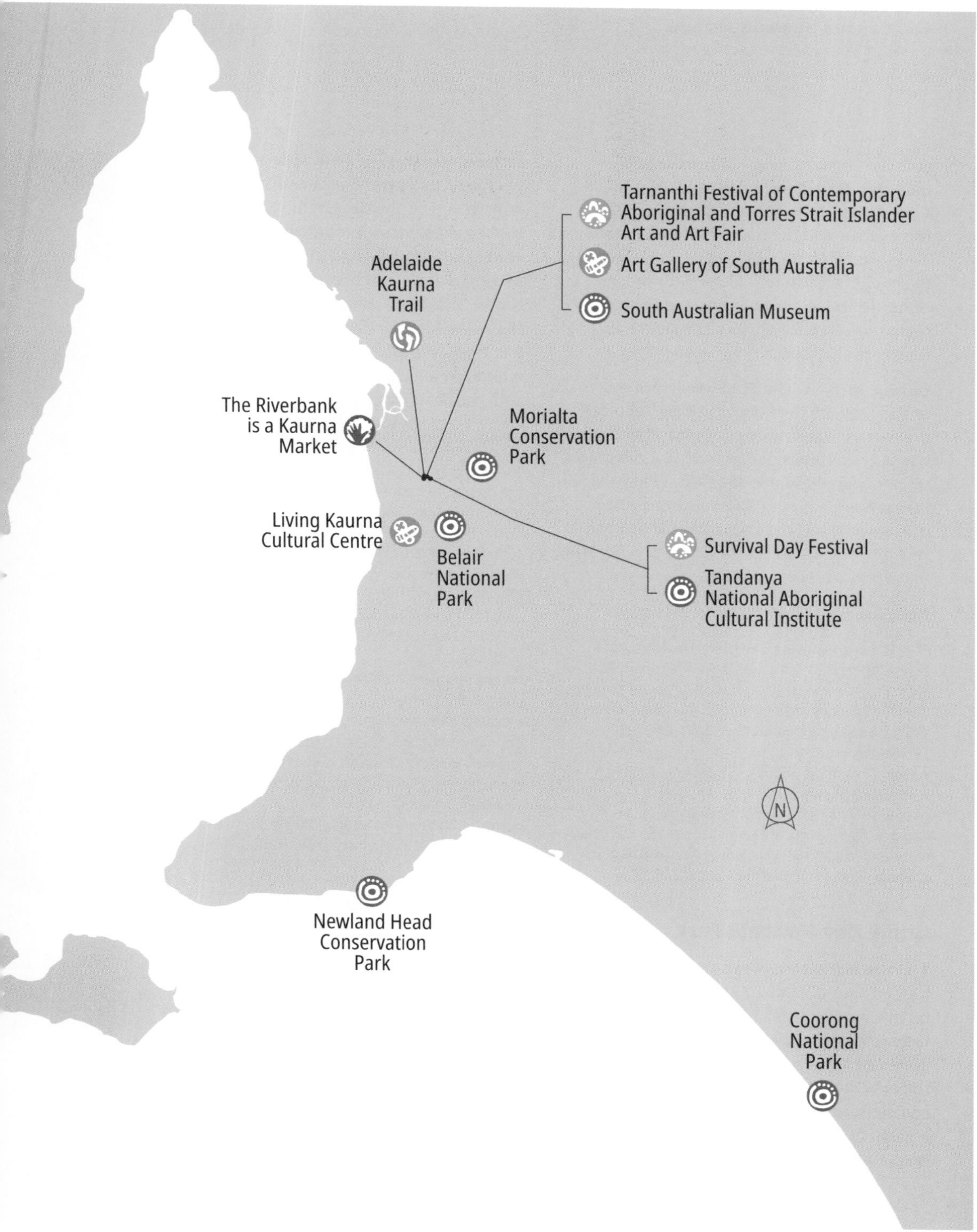

Tarnanthi Festival of Contemporary Aboriginal and Torres Strait Islander Art and Art Fair
Art Gallery of South Australia
South Australian Museum
Adelaide Kaurna Trail
The Riverbank is a Kaurna Market
Morialta Conservation Park
Living Kaurna Cultural Centre
Belair National Park
Survival Day Festival
Tandanya National Aboriginal Cultural Institute
N
Newland Head Conservation Park
Coorong National Park

yourself hiking, taking a leisurely stroll or mountain biking around it. Belair National Park is one of the oldest national parks in the world – and the first in South Australia. Treasured for its historic value and referred to simply as 'the national park' for much of its life, Belair has long been a favourite recreation area for visitors and Adelaide residents alike and is open year-round.

CULTURAL HERITAGE: The Traditional Owners of this area are the Kaurna people, who call the narrow coastal plain of Belair Piradli, which translates as 'baldness' or 'bald like the moon', referencing the sparse vista from the Adelaide Plains. Kaurna descendants maintain their cultural practice and language, and still play an active role in Caring for Country, requesting that visitors respect the area.

THINGS TO DO

The park is open every day from 8 am to sunset, except on days of total fire ban, with its excellent facilities including an adventure playground to keep the little ones amused, ovals, tennis courts, shelters and heritage pavilions that can be hired up to 12 months in advance.
WHERE: The park is about a 20-minute drive (13 km) south-east of Adelaide.
CAMPING: There is no camping available in this area.
PERMITS: Park passes are required; see the National Parks and Wildlife Service South Australia website.
CONTACT: Belair National Park: 08 8278 5477

Coffin Bay National Park

This pristine scenic coastal park covers a rugged spur of land jutting west from the tip of Eyre Peninsula into the Southern Ocean. Wild surf beaches, massive mobile dunes and eroded limestone cliffs are for the adventurous, while the park's northern coastline, with its charming, sheltered bays and inlets, offers perfect places for picnics or camping holidays.

CULTURAL HERITAGE: The Barngarla and Nauo people of the lower Eyre Peninsula coast have occupied this abundant region for thousands of years, embracing all that the waters and land have to offer. The park was accepted as part of the Nauo-Barngarla Native Title lands, offering protection to the many Aboriginal cultural sites including fish traps, shell middens and campgrounds, which remain cared for in consultation with the Traditional Owners.

THINGS TO DO

The enclosed sheltered waters of Little Yangie Bay are the perfect spot for paddling a canoe or kayaking. While this area is ideal for birdwatching and surfing, Coffin Bay is also suited to the more adventurous, with day-visit areas accessible by 2WD at Point Avoid, Long Beach, Almonta Beach and Little Yangie Bay. Much of the national park is accessible to 4WD only (a 40 km speed limit applies). Check tide times for 4WD beach tracks and avoid driving above the high-water mark.
WHERE: The park is about a 1-hour drive (50 km) west of Port Lincoln.
CAMPING: Multiple camp sites are available in the park. Bookings are essential, see the National Parks and Wildlife Service South Australia website.
PERMITS: Park passes are required; see the above website.
CONTACT: National Parks and Wildlife Services South Australia, Port Lincoln: 08 8688 3111

Coorong National Park

Coorong National Park is a long, narrow ribbon of saline wetlands, saltpans, coastal dunes and wild ocean beaches, stretching for 150 km along the Younghusband Peninsula on SA's mid-south coast. Its beaches face the blustery winds of the Southern Ocean but behind a chain of tussocky dunes is a sheltered sliver of shallow lagoons, which is an internationally recognised sanctuary for thousands of shorebirds.

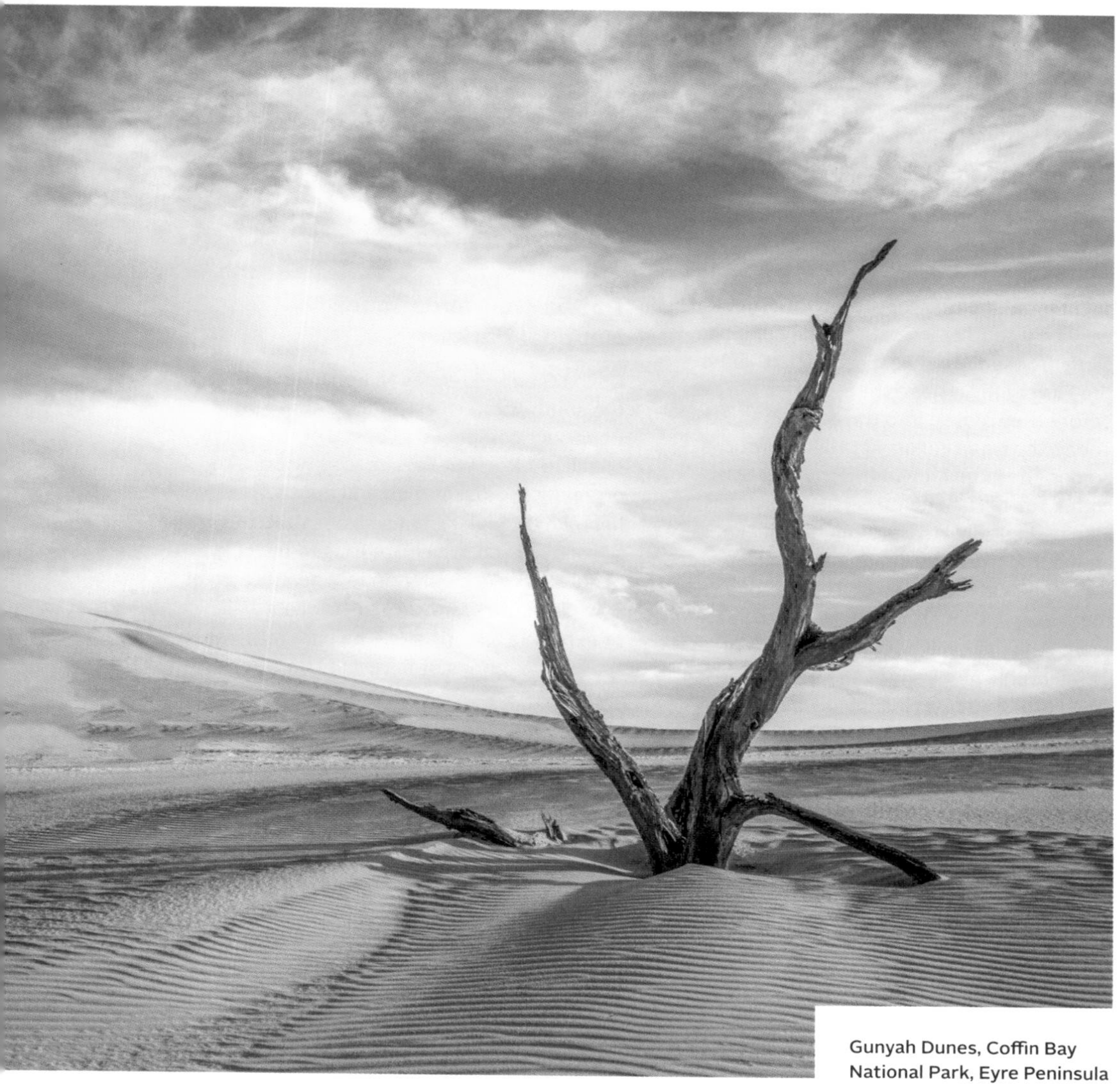

Gunyah Dunes, Coffin Bay
National Park, Eyre Peninsula

CULTURAL HERITAGE: The rich landscape of the Coorong has been home to the Ngarrindjeri people for around 6000 years. Kangaroos, wombats, snakes and goannas were traditionally hunted, while fish and shellfish were harvested. Fishing culture for Ngarrindjeri people still flourishes in this environment of saltwater lakes and lagoons. The Ngarrindjeri people travelled along the lagoons in bark and reed canoes and made substantial shelters for protection from the wild, cold southerly weather. They originally came from an Aboriginal nation further up the Murray River near the Victorian border, before they moved into the coastal country. Today, the Ngarrindjeri Aboriginal group is among the largest in Southern Australia, with a strong, rich culture. The Coorong is archaeologically and culturally significant, with burial sites, shell middens, cooking ovens and camp sites to be seen among the dunes. Although the park is open year-round, the park will be closed on days of Catastrophic Fire Danger and may be closed on days of Extreme Fire Danger. Check before you embark on your journey.

THINGS TO DO

Visitors to the Coorong can learn about Ngarrindjeri culture and beliefs from Traditional Owners and guides based at Coorong Wilderness Lodge and Camp Coorong. Nature lovers and birdwatching enthusiasts can join a 4WD Coorong Nature Tour or one of Spirit of the Coorong's eco-cruises. Walks in the park are generally easy and fairly short. Lakes Nature Trail at Salt Creek passes various habitats from ephemeral salt lakes to sand dunes to stands of mallee. Canoeing in the Coorong's sheltered waters is one of the best ways to explore the park's lagoons and islands. There are many lookouts along the eastern side of the lagoon. In the north, Pelican Point offers good birdwatching; further south, Parnka Point has scenic views up and down the lagoons with the possibility of seeing a rare orange-bellied parrot.

WHERE: 200 km south-east of Adelaide; 61 km south-east of Meningie to Salt Creek (Tea Tree Crossing).
CAMPING: Multiple camp sites are available in the park. Bookings are essential; see the National Parks and Wildlife Service South Australia website.
PERMITS: Park passes are required; see the above website.
CONTACT: Coorong National Park Information Office: (08) 8575 1200

Dhilba Guuranda-Innes National Park

Dhilba Guuranda-Innes National Park, at the south-western extremity of the Yorke Peninsula, comprises a coastal environment of saline lakes, salt flats, mallee woodlands, drooping she-oak groves and dense heathlands. High cliffs rise from stretches of sandy beach, which are fringed by rocky headlands of ancient granite. There are great places to surf, swim, dive, fish, take a walk or explore a historic site. The park features seasonal offerings of flora and fauna.

CULTURAL HERITAGE: The Yorke Peninsula land and waters belong to the Narungga Nation, which is made up of four clan groups: the Kurnara in the north of the peninsula; Windera in the east; Wari in the west; and Dilpa in the south. The Narangga traded with the neighbouring Kaurna people to the north. Around the coast and lakes of Innes there are old campsites and shell middens, reminders of where the Dilpa people lived and fished. The Narangga retain an ongoing connection with the park.

THINGS TO DO

There are cliff-top walks at The Gap and many other places to relax and enjoy the pristine coastline.The park has excellent fishing spots, with the jetty at Stenhouse Bay being a great place to start. Pondalowie Bay, known as Pondy, and

Chinamans Hat beach are among the state's top surfing locations.
WHERE: The park is about a 3.5-hour drive (300 km) from Adelaide.
CAMPING: Multiple camp sites are available in the park. Bookings are essential; see the National Parks and Wildlife Service South Australia website.
PERMITS: Park passes are required; see the above website.
CONTACT: Dhilba Guuranda-Innes National Park Visitor Information Centre: 08 8854 3200

Ikara–Flinders Ranges National Park

Ikara–Flinders Ranges National Park is one of SA's most popular tourist destinations. The 95,000 hectare park takes in rugged mountain ranges, dramatic gorges, peaceful creeks lined with river red gums, and an abundance of seasonal wildlife. It includes Heysen Range, Bunyeroo and Brachina gorges and the vast mountains that make up Ikara or Wilpena Pound. It is also renowned for its Aboriginal rock-art sites and a rich and well-preserved cultural heritage. Although open year-round, the park will be closed on days of Catastrophic Fire Danger and may be closed on days of Extreme Fire Danger. Check the NPWS SA website before you embark on the journey.

CULTURAL HERITAGE: The Traditional Owners of the land on which the park is located, the Adnyamathanha people, have a connection to the land that goes back many thousands of years. The Traditional Owners co-manage the park with representatives from the Department of Environment, Water and Natural Resources. While the Traditional Owners are very proud to share its cultural treasures, including ancient rock paintings and engravings, they do ask for all visitors to show the utmost respect for these culturally significant places to assist in protecting them for future generations.

THINGS TO DO

There are numerous walking trails in the park, with a number including Aboriginal art of cultural significance. Sacred Canyon walk (500 m, 30 minutes return, easy); from the Sacred Canyon carpark follow a short, gum-lined creek to an ancient rock-art site found on sandstone walls. The art depicts animal tracks, people and waterholes. The best time to visit is during the soft morning or afternoon light, as some paintings are weathered and hard to see. Arkaroo Rock walk (3.1 km circuit, 2 hours return, moderate) to the Akaroo rock shelter is a significant cultural site for the Adnyamathanha people. The site features ochre and charcoal rock paintings of the Yura Muda or the Dreaming for Ikara. While paintings are best seen in morning light, at sunset there are spectacular views of the Chace Range.

The park offers fantastic mountain-bike opportunities for visitors, which take in some of the most stunning scenery of the park. The Mawson trail is a long-distance cycling trail that includes spectacular views as it traverses the park. Contact the visitor centre for more information about the cycle loops. Several spectacular scenic drives are on offer in the park. Highlights include the Brachina Gorge Geological trail, which passes through 130 million years of the earth's history over a 20-km distance. Signs along the way provide information about the formation of the ranges, past climates and the evolution of early life forms.
WHERE: Ikara–Flinders Ranges National Park is in the central Flinders Ranges, about 450 km north of Adelaide. Caution is advised on unsealed roads, which may be affected by changing weather conditions throughout the year.
CAMPING: Multiple camp sites are available in the park. Bookings are essential; see the National Parks and Wildlife Service South Australia website.
PERMITS: Park passes are required; see the above website.
CONTACT: Natural Resource Centre, Port Augusta: 08 8648 5300

Innamincka Regional Reserve

Surrounded by trackless desert and forbidding gibber plains, the beautiful verdant wetlands of the Cooper Creek in Innamincka Regional Reserve and the Coongie Lakes in Malkumba-Coongie Lakes National Park form the core of a remote, vast and protected area. Picturesque waterholes shaded by coolibah trees provide a habitat for a surprising number of wetland birds and aquatic creatures.

CULTURAL HERITAGE: The Yandruwandha, Yawarrawarrka and Dieri people have lived in the region for thousands of years, with Cooper Creek being a main trade route for Aboriginal people in the area – the name Innamincka is believed to mean 'meeting place' or 'dark hole'. The area remains a spiritual place for the Traditional Owners, who continue to protect the land and waters. Stone engravings, middens, scattered artefacts in toolmaking sites, camp sites, quarries and stone arrangements are common around the Coongie Lakes and along the Cooper, especially the North West Branch. These remains give an insight into the abundance provided by the area for thousands of years. Seasonal offerings of flora and fauna are an additional pleasure.

THINGS TO DO

Innamincka Regional Reserve offers a rare combination of desert camping and wetland activities. Among the recreational pursuits, visitors can enjoy a quiet paddle or leisurely swim in Australia's largest billabong – Cullyamurra Waterhole

WHERE: The reserve is about a 15.5-hour drive (1200 km) from Adelaide.

CAMPING: Multiple camp sites are available in the park. Bookings are essential; see the National Parks and Wildlife Service South Australia website.

PERMITS: Park passes are required; see the above website.

CONTACT: Innamincka Regional Reserve Visitor Information Centre: 08 8675 9909

Kati Thanda–Lake Eyre National Park

Kati Thanda-Lake Eyre National Park encircles a desolate landscape of saltpans and waterless tracts of red desert. On rare occasions, the generally dry salt-encrusted lake surfaces are transformed to massive wetlands that attract thousands of birds, fish and other aquatic organisms. It is well worth the trip to visit one of the country's great outback destinations. In 2012, a partnership was formed between the Arabana Aboriginal Corporation and the Department of Environment, Water and Natural Resources to share responsibility for the management of the Kati Thanda-Lake Eyre National Park.

CULTURAL HERITAGE: Once Kati Thanda dried up, the Country appears to have been unoccupied until around 5000 years ago. At this time, the Arabana on the lake's western shores and the Dieri people living around the lower reaches of the Warburton and Cooper rivers relied on mound springs for water. When the lake was full, abundant food resources allowed people to move across the land with ease, conducting trade and ceremonial business with neighbouring groups. When the lake was dry, the people gathered around the springs and waterholes. Dieri Country was a crossroads for major trade routes: pituri traded from the north, stones from the east and west, ochre from the south, and even pearl shell from Cape York reached this far south. After a long Native Title battle, the Arabana people have now regained ownership of land to the west of Kati Thanda, a significant part of their homeland and heritage.

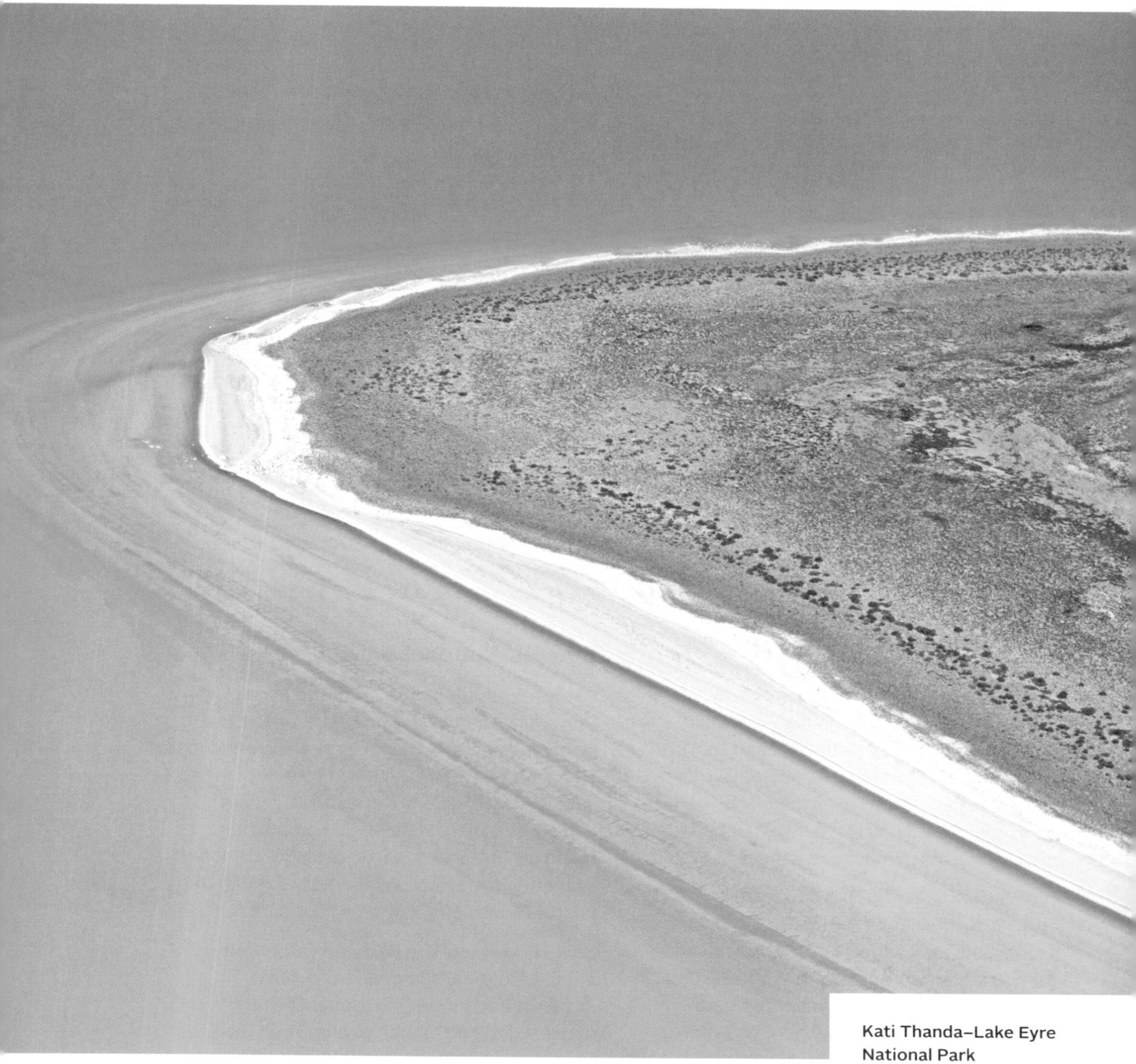

Kati Thanda–Lake Eyre National Park

THINGS TO DO

The park offers incredible sights, photography, bush camping and birdwatching. There are views over Kati Thanda South from the Oodnadatta Track at Bopeechee, but one of the best perspectives is from the air. Scenic flights are available, and all visitors are asked to avoid driving on the lake's fragile surface.
WHERE: The park is about a 1.5-hour drive (60 km) east of William Creek and a 2-hour drive (95 km) north-west of Marree.
CAMPING: Multiple camp sites are available in the park. Bookings are essential; see the National Parks and Wildlife Service South Australia website.
PERMITS: Park passes are required; see the above website.
CONTACT: National Parks Wildlife Service South Australia, Port Augusta: 08 8648 5328

Lake Torrens National Park

Transitory Lake Torrens is starkly photogenic. Protected within Lake Torrens National Park is Australia's second largest lake, which has filled with water only once in the past 150 years. Infrequent thunderstorms do provide a little relief, sometimes turning a hard-packed salt crust to boggy brown mud. Numerous birds call the lake home, including banded stilts that arrive in flocks to feast on brine shrimp. Vegetation around the lake is sparse, consisting mainly of saltbush, bluebush and samphire. Although the park is open daily, it will be closed if there is extreme fire risk or catastrophic fire danger.

CULTURAL HERITAGE: The land and water at Lake Torrens is the traditional lands of 4 Aboriginal groups: the Barngarla, Kokatha, Kuyani and Adnyamathanha people. In the off seasons the people stayed near the springs and waterholes; in good times there was more movement – particularly for trade and ceremonial purposes. It is sacred territory crossed by many Dreaming tracks and there are many rock engravings sites. In 2016, the Supreme Court did not grant Native Title to any of the 4 Aboriginal groups, and in January 2021, despite opposition from the Traditional Owners, the South Australian Government approved mineral drilling of the lake.

THINGS TO DO

This park is really best for those seeking an observatory experience, as driving on the lake surface is not permitted because of the damage caused by deep wheel ruts and scars. In some spots, soft patches make it quite easy to bog or even roll your vehicle, and this can quickly become a life-or-death situation in a place as remote as this. Access to the national park is via Mulgaria or Andamooka stations (permission required for private roads).
WHERE: Lake Torrens National Park is a 4.5-hour drive (345 km) north of Adelaide. Permission must be obtained before entering this park.
CAMPING: Not permitted at Lake Torrens National Park.
PERMITS: Park passes are required; see the National Parks and Wildlife Service South Australia website.
CONTACT: National Parks Wildlife Service South Australia, Port Augusta: 08 8648 5300

Lincoln National Park

Easily accessible at the tip of the Eyre Peninsula, Lincoln National Park protects a sweeping plain of coastal mallee surrounded by bays and ocean beaches. The quiet coves with sparkling blue waters, storm-carved limestone cliffs and massive white dunes are relatively untracked, particularly the declared Wilderness Area around Memory Cove in the pristine south-east corner of the park.

CULTURAL HERITAGE: The Barngarla and Nauo people are the traditional custodians of this country. The Traditional Owners mastered the art of harvesting freshwater from underground and coastal springs, with shellfish, fish, reptiles, mammals and edible plants having supplied a bountiful larder; throughout the park there are fish traps of arranged stones, shell middens and artefacts located in areas where stone was once worked. Open year-round, the park has seasonal offerings of flora and fauna.

THINGS TO DO

Lincoln offers a variety of activities along its beautiful coastlines, including beachcombing, fishing, swimming and sightseeing. Cliff edges are unstable or undercut in places, so extreme care should be taken when walking in coastal areas and when fishing or driving. Ocean conditions can become hazardous so it is best to check the tides before taking a swim or going for a paddle.

WHERE: The park is approximately a 7.5-hour drive (650 km) west of Adelaide; a 40-minute drive (20 km) south of Port Lincoln; a 3.5-hour drive (290 km) south-east of Streaky Bay.

CAMPING: Multiple camp sites are available in the park. Bookings are essential; see the National Parks and Wildlife Service South Australia website.

PERMITS: Park passes are required; see the above website.

CONTACT: National Parks and Wildlife Service South Australia, Port Lincoln: 08 8688 3111

Morialta Conservation Park

Morialta Conservation Park has rugged, red cliffs and 3 grand waterfalls along Fourth Creek that crash into rock pools, providing a habitat for small reptiles, frogs and birds. Away from the gorge, woodlands cloak the hills, and are a refuge for honeyeaters, thornbills and many other birds, while spindly she-oaks and yaccas cling to the steepest slopes. Although open year-round, it is best to visit the park during winter and spring and to see the waterfalls in full force.

CULTURAL HERITAGE: This area is part of the traditional lands of the Kaurna people, who hunted possums, bandicoots, kangaroos, fish and lizards, and made extensive use of fire to manage the land. Descendants of these people still live in Adelaide and, with other Kaurna people, have been reviving their culture and language. An initial 218 hectares donated in 1913 was supplemented by land purchases in the 1960s and renamed Morialta Conservation Park in 1972 after the Kaurna word morialta, meaning 'ever-flowing'.

THINGS TO DO

Soaring eucalyptus trees shade the grassy area near the park entrance for visitors accessing the barbecues, picnic tables and toilets. Take a relaxed saunter along the wheelchair-friendly Valley Walk, past Giants Cave to the base of First Falls, or climb to Deep View Lookout to marvel at the view down the valley to Adelaide and the coast.

WHERE: Morialta Conservation Park is about a 20-minute drive (10 km) north-east of Adelaide.

CAMPING: Not permitted in this park.

PERMITS: Park passes are required; see the National Parks and Wildlife Service South Australia website.

CONTACT: Black Hill National Park and Wildlife Service: 08 8336 0901

Mount Remarkable National Park

Meander through the foothills of these scented woodlands comprising northern cypress pine, acacia and eucalypt, located in the southern reaches of the Flinders Ranges. This enchanting bushland park hosts steep wooded valleys and rugged, red quartzite gorges. The park conserves part of an important geological region of high diversity, where arid zone and temperate species overlap. It is best to visit the park in the milder temperatures from April to October, as the warmer months can bring extreme heat and heavy rainfall.

CULTURAL HERITAGE: The Nukunu people have traditional ties with this region, and sites in the park reveal their use of chert (very hard sedimentary rock used to make spearheads) and quartzite. The

The view from Morialta Conservation Park

Nukunu now live in several centres around Mount Remarkable and retain strong links to Country. Nukunu continue to practise culture and language on Country with further knowledge of the cultural heritage of the region remaining unknown, as it may be privileged to selected Nukunu people and therefore not recorded for public use.

THINGS TO DO

With 100 km of trails, Mount Remarkable National Park provides lots of opportunities for bushwalking. When you are ready to put your feet up and have a feed, picnicking in the shady areas with facilities alongside the creek at Mambray and at Blue Gum Flat in Alligator Gorge is a pleasant way to take in the surrounds.

WHERE: The park is about a 1-hour drive (45 km) north of Port Pirie.

CAMPING: Multiple camp sites are available in the park. Bookings are essential; see the National Parks and Wildlife Service South Australia website.

PERMITS: Park passes are required; see the above website.

CONTACT: National Parks and Wildlife Service South Australia, Yorke and Mid North: 08 8841 3400

Murray River National Park

Located alongside the peaceful waters of the lower reaches of the great Murray River, this national park embraces 3 separate areas of braided creeks, shady riverbanks and riverine floodplains that include some of the most striking river environments in Australia. Enjoy the seasonal offerings of flora and fauna. Historical sites in the area demonstrate the strong cultural connections Traditional Owners have with this fertile region. Although Murray River National Park can be visited year-round, heat can become extreme in January and February, so it is always best to check before visiting.

CULTURAL HERITAGE: The river region in South Australia belongs to the Ngawait, Erawirung, Ngintait, Maraura and Danggali people. The plentiful water and food resources enabled populations to flourish, with the river forming a natural highway along which groups could travel by canoe. Numerous scarred trees along the Murray show the history of prolific canoe-making in this area. Edible plants and roots were foraged, while animal meat, mussels, waterbirds and tortoises were caught with nets and spears. There are countless cultural and historic sites along the river, including shell middens, burial grounds, camp sites and scarred trees.

THINGS TO DO

Visitors to the park can bush camp or stay in a houseboat, relax under shady river red gums, swim in Australia's largest river, canoe along the backwaters, watch out for birds, and enjoy some good fishing.

WHERE: Travel times from Adelaide vary from a 2.5-hour to 4-hour drive (200 km–300 km) depending on which entrance of the park is used; see the National Parks and Wildlife Service South Australia website for more details.

CAMPING: Only permitted at dedicated sites; Bookings are essential, see the above website.

PERMITS: Park passes are required; see the above website.

CONTACT: National Parks Wildlife Service South Australia, Berri: 08 8580 1800

Newland Head Conservation Park

Surrounded by rocky headlands, Newland Head Conservation Park protects 2 long beaches that follow walking trails leading to observatory gems. The mouse-sized southern pygmy possum feeding on bugs and nectar from banksia flowers is a delight for visitors. Fur-seals, whales and little penguins are sometimes spotted in the water, while the vegetation includes mallee heath and coastal dune flora, and around the Waitpinga Creek estuary are samphire and wetland species. Although open year-round, the park will be closed if there is a fire risk, so it is best to check before visiting.

CULTURAL HERITAGE: Newland Head Conservation Park, just west of Victor Harbor on the Fleurieu Peninsula, protects Waitpinga and Parsons beaches, Newland Headland, the Waitpinga Cliffs coastal reserve and a number of important social and cultural sites belonging to the Ramindjeri, one of the 18 clans making up the Ngarrindjeri nation.

THINGS TO DO

Activities in the park include leisurely beach strolls or bushwalks that offer some magnificent views. Keen walkers can take the challenging Newland Head Nature Hike (15 km, 7 hours, medium difficulty) that follows a section of the Heysen Trail along the cliff tops. The water is too treacherous for swimming and is best left to expert surfers, but it can offer up treasures for beachcombers. Gutters formed by huge surf on Waitpinga and Parsons beaches create excellent fishing, with mullet, mulloway and salmon the target fish. The rocky headlands at the ends of both beaches are prone to wild surf and freak waves so rock fishing can be extremely dangerous.
WHERE: Newland Head Conservation Park is approximately a 2-hour drive (91 km) south of Adelaide.
CAMPING: Not permitted in this park.
PERMITS: Park passes are required; see the National Parks and Wildlife Service South Australia website.
CONTACT: National Parks and Wildlife Service South Australia, Victor Harbor: 08 8552 0300

Nullarbor National Park, Wilderness Protection Area and Regional Reserve

The serene and isolated beauty of the Nullarbor National Park, Wilderness Protection Area and Regional Reserve is unforgettable. This strip of the famous Nullarbor Plain stretches from the head of the Great Australian Bight to the border of Western Australia. Along its southern edge, soaring-high cliffs drop to the deep blue of the Great Australian Bight Marine Park. In the north, the park joins the massive Nullarbor Regional Reserve, which extends to the Trans Australian Railway. The park is now co-managed by the Traditional Owners and National Parks and Wildlife staff. Although open year-round, it is best to visit between May and October to catch a glimpse of whale migration.

CULTURAL HERITAGE: The Mirning people, members of the A<u>n</u>angu Pitjantjatjara group, are the Traditional Owners of the Nullarbor parks. There are 60 known archaeological sites on the plain, including handprints, hearths, stone implements and paintings, with many indicating over 40,000 years of connection to Country. Today the Mirning people live in several centres around the park and traditional customs remain strong, with many people living on their traditional lands, hunting game meats such as malu (kangaroo), kilpara (Australian brush-turkey) and wadu (wombat) as important food sources.

THINGS TO DO

Bask in the majestic southern views where whales perform their yearly migrations. The park offers sightseeing, caving, 4WD touring and whale-watching. There are also scenic flights from Nullarbor Roadhouse. Travel in more remote parts of the park requires considerable expertise and preparation as there are no facilities. Cliff edges are extremely steep and undercut in places. Be prepared for extreme conditions.
WHERE: Nullarbor National Park and Regional Reserve is about a 4-hour drive (300 km) west of Ceduna.
CAMPING: You can camp under the stars at the Nullarbor Wilderness protection area. Bookings are essential; see the National Parks and Wildlife Service South Australia website.

PERMITS: Park passes are required; see the above website.
CONTACT: National Parks and Wildlife Service South Australia, Ceduna: 08 8625 3144

Vulkathunha-Gammon Ranges National Park

At the northernmost end of the Flinders, the windswept Vulkathunha–Gammon Ranges are the last cluster of ancient mountains before the vast plains of central Australia. Few travellers venture here compared to national parks further south, but this place has a unique pull, with rugged twisted ridges, rock-strewn valleys, sheer cliffs, with hidden plunge pools and rocky creeks to be found under sheltered gorges. Although the park is open daily, to allow for hunting in this area the cultural-use zone by Lake Frome is closed to the general public from 3 pm to 5 am daily.

CULTURAL HERITAGE: Adnyamathanha songlines traverse the area, and the natural features of the Country are woven into Adnyamathanha traditional stories, having great significance for all phases of life from birth through to death. They tell of places that are munda, or dangerous, to visitors and where access is prohibited. Today, the Adnyamathanha live at Nepabunna, Nantawarrina, Mount Serle and other locations throughout the ranges; their knowledge, language, ceremonies, kinship systems, traditional cultural sites, and hunting and food gathering techniques are being passed on to new generations. As custodians, the Adnyamathanha people jointly manage the Vulkathunha–Gammon Ranges National Park and continue to conduct cultural activities within its boundaries. A cultural-use zone has been established between Balcanoona and Lake Frome specifically for this purpose.

THINGS TO DO

The park offers sightseeing and camping in a remote outback terrain; due to the isolation of this location, bushwalking is generally for experienced wilderness walkers only. The area has Aboriginal cultural importance, which can be seen at Iga Warta, just outside the park in the south-west.
WHERE: Vulkathunha–Gammon Ranges National Park is about an 8-hour drive (660 km) north of Adelaide, and a 1.5-hour drive (100 km) east of Leigh Creek. Not all areas are suitable for 2WD vehicles, so it is best to check before visiting the park.
CAMPING: Multiple camp sites are available in the park. Bookings are essential; see the National Parks and Wildlife Service South Australia website.
PERMITS: Park passes are required; see the above website.
CONTACT: National Parks and Wildlife Service South Australia, Port Augusta: 08 8648 5300

Wabma Kadarbu Mound Springs Conservation Park

Wabma Kadarbu Mound Springs Conservation Park is a place of transcendent natural mound springs and ancient cultural Dreaming. Surrender your inner adventurer and soak in the surrounds with a calm and reflective wander through the historical plains and mystical waters.

CULTURAL HERITAGE: Wabma Kadarbu Mound Springs Conservation Park is located on Arabana Country and is a Dreaming site that literally translates to 'snake-head'. The Traditional Owners welcome visitors to this area to learn about the stories and culture that has survived for thousands of years. In sacred places that hold spiritual significance, please take note of signs and refrain from touching anything out of respect for the Traditional Owners' ongoing connection to this place.

THINGS TO DO

Wabma Kadarbu Mound Springs Conservation Park is a place to take in the atmosphere at a leisurely pace and is not ideal for more adventuristic types. Absorb the surrounding plains and natural mound springs in a meditative-like fashion. If you do decide to 4WD in this area, please follow the strict instructions on the National Parks and Wildlife Service South Australia website.
WHERE: Wabma Kadarbu Mound Springs Conservation Park is a 6-hour drive (498 km) north of Port Augusta.
CAMPING: Not permitted in this park.
PERMITS: Park passes are required, see the National Parks and Wildlife Service South Australia website.
CONTACT: National Parks Wildlife Service South Australia, Port Augusta: 08 8648 5328

Witjira National Park

One of 3 parks stretching east–west across the north-east of the state, adjacent to the border with the Northern Territory and Queensland – Witjira National Park is most famous for its striking diversity. In the west is the largest collection of artesian springs in Australia, circled by stunted ti-trees, century-old date palms and wetlands attracting 60 species of bird. This place is a wonderland for wildlife. Further east there is the largest parallel dune desert in the world, with brilliant red sandhills, glistening silver saltpans, stony tablelands, harsh gibber plains and ephemeral lakes. The best time to visit the park is between April and September.

CULTURAL HERITAGE: Part of the traditional lands of several Aboriginal groups, Witjira National Park is co-managed with the Irrwanyere Aboriginal Corporation representing the Lower Southern Arrernte, Wangkangurru, Arabunna and Luritja people. This arrangement includes provision of permanent living areas within the park so Aboriginal people can effectively manage their land. Archaeological evidence in the parks suggests Aboriginal occupation stretching back thousands of years. The springs have always been central to life and culture, determining the lines of important trade routes through the desert. The Witjira National Park co-management board is proud to work in collaboration with other conservationists to support the natural environment by using collective expertise.

THINGS TO DO

These desert parks offer captivating natural features and historic sites to trek around. This is remote Country so you will need to be prepared and self-sufficient and carry plenty of food, water and fuel. Outback camping and 4WD touring are also popular activities on this Country.
WHERE: Witjira National Park is located approximately 9.5 hours (885km) north-west of Port Augusta.
CAMPING : Multiple camp sites are available in the park. Bookings are essential; see the National Parks and Wildlife Service South Australia website.
PERMITS: Park passes are required; see the above website.
CONTACT: National Parks Wildlife Service SA, Port Augusta: 08 8648 5300

TOURS AND STAYS

Aboriginal Cultural Tours SA

A tour operator located on Adjahdura Land on the Yorke Peninsula, Aboriginal Cultural Tours is run by Quenten Agius, who is a Traditional Owner, and chairperson and Senior Heritage Monitor for the Adjahdura Narungga Heritage group. The lands are significant cultural sites for Aboriginal communities in the area and were the site of the Point Pearce Aboriginal Mission, built in 1867. The township still survives, and, unlike most missions, Point Pearce is remembered by local Elders as an Aboriginal sanctuary. Aboriginal Cultural Tours SA offers 10 single-day and multi-day bush, coastal and combination tours through Ngadjuri Country and Adjahdura land, and has a focus on supporting local businesses, accommodation providers and produce. The company has won multiple tourism awards over the past decade that reflect the quality of this operation.

WHERE: 46 Maitland Rd, Point Pearce.
CONTACT: 0429 367 121

Adelaide Kaurna Trail

Take a journey though time and celebrate the Kaurna past, present and future by taking a 2–3-hour heritage stroll through the traditional lands of the Kaurna people of the Adelaide Plains. The Kaurna trail is optimal when you're not in a rush, as the rich historic significance is worthy of your time and attention. You will learn about the Traditional Owners and discover stories from Elders through the writing and Indigenous art seen along the way. There is a total of 24 sites to visit including Red Kangaroo Dreaming, or Tarndanyangga, with the trail being a restorative way to reflect on the past and learn about the adapting and thriving Kaurna culture today. The 9.7-km trail is recommended for those with a moderate fitness level and is suitable by foot or with a bicycle.

WHERE: Centred around the Adelaide CBD.

Adelaide Ocean Safari

Multi-award-winning business Adelaide Ocean Safari will have you exploring all that the Glenelg waters have to offer. Adelaide Ocean Safari offers a cultural tour, curated by Traditional Owners, that takes guests on a journey to areas only observable by water; this option is ideal for those who want to learn from someone with deep cultural insight of the region. With a knowledgeable team at the helm, your experience can include snorkelling and swimming – with dolphins if the timing is right – or for those more land oriented, the comfortable vessels will ensure your experience is a relaxing one. Take in the extensive coastline of Kangaroo Island on a special 75-minute cruise, with the chance to see birdlife and wildlife, such as seals or majestic whales, over the winter months. The Seafood and Wine Safari offers an indulgence of the senses, with fresh local produce and wine from the Barossa to enjoy while you sit back and enjoy the deep blue surrounds.

WHERE: Christmas Cove Marina Pier, Penneshaw, Kangaroo Island.
CONTACT: 0417 551 444

Take in the extensive coastline of Kangaroo Island with Adelaide Ocean Safari

Iga Warta

The Adnyamathanha people are the Traditional Owners of the Northern Flinders Ranges. Iga Warta tours are proudly Aboriginal owned and operated, aiming to keep culture alive by sharing knowledges and generously including visitors in historical teachings about the area. Visitors can immerse themselves in the surrounding plants, animals, mountains and culturally significant sites that hold ancient and lively stories. Maintaining cultural practice is an important element of this experience, as it shows visitors how the land was managed (pre-colonisation) and how the Adnyamathanha people thrived over thousands of years. Overnight stays are in tents and swags so that guests experience the true nature of the area, while learning the rules of the Muda (Dreaming) and engaging in how the Adnyamathanha people have adapted and continue to thrive on the land. The Ochre Pit tour teaches guests about the uses of ochre and how each colour is significant for various reasons, while the

A sunset tour at Wilpena Pound Resort

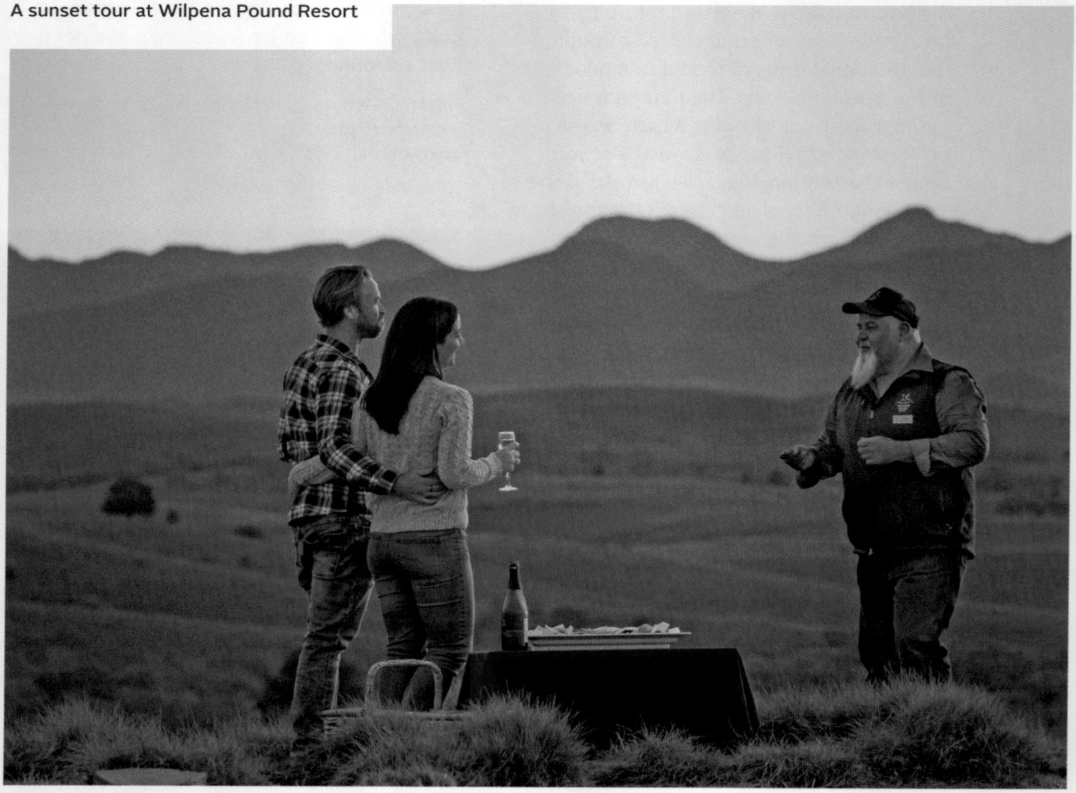

Red Gorge Tour takes guests to a site that is 80,000 years old, where you can learn about the historical connection to the sacred site. For those led by their stomachs, there is a Mai (food) tour that provides visitors with the opportunity to see how bush tucker is cultivated and cooked using traditional methods. There is a tour for all interest at Iga Warta, if for no other reason than immerse yourself in the exquisite surroundings, this is well worth a visit.

WHERE: Via Copley.
CONTACT: 08 8648 3737

Wilpena Pound Resort

Located within the Ikara–Flinders Ranges National Park, Wilpena Pound Resort was purchased in 2012 as a joint venture by Indigenous Business Australia (IBA) and the Adnyamathanha Traditional Lands Association (ATLA), to provide a sustainable economic future for the local Adnyamathanha people. The resort offers a number of activities to visitors to Adnyamathanha Country, including Aboriginal culture walks, 4WD tours, and scenic flights around the park and over Lake Eyre. Accommodation ranges from hotel rooms to luxury safari tents and camping grounds; see the resort website for details. Partial park closures are implemented during the summer months, so check the website for changes to activities.

WHERE: Ikara–Flinders Ranges National Park is located 429 km north of Adelaide and is accessible by car or scenic flight transfer (must be arranged in advance). Buses run from Adelaide to the town of Hawker, with transfers available from Hawker to the resort if booked in advance.
CONTACT: Resort reception: 08 8648 0004; reservations: 1800 805 802; campground bookings: 08 8648 0048

ART GALLERIES, CULTURAL CENTRES AND MUSEUMS

Art Gallery of South Australia

The Art Gallery of South Australia houses some of the most important collections of Aboriginal and Torres Strait Islander art in the country. As well as its outstanding permanent collections, the gallery has a calendar of exciting temporary exhibitions and events throughout the year, including the Tarnanthi Festival and educational programs for school children, with many focusing on Indigenous art. Although general admission is free, fees apply for some special exhibitions.

WHERE: North Tce, Adelaide.
CONTACT: 08 8207 7000

Arts Ceduna

Arts Ceduna sells artworks by more than 100 artists from the far-west region of South Australia. The artists from this region have strong ties to Country and the influence of the environment is clearly seen in their work. Surrounding Ceduna is the largest untouched mallee and spinifex country to the north, ancient rock formations, such as the Gawler Ranges, to the east, the pristine waters of the Great Australian Bight to the south, and the vast Nullabor Plains to the west. This diverse country accounts for the equally diverse and unique range of artworks displayed and sold at Arts Ceduna.

WHERE: Ceduna Arts and Cultural Centre, 2 Eyre Hwy, Ceduna. Ceduna is located 786 km north-west of Adelaide on the Eyre Peninsula. Bus services operate between Adelaide and Ceduna in both directions.
CONTACT: 08 8625 2487

Kuju Aboriginal Arts

Kuju Aboriginal Arts showcases Indigenous art from Port Lincoln and the Wangka Wilurrara region. The works exhibited come from a range of artists and reflect the culture, stories and lifestyle of the region. Local artists explore traditional and contemporary mediums, giving the artworks a unique look. Kuju is Aboriginal-owned and operated, aiming to provide artists with a source of income and economic independence.

WHERE: 30 Ravendale Rd, Port Lincoln. The coastal city of Port Lincoln is located on the south-east point of the Eyre Peninsula in SA.
CONTACT: 08 8682 6677

Living Kaurna Cultural Centre

The Living Kaurna Cultural Centre is located at the Warriparinga Wetlands, which have been a gathering place for the Kaurna people for thousands of years. The centre is operated by Kaurna-owned business Southern Cultural Immersion, striving to promote and nurture reconciliation and cultural respect towards First peoples within Australia.

The Living Kaurna Cultural Centre is open to visitors, and features an art gallery and retail space set in the sprawling grounds. The grounds feature stunning art instillations and natural flora and fauna, all surrounding the Sturt River.

The Living Kaurna Cultural Centre also hosts major First peoples celebrations, including music performances and markets. Cultural training, community engagement, art and cultural workshops and cultural tours are all on offer.

WHERE: Warriparinga Way (off Sturt Rd), Bedford Park, Adelaide.
CONTACT: 08 8357 5900

Top: Art installation at the entry to the Warriparinga grounds, Living Kaurna Cultural Centre

Bottom: Living Kaurna Cultural Centre

Pwerle Gallery

With familial legacy at its heart, Pwerle Gallery is an Aboriginal family-owned and operated business with most of the artists on the roster being connected through ancestral ties. Jade Torres founded the gallery in 2015, following in the footstep of her father, renowned art dealer Fred Torres. Jade is the granddaughter of celebrated artist Barbara Weir and great-granddaughter of Minne Pwerle, the namesake of the gallery, who took up painting at the age of 80 and went on to become a revered artist. The gallery is extensive, presenting over 300 exhibitions at exclusive galleries across the world, and actively promotes Indigenous art in publications around the globe. Pwerle Gallery has also introduced works to new audiences through collaborations with fashion labels, wine companies and media projects that have expanded the reach of the distinctive Utopian style. Artworks for sale can be viewed on the website and information about each one is detailed and easily accessible, though if you seek a more tactile experience, appointments can be arranged.

WHERE: Online at the Pwerle Gallery website.
CONTACT: 0412 104 797

South Australian Museum

The South Australian Museum cares for the most expansive collection of Aboriginal and Torres Strait Islander material in the world. With extraordinary collections of art and culture, archival and archaeological records, the museum tells stories of thousands of years of Aboriginal creativity, technologies and ingenuity. The museum works closely with Aboriginal people to ensure collections are activated and accessible, and that stories are relevant and truthful. It engages with Aboriginal groups across Australia to co-create and collaborate on research projects, exhibitions and public programs. The museum is also active in repatriation of human remains and sacred objects by working with communities to return remains and objects to their place of origin, a primary responsibility for reconciliation. The museum is committed to working closely with communities to ensure that truth-telling (including about the museum's own history) is an active part of the stories it shares with the public.

WHERE: North Terrace, Adelaide.
CONTACT: 08 8207 7500

Tandanya National Aboriginal Cultural Institute

Tandanya is the oldest Aboriginal-owned and managed multi-arts centre in Australia and features traditional and contemporary Aboriginal and Torres Strait Islander visual and performing arts. In the Kaurna language, Tandanya means 'place of the red kangaroo', referring to the centre's location on Kaurna land, within the location of the traditional Red Kangaroo ceremony. Several gallery spaces display about 12 exhibitions annually, which seek to reflect the vibrant and diverse culture existing within Aboriginal and Torres Strait Islander communities. Throughout the year, Tandanya also hosts community events and festivals, including Survival Day in January and the Spirit Festival in March. The visual arts program includes free and ticketed shows.

WHERE: 253 Grenfell St, Adelaide.
CONTACT: 08 8224 3200

The Tjatu Gallery

Tjatu Gallery is a partnership between Mimili Maku, Iwantja Arts and Marla Travellers' Rest. Tjatu means 'together' in Yankunytjatjara.

Top: APY Women's Collaborative, Amata, 2017

Bottom: Delquade Dunnett and Otis Ken, Amata, with APY Art Centre Collective, 2017

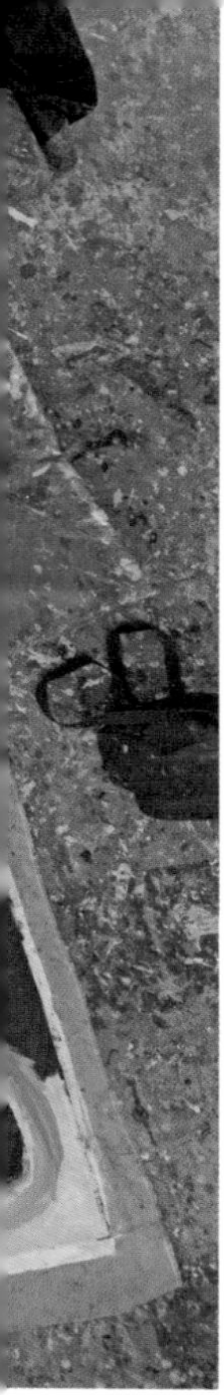

The partnership enables the artworks, and the various stories told through them, to be displayed in a gallery space that is more easily accessible to tourists than some others in the APY Lands. In the future, the gallery plans to hold artists' talks and meet-the-artist markets to provide a direct link between tourists, passers by and visitors to the Aboriginal people of these remote areas.

WHERE: Marla is a small service town on the Stuart Hwy, 159 km south of the NT border and 676 km north of Port Augusta. It offers a range of facilities for travellers including accommodation, a restaurant, bar, service station and supermarket.
CONTACT: 08 8956 2984

PLACES

The Riverbank is a Kaurna Market

In 2018, Kaurna Aboriginal artist and architect, Paul Herzich designed the Riverbank is a Kaurna Market. An installation of imagery and writing created in sandblasted concrete and acrylic paint, this 2D work explores the past, present and future footsteps taken by Kaurna people in this exact locale. It allows visitors to take a journey through ancient Kaurna culture by literally walking on the same path between the riverbank and the Adelaide Central Market, a route that has been taken by Kaurna people over thousands of years. The work was created to elicit feelings of recognition for Kaurna culture, language and practice into the future. An experience that is monetarily free but will leave you abundant with knowledge and respect for the Kaurna people and culture.

WHERE: Topham Mall, Adelaide
CONTACT: Via the Explore Adelaide pages on the City of Adelaide website.

ART CENTRES

APY Art Centre Collective

The APY Art Centre Collective is a group of 10 remote Aboriginal-owned arts enterprises that collaborate on projects and progress strong business initiatives by and for the people of the Anangu Pitjantjatjara Yankunytjatjara (APY) Lands, in remote South Australia. The collective aims to support every young person in the APY communities to be strong and proud in their culture and to succeed in both the Indigenous and non-Indigenous worlds.

The collective runs not-for-profit galleries in Sydney and Adelaide, which allow its emerging Indigenous artists to connect with a wide audience outside of their remote communities, gain professional development opportunities and build a network supporting them to pursue successful careers in the arts. These young artists have watched, listened to and learned from their grandparents, the senior men and women of the APY Lands, and are now taking their turn to find new ways of sharing these traditions and stories. The APY galleries showcase artists working across mediums including painting, traditional punu (wood) carving, weaving, textiles, new media and digital photography.

SYDNEY: 45 Burton St, Darlinghurst
CONTACT: 02 9368 1173
ADELAIDE: 9 Light Sq
CONTACT: 08 8212 4743
APY ART CENTRES:

Mimili Maku
Tjungu Palya
Ninuku Arts
Tjala Arts
Iwantja Arts
Kaltjiti Arts
Tjanpi Desert Weavers

Iwantja Arts

Iwantja Arts is named after Iwantja Creek, where the Indulkana community was first formed. The history of Iwantja Arts is rich in printmaking. In the early 1980s two artists travelled to Canberra campaigning for funding to establish a printmaking workshop and painting studios. Many of the early limited-edition prints from Iwantja Arts are now held in the South Australian Museum in Adelaide and the National Gallery of Australia in Canberra. Today, the centre supports artists working across a range of mediums, both individually and collaboratively. It is a not-for-profit, Aboriginal-owned and run centre aiming to provide opportunities, training and career development for artists. At the time of writing, Iwantja Arts was closed to the public, so check the website and make contact before planning a visit.

WHERE: Indulkana community is close to the Stuart Hwy, about 575 km south of Alice Springs. It sits in a small ridge on the edge of the Indulkana Ranges.
CONTACT: 08 8670 7722

Kaltjiti Arts

A member of the APY Art Centre Collective, Kaltjiti Arts is the heart of the Fregon community. Established in 1961, it is now a place of dynamism, creativity and artistic excellence, focusing on cultural maintenance and economic sustainability through the arts. Kaltjiti is known for high-quality artworks that tell the stories of the region's sacred Tjukurpa. Artistic expression is a way for senior Elders and artists to transfer knowledge from the ancestors to younger generations, maintaining the living culture of the Anangu. Kaltjiti paintings are bold, bright and contemporary.

WHERE: Fregon community, APY Lands.
PERMITS: Permits are required from the APY Administration when visiting the APY Lands.
CONTACT: 08 8956 7720

Mimili Maku Art Centre

Mimili Maku Art Centre is named after the witchetty grub, maku, which is found in the roots of *Acacia kempeana*. The Maku Tjukurpa is the witchetty grub songline, a story of great cultural and historical significance in this area. Artworks feature traditional narrative, imagery and symbols, juxtaposed with abstract designs and bold colours. The complex depiction of Country and the Maku Tjukurpa is of particular interest to art collectors nationally and overseas. The art centre involves and supports artists from the Mimili community as well as Perentie Bore, Wanmara, Blue Hills and Sandy Bore homelands in the surrounding area.

WHERE: Mimili is about 645 km south of Alice Springs. It lies at the base of the Everard Ranges.
WHEN: To make an appointment to visit Mimili Maku Arts, please contact the manager: info@mimilimaku.com
CONTACT: 08 8956 2984

Ninuku Arts

Ninuku Arts, established in 2006, is located in the Kalka community, in the far north-west corner of South Australia, in the APY Lands. It supports roughly 40 Pitjantjatjara and Ngaanyatjarra artists from both Kalka and Pipalyatjara, the two most remote of the APY communities. The art centre is the cultural and social heart of the communities, with artists working and connecting with one another daily. Artworks have been exhibited nationally and internationally.

The origins of art from the area lie in the Western Desert dot painting, but over time the artwork has grown to include different brush techniques, as well as tjanpi (grass), kalawatjanga (glass) and punu (wood) sculptures. Today, artists are renowned for their use of striking colour palettes and a wide diversity of techniques, styles and mediums, which they use to tell the stories from their Country and lives. Ninuku women are also known for creating wearable art and jewellery, made from painted and decorated tatu (gumnuts), initinti tree seeds, and quandong from the bush. Due to their handmade nature, each piece is unique.

WHERE: Kalka, APY Lands (262 km from Uluṟu–Kata Tjuṯa).
PERMITS: Permits are required when visiting the APY Lands. Information can be obtained by contacting the art centre.
CONTACT: manager@ninukuarts.com.au

Tjala Arts

Tjala Arts is one of the 10 largest Australian Aboriginal art centres. Founded by local women of the Amata community in 1997, the art centre now includes both male and female artists and has been described as the heartland of the Amata community. The works have a strong focus on Tjukurpa: the stories, Law and Dreaming of the region. Tjala means 'honey ant' in Pitjantjatjara. The ant is both a traditional bush food and the Tjukurpa Creation story for the Amata area. Tjala Arts is renowned for a diverse range of styles, including rich colours and energetic brushstrokes. Artist's work across a variety of media, including traditional woodwork, sculptural fibre weaving, acrylic painting on linen and, for some of the younger artists more contemporary mediums such as film and photography.

WHERE: The Amata community is about 115 km due south of Uluṟu-Kata Tjuṯa, and 14 km south of the NT border, in SA. It is located on the western side of the Musgrave Ranges.
CONTACT: 08 8956 2899

Tjungu Palya

Tjungu Palya means 'good together', and the art centre is the result of the collaboration of artists from the Nyapari community and the neighbouring homelands of Kanpi and Watarru. Founded in 2006, the art centre is now a dynamic and innovative space supporting many local artists through various mediums.

WHERE: Nyapari is located at the base of the Mann Ranges, 20 km south of the NT border and about 450 km south of Alice Springs.
CONTACT: 08 8956 7111

6 QUEENSLAND

FESTIVALS

Cairns Indigenous Arts Fair

The Cairns Indigenous Arts Fair (CIAF), one of the most highly acclaimed art festivals in Australia, was established by the Queensland Government in 2009 , becoming an independent company limited by guarantee in 2014. The event provides a rare opportunity for visitors to engage in an immersive program of storytelling through an array of arts mediums in a way not offered anywhere else in the world, and via both physical and digital platforms. It is the perfect family event and caters to all interests. With art exhibitions, fashion, dance, theatre, film and music programs, there is plenty to do over this 3-day celebration of Queensland Aboriginal and Torres Strait Islander cultures.

CIAF showcases Queensland visual art and performance, with a focus on offering an ethical marketplace, attracting national and international collectors and curators, commissioning new work and providing pathways for emerging artists. Most events are free, but check the website for information about the program and any ticketed events.

WHERE: Cairns Convention Centre and Munro Martin Parklands as well as at key arts and cultural hubs throughout the city (Cairns Art Gallery, Bulmba-ja Arts Centre, Tanks Arts Centre, Cairns Performing Arts Centre).
WHEN: Annually in August
CONTACT: 07 4252 6312

Laura Quinkan Dance Festival

The Laura Quinkan Dance Festival is a celebration of Aboriginal culture held in Western Yalanji Country in North Queensland. It is a vibrant and unique way for tourists to experience this ancient and ongoing culture through powerful performances of the songs and dances of many Indigenous nations from the Cape York region. This biennial festival, which was cancelled in 2020 but was back in 2021, is one of Queensland's largest cultural gatherings. It has attracted crowds of visitors from Australia and around the world for the last 25 years.

WHERE: Held 15 km south of Laura, at the Ang-Gnarra Festival Grounds, or meeting grounds, of Cape York.
WHEN: Usually held the weekend of the end of June/ start of July.
CAMPING: The festival sets up a campground for visitors, with facilities including showers and toilets, and a range of stalls selling food and crafts.
CONTACT: 0473 491 540

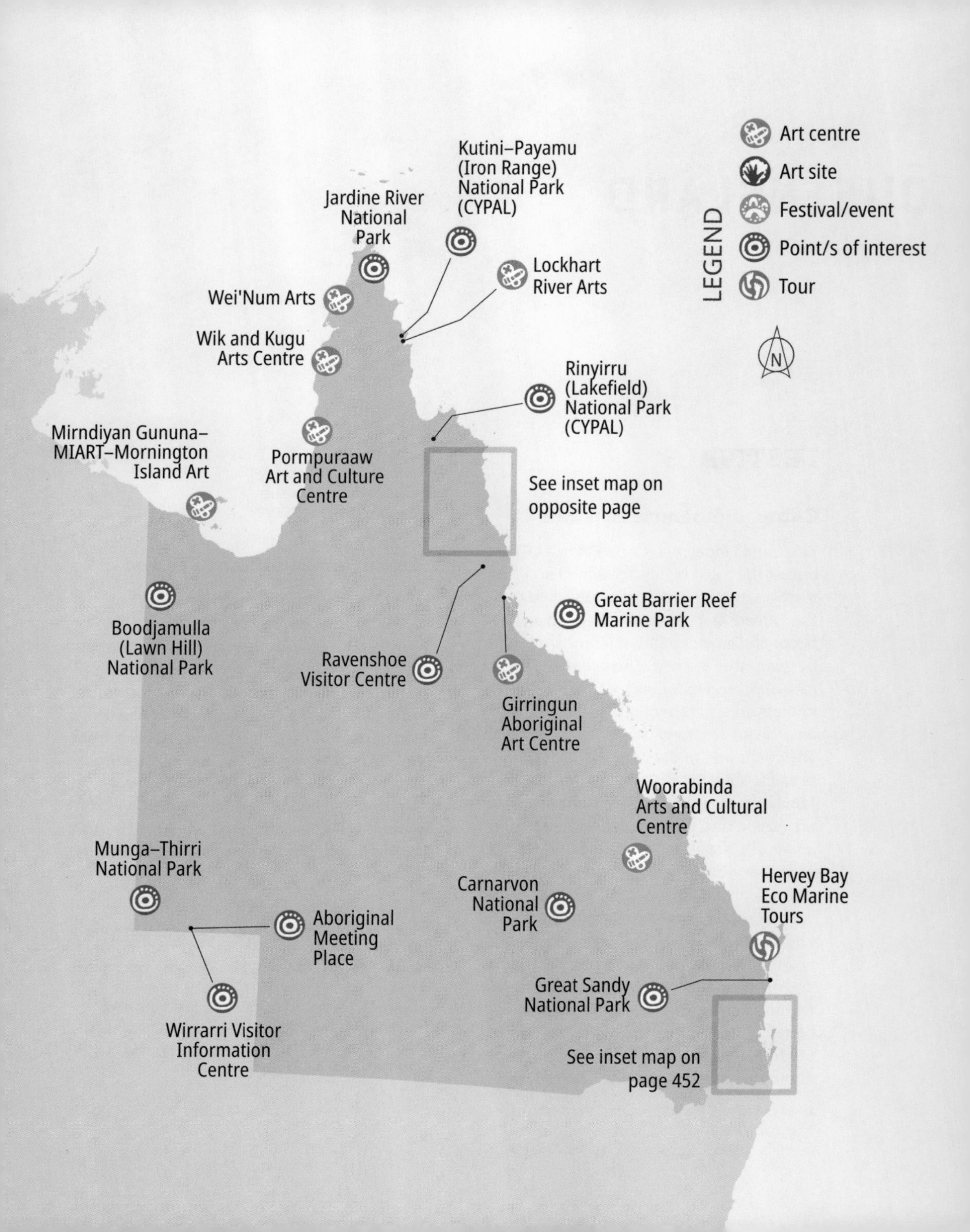

LEGEND
Art centre
Art site
Festival/event
Point/s of interest
Tour
N
Kutini–Payamu (Iron Range) National Park (CYPAL)
Jardine River National Park
Lockhart River Arts
Wei'Num Arts
Wik and Kugu Arts Centre
Rinyirru (Lakefield) National Park (CYPAL)
Mirndiyan Gununa–MIART–Mornington Island Art
Pormpuraaw Art and Culture Centre
See inset map on opposite page
Great Barrier Reef Marine Park
Boodjamulla (Lawn Hill) National Park
Ravenshoe Visitor Centre
Girringun Aboriginal Art Centre
Woorabinda Arts and Cultural Centre
Munga–Thirri National Park
Carnarvon National Park
Hervey Bay Eco Marine Tours
Aboriginal Meeting Place
Great Sandy National Park
Wirrarri Visitor Information Centre
See inset map on page 452

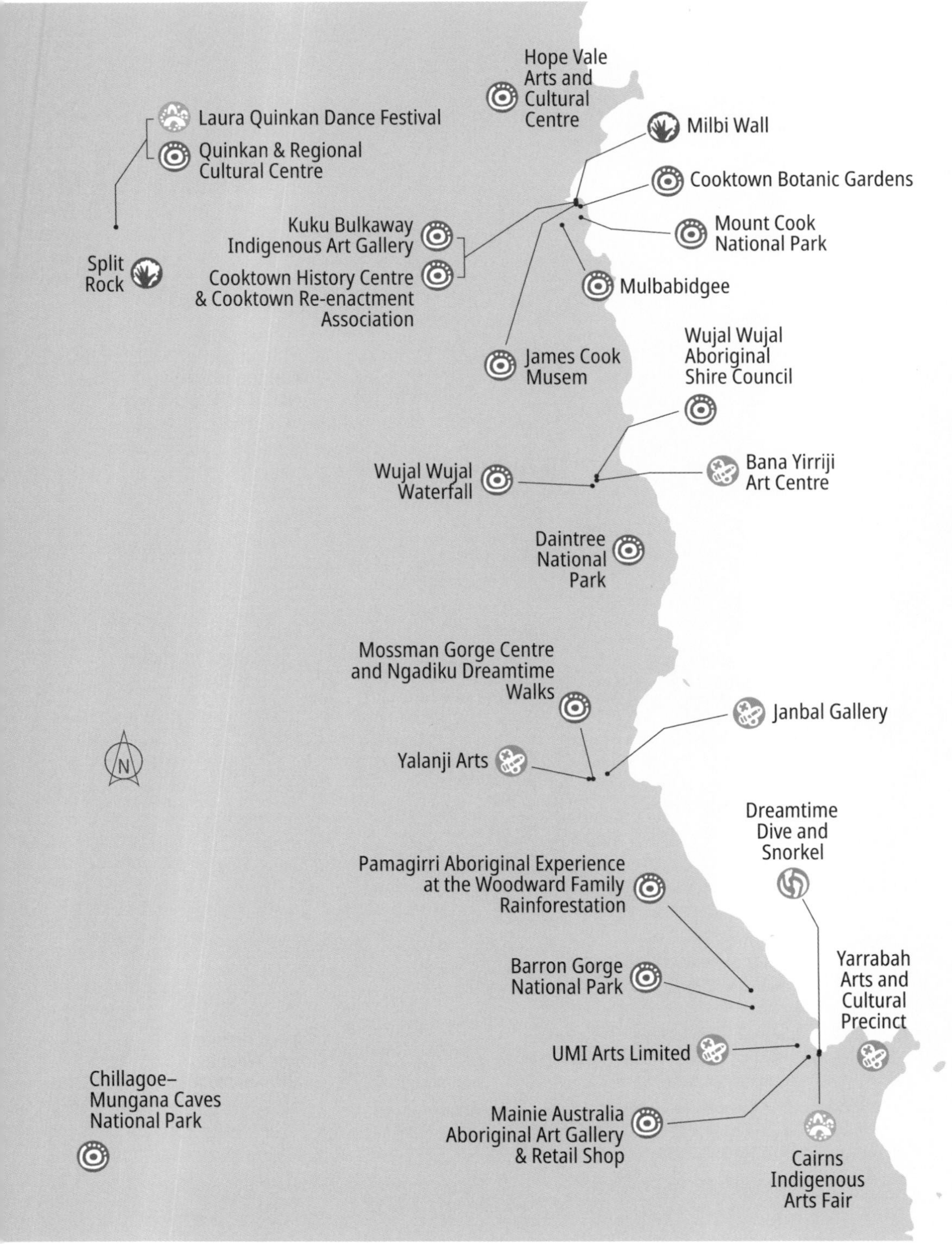
Hope Vale Arts and Cultural Centre
Laura Quinkan Dance Festival
Quinkan & Regional Cultural Centre
Milbi Wall
Cooktown Botanic Gardens
Kuku Bulkaway Indigenous Art Gallery
Mount Cook National Park
Split Rock
Cooktown History Centre & Cooktown Re-enactment Association
Mulbabidgee
James Cook Musem
Wujal Wujal Aboriginal Shire Council
Wujal Wujal Waterfall
Bana Yirriji Art Centre
Daintree National Park
Mossman Gorge Centre and Ngadiku Dreamtime Walks
Janbal Gallery
N
Yalanji Arts
Dreamtime Dive and Snorkel
Pamagirri Aboriginal Experience at the Woodward Family Rainforestation
Barron Gorge National Park
Yarrabah Arts and Cultural Precinct
UMI Arts Limited
Chillagoe–Mungana Caves National Park
Mainie Australia Aboriginal Art Gallery & Retail Shop
Cairns Indigenous Arts Fair

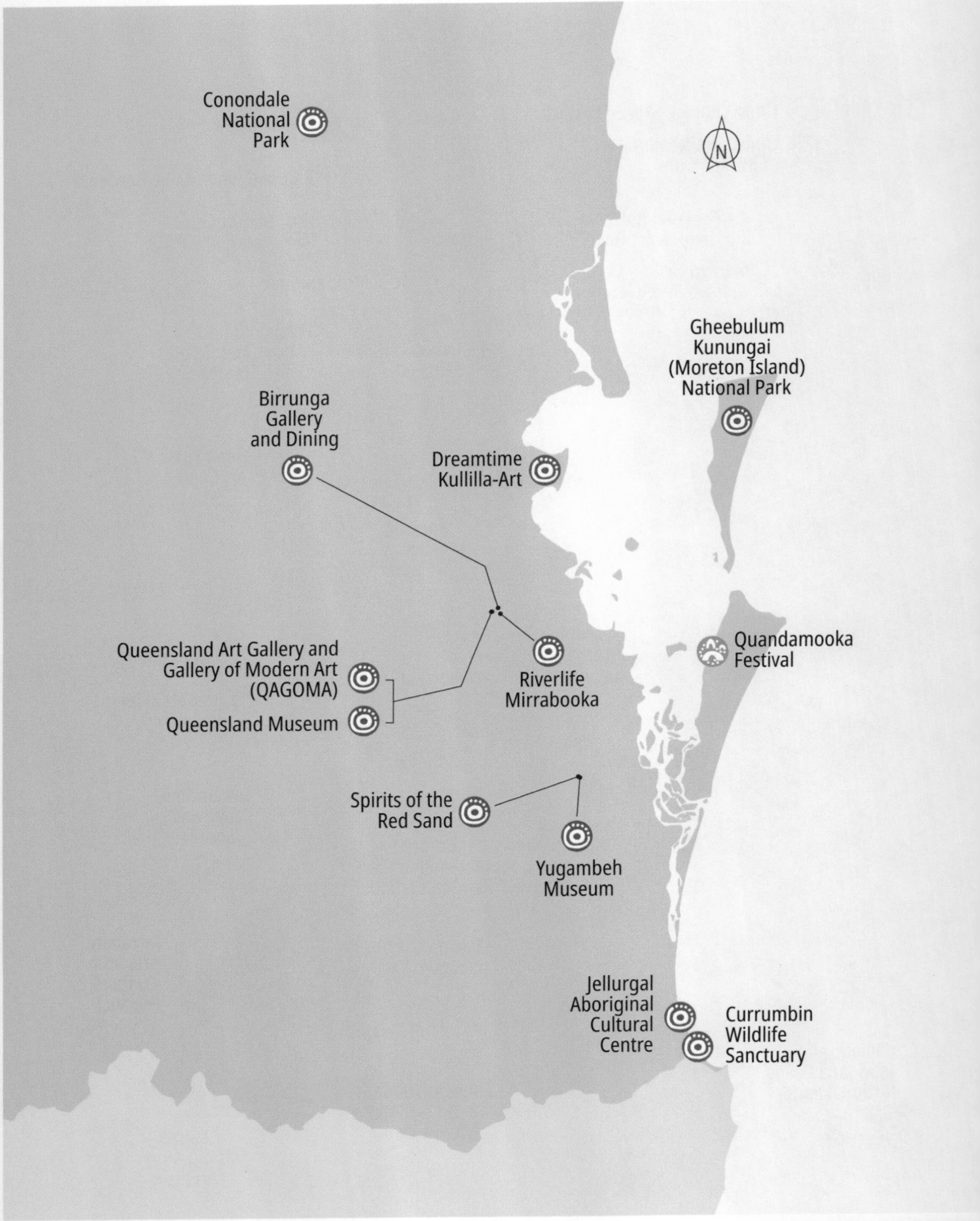
Conondale National Park
N
Gheebulum Kunungai (Moreton Island) National Park
Birrunga Gallery and Dining
Dreamtime Kullilla-Art
Queensland Art Gallery and Gallery of Modern Art (QAGOMA)
Queensland Museum
Riverlife Mirrabooka
Quandamooka Festival
Spirits of the Red Sand
Yugambeh Museum
Jellurgal Aboriginal Cultural Centre
Currumbin Wildlife Sanctuary

Quandamooka Festival

The South East Queensland clans of Nughi, Nunukul and Goenpul are collectively known as the Quandamooka people, and their culture, Country and people are celebrated at this special festival. In 2019, the festival ran for 3 months, with experiences such as music, visual arts, workshops, bush-tucker dining, whale watching cultural tours, kunjiel (corroborees), dynamic dance, storytelling, Indigenous sports, and insights into cultural heritage and Caring for Country. The 2020 festival was cancelled because of the COVID-19 pandemic, but Quandamooka will return bigger and better than ever in forthcoming years. The festival celebrates the significance of the Indigenous connection to land – which is woven through the various and diverse events.

WHERE: Minjerribah (North Stradbroke Island) and Winnam (Wynnum). Access the island by water taxi, or vehicle ferry from Toondah Harbour, Cleveland by car or connecting train and bus service. On the island, bus transport is regular and affordable from Goompi (Dunwich) to Pulan Pulan (Amity Point) and Mooloomba (Point Lookout). Scooter hire is also available.
WHEN: The festival ran in August in 2019; check the website for yearly details.
GETTING AROUND: 4WDs are not required on the island unless you are planning to drive off-road or on the beaches.
CONTACT: 07 3415 2816

NATIONAL PARKS

Barron Gorge National Park

Barron Gorge National Park is part of the Djirri Nyundu Nyrrumba area, where the Djabugandgi Bama (Djabugay people) are the traditional owners. In 2004, the Federal Court of Australia recognised the Djabugay people's Native Title over the land, and a formal Indigenous Land Use Agreement exists so that the park's cultural importance can be aligned with the state's conservation efforts. The Djabugay people believe that all the rivers and creeks in the national park were created by the carpet snake ancestor Budaadji.

Rugged mountains with steep ravines are covered by tropical rainforests, broken up with striking waterfalls and the main natural feature of the park – Barron Gorge. You can explore the park by scenic railway, cable car or by foot along one of the numerous walking trails. The trails range from easy strolls to challenging tracks, from 20 minute walks to 7 hour climbs. There are 2 railway/cable trips. The historic Kuranda train winds its way up the steep slopes of the MacAlister Range and affords spectacular views of the gorge, where it stops briefly. It runs daily from Cairns to the picturesque heritage station at Kuranda. The cable car offers another perspective of the rainforest, departing from Kuranda station then riding high above the canopy, stopping at Barron Falls (and the Rainforest Interpretive Centre) and at the top of Red Peak (where there is a boardwalk through rainforest ferns), before dropping down to the Caravonica terminal in Smithfield, 14 km north of Cairns. Water activities include canoeing and whitewater rafting.

WHERE: 18 km north-west of Cairns.
CAMPING AND ACCOMMODATION: Camping is not permitted in the national park, but there is a campground in the adjacent Speewah Conservation Park. This 15.2 ha camping area is also the trailhead for all the main walks in Barron Gorge National Park. It has modest facilities, but visitors must bring all supplies and water with them. Nearby Cairns has accommodation for a broad range of budgets and tastes, while Kuranda offers more low-key and charming B&B accommodation.

PERMITS: Permits and fees only apply for camping at the Speewah Conservation Park.
CONTACT: Cairns: 07 4051 3588, 1800 093 300; Kuranda: 07 4093 9311, 0407 758 645

Boodjamulla (Lawn Hill) National Park

Multicoloured sandstone cliffs tower over the oasis centre of Lawn Hill Gorge, in the middle of Boodjamulla (Lawn Hill) National Park. Boodjamulla is one of the most scenic parks in the state. Essentially wilderness grounds, only the gorge and its immediate surrounds are accessible to visitors. The palm-fringed river can rise dramatically in the Wet season so visits between April and September are recommended. This remote area has little reception, so you must be self-sufficient.

This area was home to vast cattle stations from the 1860s and was given to the government in 1984 to be held as a national park. Riversleigh's fossil fields are within the park, an hour's drive (51 km) south of Lawn Hill Gorge. Signage and a self-guided interpretive trail (800 m loop) at the fossil fields provide you with information, but there is not much left to see. You can gain a stronger understanding of the mammal and marsupial fossil discoveries in Boodjamulla by taking a guided tour, which departs from Adels Grove.

CULTURAL HERITAGE: There are stone relics, rock art and mussel middens, which have been left as the legacy of the Waanyi people over the last 17,000 + years. They know Boodjamulla as the rainbow serpent, who created the land, as well as the permanent springs flowing into the creek to keep his skin wet. This land is sacred and has been used by the Waanyi as ceremonial and celebratory space only. The Waanyi help manage the park and own 50 per cent of the Lawn Hill Riversleigh Pastoral Holding Company.

THINGS TO DO

There are many options for bushwalking – with long and short trails of all different fitness levels open to the public (the Waanyi ask that, as a sign of respect, the rock art is not photographed). The walks often lead to a variety of swimming springs, dams and waterfalls. There are beautiful views, and plenty of animals to enjoy in their natural habitat. Freshwater crocodiles inhabit the middle and upper sections of the gorge but are considered harmless if left alone. Canoe hire is available (you may also bring your own) to enjoy in the Duwadarri Waterhole, a 6 km return trip at the top of Lawn Hill Gorge.
WHERE: Wills Rd, Lawn Hill.
CAMPING AND ACCOMMODATION: There are 2 camp sites in the area, one at Lawn Hill Creek on the banks of the Lawn Hill Section, and another on the banks of the Gregory River. Both have basic facilities so visitors must be self-sufficient, bringing all supplies. The closest accommodation is 10 km away at Adels Grove, where camping (BYO or provided erect tents) and rooms are available, although there are no powered sites. There is a bar, restaurant and swimming hole on site. Call 07 4748 5502 to book.
PERMITS: Camping permits are required and fees apply.

Carnarvon National Park

Carnarvon National Park is the region's most popular tourist attraction, and is over 160 million years old. Carnarvon Gorge is the most visited section of the park, and houses fascinating Aboriginal rock art in its towering white sandstone cliffs and side gorges. Less easy to access but equally worth exploring are Mt Moffatt, Ka Ka Mundi and Salvator Rosa, which offer a remote wilderness experience. The area was declared a national park in 1932, as pastoralists were lobbied by the Royal Geographical Society of Queensland to abandon their leases. This move excluded the Ka Ka Mundi section, which was not included as part of the national park until 1974.

The Bidjara people hold Carnarvon Gorge as a significant Dreaming area, as

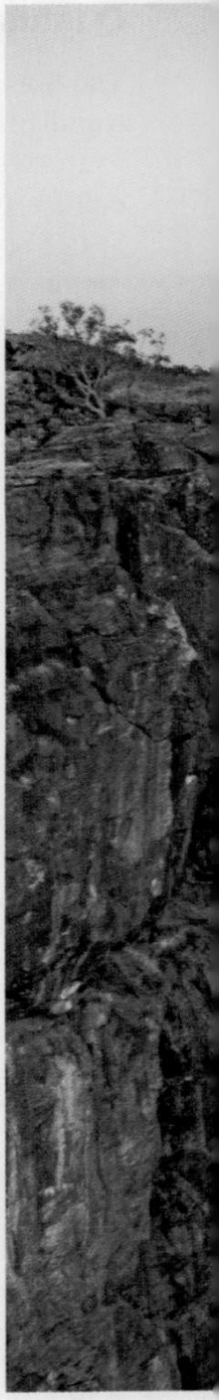

Boodjamulla (Lawn Hill) National Park

Mundagurra – the rainbow serpent – travelled through the creeks of the area and carved the gorge out of the rock on its travels. There are many bushwalking trails throughout the park, and campers and explorers of all levels will be able to find something to suit. The rock art sites are enormously culturally significant, and very old and fragile (so please keep to the boardwalks, and do not touch the art). The art can be found in many of the self-guided walks, and have descriptive and interpretive signs.

WHERE: 550 km north-west of Brisbane; 270 km north of Roma; 196 km south-east of Emerald.
CAMPING AND ACCOMMODATION: There are 4 sections of the park which have camping areas, and facilities vary. Carnarvon Gorge offers restricted camping options – a small camping area with basic facilities, accessible only by a 9.7 km walk, or camping at the mouth of the gorge outside the visitor centre, only during specific holiday periods. Both options require advance bookings and are quite busy. There are also 2 private options for accommodation, one offering cabins, safari tents and powered camp sites suitable for caravans and campervans and the other offering boutique cabins. The other 3 sections of the park offer less competitive, much larger camping areas, though the facilities are outdated. Campers in Ka Ka Mundi and Salvator Rosa must be self-sufficient as there are no facilities, though you can set up anywhere in designated bush camping areas. Mt Moffatt has several designated camping areas, and self-sufficient bush camping is permitted in most places throughout the section. Bookings are essential.
PERMITS: Camping permits are required and fees apply.
CONTACT: Roma 07 4622 8676; Injune 07 4626 0503

Chillagoe–Mungana Caves National Park

The rugged Chillagoe–Mungana Caves National Park is rich in natural and cultural heritage. Its outstanding features include spectacular limestone caves, small galleries of Aboriginal rock art engraved in the ancient limestone, jagged limestone outcrops, and a historically significant mining site.

There are several walking trails to explore, such as the Balancing Rock track that leads to an impressive limestone tower, and the Royal Arch track, an easy 9 km walk, which passes through the Wullumba rock-art site and leads to the area's largest cave system. Daily ranger-led tours take groups into the fascinating and stunning limestone caves with beautiful cave decorations. Visitors can also explore self-guided caves (Pompeii and Bauhinia caves) on their own. The Chillagoe-Mungana Caves National Park Directory Guide provides more information and can be downloaded from the Department of Environment and Science website.

WHERE: About a 3-hour drive (215 km) west of Cairns. The Hub, 21–23 Queen St, Chillagoe.
ACCOMMODATION: Camping is not permitted in the park; however, there is accommodation located in the nearby town of Chillagoe.
CONTACT: The Hub: 07 4094 7111; Queensland Parks and Wildlife Service: 13 74 68

Conondale National Park

The Gubbi Gubbi people are the Traditional Owners of this area, and are still strongly connected to the land, on which many culturally important sites sit. The bunya pine trees helped to influence the decision to make this area a national park, and they have always been an important source of food for the Gubbi Gubbi, with the nuts harvested to use in many celebrations and culturally significant events. There are various bushwalking options available, from a 500 m return, stretch of the legs walk, to the 56 km Conondale Range Great Walk – a circuit route winding through the park. The development of the spectacular Conondale Range Great

Walk could not have happened without substantial input from the local Aboriginal people. The park boasts the Queensland Horse Trail Network, and is one of the few national parks where horse riding is allowed. Conondale has a network of gravel roads suitable for 4WD vehicles, which thread throughout (and also to the Imbil State Forest, which is adjacent) and give visitors access to some spectacular views.

WHERE: 130 km north of Brisbane; 37 km west of Nambour.
CAMPING AND ACCOMMODATION: Basic facilities are available at the 3 camping areas near the Booloomba Creek, and at the walkers camps along the Conondale Range Great Walk (these are for hikers only). Maleny is close by, and offers a range of B&B accommodation, and rural farmstays. Bookings are essential.
PERMITS: Camping permits are required and fees apply.
CONTACT: Maleny Hinterland: 07 5499 9788; Montville: 07 5478 5544

Daintree National Park

With its stunning scenery of rainforest-clad mountains sweeping down to long sandy beaches, Daintree National Park is one of the most revered parks in Australia. Its Cape Tribulation section is the only place on Earth where 2 World Heritage areas exist side by side, with the Daintree rainforest meeting the Great Barrier Reef. The 2 sections of the park – Mossman Gorge and Cape Tribulation – are valued for their equally striking scenery and biodiversity, and were declared national parks in 1967 and 1981 respectively, before being amalgamated in 1981 as the Daintree National Park. The Eastern Kuku Yalanji people are the Traditional Owners here, and survived off the abundance of food and wildlife for tens of thousands of years. Many of the natural features in the park are spiritually important to them, and the park has an access and use agreement with the Eastern Kuku Yalanji.

The only place in the park with barbecue facilities is Dubuji, though Jindalba and Kulki also offer picnic tables and spaces. These 3 areas have toilet facilities, as does the carpark at the entrance to the Mossman Gorge section of the park. Swimming is not recommended for humans, as crocodiles and jellyfish spend time in the ocean during much of the year. Much of Mossman Gorge is inaccessible to anyone except experienced, well-equipped bushwalkers (who must inform the ranger before departure), but the Rex Creek circuit and Barral·Marrjanga boardwalk are easy and offer fantastic views.

The Cape Tribulation section of the park has 4 short walks, each offering slightly different views and information. All of these include a boardwalk, and 3 are fully wheelchair accessible. Guided walking tours are available with commercial operators, and the day hike on the steep Mt Sorrow Ridge Trail is self-guided.

Walu Wugirriga (Mt Alexandra Lookout) is 5 km north of the Daintree River in the Cape Tribulation section of the park. It is a stunning way to enjoy breathtaking views of the coast and mouth of the Daintree River, as you finish your trip to the park.

WHERE: 80 km north of Cairns (Mossman Gorge); 110 km north of Cairns (Cape Tribulation).
CAMPING AND ACCOMMODATION: Noah Beach in the Cape Tribulation section of the park is the only place where camping is available. These basic sites are numbered and must be booked in advance. If you have access to a boat, Snapper Island in the Hope Islands National Park is a nearby alternative, and must also be booked in advance. Cape Tribulation and Mossman Gorge are nearby, and both offer many accommodation options. Bookings are essential.
PERMITS: Camping permits are required and fees apply.
CONTACT: Cairns: 07 4051 3588

Gheebulum Kunungai (Moreton Island) National Park

The Ngugi people were the original inhabitants of Mulgumpin (Moreton Island) and evidence shows that they have lived on the island for at least the last 2000 years. The abundant marine life would have contributed to their diets, with fish, shellfish, dugong and turtle still swimming in large numbers. Limited development on the island means the heritage has been well preserved, and over 300 cultural sites have been recorded here. Mulgumpin is a standout in the already remarkable Moreton Bay islands, and boasts long sandy beaches, freshwater lagoons with clear water, some of the world's highest sand dunes, and wildflower heaths. Historical places of interest include Cape Moreton Lighthouse, which was built in 1857 and is still in operation as Queensland's oldest lighthouse. Concrete bunkers at Cowan Cowan and Toompani Beach are all that remains of some World War Two army forts. Walking and 4WD are the only transport options on this sandy island, but there is so much to do regardless – hikes ending in panoramic views, birdwatching, swimming and fishing.

WHERE: 40 km north-east of Brisbane.
CAMPING: There are 5 camp sites on the island, all of which have facilities including water and showers. Camping is also permitted at 5 specific camping zones along the eastern and western beaches. All but 2 of the camping areas and camp sites allow open fires (bring your own firewood, and use existing sites) but fuel or gas stoves are preferred. Bookings are essential.
PERMITS: Camping and 4WD permits are required and fees apply.
CONTACT: Wynnum Manly: 07 3348 3524; Brisbane: 07 3006 6290

Great Barrier Reef Marine Park

The Great Barrier Reef is one of the 7 natural wonders of the world. Stretching for more than 2300 km along the Queensland coast and covering 35 million hectares, it features brilliantly coloured corals living beneath aquamarine waters, a profusion of tropical islands and a wealth of marine creatures and birdlife. The Great Barrier Reef was designated as a World Heritage area in 1981, and was the first coral reef ecosystem in the world to receive this status. It is the world's largest and most famous coral formation.

The Great Barrier Reef is the leading tourist attraction in Queensland, and one of the world's foremost tourist destinations, particularly for diving and snorkelling. Breathtakingly beautiful just below the surface of the water, the Reef has a complex ecosystem – more than 1500 species of fish coexist with 4000 species of molluscs, 400 species of sponge and over 400 species of hard corals, as well as sea turtles, manta rays, sharks, dolphins and whales. Extensive seagrass beds provide a home for the threatened dugong; threatened green and loggerhead turtles nest on islands in the Reef; and humpback whales migrate there to give birth. Birdlife is also abundant, and hundreds of species nest in the Reef islands.

Aboriginal and Torres Strait Islander peoples are the Traditional Owners of the Great Barrier Reef region, and there are significant cultural sites on many of its islands. The strong ongoing links between the Traditional Owners and their sea Country was recognised in the Great Barrier Reef's World Heritage listing and contributes to its Outstanding Universal Value. The cultural and ecological knowledge of the Traditional Owners will be essential to delivering the Reef 2050 Plan, which is the blueprint for

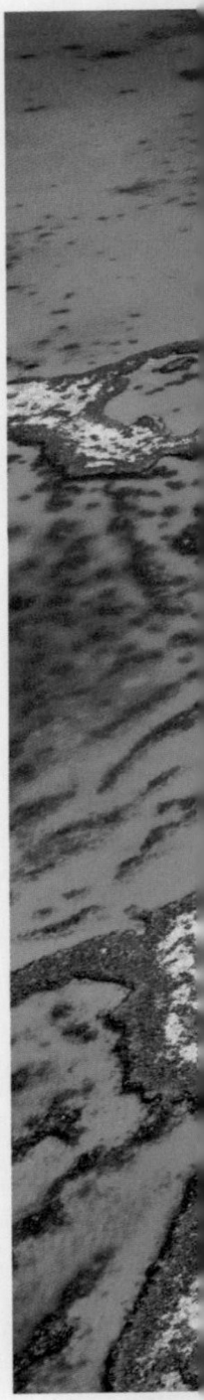

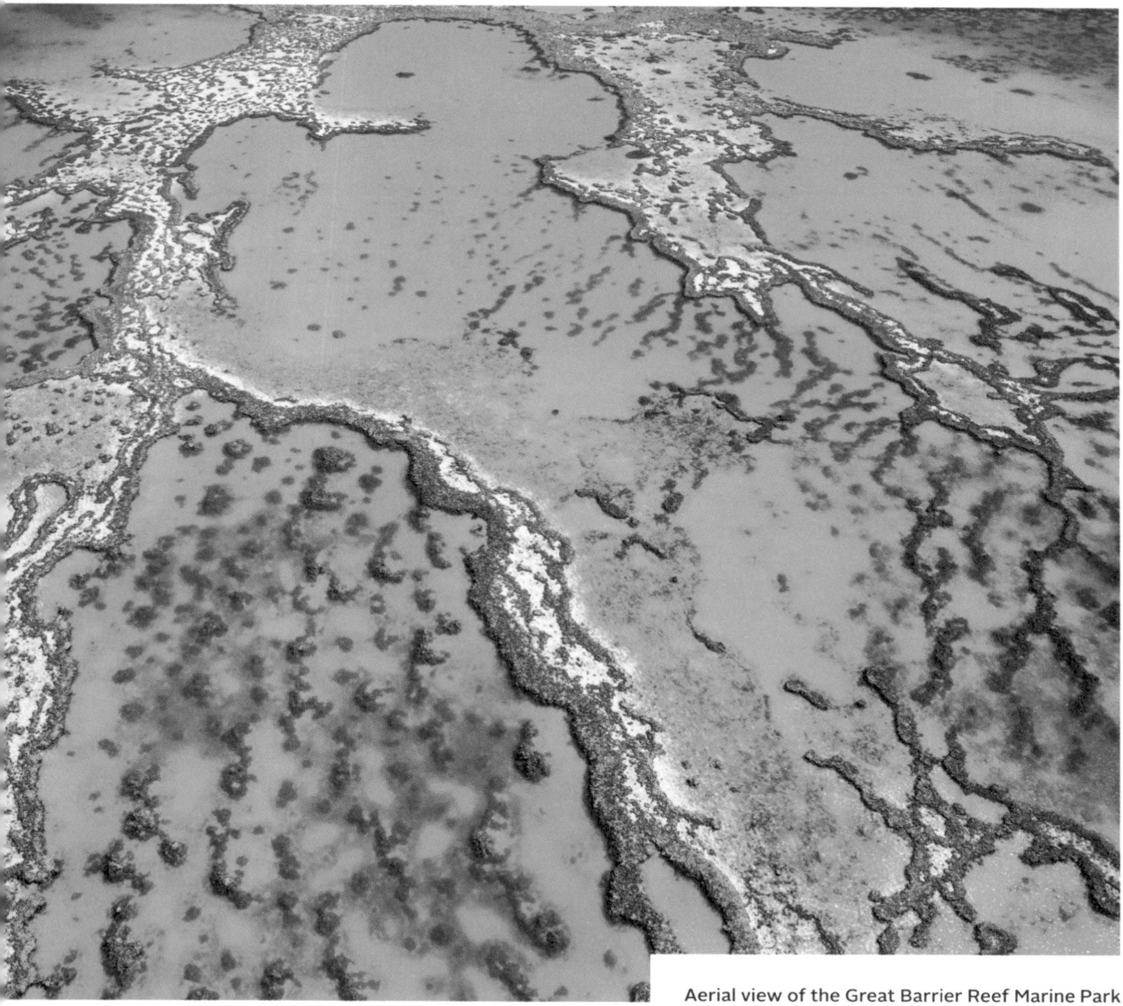

Aerial view of the Great Barrier Reef Marine Park

protecting and managing the Reef and designed to be implemented in a collaborative partnership. The Plan was released by the Australian and Queensland governments in 2015, and a statement from the Department of Environment and Energy noted that, 'With input from scientists, communities, Traditional Owners, industry and non-government organisations, a key principle of the Plan is developing the Reef's resilience in the face of a variable and changing climate.' Australians and people all around the world are gravely concerned for the health of the Reef, and UNESCO has identified that climate change is a challenge to the Reef now and will be increasingly so over the next few decades.

Scattered throughout the Reef are more than 900 islands, many of which are protected as national parks. Each of the Reef's island national parks provides very different experiences for visitors. Some offer luxury resort-style accommodation with a range of recreational activities; others are remote and rugged with bush camping only (dozens of islands in these national parks permit camping). There are islands with strong Aboriginal cultural links, and islands that provide important breeding grounds for birds.

SOUTHERN REEF ISLANDS: The southern part of the Reef stretches from just north of Hervey Bay to the southern reaches of the Coral Sea, north of Yeppoon. Access to the islands in this area is from the major population centres of Gladstone and Yeppoon, east of Rockhampton, and various smaller places along this coast.

ISLANDS OF THE WHITSUNDAY COAST: Off the central Queensland coast from south of Mackay to Bowen are hundreds of islands, many grouped together and protected under national park status. The main access is by boat from Mackay in the south and Shute Harbour or Airlie Beach in the north. Airports are at Mackay, Proserpine and Hamilton Island.

TROPICAL NORTH ISLANDS: The islands in this region lie offshore from just south of Townsville to Cape York. They are generally accessible from the main population centres of Townsville and Cairns, both of which have major airports. Cairns has an international airport and services a range of tours to the outer reef.

The Queensland Parks and Wildlife Service (tel: 13 74 68) together with the Great Barrier Reef Marine Park Authority (07 4750 0700) are responsible for managing the Reef and associated island national parks along its length.

PLANNING YOUR TRIP TO THE GREAT BARRIER REEF

When planning your visit to the Reef you will find useful information on the Great Barrier Reef Marine Park Authority website.

To find out about the national parks in the area visit the parks and forests section of the Department of Environment and Science website.

The Cairns Visitor Centre provides information about Indigenous-owned and operated Reef tours: 07 4036 3341 or visit its website.

To read the UNESCO World Heritage listing for the Reef visit the UNESCO website.

The Queensland Parks and Wildlife Service manages over 300 national parks in the state. In addition to the ones included here, visitors can find out about the other parks on the website.

Great Sandy National Park

Great Sandy National Park comprises 2 parts. Cooloola is on the coast between Rainbow Beach in the north and Noosa Heads in the south. K'gari (Fraser Island) is the world's largest sand island, north of Rainbow Beach. The famous coloured sands, pristine blue water, plentiful marine life, and lush rainforests are some of the features visitors will find at Great Sandy National Park, one of Queensland's largest national parks. Aboriginal people have lived in the Great Sandy area for at least 5000 years according to archaeological evidence, but they may have been there far longer. The Butchulla people lived on K'gari (Fraser Island) and the nearby mainland. Their heritage sites of spiritual, social and archaeological significance are found on the island, as well as their middens, artefacts, scarred trees and camp sites. The Butchulla led a complex, self-sufficient way of life intrinsically connected to the seasons, the land, and life on it and in the surrounding ocean. Soon after European settlement of the area in the 1840s the Indigenous people were forced off their land, and by the late 1800s their lifestyle had been destroyed and the Aboriginal people from around the region were relocated to a mission on Fraser Island. Today, descendants of these people who live in the area are working to protect and share their culture and way of life, which is so closely tied to this beautiful and bountiful natural environment.

WHERE: Cooloola lies between Noosa Heads and Rainbow Beach. Noosa Heads is about 155 km (about a 3-hour drive) and Rainbow Beach is about 240 km (about a 3-hour drive) north of Brisbane. Fraser Island is about 300 km north of Brisbane and 15 km off the coast of Hervey Bay and Maryborough.
CAMPING: There is an exciting range of camping options in the park. Details are available on the Department of Environment and Science website.
COST: Driving on the beaches and some inland sand tracks requires a Vehicle Access Permit (VAP). The cost of the VAP depends on which area of the Great Sandy National Park. Camping fees also apply.
CONTACT: Queensland Parks and Wildlife Service: 13 74 68

Jardine River National Park

On the northern tip of Cape York Peninsula, Jardine River is the largest perennial river in the state, and the national park surrounds it. There are many uncommon species to see here, including the spiny knob-tailed gecko, palm cockatoo and common spotted cuscus. This land has traditionally been owned by the Atampaya, Angkamuthi, Gudang, Wuthathi and Yadhaykenu people, who now jointly manage the park. There are many beautiful and scenic falls, and beach fishing is allowed at Captain Billy Landing and Ussher Point, but these locations are part of the Great Barrier Reef Marine Park so fishing restrictions apply, and crocodile warnings must be respected.

WHERE: 920 km north of Cairns via Peninsula Developmental Rd; 4WD access only.
CAMPING AND ACCOMMODATION: Two bush camping sites, with several in nearby resources reserves. Visitors must be self-sufficient. Bookings are essential. North of the park, Resort Bamaga has 4-star accommodation; Seisia has a campground with self-contained units. Visit only during the Dry season, from May to October.
PERMITS: Camping permits are required and fees apply.
CONTACT: Cooktown and Cape York Peninsula: 07 4069 6004

Kutini–Payamu (Iron Range) (CYPAL)

Pristine lowland rainforest is protected here, with over 320 plant species acting as a haven for many types of wildlife. The Kuuku Ya'u people are the Traditional Owners, and although a mission was established in nearby Lockhart, the Kuuku Ya'u people have continued their traditional hunting, gathering and fishing practices along the coast, with a 2024 vision released to confirm intentions to manage the Ngaachi land according to historic culture and traditions. Fishing is only allowed at Chilli Beach; steer clear of any of the freshwater creeks or rivers. There are a few significant walking trails in the park, and none of them are considered difficult. Visitors must be self-sufficient, and bring any supplies they need. This park is a wildlife enthusiasts' paradise.

WHERE: 752 km north of Cairns.
CAMPING: There are 4 bush camping sites: Chilli Beach Camping Area, Cooks Hut Camping Area, and Rainforest and Gordon Creek Camping areas. Only Chilli Beach and Cooks Hut have toilets. Bookings are essential
PERMITS: Camping permits are required and fees apply.
CONTACT: Cooktown and Cape York Peninsula: 07 4069 6004

Mount Cook National Park

This area covers the northern boundary of the traditional lands of the Eastern Kuku Yalanji Aboriginal people, including the Yuku Baja Muliku, Kuku Bididji and Kuku Nyungkul clans, and the southern boundary of the Gungarde and Guugu Yimithirr Aboriginal people, including the Waymbuurr and Gamay clans. The area's diverse ecosystem has always provided food and resources for the Traditional Owners, and though people have moved out to the communities of Hopevale and Wujal Wujal, the spiritual connection to Country remains strong. The park is home to a range of wild animals, including northern quolls, buff-breasted paradise-kingfishers, pied imperial-pigeons, and amethystine pythons – which is at the centre of the Guugu Yimithirr Dreaming of the area. They believe that the Wahalumbaal birrir (Endeavour River) was created by the Mungurru (amethystine python) while travelling down to the ocean. The park is undeveloped and diverse, and animals are everywhere, so bring your binoculars to help you spot any that are camouflaged.

WHERE: Ida Street, Cooktown.

Munga–Thirri National Park

Since 2019, the head owner of this national park has been Wangkangurru Elder Don Rowlands OAM, who lives in Birdsville. Aboriginal people survived in this extreme climate by digging soaks, and respecting the power of the land. This is the largest national park in Queensland, and was formerly known as the Simpsons Desert Park. The park is closed to visitors in December–March, as the extreme heat in the hottest part of Australia is unsuitable for travel; wet weather during the year may also cause temporary closures, as the tracks are impassable. It is essential that only prepared, fully-equipped, experienced drivers take on this exploration. Large sand dunes have formed over 30,000 years, the tallest is 50 m and the longest is 200 km. Other awe-inspiring natural features include salt lakes and claypans. Many animals live in this space, with over 180 bird species and regular sightings of dingoes, wild camels, bats, burrowing lizards and geckos.

WHERE: 79 km west of Birdsville.
CAMPING: Camping is permitted within 500 m of the QAA line. Rangers encourage visitors to bring gas stoves, as there is a depletion of wood that is harming flora and fauna.
CONTACT: 07 4656 3272

Rinyirru (Lakefield) National Park (CYPAL)

This land was returned to the Aboriginal clans of the Lama Lama and Kuku Thaypan in 2011, and the Traditional Owners now jointly manage the park. Situated on the Cape York Peninsula, this is Queensland's second largest park. Renowned for its immense river systems and remarkable wetlands, Rinyirru's standout features include the rainforests growing along different sections of the Normanby and Kennedy rivers, and the Kalpowar Discovery Walk at Kalpowar Crossing, which is the only walk in the park. Because of the Wet season, visitors are welcome between 1 June and 30 November each year. Fishing is allowed; hopefuls can look for mangrove jack, fingermark, cod, trevally, queenfish and salmon in the saltwater areas, and barramundi, tarpon, catfish and archerfish in the freshwater regions. Recreational fishing is also allowed at all camp sites. Make sure you don't prepare food or clean the fish at the water's edge, as crocodiles will make themselves known. Rarda-Ndolphin is an important ceremonial site which can be seen from the carpark and the viewing area, and there will be other areas which you will be asked not to enter due to cultural significance at various times, so please remain respectful of Country and its people.

WHERE: 340 km north-west of Cairns; 118 km west of Cooktown; 27 km north of Laura.
CAMPING: The 22 bush camp sites throughout the park are all for experienced, self-sufficient campers, as they do not have facilities. Modest facilities can be found at the 2 camp sites near Hann and Kalpowar crossings. Roads are rough. Bookings are essential.
PERMITS: Camping permits are required and fees apply.
CONTACT: Cooktown and Cape York: 07 4069 6004

TOURS AND STAYS

Adventure North Australia

Adventure North Australia has been operating out in the Daintree region of north-east Queensland since 2004, and developed its Bama Way Aboriginal Tours in 2007 in partnership with several Indigenous-owned tour companies and cultural centres. Tours run by Adventure North are created in partnership with, and guided by, Traditional Owners of the lands and immerse visitors in the natural and cultural beauty of the area. Guests can choose from 1- and 2-day Daintree Dreaming or Dreamtime Walk tours, a 2-hour coastal walk along Cooya Beach, or 30-minute walking tours to Bloomfield Falls. All tours have an emphasis on the rich Aboriginal cultures of the area and guides provide demonstrations, teach traditional skills and share their cultural knowledge.

WHERE: 26 Redden Street, Cairns.
CONTACT: 07 4047 9075

Dreamtime Dive and Snorkel

On this day tour to two spectacular Great Barrier Reef sites – Moore Reef and Milln or Flynn Reef – Indigenous sea rangers give visitors the opportunity to see how the world's oldest living culture is incorporated in to some of Australia's most spectacular marine life. Traditional Owners have passed down their Dreaming stories for tens of thousands of years and now the Gimuy Walubara Yidinji, Mandingalbay Yidinji, Yirrganydji and Gunggandji people (the Traditional Owners of the sea Country on which the business operates) share their knowledge with visitors who come to explore this beautiful area. Additional experiences, such as introductory and certified diving, and guided snorkel tours, can also be booked in advance or while on the boat. Spend a relaxing 5 hours exploring and gaining a deeper cultural understanding of this diverse ecosystem and our Indigenous heritage.

WHERE: Check-in counter is located in Cairns Reef Fleet Terminal, 1 Spence St, Cairns.
CONTACT: 07 4030 7920

Hervey Bay Eco Marine Tours

Operating on Butchulla Country, Hervey Bay Eco Marine Tours offers tours on Milbi (Butchulla for 'sea turtle'), a 12 m-long, glass-bottomed sea vehicle, that gives guests the chance to experience local islands, snorkel, learn about the Great Sandy Straits with an Aboriginal tour guide/s, and search for reef fish, turtles, dugongs and dolphins. The tours they offer are as relaxed as you want them to be, with swimming, snorkelling and exploring optional. The land and sea custodians of this area have been here for many thousands of years and this is a unique opportunity to learn and be welcomed to their Country.

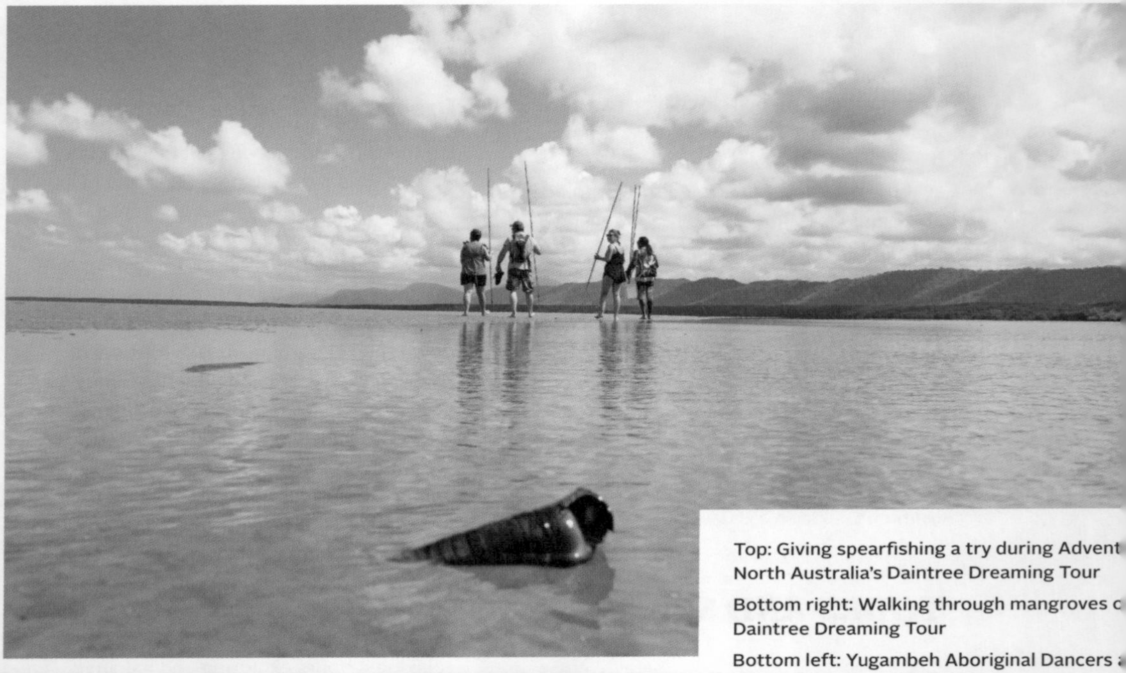

Top: Giving spearfishing a try during Advent
North Australia's Daintree Dreaming Tour

Bottom right: Walking through mangroves c
Daintree Dreaming Tour

Bottom left: Yugambeh Aboriginal Dancers
Currumbin Wildlife Sanctuary

WHERE: The *Milbi* departs from Berth 5, Great Sandy Straits Marina, Buccaneer Drive, Urangan – but you will need to check-in at Shop 6/17 Buccaneer Drive, Urangan, Hervey Bay, on the marina just opposite Cafe Balaena, where fittings for the snorkelling gear (included as part of the tour) are carried out. You will then be walked down to the boat.
CONTACT: 07 4125 6888

Jarramali Rock Art Tours

Jarramali Rock Art Tours is family owned and operated by friendly and experienced Kuku Yalanji Traditional Owners who aim to give visitors the opportunity to experience the significant rock art, tree carvings, grindstones and engravings at each of the remarkable sites they visit. This is an invaluable opportunity to view Quinkan rock art, regarded by UNESCO as one of the ten most significant bodies of rock art in the world. Each of the tours highlights a connection to land, intertwined in the stories that the Kuku Yalanji people hold dear. Groups and individuals are treated to an Aboriginal cultural tour experience that encompasses European, Chinese and Aboriginal history.

WHERE: Jarramali Rock Art Tours is located 5.5 hours north of Cairns on the Mulligan Hwy and Peninsula Developmental Rd, near the township of Laura. Passengers can be picked up from Cairns or Port Douglas. 4WD tag-along tours can meet and leave from Laura. Heli tours leave from Cairns or Laura.
CONTACT: 0402 805 821

Journey into Olkola Country

Over 6 days, visitors have an incredible opportunity to experience the rugged wilderness of Olkola Country in Cape York Peninsula through a safe and expertly guided tour operated by Intrepid Travel. A harmonious combination of exploring nature and learning about Aboriginal culture makes this tour unforgettable and special. The Traditional Owners are willing to share their ancestral lands with visitors eager to learn about the richness of Aboriginal culture. With more than 1 million hectares of biodiverse savannah woodlands, river systems, lagoons and rocky escarpments to explore, visitors will walk and drive through places of great significance for the Olkola. The tour does not require a high level of fitness. Basic camping facilities are provided along with breakfast, lunch and dinner. This tour offers a unique cultural and travel experience. Tours run from late August through to early September. Visitors must be respectful of the experience and open to learn about Aboriginal culture. There is no wi-fi or phone coverage.

WHERE: The tour starts and ends in Cairns and travels up to the town of Laura in Cape York Peninsula and on to Olkola Country.
CONTACT: 1300 797 010

Kuku Yalanji Cultural Habitat Tour

The tour Kuka Yalanji Traditional Custodians offer at Cooya beach, just north of Port Douglas, is on their traditional homeland, where they continue to practice their cultural activities and maintain their cultural heritage. After explaining the importance of this Country, guides introduce guests to their traditional fishing activity of spear throwing and handling as it is still practised today. Then, each with a spear, visitors follow their cultural guide along Cooya beach observing cultural medicine and food plants. The guides then take guests with them into the mangroves and onto the mudflats as they continue their daily spear fishing and gathering for their families. After about 2 hours of cultural activities and coastal walking, guests return with the guides to see Kuku Yalanji artefacts and share rare stories from the guides' traditional land while they prepare their daily food for their families. A minimum number of 4 adults is required to operate the tour.

In a separate tour, you can experience night-time fishing, still a common traditional activity, with a local family. New lighting technology is sure to make your hour-long experience one to remember. A minimum number of 2 adults is required to operate the tour.

For both these tours, a medium to high level of fitness is required, and you will need to bring drinking water and insect repellent, and wear beach shoes and comfortable clothing for walking through water, mudflats and mangroves. The Coastal Beach and Mangrove Walk departs twice daily and bookings are essential; the Coastal Beach Night Time Walk departs on request at 7.30 pm and bookings are essential.

WHERE: Cooya Beach, Mossman.
CONTACT: 07 4098 3437

Mandingalbay Ancient Indigenous Tours (MAIT)

The 4 tour experiences available – a 3-hour guided eco cultural tour, the Deadly Dinner (requiring a minimum of 30 guests), the overnight stay, or an opportunity to design your own experience – provide an unforgettable engagement with ancient lands and Indigenous traditions. The Mandingalbay Yidinji people (MY People) are direct descendants of Jubalum and have held onto the ancient ways of caring for and sustainably governing and interacting with Country. Experienced tour guides share Mandingalbay Yidinji's timeless culture and connection with Country with visitors, ensuring a future for their generation and many more. Through all of the changes and displacement of the last hundred years, the MY People's identity has remained strong and intact, and their inherited cultural rights and responsibility to Country have not diminished. Mandingalbay Ancient Indigenous Tours aim to share the history, environment and cultural values of the people and land to all who wish to experience it. The MAIT travel from the Cairns Reef Terminal, across Trinity Inlet, and up to Hills Creek. The rainforest mountains of the Mandingalbay Yidinji lands are abundant with medicinal plants (edible flowers, native herbs and sweet fruit). Each experience is informative and awe-inspiring.

WHERE: 1928RN Yarrabah Rd, Bessie Point.
CONTACT: 07 4056 8283

Mossman Gorge Centre and Ngadiku Dreamtime Walks

The Mossman Gorge Centre is a wonderful starting point from which to visit Mossman Gorge and the Daintree rainforest. The centre contains an Indigenous art gallery, a gift shop and the Mayi Cafe and Restaurant, and runs guided and self-guided walks through the surrounding world heritage–listed rainforest. The Mossman Gorge Centre is committed to limiting the damage that can be caused by tourism. An example of how they are achieving this is through their low-emission shuttle bus, which departs every 15 minutes and transports visitors from the centre to the heart of Mossman Gorge and back for a small cost, eliminating unpoliced car traffic through the area.

Ngadiku (Nar-di-gul) means 'stories and legends from a long time ago' in the local Kuku Yalanji language. The Indigenous people from the Mossman Gorge area in North Queensland offer visitors a unique experience, guiding them on the Dreamtime Gorge Walk where the local people have exclusive access to Kuku Yalanji land. The walk starts with a smoking ceremony then winds through stunning rainforests, visiting culturally significant sites and special places, passing traditional bark shelters and walking over cool, clear streams. The Indigenous guide demonstrates traditional plant use, identifies bush foods and medicines, and shares the Kuku Yalanji people's stories about the rainforest, explaining their special relationship with this unique tropical environment. At the end of the tour, guests are invited to enjoy bush tea and damper.

WHERE: Mossman Gorge Centre, 212 Mossman Gorge Rd, Mossman; 77 km from Cairns; 20 km from Port Douglas.
CONTACT: For enquiries about the Mossman Gorge Centre and about the Ngadiku Dreamtime Walk: 07 4099 7000

Mungalla Aboriginal Tours

The Nywaigi people are the Traditional Owners of the lands around Ingham in North Queensland. On the 3–4 hour Mungalla tours, visitors learn about the rich culture and history of the Nywaigi, and hear about the often brutal conflict between the Aboriginal people and the European settlers who shaped the destiny of North Queensland. The tour allows visitors to witness some of the birdlife of the area, with 230 species having been recorded. The tours start and finish at the grand Mungalla station homestead site, where visitors can see historic artefacts and try their hand at throwing a boomerang. Then the tour goes by bus to the original homestead, where the guide shares stories of the first European settler on Mungalla in 1882, James Cassady, and rich and fascinating stories of the Nywaigi people and the beautiful tropical area that is their land. If they wish, visitors can enjoy a country BBQ lunch or a Kup murri dinner, where the food is cooked in the ground.

The Mungalla Aboriginal Business Corporation and its parent body, The Nywaigi Aboriginal Land Corporation, which holds the title to Mungalla station, are committed to improving the economic and social position of the Nywaigi people. They are working to achieve these aims by sharing the history of Mungalla station and its stunning environment through these fascinating tours.

WHERE: Mungalla station is located outside of Ingham, 128 km north of Townsville.
CONTACT: 07 4777 8718

Nyanda Cultural Tours

An authentic experience offering visitors a connection to a special and culturally significant place. The local Aboriginal tour guides lead guests around Brisbane's Nudgee Waterholes, Bora Ring and Bush Food Gardens site, with the tour presenting Aboriginal history, cultural performances, insights and stories. The 1.5-hour tour includes a smoking ceremony, seasonal bush food tasting and participation in weaving and ochre-making. A morning tea of wattleseed damper with rosella, wild lime and lilly pilly jams is served, with a one-of-a-kind Nyanda lemon myrtle cordial. The tours are by appointment only.

WHERE: Nyanda, 52 Childs Rd, Nudgee, Brisbane. Parking is available at Banyo Devils Rugby League Club.
CONTACT: 07 3868 1244

Pamagirri Aboriginal Experience at Rainforestation Nature Park

The award-winning Rainforestation Nature Park, located in Kuranda's World Heritage Rainforest, offers 3 unique experiences: the Pamagirri Aboriginal Experience, tours of the rainforest aboard an amphibious World

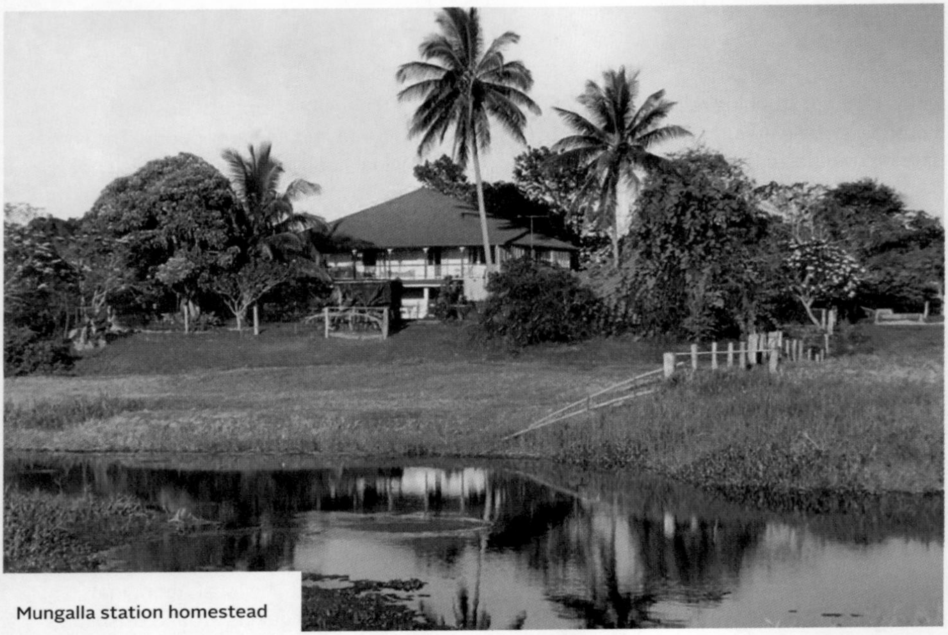

Mungalla station homestead

War Two Army Duck, and the Koala and Wildlife Park. It is open year-round except Christmas Day.

Rainforestation Nature Park first introduced an element of Aboriginal cultural experience in 1987, giving guests the chance to learn to throw a boomerang while waiting for an Army Duck tour. In 1993, an expansion was made in response to the growing interest in Aboriginal and Torres Strait Islander culture, with the formation of the Pamagirri Aboriginal Dance Troupe. The Pamagirri Performers took out the Gold Award in the 2019 Queensland Aboriginal and Torres Strait Islander Tourism Awards, and a Bronze in the same category at the National Awards.

Pamagirri means 'silent snake', and is symbolic of the Rainbow Serpent, responsible for the creation of the mountains and rivers in Aboriginal Dreaming stories.

The Dreamtime Walk was also introduced in 1993, with spear throwing demonstrations, didgeridoo playing and lessons in boomerang throwing. The Dreamtime Walk leads visitors to the rainforest amphitheatre, which provides a beautifully natural backdrop to the Pamagirri Dance Performance. The rainforest serves as the theatre walls, and the sounds of the forest accompany the sounds of didgeridoo, chanting and clapsticks. The performance depicts the unique animals, traditional history, and food gathering of this ancient culture.

The development of the Rainforest Walkabout in 2017 saw the Aboriginal experience further expanded. This 45-minute fully guided walk through the rainforest introduces traditional bush foods and medicines along with hunting tools, weapons and traditional Dreaming stories. Each tour is

Introduction to culture and collecting ochre with Pamagirri Aboriginal Experience at the Rainforestation Nature Park, Kuranda

slightly different, as each guide tells some of their own personal stories.

COVID-19 brought both challenges and opportunities in 2020. Rainforestation Nature Park and the Pamagirri Performers have developed a brand-new product called the Pamagirri Mini Mob during this time. This fun personal experience combines the Rainforest Walkabout with giving the kids their own PVC didgeridoo to paint, and a first lesson on how to play it. Guests leave with new knowledge, new skill – and a new didgeridoo!

In 2020, Rainforestation Nature Park hosted the inaugural Pamagirri Art Market for Emerging Indigenous Artists. This market gives Rainforestation's own artists, as well as other local Indigenous artists, the opportunity to sell their artwork.

The Pamagirri Art Market was developed out of an idea to support artists who had limited opportunities to sell their artwork due to the COVID-19 pandemic. With no cost to have a stall, no commissions being taken, and visitors not being charged an entrance fee to the art market, this is truly a show of support to these emerging artists, with the market planned to become an annual event that will continue to grow and develop over the years.

WHERE: Kennedy Hwy, Kuranda. Rainforestation is accessible by shuttle bus from Kuranda Village. Alternatively, there is parking onsite if arriving by car.
CONTACT: 07 4085 5008

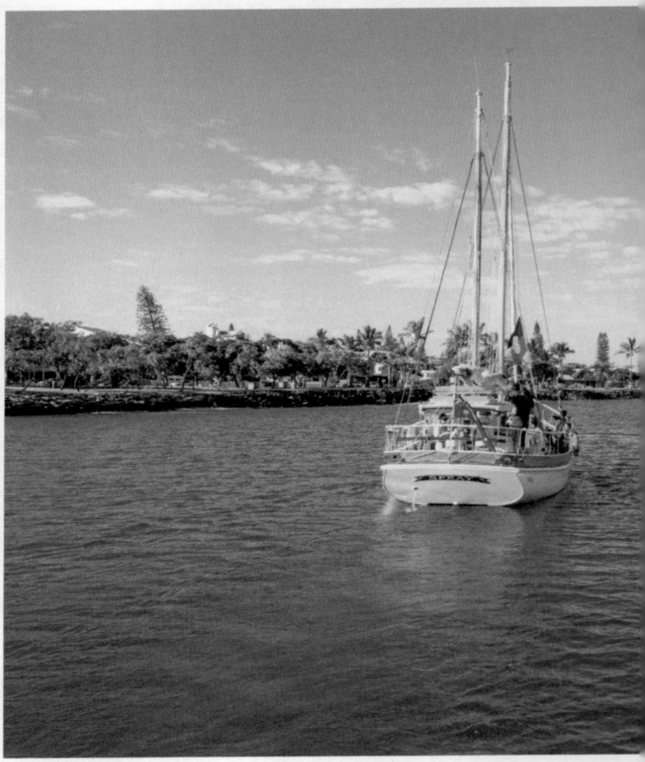

Saltwater Eco Tours onboard the historical vessel *Spray of the Coral Coast*, on the Mooloolah River, Sunshine Coast

Saltwater Eco Tours

Based on the Sunshine Coast, these unique experiences operate on the traditional waters of the Kabi Kabi/Gubbi Gubbi people to help forge a deeper connection to Indigenous culture and the ocean. Realising the vision of young Indigenous man Simon Thornalley, who restored a traditional timber sailing vessel *Spray of the Coral Coast*, the tours

offer delicious bush tucker–infused food, local storytelling and interactive demonstrations relating to the ancient culture of the local saltwater people. Sunset tours with live music are regularly offered.

WHERE: Penny Lane Jetty, Mooloolaba.
CONTACT: 0484 221 335

South West Queensland Indigenous Cultural Trail

South West Queensland Indigenous Cultural Trail (SWQICT) will take you on a journey across 7 communities that hold significant meaning to the local Indigenous people. The trail comprises a number of different cultural heritage sites across the towns. The Indigenous groups within this network each hold their own stories, and have important sites and healing places. This self-drive tour leads you through a unique area of undisturbed natural bushland, wildlife, lagoons and ancient waterways. The preservation of sites, stories and heritage through documentation and the creation of Indigenous artefacts, dance, literature and arts has enabled these communities to build on their local knowledge, and celebrate and share their culture.

WHERE: Looping from Dirranbandi to St George and Surat, to Roma, Mitchell and Charleville, then through Cunnamulla back to St George.

Straddie Adventures

Straddie Adventures is owned and operated by Traditional Owners of North Stradbroke Island and is a registered Authentic Aboriginal Cultural Experience. Owner Mark Jones is passionate about sharing his 'Kulcha' with visitors and passing down to new generations the invaluable knowledge he has received from his predecessors. Mark offers kayaking, sandboarding and 4W driving experiences that extend from 2 hours up to many days, all with a cultural element. There are also combo packages available, such as the 5-hour long Sandboard & Kayak Kulcha Experience, or the 2-day Kayak & 4WD Safari. Children can participate in all the tours as well, with ticket prices for tours and packages varying depending on age.

WHERE: 34 Dickson Way, One Mile, Stradbroke Island.
CONTACT: 0433 171 477

Two Boys Dreaming

This short, self-guided walking trail on the outskirts of town tells the creation story of how water wells were formed in the Simpson Desert. Check with the Wirrarri Visitor Information Centre before visiting, as floods and other conditions can affect access.

WHERE: Windorah Rd, Birdsville.
CONTACT: (Wirrarri Visitor Information Centre) 07 4564 2000

Walkabout Cultural Adventures

Owned and operated by Juan Walker, a descendant of the Eastern Kuku Yalanji people, Walkabout Cultural Adventures was created in 2008. Juan is passionate about sharing the stories, history and culture of Kuku Yalanji Country, located between Port Douglas and Cape Tribulation, and showcases bush foods and medicines, and traditional practices. The day tours on offer primarily take place within the Daintree, Cape Tribulation and Mossman, including Mossman Gorge and Cooya Beach areas. The tours operate as full and half-day experiences, and are run in small groups (maximum of 11 people); private personalised tours are also available, where guests can choose which

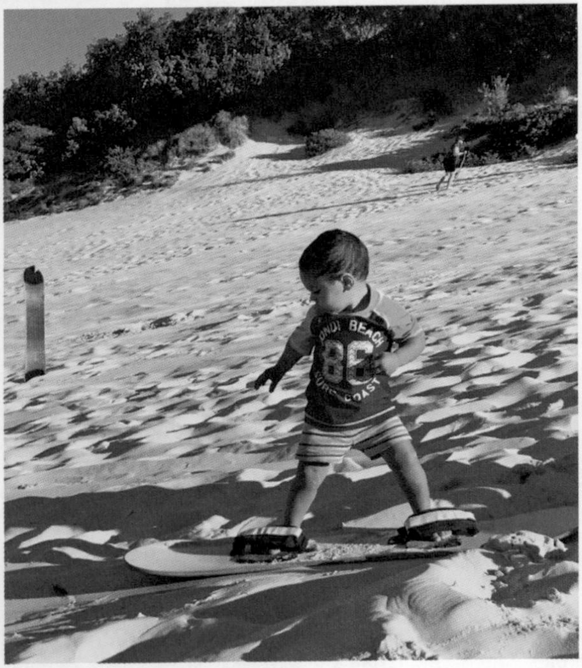

Top: Kayaking through the remains of a ship wreck off the coast of Straddie

Above: Sandboarding with Straddie Adventures on beautiful Straddie

sites and experiences they would like to explore. Tours run Monday–Saturday.

As some tours include water-based activities, it is a good idea to bring shoes appropriate for walking in water (reef walkers, etc.), along with swimwear, a towel, sunscreen, a hat and insect repellent.

WHERE: Guests staying in Port Douglas (1 hour north of Cairns), Mossman and the Daintree will receive transfers to and from their accommodation. Those staying elsewhere should make their own way to Port Douglas and Mossman for collection.
CONTACT: 0429 478 206

Wirrarri Visitor Information Centre

Full of up-to-date information on roads, tracks and the weather, this centre is a must visit if you are planning on heading anywhere remote. Get some travel tips, have a browse at the local artists' work in the extensive gallery, and take in an informative documentary in the theatrette. Wireless internet access, maps, souvenirs and a small library round out this space.

WHERE: 29 Burt St, Birdsville.
CONTACT: 07 4564 2000

Wujal Wujal Aboriginal Shire Council

Call in to the council before exploring the tracks and trails of the Wujal Wujal region, where a special Welcome to Country ceremony can be arranged. You can register for road, weather and emergency updates, gain local tips and tricks, and plan your adventure with the locals of Wujal Wujal. Straddling the rainforests and the reef, between two UNESCO World Heritage Sites, drive and explore so many beautiful areas with awe-inspiring surroundings. Located in the centre of town, the council office can provide inspiration

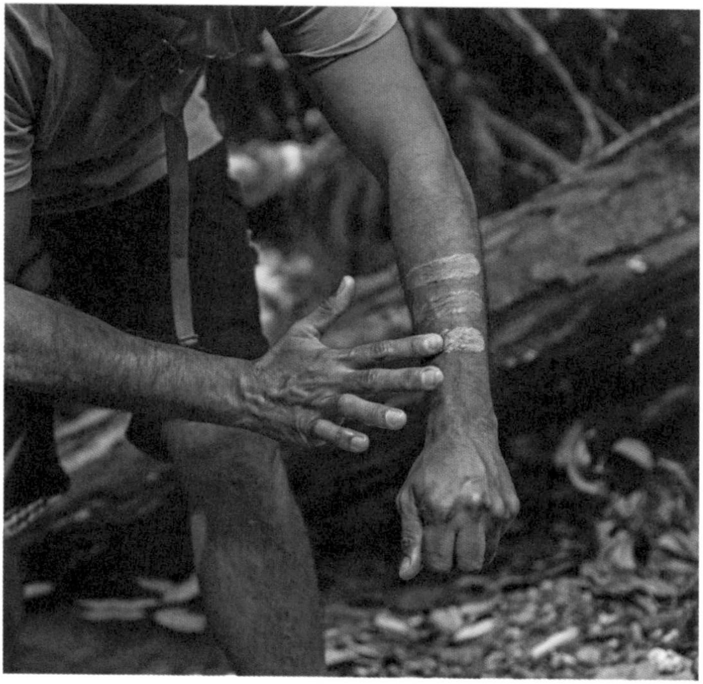

Walkabout Cultural Adventures takes visitors through Kuku Yalanji country, exploring tropical Daintree rainforest, waterways and mangroves, teaching about the environment, bush foods and medicines and ochre painting and information for any adventures in the area.

WHERE: Lot 1, Hartwig St, Wujal Wujal.
CONTACT: 07 4083 9100

Yindilli Camping and Tours

The crystal clear waters of Bairds Creek act as the background to the Yindilli Camping Ground. Guests will immediately be drawn by the serenity of the natural bushlands and the beautifully maintained gardens, walkways and amenities. Colin 'CJ' and Helen Fischer own and operate this camping ground, and CJ will act as host for any of the many guided walks available. His commentary includes traditional stories of cultural and spiritual significance for Buru and its people, and identification of local bush tucker and an explanation of its uses – both as a food source and medicinally. All bush walks are taken at a pleasant, leisurely pace, with nature forming a perfect backdrop as you enjoy a picnic lunch.

Yindilli Camping Ground has toilet facilities, fireplaces (for cooking etc.) and dry firewood. You must provide your own camping gear and food. Minimal refreshments are available from the main house/office.

Guided walks include the Rainforest Walk of approximately 1 hour, and the full-day Cultural Sites Walk, for which bookings are essential. The Rainforest Walk takes visitors through nearby rainforest and includes a Welcome smoke ceremony, stories and identification of bush tucker, as well as damper and tea. The Cultural Sites Walk commences with a walk of approximately 1 hour to a site of cultural and spiritual significance to the Kuku Yalanji people. This walk includes a Welcome smoke ceremony, stories, face and body painting with traditional clays, bush-tucker demonstrations, and bathing in the healing waters of the pristine Meg River. A picnic lunch and refreshments are provided.

WHERE: CREB Track, Chinacamp, via Wujal Wujal.
CONTACT: 07 4098 6248

ART GALLERIES, CULTURAL CENTRES AND MUSEUMS

Birrunga Gallery & Dining

At this sanctuary in the heart of the Brisbane CBD, as soon as you enter the basement-level, open-plan gallery, cafe and bar, you are in for a refreshing, ambient change. The gallery hosts a curated presentation of First peoples art and artefacts, with original artworks, including prints, textiles, weapons, didgeridoos, boomerangs, baskets and coolamons, for sale. It also offers guided workshops on carving or weaving. The cafe menu is heavily influenced by bush tucker and local indigenous cuisines with fresh, native ingredients in modern dishes. A First Nations Artisan Market is held fortnightly, and music, dance and a variety of other classes can be held in this space.

WHERE: 300 Adelaide St Basement Level Brisbane City.
CONTACT: 07 3705 5742

Cooktown History Centre and Cooktown Re-enactment Association

Cooktown Re-enactment Association was established with 3 clear intentions: to stage a culturally and historically accurate re-enactment of the arrival of Captain Cook's ship *Endeavour* at Waalmbal Birri

(Endeavour River) in 1770 and the following 48 days in Waymburr (now known as Cooktown); to share the history of the Guugu Yimithirr Bama (people) and the sailors of the HMB *Endeavour*, during this period of time when what is considered to be the first act of reconciliation in Australia occurred; and to explain many other significant events that took place. The association encourages cultural appreciation, historical awareness, community pride and economic development through events and activities that provide opportunities to fundraise, promote and educate. The staff in the centre are knowledgeable and committed to sharing the stories which they help to preserve. Waalmbal Birri Heritage and Culture Centre has evolved from these activities where the 48-days story is told through graphic murals.

WHERE: 121a Charlotte St, Cooktown.
CONTACT: 07 4069 6861

Dreamtime Kullilla-Art

Step into a world of colour, stories and ancient Indigenous culture at Dreamtime Kullilla Art. This family-owned Indigenous art gallery and retail shop, located on the Redcliffe Peninsula, stocks genuine, quality, royalty-paid Aboriginal art products, allowing you to shop with confidence. A diverse range of ethically sourced and honestly priced products are available to browse, from keyrings, tablecloths, laptop bags, coffee cups and jewellery to 'proper' boomerangs, books, maps, bush tucker and medicine. These product are perfect for gifts or souvenirs.

Meandering up the stairs from the retail shop, you will discover the Dreamtime Kullilla Art Gallery and the studio space of resident artist and business owner Michael Connolly. From Charleville, south-west Queensland, Michael is a descendant, on his father's side, of the Kullilla tribe from the Thargomindah and Eulo region and, on his mother's side, of the Muruwari people from the Goodooga and Brewarrina region of north-west New South Wales. With this rich Indigenous background and a unique way of interpreting his cultural heritage, Michael is able to represent a unique perspective in the visual and performing arts, which informs his significant work in cross-cultural contexts. He is also an accomplished didgeridoo player and performer. Michael uses the artist name of Munda-gutta Kulliwari, which means 'you know me before you see me'.

The gallery space of Dreamtime Kullilla Art Gallery is a truly immersive cultural experience, with Michael, or a member of staff, on hand to walk visitors through the stories behind the works, including Michael's own work – and happy to share the cultural background of each of the artists exhibited.

WHERE: 1/349 MacDonnell Rd, Clontarf.
CONTACT: 0417 385 398 | 0419 700 092

James Cook Museum

Housed in the Sisters of Mercy convent school building, the museum includes a large collection of local Guugu Yimithirr artefacts, as well as an Indigenous gallery, where the culture and history of the Guugu Yimithirr people is recorded in a range of mediums. The stories and history, both Indigenous and non-Indigenous, that you will find in the museum, including a story about what is considered to be the first act of reconciliation in this country, between the local Bama people and Captain James Cook will interest the whole family. An original anchor and cannon from HMB *Endeavour* form part of the museum collection. The verandah of

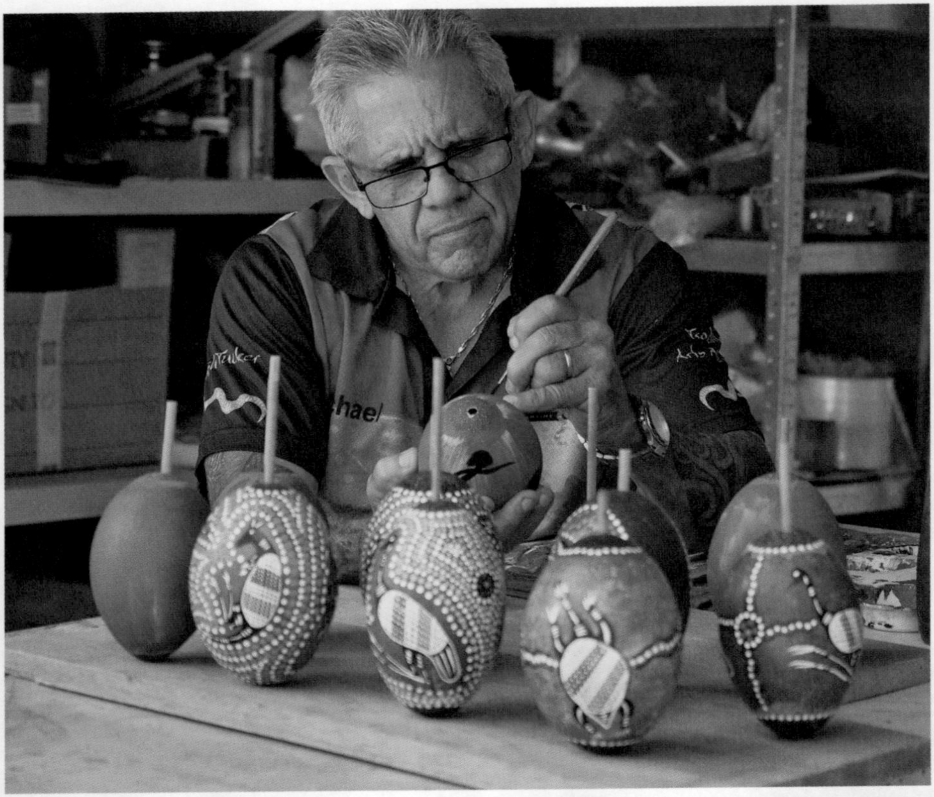

Michael J Connolly (Munda-gutta Kulliwari) handpainting a didgeridoo and emu eggs at Dreamtime Kullilla-Art Gallery

the 3-storey building provides magnificent views over Cooktown and the banks of the Endeavour River.

WHERE: 50 Helen St, Cooktown.
CONTACT: 07 4069 5386

Janbal Gallery

Janbal Gallery, located on Kuku Yulanji Country in Mossman, just north of Cairns, is run by local Aboriginal artist Brian 'Binna' Swindley. It is named after his late mother, acclaimed Aboriginal artist Shirley 'Janbal' Swindley, whose name referred to the rare blue quandong that grows in the Mossman region. The gallery exclusively showcases hand-painted originals, completed on site by Binna himself, including didgeridoos and artefacts. Brian's Aboriginal name, Binna, means 'hearing impaired', pointing to the severe hearing impairment that he was born with. Binna has taught himself to speak and lip read, and runs daily hour-long private art classes for visitors, during which he talks about his culture and the legacy his mother left him. The private classes give guests the chance to paint either canvases or boomerangs and can be booked on the website.

WHERE: 5 Johnston Rd, Mossman, a 1-hour drive north of Cairns when travelling along the Captain Cook Hwy.
CONTACT: 07 4098 3917. Due to Binna's hearing impairment, it is preferred that enquiries be made by email: info@janbalgallery.com.au

Jellurgal Aboriginal Cultural Centre

Jellurgal Aboriginal Cultural Centre is located at the base of Burleigh Head National Park in Burleigh Heads on the Gold Coast, alongside pristine Tallebudgera Creek. At the centre, you can browse through artwork from local Indigenous artists in the art gallery and see Aboriginal artefacts such as dilly bags, shields, tools, boomerangs, nulla nullas, didgeridoos and other tools and instruments that were part of everyday life for the Traditional Custodians of the Gold Coast for thousands of years. You can embark on a journey of discovery into Aboriginal culture by taking one of the centre's renowned Jellurgal tours, a guided walk along a picturesque beachside rainforest walkway wrapped around the magical mountain, Jellurgal. Learn about the Aboriginal history and culture of the Gold Coast, meet a Traditional Custodian and hear the Dreaming stories associated with the creation of Jellurgal. You can also hear about the traditional life, bush tucker, fishing, hunting and the important ecological practices and connection to the land embraced by the Yugambeh-speaking people for thousands of years. Take along your beach attire and head to the pristine Tallebudgera Creek, recently named one of Australia's best swimming spots, after your visit to Jellurgal.

WHERE: 1711 Gold Coast Hwy, Burleigh Heads.
CONTACT: 07 5525 5955

Kuku Bulkaway Indigenous Art Gallery

The Yuku Baja Muliku people own and operate this gallery, and each piece of art has a unique story. The artists are inspired by the land and sea, and the connection to land. This inspiration comes from all around – the plants, animals, bush food and life in the Cape York area are all represented. Local ancient culture and more recent traditions are also displayed.

Yuku Baja Muliku run an Indigenous ranger program on Country, and found that issues staff faced were taking a toll on the their mental health, so they were encouraged to share their stories, to express themselves through art, with incredibly beneficial results. When experienced artists in the community saw how painting, drawing, writing stories and making tools became such a helpful aid to staff wellbeing, they supported the program through sharing their skills and techniques. Kuku Bulkaway Arts was launched and has been a huge success. It has melded the rangers' sea and land management work and their artistic sides, and many of the staff have been with the company for over a decade.

WHERE: 142 Charlotte St, Cooktown.
CONTACT: 07 4069 6957

Mainie Australia Aboriginal Art Gallery & Retail Shop

Aboriginal owned and operated, this fashion and gift collection melds two ancient artistic cultures: the historic Silk Cities of China and the Aboriginal arts heritage of Australia. Mainie pays royalties from every sale to the Aboriginal artists and their families, and each piece is presented in a handmade box with information included about the original artwork, the artist's story, and the land it was created on. The silk is handmade in Suzhou and Hangzhou, and the designs are depictions of ancient Dreaming stories which the Aboriginal artists have inherited from their ancestors. The company embraces Fair Trade ethics and is an approved dealer member of the Indigenous Art Code.

WHERE: 77–91 Scott St, Bungalow, Cairns.
CONTACT: 07 4030 2186

Top: Visitors enjoy a Jellurgal Walkabout tour at Burleigh Heads on the Gold Coast

Bottom: Jellurgal Walkabout tours include Dreaming stories associated with popular Gold Coast locations including Tallebudgera Creek

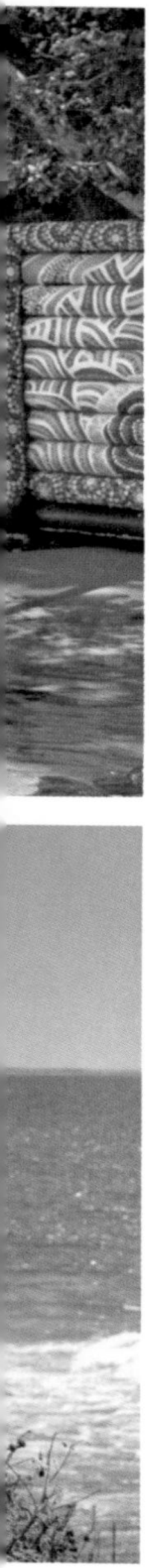

Queensland Art Gallery and Gallery of Modern Art (QAGOMA)

These galleries are one institution, QAGOMA, located on 2 sites in the Cultural Precinct of South Bank, across the river from the centre of Brisbane. Their combined vision is to be the 'leading institution for the contemporary art of Australia, Asia and the Pacific', and the Asia Pacific Triennial is one way they achieve it. This major exhibition, held in both galleries, displays works across many mediums by Aboriginal and Torres Strait Islander artists as well as artists from other countries and cultures in Asia and the Pacific.

The permanent collection and annual calendar of temporary exhibitions and events also celebrate the art and culture of Aboriginal and Torres Strait Islanders. GOMA has a focus on collecting and displaying contemporary Indigenous art, while the Queensland Art Gallery shows and collects traditional Indigenous works as well. Throughout the year, GOMA's Children's Art Centre runs a free program for kids that is dynamic and fun, and that parents will enjoy too.

Visitors can spend the day visiting the 2 galleries, dining in their cafes and restaurants, and sitting by the river and smelling the flowers of the frangipani trees that grow along its banks.

WHERE: Stanley Place, Cultural Precinct, South Bank, Brisbane.
CONTACT: 07 3840 7303

Queensland Museum, Brisbane

The museum considers the cultural material of Queensland's Aboriginal Peoples and Torres Strait Islanders to be the most important part of its collections, and in particular the links this cultural material reveals between adjacent regions, including the Northern Territory and the Western Pacific's Papua New Guinea, the Solomon Islands and Vanuata. Cultures and histories research and community engagement activities play a key role at the museum in fostering respect and recognition of Aboriginal, Torres Strait and Australian South Sea Islander peoples in the broader Queensland community.

WHERE: Cnr Grey & Melbourne sts, South Brisbane.
CONTACT: 07 5525 5955

Quinkan & Regional Cultural Centre

Owned and operated by the local Aboriginal community, the cultural centre provides information on attractions, accommodation and travelling conditions throughout the area. The Laura region, where the cultural centre is situated, is renowned as a highly significant rock art site, with World Heritage and UNESCO listings. It has been given the name Quinkan Country, after the Quinkan spirit figures depicted in the rock art – and hence the name of the cultural centre. The centre presents a display of local Aboriginal ancient culture and recent traditions and changes, as well as a DVD showcasing the Laura region. Local Indigenous guides are available for tours, and a selection of Aboriginal arts and crafts are available. There is a small cafe in the centre.

WHERE: 2 Peninsula Developmental Rd, Laura.
CONTACT: 07 4060 3457

Ravenshoe Visitor Centre

This one-stop shop for travel information is staffed by skilled and knowledgeable local volunteers who can provide advice on what to do, things to see, and places to stay and eat. The centre houses a small museum dedicated to the history of the area, and the

Nganyaji Interpretive Centre – a spectacular presentation of local Indigenous artefacts and the Jirrbal rainforest people's knowledge system. This centre was opened in 2002, with the Ravenshoe Heritage Gallery a more recent addition.

WHERE: 24 Moore St, Ravenshoe.
WHEN: Open 365 days a year.
CONTACT: 07 4089 2243

Yugambeh Museum

The Yugambeh Museum Language and Heritage Research Centre holds information and records on traditional knowledge, including ancient and more recent artefacts, family history records, photographs and archival records, and an extensive library of books, audio, CDs and tapes of the European and Aboriginal history of the region – stretching through Tweed River, Logan and the Gold Coast. The museum works with the community to bring together cultural and education exchanges through many initiatives, so that future generations will also be able to truly connect with the Indigenous legacy of the region.

WHERE: 2 Plantation Road, Beenleigh.
CONTACT: 07 3807 6155

PLACES

Aboriginal Meeting Place

This traditional women's meeting place now has a rotunda with stone seats and a mosaic floor made by 2 artists, Joyce Crombie and Jean Barr. It's part of several large-scale sculptures in the Diamantina Shire made by local artists linking Country, community and stories. It's also one of the stops on the Footprints in Time Indigenous arts trail around Birdsville.

WHERE: Maps for locating the meeting place are available at the Wirrarri Visitor Information Centre, 29 Burt St, Birdsville.
CONTACT: (Wirrarri Visitor Information Centre) 07 4564 2000

Cooktown Botanic Gardens

Established in 1878, the gardens are located within the Gallop Botanic Reserve, and house 5 major plant collections, including species traditionally used by local Aboriginal people. The gardens have undergone a recent development and now include the First People's Grove and Yarning Circle. This is a peaceful place to learn about local flora and fauna, while being close to town, and connected to bushland reserves.

WHERE: Walker St, Cooktown, 1.5 km from the centre of town.

Currumbin Wildlife Sanctuary

Located in the heart of Currumbin, the sanctuary is the perfect place to connect with nature. With over 27 hectares of wide-open spaces featuring lush rainforest and the Australian bushland, the iconic Currumbin Wildlife Sanctuary is a beautiful environment to visit and for getting back to nature. Visitors can feed wild lorikeets, and see mammals, reptiles, birdlife, exotic species and live shows. To celebrate the rich local Aboriginal culture at Currumbin Wildlife Sanctuary, the Yugambeh Aboriginal Dancers perform daily, showcasing the culture of the Yugambeh people, and the Traditional Owners of the Gold Coast region.

Currumbin Wildlife Sanctuary is a not-for-profit organisation that invests all proceeds back into caring for wildlife and various conservation programs. It offers great cafes and food outlets, gift shops and photo opportunities to capture special moments.

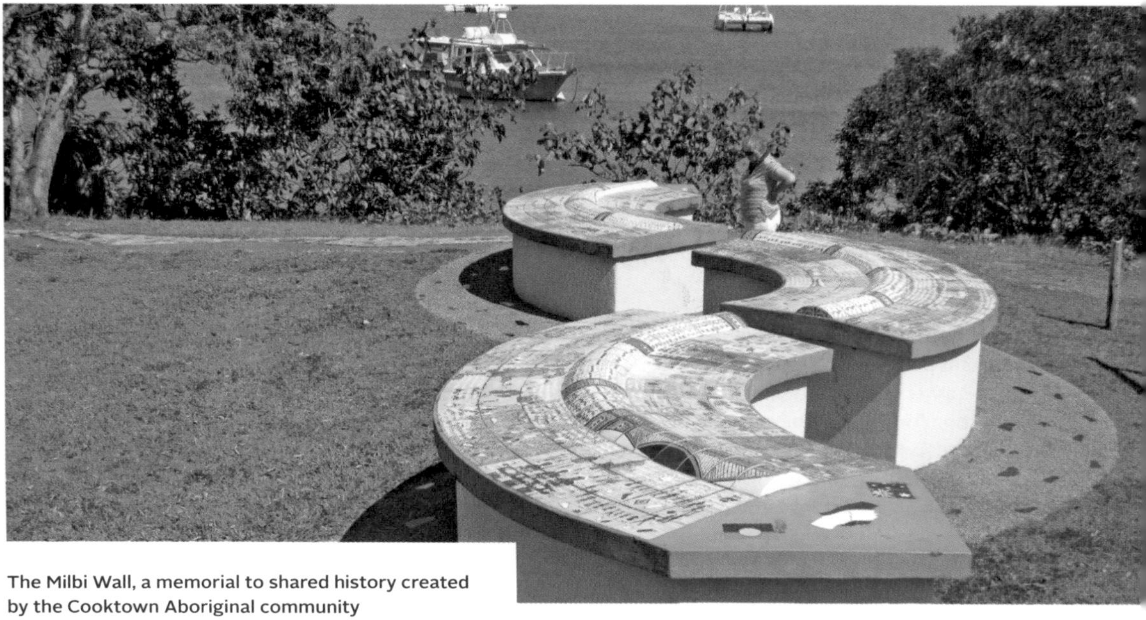

The Milbi Wall, a memorial to shared history created by the Cooktown Aboriginal community

The CWS app helps visitors plan their day in advance, get showtime alerts, and much more.

WHERE: 28 Tomewin St, Currumbin. The sanctuary is a 10-minute drive by car or bus from the Gold Coast airport, on the Gold Coast Hwy, or the route 700 bus will take visitors straight to the sanctuary.
CONTACT: 07 5534 1266

Flames of the Forest

A dining experience like no other – storytelling and music accompanies a 4-course tropical tasting menu (available on limited Tuesdays). The Aboriginal Cultural Experience features 2 brothers sharing their culture through storytelling, didgeridoo playing and song.

Set beneath the canopy of the oldest rainforest in the world, this captivating experience provides memories for a lifetime. Culture and cuisine are melded together under this enchanting rainforest setting.

WHERE: Mowbray River Road, Port Douglas. Return pick-up is available from most accommodation houses in Port Douglas or Thala Beach Nature Reserve. There is no self-drive available.
WHEN: Tuesday and Thursday evenings.
CONTACT: 07 4099 3144

Milbi Wall

Cook Shire Council wanted to acknowledge the significance of the first known contact of the local Aboriginal people with Europeans, from the Guugu Yimithirr point of view. Milbi (story) wall was developed at the spot where Captain Cook and his crew first stepped foot in 1770, with a well-known potter and the Gungarde Aboriginal Corporation collaborating with local Aboriginal artists and storytellers to create a 12 m-long, ceramic tile 3-part story. It covers significant events including the Creation story, the meeting of Captain Cook, the 1967 Referendum, and many varied and important details in between. Allow plenty of time to truly soak in the details, and show this work the attention it deserves. The wall was opened in 1998.

WHERE: Foreshore, Charlotte St, Cooktown.

Mulbabidgee

For thousands of years, Mulbabidgee was an important place for the local Gungarde people to gather resources through hunting, and collecting food and medicine. The seasonal wetland sits at the top of Meldrum Creek, about 8 km south of Cooktown. Lush tropical woodland, abundant birdlife, and an expansive picnic area make this place endlessly fascinating, though the mosquitos will take every chance they can to get at your exposed skin, so dress accordingly. The local Gungarde Aboriginal Corporation worked in collaboration with Queensland Parks and Wildlife Service to develop a 1.5 km boardwalk and walking track around the edge of the bird sanctuary, where thousands of waterbirds take refuge (especially during the dry season). There is a 390 m path which leads to the picnic area, passing through the melaleuca forest – keep an eye out for signs along the path, as some of the trees are numbered and named. There is a self-guided trail through the park, and an informative brochure about the Aboriginal culture of the area is available from the QPWS offices in Cairns or Cooktown.

WHERE: 5 km south of Cooktown, along the Mulligan Hwy.
CONTACT: 07 4069 5444

Riverlife Mirrabooka

At Riverlife Mirrabooka, visitors can sit outside by the river at Kangaroo Point, Brisbane, and watch performances by the Yuggera Aboriginal Dancers, who have performed for audiences around Australia and internationally. There are also opportunities for visitors to get involved and participate in traditional song and dance passed down over many generations, learn traditional fire-starting techniques and boomerang throwing, taste Indigenous bush tucker, or paint a boomerang. Also, listen to musicians playing Aboriginal instruments and gain insights into Aboriginal life and history through fascinating and educational talks. Riverlife Mirrabooka is perfect for visitors who enjoy learning through interactive experiences.

Riverlife Mirrabooka is in the Queensland Tourism Awards Hall of Fame for the Best Indigenous Product in Queensland, Australia.

WHERE: Naval Stores, Kangaroo Point, Brisbane.
CONTACT: 07 3891 5766

Spirits of the Red Sand

Launched in 2018, and based on true events that occurred at the start of the 20th century, Spirits of the Red Sand explores 60,000 years of Aboriginal culture, giving guests the opportunity to journey from Dreaming times to 1800s Australia in a unique roving theatre and dinner experience where history is brought to life.

The performances are raw, emotional and immersive, turning a truthful and unflinching eye on Aboriginal and colonial history. The historical re-enactment follows the journey of three Aboriginal brothers set to meet the British newcomers for the first time. This world-first in authentic Aboriginal storytelling is followed by a 3-course dinner, where you will meet the modern-day Aboriginal cast, direct descendants of the very story you just journeyed through. A yuweii (never a complete goodbye but a see you soon) song and dance ends the evening.

Spirits of the Red Sand by day offers cultural tours, workshops and experiences for education and corporate groups: from the Welcome to Country Aboriginal Experience, an interactive tour that shares ancient traditions and ceremonies along with boomerang painting, bush-tucker tasting and didgeridoo playing, to cultural awareness workshops and team building incentives. Also on offer is function space for hire, a cafe and a thriving events calendar.

WHERE: 205 Main St, Beenleigh.
CONTACT: 07 3801 8198

Split Rock

The walk to Split Rock is short but worthwhile. Many of the walks in the Laura area have rock art to display, but Split Rock does not require a guide. The site is directly off the Peninsula Development Road, and can be accessed any time (although, the road occasionally closes due to flooding in the Wet season). This natural, well-maintained trail is easy to walk but does include some sections of stone steps. The main gallery area at the peak of the walk shows painted and engraved Indigenous art, with interpretive signs. There are some areas signposted as restricted, so please respect the wishes of the Traditional Owners.

WHERE: Peninsula Developmental Rd, Laura.

Wujal Wujal Waterfall

Less than 2 km south of Wujal Wujal community, home of the Kuku Yalanji, Kuku Nyungkul and Jalunji clans, this important cultural site has a short track leading to the falls, which are about 40 m tall. Walk from town, or park at the start of the track – limited parking available.

WHERE: Bloomfield River, Daintree National Park.

ART CENTRES

Bana Yirriji Art Centre

Bana Yirriji Art Centre supports the artistic expression and cultural knowledge of the Eastern Kuku Yalanji peoples of Wujal Wujal. The centre's artists are renowned nationally and internationally for a unique art style influenced by their heritage as rainforest people, with individual motifs reflecting the land, rivers, seas and wildlife of their Far North Queensland Country. Artists work in a range of mediums including natural seed jewellery, prints, paintings, artefacts and textiles. Bana Yirriji includes an art gallery, artist studio and shop.

WHERE: Wujal Wujal (70 km from Cooktown).
CONTACT: 07 4060 8333

Girringun Aboriginal Art Centre

Girringun Aboriginal Art Centre was established in 2008, to support the artists from the 9 Traditional Owner groups in and around Cardwell, in Far North Queensland – the Nywaigi, Gugu Badhan, Warrgamay, Warungnu, Bandjin, Girramay, Gulngay, Jirrbal and Djiru peoples, whose collective traditional Country spans some 25,000 square kilometres. The distinct Aboriginal rainforest culture and artistic traditions of the Girringun region are brought to life through a range of mediums, including weaving, painting, pottery, textile design and traditional artefacts. Artists from Girringun are multi-award-winning and are attracting attention far and wide.

WHERE: 235 Victoria St, Cardwell.
CONTACT: 07 4066 8300

Hope Vale Arts and Cultural Centre

Hope Vale Arts was opened in 2009 to ensure the promotion and preservation of the unique Guugu-Ymithirr culture of Far North Queensland. The centre is an open and accessible space for all members of the Hope Vale community to pursue their artistic expression. In 2016, Hopevale artists expanded their knowledge of textile printing and design, exploring a new medium of storytelling. They are now nationally and internationally renowned for their striking textiles, which have been showcased in collaborative fashion collections at the Cairns Indigenous Art Fair, Darwin Aboriginal Art Fair and fashion shows in Canberra.

WHERE: 1 Flierl St, Hope Vale.
CONTACT: info@hopevaleart.org.au

Lockhart River Arts

Established in 1995, Lockhart River Arts Centre is a prominent Indigenous Australian art centre located on the eastern side of the Cape York Peninsula. The art centre supports, promotes and represents Lockhart River artists with their vibrant and diverse artistic expression and cultural preservation. Artworks include painting, ceramics, prints, basket weaving and other traditional crafts.

The art centre has established active working relations with galleries both nationally and internationally to exhibit and showcase Lockhart River Arts. The art centre also participates annually at both the Cairns Indigenous Art Fair and the Darwin Aboriginal Art Fair.

WHERE: 1 Piiramo St, Lockhart River.
CONTACT: 07 4060 7341

Pormpuraaw artists painting a mural

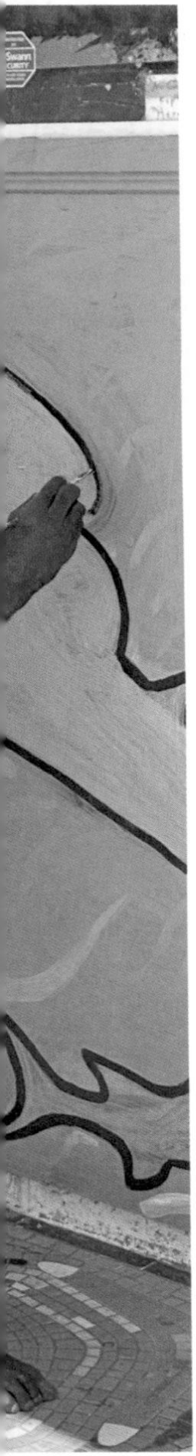

Mirndiyan Gununa – MIART – Mornington Island Art

MIART forms part of the Mirndiyan Gununa Aboriginal Corporation on Mornington Island, which lies in the remote Gulf of Carpentaria, northern Australia. One of the first art and cultural organisations established in Aboriginal Australia, Mirndiyan Gununa is fully owned and controlled by an Indigenous board, with its Indigenous-majority staff delivering the locally relevant programs that produce internationally renowned artwork.

Mirndiyan Gununa's primary purpose is to maintain and develop the cultures of the Lardil and Kaidilt people. The creative practice of the MIART Studios is built on the groundbreaking work of Lardil artist Goobalathaldin Dick Roughsey and Kaidilt artist Mirdidingkingathi Juwarnda Sally Gabori. Mornington Island's remote location gives artists a strong focus on cultural and spiritual subject matter, with language integral to the art centre's creative activities. Artists explore their connection to Country while working in mediums that range from painting to music and dance to storytelling.

WHERE: Mornington Island (440 km north of Mount Isa and 28 km off the coast of mainland Australia).
CONTACT: 0418 224 953

Pormpuraaw Art and Culture Centre

Located on the western coast of the Cape York Peninsula, Pormpuraaw community and its surrounds is the Country of the Thaayorre people. It is also home to the Wik and Kugu people, whose traditional lands are adjacent. Pormpuraaw is a Thaayorre word meaning 'entranceway to a house'. Pormpuraaw Art Centre is the hub of community life, and brings people together from all across the region. Each clan and individual is connected to one or two major totems, and multiple minor ones, representing a clan's ancestral homeland. For Pormpuraaw itself, the main totems are the crocodile and barramundi. They feature in many stories from the area, along with other spirits of the Creation time. Artistic expression for Pormpuraaw artists is a fun way to engage with their heritage and traditional law, and to share this with the outside world.

Art from Pormpuraaw is diverse, powerful and colourful. It includes the traditional forms, such as painting on bodies, tools, weaving, dance and song, as well as the contemporary representation of ancient storytelling, such as ghost-net sculpture, painting, prints and carvings. Pormpuraaw is well known for its master ghost-net weavers, who recycle washed-up commercial fishing nets and other materials into meaningful art, often representing clan totems. Ghost-net sculptures from the area are popular nationally and internationally.

WHERE: 2 Thinarrin St, Pormpuraaw (494 km from Cooktown).
CONTACT: 0437 172 758

UMI Arts Limited

The peak Aboriginal and Torres Strait Islander arts and cultural organisation for Far North Queensland, UMI supports artists from north of Cairns, including the Torres Strait Islands, south to Cardwell, and west to Camooweal, including the Gulf and Mount Isa regions. Established in 2005, the Indigenous-led organisation assists Aboriginal and Torres Strait Islander peoples to participate in the maintenance, preservation and protection of cultural identity. UMI is a creole word meaning 'You and ME', reflecting the importance of working together to keep culture strong.

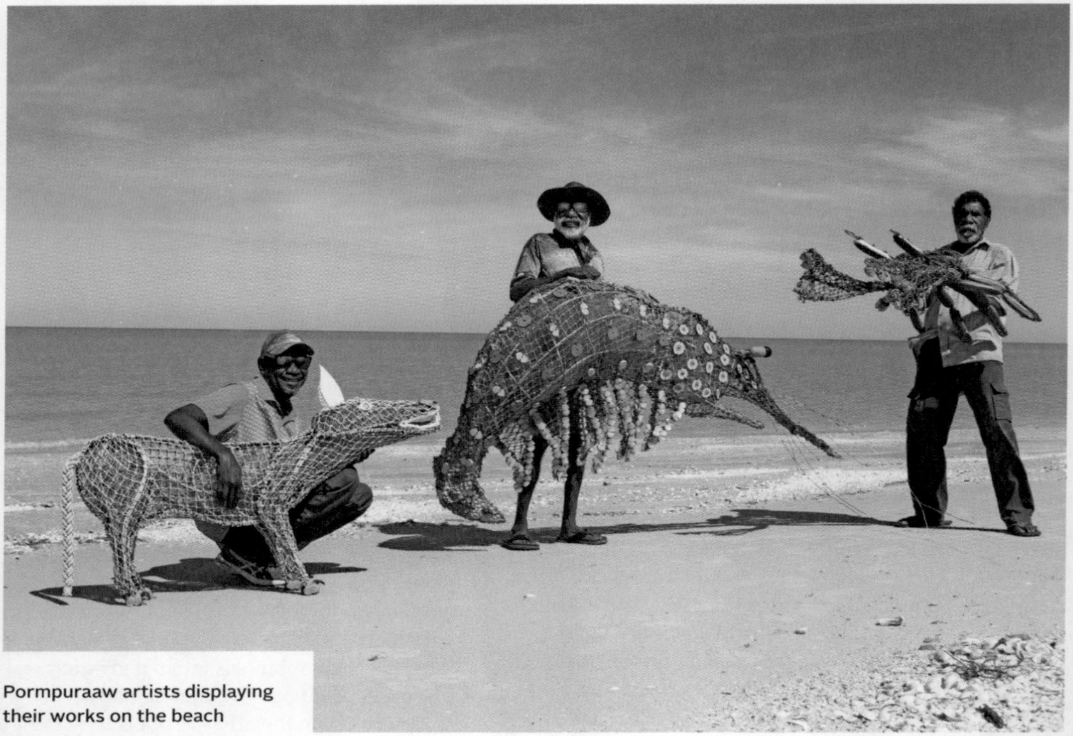

Pormpuraaw artists displaying their works on the beach

The annual program of events and activities run by UMI brings people together to share stories and strengthen Indigenous cultural practices.

UMI also operates as the Cairns Indigenous Art Centre, supporting Indigenous artists who live and work in Cairns.

WHERE: Shop 4/1 Jensen St, Manoora, Cairns.
CONTACT: 07 4041 6152

Wei'Num Arts

Wei'Num Arts supports Indigenous artists throughout the Western and Northern Cape York region, focusing on fine arts and traditional crafts, arts education and training, arts business and marketing and promotion of the diverse cultural histories of the region.

WHERE: Weipa Rd, Mapoon (88 km from Weipa).
CONTACT: admin@weinumarts.com.au

Wik and Kugu Arts Centre

Wik and Kugu started in the 1990s as an independent arts initiative, before being officially established as an arts centre in 2001 to service artists from the five Aurukun clan groups, Apalech, Puch, Sara, Wanam, and Winchanam. The art centre is located on the eastern edge of the Gulf of Carpentaria in remote Far North Queensland, with a men's art studio and workshop, a women's art studio, named after respected artist Akay Koo'Oila, and a gallery space.

The men are renowned for exquisite wooden sculptures that are related to animal totems and extend traditional cultural practices. Additionally, the men produce bold ochre and charcoal works referencing traditional body painting designs, among other contemporary prints. Likewise, the women are well-known for their ochre-based paintings, pandanus fruit bowls and feather flower arrangements.

WHERE: Aurukun (178 km from Weipa).
CONTACT: 07 4060 6843

Woorabinda Arts and Cultural Centre

Woorabinda Arts and Cultural Centre (WACC) was born as a concept in 2018, opening publicly in March 2021. WACC is home to cultural development and presentations of oral histories, performance and visual arts produced by First peoples artists of Central Queensland. A multi-faceted cultural space, WACC provides a permanent centre for artists and the community to create and present their artistic work, intending to support and heal; enhancing and fostering collaboration. Home to a gallery space, workshop rooms and gift shop, WACC presents publicly and facilitates the opportunity to purchase directly from First peoples artists of Central Queensland.

Situated on the lands of the Wadja Wadja/Wadjigal people in the regional town of Duaringa, Queensland, WACC is located 60 km north-east of Woorabinda Aboriginal community. WACC ensures that for the first time, First peoples of Central Queensland have a dedicated space for the development and presentation of cultural and creative outcomes.

WACC takes a grassroots perspective of training, development and management, placing First peoples at the heart of the Cultural Centre. Managed and operated by entirely First peoples, WACC has the vision to become a leading First peoples art and cultural centre.

WHERE: Former Duaringa CWA Hall, Edward St, Duaringa (111 km from Rockhampton).
CONTACT: info@woorabindaartscentre.com

Yalanji Arts

Yalanji Arts supports Kuku Yalanji artists of the Mossman Gorge region to showcase their culture through artistic expression. The eastern Kuku Yalanji Country stretches from Black Mountain in the north, along the coastal plain to Mowbray in the south. Artists celebrate their culture and the deep respect, knowledge and connection to the richly diverse rainforest and ocean environments of their Country. A range of quality artworks are produced at Yalanji Arts, including stunning handmade and on-site fired ceramics, acrylic paintings, traditional artefacts, contemporary wooden sculptures and hand-dyed and screen-printed textiles.

WHERE: Mossman Gorge (70 km from Cairns).
CONTACT: 07 4098 1305

Yarrabah Arts and Cultural Precinct

Yarrabah community lies on the traditional lands of the Gunggandji people. The Yarrabah Arts and Cultural Precinct, including the Yarrabah Arts Centre and a rainforest boardwalk, showcases Aboriginal culture, art, identity and history. Artists create handmade pottery, paintings, woven baskets, placemats and textiles. Another part of the precinct is the Menmuny Museum, a nationally significant historical collection showing the traditions and impact of Christianity on the local community.

WHERE: Yarrabah (60 km from Cairns by road).
CONTACT: 07 4056 9249

7 TASMANIA

FESTIVALS

Ballawinne Festival

Taking place on Melukerdee Country, the Ballawinne (red ochre) festival and cultural day celebrates Tasmanian Aboriginal philosophies, literature and ongoing connection to Country. The South East Tasmanian Aboriginal Corporation, in conjunction with Weetapoona Aboriginal Corporation, hold annual cultural festivals around the south-east of Tasmania that are open to the whole community, with the cultural theme differing each year based on the current community needs. Empowering the south-east Tasmanian Aboriginal community through self-determination, this festival facilitates relationship building and establishes strong connections with the wider community in an inclusive and safe environment. Patrons can listen, learn and even take part in creating local cultural practices such as basket weaving, tool making and visual artworks. Renowned guest speakers take the festival stage each year to share their knowledge and contribute to this welcoming community.

WHERE: Port Cygnet
CONTACT: 03 6295 0004

Nayri Niara Good Spirit Festival

The Nayri Niara Good Spirit Festival is held on Bruny Island every 2 years. The festival aims to bring people from all backgrounds together to celebrate Aboriginal culture and to honour the traditional custodians in a safe and supportive environment. Various ceremonies are held during the festival, as well as live music performances and contemporary celebrations of culture and diversity. Many different social enterprises run stalls over the weekend and feature music, food, weaving and arts and crafts. The focus of the festival is on creating positive social change and bringing joy to the festival participants. Most of the festival events are free, however some may charge admission. Information about the program and ticket sales is released closer to the event date. Temperature and weather conditions on Bruny Island can change quickly and dramatically. Visitors should dress accordingly and bring adequate supplies of water. Drinking alcohol and drug use is not permitted at the festival. Camping is not available.

WHERE: Great Bay, Bruny Island. A ferry service operates; for more information on getting there, see the festival website.
WHEN: Every 2 years; the most recent festival was held in March 2019.
CONTACT: Via the festival website.

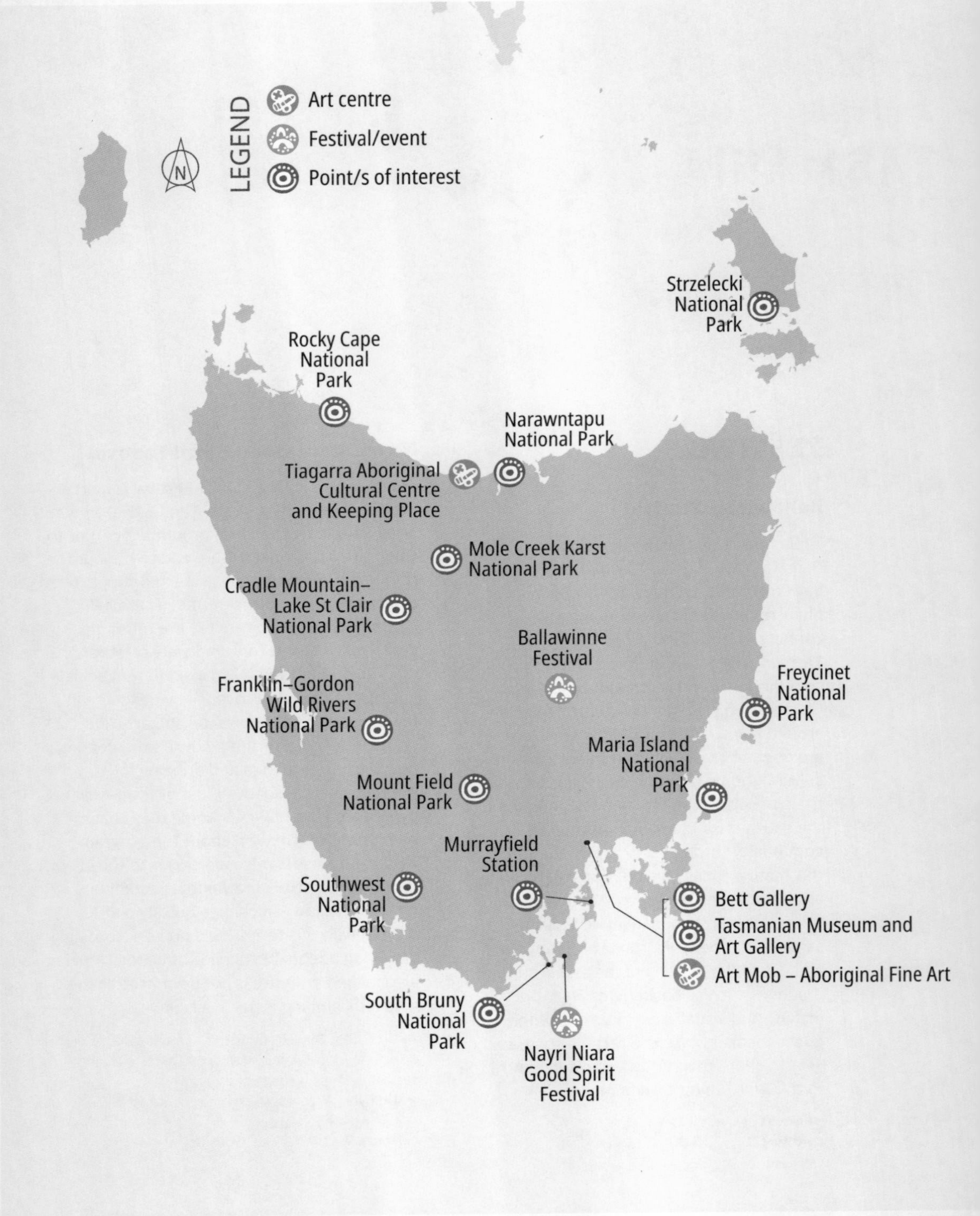
LEGEND
Art centre
Festival/event
Point/s of interest
N
Strzelecki National Park
Rocky Cape National Park
Narawntapu National Park
Tiagarra Aboriginal Cultural Centre and Keeping Place
Mole Creek Karst National Park
Cradle Mountain–Lake St Clair National Park
Ballawinne Festival
Freycinet National Park
Franklin–Gordon Wild Rivers National Park
Maria Island National Park
Mount Field National Park
Murrayfield Station
Southwest National Park
Bett Gallery
Tasmanian Museum and Art Gallery
Art Mob – Aboriginal Fine Art
South Bruny National Park
Nayri Niara Good Spirit Festival

NATIONAL PARKS

Cradle Mountain–Lake St Clair National Park

Part of the Tasmanian Wilderness World Heritage Area, Cradle Mountain–Lake St Clair National Park is a rugged wilderness. It is one of the most popular places to visit in Tasmania and is known widely for its jagged terrain and icy lakes and streams.

The Aboriginal custodians of Lake St Clair, or leeawuleena (meaning 'sleeping water'), are the Larmairremener of the Big River clan, while Cradle Mountain and Lake Dove, or Weebonenetiner, are part of the traditional lands of the North tribe.

Plains of buttongrass around Lake St Clair and in the Cradle Valley indicate where Aboriginal people used fire to manage grazing lands and attract a good supply of game animals. The relationship between palawa (Tasmanian Aboriginal people) and their land is the inspiration behind the Lake St Clair Visitor Centre's natural fibre sculpture. Woven by 3 Indigenous artists using buttongrass, sedges and dodder vine from the leeawuleena–Lake St Clair area, it pays respect to the 9 Tasmanian Aboriginal tribes and complements the nearby Larmairremener tabelti Walk. Creative interpretation panels along this cultural heritage walk tell visitors about the life of the Larmairremener, the Indigenous people of this region. The walk goes through a wide variety of vegetation, such as banksias, buttongrass, ti-tree thickets, Tasmanian waratahs, rainforest ferns and tall eucalypt stags. The track follows ancient ridges, called moraines, which were formed by retreating glaciers during the ice ages. It leads to a viewpoint above the Hugel River, then descends to a rainforest and joins the Watersmeet Track, where the Hugel and Cuvier rivers meet.

THINGS TO DO

Cradle Mountain–Lake St Clair National Park offers walking trails, camping, cabins, short and overnight walks. For more information on activities, see the Parks and Wildlife Tasmania website.

WHERE: Cradle Mountain is a 90-minute drive from Launceston. Walks start from both the northern and southern visitor centres. In the north, visitors need to catch a shuttle bus to Dove Lake where many walks begin.

CAMPING: Bookings are essential; see the Parks and Wildlife Tasmania website.

PERMITS: Park passes are required; see the above website.

CONTACT: Cradle Mountain Visitor Centre: 03 6492 1110; Lake St Clair Visitor Centre: 03 6289 1115

Franklin–Gordon Wild Rivers National Park

Situated at the heart of Tasmania's 1.38 million ha Wilderness World Heritage Area, the Franklin–Gordon Wild Rivers National Park spans a vast region of pristine temperate wilderness in the centre of western Tasmania.

CULTURAL HERITAGE: The area holds great cultural significance for Aboriginal communities, with a number of sites, including the Kutikina Cave, having been returned to the Traditional Owners under the *Aboriginal Lands Act 1995*. For at least 39,000 years, Wild Rivers Country has been occupied by the Lowreenner, Minemegmer and Lumnermareerme bands of the South West tribe. Tasmanian Aboriginal people retain strong cultural ties with the Franklin–Gordon Wild Rivers region and maintain considerable responsibility for the park's management.

1983 marked a decision of great significance for Aboriginal identity in Tasmania and the nation more widely. The *Commonwealth of Australia v. Tasmania* case was initiated in 1978 following the proposal to construct a dam on the Gordon River. The Hydro-Electric Commission (an organisation owned by the Tasmanian Government) had proposed to develop power generation in this area. The Commonwealth Government, alongside some non-Indigenous environmentalists and many Tasmanian Aboriginal people, rallied against the development, as it would necessitate the destruction of much of the natural environment in the region. The wider environmental argument against the dam then expanded into a cultural one.

The Commonwealth argued that the proposed development area held cultural significance for Tasmanian Aboriginal people and that the altering of this locale would destroy the historical connection between the people and the land. This then created an opportunity to open a dialogue about Tasmanian history before colonisation about what was considered significant, and by whom. The area was designated a World Heritage Site, and construction of the dam was denied.

THINGS TO DO

There are a range of activities to engage in, such as bushwalking and rafting. Rafting is very dangerous on this river and it is essential to have a high level of experience or go with a company on a guided tour. For those wanting some leisurely enjoyment of the pristine surrounds, the Franklin Nature Trail is lovely, and wheelchair friendly. The Mt King William walk has views to Mt Rufus in the north; Donaghys Hill lookout platform, a moderately steep 20-minute walk from the Lyell Hwy, has views to the upper reaches of the Franklin River and Frenchmans Cap. In the shallows of the river, platypus can be spotted, while echidna can be seen walking along the park floors. Many activities are weather dependent, and conditions can deteriorate rapidly, including roads that are subject to ice and snow, so it is best to keep watch of changing conditions in the area.

WHERE: The park is approximately a 2.5-hour drive (190 km) west of Hobart and roughly a 2-hour drive (175 km) south of Launceston. This area is abundant with wildlife, so it is requested that you do not travel in the evenings.

CAMPING: There is no camping available in this national park. The area is fuel-stove only, with no campfires permitted.

PERMITS: Park passes are required; see the Tasmania Parks and Wildlife Service website.

CONTACT: Tasmania Parks and Wildlife Service: 1300 827 727; Visitor Centre: 03 6289 1115

Freycinet National Park

Located in the territory of the Paredarerme (Oyster Bay) Nation, Freycinet National Park protects a whole peninsula of rugged mountains which is fringed with sea cliffs and scenic white-sand beaches, including the renowned Wineglass Bay. Eucalypt woodlands and coastal wetlands as well as dramatic pink-granite peaks reveal an abundance of animal and birdlife, which matches its scenic beauty.

CULTURAL HERITAGE: Freycinet National Park is a place of deep cultural significance for the Toorernomairremener clan (part of the Paredarerme Nation), who seasonally shared this hunting land with neighbouring Linetemairrener and Loonititetermairrelehoinner groups. palawa people of this area maintain a strong and continuing connection . A variety of seasonal foods were enjoyed, from ducks, swans, sea vegetables, birds and shellfish in the coastal lowlands, to wallabies and kangaroos inland. Middens on the coast indicate where food was harvested and stone tools were manufactured.

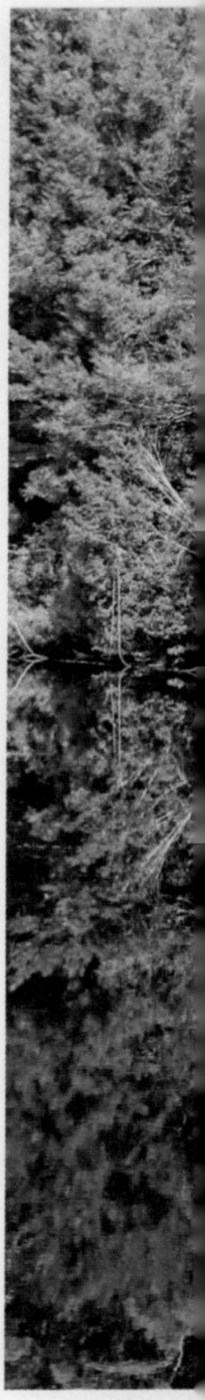

Gordon River in Franklin-Gordon Wild Rivers National Park

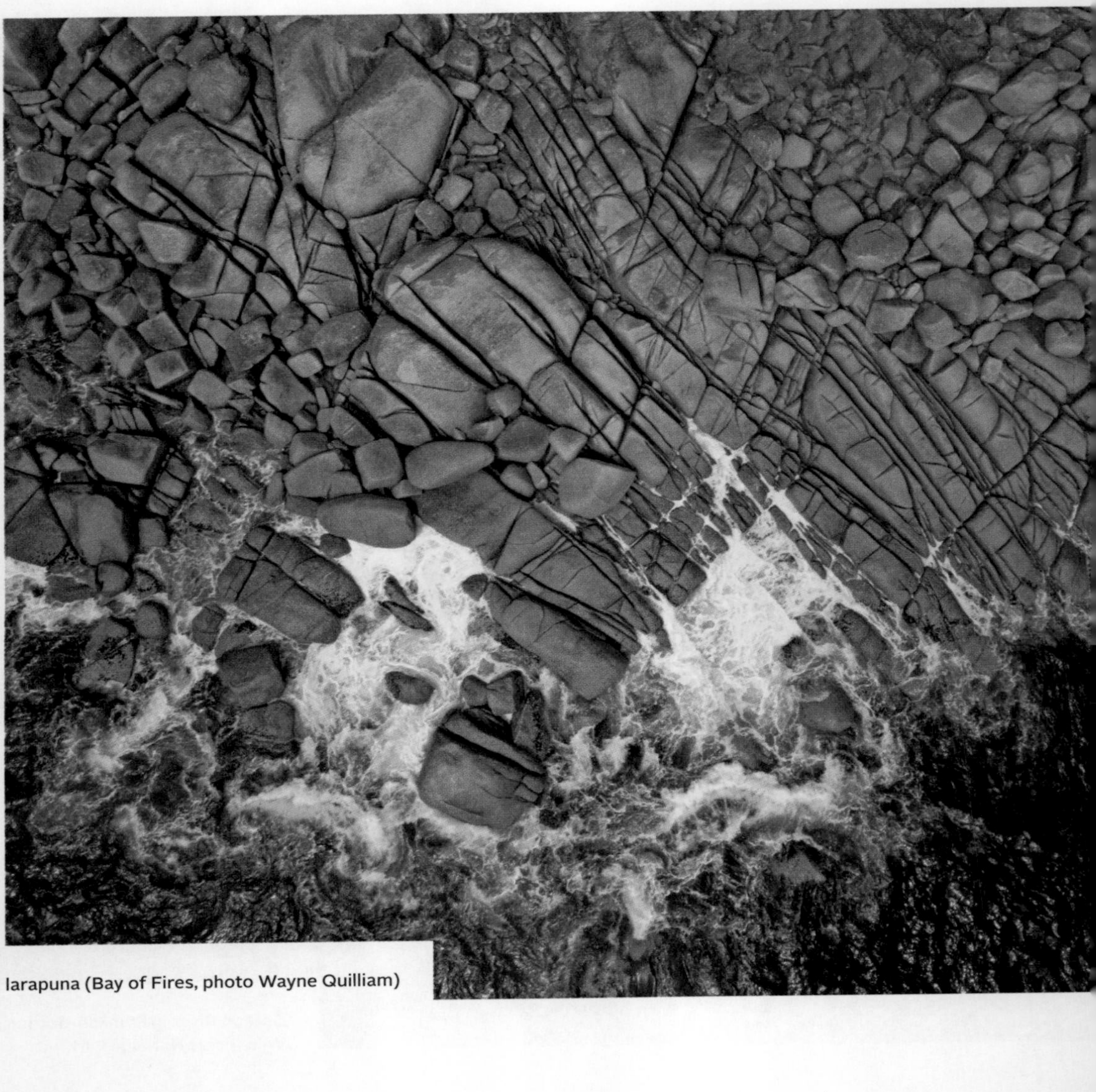

larapuna (Bay of Fires, photo Wayne Quilliam)

THINGS TO DO

Circular bays, white-sand beaches and lichen-clad boulders entice bushwalkers and more leisurely strollers to enjoy the hiking trails, ranging from walks of a few minutes to several days. Kayaking and fishing can also be enjoyed in this area. There are some wheelchair-accessible paths. There is also a gentle hike that provides sublime coastal views.
WHERE: The park is approximately a 3 hour-drive (200 km) north-east of Hobart and roughly a 2.5-hour drive (150 km) south-west of Launceston.
CAMPING: Camping is permitted in this area, including for Freycinet overnight walkers, and at Friendly Beaches, as well as Richardsons Beach, Honeymoon Bay and Ranger Creek. Bookings are required, see the Tasmanian Parks and Wildlife website.
PERMITS: Park passes are required; see above website. The Tasmanian Aboriginal community ask visitors to appreciate this area and travel through it with respect and consideration.
CONTACT: Tasmania Parks and Wildlife Service: 1300 827 727; Freycinet Field Centre: 03 6256 7000

Maria Island National Park

This serene locale with adjoining majestic cliff faces and rolling hills is a place where the past meets present. Bright blue waters accommodate seals, dolphins and seabirds.

CULTURAL HERITAGE: For more than 35,000 years, this area has belonged to the Paredarerme (Oyster Bay Nation) and is known to local Aboriginal communities as Wukaluwikiwayna – a place of great cultural significance for Puthikwilayti or Tasmanian Aboriginal people from the area. Regular canoe crossing and clan exchange took place on Maria Island, ensuring an abundant supply of seafood and game. Smoke from fires and dome-shaped burial mounds were a regular sight for onlookers.

THINGS TO DO

Bushwalking to the summit of Bishop and Clerk past the Fossil Cliffs is a popular activity in this area, providing a majestic look at this geological and spiritual past – and present. Snorkelling around the rock pools is also a valued experience in this area.

This area can be visited year round, but, with no shops nearby, make sure you take with you any food you will need and appropriate all-weather clothing.
WHERE: A 45-minute passenger ferry ride from Triabunna is the most common mode of transport for visiting this area. Triabunna is about 1.5 hours' drive (85 km) from Hobart and a 2.5-hour drive (180 km) from Launceston. Vehicle access is not permitted, but access via bike and foot is allowed.
CAMPING AND ACCOMMODATION: Maria Island is a haven for campers, with many camp sites available for walkers trekking for more than a day – and they're just a short trip from beaches. Fires are permitted in some locations, so you will need to check before you set out. There is also bunk-house style accommodation available at nearby Darlington.
PERMITS: Park passes are required; see the Tasmania Parks and Wildlife Service website. The Tasmanian Aboriginal community ask visitors to appreciate this area and travel through it with respect and consideration.
CONTACT: Tasmania Parks and Wildlife Service: 1300 827 727; Maria Island Field Centre: 03 6257 1420

Mole Creek Karst National Park

Gleaming crystals, stalactite pools, underground streams, flowstone formations and a most impressive glow-worm display are among the breathtaking features at Mole Creek Karst National Park. Marakoopa Cave (one of the 2 sites accessible to visitors) is now included as a Tasmanian Wilderness World Heritage Area. The King Solomons Cave tour reveals a colourful 228-m-long cave with a majestic range of formations including shawls, stalagmites and calcite crystals known as King Solomon's Diamonds.

CULTURAL HERITAGE: The Mole Creek karst system, or Kooparoona Niara, is a place of cultural practice for Aboriginal people from the northern nations. The area was used for ceremonial purposes, art practice, hunting and trading. Is it widely acknowledged that Aboriginal people sourced ochre from Toolumbunner or Gog Range via a complex track system maintained by fire burning.

THINGS TO DO

Look for rare white gums, wedge-tailed eagles and grey goshawks. Bats are found around cave entrances and pademelons, while wallabies and wombats' rustle through the bush. Arguably, the most unique creatures live underground: spider-like cave harvestmen, cave beetles and cave pseudoscorpions are rare and vulnerable species found only here; and Tasmanian cave spiders belong to a group that may be the ancestors of modern spiders. There are short nature walks, and easy walks in the nearby Alum Cliffs and Devils Gullet state reserves.

Mole Creek Karst National Park is only accessible by booking a tour in advance. Cave temperatures can drop to around 9°C, so shoes and warm clothes are recommended.

WHERE: The park is approximately a 3.5-hour drive (275 km) south-west of Hobart and roughly a 1.5-hour drive (90 km) north-east of Launceston. Please be alert when driving at night, as the roads are shared with precious wildlife.

CAMPING: No camping is available in this area.

PERMITS: Park passes are not required to enter the caves, though they are needed for other areas of the national park, so it is best to obtain one; see the Tasmania Parks and Wildlife Services website.

CONTACT: Tasmania Parks and Wildlife Service: 1300 827 727; Mole Creek Caves: 03 6363 5182

Mt Field National Park

The original custodians of the land where Mt Field National Park is located are the Pangerninghe people of the Big River tribe. Mt Field National Park supports a vast range of vegetation, from swamp-gum forests to rainforests, and even alpine moorlands at the higher elevations. The original custodians traditionally hunted for wombat, platypus and Bennett's wallaby across this diverse landscape. Trading with other groups for coastal resources and ochre also regularly took place. The park has several cultural sites with artefacts dating back 10,000 to 30,000 years, though these are not publicly accessible.

THINGS TO DO

Scenic attractions include panoramic views, Russell Falls, Lake Dobson, bushwalks and skiing areas. Mt Field National Park is part of the Tasmanian Wilderness World Heritage Area.

WHERE: Mt Field National Park is just over an hour's drive from Hobart via New Norfolk. The park is also accessible by public transport.

CAMPING: There are multiple camping sites; some are powered with electricity and gas. Bookings are not taken, so it is best to get there early and grab a spot.

PERMITS: Park passes are required, see the Parks and Wildlife Services Tasmania website.

CONTACT: Mt Field Visitor Centre: 03 6288 1149

Narawntapu National Park

The vegetation in this park is largely heath and coastal wattle, commonly known as boobyalla, which share this wilderness with the patches of ti-tree and silver banksia that are visible around the lagoons. One distinctive plant to look out for is the miniature trigger plant, while Forester kangaroos, Bennett's wallabies, Tasmanian pademelons, Tasmanian devils and wombats can all be discovered while visiting the park.

CULTURAL HERITAGE: Middens indicate that local communities regularly consumed a diet of mussels and shellfish. Aboriginal history dates back 30,000 years, with artefacts such as tools revealing a continuing and strong cultural connection to Narawntapu. Many sites are protected under the *Aboriginal Heritage Act 1975* and remain undisturbed.

A wombat in Narawntapu National Park

THINGS TO DO

Enclosed in a 20 km strip of coast with long, sandy beaches, dunes and freshwater lagoons, dissected by a sandstone range rising, Narawntapu has ranger-led walks and talks that are a highlight in summer. Springlawn, Bakers Point and Badger Head are well set up for picnics, as well as having excellent fishing off the shelf or in the estuary. Bakers and Badger beaches offer safe swimming, though it is best to keep an eye out for changing weather conditions. Narawntapu National Park can be visited year-round, though a section of Springlawn Beach is reserved for waterskiers from November to April.

WHERE: Narawntapu National Park is approximately a 3.5-hour drive (270 km) from Hobart and roughly a 1-hour drive (75 km) from Launceston. Please be alert when driving at night, as the roads are shared with precious wildlife.

CAMPING: Bookings are essential for camping; see the Tasmania Parks and Wildlife Service website.

PERMITS: Park passes are required; see the above website.

CONTACT: Tasmania Parks and Wildlife Service: 1300 827 727; Mersey Field Centre: 03 6428 6277

Rocky Cape National Park

Rocky Cape National Park lives up to its name, with colourful rock formations found along its coastline and inlets. Caves in the park contain Aboriginal middens, made up of the ancient remains of shellfish, seals, scale fish, grass trees and ferns. These middens are evidence of the continuous occupation of this area over 8000 years. Rocky Cape National Park is a wonderful place for visitors who enjoy adventure, and climbing and scrambling over rocks, as well as bushwalking, swimming, fishing and relaxing.

The Tasmanian Aboriginal people from the Rocky Cape region continue a close spiritual and recreational connection to this area. Visitors are respectfully requested not to enter North, South or Lee Archer caves.

WHERE: Rocky Cape National Park is situated on the north-west coast of Tasmania about a 2-hour drive west of Launceston.
CAMPING: Rocky Cape National Park is only a day park, so camping is not permitted.
PERMITS: Park passes are required; see the Tasmania Parks and Wildlife Service website.
CONTACT: Rocky Cape National Park Visitor Centre: 03 6458 1480

South Bruny National Park

South Bruny National Park is perfect for anyone who enjoys going for a bushwalk accompanied by the sound of crashing waves and a wide variety of birdsong. With its abundant wildlife, the area was an important hunting ground for the Traditional Owners; Bennett's wallabies, Tasmanian pademelons, brush-tailed possums and echidnas are just some of the animals that roam the forests here. The ocean surrounding Bruny Island is home to fur seals and migrating whales, with occasional visits from leopard seals. Cape Bruny Lighthouse is a popular destination.

WHERE: Bruny Island is about 50 km south of Hobart. D'Entrecasteaux Channel separates the island from mainland Tasmania. A vehicular ferry departs from Kettering at regular intervals throughout the day. The ferry goes to Roberts Point, on north Bruny Island. From there, drive on sealed and unsealed roads to the southern part of the island.
CAMPING: Bookings are essential; see the Parks and Wildlife Tasmania website.
PERMITS: Park passes are required; see the above website.
CONTACT: South Bruny National Park Visitor Centre: 03 6293 1419

Southwest National Park

The distinctive ecosystem of Southwest National Park offers the largest expanse of Tasmanian wilderness. This World Heritage area is vast and wild, inviting visitors to marvel at the huon pines and bask in the forest scents. A land of contrast, this area provides white-sand beaches, mountainous cliffs and buttongrass plains worthy of any sightseer's attention.

CULTURAL HERITAGE: Tasmanian Aboriginal people from 2 major tribes lived in the area: the Needwonne and Ninene clans occupied coastal country around Port Davey, the Kumtemairrejner clan lived in the Huon River valley and the Lumnermareeme people lived further north around Mount Anne. Coastal settlements were substantial, with permanent dwellings comprising branch-and-leaf huts, and people lived well, harvesting seals, waterbirds and shellfish. In the 1980s, 2 rock-art sites were discovered in Ballawinne (meaning 'ochre') Cave, with 23 hand stencils depicted in red ochre found on the dolomite rock of the cave walls; these predated the last ice age, proving that Aboriginal people utilised caves in the south-west as long ago as 35,000 years, with art sites here among the earliest known in the world. At Wagarta Mina (meaning 'my blood'), another array of hand stencils in red ochre have been dated at more than 12,000 years old. The ochre in this case had been mixed with blood. Both these caves are now owned and cared for by the Aboriginal community, and a permit is required to visit them.

THINGS TO DO

This area is remote and subject to extremes of weather, so anglers and walkers must be prepared and equipped for all conditions. A scenic flight is a particularly exciting way to see the complexity of this unspoiled grandeur.

CAMPING: Camping is most popular at the northern entrance to Southwest National Park, where powered sites and showers are located. The area is fuel-stove only and no campfires are permitted.
PERMITS: Park passes are required; see the Tasmania Parks and Wildlife Service website.
CONTACT: Tasmania Parks and Wildlife Service: 1300 827 727; Mount Field Visitor Centre: 03 6288 1149

Strzelecki National Park

This remote national park along the Bass Strait offers 360-degree views of ancient granite mountains. Marvel at stunning ocean views or relax on sandy beaches filled with turquoise water and fringed with orange lichen–covered rocks. Tasmanian pademelons, long-nosed potoroos, 2 species of burrowing crayfish, the endangered forty-spotted pardalote and a wealth of birdlife feed amid the white and blue gums.

CULTURAL HERITAGE: Strzelecki National Park is a place of deep cultural significance dating back 40,000 years, with many artefacts, shell middens and cave deposits highlighting the connection to place for Tasmanian Aboriginal people from the area. Aboriginal people from across Tasmania were removed from traditional living and placed at Wybalenna (meaning 'black man's houses' in English), a place mostly home to the Ben Lomond Nation, who are the largest Aboriginal nation of the area. These sites are protected under the *Aboriginal Relics Act 1975*.

THINGS TO DO

Trouser Point Reserve, a low granite headland, rises up between sandy beaches, with great opportunities for short walks, swimming, snorkelling, scuba diving and rock fishing. There is a picnic area with tank water, barbecues and fireplaces for visitors to enjoy. The most spectacular bushwalk is the 5-hour return trek up Mt Strzelecki Peak (756 m), the island's highest mountain. Strzelecki National Park can be visited year round. With its cool maritime climate, weather is susceptible to change, so please check before you arrive to ensure you will be comfortable.
WHERE: This area can be accessed by air or sea, with flights of about 1 hour from Melbourne or 35 minutes from Launceston. There is no public transport in the area, so it is best to have a hire car organised.
CAMPING: There is a beachside campground at Trousers Point; bookings cannot be made in advance.
PERMITS: Park passes are required; see the Tasmania Parks and Wildlife Services website.
CONTACT: Tasmania Parks and Wildlife Service: 1300 827 727; Furneaux Field Centre: 03 6359 2217

TOURS AND STAYS

Kooparoona Niara Tours

Be guided by local Aboriginal people from the Kooparoona Niara region (the Great Western Tiers) of northern Tasmania and learn about the 10,000-year connection to Country that continues to flourish. The Kooparoona Niara region was a traditional meeting place for 3 Aboriginal nations and has great cultural significance for people of the north tribe. These exclusive tours are not only educational but also uniquely inclusive, taking you on a journey that encapsulates personal stories and knowledge of the historical sites and surrounds. Inhale the crisp northern air and embrace the lush mountainous wilderness as you sample some of the finest local produce the region has to offer. Full-day and half-day tours are available, with tour guides kindly collecting you from your accommodation and allowing you to completely surrender to the beauty that encircles northern Tasmania.

WHERE: Kooparoona Niara region in Northern Tasmania. Guests will be picked up from their accommodation.
CONTACT: 0417 529 889

Misty mountain ranges in western Tasmania (photo Wayne Quilliam)

Needwonnee Walk

Isolation has never been more inviting with Needonnee Walk, located in the Tasmanian wilderness of Melaleuca, giving visitors an intimate and visual Aboriginal cultural interpretive experience. The Melaleuca region is the traditional lands of the Needwonnee people, who lived in this area in hut-like dwellings.

WHERE: This remote area can only be reached via air or water, there is no road access to this region.
CAMPING: Only available for those on extended bushwalks. The area is designated Fuel Stove Only with no campfires permitted.
PERMITS: Park passes are required and can be obtained from the Parks and Wildlife Services Tasmania website.
CONTACT: Huonville Field Centre: 03 6121 7026

wukalina Walk

This Aboriginal-owned-and-operated guided walk takes visitors on a 3-night, 4-day walk through the magnificent natural landscape of larapuna (Bay of Fires) and wukalina (Mt William) in north-east Tasmania, the cultural homeland of the palawa (Tasmanian Aboriginal people). For visitors, the wukalina Walk is a significant experience that aims to deepen your understanding of palawa (Tasmanian Aboriginal) culture and community history, while immersing yourself in the natural and rugged beauty of the area. Walk with palawa guides in the footsteps of the Traditional Owners on the cultural homeland of wukalina and larapuna. The guide shares palawa Creation stories and invites visitors to participate in cultural

practices that have been passed down for hundreds of generations.

Guests spend 2 nights in comfortable domed huts and 1 night in the meticulously renovated Lighthouse Keepers Cottage at larapuna. The magnificent natural landscape of north-east Tasmania is the perfect place for visitors to learn about the cultural history of place and Country. For information on when the walks are run, see the wukalina Walk website.

WHERE: The walk starts at the Aboriginal Elders Council of Tasmania Centre, 163 St John St, Launceston.
CONTACT: 0447 244 727

ART GALLERIES, CULTURAL CENTRES AND MUSEUMS

Art Mob – Aboriginal Fine Art

Art Mob, Aboriginal Fine Art displays a vast and diverse range of artworks and original pieces. With around 15 exhibitions held each year, and over 100 Indigenous artists from all over the country featured annually, this art gallery offers visitors the opportunity to view and purchase artworks by emerging Indigenous artists. Art Mob is a commercial gallery and visitors are able to purchase selected artworks, prints and jewellery, with details of the artist and the artwork, including authentication, provided for all purchases. For those who are unable to visit Art Mob in person, there is also an accessible online shop. Art Mob is a member of the Aboriginal Art Association of Australia.

WHERE: 29 Hunter St, Hobart.
CONTACT: 03 6236 9200

Bett Gallery

Bett Gallery displays extensively throughout the year with a distinctive range of artworks by both renowned and emerging artists. Showcasing numerous Aboriginal and Torres Strait Islander artists from all over the country, Bett Gallery also holds pieces by local Tasmanian Aboriginal artists such as esteemed visual artist Julie Gough. Visitors can expect to be enchanted by the eclectic and diverse range of works displayed at the gallery, with many providing visitors the opportunity not only to sight but also purchase works by established and developing artists. Bett Gallery meticulously selects high quality Aboriginal and Torres Strait Islander artworks and ensures that each work is accompanied with authentication. For those short on time, the website displays the works on offer so you can contact the gallery with any queries you may have regarding available works.

WHERE: Level 1, 65 Murray Street Hobart.
CONTACT: 03 6231 6511

Tasmanian Museum and Art Gallery

The Tasmanian Museum and Art Gallery is the leading historical and cultural space for visitors to learn about the Indigenous and European histories of Tasmania. The gallery hosts a permanent exhibition called ningina tunapri, which means to 'give knowledge and understanding'. The exhibition showcases both contemporary and historical displays of local Tasmanian Aboriginal art and culture. The museum and art gallery also provide educational tools and resources so visitors can learn about the history of Tasmania through an accessible platform. It runs family Discovery Days several times a year,

Top: Hermannsburg Potters, Pmara nurnaka. Urrknga nurnka. Nurna lhama pmara marra inthurra nurnakanha artitjika. Our country. Our clay. We go out on our beautiful country. A selection of works from 2019 Bett Gallery exhibition.

Bottom: Jeanette James, Palawa Echidna spine necklace, 2014, Tasmanian Echidna spine needles with woven flax string & claw toggle, 65 cm length.

Below: Julie Gough, *Some words for a change*, 2008, Tea tree sticks, paper, plastic & wax. Installed approx: 220 × 300 × 220 cm.

school-holiday programs and an annual children's festival, usually held in April.

WHERE: Dunn Pl, Hobart.
CONTACT: 03 6165 7000

Tiagarra Aboriginal Cultural Centre and Keeping Place

Tiagarra Aboriginal Cultural Centre and Keeping Place is a space of great significance for Aboriginal people in Tasmania. It is a keeping place and museum that seeks to preserve and protect Tasmanian Aboriginal history. The cultural and art centre displays ancient petroglyphs (rock carvings) that reflect what life was like for the Aboriginal people in Tasmania over thousands of years prior to colonisation. On display are weapons and tools, as well as other artefacts. Tiagarra Aboriginal Culture and Art Centre protects historical relics and uses them to educate visitors and maintain traditional knowledge. Guided tours of the centre run regularly.

WHERE: Mersey Bluff, Devonport.
CONTACT: 03 6424 8250

PLACES

Murrayfield Station

Murrayfield Station, located on Bruny Island, is a culturally and spiritually significant place for Tasmanian Aboriginal people. A windswept 14-km-long coastline, lush forest and ancient wetlands have provided an abundance of food, resources for tool manufacturing, and materials to build shelter and huts for thousands of years. This locale is a wonderous place rich in history that holds over 300 registered Aboriginal sacred sites. In 2001, the land was purchased by the Indigenous Land Corporation in recognition of the ongoing connection to the surrounding environment and cultural importance for Tasmanian Aboriginal people. In 2016, Weetapoona Aboriginal Corporation was granted the 4000-ha property, which now employs people to run the land, including a prosperous sheep farm. The Cultural Centre provides opportunity for Tasmanian Aboriginal people to come together and learn about cultural practices on land that is owned by Tasmanian Aboriginal people, a rare and incomparable experience. It welcomes visitors to learn about Tasmanian Aboriginal culture in a formal or informal capacity; a place such as this will captivate you with its beauty and is well worth a visit.

WHERE: 150 Trumpeter Bay Road, Bruny Island.
CONTACT: weetapoona@hotmail.com

palawa kilpi

For those who wish to taste the flavours of an ancient culture, palawa kilpi (Tasmanian Aboriginal food) is a one-of-a-kind dining experience. Not only does palawa kilpi create dishes that showcase delicious local produce; they are also presented in creative ways that highlight the historical and cultural utilisation of the surrounding environment. Actively bringing awareness to palawa culture and the relationship between locale and food, these dishes gently create a space for conversations that shed light on palawa culture more widely. The palawa kilpi ethos is to strengthen the community by sharing palawa food and enabling people to experience what a sustainable future could look like – one that is inclusive of the ongoing connection to Country. You can find palawa kilpi at food markets and catering is available by request.

WHERE: Available for personal catering across Tasmania.
CONTACT: 0407 988 184

8 AUSTRALIAN CAPITAL TERRITORY

NATIONAL PARKS

Namadgi National Park

A wide range of natural environments are found in the Namadgi National Park, which covers almost 46 per cent of the ACT. The park is home to an abundance of flora and fauna, including threatened species and more than 40 rare or uncommon species. There is a rich Aboriginal history in this area, with sites of cultural significance dating back 21,000 years. The region was traditionally a meeting place where the Ngunnawal people and neighbouring clans including the Ngarigo, Wolgalu, Gundungurra, Yuin and Wiradjuri nations would meet for ceremonies and marriages. At Namadgi National Park you will find scarred trees, rock art, grinding groove sites and initiation grounds, however please always be respectful by reading the signs provided.

THINGS TO DO

With 160 km of marked walking tracks that range in time from under 1 hour to 7 hours, the park is a stunning, diverse and fascinating destination for visitors who enjoy the outdoors.

WHERE: 3.5 km south of Tharwa.

CAMPING: Multiple camp sites are available; see the Access Canberra website for more details.

CONTACT: Namadgi Visitor Centre: 02 6237 5307

Tidbinbilla Nature Reserve

Located on the edge of Namadgi National Park, Tidbinbilla Nature Reserve is definitely worth visiting on the way to or from the park, or as a day trip on its own. The name Tidbinbilla is derived from the Ngunnawal (the Traditional Owners of the Canberra region) word Jedbinbilla, which means 'a place where boys were made men'. The area is rich in Aboriginal history, with artefacts and rock shelters dating back at least 21,000 years. The Birrigai Time Trail leads to the Birrigai rock shelter, one of the oldest rock shelters in Canberra and its surrounding regions. The reserve takes in wetlands, grasslands, wet forest and subalpine forests. Having such diverse environments, it is home to a wide range of animals, including kangaroos, koalas, platypus, potoroos, wallaroos, wombats, echidnas and many other species. Tidbinbilla plays a vital role in wildlife management and protection and runs breeding programs for the endangered northern corroboree frog and the southern brush-tailed rock wallaby.

THINGS TO DO

Visitors can learn about the natural and cultural history in the visitor centre or by joining a ranger-guided walk, held every weekend, school holidays and public holidays. The sanctuary at Tidbinbilla offers fabulous nature-based experiences, and it is a great

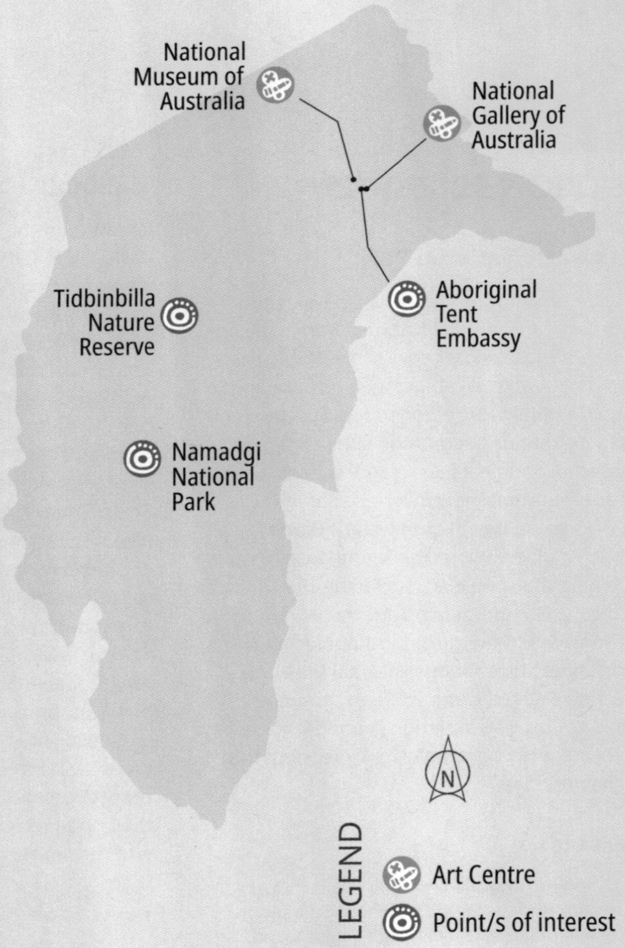
National Museum of Australia
National Gallery of Australia
Aboriginal Tent Embassy
Tidbinbilla Nature Reserve
Namadgi National Park
N
LEGEND
Art Centre
Point/s of interest

Tidbinbilla Nature Reserve

way for visitors to discover our natural world. It has wheelchair-friendly footpaths so everyone can explore the wetlands of the nature reserve and see some of the many migratory birds and reptiles that are found there. The sanctuary is also a lovely place for a picnic. There are 22 walking trails throughout the reserve, which range from easy to moderate and hard, and span from 500 m to 19 km (the average walk is 4.5 km).

WHERE: Tidbinbilla is an easy 40-minute drive to the south of Canberra.

PERMITS: Passes are required; see the Access Canberra website.

CONTACT: Tidbinbilla Visitor Centre: 02 6205 1233

TOURS AND STAYS

Dhawura Aboriginal Cultural Tours

Ngunawal man Tyronne Bell established Thunderstone Aboriginal Cultural Services in 2013. From this, the idea of providing informative services for visitors to Canberra resulted in Dhawura Aboriginal Cultural Tours. The Ngunawal people are the traditional custodians of Canberra and the surrounding areas of the Australian Capital Territory, which is where the tours operate. There are 3 categories of tours: short, half-day and full-day. The short tours are the perfect way for visitors to view the Canberra scenery from up high, touch, smell and taste local bush food and become familiar with the local wildlife, including a few endangered species. The short tours take visitors to Mt Majura, the highest peak in Canberra, standing at 888 m, or Mt Taylor, standing at 856 m, or Black Mountain, standing at 812 m. The half-day driving tours, recommended for visitors aged 12 years and over, visit various cultural sites around Canberra, such as Red Hill and Theodore and Lanyon Homestead. This tour showcases what life was like before Ngunnawal Country became the Australian Capital Territory.

On the full-day tours (run seasonally, September–March), visitors will be driven in a 4WD to some of Canberra's most scenic areas, such as Namadgi National Park and Flea Creek, located in the Brindabella Mountains region. There are many beautiful places of significance for Aboriginal people at Namadgi National Park, many dating back thousands of years, and Flea Creek is teeming with wildlife. The tour includes guided information about the historical changes to the surrounding mountains and valleys, and knowledge about bush food, artefacts and stone tool use in the area. On this tour there is the opportunity for a cool swim if the weather

Top: Breathtaking views of the National Museum of Australia, Canberra

Above: A welcome from our Ngunnawal, Ngunawal and Ngambri traditional custodians in First Australians gallery, National Museum of Australia, Canberra

is fine. Tour bookings can be made by email: dhawuratours@gmail.com.

CONTACT: 0407 517 844

Murumbung Yurung Murra Tours

Murumbung Yurung Murra Tours offers sightseers the opportunity to visit Ngunnawal Country with an experienced Aboriginal ranger. This tour provides guests with local knowledge and insight to the region's surrounding land and waters, a place where the Ngunnawal and nearby nations have gathered for thousands of years in ceremony and lore. Some tour highlights include trying your hand at tool making, learning about the local language, discovering the flora and fauna, participating in a twilight walk where you can join activities such a mixing ochre and learn how it is used in art practice, or journeying through the mountains actively listening to stories that expand your horizons. Taking a tour with Murumbung Yurung Murra will enable you to discover how this area is still a place of deep cultural significance for Ngunnawal people, all while unwinding and absorbing the beauteous surrounding wilderness.

WHERE: Exact location depends on the chosen tour.
CONTACT: 02 6207 0078

ART GALLERIES, CULTURAL CENTRES AND MUSEUMS

National Gallery of Australia

The National Gallery of Australia offers visitors the chance to immerse themselves in the work of iconic artists and artistic movements that span across time and continents. The gallery recognises that Aboriginal and Torres Strait Islander peoples have lived on the continent of Australia for tens of thousands of years, with their art and traditions among the oldest and richest in human history. Its calendar of special exhibitions always includes work by Indigenous artists and it holds a diverse permanent collection of Aboriginal and Torres Strait Islander art. The NGA also has an extensive library, study spaces, cafes, family-specific spaces and outdoor installations such as the Sculpture Garden, the Fern Garden and Skyspace. Although general admission is free, fees apply for special exhibitions.

WHERE: Parkes Place, Parkes, ACT. The NGA is located in the heart of Canberra, near Parliament House, the High Court of Australia and next door to the National Portrait Gallery. Visitors can walk through the Sculpture Garden to the NGA from the path around Lake Burley Griffin.
CONTACT: 02 6240 6411

National Museum of Australia

The National Museum of Australia explores the land, nation and people of Australia. It is committed to its focus on Indigenous histories and cultures, European settlement and the Australian people's interaction with the environment. The museum undertakes many educational and archival programs to ensure that knowledge of Australia will always be current and readily available to the public. The museum holds one of Australia's largest collections of historical artefacts and the world's largest collections of bark paintings. Educational exhibitions are a permanent fixture on the museum calendar, always featuring interesting exhibitions, with many offering insights into Indigenous life, culture and history. Although general admission is free, fees apply for special exhibitions.

WHERE: Lawson Cres, Acton Peninsula, Canberra.
CONTACT: 1800 026 132

PLACES

Aboriginal Tent Embassy

Embassies are known internationally as places of diplomatic representation of a country's government in another country. In 1972, 4 Aboriginal representatives erected the Tent Embassy in front of Parliament House, Canberra – now known as Old Parliament House. The intention of the protest has shifted over time, and now includes not only land rights but also sovereignty and self-determination. Today the Aboriginal Tent Embassy is still an extremely significant place for Indigenous Australians and remains an important physical place that represents the struggles for land rights that Aboriginal people have faced for more than 200 years, and continue to experience today.

VISITORS TO THE ABORIGINAL TENT EMBASSY SHOULD TREAT IT WITH RESPECT.
WHERE: On the lawns of Old Parliament House on King George Tce.

9

TORRES STRAIT ISLANDS

FESTIVALS

Winds of Zenadth Cultural Festival

This 4 day event is held every 2 years and showcases the rich diversity of Torres Strait culture. Visitors can witness the all-island celebrations including cultural dances, boat races, and forums. There is a focus on song, dance, art and ceremony as a way of practising and maintaining traditions.

WHERE: Victoria Pde, Thursday Island.
WHEN: In 2021, the festival was held in mid-September.
CONTACT: 07 4069 1336

TOURS AND STAYS

Peddells Thursday Island Tours

Learn about the culture and hidden past of Thursday Island with this locally guided historic tour. Visitors discover the military, maritime, pearling and cultural history of the Torres Strait with visits to the Thursday Island Museum and Japanese Pearl Divers Memorial. The 90-minute tour also includes a scenic drive around the island. Tickets must be purchased in advance. For tour times and fares, visit the website.

CONTACT: 07 4069 1551

ART GALLERIES, CULTURAL CENTRES AND MUSEUMS

Torres Strait Heritage Museum

Visitors can access the rich history of the area through a visit to this museum. Main attractions include the exploration of World War 2 stories, pearling, local art collections and Torres Strait culture and traditional stories. The museum is part of the Horn Island 'In Their Steps' World War Two tour, or can be accessed directly. The significant military history of the island is explored with genuine appreciation and carefully curated precision, the collection has largely been possible through donations received from World War Two veterans and their families, as well as local artists and people from the Torres Strait.

WHERE: 24 Outie St, Horn Island.
CONTACT: 0427 903 333

ART CENTRES

Badu Art Centre

Badu Art Centre enables the expression and renewal of Badu Island cultural practices and traditions. The artists' work reflects

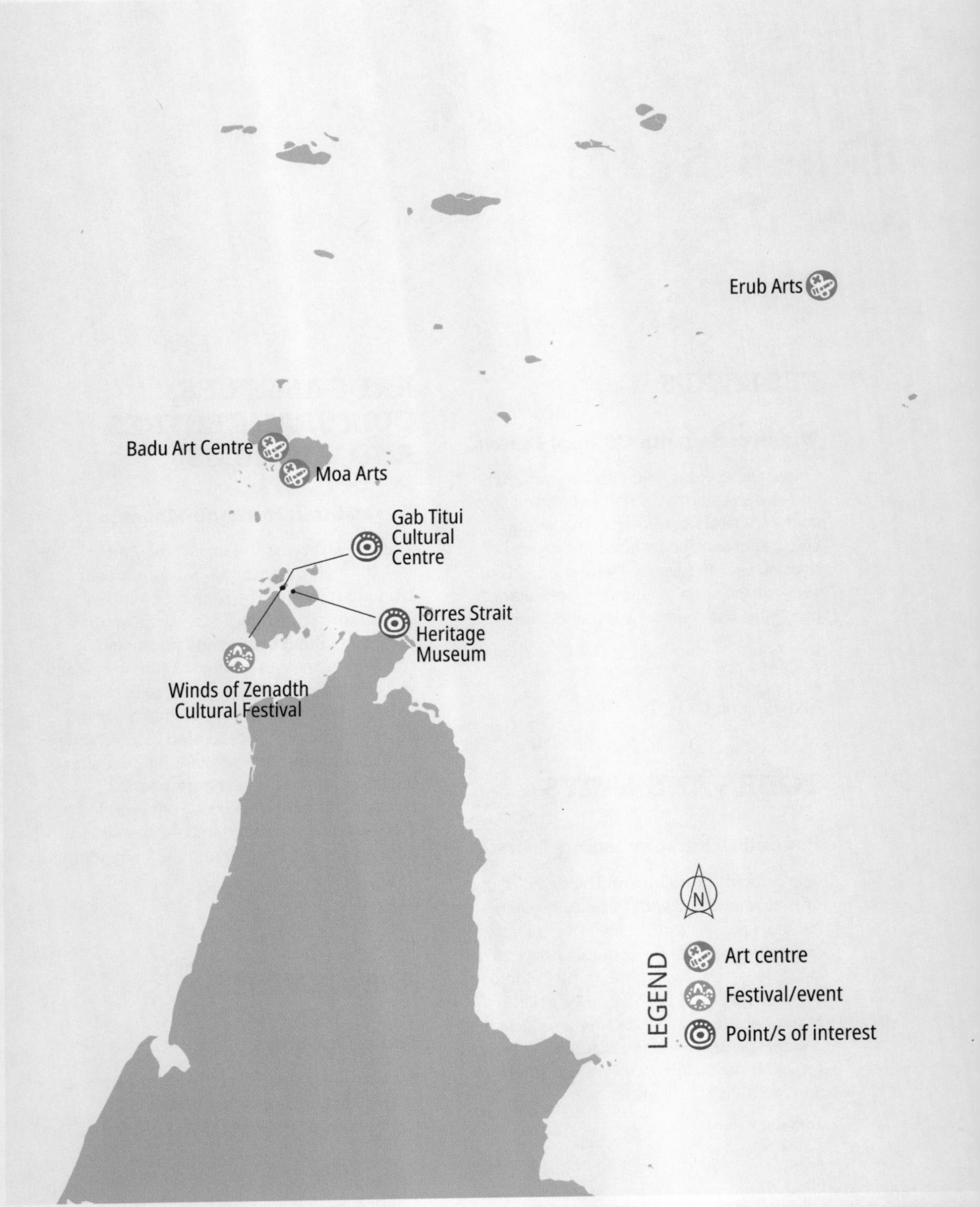

Erub Arts
Badu Art Centre
Moa Arts
Gab Titui Cultural Centre
Torres Strait Heritage Museum
Winds of Zenadth Cultural Festival
N
LEGEND
Art centre
Festival/event
Point/s of interest

Saibai Island dancers with bamboo clappers called Moerap, depicting the sound of thunder (photo Torres Strait Heritage Museum)

connection to language, the ocean, and the lands and animals of the island. The creative depth of artists is portrayed across a range of visual and creative mediums, including printmaking, etching, painting, jewellery and carving. It is also the home of the only Indigenous-owned bronze foundry in the country.

WHERE: Badu Island, Western group of Torres Strait Islands.
PERMIT: Visiting Badu island requires permission from the Art Centre Chair, and the Native Title Body, Mura Badhulgal. The art centre can receive and assist with applications.
CONTACT: 07 4090 0956

Erub Arts

Erub (Darnley) Island is the most north-eastern of the Torres Strait Islands. Erub Arts, the first incorporated art centre in the Torres Strait Islands, supports the Erubian cultural identity through the support and promotion of contemporary art. Artists are from 4 tribal groups, and their art draws influence from the sea, reef and marine life that surrounds the Torres Strait Islands and guides the seafaring way of life. Erub Arts showcases traditional and modern mediums, reflecting both age-old stories and contemporary living cultures.

Artists are renowned nationally and internationally for their distinctive ghost nets, which repurpose a globally disastrous environmental problem into large-scale collaborative installation pieces, as well as smaller art pieces. Other world-renowned artworks include hand-built ceramics, a range of works on paper, printed fabrics, as well as jewellery, t-shirts and other merchandise.

WHERE: Erub (Darnley) Island (260 km north of Cape York).
CONTACT: 07 4090 0827

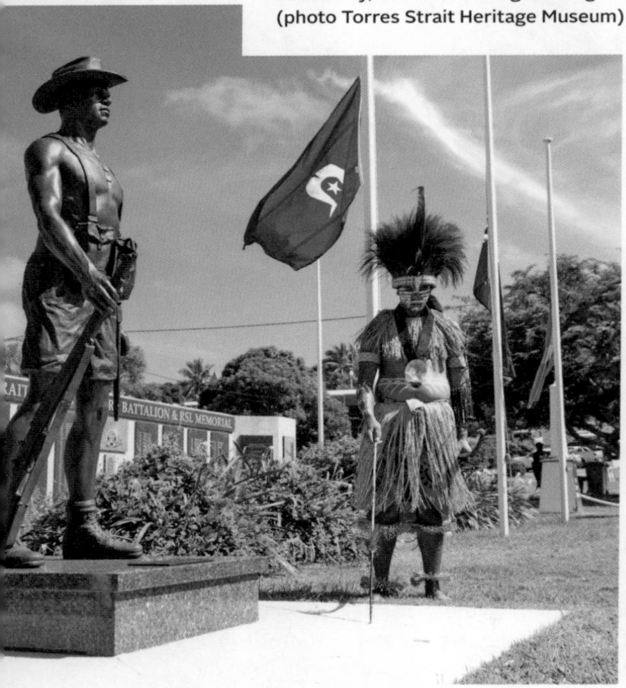

Anzac Day, Warriors through the Ages (photo Torres Strait Heritage Museum)

Gab Titui Cultural Centre

The name Gab Titui combines both eastern and western language groups of the Torres Strait region, and translates to 'Journey of the Stars'. The centre is a keeping place of historical and cultural materials from the Torres Strait, and a space to support the contemporary artistic and cultural aspirations of the Torres Strait Islander peoples. Gab Titui supports more than 100 artists from right across the Torres Strait and the northern peninsula of Australia, through arts development programs and the gallery shop, which provides a point of ethical sale and promotion of artists and their work.

The cultural centre also includes the Ephraim Bani Gallery, which aims to preserve local culture, history and heritage and present the importance of cultural identity of the Torres Strait Islander peoples, and the Wabunaw Geth Gallery, which features a rotating program of art exhibitions.

WHERE: Cnr Victoria Parade and Blackall St, Thursday Island (35 km north-west of Cape York).
CONTACT: 07 4069 0888

Moa Arts

Ngalmun Lagau Minaral (Our Island Designs), trading under the name Moa Arts, is an art centre located on Moa Island in the Torres Strait. The centre enables and supports the expression, renewal, preservation and promotion of cultural practices unique to the Mualgal people. Ancestral stories, totemic representations and connections to land, sea, sky and family inspire artistic practice, as well as the beautiful land and sea ecosystems of the island. Artists work in a range of visual and creative mediums, resulting in high-calibre works in printmaking, etching, works on paper, traditional beaded jewellery making, weaving and carving. Please contact the art centre manager to arrange a visit.

Artworks from Ngalmun Lagau Minaral are regularly exhibited in the Gab Titui Cultural Centre's Wabunaw Geth Gallery and are also available for purchase through the Gab Titui Gallery Shop.

WHERE: Kubin community, Moa Island (40 km north of Thursday Island).
CONTACT: 07 4069 4993

Top: Daua Island, part of the Murray Islands group (photo Wayne Quilliam)

Bottom: Fish traps surrounding Mer (Murray Island, photo Wayne Quilliam)

INDEX

Note: Bold page numbers refer to illustrations; NP = National Park

A Taste of Broome, Broome WA 301
A.B. Original 117, 118
Abbott, Peter 267
Abdulla, Ian 104
Aboriginal ancestral remains
  museum acquisitions of 164
  repatriation 164–8
Aboriginal and Torres Strait Islander Commission (ATSIC) 182
Aboriginal and Torres Strait Islander cultures 24, 32, 34, 175
  NAIDOC Week ceremonies and celebrations 180–3
  reconciliation improving understanding and awareness of 169–70
  respect for 40–1
  see also Aboriginal art; languages; music; performance; Torres Strait Islander art
Aboriginal and Torres Strait Islander history and culture
  reason for learning about 214
  teaching in universities and schools 8, 11, 214
Aboriginal and Torres Strait Islander peoples
  definition 34
  employment and training 28, 30, 191
  empowerment 5–6
  fairness towards 24
  frontier violence 17, 25–6, 84, 170–1, 173, 467
  government/institutional control 28–30, 32, 158, 173, 175, 176, 221
  identity 34
  location 4, 30–1
  military service 179–80
  no formal means to have a say in their futures 183–4
  no treaty with 213
  not treated as citizens 174
  population 5
  racist stereotypes of 24, 82–5
  recognition in Australian Constitution 175, 177–9
  terms 220–8
  Voice to be enshrined in the Australian Constitution 184–7, 213–14
  see also Aboriginal people; Torres Strait Islander people
Aboriginal art 86–107
  connection between being and place 88
  European artist influences 92
  exhibitions 95, 98, 104, 274
  link to Country 97–100
  spiritual beliefs/sacred symbols represented in 88–9, 94
  stories based on the landscape 95
Aboriginal artists 87–107
  colonisation impact on 87–8
  encounters with Europeans 92
  ethical dealings with 100–1
Aboriginal Arts Board of the Australia Council 96
Aboriginal Blue Mountains Walkabout, Faulconbridge NSW 383–4
Aboriginal children, forced removal of 29, 32, 158–62, 175, 226
  see also Stolen Generations
Aboriginal communities 30
  campaigns for land rights 31
  diversity 30–1
  empowerment 30, 31
  notion of 31–2
Aboriginal Cultural Tours SA, Point Pearce SA 438–9
Aboriginal deaths in custody 139, 143, 175, 214–18
Aboriginal English 44–5
Aboriginal family life 32
  see also kinship system
Aboriginal fire management 68, 69–70, 71–2
Aboriginal Heritage Tasmania 19, 20
Aboriginal Heritage Walk, Royal Botanical Gardens, Melbourne Vic. 415
Aboriginal history
  no information available for tourists about 170–1
  suppression of by settlers 171
  timelines 175
Aboriginal Land Commission 30
Aboriginal land management practices 11–12, 63, 68–73
Aboriginal Land Rights (Northern Territory) Act 1976 98, 175
Aboriginal languages *see* Indigenous languages
Aboriginal Languages Act 2017 (NSW) 43
Aboriginal medical and legal services 30
Aboriginal Meeting Place, Birdsville Qld 480
'Aboriginal Natives', social security payments 29
Aboriginal pastoralists 30
Aboriginal people 2, 220
  agricultural practices 12, 64, 66–7
  aquaculture practices 12, 15–17, 66, 67
  equal pay campaign 29–30
  forced off their land by massive land clearing 27
  honest stories of 171–2
  as hunters and gatherers 64
  incarceration rate 129, 174, 184, 216, 218
  living on the mainland for at least 65,000 years 2, 7, 8, 22, 41, 172
  population 83, 84
  ration system 27
Aboriginal protests 208–9
  see also Black Lives Matter movement and protests
Aboriginal Reconnaissance Unit in Arnhem Land 180
Aboriginal reserves 29, 30, 158, 173, 176
Aboriginal rights
  movement for 176
  national referendum (1967) 175, 176–9, **178**, **179**
  support for 179
  see also land rights
Aboriginal stories going as far back as 7000 years or more 13
Aboriginal Tent Embassy 208, 221
Aboriginal and Torres Strait Islander tour guides 169–70
Aboriginal words, in modern Australian English 52
acknowledgement of Country 221
Adelaide Kaurna Trail, Adelaide SA 439
Adelaide Ocean Safari, Penneshaw, Kangaroo Island SA 439
Adjahdura land 439
Adjahdura Narungga Heritage group 438
Adnyamathanha people/Country 429, 432, 437, 440, 441
Adnyamathanha Traditional Lands Association (ATLA) 441
Adventure North Australia, Cairns Qld 463, **464**
Agius, Quenten 438
agricultural practices 12, 64, 66–7
AIATSIS map **46–7**, 220–1
Alberts, Jada 138–9, **139**
alcohol 84
Alice Springs Visitor Information Centre, Alice Springs NT 264
Alyawarr people 251, 276
Anangu people/Traditional Owners 205–6, 282, 298
Anangu Pitjantjatjara group 436
Anangu Pitjantjatjara Yankunytjatjara (APY) Lands *see* APY Art Centre Collective
ancestors 32, 34, 222
  arrival on the mainland at least 65,000 years ago 2, 7, 8, 22, 41, 172
  influence of 34
  see also ancestral beings; Elders
ancestral 221
ancestral beings 17–18, 32–3, 227
  see also 'the Dreaming'; 'Dreamtime'
ancestral lands, Indigenous people on 31
ancestral remains 164
  repatriation of 164–8
  and the *Return, Reconcile, Renew* project 165–6
Ancestress 135
ancient art *see* rock art
Andrew, Brook Garru 102–4, 168
Andrews, Jimmy Dillon 326
Ang-Gnarra Aboriginal Corporation 121
Angkamuthi people 461
animals, skin names 57
Anindilyakwa Arts, Groote Eylandt NT 275–6
Anmatyerr people 295, 296
anthropologists 221
Anu, Christine 111
Apakatjah 116
Apalech clan 486
APY Art Centre Collective, Darlinghurst SA **88**, **444**, 445
APY Lands SA 445, 446–7
aquaculture systems and practices 12, 15–17, 66, 67, 401
Arabana people/Country 430, 437, 438
Arakwal people 395
Araluen, Evelyn 135
Araluen Arts Centre, Araluen NT 272
archaeological evidence of early Aboriginal occupation 8–9
archaeological finds 11
archaeological methods, used to explore the past of First peoples 11
Archibald Prize 102, 136
Ardler, Kane **361**
Arlpwe Art and Culture Centre, Ali Curung NT 276
Arnhem Land bark paintings 86
Arnhem Land systems (skin names) 57
Arnhemlander Cultural and Heritage Tour NT 266
Arrarrkbi people 244
Arrernte people 240, 244, 256, 290, 295, 296, 299
  section system (skin names) 57, 61
art 86–107
art centres
  Northern Territory 275–99
  Queensland 483–7
  South Australia 445–7
  Victoria 422
  Western Australia 342–50
Art Galleries Association of Australia 104

art galleries, cultural centres and museums 86–7, 501–3
New South Wales 398–400
Northern Territory 272–5
Queensland 474–80
South Australia 441–5
Victoria 417–18
Western Australia 338–9
Art Gallery of New South Wales, Sydney NSW 398
Art Gallery of South Australia, Adelaide SA 423, 441
Art Gallery of Western Australia, Perth WA 338
Art Mob – Aboriginal Fine Art, Hobart Tas. 501
art sales, Bathurst Island NT 243
Artists of Ampilatwatja, Ampilatwatja Community NT 276
Arts Ceduna, Ceduna SA 441
assimilation policies/period 29, 32, 71, 96, 114, 122, 145, 158, 175, 176, 221
Association of Northern, Kimberley and Arnhem Aboriginal Artists (ANKA) 101, 104–5
astronomical knowledge 75–9
Atampaya people 461
Atherden, Geoffrey 408
'Aunty' 56
AUSTLANG 220
Australia Commercial Galleries Association 104
Australia Day 208–12
Australian Constitution 176, 183, 226
Aboriginal people recognition in (1967 referendum) 175, 177–9, 186, 187
First Nations Voice to be enshrined in 184–7, 213–14
referenda to change 175, 186–7, 213, 226
Australian Defence Forces (ADF) 179, 180
Australian endemic land mammal extinctions 67–8
Australian Indigenous Minority Supplier Council (AIMSC) 190
Australian Institute of Aboriginal Torres Strait Islander Studies 96
map of Indigenous Australia **46–7**, 219–20
Australian Memory of the World Register 92
Australian Museum, Sydney NSW 398
Australian reconciliation movement 169
Australian War Memorial 180
Ayal Aboriginal Tours Kakadu, Kakadu NP NT 264
Ayers Rock NT *see* Uluru NT
Ayers Rock Resort NT **269**, 271

Bábbarra Women's Centre, Maningrida Community NT 277
Bach, J. 83
Bacon, Sean 139
Bad Apples Music 118
Badimia Country 350
Badu Art Centre, Badu Island Qld 511–13
Baker, Danzal (Baker Boy) 116–18, 135
Baker, Simon 141
Balanggarra Traditional Owners 17
Balit Narrun – Share the Spirit Festival, Melbourne Vic. 403
Ballardong Country 334
Ballawinne Festival, Port Cygnet Tas. 489
Baluk Arts, Mornington Vic. 422
Bama people 475
Bana Yirriji Art Centre, Wujal Wujal Qld 483
Banana Well Getaway, Broome WA 323
Bandjin people 483
Bangarra Dance Theatre 120, 121, 355
Bangerang language 416
Bani, Ephraim 110–11
Banks, Kirsten 76
Bannon-Harrison, Dwayne and Amelia 392, 401
Banubanu Beach Retreat, Bremer Island NT 264–5
Banyjima people/language group 308, 349
Barak, William 417
Bardi people 325, 326, 330, 332, 333
Bardon, Geoffrey 92–3, 95
Bardon, James 95
bark paintings 86, 92, 93, 509
Barkaa 118
Barker, Wayne Jowandi **334**
Barkly Regional Arts, Tennant Creek NT 277
Barmah NP Vic. 408–9
Barngarla people 426, 432
Barns, Greg 212
Barr, Jean 480
Barrington Tops NP NSW 356–7
Barron Gorge NP Qld 453
Barunga Festival, Barunga NT 32, 237
Barunga Statement 112
Bataluk Cultural Trail, Gippsland Vic. 415
Bawaka Homeland Highlights, East Arnhem Land NT 267
Beautiful One Day 139
Belair NP SA 423–6
Belgrave Survival Day, Belgrave Vic. 403
Bell, Ethan 135
Bell, Tyronne 507
Ben Lomond Nation 499
Bennelong **82**, 83
Bennett, Dr Lou 118
Berg, Uncle Jim 166, 167
Berndt, Catherine H. 92
Berndt, Ronald 92
Bero, Nornie 421
Bett Gallery, Hobart Tas. 501, **502**
Bibbulman Country 333
Bicentennial celebrations, Sydney Harbour (1988) 208
Bidawal people 369
Bidjara people 454–6
Bidyadanga Artists at Short St Gallery, Town Beach, Old Broome WA 342–3
Bima Wear, Wurrumiyanga, Bathurst Island NT 278
Bimson, Laurie 389
Bindi Bindi Dreaming, Perth WA 323–4
Bindi Mwerre Anthurre Artists, Alice Springs NT 278
Bindjareb Park, Pinjarra WA 324
Bininj/Mungguy people 246–7
Binskin, Mark 67
Birch, Tony 132–3, 135
Bird, Michael I. 9
Biripi people/Country 351, 356
Birrarung Marr, Melbourne Vic. 5, 415, 419
Birriliburu clan 339
Birritjama, Dawida 92
Birrunga Gallery & Dining, Brisbane Qld 474
Black Arm Band 118
Black Johnny 92
Black Lives Matter movement and protests 118, 129, 137, 214–16, 218
Black, Justice Michael 150–1
Black Olive Catering, Melbourne Vic. 194
Black Point Cultural Centre, Garig Gunak Barlu NP NT 244
Black Summer 2019-20 67–9, 70
Black Tracks, Kimberley region WA 324
Black Wars, Tasmania 170
Blackfulla Bookclub 141
Blackley, Magdalena 139
Blair, Wayne 144
Blak Markets, La Perouse and Barangaroo NSW 398–9
Blake, Andrew 99
Blue Mountains NP NSW 357–60
Blue Mud Bay High Court sea rights claim 98
body painting 120
Bond, Chelsea 135
Booderee NP NSW 360–1
Boodjamulla (Lawn Hill) NP Qld 454, **455**
Boon Wurrung people/language group 39, 406, 414, 419
Boorloo Experience, Perth WA 324
Border Ranges NP NSW 361–2
Borrgoron Coast to Creek Tour, Cygnet Bay WA 325
Borroloola Traditional Owners 298
Bosun, David 76, 78
Bouddi NP NSW 362, 388
Bourke, Chris 36
Bowali Visitor Centre, Jabiru NT 249
Boyce, James 65, 71
Bradshaw, Joseph 91
'Bradshaws' 91–2
Brambuk: The National Park and Cultural Centre, Halls Gap Vic. 410–11
Bran Nue Day 118
Brataualung people 413
Breaden, Christine 267
Brewarrina Aboriginal Cultural Museum, Brewarrina NSW 400–1
Brian Lee Tagalong Tours, Kooljaman WA 325
Briggs, Adam 118, 139
Briggs, Tony 144
Bringing them home: The 'Stolen Children' report 159–61, 185
Brisbane Ranges NP Vic. 409
Brisbane Water NP NSW 362–3
British
claim possession of Australia 149
establish settlements in Australia 172–3
invasion and conflict 17, 25–6, 84, 170–1, 172–4
British motherland, Australia's links to the 211–12
Brown, Hazel 128
Brown, Latoya 389
Browning, Daniel 109
Bryant, Rob 121
Buandig people 411
Buckley, William 92
Budawang people 365
Budj Bim Cultural Landscape, south-west Vic. 13–17, 66, 409
aquaculture system 14, 15–17
Master Plan 13, 15
volcanic landscape 14, 15
Budj Bim NP Vic. 409–10
Budj Bim Tours, Portland Vic. 416
Buku-Larr.gay Mulka Art Centre, Yirrkala NT **90**, 278–9
Bula'Bula Arts, Ramingining NT 279–80
Bularri Muurlay Nyanggan Aboriginal Corporation 388, 397
Bullawah Cultural Trail, Wangaratta Vic. 416
Bullen Bullen Cultural Tours, Kallista Vic. 416
Bundjalung NP NSW 363–4
Bundjalung people 361, 363
Bundyi Aboriginal Cultural Knowledge, Wagga Wagga NSW 384
Bundy's Cultural Tours, Kooljaman WA 326
Bungle Bungle Range, Purnululu NP WA 317, 318
Bungoolee Tours, Fitzroy Crossing WA 326–7
Bunjil (spiritual figure) 410
Bunjilaka Aboriginal Cultural Centre, Melbourne Museum, Carlton Vic. 417
Bunjil's Collective Indigenous Art Gallery and Gift Shop, Horsham Vic. 419
Bunuba people 307, 326, 347
Bunurong clan of the Kulin Nation 130, 414
Burarrwan.a, Rrikin 113
Burleigh Head NP Qld 477
burning *see* cultural burning
Burrguk Aboriginal Corporation 323
Burrinja Cultural Centre, Upwey Vic. 417
Burrungkuy area, Kakadu NP NT 248

Burrungkuy (Nourlangie) and Ubirr, Kakadu NP NT 250–1
Bush Bands Bash, Alice Springs NT 242–3
Bush Ghoodhu Wongutha Tours, Kalgoorlie WA 327
bushfires 2019-20 67–9
cultural burning as large part of the solution 68–70
loss of and threats to biodiversity 67, 68
business 188, 189–91
Butchulla people/Country 460–1, 463
buying First Australian art 104–7

Cairns Indigenous Art Centre, Cairns Qld 486
Cairns Indigenous Arts Fair, Cairns Qld 449
Calma, Tom 49, 187
Campbell, Aunty Margret 387
Campbell, Uncle Richard 135
Cape Leeuwin WA 309
Cape Leveque WA 333
Cape Naturaliste Lighthouse WA 311–12
Cape Naturaliste WA 309, 333
Cape Tribulation Qld 457, 471
Cape York Peninsula Qld 465, 486
Cardona, Joseph 37
Caring for Country 74
Carnarvon NP Qld 454–6
Cassidy, James 467
Castlemaine State Festival, Castlemaine Vic. 403
census 175, 177, 178
Central Australian art styles 86, 94–5
certificates of authenticity 106–7
Chant of Jimmie Blacksmith, The (Keneally) 211
Charcoal Lane, Fitzroy Vic. 195
Charles Darwin NP NT 243–4
Chatwin, Bruce 33
Cheetham, Deborah 122–3, **123**
child endowment payments 29
children's literature 139–40
Chillagoe–Mungana Caves NP Qld 456
Cicada Lodge, Nitmiluk NP NT 266
City of Gold 136–7
City of Parramatta cultural experiences, Parramatta NSW 384–6
clan names 34
clapsticks 108, 115
Clarke, Maxine Beneba 129
Clarkson, Chris 8
cleverman 79, 221
Cleverman (television series) 144–5
climate change 67
Clothing the Gaps, Brunswick Vic. 419
Co-Design Group (report on Indigenous Voice enshrinement) 187
Code of Ethics of the National Association for the Visual Arts 104
Coffin Bay NP SA 426, **427**
Cole, Malcolm 37
Coleman, Claire G. 131–2, **132**, 135
Collis, Paul 135
colonial invasion and conflict 17, 25–6, 84, 170–1, 172–4
see also massacres
Colony of New South Wales 173
Coloured Stone 208
Commonwealth of Australia 174, 183
Conjola NP NSW 365
Connection Shepparton, The, Shepparton Vic. 422
Connolly, Michael J (Munda-gutta Kulliwari) 475, **476**
Conondale NP Qld 456–7
convicts 172, 211
Cooee Cafe and Catering, Capel Sound 419–20
Cook, Captain James 25, 52, 378, 474–5, 481
Cooktown Botanic Gardens, Cooktown Qld 480
Cooktown History Centre and Cooktown Re-enactment Association, Cooktown Qld 474–5
Coomalie Art Centre, Batchelor NT 280–1
Cooper, Victor 264
Coorong NP SA 426–8
Corn, Aaron 58, 60, 61, 112, 113, 115
coronial inquiry into a death in custody 216–18
Council for Aboriginal Reconciliation 175, 212
Country 221–2
acknowledgement of 221
cultural burning on 71, 72–3
Indigenous rangers working on 74
link with art 97–100
listening to 22
respect for 7
Country of the Kuku Thaypan 121
Country of the Malak Malak people 292
Country to Couture (DAAF event), Darwin NT 273
Coutts, Peter 15–16
Couzens, Vicki 123
COVID-19 restrictions, impact of 104, 105–6, 197
Cox, Belinda 328
Cradle Mountain–Lake St Clair NP Tas. 491
Cragg, David 135
creoles 44–5
Crispin, Judith 95
Crombie, Joyce 480
Crown lands 149
cultural awareness for visitors 198
dress standards 204, 205
language rules 202
photographs and videos 203
questions may not always be welcome 201
showing respect for your hosts 199
signs and published cultural rules and protocols 203–7
taboos on saying the names of someone who has died recently 33, 201–2
When to use names of people and places and when not to 201–2
cultural burning 68–70, 71–3
culture 22
see also Aboriginal and Torres Strait Islander cultures
Cummeragunga (Mission) 109, 122, 144
Currumbin Wildlife Sanctuary, Currumbin Qld **464**, 480–1
Curtis, Roy Jupurrula 96

Dagoman people 275
Daintree NP Qld 457
Dale Tilbrook Experiences, Henley Brook WA 327
Dambimangari Traditional Owners 17
Dampier, William 82–3
Dampier Peninsula WA 325, 330–1
Dan, Uncle Seaman 111
dance 3, 108, 110–15, 116, 121, 149, 182, 336, 449, 464, 480, 482
traditions 119–21
Danggali people 435
Danggu Geikie Gorge NP WA 307
Dark Emu: Black Seeds: Agriculture or Accident? (Pascoe) 64–7, 80–1, 130
Aboriginal civilisation erased from Australia's national conscience 65–6
criticisms of 65–6
farming innovations 64
rejects hunter-gatherer tag 64, 65
support for 67
Darkinjung people/Country 351, 357, 363, 388
Darngku Heritage Cruises, Fitzroy Crossing WA 327–8
Darwin Aboriginal Art Fair, Darwin NT 273
Dastey, Sally 118
Davidson's Arnhem Land Safaris, Mt Borradaile NT 265
Davies, Terry 95
Davis, Jack 135
Davis, Megan 179, 214
Davis, Trevor 334, **334**
Davison, Joel 135
Day, Tanya 216–17, 218
de Heer, Rolf 52
de Napoli, Krystal 76
Deadly Funny, Melbourne 403–6
deaths in police custody 139, 143, 175, 214–18
deceased, taboo on saying the name of someone who has recently died 33, 201–2
D'Entrecasteaux NP WA 306–7
Desart 101
Desert Mob (art event), Alice Springs NT 274
Desert Pea Media 135
Devils Marbles NT *see* Karlu Karlu (Devils Marbles) Conservation Reserve NT
Dhalwaŋu clan 142
Dharawal NP NSW 365–6
Dharawal people 357, 363, 365, 378
Dharug people 357, 380, 384
Dhawura Aboriginal Cultural Tours, Canberra ACT 507–8
Dhilba Guuranda-Innes NP SA 428–9
Dhungala Children's Choir 122
Dhuwa 58, 98, 99
Dickson, Greg 44
Dieri people/Country 430
digital writing 140–1
Dilpa clan group 428
Diramu Aboriginal Dance and Didgeridoo, Bondi Beach NSW 397
discrimination against Indigenous people 29, 183, 216
Dja Dja Wurrung language group 419
Djab Wurrung people 397
Djabugandgi Bama (Djabugay people) 453
Djabulukgu Association 266
Djadawitjibi people of the Djinang group 279
Djaru language group 349
Djatpa.arri-style music 113
Djawa, Tom 92
Djigirr, Peter 52
Djilpin Arts, Wugularr (Beswick) NT 281
Djirri Nyundu Nyrrumba area 453
Djirrily Dreaming, Aboriginal Cultural Tours, Perth WA 328
Djiru people 483
Djómi museum at Maningrida Arts and Culture, Maningrida community NT 291
Djurandi Dreaming, Perth WA 329
Dodson, Mick 158–9
Donovan, Casey 118
Donovan, Clayton 195
Donovan, Emma 118
Doomadgee, Cameron 143
'the Dreaming' 33, 222
sites 437, 454–6
stories/designs 52, 96, 112, 251, 253, 314, 340, 348, 357, 363, 478
'Dreamtime' 33, 227
Dreamtime at the 'G, Melbourne Cricket Ground, Melbourne Vic. 406–8
Dreamtime Divas 40
Dreamtime Dive and Snorkel, Cairns Qld 463
Dreamtime Kullilla-Art, Clontarf Qld **89**, 475, **476**
Dreamtime Southern X, The Rocks, Sydney NSW 387
Drover's Wife: The Legend of Molly Johnson, The (Purcell) 141
Drummond, Cassmond **334**
Dumu Balcony Cafe, Bright 420–1
Dunaman, Lasey 38, 40
Dungay, David, Jr 135
Dunghutti people/Country 351, 377, 399
Dunghutti-Ngaku Aboriginal Art Gallery, Kempsey South NSW 399–400

Dunnett, Delquade **444**
Durrmu Arts Aboriginal Corporation, Peppimenarti NT 281
Dutton, Merinda 141

Eades, Diane 44
East Journey (band) 115
Eastern Guruma people 308
Eastern Kuku Yalanji people/Country 457, 462, 471, 483
Echo, Johnny 329
Echo Tours, Warmun WA 329
Eckermann, Ali Cobby 135
educational training 30, 191
Edwards, Aunty Jodi 135
Eira, Travers 123
Elcho Island 57, 117
Elcho Island Art and Craft, Galiwin'ku, Elcho Island NT 281–2
Elders 22, 33, 43, 56, 93, **94**, 95, 222
Electric Fields 116
Elkin, A. P. 221
Ella, Tim 389, **391**
Ellery Creek Big Hole, Tjoritja/West MacDonnell NP NT 257
employment and training 28, 30, 191
Enoch, Wesley 408
environment, Indigenous knowledge about the 64–7
Eora people/Country/Nation 172, 380, 392, 398
equal pay 30, 176
Erawirung people 435
Ernabella Arts Inc, Pukatja (Ernabella) community NT 282
Ernabella Arts Tour – Longitude 131°, Yulara NT 282–4
Erub Arts, Erub (Darnley Island) Qld 513
Erub dialect 45
Eseli, Peter 76, 78
Etherington, Ben 131
ethical dealings in First Australian art 100–1, 106
Euahlayi people 78
Eumeralla Resistance Wars 17, 123
Eurobodalla NP NSW 366
European artists 92
European colonialists, perceive Indigenous peoples as 'backward people' 8, 82–3, 85
Explore Byron Bay, Byron Bay NSW 388

fake art 100–1, 107
Farmers or Hunter-Gatherers? The Dark Emu Debate (Sutton and Walshe) 65
  criticism of 65–7
farming innovations implemented by precolonial Aboriginal societies 64
Federal Council for the Advancement of Aborigines (FCAA) 176
Federal Council for the Advancement of Aborigines and Torres Strait Islanders (FCAATSI) 176
federation 174, 183
Fernando, Todd 39
festivals
  New South Wales 351–5
  Northern Territory 32, 196–7, 203–5, 237–42
  Queensland 3, 121, 449–53
  South Australia 423
  Tasmania 489
  Torres Strait Islands 511
  Victoria 403–6
  Western Australia 301–4
film
  early 110
  made in First Languages 52
film and television storytellers 141–2
Finke Gorge NP NT 244
fire
  importance in religious rituals and ceremonies 70–1
  in land management 68–70, 71–3
  use of on Country 71–3
firestick farming 71
First Australian art
  advice on buying 104–7
  ethical dealings in 100–1, 106
  in the global market 102–4
  see also Aboriginal art; Torres Strait Islander art
First Australians 220
  exclusion from Australian constitutional, political, social and economic life 212
  forced off their land by massive land clearing 27
  frontier violence 17, 25–6, 84, 170–1, 173, 467
  institutional control of 28–30
  massacres of 25–6, 84, 123, 141–2, 317
  truth-telling to acknowledge history about 184, 185
  see also Aboriginal and Torres Strait Islander peoples
First Eleven team (Australia's first international test cricket team) **408**
First Languages 42–53
  films in 52
  music in 52
First Languages Australia, resources 49
First Nations people *see* First Australians
First Nations Rainbow 37
First Nations Voice to be enshrined in the Constitution 184–7, 213–14
Fischer, Colin and Helen 474
fishing protocols 207
5 Lands Walk, Central Coast NSW 351
Flames of the Forest, Port Douglas Qld 481
Florek, Stan 165
Floyd, George 214
Fogarty, Lionel 136
Forrest, Andrew 191
Foxx, Felicia **38**, 40
Frank, Imiyari **299**
Franklin–Gordon Wild Rivers NP Tas. 491–2, **493**
Fraser Island Qld 460
fraudulent art 100–1, 107
Freedom Ride 226
freehold title 149, 151, 153, 222
Fremantle Arts Centre – Revealed, Fremantle WA 343–4
Freycinet NP Tas. 492–5
frontier violence 17, 25–6, 168, 173, 467
  Black Wars, Tasmania 170–1
  see also massacres
Fry, Declan 135
'full-bloods' 29, 158
Fuller, Robert 78
funeral ceremonies 119
The Furnace 141, 142

Gaambera people *see* Wunambal Gaambera people/language group
Gab Titui Cultural Centre, Thursday Island Qld 514
Gabori, Mirdidingkingathi Juwarnda Sally 485
Gadigal people 5, 84, 392, 398
Gagadju people 246
Gajirrabeng people 252
Galiwin'ku, Elcho Island 57
Gamboola Resources Pty Ltd 152–3
Gamilaroi people 381
Gammage, Bill 214
  The Biggest Estate on Earth: How Aborigines Made Australia 11, 64, 71, 84
Gammeraigal people 5
Ganambarr, Baykali 142
Ganinya community 345
Gapuwiyak Culture and Arts Aboriginal Corporation, Gapuwiyak NT 284–5
Garig Gunak Barlu NP NT 244–5
Garigal NP NSW 366–7
Garimara, Doris Pilkington 145
Gariwerd (Grampians) NP Vic. 197, 410–11, **410**
Garma Festival, Gulkula NT 32, 196–7, 237–40, **241**
  behaviour protocols 203–5
Garma Forum 97
Garma Statement on Indigenous Music and Dance 111–15
Garrett, Peter 112
Garrigarrang language 398
Garrwa people 298
Gawurra 116
gay rights 36
Gayarra Wanjina Aarwarrndju 18
gender identities 34–5
George, Tommy 72, 73
Gheebulum Kunungai (Moreton Island) NP Qld 458
Ghillar, Uncle (Euahlayi Elder) 78
Giddy, Allan 135
Giingan Gumbaynggirr Cultural Experience, Korora NSW 388
Gija art, language and culture 349, 350
Gilbert, Kevin 135
Gillick, Declan Furber 135
Gimuy Walubara Yidinji people 463
Gina, Nova 40
Ginibi, Ruby Langford 135
Giraiwurung people 413
Giro Giro 94
Girramay people 483
Girri Girra, Central Coast NSW 388
Girringun Aboriginal Art Centre, Cardwell Qld 483
Girriyoowa community 345
Githabul people/language group 361
glossary 219–28
Gnylmarung Retreat, Gnylmarung WA 329
Go Cultural Aboriginal Tours and Experiences, Perth WA 329–30
Godinymayin Yijard Rivers Arts and Cultural Centre, Katherine East NT 285
Goenpul clan 453
Goodes, Adam 102, 134
Goodrem, Delta 117
Goolamwiin, Perth WA 330
Goolgaradah community 345
Goombaragin Eco Retreat, Pender Bay, Dampier Peninsula WA 330
Gooniyandi people/Country 345, 347
Goorawal people 368
Goori people 400
Goreng people 320
Gosse Bluff NT *see* Tnorala (Gosse Bluff) Conservation Reserve NT
Gostelow, Tia 116
Gough, Julie 501, 502
Goulburn River NP NSW 391
gourmet food and culinary tourism 194–6
government control policies 28–30, 32, 158, 173, 175, 176, 221
  see also Aboriginal reserves; assimilation policies/period; missions/missionaries
government procurement, through Indigenous businesses 190–1
Graetz, Ben 37
Graham, Trevor 147
grain production 64
Grampians *see* Gariwerd (Grampians) NP Vic.
Grant, Stan 34, 134, 209, 216
  Australia Day 209–11
  On Identity 34
graphic novels 140

Great Barrier Reef Marine Park Qld 458–60, **459**
Great Sandy NP Qld 460–1
Grey, Sir George 91
Griffen, Ryan 144–5
Griffiths, Billy 125–6
Gubbi Gubbi people 456, 470
Gudang people 461
Gudanji people 298
Gugu Badhan people 483
'gulag archipelago' 28
Gulngay people 483
Gulpilil, David 52, 145
Gululu Day Tour, East Arnhem Land NT 267
Guluyambi Cultural Cruise, Kakadu NP NT 266
Gumatj clan/language 52, 213
Gumbanan Wilderness Retreat, Dampier Peninsula WA 330–1
Gumbaynggirr people/Country 351, 382, 388, 397
Gumbula, Joe 58
Gunai-Kurnai people 414, 415
Gunbalanya, Arnhem Land 266, **270**, 289
Gundabooka NP NSW 367
Gunditj Mirring Traditional Owners Aboriginal Corporation 13, 16–17
Gunditjmara people/Country 17, 409, 411, 416
  Budj Bim Cultural Landscape, south-west Vic. 13–17, 409
Gundungurra people 357, 505
Gungaletta people 149
Gungarde Aboriginal Corporation 481, 482
Gungarde people 482
Gunggandji people 463, 487
Gupapuyngu clan 284
Gurindji people 118, 175, 288–9, 344
Guringai Aboriginal Tours, Ku-ring-gai Chase NP NSW 389
Guringai people 389
gurrutu (Yolŋu kinship) 58–61, 98, 222
Guugu Yimithirr people/language 52, 475, 481, 484
Gweagal people 368
Gwion Gwion **9**, 94

Haddon, Alfred C. 110
Halls, Aunty Sharyn 135
Hamercher, Duane 75, 76
Harrow Discovery Centre and Unaarramin (Johnny Mullagh) Interpretive Centre, Harrow Vic. 407–8, **407**
Harvey Norman Rugby League All Stars Match 355–6
Hawk Dreaming Wilderness Lodge, Kakadu NP NT 266
Hawke, Robert 112
Healing Foundation, Canberra ACT 162
Heathcote–Graytown NP Vic. 411
Heffernan, Matthew 135, 136
Heiss, Anita 133–4
Hermannsburg Potters, Hermannsburg NT 286, **502**
Hermannsburg school NT 122, 272, 286, 287
Hervey Bay Eco Marine Tours, Urangan, Hervey Bay Qld 463–5
Herzich, Paul 445
Higgins, Missy 118
High Court
  Claim Group (Ngaliwurru and Nungali peoples) case 156–7
  dismisses idea of terra nullius 147, 148
  Mabo case 146–7, 148
  on Native Title rights 147
  rules *Queensland Coast Islands Declaratory Act 1985* invalid 147
High Ground 141–2
Hobart Museum 164
Hohnen, Michael 117
Holmes, Rosita 18
Holt, Yvette 136
homosexuality 36
Honey Ant Dreaming 93, 257
Hope Vale Arts and Cultural Centre, Hope Vale Qld 484
Howard, John 161, 182
human migration 89, 172
Human Rights and Equal Opportunity Commission 29
Human Rights Law Centre 216, 218
Hunter, Ruby 116
Hunter, Terry 325
hunters and gatherers 64
Hurley, David 180

Ian Potter Centre, The: NGV Australia, Melbourne Vic. 418
Ice Age 9, 12, 13
identity 34
  see also gender identities; kinship systems
Iga Warta, via Copley SA 440–1
Ikara–Flinders Ranges NP SA 429, 441
Ikuntji Artists, Haasts Bluff NT 286
Ilan-style music 111
Ilbijerri Theatre Company 139
Ilkurlka Roadhouse, Beadell WA 341
Ilkurlka Visitor Centre, Beadell WA 340–1, **340**
Iltja Ntjarra (Many Hands) Art Centre, Alice Springs 286–7
Inala (Brisbane) Qld 30
incarceration rate 129, 174, 184, 216, 218
indentured 223
Indigenous Art Code (IartC) 104, 105, 106–7
Indigenous Australia, looking to the future for 208–18
Indigenous Australian, definition 223
Indigenous Australian Art Commercial Code of Conduct 107
Indigenous business 188, 189–91
  and government procurement policy 190–1
Indigenous cultural groupings *see* Aboriginal people; Torres Strait Islander people
Indigenous Land Use Agreements 10, 151, 223, 453
Indigenous languages 42–53, 198, 224
  benefits of maintaining 47
  cultural association with the land 42
  number of 42
  perilous state of 47
  preservation 42–3
  protection and promotion, NSW 43–4
  and rights under UN Declaration on the Rights of Indigenous Peoples 43, 48–9
Indigenous LGBTQIA+ cultural life 35–40
  acceptance and empowerment of brothers and sisters 39–40
  development 36–7
  First peoples contributions 37–40
  Jessie Lloyd's views 38–9
Indigenous people
  Australia *see* Aboriginal and Torres Strait Islander peoples
  collecting of their ancestral remains 167
  Native Title in Canada, US and New Zealand 150, 213
Indigenous protests 208–9
Indigenous rangers, working on Country 71, 74
Indigenous tourism sector 3–5, 188, 192–4
'Indigenous Voice' to be enshrined in Australian Constitution 184–7, 213–14
IndigenousX Pty Ltd 127, 140–1
Indulkana community SA 446
Injalak Arts Gunbalanya, Gunbalanya NT 266, 287
Injalak Rock Art Tours, Gunbulanya NT 266
Innamincka Regional Reserve SA 430
Innawonga people 308
institutional control 28–30, 32, 158, 173, 175, 176, 221
Irrwanyere Aboriginal Corporation 438
Iwantja Arts, Indulkana community SA 446

Jabiru area, Kakadu NP NT 249
Jalunji clan 483
James Cook Museum, Cooktown 475–7
James, Jeanette 502
Jaminjung people 245
Janbal Gallery, Mossman Qld 477
Jandamarra 166
Jandany, Hector 349
Janke, John Paul 182
Janke, Terri 101
Jannawi Dance Clan, Sydney NSW **182**
Jardine River NP Qld 461
Jardwadjali people 197
Jarndu, Nagula 348
Jarramali Rock Art Tours, Laura Qld 465
Jaru people 317
Jawi people 325, 330, 333
Jawoyn people 254–5, 275, 281
Jellurgal Aboriginal Cultural Centre, Burleigh Heads Qld 477, **478**
Jetty to Jetty Trail, Broome WA 331
Jilamara Arts and Crafts, Milikapiti, Melville Island NT 287–8
Jilamara Arts and Crafts Association, Bathurst Island NT 143
Jim Jim Falls area, Kakadu NP NT 248
Jirrbal people 480, 483
Johnson, Carole J. 121
Johnson, Patricia 183
Johnson, Steven Maxwell 141
Jones, Mark 471
Jones, Rhys 71
Journey into Olkola Country, Cairns Qld 465
Jubalum 466
Judbarra–Gregory NP NT 245–6
Jukurrpa 96
Jupurrurla, Richard Long 288
Juukan Gorge caves, destruction, Pilbara WA 10–11
Juwalinny language group 342

Kaarak Dreaming, Dwellingup WA 331
Kabi Kabi people 470
Kadoo Indigenous and Historical Tours NSW 389, **390**
Kahua, Mahealani 169
Kaidilt people 485
Kaiela Arts Shepparton, Shepparton Vic. 422
Kakadu Cultural Tours, Kakadu NP NT 266–7
Kakadu National Park NT 246–51
  tours 264, 266–7, 271–2
Kakadu Tourism Adventure Tours, Kakadu NP NT 267
Kala Lagaw Ya (language) 45
Kalaw Kawaw Ya (language) 45
Kaltjiti Arts, Fregon community, APY Lands SA 446
Kaltukatjara Art, Kaltukatjara WA 349, 350
Kamay Botany Bay NP NSW 367–8
Kamilaroi people 78
Kanabygal 166
Kangeang people 328
Karajarri people 342
Karenggapa people 379
Karijini Eco Retreat, Karijina NP WA 332
Karijini NP WA 307–9
Karijini Visitor Centre, Karijina NP WA 309
Kariyarra langugage group 349
Karlu Karlu (Devils Marbles) Conservation Reserve NT 251
Karrangpurru people 245

Karrke Aboriginal Cultural Experiences, Watarrka NP NT 267
Karungkarni Art and Culture, Kalkarindji NT 288–9, 344
Kata Tjuṯa NT 259–62
Katherine Gorge NT 254–5
Kati Thanda–Lake Eyre NP SA 430–2
Kaurna people/language 426, 433, 439, 442, 443, 445
Kawrareg (language) 45
Kay, Aunty Delta 395, **396**
Kaytetye people 251
Kearing, Karrie-Anne 324
Keen, Ian 65
Keep River NP NT 252–3
Kelly, Paul 112, 118
Ken, Ilawanti Ungkutjuru **299**
Ken, Otis **444**
Kennedy, Aunty Joy 140
Keringke Arts, Santa Teresa community NT 289–90
K'gari (Fraser Island) Qld 460
Kija people 317
Kimberley Cultural Tours, Broome WA 333
Kimberley Girl, Broome WA 305
Kimberley rock art 9, 17–18, 326–7, 342
Kinchega NP NSW 368–9
King, Aunty Leanne **385**, **396**
Kings Canyon NT *see* Watarrka (Kings Canyon) NP NT
kinship systems 32, 34, 54–61, 223
Kira Kiro Artists, Kalumburu WA 344–5
knowledge systems and traditions 6–7, 12–13, 62–85, 101, 223
Kokatha people 432
Kooljaman at Cape Leveque WA **332**, 333
Koomal Dreaming Tours, Yallingup WA 195–6, **332**, 333
Koongurrukun clan 253
Koo'Oila, Akay 486
Kooparoona Niara Tours, northern Tasmania 495, 499
Koorah Koorah Cultural Tours, Ballardong Country, Wheatbelt WA 334
Koori Kulcha Experience, Bowral NSW 401
Koori people 360, 400
Koorie Heritage Trust, Melbourne Vic. 5, 417–18, **418**
Kosciuszko NP NSW 369–70
Kow Swamp ancestral remains 8
repatriation 166–7
Kriols 44–5, 223
Ku-ring-gai Chase NP NSW 371, 389
Ku'arlu Mangga (Good Nest), Northampton WA 345
Kuju Aboriginal Arts, Port Lincoln SA 432
Kukatja language group 349
Kuku Bididji clan 462
Kuku Bulkaway Indigenous Art Gallery, Cooktown Qld 477–8
Kuku Nyungkul clan 462, 483
Kuku Thaypan clan 462
Kuku Yalanji Cultural Habitat Tour, Mossman Qld 465–6
Kuku Yalanji people/Country 462, 465, 466–7, 473, 477, 483, 487
Kulilla tribe 475
Kulin Nation 130, 414, 419
Kulkalgau Ya (language) 45
Kullarri NAIDOC Festival, Broome WA 301
Kulumindini Arts, North Camp, Elliott, NT 290
Kumtemairrejner clan 498
Kungarakan people 280
Kunibidji Country in Arnhem Land 290
Kupka, Karel 92
Kurinyjarn community 345
Kurnara clan group 428
Kurrah Mia, Albany WA 334
Kutini–Payamu (Iron Range) (CYPAL) Qld 461
Kuuku Ya'u people 461
Kuyani people 432
Kwini people 344

Laarri Gallery, Yiyili community WA 345
Lajamanu, NT 96
Lake Bolac Eel Festival – Kuyang Lapakira, Lake Bolac Vic. 406
Lake Condah Vic. 15, 16
Lake Mungo burials NSW 8, 374
Lake Torrens NP SA 432
Lama Lama clan 462
Land Bilong Islanders 147–8
land rights 31, 96–7, 98, 175, 176, 224, 509
see also Native Title
Langford, Rosalind 165
Langton-Batty, Ruby 39–40
language groups 224
languages 42–53
Aboriginal English 44–5
benefits of learning another language 48
grammars and dictionaries 198
language work of Ngangkari healers 50, **51**
rules on use in Aboriginal society 202
of the Torres Strait Islands 45
Larapinta Trail NT 258–9
Lardil people 485
Larmairremener of the Big River clan 491
Larrakia Nation Arts, Darwin NT 290
Larrakia people 243, 290
Laura, NT 72, 73, 121, 479
Laura Aboriginal Dance Festival **3**, 121
Laura Quinkan Dance Festival, Laura Qld **3**, 121, 449
Lawson, Sue 140
Leane, Jeanine 135
Leeuwin–Naturaliste NP WA 309–12
Lefler, Dub 139
Legal, Bailey **38**, 40
Levett, Aunty Trish 135
Lewis, Niningka **299**
LGBTQIA+ people, fight for rights 36
Liberto, Ivan and Pamela Yvonne 101
Lillipad Cafe, The, Glebe NSW 401
Limilngan-Wulna Cultural Tour, Darwin NT 268
Limilngan-Wulna people 268
Lincoln NP SA 432–3
Linetemairrener group 492
Lingiari, Vincent 118, 344
Lirrwi Tourism, East Arnhem Land NT 267–8
listening to Country 22
Litchfield NP NT 253–4
Little Flower Black Mission School, Alice Springs NT **174**
Living Kaurna Cultural Centre, Adelaide 442, **442**
Lloyd, Jessie 38–9, 114, **115**
Lockhart River Arts, Lockhart River Qld 484
Long, Michael 407
Loonititetermairrelehoinner group 492
Loos, Noel 146
lore 224
Lourandos, Harry 16
Love-Johnson, Crystal 40
Lowe, Doug 164, 165
Lower Glenelg NP Vic. 411
Lower Southern Arrernte people 438
Lowreenner band of the South West tribe 491
Lucashenko, Melissa 128–9, **129**
Lui, Nakkiah 137–8
Lumnermareerme band of the South West tribe 491, 498
Luritja people/Elders 93, 262, 267, 295, 296, 299, 438

Maalinup Aboriginal Gallery, Henley Brook WA 338
Mabo, Eddie Koiki 146, 148, **148**
Mabo No. 2 case 146–8
debate over impact on Australian land ownership 148–9
and property law 149
Mabu Mabu, Melbourne and Yarraville Vic. 421
Mabu Mayi Cafe, Cable Beach WA 342
Mabuyag Island (Jervis Island) 111
Mabuyag (language) 45
MacDonald, Norma 139
McGuire, Walter and Meg 329
Mackay, Roderick 142
McKay, Roger 36–7
McKenna, Brenton 140
McKenna, Mark 208, 216
McKenzie, Queenie 349
McLeod, Bobby 136
McLeod, Michael 190
McNiven, Ian 15
McNiven, Liz 110
McQuire, Amy 139
Madarrpa clan 97
MadB **38**, 40
Mader, Stacy 76
Mahbilil Festival, Jabiru NT 240
Mailman, Deborah 109, 144
Mainie Australia Aboriginal Art Gallery & Retail Shop, Cairns Qld 478
makarrata 184, 224
Makarrata Commission 184, 185, 214
Maku Tjukurpa (witchetty grub songline) 446
Malek, Ahmed 142
Malyangapa people 376, 379
Mandingalbay Ancient Indigenous Tours (MAIT), Bessie Point Qld 466
Mandingalbay Yidinji people 463, 466
Mandjoogoordap Dreaming, Mandurah WA 335
Mandurah Performing Arts Centre, Mandurah WA 335
Mangala language group 342
Mangkaja Arts Resource Agency, Fitzroy Crossing WA 345–6
Mangolamar, Sylvester 9
Manikay singing style 52, 115, 224
Maningrida Arts and Culture, Maningrida community NT 290–1
Manyjiljarra language group 349
map of Indigenous Australia **46–7**, 219–20
Maraura people 435
Marawili, Baluka 90
Marawili, Djambawa 97–8, 99
Marawili, No.girr.a 90
Mardudhunera people 315
Mari Nawi (Big Canoe), Sydney 5, 395
Maria Island NP Tas. 495
Marika, Witiyana 141–2
Marimowa, Esmeralda 141
Marra people 298
Marranunggu clan 253
Marrawuddi Gallery, Bowali Visitor Centre NT 249
marriage 29, 55–6, 58, 60, 61, 98
marrnggitj 79, 224
Martin, Anne 182, 183
Martin, Justin 329
Martu people/language group 348, 349
Martumili Artists, Newman WA 348
Maruku Arts, Uluṟu–Kata Tjuṯu Cultural Centre NT 291
Mary River area, Kakadu NP NT 248
massacres
ancestral remains from massacre sites 166
of colonists 26
of First Australians 25–6, 84, 123, 141–2, 317
memorialisation 168
Mauboy, Jessica 109, 118, 144, 243
Mayi Harvests, Broome WA 334, 335

Mayor, Thomas 139, 184, 186
Meggitt, Mervyn 96
Melbourne's LGBTQIA+ MIDSUMMA 39 Festival, Melbourne Vic. 39
Melukerdee Country 489
Mengang Noongar people 334
men's ritual groups 34–5
Mer Island (Murray Island) 110, 146
Meriam Mir (language) 45
Meriam people of Mer island, Native Title rights 146–7, 148, 149
Merrepen Arts Centre, Nauiyu community NT 292
Mia, Kurrah 334
middens 19–21, 224
Midnight Oil 116
Miiesha 118
Milan Dhiiyaan NSW 389–91, **390**
Milbi Wall, Cooktown Qld 481–2
Milingimbi Art and Craft Centre, Milingimbi NT 292
Milirrpum v Nabalco 98
military service 179–80
Millstream–Chichester NP WA 312–13
Mimi Aboriginal Arts and Crafts, Katherine NT 292
Mimili Maku Art Centre, Mimili SA 446
Mimosa Rocks NP NSW 372
Minang people 320, 321
Minemegmer band of the South West tribe 491
Minga Cultural Experiences, Yuin Country NSW 391
mining companies 10, 153–4, 190
Minjungbal Aboriginal Cultural Centre, South Tweed Heads NSW 400
Minter, Peter 134
Mirarr people 240
Mirima NP WA 313
Miriwoong Creation era 348
Miriwoong people 252, 253, 313, 348–9
  seasonal calendar 74–5, **75**
Mirndiyan Gununa – MIART – Mornington Island Art, Mornington Island Qld 485
Mirning people 436
Mirritya Mundya, Callala Bay NSW 401
Miss First Nation Australia pageant **38**, 40
Mission Songs Project 114–15
missions/missionaries 30, 91, 92–3, 102, 141, 174, 176, 195, 224–5, 438
  ration distribution to Aboriginal people 27
Mitchell, Ben 182, 183
Mitchell River NP WA 313–14
Moa Arts, Moa Island Qld 514
'mob' names 34
Moffatt, Tracey 102
moities 225
Mole Creek Karst NP Tas. 495–6
Moongardie community 345
Morialta Conservation Park SA 433, **434**
Morris, Jacob 135
Morrison, Scott 186
Morton NP NSW 372–3
'mosaic' pattern of burning 71
Mossman Gorge, Daintree NP Qld 457, 471
Mossman Gorge Centre and Ngadiku Dreamtime Walks, Mossman Qld 466–7
mother tongues, freedom to speak 48–9
Mount Augustus NP WA 314
Mount Cook NP Qld 462
Mount Field NP Tas. 496
Mount Remarkable NP SA 433–5
Mowanjum Aboriginal Art and Culture Centre, Derby WA 18, 304, 338
Mowanjum Festival, Derby WA 304, 338
Mua Island, Torres Strait Qld 76, 78
Muecke, Stephen 125
Muir, Aunty Fay 140
Mulbabidgee, Cooktown Qld 482
Mulgumpin (Moreton Island) Qld 458
Mullagh, Johnny **407**
Mungalla Aboriginal Business Corporation 467
Mungalla Aboriginal Tours, Ingham Qld 467
Mungalla station homestead, Ingham Qld 466, **467**
Munga–Thirri NP Qld 462
Mungo Man and Mungo Woman (Aboriginal skeletons) 374
Mungo NP NSW 373–5, **374**
Munu.gurr, Barayuwa 100
Mununggurr, Sean 141
Mununggurr-Williams, Melanie 135
Munupi Art Centre, Munipi, Melville Island NT 292–3
Murgha, Letitia 19–20
Murramarang NP NSW 375
Murray River NP SA 435
Murrayfield Station, Bruny Island Tas. 503
Muru, Evan Yanna 383
Murujuga Aboriginal Corporation (MAC) 315
Murujuga NP WA 314–16
Murumbung Yurung Murra Tours, Canberra ACT 508
Muruwari people 475
museums
  acquisition of ancestral remains for 'scientific purposes' 164, 166
  return of ancestral remains and sacred objects 164–7
  see also art galleries, cultural centres and museums
Musgrave, George 72, 73
music 108–18, 242–3
  early recordings 108–10
  in First Languages 52
  National Indigenous Music Awards (NIMAs) 52, 116, 243
  protecting traditional styles 111–16
  today 116–18
musical instruments 108, 111, 115
Mutawintji Eco Tours, Mutawintji NP NSW 391–2
Mutawintji NP NSW 375–6, 391–2
Mutti Mutti people 374
Myers, Fred 94

Nagula Jarndu Designs, Broome WA 348
NAIDOC 225
NAIDOC Committee 182–3
  'Voice Treaty Truth' theme 183, 184, 186
NAIDOC Week 180–3
  themes 182–3
Namadgi NP ACT 505
Namatjira, Albert 102, 272
Namatjira, Vincent 102, 103
Nambung NP WA 316
Nanguluwurr, Kakadu NP 250
Nani, Ephraim 110–11
Nannup, Mark 39
Narana Aboriginal Cultural Centre, Geelong Vic. 418, **420**
Narawntapu NP Tas. 496–7, **497**
Narlijia Experiences Broome, Broome WA 335
Narragunnawali 212–13
Ŋarritj (white corella) 57
Narungga (Narangga) Nation 428
National Aboriginal and Torres Strait Islander Art Award (NATSIAA), Darwin 274–5
National Apology to the Stolen Generations 145, 161–2, 226
national day 208–12
National Gallery of Australia, Canberra ACT 101, 446, 509
National Gallery of Victoria, Melbourne Vic. 104
National Indigenous Art Fair, Circular Quay, Sydney NSW 400
National Indigenous Constitutional Convention (Uluru, May 2017) 184–6, 213–14
National Indigenous Fashion Awards, Darwin NT 273
National Indigenous Music Awards (NIMAs), Darwin NT 52, 116, 243
National Inquiry into the Separation of Aboriginal and Torres Strait Island Children from their Families 158–60
National Museum of Australia, Canberra ACT 96, **508**, 509
National Native Title Tribunal 151–2, 153, 154
national parks
  Australian Capital Territory 505–7
  New South Wales 356–83
  Northern Territory 244–59, 262
  Queensland 453–63
  South Australia 423–38
  Tasmania 491–9
  Victoria 408–14
  Western Australia 306–23
National Recording Project for Indigenous Performance in Australia 111
National Resting Place for unprovenanced Aboriginal and Torres Strait Islander ancestral remains 168
National Sorry Day 161, 162
Native Title 146–56, 213, 225
  application procedure 151–2
  applications based on 'past acts' and 'future acts' 153–4
  as 'bundle of rights' 149
  Canada, US and New Zealand 150, 213
  compensation claims 156–7
  'consent determinations' 154–6
  impact on the lives of Australians 151
  and mining companies 153–4, 190
  negotiation of agreements 156
  and Traditional Owners' ongoing connection with their land 149, 150
Native Title Act 1993 (Cth) 149, 152–3, 154–5
Native Title cases/claims/rights/agreements
  Arabana people, lands west of Kati Thanda SA 430
  Bundjalung people, Bundjalung NP NSW 363
  Claim Group (Ngaliwurru and Nungali peoples) case 156–7
  Djabugay people, Barron Gorge NP Vic. 453
  Githabul people, Border Ranges NP NSW 361
  Mabo No. 2 case and the High Court 146–8
  Nauo-Barngarle people, Coffin Bay NP SA 426
  Puutu Kunti Kurrama and Pinikura peoples, Pilbara WA 10
  Spinifex Traditional Owners, Great Victoria Desert WA 341
  Yolŋu people NT 96–7
  Yorta Yorta case 150–1
  see also Indigenous Land Use Agreements
Native Title determinations 152
natural disaster resilience, and Indigenous land and fire management practices 68–70
Nauo people 426, 432
Nayinggul, Jacob Junior 141
Nayombolmi 250
Nayri Niara Good Spirit Festival, Bruny Island Tas. 489
Needwonnee people 498, 500
Needwonnee Walk, Melaleuca Tas. 500
Nelson, Paddy Jupurrula 95
Neuenfeldt, Karl 111
Never Again report 11
New South Wales, protection and promotion of Aboriginal languages 43–4
Newland Head Conservation Park SA 435–6
Ngaachi land 461
Ngaanyatjarra artists 446
Ngaanyatjarra Lands of Western Australia 348

Ngaanyatjarra people/language group 348, 349
Ngaanyatjarra Pitjantjatjara Yankunytjatjara *see* NPY
Ngadjuri Country 439
Ngaliwurru people 156–7, 245
Ngalmun Lagau Minaral (Our Island Designs) 514
Ngambri people 508
Ngan'gi language group 292
Ngan'gikurrunggurr people 281
ngangkari 79, 225
Ngaran Ngaran Cultural Awareness, Narooma NSW **391**, 392, **393**
Ngarda-Ngarli 315
Ngardi language group 349
Ngarigo people 369, 505
Ngarinyman people/language group 245, 301, 338
Ngarluma people 315
'Ngarra Burra Ferra' (song) 109
Ngarranggarni 348–9
Ngarrindjeri artists 104
Ngarrindjeri people/nation 428
Ngawait people 435
Ngemba Country 367
Ngintait people 435
Ngiyampaa people 374
Ngugi people 458
Ngukurr Arts, Ngukkur NT 294
Ngunnawal (Ngunawal) people 505, 507, 508
Ngunnhu (Fish Traps), Brewarrina NSW 401
Ngurrungurrdjba (Yellow Water), Kakadu NP NT 249
Nicholls, Sir Doug 406, 417
Nielsen, Rasmus 172
Ninene clan 498
Ninuku Arts, Kalka, APY Lands SA 446–7
Nitmiluk NP NT 254–6, 265
Njarra, Iltja 287
No Fixed Address 116, 208
non-Indigenous 225
non-indigenous guides 169–72
policeNoon, Karlie 76
Noongar people/language group 196, 306, 309, 320, 321, 328, 329, 333, 336, 339, 349
Noongar Radio/ Kuditj Kitchen, Perth WA 342
Noonuccal, Oodgeroo 135
Norris, Ray P. 76
North tribe 491
northern Australia, fire management practices 71–2
NPY Women's Council 50, 80
  language work of Ngangkari healers 50–1
  Tjanpi Desert Weavers 297–8
Nughi clan 453
Nukunu people 433–5
Nullarbor National Park Wilderness Protection Area and Regional Reserve SA 437–8
Numbulwar Numburindi Arts, Numbulwar NT 294
Nungali people 156–7, 245
Nunn, Patrick 12
Nunukul clan 453
Nura Gunyu, Morton NSW **200**, 392, 393
Nyamal language group 349
Nyamba Buru Yawuru Limited (NBY), Cable Beach WA 331, 338–9
Nyanda Cultural Tours, Nudgee, Brisbane Qld 467
Nyinda, Wula Gura 337
Nyinkka Nyunyu Art and Culture Centre, Tennant Creek NT 294
Nyiyarparli language group 349
Nyungamarta language group 342, 349
Nyungar people/language 324, 329, 330, 335
Nyungar Tours with Kerry-Ann Winmar, Perth WA 335–6
Nywaigi Aboriginal Land Corporation 467
Nywaigi people 467, 483

Ochre pits, Tjoritja/West MacDonnell NP NT 257–8
Old People 33–4, 225
  repatriation 165–7
Olive, Mark 194, 195
Oliver, Steven 40, 135
Olkolo people/Country 153, 465
Olney, Justice 150
O'Loughlin, Michael 134
oral histories/oral traditions 225
Ormiston Gorge and Pound, Tjoritja/West MacDonnell NP NT 258
Orr, Ricky 268
'out-of-Africa' thesis of human migration 172
Outback Cafe, The 194–5
Outstation Gallery, Darwin NT 295
Oxley Wild Rivers NP NSW 376–7

Paakantji people 368, 374
Packing Room Prize 136
Page, Stephen 120, 121, 355
palawa kilpi Tas. 503
palawa people 164–5, 171, 492, 500
Palm Island 114, 139
Palngun Wurnangat, Wadeye NT 295
Pamagirri Aboriginal Dance Troupe, Kuranda Qld 468
Pamagirri Aboriginal Experience at Rainforestation Nature Park, Kuranda Qld **6**, 467–70, **469**
Pamagirri Art Market, Kuranda Qld 470
Pan, Mary Katatjuku **299**
Pangerninghe people of the Big River tribe 496
Pantyikali people 376
Papulankutja Artists, Papulankutja (Blackstone) WA 348
Papunya art movement 92–4, 95
Papunya Tjupi Aboriginal Arts, Papunya NT 295
Papunya Tula Artists Pty Ltd, Alice Springs NT 93, 95, 296, 349
Paredarerme (Oyster Bay) Nation 492, 495
Parker, Captain Phillip 321
Parrtjima Festival, Alice Springs NT 240–2, **241**
Pascoe, Bruce 84, 130–1, **130**, 135, 139, 216
  criticisms of his *Dark Emu* views 65–6
  Dark Emu: Black Seeds: Agriculture or Accident? 12, 64–7, 80–1, 130
Passi, Fr Dave 14, 146
pastoral stations 27, 30
Pathways 220
Paton, Nicholas 135
Pearson, Luke 37–8, 127, 140
Pearson, Noel 183, 216
Pecan Summer (opera) 122–3
Peddells Thursday Island Tours, Thursday Island Qld 511
Pederson, Aaron 139
Peedamulla Campground, Karratha WA 336
Pemulwuy 84, 166
pensions 29
performance 108–23
  New South Wales 355
  Western Australia 305
  see also dance
Perkins, Charlie 226
Perkins, Rachel 118, 142, 143
Pertame Southern Arrernte people 267
Phillip, Captain Arthur 25, 83–4, 149, 172–3, 211
photographs and videos 203
Pigram, Bart 335
Pila Nguru Aboriginal Corporation 340
Pinikura people 10
the Pinnacles 316
Pintupi art movement 86, 95
Pintupi Elders 93
Pintupi people/language group 295, 296, 349
Pitjantjatjara A̲nangu 259, 260
Pitjantjatjara artists 446
Pitjantjatjara Elders **94**
places
  Australian Capital Territory 509
  New South Wales 400–2
  Queensland 480–3
  South Australia 445
  Tasmania 503
  Victoria 419–22
  Western Australia 340–2
Plum, Thelma 118
poetry 134–6
Poetry in First Languages (PIFL) program 135
Point Pearce Aboriginal Mission, Point Pearce SA 438
Pormpuraaw Art and Culture Centre, Pormpuraaw Qld **484**, 485, **486**
Port Campbell NP Vic. 413
Poulson, Clarise Nampijinpa **96**
Poulson, Michael Japangardi **96**
Praten, Annie 36
precolonial history 8–23
Pride marches 36
'property'
  and 'bundle of rights' 149
  and Native Title 149
protection and segregation era 30, 114, 226
Provocalz 135
Puch clan 486
Pudakul Aboriginal Cultural Tours NT 268
Purcell, Leah 133, **133**, 141
Purnululu NP WA 317–20
Puthikwilayti people 495
Puutu Kunti Kurrama people 10
Pwerle Gallery SA 443

Quandamooka Festival, Minjerribah (North Stradbroke Island) and Winnam (Wynnum) Qld 453
Quandamooka people 453
Queensland Art Gallery and Gallery of Modern Art (QAGOMA), Brisbane Qld 479
Queensland Coast Islands Declaratory Act 1985 147
Queensland Museum, Brisbane Qld 479
Quinkan & Regional Cultural Centre, Laura Qld 479
Quinn, Belinda 141

Rabbit-Proof Fence 62, 145
racial discrimination 29, 183, 216
Racial Discrimination Act 1975 (Cth) 147
racial segregation 30, 209, 226
racism 29, 169, 216
racist agenda in media attacks on Pascoe 66–7
racist policies 176
racist stereotypes 6, 82–5
Rainbow Serpent 247, 290, 454, 456, 468
Rainbow Valley Cultural Tours NT 268
Rainboy Valley Conservation Reserve NT 264, 268
Rainforestation Nature Park, Kuranda Qld 467–70
Ramindjeri clan 436
Ramo, Ziggy 118
Ranuntja, Wenten 112
rappers 116, 118
ration system 27
Ravenshoe Visitor Centre, Ravenshoe Qld 480
reconciliation 24, 169–70, 175, 225, 475
Reconciliation Action Plans (RAP) 189–90, 213
Reconciliation Australia 189, 212
  work of 212–13
Reconciliation Place 208, 225
Red Room Poetry 135
Redbank Gorge, Tjoritja/West MacDonnell NP NT 258
Redfern (Sydney) NSW 30

Reece, Nicholas 211
referendums 175, 176–9, 186–7, 226
Reid, Janice
  Body, Land and Spirit: Health and Healing in Aboriginal Society 81–2
  Sorcerers and Healing Spirits: Continuity and Change in an Aboriginal Medical System 81
Reid, Nicholas 12
Reid, Teela 141
religious art 93
religious beliefs and rituals 32–4, 89
  expressed through art and culture 89, 120
  see also ancestral beings
republican 226
reserves *see* Aboriginal reserves
respect
  for Country 7
  for Indigenous traditions and cultures 40–1
  for spiritual Old People 33–4
  for Traditional Owners 272
  for your Indigenous hosts 188
Reynolds, Henry 146, 171
Rice, James 146, 148
Ridgeway, Aden 182
Riley, Grant and Anne 337
Riley, Kumalie (Rosalie) 275
Rinyirru (Lakefield) National Park (CYPAL) Qld 462–3
Rio Tinto 10
Riverbank, The, is a Kaurna Market, Adelaide SA 445
Riverlife Mirrabooka, Brisbane 482
Roach, Archie 116, 118, 135, 243, 305
Roberts, Rhonda 188
Robinson, Laurel 144
rock art 89–91
  Burrungkuy (Nourlangie) and Ubirr, Kakadu NP 250–1
  Carnarvon NP Qld 456
  Chillagoe–Mungana Caves NP Qld 456
  European interpretation 202
  Gariwerd (Grampians) NP Vic. 197
  Ikara–Flinders Ranges NP SA 429
  Injalak Hill NT 266
  Jarramali Rock Art Tours Qld 465
  Judbarra–Gregory NP NT 245
  Kalumburu WA 344
  Kamay Botany Bay NP NSW 367–8
  Keep River NP NT 252
  Kimberley WA 9, 17–18
  Ku-ring-gai Chase NP NSW 371, 389
  Lake Torrens NP SA 432
  Murujuga NP WA 314–15
  oldest known, Kimberley region WA 9
  Southwest NP Tas. 498
  Wanjina (Wandjina) figures 17–18, 91, 228
  Windjana Gorge Rock Art Tour, Fitzroy Crossing WA 326–7
  Wunambal Gaambera Country, Uunguu Indigenous Protected Area WA 342
  Wurre (Rainbow Valley) Conservation Reserve NT 264
rock music 116, 117, 118
Rocky Cape NP Tas. 497–8
Rocky Springs community 345
Roelands Mission, Roelands WA 195
Roelands Village, Roelands WA 195
Roughsey, Goobalathaldin Dick 485
Rowlands, Don 462
Rowley, Charles 28
Royal Botanic Garden Sydney Aboriginal Heritage Experiences, Sydney NSW 392–3
Royal Commission into Aboriginal Deaths in Custody 81, 175, 212, 214–16
  recommendations 218
Royal Commission into National Natural Disaster Arrangements 67, 68
  recommendations on use of Aboriginal fire management practices 68–70
Royal NP NSW 378–9
Rudd, Kevin
  apology to Stolen Generations 145, 161–2, 226
  petition to recognise the right of Yolŋu clans in the Constitution 213
Ruiz de Luzuriaga, Mojo 135
Rush, Geoffrey 118
Russell, Dug 190
Ryan, Lyndall 35–6, 171

sacred ancestral beings *see* ancestral beings
sacred sites 98, 121, 205, **206**
  destruction, Pilbara WA 10–11
sacred symbols/designs/objects 94–5, 96, 97
Saddler, Mark 384
safety signs 204, 205–7
Saffioti, Trina 139
Salee, Celuia Mapo 146, 148
saltwater crocodiles 207
Saltwater Eco Tours, Mooloolaba Qld 470–1, **470**
Saltwater Freshwater Aboriginal Cultural Festival, Mid North Coast NSW 351, **352**
Sand Dune Adventures, Williamtown NSW 394
The Sapphires 109, 144
Sara clan 486
Saunders, Kirli 140
Sayers, Andrew 92
Scott, Kim 128
scriptwriting 136–9
sea-level changes 12, 13
seasonal calendars and knowledge 74–5, 78, 196, 226
Sebbens, Shari 109, 137, 144
segregation 30, 209, 226
SEIT Outback Australia NT 268–9
Selwyn, Tim 388
Sentance, Nathan 124
Sentina, Maiko 101
Serpentine Gorge, Tjoritja/West MacDonnell NP NT 257
shell middens 19–21, 224
Shoemaker, Adam 124, 125
Short Black Opera 122
Shukuroglou, Vicky 130
Simms, Graham 37
Simpsons Gap, Tjoritja/West MacDonnell NP NT 257
Sims, Paddy Japaljarri 95
'Sistergirls' 39, 40
skin names 56–7, 60–1, 226
sky, observations of the 75–9
Skye, Alice 118
small towns and settlements, Indigenous people in 30–1
Smede, Nicole 135
Smith, Fanny Cochrane 108–9
Smith, William Ramsay 125, 126
social order 226
social security payments 29
Soft Sands (band) 115
solar points in Torres Strait Islander astronomical knowledge 76–8
Solis, Prof. Gabriel 109
song series/songlines 33, 226, 340, 446
songs
  early 108–9, 110
  protecting traditional styles 111–15
'Source of Fire' (Djambawa Maraawli) **97**
South Alligator River area, Kakadu NP NT 248–9
South Australian Museum, Adelaide SA 96, 443, 446
South Bruny NP Tas. 498
South East Tasmanian Aboriginal Corporation 489
South, John 76
South West Boojarah people 306
South West Queensland Indigenous Cultural Trail, St George Qld 471
Southbound Escapes, Narooma NSW 394
Southwest NP Tas. 498–9
Spencer, Larry Jungarrayi 95
Spinifex Arts Project 341
Spinifex families of Tjuntjuntjara 340–1
Spinifex Hill Studio, South Hedland WA 349
Spirits of the Red Sand, Beenleigh 482–3
spiritual beings 17–18, 32–4, 227
  see also 'Dreaming'; 'Dreamtime'
spirituality *see* religious beliefs and rituals
Split Rock, Laura Qld 483
sport 243
  New South Wales 355–6
  Victoria 406–8
Stack, Kerry 330
Stack, Trevor 330
stage production 136–9
'Stand strong for who you are, 2020' (Vincent Namatjira) **103**
star maps 78–9
The State of Reconciliation in Australia Report 24
Steffensen, Victor, *Fire Country: How Indigenous Fire Management Could Help Save Australia* 72–3
Stevens, William 76
Stewart, Dean 5
Stewart, Paddy Japaljarri 95, 96
Stiff Gins 118
Stirling Range NP WA 320–2
Stolen Generations 116, 122, 145, 158–68, 195, 226
  Bringing them home: The 'Stolen Children' report 159–61, 175
  commemorative plaques 162
  compensation claims 161
  and John Howard's refusal to offer an apology 161
  Kevin Rudd's apology to 145, 161–2, 226
  Memorials and Memorial Gardens 163
  significance of the apology 162
Stone, Cheryl 121
Stonewall riots, New York 36, 37
storytelling 22, 124–45
  is culture 145
  through performance 121
Straddie Adventures, One Mile, Stradbroke Island Qld 471, **472**
Street Feast Food Truck and Catering Vic. 421
Strzelecki NP Tas. 499
Sturt NP NSW 379–80
subsection systems (skin names) 57
Sultan, Dan 118
Sun 78
Supply Nation 190–1
Survival Day Festival, Adelaida SA 423
Sutton, Peter 65–6
Sweet Country 143–4
Swindley, Brian 'Binna' 477
Sydney Harbour NP NSW 380–1
Sydney Mardi Gras (Sydney Gay and Lesbian Mardi Gras) 36, 37
  Luke Pearson's views 37–8

taboos on saying the names of someone who has died recently 33, 201–2
Tandanya National Aboriginal Cultural Institute, Adelaide SA 443
Tanderrum people 416
Tangentyere Artists, Alice Springs NT 296
Tapatjatjaka Art and Craft Centre, Titjikala community NT 296
Tapaya, Tjunkaya **299**
Tapsell, Miranda 39, 109, 138, 144

Tarnanthi Festival of Contemporary Aboriginal and Torres Strait Islander Art and Art Fair, Adelaide SA 423, 441
Tarra-Bulga NP Vic. 413
Tasmanian Aboriginal people
  Black Wars 170–1
  genocide 164
Tasmanian Aboriginal songs 108
Tasmanian Museum and Art Gallery, Hobart 501–3
Taungurung people/language group 411, 419
Telstra NATSIAA, Darwin 274–5
Ten Canoes 52
terra nullius 146, 147, 148, 227
Thamarrurr Men's Shed (Thamarrurr Development Corporation), Wadeye NT 296–7
The Connection Shepparton, Shepparton Vic. 422
The Ian Potter Centre: NGV Australia, Melbourne Vic. 418
The Lillipad Cafe, Glebe NSW 401
The Olgas NT *see* Kata Tjuṯa NT
The Outback Cafe 194–5
The Riverbank is a Kaurna Market, Adelaide SA 445
The Tin Humpy, Redfern NSW 402, **402**
Thomas, Madigan 349
Thomas, Rover 101, 349
Thompson, Jack 142
Thomson, Donald 180
Thornalley, Simon 470
Thornton, Warwick 142, 143–4
Three Sisters, Blue Mountains NP NSW 357
Tiagarra Aboriginal Cultural Centre and Keeping Place, Devonport Tas. 503
Tidbinbilla Nature Reserve, Tidbinbilla ACT 505–7
Tiddas 118
Timberlina **38**, 40
Tin Humpy, The, Redfern NSW 402, **402**
Tindale, Norman B. 221
Tinkerbee Arrernte Art & Cultural Workshop NT 275
Tiwi By Design Tours, Darwin NT 297
Tiwi Design, Wurrumiyanga, Bathurst Island NT 297
Tiwi Islands Grand Final and Art Sale, Bathurst Island NT 243
Tiwi people 278, 292–3, 297
Tjakamarra, Long Jack Phillipus 93
Tjala Arts, Amata community SA 447
Tjanpi Desert Weavers, Alice Springs NT 297–8, 348
Tjapaltjarri, Billy Stockman 93
Tjarlirli Art, Tjukurla, Ngaanyatjarra Lands WA 239
Tjatu Gallery, Marla SA 443–5
TJay and Dallas 40
Tjoritja/West MacDonnell NP 256–9
Tjukurba Gallery, Wiluna WA 339
Tjukurrpa 33, 227
Tjungu Palya, Nyapari SA 447
Tnorala (Gosse Bluff) Conservation Reserve NT 259
Toorernomairremener clan 492
Top Didj Cultural Experience and Art Gallery, Katherine NT 275
Top End Wedding 39
Torres, Jade 443
Torres, Pat Mamanyjun **334**, 335
Torres Strait Creole 45
Torres Strait Heritage Museum, Horn Island Qld 51
Torres Strait Islander art 86
Torres Strait Islander languages 45
Torres Strait Islander people 2, 220, 227
  arrival on the islands 2
  astronomical knowledge, solar points in 76–8
  claims to land 146–7
  music and dance 110–11
Torres Strait Islanders (1898) (exhibition) 110
Torres Strait Islands 509–15
totems 227
tour guides, what if your guide is not indigenous? 169–70
tourism 3–5, 188, 192–4
  gourmet food and culinary tourism 194–6
  immersive cultural experiences 196–7
  outback: the landscapes if Indigenous Australia 197
tourists
  crudely manufactured art sold to 100, 107
  lack of information about Aboriginal history 170–1
  what you should know when visiting Australia 172–5
tours and stays
  Australian Capital Territory 507–8
  New South Wales 383–98
  Northern Territory 264–72
  Queensland 463–74
  South Australia 438–40
  Tasmania 499–501
  Torres Strait Islands 511
  Victoria 415–16
  Western Australia 323–37
Tower Hill Visitor Centre, Warrnambool Vic. 416
trackers 62, **63**
trade routes 12
traditional, definition 227
traditional Aboriginal medicine 80, 81
traditional healers 79–80, 221, 224
  books about 80–1
  language work 50–1
Traditional Owners 2, 4, 68, 71, 227
  cultural rules and protocols laid down by 203–7
  laws and system of governance 146
  ongoing connection with their land 149
  respect for 272
Treaties with Indigenous Australians 112
'Treaty', as new anthem 112–13, 117
Trevorrow, Bruce 161
'tribal' groups 34
Tribal Warrior Cultural Cruises, Sydney NSW 5, 395
Truganini 164–5, **164**
  remains at Hobart Museum 164
  remains returned to palawa community, cremated and ashes scattered in D'Entrecasteaux Channel 164–5
Tumut Brungle Gundagai Area Aboriginal community 369
Turpin, Myfany 143
Tutt, Corey 139
Twelve Apostles, Port Campbell NP Vic. 413
Two Boys Dreaming, Birdsville Qld 471

Ubirr, Kakadu NP NT 250
Uluṟu NT 259–62, 269
'Uluṟu Statement from the Heart' 184–5, 213, 214
  three pillars 184
Uluṟu-Kata Tjuṯa NP NT 259–62
  ban on tourists climbing on Uluṟu 205–6
Uluṟu-Kata Tjuṯu National Park Board of Management 205
Umbagai, Leah 18
Umbarra Aboriginal Cultural Centre, Wallaga Lake NSW 400
UMI Arts Limited, Cairns Qld 485–6
UN Declaration on the Rights of Indigenous Peoples, Article 13 43, 48–9
Unaipon, David 125–7
  on Australian $50 note **126**
'Uncle' 56
University of Melbourne
  Ian Potter Museum 97
  returns ancestral remains for proper burial 167
urban Indigenous people/communities 30
Us Mob 116, 208
Uti Kulintjaku Project 50

van Neerven, Ellen 133–4, **133**, 135
Venture North Safaris NT 269–70
Veth, Peter 17
Victorian Aboriginal Cultural Heritage Act 167
Victorian Aboriginal Heritage Council 166, 167
Vision Walks: The Bush Tucker Walk with Aunty Delta, Federal NSW 395, **396**
Vocale, Dale 421
Voice to be enshrined in the Australian Constitution 184–7, 213–14
'Voice, Treaty, Truth' 183, 184, 186, 213
Voller, Dylan 135
von Guérard, Eugene 92
voting rights 175
Voyages Indigenous Tourism Australia – Ayers Rock Resort NT 271
Vulkathunha-Gammon Ranges NP SA 437

Waanyi people 131, 454
Wabma Kadarbu Mound Springs Conservation Park SA 437–8
Wadandi Country 333
Wadja Wadja people 487
Wadjigal people 487
Wadumbah Indigenous Dance, Perth WA 336
Wagadagam clan 111
Wailu, Jack **148**
Wajaana Yaam Gumbaynggirr Adventure Tours, Coffs Harbour NSW 397
Wajarri people/Country 314, 350
Walangari Karntawarra, Bondi Beach NSW 397
Walkabout Cultural Adventures, Mossman Qld **4**, 471–2, **473**
Walkatjara Art Centre, Uluṟu-Kata Tjuṯu NP NT 298
Wallace, Allen 165
Walley, Olman and Sharna 324
Wallumedegal people 5
Walmajarri people/language group 347, 349
Walshe, Kerryn 65–6
Walyalup Aboriginal Cultural Centre, Fremantle WA 339
Walyunga NP WA 322–3
Wanam clan 486
Wangal people 5
Wangarr 228
Wangkajunga people/language group 347, 349
Wangkangurru people/Elders 438, 462
Wangkumara people 379
Wanjina (Wandjina) 17–18, 91, 228
Wanjina Wunggurr culture 342
Warakurna Artists, Warakurna community WA 350
Waralungku Arts, Borroloola NT 298
Waray clan 253
Wardaman people 245
Wardandi Bibbulmun people 327
Wardarnji – Fremantle Arts Centre, Fremantle WA 304
Wari clan group 428
Waringarri Aboriginal Arts, Kununurra WA 348–9
Warlayirti Artists Aboriginal Corporation, Wirrimanu (Balgo) community WA 349
Warlpiri artists 95, 96
Warlpiri Elders 95
Warlpiri people 251, 275, 295, 296, 298, 349
  skin names 61
Warlpiri style music 116
Warlukurlangu Artists Aboriginal Corporation, Yuendumu NT 95, 96, 298

Warmun Art Centre, Warmun community WA 329, 349–50
Warnayaka Art & Cultural Aboriginal Corporation, Lajamanu NT 298–9
Warnman language group 349
Warradjan Aboriginal Cultural Centre, Kakadu NP NT 249–50
Warrai people 280
Warrgamay people 483
Warrumbungle NP NSW 381
Warumpi Band 116
Warumungu people 251, 294
Warungnu people 483
Watarrka (Kings Canyon) NP NT 262, 267
Watego, Chelsea 140–1
Waterman, Richard 113
Wathaurung people/language group 409, 419
Watjan Guided Tours NT 271
Watson, Sam Wagan 135
Wave Hill Walk-Off 344
'We Have Survived' Festival 208
weather knowledge 74–5, 76
Weetapoona Aboriginal Corporation 489
Weilwan people 381
Wei'Num Arts, Mapoon Qld 486
Weir, Barbara 443
welcome ceremonies 33
Welcome to Country ceremonies 32, 33, 228
Wenham, David 142
Wentworth, William (Bill) **43**
Werat clan 253
West, Aunty Ida 165
Western Aranda people 257–8
Western Australian Museum Boola Bardip, Northbridge WA 339
Western Desert acrylic art styles 86, 94
Western Desert songlines 340
Western Yalanji Country 449
Wettenhall, Gib 17
Whadjuk Country 343
Whadjuk Noongar people 338
Whiteland, Josh 195–6, **332**
Whitlam, Gough 175
Whittaker, Alison 135
Wik and Kugu Arts Centre, Aurukun Qld 486–7
Wild Kitchen 195
Willandra Lakes Region World Heritage Area NSW 373–4
Williams, Gina 118
Willoughby, Bart 208
Wilpena Pound Resort, Ikara–Flinders Ranges NP SA 441
Wilson, Rohan 128
Wilson, Sir Ronald 158, 159
Wilson, Sammy 205
Wilsons Promontory NP Vic. 413–14
Winch, Tara Jane 127–8, **127**
Winchanam clan 486
Windera clan group 428
Windjana Gorge Rock Art Tour, Fitzroy Crossing WA 326–7
Winds of Zenadth Cultural Festival, Thursday Island Qld 511
Winhangaduringya Healing Space (travelling exhibition) 389, **391**
Winmar, Kerry-Ann 335–6
Winmar, Nicky 417
Wiradjuri artists 102–4
Wiradjuri language, introduction into state school system 43–4
Wiradjuri people 211, 357, 381, 505
Wirnda Barna Art Centre, Mount Magnet WA 350
Wirrarri Visitor Information Centre, Birdsville Qld 471, 472
Witjira NP SA 438
Woiwurrung people/language group 406, 419
Wolgalu people 505
Wollombi Aboriginal Cultural Experiences and Consultancy, Wollombi NSW 396, 397–8
women's societies 34–5
Wongutha people 327
Wonnarua people 356, 357
Woodward, Sir Edward 97
Woody, Michelle **288**
Woolkabunning Kiaka Incorporated 195
Woon-goott-oo people 315
Woorabinda Arts and Cultural Centre, Duaringa Qld 487
Worimi Local Aboriginal Land Council 394
Worimi people/Country 351, 356, 394
Working on Country programs 73
World Heritage sites/areas
  Barrington Tops NP NSW 356
  Border Ranges NP NSW 361
  Budj Bim Cultural Landscape Vic. 13–14, 15, 66, 409
  Daintree NP Qld 457
  Franklin–Gordon Wild Rivers NP Tas. 492
  Great Barrier Reef Marine Park Qld 458
  Greater Blue Mountains NSW 357, 382
  Kakadu NP NT 246, 271
  Mole Creek Karst NP Tas. 495
  Murujuga NP WA 314
  Oxley Wild Rivers NP NSW 376
  Purnululu NP WA 317
  Uluṟu–Kata Tjuṯa NP NT 260
  Willandra Lakes Region NSW 373
WorldPride festival 37
Worn Gundidj at Tower Hill, Warrnambool Vic. 416
Worrorra people/language group 18, 301, 338
Wotjobaluk people 414
Wright, Alexis 128, 130, 131, **131**, 135, 136
Wright, Leo Leeko 399
Wuddi Cultural Tours and Cultural Centre, Dumbleyung WA 336–7
Wujal Wujal Aboriginal Shire Council, Wujal Wijal Qld 472–4
Wujal Wujal Waterfall, Daintree NP Qld 483
wukalina Walk, Launceston Tas. 500–1
Wula Gura Nyinda Eco Cultural Adventures, Shark Bay WA 337, **337**
Wunambal Gaambera Country, Uunguu Indigenous Protected Area WA 342
Wunambal Gaambera people/language group 9, 18, 91, 301, 314, 338
Wurramara, Emily 116, 118
Wurre (Rainbow Valley) Conservation Reserve NT 264, 268
Wurundjeri Elders 407
Wurundjeri Woi Wurrung Cultural Heritage Aboriginal Corporation 416
Wuthathi people 461
Wuuyuru (Bigge Island) **18**
Wyatt, Ken 186, 187, 214
Wyatt, Meyne 136–7
Wyperfeld NP Vic. 414

Yabun Festival, Camperdown NSW 208, 355
Yaburara people 315
Yadhaykenu people 461
Yagan 166
Yalanji Arts, Mossman Gorge Qld 487
Yaluk-ut Weelam Ngargee, St Kilda Vic. 406
Yamaji Art, Geraldton WA 350
Yamati language group/Country 349, 350
Yandruwandha people 430
Yankunytjatjara people 259, 260
Yanyuwa people 298
Yarrabah Arts and Cultural Precinct, Yarrabah Qld 487
Yarrenyty Arltere Artists, Alice Springs NT 299
Yawarrawarrka people 430
Yawuru people/language 331, 335, 338–9, 342, 348
Yaygirr language group 382
Yellow Water Cruises, Kakadu NP NT 271–2
Yengo NP NSW 382, 397
yiḏaki (didgeridoo) **100**, 108, 115, 228
Yindilli Camping and Tours, Chinacamp via Wujil Wujil Qld 474
Yindjibarndi people/language group 312, 315, 349, 350
Yinjaa-Barni Art, Roebourne WA 350
Yirra Yaakin Theatre Company, Subiaco WA 305
YIRRAMBOI, Melbourne Vic. 406
Yirrganydji people 463
Yirritja 58, 98, 99
Yirrkala 112, 113
Yirrkala Bark Petitions 98, **99**
Yirrmal 116
Yolŋu people
  art and artists 99–100, 116, 278–9, 284
  clan groupings 52, 58–60, 98, 284
  cultural tours 267–8
  Dhuwa and Yirritja classifications 58, 98, 99, 100
  Garma Festival 32, 196–7, 203–5, 237–40
  kinship (gurrutu) 58–61, 98
  law explained through paintings 98–100
  marriage rules 58–9, 98
  matha (language) 52, 57
  medicine 81
  music and musicians 52, 111, 112–13, 116–17
  Native Title case 96–7
  petition to Kevin Rudd on their rights 213
  relationships between different clans 60, 98
  sacred ancestral entities 52, 58
  sea rights claim 98
Yorta Yorta people/Nation 408, 422
  land rights case 150–1
Yothu Yindi 52, 112, 113, 115, 116, 117, 141, 142, 243
Yothu Yindi Foundation 197
Yuendumu school NT, artwork on doors 95–6
Yugambeh Aboriginal Dancers, Currumbin Qld **464**, 480
Yugambeh Museum, Beenleigh Qld 480
Yugambeh people/language 477, 480
Yuggera Aboriginal Dancers, Brisbane Qld 482
Yugul Mangi people 294
Yuin people/Country 365, 366, 372, 373, 391, 392, 505
Yuku Baja Muliku people 462, 477–8
Yulparitja language group 342
Yunupiŋu, Galarrwuy 112, 142, 213
Yunupiŋu, Gurrumul 117, 243
Yunupiŋu, Dr Mandawuy 52, 112, 113, 141, 142
Yunupiŋu, Mungurrawuy 112
Yuraygir NP NSW 382–3
Yurri Catering, Shepparton Vic. 422

Zodiac **38**, 40

ABOUT THE AUTHOR

Professor Marcia Langton AO PhD Macq U, BA (Hons) ANU, FASSA is one of Australia's most important voices for Indigenous Australia. As an anthropologist and geographer, she has made a significant contribution to government and non-government policy as well as to Indigenous studies, native title and resource management, art and culture, and women's rights. Professor Langton has held the Foundation Chair of Australian Indigenous Studies at the University of Melbourne since February 2000. In 2016, she was honoured as a Redmond Barry Distinguished Professor, and was then appointed as the first Associate Provost at the University of Melbourne in 2017. She has received many other accolades, including the Officer of the Order of Australia award in 2020.

Acknowledgements

In writing this introduction to travelling in Indigenous Australia, I was fortunate to be assisted by several Aboriginal women whose research comprised entries on each recommended place or event. I am grateful to Nina Fitzgerald, Marly Wells, Tahlia Eastman, Ruby Langton-Batty and Rebekah Hatfield for their very significant contributions. I thank Dino Hodge for his research and Wayne Quilliam for the use of his photographs. Thanks also to Aaron Corn for his reading of sections and corrections. The staff at Hardie Grant have also contributed substantially – and must be credited as co-curators. I acknowledge their dedication and attention to detail in guiding me to produce the text and in choosing the images that bring the text to life. I especially give my thanks to the editors Marg Bowman and Nikki Lusk.

ABOUT THE RESEARCHERS

Nina Fitzgerald is a proud Aboriginal and Torres Strait Islander woman whose family hails from Kakadu, Moa Island in the Torres Strait and the Wuthathi people of Shelbourne Bay in Far North Queensland. As an active participant and observer in the Australian Indigenous Arts space her entire life, Nina is increasingly passionate about the continued elevation and inclusion of Indigenous Arts and Culture in the broader Australian narrative. Her work spans the fashion and creative sectors with roles in Creative Direction, curation and writing.

Marly Wells has Warlpiri and white Australian ancestry. She grew up in Mparntwe (Alice Springs), studied at the University of Melbourne, and has also lived in the UK. She currently works in early childhood engagement policy and strategy. Marly is passionate about reading, Saturday morning quizzes, system reform and equity for all.

Tahlia Eastman is currently a Research Fellow in the Indigenous Studies Unit at the University of Melbourne. She has Palawa and European ancestry. As a PhD candidate, Tahlia is investigating the impact of transgenerational racial and cultural passing in Tasmania. She previously worked in Aboriginal and Torres Strait Islander health policy as Research Advisor at the Lowitja Institute, where she led, and contributed to many key research projects.

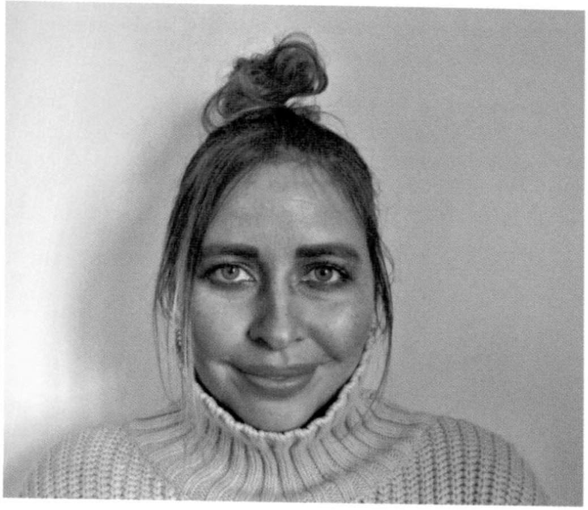

Rebekah Hatfield All-round creative and storyteller Rebekah hails from the quaint regional town of Grafton in the Northern Rivers Region of NSW, where she lives now after spending nearly a decade in Sydney. She is a proud Bundjalung-Yugambeh-Darumbal-Wiradjuri woman and has strong family connections to the communities of Fingal Head on the NSW and Qld border, Rockhampton and Wooribinda in Central Qld and several communities in Western NSW along the Darling and Barwon rivers.

Dino Hodge is an Honorary Senior Fellow with the Centre for Indigenous Studies at the University of Melbourne since 2016. Previously he has worked with the Human Rights and Equal Opportunity Commission, and as a consultant to ATSIC. His collaborative books with First Nations communities include *Did You Meet Any Malagas?* (1993), *You Don't Get Degrees in Weetbix Boxes* (1994), and *Colouring the Rainbow: Blak Queer and Trans Perspectives* (2015). In 2017 Dino received the Northern Territory Human Rights Social Change Award. He has a PhD in history, and each year works in remote NT communities as a paediatric audiologist.

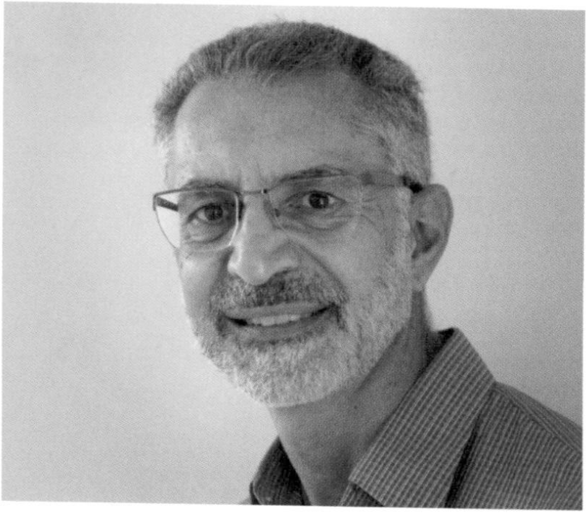

Published in 2021 by Hardie Grant Explore, an imprint of Hardie Grant Publishing

Hardie Grant Explore (Melbourne)
Wurundjeri Country
Building 1, 658 Church Street
Richmond, Victoria 3121

Hardie Grant Explore (Sydney)
Gadigal Country
Level 7, 45 Jones Street
Ultimo, NSW 2007

www.hardiegrant.com/au/explore

A catalogue record for this book is available from the National Library of Australia

Hardie Grant acknowledges the Traditional Owners of the Country on which we work, the Wurundjeri people of the Kulin Nation and the Gadigal people of the Eora Nation, and recognises their continuing connection to the land, waters and culture. We pay our respects to their Elders past and present.

Marcia Langton: Welcome to Country 2nd ed
ISBN 9781741177435

10 9 8 7 6 5 4 3 2 1

Publisher
Melissa Kayser
Project editors
Marg Bowman, Nikki Lusk
Editorial assistance
Rosanna Dutson, Rachel Rawling
Researchers
Nina Fitzgerald, Marly Wells, Tahlia Eastman, Rebekah Hatfield, Dino Hodge, Ruby Langton-Batty
Proofreader
Ella Woods
Design
Pfisterer + Freeman
Typesetting
Megan Ellis
Cartography
Emily Maffei
Map symbols design
Relative Creative
Index
Max McMaster
Tourism information
Supplied with thanks to Jason Eades and Tim Sculthorpe of welcometocountry.com

Cover artwork by Barbara Moore, born 1964, Anmatyerre people, Northern Territory
Ngayuku ngura-My Country, 2020
Synthetic polymer paint on linen, 197×198cm
Image courtesy of Tjala Arts

Colour reproduction by Megan Ellis and Splitting Image Colour Studio

Printed and bound in China by LEO Paper Products LTD.

FSC www.fsc.org MIX Paper from responsible sources FSC® C020056

The paper this book is printed on is certified against the Forest Stewardship Council® Standards and other sources. FSC® promotes environmentally responsible, socially beneficial and economically viable management of the world's forests.

Photography credits (left to right, top to bottom where more than one image appears on a page)

Page 3, 4, 10, 12, 14, 23, 31, 32, 41, 44, 49, 53, 55, 56, 79, 87, 109, 110, 116, 119, 120, 151, 152, 155, 159, 160, 170, 177, 181, 189, 190, 191, 199, 209, 215, 217, 236, 245, 252, 258, 263, 300, 310, 315, 319, 322, 364, 370, 378, 412, 488, 494, 500, 510, 210a,b, 410a, 515a,b Wayne Quilliam; 5, 270a, 332a, 473a James Fisher/TA; 6, 192, 469a, 469b Rainforestation Nature Park; 9 Peter Randolph/Western Australian Museum/Wunambal Gaambera Aboriginal Corporation; 11 K Dicker/National Archives of Australia; 18 Wunambal Gaambera Aboriginal Corporation; 21 Melinda Sawers; 25, 63, 94, 96, 147, 173, 174, 27a National Archives of Australia; 27b Australian News & Information Bureau/John Tanner/National Archives of Australia; 28 W Pedersen/National Archives of Australia; 35 courtesy of the NT AIDS & Hepatitis Council; 38 Joseph Mayers/Miss First Nation Australia; 43 Courtesy of AIATSIS, Barbara Wentworth Collection, item WENTWORTH.B03.CS-000168946; 47 Aboriginal Studies Press/AIATSIS/David R Horton; 51a Illustrator: Joshua Santospirito/NPY Women's Council; 51b Illustrator: Katelyn Griffin/NPY Women's Council; 51c NPY Women's Council; 59a, 59b, 61a,b,c Aaron Corn 2003 'Dreamtime Wisdom, Modern-Time Vision,' Vol. II, pp. 148–150, PhD thesis, The University of Melbourne; 60 Aaron Corn 2003 'Dreamtime Wisdom, Modern-Time Vision,' Vol. I, p. 219, PhD thesis, The University of Melbourne; 66 Department of Agriculture, Water and the Environment (DAWE); 68 Courtesy of AIATSIS, Sylvie Poirier Collection, item POIRIER.S09.CS-000115846; 70 courtesy of Victor Steffensen; 75 Mirima Dawang Woorlab-gerring Language and Culture Centre (MDWg); 82 Courtesy of AIATSIS, Aldo Massola Collection, item MASSOLA.A01.BW-N02450_11; 88, 444a,b Rohan Thompson; 89 Dreamtime Kullilla-Art/Greg Dries; 90, 97, 100, 102 Buku-Larrŋgay Mulka Centre; 93 Australian News & Information Bureau/National Archives of Australia; 99 House of Representatives/Commonwealth Parliament of Australia; 103 Vincent Namatjira/Iwantja Arts/THIS IS NO FANTASY/Art Gallery of NSW; 105 LuGu Productions; 114 Luke David/Mission Songs Project; 123 Courtesy of Short Black Opera; 126 Richard McDowell/Alamy Stock Photo; 127 Tyler Freeman Smith; 129 LaVonne Bobongie; 130a Linsey Rendell; 130b Vincent Long; 131 Lily Marc; 132a courtesy of Leah Purcell; 132b courtesy of Ellen van Neerven; 135 courtesy of Desert Pea Media; 138 courtesy HLA Management; 144 Taylor Hill/FilmMagic/Getty Images; 148 Trevor Graham Yarra Bank Films Pty Ltd/National Archives of Australia; 164 Courtesy of AIATSIS, Royal Commonwealth Society of Tasmania Collection, item RCS.001.BW-N00701_07; 150 Courtesy of AIATSIS, Aboriginal and Torres Strait Islander Commission (ATSIC) Collection, photographer Peter Smith, item ATSIC.006.CN-E00011_03; 178 Courtesy of AIATSIS, Jean Horner Collection, item HORNER2.J01.BW-N04612_12; 179 Courtesy of AIATSIS, Department of Aboriginal Affairs (DAA) Collection, item DAA.003.BWN04528; 182 Mark Metcalfe/City of Sydney; 184 Jimmy Widders Hunt; 194 Russell Ord/Koomal Dreaming; 196, 241a Melanie Faith Dove/Yothu Yindi Foundation; 200, 393b Nura Gunyu; 202 Michele and Tom Grimm/Alamy Stock Photo; 204 Jeff Greenberg/Contributor/Getty Images; 206 Wim Wiskerke/Alamy Stock Photo; 217 courtesy of Belinda Stevens; 228 Teagan Glenane/Yothu Yindi Foundation; 241b Parrtjima; 269 Voyages Indigenous Tourism Australia; 270b SEIT Outback Australia; 274 Georges Antoni for marie claire; 278 George Fragopoulos; 280 Roy Burnyila; 283 Baillie Lodges; 284 Gapuwiyak Culture and Arts Aboriginal Corporation; 285 Tamara Penniket; 288 Jilamara Arts and Crafts; 289 Penny Smith; 293 Cathy Laudenbach Merrepen Arts; 299 Rhett Hammerton/Tjanpi Desert Weavers; 304a,b,c Goolarri Media Enterprises; 305 Dana Weeks; 325a,b Boorloo Experience; 326 Kristi O'Brien/TA; 328 Jade Kingston; 332b,c Koomal Dreaming; 334a Mayi Harvests; 334b As One Nyitting; 337 Anson Smart/TA; 340, 341 Liam Byrne; 343 Short St Gallery; 347 Bobbi Lockyer; 348 Tjarlirli Art; 354a And the trees photography (Jay Black) courtesy of Saltwater Freshwater Arts Alliance; 354b Hilda Bezuidenhout; 358 Filippo Rivetti/DNSW; 361 Parks Australia; 374, 387 DNSW; 385a,b Sasa Kennedy; 390a Kadoo Indigenous and Historical Tours; 390b Isabella Moore; 391 Mark Bond; 390c, 393a Ngaran Ngaran Cultural Awareness; 394 Archie Sartracom/TA; 395a John Slaytor Photography; 395b Belinda Pratten; 396a,b Wendy Bithell; 397 Wollombi Aboriginal Cultural Experiences and Consultancy; 399 Alan Guihot; 402a,b Terence-Kent Ow; 407, 408a,b Harrow Discovery Centre; 410b Robert Blackburn/VV; 418 Nicole Cleary; 420a Narana Aboriginal Cultural Centre; 420b,c Dale Champan/My Dilly Bag; 427 Goin' Off Safaris/Fran Solly/TA; 431 Grant Hunt Photography/TA; 434, 439, 459, 493, 497, 504, 507 TA; 440 Wilpena Pound Resort; 442a,b Living Kaurna Cultural Centre; 448 Tourism Port Douglas and Daintree; 455 TEQ; 464a,c Adventure North Australia; 464b Currumbin Wildlife Sanctuary; 468 Mungalla Aboriginal Tours; 470 Jesse Lindemann/TEQ; 472a,b Straddie Adventures; 473b Ewen Bell/Lonely Planet; 473c Jilara Kuch/Tourism Tropical North Queensland; 476a,b Dreamtime Kullilla-Art; 478a,b Courtney Atkinson/TEQ; 481 Ian Bevege for Milbi Wall (QLD); 484 Paul Jakubowski/Pormpuraaw Art; 486 Faye Atkinson/Pormpuraaw Art; 502a,b,c Bett Gallery; 508a,b National Museum of Australia; 513, 514 Liberty Seekee.

Abbreviations

DNSW Destination New South Wales
TA Tourism Australia
TEQ Tourism and Events Queensland
VV Visit Victoria